The
Index

JAMES CAMERON-WILSON

Grosvenor House
Publishing Limited

James Cameron-Wilson is hereby identified as author of this
work in accordance with Section 77 of the Copyright, Designs
and Patents Act 1988

The book cover design is copyright to James Cameron-Wilson
Aardvark illustration on back cover kindly created by Julian Mulock

This book is published by
Grosvenor House Publishing Ltd
28-30 High Street, Guildford, Surrey, GU1 3HY.
www.grosvenorhousepublishing.co.uk

A CIP record for this book
is available from the British Library

ISBN 978-1-907652-45-5

To Vivienne,
for her indefatigable encouragement

Introduction

It all began when I forgot the word for "a fear of the number thirteen." Personally, I think it's wonderful that such a word exists in the English language and I was determined to be able to conjure it up at will. "So, I gather you're a tad triskaidekaphobic then?" I would enquire of some superstitious unfortunate, expressing a degree of faux concern. I was also partial to the adjective that described a person with really attractive buttocks. I don't know if there's the French equivalent of the term callipygian, but I'm proud that we have it in the Oxford English dictionary.

For the most part I could recall these words at will, but occasionally I would forget a gem. So I started to jot them down on the computer. Then these entries became pages, so I alphabeticised them under the noun to which they belonged. Therefore callipygian would be found under "buttocks, endowed with particularly beautiful ones," just above "buttocks, endowed with particularly hairy ones: dasypygal."

The file continued. If feline is the adjective for cat, I wondered, what is the adjective for goose? So I located the offending omission (anserine) and added it to the list, sensibly parked under the entry marked "goose". Interestingly, I found that while most people seem to know the adjective for cat (feline), few knew the collective noun (a clowder of cats), just as they seemed quite acquainted with a gaggle of geese, but not the adjective anserine. I was adamant that I would have the answer at my fingertips. And so my treasury of unusual and fascinating words grew, each verbal jewel alphabetically catalogued under the pertinent noun. And as the pages bred, so I became aware of a burgeoning interest from friends and fellow journalists. I was producing a source of information they wanted to access.

Alongside my infatuation with words lies my fixation with famous people. Be it the drummer from Aerosmith, the actress who played Miss Ellie in TV's *Dallas* or the patron saint of death, I wanted the name immediately. After all, I'm a crossword fanatic, a writer, the father of an undergraduate, a devotee of TV and pub quizzes and a listaholic. Thus, over the years, I collated a prodigious catalogue of the famous, cross-referenced by profession, demise and any distinguishing quirks. Accordingly, you will find Frida Kahlo under the headings "amputees," "bisexuals," "feminists," "Mexican and famous," "Mexican painters," "moustached painter, female" and "painters, female." The drummer Joey Kramer you will find under "Aerosmith."

And so began the task of drawing up biographical rosters, lists that demanded inclusion in my book: German composers, Italian painters, Australian actors, Japanese novelists. A list of American actors, say, would have been pointless (and endless), just as a collection of Swiss naval officers would have been redundant.

Some of the lists are longer than others. Whilst I could have added substantially to, say, the inventory of Absurdists, I had to consider the question of space. True, I got carried away with architects and poets, but then I started those lists earlier on in this book's genesis and felt that, having compiled them, how do I jettison Pam Ayres in favour of Solon? In the great scheme of history, Solon is by far the more important scribe, but to today's pop-cultural readership Pam Ayres is probably better known and rather more user-friendly.

1

I have also included acronyms that have recently crept into the cultural lexicon, both as shorthand in text-messaging (LOL for laugh-out-loud) and ones adopted by the media (Asbo for anti-social behaviour order), while embracing others for the pure fun of it (for example AAAA for the Association Against Acronym Abuse). More traditional acronyms such as SOS and OTT I have shunned as they are already well documented.

Eventually, the book began to write itself, with me at the rudder, guiding it through the pertinent currents. Experts in various fields (music, cricket, architecture) were consulted (I'm not a total polymath), and the lists rounded themselves out. Some I had to rein in, others I became obsessed with (such as my compilation of famous siblings) because I fell in love with the idea and knew of no other comparative stockpile in print.

So, *The Index*, in contrast to *Roget's Thesaurus*, *Chambers' Biographical Dictionary* and other worthy references, has become a mammoth miscellany of the obscure, the eccentric and the pop cultural, but one arranged in alphabetical order so as to make it a useful handbook in its own right. Logophiles, crossword addicts, amateur academics, journalists, schoolchildren, writers and collectors of ephemera should not only find it seductive reading but also a unique enchiridion.

Occasionally one will come across inexplicable pieces of information that may not seem to fit in with the tone of the rest of the book. These are here because they pop up so frequently in crosswords that I felt it useful to have them at hand. In addition, I have included some lists of synonyms for words I find particularly problematic. For instance, the common adjective "beautiful" can quickly become banal and meaningless when such variants as "pulchritudinous" or "babelicious" may give the definition a fresh spin. And for the same idiosyncratic reasons listed above, I have included buildings, cities, countries, dates, events, nicknames, operas, patron saints, popular slogans and, to be totally subjective, favourite quotes.

So, like every reference, *The Index* will have its strengths and its weaknesses, but I trust its usefulness will outweigh any profoundly dramatic irritations.

James Cameron-Wilson

The Index

A

AAAA: Association Against Acronym Abuse
aardvark, adjective: edentaleff
aardvark, collective noun: armoury
aardvark, famous: The Aardvark (TV cartoon featured on *The New Pink Panther*), Cerebus (comic-strip character)
aardwolf, adjective: protelidf
ABBA: enormously popular Swedish pop group formed in Stockholm in 1970; comprised of: Agnetha Fältskog (vocals), Benny Andersson (vocals, keyboards, synthesiser), Bjorn Ulvaeus (vocals, guitar) and Anni-Frid Lyngstad (vocals). Formerly known as The Festfolk Quartet: 'Abba' is an acronym made up of the initials of the members' first names
abbess, adjective: abbatial
abbey, adjective: abbatial
Abbey Theatre: theatre in Dublin, opened in 1904; destroyed by fire in 1951; re-opened in 1966
abbot, adjective: abbatial
abdicators: Pope Benedict IX, Charles IV of Spain, Charles X of France, Christina of Sweden, Edward II, Edward VIII, Ferdinand of Austria, Pope Gregory VI, Isabella II of Spain, James II, Louis-Philippe of France (France's last king), Mary Queen of Scots, Napoleon Bonaparte, Nicholas II of Russia, Richard II
abductees: Barbara Blandish (from the James Hadley Chase novel *No Orchids For Miss glandish*), Lorna Doone, Ganymede, Eugene Paul Getty II, Patty Hearst, Helen of Sparta, Natascha Kampusch (Austrian ten-year-old girl held captive in a window-less cell for over eight years), Brian Keenan, Shannon Matthews, John McCarthy, Daniel Pearl (American journalist murdered in Karachi, Pakistan), Persephone, Matthew Scott, Frank Sinatra Jr, Terry Waite, Tammy Wynette - see escapees and kidnapping victims
Aberdeen, birthplace of: Alexander Calder (sculptor), Dame Evelyn Glennie (percussionist), Annie Lennox, James Clerk Maxwell (physicist)
Aberdeen, rivers: Dee, Don
abolitionists: John Brown, Frederick Douglass, Olaudah Equiano, William Lloyd Garrison, Elizabeth Palmer Peabody, Wendell Phillips, Ignatius Sancho, Harriet Beecher Stowe, Harriet Tubman, David Walker, William Wilberforce
Abominable Snowman: yeti
Aboriginal actor: David Gulpilil
Aboriginal club: nullah
Aboriginal languages: Adnyamathanha, Aranda, Baagandji (now extinct), Wathawurung (now extinct), Wemba-wemba, Wiradhuri, Yagara (now extinct), Yindjibarndi (of Western Australia), Yuwaalaraay (of New South Wales)

3

Aboriginal manhood rite: bora
Aboriginal medicine man: koradji
Aboriginal politician: Neville Bonner (the first to be elected to the Australian
    Parliament)
Aboriginal singer: Geoffrey Gurrumul Yunupingu
Aboriginal wind instrument: didgeridoo
Aboriginal tribe: Aranda, Yolngu
Aboriginal woman: lubra
Aborigine: Abbo (Australian slang), binghi (Australian slang)
abortion: first legalised in 1920, in the USSR
abortion, legalised in Britain: 27 April 1968 (introduced by the Liberal MP David
    Steel)
Absolutely Fabulous: TV sitcom written by Jennifer Saunders, later turned into a French
        film, *Absolument Fabuleux* (2001), starring Josiane Balasko and Nathalie Baye
    broadcast 12 November 1992 (on BBC2) - 25 December 2004 (BBC1)
    cast: Jennifer Saunders (Edina 'Eddy' Monsoon), Joanna Lumley (Patsy
        Stone), Julia Sawalha (Saffron Monsoon), Jane Horrocks (Bubble/Katy
        Grin), June Whitfield (Mother)
absorbtion, adjective: sorbefacient
abstainer: "A weak person who yields to the temptation of denying himself a
    pleasure" – Ambrose Bierce
abstract painters: Cecily Brown, Judy Cassab, Lyonel Feininger, Wassily
    Kandinsky, Franz Kline, Piet Mondrian, Robert Motherwell, Barnett Newman,
    Ben Nicholson, Kenneth Noland, Jackson Pollack, Bridget Riley, Mark Rothko,
    Kurt Schwitters, Frank Stella, Cy Twombly
Absurdists: Arthur Adamov, Edward Albee, Samuel Beckett, Albert Camus, Jean
    Genet, Daniel Handler, Joseph Heller, Eugène Ionesco, Franz Kafka, Søren
    Kierkegaard, Harold Pinter, Tom Robbins, Tom Stoppard, Patrick Süskind
abyss, adjective: abyssal
ACAB: all coppers are bastards; always carry a Bible
academics, patron saint of: Thomas Aquinas
Acas: Advisory, Conciliation and Arbitration Service
accents, British – see dialects, British
accidents, fact: 20% of accidents on British motorways are caused by drivers falling
    asleep
accidents, fear of: dystychiphobia
accident prone characters: Inspector Jacques Clouseau, Monsieur Hulot (played
    by Jacques Tati), Frank Spencer (from TV's *Some Mothers Do 'Ave 'Em*)
accordion: patented in May 1829 by Cyril Demian, although other sources suggest
    the musical instrument was invented in 1822 by C.F.L. Buschmann of Berlin
accordion players: Martin Jacques, Chango Spasiuk
accountant: "Someone who knows the cost of everything and the value of
    nothing"; "Someone who solves a problem you didn't know you had in a way
    you don't understand"; and another joke: "What does an accountant use for
    birth control? His personality"
accountant, collective noun: audit
AC/DC: hard rock band formed in Sydney, Australia, in 1973; comprised of
    Malcolm Young (guitar), Angus Young (lead guitar), Ronald Belford 'Bon'
    Scott (vocals; died: 19 February 1980), Phil Rudd (drums) and Mark Evans
    (bass). Earlier group members consisted of Dave Evans (vocals), Larry Van
    Knedt (bass), Colin Burgess (drums), and Rob Bailey and Peter Clark (rhythm
    section)

achievement: "The way to get things done is not to mind who gets the credit for doing them" – Benjamin Jowett; "Accomplishing the impossible means only that your boss will add it to your regular duties" - Gary Larson

achilles tendon: tendo-calcaneus

acorn-bearing: balaniferous

acorn-shaped: balanoid

acre: first defined in 1305 (as 4,840 square yards)

acrobat: Joseph Grimaldi

acrobat, collective noun: troupe

acronym: A Clever Reminder Often Nudges Your Memory

acrostic: invented in 328 AD by Porphyrius Optaliamus

acting: "The art of keeping a large number of people from coughing" - Ralph Richardson

acting, adjective: roscian

acting gurus: Stella Adler, Uta Hagen, Sanford Meisner, Konstantin Stanislavski, Lee Strasberg

action painter: Jackson Pollack

activist, collective noun: cadre

activists: Rudolf Bahro, Josephine Baker, Steve Biko, Chastity Bono, Breyten Breytenbach, Anita Bryant, Stokely Carmichael, Sir Roger Casement, Erskine Childers, Noam Chomsky, Eldridge Cleaver, Rachel Corrie (23-year-old American who in 2003 was crushed to death under the tracks of an Israeli army bulldozer), Charles Coughlin, Dame Kathleen Courtney, Angela Davis, Emily Davison, Dorothy Day, Mahadev Desai, Phoolan Devi, Bernardine Dohrn, Jean Dominique, Rudi Dutschke, Louis Farrakhan (organiser of the Million Man March in Washington on 16 October 1995), Dr Spencer Fitzgibbon, Jane Fonda, Marcus Garvey, Ben Hartley, Tom Hayden, Abbie Hoffman, George Jackson, Leila Khaled, Dame Anne Loughlin, Miriam Makeba, Malcolm X, Winnie Mandela, James Mawdsley (who was sentenced to 17 years in a Burmese jail for handing out pro-democracy leaflets in Rangoon), Russell Means, Harvey Milk, Ralph Nader, Huey P. Newton, Rosa Parks, Vanessa Redgrave, Paul Robeson, Bobby Seale, Rev. Al Sharpton, Susan Sontag, Aung San Suu Kyi, Helen Suzman, Swampy (aka Daniel Hooper), Morgan Tsvangirai, Desmond Tutu, Wat Tyler, Orlando and Claudio Villas-Boas, Mary Whitehouse, William Wilberforce

actor: "An emotional athlete" - Al Pacino; "Method actors give you a photograph. Real actors give you an oil painting" - Charles Laughton; "Scratch an actor and you will find an actress" - Sophia Myles

actor, collective noun: cast, company, cry, troupe

actors – see Australian actors, Italian actors, knights theatrical, Shakespearean actors

actors, in film, fact: eighty per cent of Screen Guild members earn less than $5,000 per year

actors, patron saint of: Genesius of Rome

actress: "Babe, District Attorney and *Driving Miss Daisy* – the three stages of an actress's career" – Goldie Hawn

actuary: an accountant without the sense of humor

acupressure: shiatsu

ADAS: Agricultural Development and Advisory Service

ADD: Attention Deficit Disorder

Addams Family, The: eccentric, beloved sitcom featuring a macabre nuclear family, based on the cartoon by Charles Addams; later made into two extremely successful feature films, *The Addams Family* (1991) and *Addams Family Values* (1993) created by David Levy

broadcast: 18 September 1964–8 April 1966

cast: Carolyn Jones (Morticia Addams), John Astin (Gomez Addams), Jackie Coogan (Uncle Fester), Blossom Rock (Grandmama), Ken Weatherwax (Pugsley Addams), Lisa Loring (Wednesday Addams), Felix Silla (Cousin Itt), Ted Cassidy (Lurch)

addiction-breaking drug: ibogaine (extract from an African shrub)

Aden: former name for Yemen

ADHD: Attention Deficit Hyperactivity Disorder

ADHD drug: Methylphenidate, Ritalin

Adityas (sun gods of Hindu mythology): Ansa, Aryman, Bhaga, Daksha, Dhatri, Indra, Mitra, Ravi, Savitri, Surya, Varuna and Yama

admirals: George Anson, Sir David Beatty, John Benbow, John Fisher, Sir John Hawkins, Horatio Hornblower, Sir John Jellicoe, Husband Kimmel (commander-in-chief of the US Pacific Fleet during the Japanese attack on Pearl Harbour), Earl Louis Mountbatten, Horatio Nelson, Robert Peary, William Penn - see naval officers

admiral, collective noun: bridge

Admiralty Arch, The Mall, London SW1: structure built in 1910 as part of the Queen Victoria memorial scheme

ADR: automated dialogue replacement (in sound editing on film)

adults: "Adults are just children who owe money" - Kenneth Branagh in *Peter's Friends* (1992 film)

adult performers – see porn stars

adulterer: bedswerver

adulterers: Mark Antony, Paddy Ashdown, Pope Alexander VI, David Blunkett, Prince Charles, Bill Clinton, Robin Cook, David (who had a fling with Bathsheba, before making an honest woman of her), Angus Deayton, Edward VI, Edward VII, Desiderius Erasmus, Dan Gallagher (played by Michael Douglas in *Fatal Attraction*), Gary Hart, Henry VIII, Boris Johnson, Pope Julius II, John F. Kennedy, Martin Luther, Sir John Major, David Mellor, Cecil Parkinson, John Prescott, John Profumo, Pope Sixtus IV

adultery, fact: 80% of men who die during intercourse are committing adultery at the time

adultery victims, patron saint of: Monica

adulteresses: Bathsheba, Catherine de Médicis, Lady Chatterley, Cleopatra, Clytemnestra, Edwina Currie, Alex Forrest (played by Glenn Close in *Fatal Attraction*), Helen of Troy, Anna Karenina, Lady Caroline Lamb

adventurers: Major James Bigglesworth DSO MC (aka 'Biggles'), Jack Colton (as played by Michael Douglas on film), Gabriele D'Annunzio, Sir Francis Drake, Bulldog Drummond, 'the Falcon,' Steve Fossett (the first person to stage a solo balloon flight around the world), Richard Hannay (creation of John Buchan), Sir Edmund Hillary, Horatio Hornblower, Ivanhoe (full name: Wilfred of Ivanhoe), Indiana Jones, Robert Peary, Dirk Pitt, Allan Quartermain, Sir Walter Raleigh, John Smith, Robert Louis Stevenson

advertising: "Advertising may be described as the science of arresting the human intelligence long enough to get money from it" – Stephen Leacock

advertising executives: William Bernbach, Jerry Della Femina, Frank Lowe, David Ogilvy, Charles and Maurice Saatchi, Michael Steadman (played by Ken Olin in TV's *thirtysomething*)

advice: "A good scare is worth more to a man than good advice" – Edgar Watson Howe
advisor, collective noun: council
AEA: Association of European Airlines
AEP: Attenuating Energy Projectile (plastic bullet that collapses on impact)
aerial navigation, adjective: aeropleustic
aeronautical engineers: Sir Barnes Wallis, Sir Frank Whittle
aeroplane: first heavier-than-air craft successfully launched in 1886 by Orville and Wilbur Wright at Kitty Hawk in North Carolina
aeroplane: the first steam-powered aircraft, the *Eole*, was built by Clement Ader in 1890 in France
aeroplane, collective noun: flight, squadron
aeroplane victims – see plane crash, killed in
aeroplanes, dread of: aeronausiphobia
aerosol (spray can): invented in 1926 by the Norwegian Erik Rotheim
aerosol, first patented in the US: 1941
Aerosmith: US rock group formed in New Hampshire in 1970; comprised of Steven Tyler (vocals; real name: Steven Talarico), Joe Perry (lead guitar), Brad Whitford (rhythm guitar), Tom Hamilton (bass) and Joey Kramer (drums)
Afars and the Issas, Territory of the: former name for Djibouti (until 1977)
affair: ding-dong, extracurricular activity, fling, matinee, nooner, unholy bedlock
Afghanistan: republic in central Asia
  capital: Kabul
  currency: afghani
  language: Pashto and Dari (Persian), Tajik
  religion: Muslim
  fact: the world's main supplier of heroin, accounting for 93% of the total global output (as of August 2007)
  1996: Taliban government imposed by force
  7 October 2001: date of the first strikes by the USA and UK on the Taliban's military targets (63 days after which the Taliban fleed Kandahar)
Afghan Civil War and Soviet invasion: 1979–1988
Afghan singer: Mahwash
afloat: natant
Africa, the smallest country in: The Gambia
Africa, three largest countries (out of 53): 1) Sudan 2) Algeria; 3) Democratic Republic of the Congo
African cities, largest (by population): 1) Cairo; 2) Lagos; 3) Kinshasa; 4) Addis Ababa; 5) Nairobi; 6) Johannesburg; 7) Alexandria; 8) Casablanca; 9) Abidjan; 10) Kano
African countries, number of: 53
African violet: saintpaulia
African-Americans, patron saints of: Benedict the African, Peter Claver and Martin de Porres
African-American dialect: Ebonics
African-American holiday: Kwanzaa (a non-religious, cultural holiday celebrated December 26-January 1)
African-American writers: Maya Angelou, James Baldwin, Charles Waddell Chesnutt, Countee Cullen, William Du Bois, Ralph Ellison, Alex Haley, Virginia Hamilton, Chester Himes, Langston Hughes, Nella Larson, Toni Morrison, Gloria Naylor, Gordon Parks, Faith Ringgold, Alice Walker, Booker T. Washington, Richard Wright

after shave: Blue Jeans, Escape, Eternity (Calvin Klein), Extreme Man, Factor
  for Men, Gucci Envy, Hai Karate, Maculine (Dolce & Gabbana), Obsession
  (Calvin Klein), Old Spice, paco rabanne, Seaward, Stetson, Wings For Men, XS
  - see cologne

afterlife, ruler of: Osiris (Egyptian mythology)

afternoon, adjective: postmeridian

age: "A very high price to pay for maturity" – Tom Stoppard

ageing: "Being an old maid is like death by drowning, a really delightful sensation
  once you cease to struggle" - Edna Ferber

ageing, study of: geriatrics, gerontology

agents, theatrical: Creative Artists Agency (CAA), International Creative
  Management (ICM), Swifty Lazar, William Morris, Peggy Ramsay

Agincourt, battle of: 25 October (St. Crispin's Day)1415

agony aunts: Katie Boyle, Dear Abby, Ann Landers, Marjorie Proops, Anna
  Raeburn, Claire Rayner, Miriam Stoppard, Dr Ruth Westheimer

agreement, goddess of: Harmonia (Greek mythology), Concordia (Roman)

agriculture, adjective: geoponic

agriculture, god of: Cronus (Greek), Saturn (Roman), Rindr (Norse)

agriculture, goddess of: Ceres (Roman), Demeter (Greek), Rindr (Norse)

agricultural products, collective noun: show

agronomists: Trofim Denisovich Lysenko, Antoine Parmentier

Aida: opera by Giuseppe Verdi, first produced in Cairo in 1871

Aids: Acquired Immune Deficiency Syndrome
  first reported by Dr Michael Gottlieb in 1980
  first reported Aids victim: Margrethe P. Rask, a Danish physician who died
    from the condition on 12 December 1977

Aids, fact: when South Africa unveiled plans to manufacture cheaper drugs to fight
  Aids, drug companies in the West took legal action

Aids patients, patron saint of: Aloysius Gonzaga and Peregrine Laziosi

Aids victims: Peter Allen, Néstor Almendros (cinematographer), Reinaldo Arenas,
  Arthur Ashe, Isaac Asimov, Michael Bennett (choreographer), Gia Carangi
  (supermodel), Ian Charleson (actor), Bruce Chatwin (novelist), John Curry,
  Denholm Elliott, Kenny Everett, Keith Haring (artist), Jim Henson, Terrence
  Higgins, John C. Holmes, Rock Hudson, Derek Jarman (filmmaker), Fela Kuti
  (musician), Liberace, Robert Mapplethorpe (photographer), Freddie Mercury,
  Rudolf Nureyev, Anthony Perkins, Tony Richardson (filmmaker), Chris Smith
  (British politician)

Aids-fighting agent (protein): chemokine

air, adjective: pneumatic

air, divination by: aeromancy

air, fear of: aerophobia

air, god of: Shu (Egyptian mythology)

air force officer: Henry H. Arnold
  - see aviators, pilots, fighter pilots

air kiss: Park Avenue Grunt

air spirit: sylph

air stewardess: cow pilot, flight attendant, stew

air travel fatalities: on average, six Britons die a year in airline crashes

aircraft: aerocraft (largest airborne vessel ever produced), B52 (bomber), Cessna
  180, Concorde, F-117 Stealth fighter, Harrier, F17, jumbo jet, Lear jet, LoFlyte
  (aka a "wave rider," an aircraft shaped like a mantra ray that can fly more than
  twice the speed of Concorde), MiG, Pan Am Boeing 747, Stealth fighter
  - see bombers

aircraft, collective noun: wing

aircraft, surgical operation carried out on: Hong Kong to London flight, utilising a coat hanger, a pair of scissors and a glass of brandy to free air from the collapsed lung of Paula Dixon. The operation was performed by the passengers Professor Angus Wallace and Dr Tom Wong

aircraft designers: Marcel Dassault, Howard Hughes, Sergei Korolev, Reginald Mitchell (conceived the Spitfire), Sir Thomas Sopwith, Sir Barnes Wallis

aircraft manufacturer: William Boeing

airfield, first: Huffman Prairie, Ohio, set up in 1904 by the Wright brothers

airline founders: Sir Richard Branson, Howard Hughes, Sir Freddie Laker, Juan Trippe

airliner, biggest: Airbus A380 (launched in April 2005)

airlines, low-cost: Buzz, easyJet, Go, Ryanair

airmail stamp collecting: aerophilately

airman: Major James Bigglesworth DSO MC (aka 'Biggles')
- see aviators, fighter pilots, pilots

airplanes, killed in – see plane crash, killed in

airport, world's busiest: O'Hare, Chicago (handles 66.4 million passengers per annum)

airport, Europe's busiest: Heathrow, London

airport, world's largest: Denver International, Colorado

airports: "When efficiency of operation is combined with the best architecture going, then these usually indeterminate places become something other than vessels of anxiety and boredom" – Hugh Pearman

airports named after famous people: Bob Hope (Burbank), Charles de Gaulle (Paris), Don Quixote (South Madrid), George Best (Belfast City), John F. Kennedy (New York), John Foster Dulles (Washington DC), John Lennon (Liverpool), John Paul II (Kraków), John Wayne (Santa Ana), Josef Strauss (Munich), Kochi Ryoma (Kochi, Japan - named after the samurai Ryoma Sakamoto), Leonardo Da Vinci (Rome), Lester B. Pearson International (Toronto), Marco Polo (Venice), Mozart (Salzburg), Princess Beatriz (Aruba), Queen Alia International Airport (Amman), Ronald Reagan (Washington DC), Simón Bolívar (Caracas), V.C. Bird (Antigua), Will Rogers (Oklahoma City)

AK: postcode for Alaska

AL: postcode for Alabama

Alabama, 22nd state (1819), Heart of Dixie, Camellia State

    capital: Montgomery

    birthplace of: Hank Aaron (baseball player), Tallulah Bankhead, Johnny Mack Brown, Jimmy Buffett, Nat King Cole, Angela Davis, Joe Louis, Helen Keller, singer Shelby Lynne, Wilson Pickett, Condoleezza Rice, Percy Sledge, Candi Staton, George Wallace, Dinah Washington (blues singer), Hank Williams formerly known as the Cotton State (until the boll weevil killed the cotton)

    motto: 'We dare defend our rights'

    state bird: yellowhammer

    state flower: camellia

    state tree: Southern pine

    tourist attractions: Jefferson Davis' 'first White House' of the Confederacy, Helen Keller's birthplace

fact: the state only abolished the firing squad in 2002 (replacing its mode of capital punishment with lethal injection)

Alamo, Battle of: 23 February-6 March 1836

Alamo, Battle of, victims: Jim Bowie, Davy Crockett

Alamo, Battle of, victor: Antonio López de Santa Anna

alarm bell: tocsin

Alaska, 49th state (1959), The Last Frontier (unofficial)
> **capital:** Juneau
> **motto:** 'North to the future'
> **native Alaskan:** Aleut (see Eskimo)
> **state bird:** willow ptarmigan
> **state flower:** forget-me-not
> **state tree:** sitka spruce
> **tourist attractions:** Portage Glacier, Mendenhall Glacier, Glacier Bay National Park
> **fact:** Alaska boasts the most northern, eastern and western points of the United States

Albania: republic in south-eastern Europe
> **capital:** Tirana
> **currency:** lek
> **language:** Albanian
> **nickname:** Land of the Eagles
> **religion:** Muslim

Albanian and famous: Jim Belushi (of Albanian extraction), John Belushi (of Albanian extraction), Pope Clement XI, Bekim Fehmiu (film actor), Enver Hoxha (dictator), Ismail Kadare (writer and poet), Scanderbeg (patriot), Mother Teresa (of Albanian extraction)

albatross, adjective: procellariid

Albert Bridge, London: opened in 1873; constructed by R.M. Ordish

Albert Hall, Kensington Gore, London SW7: opened in 1870; designed by Captain Francis Fowke and Colonel H.Y. Darracott Scott; previously known as the Hall of Arts and Sciences, the building had its name unexpectedly changed when, in 1868, Queen Victoria laid the foundation stone at the rear of the stalls

albinos: Edward the Confessor (English king), Elric of Melniboné (from a series of novels by Michael Moorcock), Salif Keita (Malian musician), Silas (from *The Da Vinci Code*), Edgar Winter and Johnny Winter (musicians)

album, best-selling in US: 1) Eagles - *Their Greatest Hits 1971–1975*; 2) Michael Jackson – *Thriller*; 3) Led Zeppelin - *Led Zeppelin IV*; 4) Pink Floyd - *The Wall*; 5) Billy Joel - *Greatest Hits Volume I & Volume II*; 6) AC/DC - *Back In Black*; 7) Shania Twain – *Comer On Over*; 8) Garth Brooks – *Double Live*; 9) The Beatles - *The Beatles*; 10) Fleetwood Mac – *Rumours*

alchemists: Heinrich Cornelius Agrippa, Roger Bacon, Sir Isaac Newton, Paracelsus, Plato, August Strindberg

alchemy, adjective: spagyric

alcohol: "Can both raise and lower the blood pressure, cure infant colic, lift a hangover, prevent a heart attack, nip a cold in the bud, ensure a good night's sleep and serve as both an anaesthetic and antiseptic" – James Le Fanu; "The most helpful and hygienic of beverages" - Louis Pasteur; "Alcohol may be man's worst enemy, but the Bible says love your enemy" - Frank Sinatra

alcohol, fact: alcohol is the cause of 13 deaths a day in the United Kingdom: that is 4,000 deaths a year and – indirectly –28,000 deaths per annum, largely from accidents

alcohol, first large-scale production of: in Modena, Italy, in 1320

alcohol, last drop in the glass: heeltap

alcohol, world's top consumer of: France (1999)

alcohol-consuming nations, per capita: 1) Luxembourg; 2) France; 3) Portugal

alcoholic psychosis: delirium tremens

Alcoholics Anonymous: started by Bill W (William Wilson), on 12 May 1945, in Akron, Ohio

alcoholics, patron saint of: Venerable Matt Talbot and Monica

alcoholism: "My first wife drove me to drink. It's the only thing I'm indebted to her for" – W.C. Fields

ale: Daily Mail (Cockney Rhyming Slang)
– see beer

Alexandra Palace, Muswell Hill, London N22: opened in 1862

alfalfa: lucerne

algebra: appeared around 250 AD

algebra, fact: first book on algebra said to have been written by Diophantus of Alexandria

Algeria: republic in north-west Africa
  capital: Algiers
  currency: dinar
  language: Arabic (official); Berber, French
  religion: Muslim

Algonquin Hotel Round Table, members: Franklin P. Adams, Robert Benchley, William Faulkner, George Kaufman, Alan Jay Lerner, Frederick Loewe, Dorothy Parker, Robert Sherwood, James Thurber

Alien (1979 film), selling line: "In space no one can hear you scream"

aliens: E.T. (The ExtraTerrestrial), Mork (of TV's *Mork and Mindy*), Mr Spock

alien abduction, fact: 20% of Americans claim to have been abducted by aliens (according to *The Mail On Sunday*)

alien life forms, fact: 58% of British men and 43% of British women believe that aliens exist

All About Eve (1950 film), famous line: Margo Channing (Bette Davis): "Fasten your seat belts. We're in for a bumpy night"

All Saint's Day: festival celebrated 1 November

All Souls' Day: festival celebrated 2 November

allergy, fact: reaction usually caused by the protein Fed d 1 which is secreted onto a cat's fur

alligator, adjective: eusuchian

alligator, Cockney Rhyming Slang: later

alligator, collective noun: congregation

alligator, famous: Elvis (as featured in NBC TV's *Miami Vice*, being the pet of Det. Sonny Crockett), Wally Gator (the 'swinging alligator of the swamp')

alligator sound: peep

alligator young: hatchling

allspice (tree): pimento

Ally McBeal: TV comedy-drama set in a Boston legal firm created by David E. Kelley
  broadcast: 8 September 1997 (pilot) - 20 May 2002
  cast: Calista Flockhart (Ally McBeal), Courtney Thorne-Smith (Georgia Thomas), Gil Bellows (Billy Alan Thomas), Greg Germann (Richard Fisherman), Lisa Nicole Carson (Renee Radick), Robert Downey Jr (Larry Paul), Jane Krakowski (Elaine Vassal), James LeGros (Mark Albert), Peter

MacNicol (John Cage), Portia de Rossi (Nelle Porter), Lucy Liu (Ling Woo), Dyan Cannon (Judge Whipper Cone), Vonda Shepard (herself)

almond, adjective: amygdaline

almond-shaped: amygdaloid

alms, adjective: eleemosynary

alone, fear of being: monophobia

alpaca, offspring: cria

alphabets: A for 'orses, Devanagari (Sanskrit, Hindi, etc), finger alphabet, Greek, Hebrew, Morse, NATO Phonetic (see), ogham (Old Irish), phonetic, Runic, sign language, Western Union Phonetic (see)

alphabet, teacher of: abecedarian

alphabetically arranged: abecedarian

Alpine orphan: Heidi

Alpine peak: aiguille

Alps, disaster: November 2000: in which 156 skiers and snowboarders were burnt alive while travelling on a funicular train through the two-mile tunnel to the slopes above Kaprun, Austria

altar servers, patron saint of: John Berchmans

alter egos: Catwoman (Selina Kyle, Patience Philips), Puff Daddy (Sean Combs), P. Diddy (Sean Combs), Dame Edna Everage (Barry Humphries), Aladin Sane (David Bowie), Slim Shady (Eminem), Ziggy Stardust (David Bowie), The Thin White Duke (David Bowie)
- see pen names

alternative medicine: acupressure, acupuncture, Alexander technique, aromatherapy, Ayurvedic healing, chiropractic medicine, crystal healing, cupping, Feldenkrais, flower remedies, herbalism, holistic, homoeopathy, iridology, kinesiology, magnetic healing, massage, naturopathy, osteopathy, psychic healing, reflexology, reiki, shiatsu, therapeutic touch

alternative therapies: acupuncture, facials, Frigo Thalgo body wrap, high pressure blitz water jet, homoeopathy, massage, Phoenix Rising yoga, reflexology, reiki, yoga

altruists – see philanthropists

Alzheimer's disease: identified by the German psychiatrist and neuropathologist Alois Alzheimer (1864–1915)

Alzheimer's disease, fact: it is estimated that between 290,000 and 380,000 suffer from the disorder in England and Wales and five million people in the United States. Latest studies reveal that the disease now attacks twenty per cent of people between the ages of 75 and 84 (and nearly half of those over 85) in the West

Alzheimer sufferers: Dana Andrews, Charles Bronson, Winston Churchill (a mild casualty), Perry Como, Aaron Copland, Willem De Kooning (abstract painter), Ralph Waldo Emerson, Henry Ford, Rita Hayworth, Charlton Heston, W. Somerset Maugham, Iris Murdoch, Edmund O'Brien (actor), Maurice Ravel (French composer best known for his *Bolero* composition), Ronald Reagan, Sugar Ray Robinson, Jonathan Swift (satirist who wrote *Gulliver's Travels*), E.B.White (essayist and children's novelist)

Amazon rain forest, fact: the jungle still covers 86% of the land it covered in the 1950s

Amazon.com, founder: Jeff Bezos (pronounced Beezoss)
  headquarters: Seattle
  started operation: July 1995
  motto for employees: "work hard, have fun and make history"

Amazonian queen: Hippolyta

ambassador, mode of verbal address: Your Excellency

ambition: "Don't climb up too close to God. He might shake the tree" – line spoken by Caroline Goodall in the 1994 American film *Disclosure.*

ambivalence: "They say the definition of ambivalence is watching your mother-in-law drive over a cliff in your new Cadillac" – David Mamet

ambulance: first appeared in the 1500s

ambulance driver: Nick Adams

America: "America was a country that went from barbarism to decadence without an intervening period of civilisation" – Georges Clemenceau (1841–1929)

America's sweetheart: Mary Pickford

American Civil War: 1861–1865

American Civil War characters (symbolically speaking): Billy Yank (representing the Union North) and Johnny Reb (the Confederate South)

American composers: John Adams, Samuel Barber, Leonard Bernstein, Ernest Bloch (born in Geneva, Switzerland), Earle Brown, Dave Brubeck, John Cage, Elliott Carter, Aaron Copland, Chick Corea, Henry Cowell, Morton Feldman, Rudolf Friml, George Gershwin, Philip Glass, W.C. Handy, Victor Herbert, Charles Ives, Stan Kenton, Erich Wolfgang Korngold, Harry Partch, Steve Reich, Terry Riley, Richard Rodgers, William Schuman, John Philip Sousa, Kurt Weill

American conflicts: Spain (1898), Cuba, Haiti, Dominican Republic, Mexico, Nicaragua, First World War, Second World War, Vietnam, Haiti, Gulf War, Bosnia, Kosovo, Iraq, Afghanistan

American footballers: Terry Crews, Otto Graham, Ray Lewis (a Baltimore Ravens linebacker and three-time NFL All-Pro accused of murder), Dan Marino, Joe Montana, Joe Namath, Fritz Pollard, Gale Sayers, O.J. Simpson, Hines Ward, Ricky Williams

American-Mexican War: 1846–1848

American painters: Josef Albers, Jean-Michel Basquiat, Mary Cassatt, Judy Chicago, Thomas Cole, Willem de Kooning, Marcel Duchamp (born in France), Thomas Eakins, Adolph Gottlieb, Edward Hicks, Winslow Homer, Edward Hopper, Jasper Johns, Franz Kline, Jacob Lawrence, Roy Lichtenstein, Robert Motherwell, Kenneth Noland, Georgia O'Keeffe, Maxfield Parrish, Charles Wilson Peale, Joseph Pickett, Jackson Pollock, Maurice Prendergast, James Rosenquist, Mark Rothko, Albert Ryder, John Singer Sargent, Julian Schnabel, Ben Shahn, Charles Sheeler, Frank Stella, Yves Tanguy, Cy Twombly, Andy Warhol, Tom Wesselmann, Benjamin West, James Whistler, Grant Wood (*American Gothic*), Andrew Wyeth (*Christina's World*, the Helga portraits)

American playwrights: Edward Albee, Maxwell Anderson, Jon Robin Baitz, James Baldwin, S.N. Behrman, Marc Connelly, John van Druten, Christopher Durang, T.S. Eliot, Julius J. Epstein, Horton Foote, Paul Green, John Guare, Moss Hart, Alfred Hayes, Lillian Hellman, Beth Henley, Sidney Howard, Langston Hughes, William Inge, Robinson Jeffers, George S. Kaufman, Sidney Kingsley, Neil LaBute, James Lapine, Warren Leight, Kenneth Lonergan, Craig Lucas, Charles MacArthur, David Mamet, Elaine May, Terrence McNally, Arthur Miller, Toni Morrison, Clifford Odets, Eugene O'Neill, John Patrick, David Rabe, Elmer Rice, Paul Rudnick, William Saroyan, Sam Shepard, Martin Sherman, Robert E. Sherwood, Neil Simon, Donald Ogden Stewart, Wendy Wasserstein, Thornton Wilder, Tennessee Williams, August Wilson, Lanford Wilson

American-Spanish War: 1898

American War of 1812 (1812–1815)

American War of Independence (1775–1783), military figures: Charles
   Cornwallis, George Washington

Americans: "The American in your living room is 90 per cent California, five per
   cent slum-dweller and five per cent banjo-playing incest victim" - A.A. Gill;
   "Americans go deeply into the surface of things"- Henry Ward

amnesia, fear of: amnesiophobia

Amnesty International: human rights organisation founded in 1961 by Peter
   Benenson

amphibian, largest in the world: Chinese giant salamander

amphibians, fear of: batrachophobia

amputation during surgery: first carried out in 1679

amputees: Captain Ahab, Dave Allen (just minus a finger), Rick Allen (one-armed
   drummer for Def Leppard), Sir Douglas Bader, Sarah Bernhardt, John Wayne
   Bobbitt (whose penis was hacked off by his wife, Lorena Bobbitt), Tycho Brahe
   (who lost his nose in a duel), Art Buchwald, Max Cleland, Guillaume Depardieu,
   Terry Fox (marathon runner), Jane Froman (singer), Jerry Garcia (missing half
   of a middle finger), Abu Hamza, Daryl Hannah (lost the tip of an index finger
   in a childhhod accident), Captain Hook, Marmaduke Hussey (former BBC
   chairman who lost a leg in World War II), Frida Kahlo, Alison Lapper (actually
   born without arms), Long John Silver, Edouard Manet (whose leg was
   amputated as he underwent the final stages of syphilis), John Martyn, Heather
   Mills (formerly Mrs Paul McCartney), Horatio Nelson, Cole Porter (whose right
   leg was amputated in 1958, the same year he wrote his last song, *Wouldn't it
   Be Fun?*), Arthur Rimbaud, Harold Russell (Oscar-winning actor), Peter
   Stuyvesant (Dutch colonial governor), Uranus (castrated by his son Cronus),
   Earl of Uxbridge (of the Battle of Waterloo fame), Vincent Van Gogh (cut off
   part of his own ear), Josiah Wedgwood (leg amputated just below the knee),
   Paul Wittgenstein

amputees, sexual arousal derived from: teratophilia

amusement parks, UK: Alton Towers, Blackpool Pleasure Beach, Chessington
   World of Adventures, Drayton Manor Park, Oakwood, Pleasureland Southport,
   Thorpe Park

amusement/leisure parks/piers, most popular in Britain: 1) Blackpool Pleasure
   Beach; 2) Palace Pier, Brighton; 3) Segaworld, The Trocadero, Piccadilly
   Circus; 4) Eastbourne Pier; 5) Alton Rowers, Staffordshire; 6) Pleasureland,
   Southport; 7) Peter Pan's Adventure Island, Southend; 8) Legoland, Windsor;
   9) Chessington World of Adventures; 10) Pleasure Beach, Great Yarmouth

anaesthetic: first used during a surgical operation in 1842 by Dr Crawford W. Long
   of Georgia, USA. He applied ether to his patient

anaesthetic, fact: one in 500 patients under anaesthetic retain a degree of
   consciousness

anaesthetic, first patient to benefit from: James Venable (in 1842)

anaesthetists, patron saint of: René Goupil

anagram: invented by Lycrophon in 280 BC

anal intercourse: ace-fucking, back-scuttling, brown holing, buggery, chocolate
   cha-cha, Greek, tubing

anal passage: exhaust pipe, Marmite motorway, rectum

anarchists: Mikhail A. Bakunin, Noam Chomsky, Matt Drudge (famous for
   disseminating politically censored pictures on the Internet), Buenaventura

Durruti, Sebastien Faure, Emma Goldman, Daniel Guerin, the Haymarket
Martyrs, Ivan Illich, Peter Alexeyevich Kropotkin, Lucy Parsons, Pierre-Joseph
Proudhon, Nicola Sacco, Henry David Thoreau (author of *Civil Disobedience*),
Bartolomeo Vanzetti, Adolph Verloc (eponymous hero of Joseph Conrad's novel
The Secret Agent), Emiliano Zapata

anatomists: Raymond Dart, Galen, Henry Gray, Herophilus, Sir Richard Owen,
Andreas Vesalius

anatonyms (words that use part of the body as a verb): back (a project), eye
(a prospect), face (the music), finger (a suspect), foot (the bill), hand (in your
notice), head (a corporation), knuckle (down to work), neck (a member of the
opposite sex), rib (a colleague), shoulder (a responsibility), stomach (a horror
film), toe (the line)

ancestor, earliest: primogenitor

anchor: invented by Anacharis the Scythian in 592 BC

anchovy, adjective: engraulid

'and' symbol: ampersand (&)

Andorra: small European principality, situated in the Pyrenees between France
and Spain
  capital: Andorra la Vella
  currency: euro; formerly: French franc and Spanish peseta
  language: Catalan (official), French, Spanish
  religion: Roman Catholic
  status: semi-feudal co-principality
  population: 61% Spanish; 30% Andorrean, 6% French

androids: Frankenstein's monster, humanimal (from H.G. Wells' *The Island of
Dr Moreau*)

angel, adjective: angelic

angel, collective noun: chorus, host

angel experts: Theolyn Cortens, Doreen Virtue

Angel of Death: nickname for the Nazi concentration camp doctor Josef Mengele

angels, nine choirs of (as described in Christian tradition): seraphim, cherubim,
thrones, dominations, virtues, powers, principalities, archangels and angels

angelfish, adjective: squatinid

anger, extreme: apoplexy

anger, internalised: inrage

Angkor Wat: vast Hindu complex in Cambodia, arguably the largest religious
facility ever built. Constructed in the 12th century for King Suryavarman II, the
site boasts the longest running bas-relief in the world

angle, instruments for measuring: graphometer, protractor

angler, collective noun: exaggeration (joc.)

Angola: a republic in South-West Africa
  capital: Luanda
  currency: kwanza
  language: Portuguese (official), Bantu dialects
  religion: Christian

Angolan guerrilla war: 1961–1975

angry and famous: Achilles, Ludwig van Beethoven, Gordon Brown, Naomi
Campbell, Russell Crowe, God, Adolf Hitler, John McEnroe, Sean Penn, Queen
of Hearts (% Lewis Carroll), Gordon Ramsay, John Sweeney (investigative
journalist who lost his temper big-time with a Scientology representative on the
BBC's *Panorama* programme)

Angry Young Men: clique of British writers who emerged in the 1950s to express somewhat controversial viewpoints. They included Kingsley Amis, John Osborne, John Wain and Colin Wilson
animal, adjective: zoic
animal, dead, adjective: necrogenic
animal, first in space: a Russian dog called Laika (on 3 November 1957); second animals in space: two American mice called Laska and Benjy (on 13 December 1958)
animal, largest living: blue whale
animal, largest living on land: elephant
animal, longest: the ribbon worm, known to exceed 180 foot
animal, longest surviving: lingula, a marine animal that has been in existence for half a billion years
animal, sexual excitement derived from contact with: zooerasty, zoolagnia, zoophilia
animal authorities: Joy Adamson (lions), David Attenborough, David Bellamy, Dian Fossey (gorillas), Jane Goodall (chimpanzees), Steve Irwin (fierce creatures), Janet Mann (dolphins), Virginia McKenna (lions), Johnny Morris, Rick West (tarantulas)
animal behaviour, science of: ethology
animal communication, study of: zoosemiotics
Animal Crackers (1930 film), famous lines: Captain Spaulding (Groucho Marx) to Mrs Teasdale: "Why, you're one of the most beautiful women I've ever seen, and that's not saying much for you." Spaulding: "Well, you go Uruguay, and I'll go mine." Spaulding: "One morning I shot an elephant in my pyjamas. How he got in my pyjamas I dunno... But that's entirely irrelephant to what I'm talking about."
animal hide, aversion to: doraphobia
animal lover: philotherian
animal medal: Dickin Medal (the zoic equivalent of the Victoria Cross)
animal noises, involuntary blurting out of: aboiement (pronounced ah-bwah-mahn)
animal painters: Théodore Géricault, Sawrey Gilpin, Sir Edwin Landseer, Henri Rousseau, George Stubbs, Richard Symonds
animal rights bodies: American Humane Association (established in 1940), People for the Ethical Treatment of Animals (Peta)
animals, fear of: zoophobia
animals, patron saint of: Francis of Assisi
animals in advertising, most popular: 1) dog; 2) cat; 3) pig; 4) horse; 5) lion; 6) chimpanzee and other apes; 7) dolphin; 8) cow; 9) penguin; 10) elephant
animated actor: synthespian
animated cartoon, first: *Humorous Phases of Funny Faces* (1907)
animation terms: cartoon, cel, CGI, claymation, computer animation, digital, hand-drawn, layout, motion-capture, performance capture, stop-motion, 2-D, traditional cel animation, tradigital animation
animation, father of: Winsor McCay
animators: Aardman, Tex Avery, Joseph Barbera, Don Bluth, Walt Disney, Max Fleischer, Studio Ghibli, William Hanna, Hanna-Barbera, Ray Harryhausen, John Hubley, Chuck Jones, John Lasseter, Winsor McCay, Norman McLaren, Otto Messmer, Hayao Miyazaki, Nick Park, Pixar, Oliver Postgate, Nicholas and Stephen Quay, Lotte Reiniger, Jan Svankmajer, Frank Tashlin, UPA (United Productions of America)

ankle bones: malleolus, talus, tarsus (including the heel)

Ann Summers: retail chain specialising in lingerie and other sexually-related merchandise; first outlet opened in 1970

Annie Hall (1977 film), famous lines: Alvy Singer (Woody Allen): "I would never want to belong to any club that would have someone like me for a member"; Annie Hall (Diane Keaton): "Well, la-di-da"; Alvy Singer: "Hey! Don't knock masturbation. It's sex with someone I love"; Alvy Singer: "That was the most fun I've ever had without laughing"; Alvy Singer: "A relationship, I think, is, is like a shark, you know. It has to constantly move forward or it dies, and I think what we got on our hands is a dead shark"

anorexia, celebrity killed by: Karen Carpenter

ant, adjective: formic, formicine, myrmicine

ant, collective noun: army, colony, swarm

ant, crawl like an: formicate (verb)

ant, fact: the insect has the largest brain in proportion to its body than any other living creature

ant, young: antling

ant hill: formicarium, formicary

ant hill, adjective: formicarian

ant nest: formicary

ants, British: black ant, meadow ant, parasitic ant, red ant, slave-making ant, wood ant

ants, famous: Ant (from the *Ant and Bee* books for small children), Z-4195 (voiced by Woody Allen in the animated film *Antz*)

ants, fear of: myrmecophobia

ants, study of: myrmecology

ant bear: aardvark

Antarctic, explored by: Roald Amundsen (the first man to reach the South Pole), Richard Evelyn Byrd, Captain James Cook, Sir Edmund Hillary, Sir James Clark Ross, Robert Falcon Scott (played on film by John Mills)

anteater, adjective: myrmecophagine

antelope, adjective: alcelaphine, bubaline

antelope, collective noun: herd

antelope, young: calf, kid

anthology: florilegium

anthrax attacks in US: September 2001, when five people were killed

anthropologists: Carlos Castaneda, Mary Douglas, Edward Evans-Pritchard, Tom Harrisson, Thor Heyerdahl, Alfred Kinsey, Claude Lévi-Strauss, Margaret Mead, Desmond Morris, Knud Johan Victor Rasmussen, Clark Wissler

anthroposophy: spiritual movement founded by Rudolf Steiner

anticipation: prolepsis

antidepressant: happy pill, Prozac, Seroxat, SSRI

Antigua and Barbuda: a state in the Caribbean
    capital: St John's
    currency: East Caribbean dollar
    language: English
    religion: Christian

antiquary: Sir Robert Cotton

antiques authorities: David Dickinson, Arthur Negus, Hugh Scully

antiques dealer: Lovejoy

Antiques Roadshow: half-hour TV series examining the value of the public's possessions

first broadcast: 1979 on BBC1

presented by: Bruce Parker, Angela Rippon, Arthur Negus, Max Robertson, Hugh Scully, Michael Aspel and Fiona Bruce

antiseptic: first used in 1865

antiseptic, types of: acriflavine, borax, creosote, eucalyptus oil, iodine, phenol, thymol

Antwerp: diamond-cutting capital of the world

anus: asshole, bung, Cadbury channel, chocolate eye, chocolate runway, chocolate starfish, Elephant and Castle (Cockney Rhyming Slang for 'arse-hole'), exhaust pipe, hoop, kazoo, Khyber Pass (Cockney Rhyming Slang), manhole, north pole (Cockney Rhyming Slang for 'hole'), servant's entrance, third eye

anus, adjective: anal, proctal

anus, doctor of: proctologist

anus, science of: proctology

anus licking: anilingus

anvil of a blacksmith: stithy

Anzio Operation: campaign in Italy, 22 January 1944

AOB: any other business

AOC: appellation d'origine contrôlée (French guarantee of authenticity in food and wine)

AONB: Area of Outstanding Natural Beauty

AOR: adult-orientated rock (music)

Apache renegade: Geronimo

ape, adjective: simian

ape, ancestor: hominid

ape, collective noun: shrewdness

ape, sound: gibber

ape, young: infant

- see chimpanzees, monkeys, etc

aphrodisiacs: dewberry (as mentioned in *A Midsummer Night's Dream*), fennel, ginseng, hops, liquorice, mandrake, oysters, yohimbine bark

aphrodisiac drink: philtre

APK: audio press kit

Apocalypse Now (1979 film), famous lines: Lt. Col. Kilgore (Robert Duvall): "I love the smell of napalm in the morning... smells like victory;" Col. Kurtz (Marlon Brando): "The horror! The horror!" [last line]

Apocryphal books: Baruch, Esdras, Judith, Tobit

Apollo 13 (1995 film), famous line: Jim Lovell (Tom Hanks): "Houston, we have a problem"

apostles: Simon, Andrew, James, John, Philip, Bartholomew, Thomas, Matthew, James, Thaddaeus, Simon the Zealot, Judas Iscariot, Matthias

Apostrophe Protection Society: founded by John Richards

apothecary: Nostradamus

appeal, adjective: appellate (especially in a court of law)

appetite, enormous: polyphagia

appetite region of the brain: appestat

applause, professional provider of: claqueur

apple (of which there are over 6,000 varieties): Apple-john, Arkansas Black, Bastard Rough Coat, Belle de Boskoop, Bitterscale, Black Wilding, Blenheim Orange, Bloody Turk, Braeburn, Bramley, Bramley Seedling, Bringewood Pippin, Broadtail, Brown Cockle, Burr Knot, Claygate Pearmain, Cox's Orange,

Crab apple, D'Arcy Spice, dessert apple, Devonshire Quarrenden, Duck's Bill, Edwards VII, Eggleton Styre, Egremont Russett, Ellison's Orange, Extraordinaire, Fireside, First and Last, Foxwhelp, Freedom (USA), Gala, Golden Delicious, Golden Knob, Granny Smith, Great Expectations, Greensleeves, Grenadier, Hagloe Crab, Hoe, Hogshead, Idared LA, Irish Peach, James Grieve, Jazz, John-apple, Kenneth, Kentucky Redstreak, Laxton's Fortune, Laxton's Superb, Lord Derby, Lord Lambourne, McIntosh, Miller's Seedling, Monstrous Pippin, Newton Wonder, Pearmain (the first recorded apple variety in Britain), Peasgood's Nonesuch, Pink Lady, Pippin, Pitmaston Pineapple, Pride of Kent (aka Flower of Kent and Newton Apple), Red Delicious, Red Ingestrie, Reverend W. Wilkes, Ribston Pippin, Royal Gala, Sheep's Snout, Slack-my-girdle, Spartan, Starking, Sturmer, Sundowner, Suntan, Sweeting, Tom Putt, Tudor, Worcester Pearmain, Wyken Pippin

apple, fact: of the apples sold in the United Kingdom, only 20 per cent are indigenous

apple, Sir Isaac Newton's (which led to his exploration of gravity): Pride of Kent (aka Flower of Kent and Newton Apple)

apple brandy: calvados

apple-shaped: pomiform

apples crushed for cider-making: pomace

Aqua Libra: drink comprised of mineral water and fruit juice

aqueduct, longest in world: the 825-mile long Water Project in California (built in 1974)

AR: postcode for Arkansas

Arab: camel jockey, dune coon, sand nigger, towel head

Arabic words: couscous, fakir, harem, hashish, imam, jehad, kasbah, mufti, nadir, sheikh, yashmak

archaeologists: Hiram Bingham, Howard Carter, Sir Arthur Evans, Giuseppe Fiorelli, Jacquetta Hawkes, Indiana Jones, Alfred Kidder, Julian Richards, Heinrich Schliemann, John Lloyd Stephens, Sir Mortimer Wheeler, Sir Charles Woolley

archaeologists, patron saint of: Helen

archangels: Chamuel, Gabriel, Jophiel, Michael, Raphael, Uriel, Zadkiel

arch-shaped: arciform

archbishop, black (first in the Church of England): John Sentamu (Bishop of Birmingham)

archbishop, mode of verbal address: Your Grace

Archbishops of Canterbury: Augustine (first), Thomas Becket, George Carey, Donald Coggan, Thomas Cranmer, Geoffrey Fisher, William Laud, Michael Ramsey, Robert Runcie, Rowan Williams

archer: toxophilite

archers, famous: Apollo, Cupid, Eros, Legolas (from *The Lord of the Rings*), Pandarus, Paris, Philoctetes, Robin Hood, Sagittarius, William Tell

Archers, The: long-running radio soap

    location: Ambridge, just off the B3980, six miles south of Borchester and 17 miles west of Felpersham

    debut (in the Midlands): Whitsun, 1950

    national debut: Monday, 1 January 1951

    lead character: Eddie Grundy (played by Trevor Harrison)

    appreciation society: Archers Addicts (formed in 1990)

archery: toxophily

archery, adjective: toxophilite

archery lover or student: toxophilite

archery manufacturer: artillator

archery terms: American round, animal round, archer's paralysis, arm guard, barebow, battle clouts, belly (the side of the bow closest to the bow string), bowsight, broadhead, bullseye, clout, crest, crossbow, draw weight, drift (deviation of an arrow's trajectory due to wind), field archery, fingerstall, fletching, flight shooting, foot bow, green, King's round, longbow, Mediterranean draw, Mongolian draw, nock, petticoat (the outer fringe of a target), popinjay shooting, quiver, string dampener, wand, wand shooting

architects: Alvar Aalto, Sir Patrick Abercrombie, James Adam, Robert Adam, William Adam, Dankmar Adler, Leon Battista Alberti, Will Alsop, Tadao Ando, Thomas Archer, Sir Charles Barry, John Francis Bentley, Gian Lorenzo Bernini, Francis Bindon, G.F. Bodley, Francesco Borromini, Mario Botta, Donato Bramante, Lancelot Brown, Sir William Bruce, Isambard Kingdom Brunel, Filippo Brunelleschi, Daniel Burnham, Callicrates, John Carr, Hugh Casson, Richard Castle, Sir William Chambers, David Childs, Sir David Chipperfield, Charles Robert Cockerell, Sir Ninian Comper, Lucia Costa, George Dance, Philibert Delorme, Jeremy Dixon, Sir Terry Farrell, Hassan Fathy, Sir Norman Foster (aka Lord Foster of Thames Bank), Buckminster Fuller, James Gandon, Antoni Gaudí, Frank Gehry, James Gibbs, Cass Gilbert, Bruce Goff, Michael Graves, Walter Gropius, Zaha Hadid, Jules Hardouin Mansart, Nicholas Hawksmoor, Christine Hawley, Robert Hooke (largely responsible for the re-mapping of London after the Great Fire), Sir Michael Hopkins, Ictinus, Imhotep, Helmut Jahn, Sir Joshua Jebb (prison architect), Philip Johnson, Edward Jones, Sir Horace Jones, Inigo Jones, Louis I. Kahn, Jan Kaplický, William Kent, Kisho Kurokawa, Morris Lapidus, Sir Denys Louis Lasdun, (Charles) Le Corbusier, Daniel Libeskind, Adolf Loos, Sir Edwin Lutyens, Charles Rennie Mackintosh, Fumihiko Maki, Michelangelo Buonarroti, Ludwig Mies van der Rohe, John Nash, Oscar Niemeyer, Andrea Palladio, Sir Joseph Paxton, IM Pei, Cesar Pelli, Auguste Perret, Renzo Piano, Augustus Pugin, Sir Richard Rogers (aka Lord Rogers of Riverside), Eero Saarinen, Karl Friedrich Schinkel, Sir George Gilbert Scott, Sir Giles Gilbert Scott, Richard Norman Shaw, Sir Robert Smirke, Sir John Soane, Solness (from Ibsen's *The Master Builder*), Albert Speer, Sir Basil Spence, Sir James Stirling, Edward Stone, Louis Sullivan, Kenzo Tange, Yoshio Taniguchi, Quinlan Terry, John Utzon, Sir John Vanbrugh, Robert Venturi, Aston Webb, Philip Webb, Stanford White, William Wilkins, Sir Christopher Wren, Frank Lloyd Wright, James Wyatt

architects, patron saint of: Thomas the Apostle

architecture: "The masterly, correct and magnificent play of masses brought together in light" – Charles Le Corbusier

architecture, adjective: architectural, architectonic, oecodomic

architectural authorities: Charles Jencks, James Lees-Milne, Sir Nikolaus Pevsner

architectural prize: the Pritzker (USA)

architectural styles: Anglo-Saxon, art deco, art nouveau, arts and crafts, Aztec, baroque, Brutalist, Byzantine, classical, colonial, Corinthian, Doric, Dutch colonial, Egyptian, flamboyant, French Gothic, Georgian, Gothic, Ionic, Islamic, Japanese, Maya, modernism, organic, postmodernism, Renaissance, revival, robotic, rococo, Romanesque

Arctic Monkeys: rambunctious indie rock group formed in Sheffield, South Yorkshire, in 2003, comprised of Alex Turner (vocals, guitar), Jamie Cook

(guitar), Andy Nicholson (bass) and Matt Helders (drums). An overnight
success in England, the group saw their first album, *Whatever People Say
I Am, That's What I'm Not*, become the biggest selling debut in UK music
history
Ardennes Offensive: 16 December 1944 – 30 January 1945
Are You Being Served?: TV sitcom set on the Ladies' Fashions and Menswear floor
of a department store
written by Jeremy Lloyd and David Croft
broadcast: 8 September 1972–1 April 1985 on BBC1 (and adapted for the big
screen in 1977)
cast: Mollie Sugden (Mrs Slocombe), John Inman (Mr Humphries), Frank
Thornton (Captain Peacock), Trevor Bannister (Mr Lucas), Wendy
Richard (Miss Brahms), Arthur Brough (Mr Grainger), Nicholas Smith
(Mr Rumbold), Arthur English (Mr Harman)
Argentina: republic in South America
capital: Buenos Aires
currency: Argentine peso
language: Spanish
religion: Roman Catholic
patron saint: Our Lady of Lujan
waterfall: Iguaçú Falls
fact: famous for its corned beef
Argentinean and famous: Luis Bacalov (composer), Daniel Barenboim (now an
Israeli national), Jorge Luis Borges (writer), Juan Manuel Fangio (racing
driver), Leopoldo Galtieri (soldier and statesman), Carlos Gardel (pre-eminent
tango singer), Ernesto 'Che' Guevara, Ricardo Güiraldes (poet and novelist),
Mauricio Kagel (composer and dramatist), Diego Maradona, Lionel Messi
(footballer), Aristotle Onassis (born in Turkey), Ermindo Onega (footballer),
Cesar Pelli (architect), Eva Perón, Juan Domingo Perón (soldier and president),
Hugo Porta (rugby player), Manuel Puig (novelist, *Kiss of the Spider Woman*),
Juan Manuel de Rosas (dictator), Lalo Schifrin (composer), Esther Vilar
(playwright, *Speer*, etc), Guillermo Vilas (tennis player), Rafael Viñoly
(architect; Uruguayan-born)
Argentinean cruiser: Belgrano (torpedoed by the British in the Falklands' war)
argument: "Looking to each other for balance" - Kevin Costner
argument: altercation, barney, rumpus, set-to, slanging match, spat, tiff
argument, adjective: eristic
Ariadne on Naxos: opera by Richard Strauss first produced in 1912 in Stuttgart
(in a double- bill with Molière's play *Le Bourgeois Gentilhomme*)
Aristotle's school: Lyceum (established in 335 BC)
Arizona, 48th state (1912), Grand Canyon State
capital: Phoenix
birthplace of: Lynda Carter, Cesar Chavez (labour leader), Geronimo, Barry
Goldwater (politician and author), Charles Mingus, Stevie Nicks, Linda
Ronstadt
motto: 'Ditat Deus' ('God enriches')
state bird: cactus wren
state flower: saguaro cactus
state tree: palo verde
tourist attraction: Grand Canyon, the world's largest ravine
Arkansas, 25th state (1936), Land of Opportunity
capital: Little Rock

birthplace of: G. M. ('Broncho Billy') Anderson (real name: Max Aronson), Helen Gurley Brown, Glen Campbell, Johnny Cash, Eldridge Cleaver, Bill Clinton, Al Green, John Grisham, Alan Ladd, Josh Lucas (actor), Douglas MacArthur, Dick Powell (actor/singer), Billy Bob Thornton

motto: 'Regnat Populus' ('The people rule')

state bird: mockingbird

state flower: apple blossom

state tree: pine

tourist attraction: Hot Springs National Park

fact: the only state to pass a resolution on the correct way to pronounce its name (Ark-an-saw) – that is, it's illegal to pronounce Arkansas 'Ar-kansas' within the state boundaries

arm, adjective: brachial

arm bones: humerus, radius, ulna

armadillo: apar, giant armadillo, little hairy armadillo, nine-banded armadillo, peba, pink fairy armadillo, six-banded armadillo, three-banded armadillo

armadillo, adjective: dasypodid, tolypeutine, xenarthral

armadillo, fact: supposedly the only animal besides humans that can catch leprosy

armadillo plate: scute

armageddon, branch of theology dealing with the teachings of: eschatology

Armenia: republic in north-west Asia (formerly a part of Russia)

    capital: Yerevan

    currency: dram

    language: Armenian

    recent history, August 1990: establishes independence

    religion: Christian (Armenian Apostolic)

Armenians, famous: Charles Aznavour, Isabel Bayrakdarian (soprano), Erig Bogosian, Atom Egoyan (film director), Djivan Gasparyan (duduk maestro), Arshile Gorky (painter), Georgei Gurdjieff, Aram Khatchaturian (classical composer), Armen Takhtajan (botanist)

armour, entire complement: panoply

armour for the arm: vambrace

armour for the armpit: besagews

armour for the chest: breastplate

armour for the chest and back: cuirass

armour for the elbow: couter

armour for the face: visor

armour for the foot: sabaton

armour for the hand: gauntlet

armour for the knee: poleyn

armour for the shin: greave

armour for the shoulders: pauldron

armour for the thigh: cuisse

armour for the throat: gorget

armour for the upper arm: brassard, rerebrace

armourer: Andrea Ferrara

armpit: axilla

armpit, adjective: axillary

armpit, fact: the Koreans and Japanese have few of the axillary scent glands indigenous to the rest of humanity

armpit armour: besagews

arms dealers: Viktor Bout (aka 'The Merchant of Death'), Andrew Undershaft (from Shaw's *Major Barbara*)

arms manufactuer: Alfred Krupp
- see firearms and munition inventors

army, adjective: military

army, Cockney Rhyming Slang: Kate Karney (once a popular music hall performer)

army, Latin: exercitus

army divisions: division> regiment> battalion> formation> brigade> unit> company> platoon (25 to 50 men)> squad (eight to twelve men)

army recruitment slogan: 'Join the army and see the world'

arrow, adjective: sagittal

arrow, collective noun: sheaf

arrow, handle: stele

arrow holder: quiver

arrow feathers: fletching

arrow maker: artillator

arrow poison: curare

arrow slot (for attaching the bowstring): nock

arrow-shaped: beloid

arse, Cockney Rhyming Slang: bottle and glass

arson, adjective: incendiary

arsonists: James Aitken (aka John the Painter), Nero

art: "Of all lies, art is the least untrue" Gustave Flaubert; "Art might hold the mirror up to nature, but it only becomes art when someone tilts the mirror" - Howard Jacobson; "The difference between a craft and an art is that art ought never to repeat itself, whilst craft ought always to repeat itself" - Jonathan Meades; "Learning to enjoy art is a bit like learning to swim: if you don't do it early in life, the fear of drowning becomes over-whelming" - Richard Morrison; "Art is a lie that makes us realise truth" – Pablo Picasso; "Skill without imagination is craftsmanship and gives us many useful objects such as wickerwork picnic baskets. Imagination without skill gives us modern art" – Tom Stoppard; "Art is what you can get away with" - Andy Warhol; "The enemy of art is the absence of limitations" - Orson Welles; "Art is making something out of nothing and selling it" – Frank Zappa

art, patron saint of: Catharine of Bologna

art authority: Sister Wendy Beckett
- see art critics

Art Basel: the biggest contemporary art fair in the world, held in Basel, Switzerland

art collectors: Samuel Courtauld, Peggy Guggenheim, J. P. Morgan, Charles Saatchi

art critics: Lawrence Alloway (who coined the term 'pop art'), Charles Baudelaire, Clive Bell, John Berger, Jean Cassou, Roger Fry, Théophile Gautier, Clement Greenberg, Hilton Kramer, Osbert Lancaster, Wyndham Lewis, Ad Reinhardt, Franz Roh, Harold Rosenberg, John Ruskin, R.A.M. Stevenson, Thomas Wainewright (also an alleged poisoner)

art dealers: Leo Castelli, Daniel Cottier, Joseph Duveen

art fairs, leading: Arco (Madrid), Art Basel, Frieze (Regent's Park, London), Venice Biennale

art forgers: Tom Keating, Han van Meegeren, Robert Thwaites, Thomas Wainewright

art galleries in Britain, most popular: Kelvingrove Art Gallery and Museum (in Glasgow), National Gallery, National Portrait Gallery, Tate Britain, Tate Modern (world's most popular, with 5.5m visitors in its first year)

art historians: Sir Anthony Blunt, Sir Kenneth Clark, Matthew Collings, Dame
Helen Cooper, E.H. Gombrich, Francis Haskell, Eric Hobsbawm, Neil
MacGregor, Sir Nikolaus Pevsner, Sir John Rothenstein, Giorgio Vasari
artery, obstruction of: embolism
Arthur, father of: Uther Pendragon
Arthur, wife of: Queen Guinevere
Arthurian characters: King Arthur, Sir Bedivere (or Bedver), Sir Bors, Sir Calidore,
Elaine, Enid, Fisher King, Sir Galahad, Gawain, Geraint, Guinevere, Kay, Lady of
Shalott, Lancelot, Merlin, Mordred, Morgana (aka Morgan le Fay), Sir Pelleas,
King Pelles, Uther Pendragon, Perceval, Sir Tristram, Uther Pendragon, Viviane
(Lady of the Lake)
artichoke: a member of the thistle family which evolved in North Africa (or possibly
Sicily). The plant was first recorded in 1466
article (in English), noun used without: anarthrous (adjective)
artist: "An artist doesn't create beauty - he simply removes what prevents us from
seeing it" – a line from the 1994 French film *Elisa*
artists, contemporary: Carl Andre (whose exhibit of firebricks at the Tate caused a
sensation), Karel Appel, Francis Bacon, Georg Baselitz, Fernando Botero,
Tracy Emin, Lucian Freud, Maggi Hambling, Patrick Heron (Britain's foremost
abstract artist, who died March 1997), Damien Hirst ("the psycho wunderkind
of modern art"), David Hockney, Gary Hume, Sacha Jafri, Jasper Johns,
Michael Landy (who systematically destroyed his possessions in a shop
window of the old C&A in Oxford Street, London), Alexandra Nechita (child
prodigy), Marc Quinn, Robert Rauschenberg, Ad Reinhardt, Gerhard Richter,
Norman Rockwell, Jenny Saville, Frank Stella, Antoni Tiapies, Cy Twombly,
Euan Uglow (English painter, died in the summer of 2000), Gillian Wearing,
Rachel Whiteread
artists, patron saint of: Luke the Apostle
artist's field: canvas, collage, composition, pallette, spectrum, texture
artist's studio: atelier
arts, god of: Ptah (Egyptian mythology)
arts, patroness of: Athene (Greek), Minerva (Roman)
art terms: abozzo, acanthus (thistle motif on Corinthian columns), action painting,
alla prima, anamorphosis, aquarelle, arabesque, art nouveau, a trois crayons,
aureole, automatism, avante-garde, bas-relief, calligraphy, camaieu, chiaroscuro
(use of shadow delineation), collage, cubism, Dada, découpage, ebauche,
filigree, gilding, hatching, impasto (the use of laying on thick strokes),
impressionism, kinetic art, op art, realism, relief, Renaissance, rococo,
scrimshaw, stipple, surrealism, tempera, tenebrism, tessellated, thumbnail
sketch, tondo, tone, topographic landscape, traction fissure, trompe l'oeil
Aruba: island in the Caribbean, a dependency of the Netherlands
chief town: Oranjestad
Asbo: acronym for "anti-social behaviour order"
ASCII: American standard code for information interchange
asexual and famous: Frédéric Chopin, Sir Isaac Newton
Ash (acronym): Action on Smoking and Health
ash, adjective: cinerial, cinereous
Ashes, The: cricket test match played between England and Australia, so named
because the winning trophy – traditionally kept at the Lord's cricket ground
in London, regardless of which country wins - contains the ashes of a cricket
stump. The trophy is actually a pottery urn, donated to the English captain

Ivo Bligh by a group of Melbourne women after England lost to Australia in the 1882–83 series

aspirin: invented in 1859 by Heinrich Kolbe

aspirin, first available on prescription: May 1899, in Germany

Asprey & Garrard, 165–166 New Bond Street, London W1: family business that supplies the royal family with art, jewellery and silverware

ass, adjective: asinine

ass, collective noun: pace

ass, female: jenny

ass, male: jackass

ass, sound: bray

ass, worship of: onolatry

assassinated and famous: Alexander II of Russia, Thomas Becket, King Birendra of Nepal (along with ten other members of the royal family), Benazir Bhutto, Julius Caesar, Caligula, Michael Collins, Phoolan Devi, Zoran Djindjic, King Faisal of Saudi Arabia, Pim Fortuyn, Archduke Franz Ferdinand of Austria, Indira Gandhi, Mahatma Mohandas Gandhi, Rajiv Gandhi, James Garfield, Ian Gow (British Conservative politician), King Henry III of France, King Henry IV of France, John F. Kennedy, Robert Kennedy, Martin Luther King, Sergey Kirov, John Lennon, Abraham Lincoln, Anna Lindh (foreign minister of Sweden), Huey P. Long, Malcolm X, Jean-Paul Marat, William McKinley, Harvey Milk, Earl Louis Mountbatten, Benito Mussolini, Airey Neave, Nicholas II of Russia, Lee Harvey Oswald, Olof Palme, Pompey the Great, Yitzhak Rabin, Grigori Rasputin, Oscar Romero (Salvadorean archbishop), Leon Trotsky, Gianni Versace, Hendrik Verwoerd, Pancho Villa, Emiliano Zapata

assassins: John Bellingham (shot the British prime minister Spencer Perceval in the Houses of Parliament), John Wilkes Booth (shot Abraham Lincoln), Brutus (Julius Caesar), Samuel Byck (attempted to kill Richard Nixon by hijacking a jet with the intention of crashing it into the White House), Mark David Chapman (John Lennon), Andrew Cunanan (Gianni Versace), Leon Czolgosz (shot President William McKinley at the Pan-American Exposition in Buffalo), Aeon Flux (from the animated TV series), Lynette 'Squeaky' Fromme (attempted to kill President Gerald Ford in Sacramento), Charles Guiteau (shot Presidential candidate James Garfield), John W. Hinckley Jr (attempted to assassinate president Ronald Reagan as he left the Washington Hilton Hotel), Ramon Mercader (Leon Trotsky), Sarah Jane Moore (attempted to assassinate President Gerald Ford in San Francisco), Lee Harvey Oswald (shot John F. Kennedy dead in Dallas, Texas), James Earl Ray (Martin Luther King), Giuseppe Zangara (attempted to assassinate President-elect Franklin D. Roosevelt in Miami's Bayfront Park) - see murderers and serial killers

Assyrian general: Holofernes

asterisk: first featured in a British publication in Sir Philip Sidney's *Arcadia*

astrologers: Jeane Dixon, Russell Grant, Liz Greene, Mystic Meg, Nostradamus (aka Michel de Notredame), Paracelsus, Michael Scott, Shelley von Strunckel, Patric Walker

astrology, muse of: Urania

astrology annual/publication: *Old Moore Almanac*

astronauts: Edwin E. 'Buzz' Aldrin (the second man to set foot on the moon), Neil Armstrong (the first man to walk on the moon), Alan L. Bean (the fourth man to walk on the moon), Gerald Carr, Eileen Collins (commanded the Space

Shuttle Columbia), Charles Conrad Jr (the third man to walk on the moon),
Charles M. Duke (the tenth man to walk on the moon), Dr Michael Foale (first
Briton to walk in space), Yuri Gagarin (Russian, the first man to travel in
space), Edward G. Gibson, John Glenn (the first American to orbit the earth),
Flash Gordon, Bernard Harris (first black man to walk in space), James B.
Irwin (the eighth man to walk on the moon), Alexei Leonov (the first man to
walk in space, on 18 March 1965), Jim Lovell (who on the abortive Apollo
13 mission, said, "Houston, we have a problem"), Dr Shannon Lucid (US
cosmonaut trapped on the Russian space station Mir), Edgar D. Mitchell (sixth
man to walk on the moon and an unquestioning believer in UFOs), Stephen S.
Oswald, William R. Pogue, Sally Ride (first US woman in space), David R.
Scott (the seventh man to walk on the moon), Helen Sharman (first Briton in
space), Alan B. Shepard (the fifth man to walk on the moon), Valentina
Tereshkova (the first woman in space), Gherman S. Titov (Russian, the second
man to orbit the earth), Edward H. White (the first American to walk in space),
Yang Liwei (China's first astronaut), John W. Young (the ninth man to walk on
the moon)
- see space travellers

astronauts, British: Michael Foale, Nicholas Patrick, Piers Sellers,. Helen Sharman
(the first Briton in space)

astronaut, female, first in space: Valentina Tereshkova (as of 16 June 1963)

astronauts, patron saint of: Joseph of Cupertino

astronomers: Archimedes, Benjamin Banneker, Friedrich Bessel, Tycho Brahe,
Richard Carrington, Nicolaus Copernicus, Sir Arthur Eddington, Eratosthenes,
Galileo Galilei, Sir Francis Graham-Smith (astronomer royal), Asaph Hall,
Edmund Halley, Gerald Hawkins (examined the phenomenon of crop circles
and argued that Stonehenge was an observatory), Caroline Lucretia Herschel,
Sir John Herschel, Sir William Herschel, Hipparchus, Jeremiah Horrocks, Sir
Fred Hoyle (author of *The Nature of the Universe*), Edwin Hubble (noted for
his investigation into the recession of the galaxies), Milton Lasell Humason,
Hypatia, Johannes Kepler (who proposed the theory of planetary motion),
Pierre-Simon Laplace, Edward Maunder, Maria Mitchell, Sir Patrick Moore,
Sir Isaac Newton, Omar Khayyám, Jean Picard, Ptolemy, Sir Martin Rees
(astronomer royal), Sir Martin Ryle, Carl Sagan, Giovanni Schiaparelli, Johann
Schröter, Dr Percy Seymour, Iosif Shklovsky, Vesto Slipher, Willem de Sitter,
Fred Whipple, Sir Arnold Wolfendale (astronomer royal), Fritz Zwicky (noted
for his study of supernovae)

astronomer's muse: Urania

astronomical distance: light year, parsec

astronomy, muse of: Urania

astrophysicists: Charles Abbot, Johannes Kepler, Georges Lemaître, Edward Milne

ATB: all the best

atheist: Richard Dawkins

Athens, birthplace of: Melina Mercouri, Plato, Timon of Athens

athletes: Kriss Akabusi, Nikolay Avilov, Fanny Blankers-Koen, Avery Brundage,
Zola Budd, Galina Bystrova, Milt Campbell, Chi Cheng, Linford Christie,
Aleksandra Chudina, Ronald Clarke, Hestrie Cloete, Sebastian Coe, Babe
Didrikson, Jonathan Edwards, Ray Ewry, Dick Fosbury, Sally Gunnell, Jürgen
Hingsen, Kinue Hitomi, Colin Jackson, Bruce Jenner, Sabine John, Rafer
Johnson, Marion Jones, Carl Lewis, Denise Lewis, Greg Louganis, Dean
Macey, Bob Mathias, Diane Modahl, Glenn Morris, Paavo Nurmi, Dan

O'Brien, Harold Osborn, Micheline Ostermeyer, Steve Ovett, Jesse Owens, Eulace Peacock, Mary Peters, Irina Press, Mary Rand, Wilma Rudolph, Kelly Sotherton, Mark Spitz, Irena Szewinska, Daley Thompson, Dame Tanni Grey-Thompson, Jim Thorpe, Jane Tomlinson, Bill Toomey, Allan Wells, Yvette Williams, Bärbel Wöckel, Yang Cguang-kwang

athlete's foot: tinea

Atlanta, birthplace of: Bobby Jones (golfer), Martin Luther King, Brittany Murphy, OutKast, Jerry Reed (C&W singer), Kelly Rowland, Steven Soderbergh (filmmaker), Kanye West

Atlanta, formerly known as Terminus (1837–1845)

Atlanta river: Chattahoochee

Atlanta tourist attraction: Stone Mountain Memorial (featuring Jefferson Davies, Robert E. Lee and Stonewall Jackson on horseback)

Atlantis: lost Utopia first described by Plato in 360 BC

Atlas's daughters: Hyades

ATM: automated telling machine

atmosphere, components of: nitrogen (78%), oxygen (21%), argon (1%), water vapour and carbon dioxide

atmosphere levels: troposphere (closest to the earth's surface), stratosphere, mesosphere, ionosphere (combining the D region, the E region and the F region, aka the Appleton layer), thermosphere, exosphere (furthest from the earth's surface)

atmosphere furthest from the earth: exosphere

atmosphere, study of: aerology

atomic constituents: electron, proton, neutron, quark, string

atrium, adjective: atrial

atrocities, fear of: teratophobia

attorney: Benjamin Matlock (from TV's *Matlock*)
    - see barristers, lawyers

attorneys, patron saints of: Thomas More and Raymond of Penyafort

aubergine: brinjal (in Indian cuisine), eggplant (USA), melitzanes (in Greek cuisine)

aubergine dish: baigan ka tikka, melanzane alla parmigiana, moussaka, ratatouille

auctioneer: John Sotheby

auctioneer houses: Bonhams, Butcher Henry International, Christie's, Cooper and Owen (specialising in entertainment), Phillips International, Sotheby's, Terrence Butts

auction web site: eBay

Audi car slogan: 'Vorsprung durch Technik' (meaning "Advancement through technology")

auditor: "Someone who arrives after the battle and bayonets all the wounded" (popular joke)

auk, collective noun: colony

Auld Lang Syne: Scottish song traditionally sung on New Year's Eve, meaning "old long since" or "the good old days". The melody first appeared around 1700 and parts of the song materialised in a 16th century poem, while the modern version was published in 1796. Robert Burns wrote two of the five verses

aunt, adjective: materteral (very rare and used sententiously)

auras: astral body (the more spiritual in nature and of greater volume), etheric double (which barely projects beyond the skin, is partially linked to the corporeal body and is consequently more visible)

Auschwitz: Nazi concentration camp in Poland responsible for the extermination of 1,100,000 human lives

Australia: country situated between the Pacific and the Indian Ocean that gained its independence from the United Kingdom in 1901

    capital: Canberra

    currency: Australian dollar

    language: English

    religion: Christian

    first prime minister: Edmund Barton

    music groups: AC/DC, Air Supply, Crowded House, INXS, Men at Work, Mental As Anything, Rocket Science, Silverchair, The Vines

    nickname: Down Under, Oz

    patron saint: Our Lady Help of Christians

    railway: the Ghan railway (a continuous 1,800-mile track between Adelaide and Darwin, opened on 18 September 2003)

    fact: in 1989, 40 per cent of Australian adults were overweight; by 1995, the figure had reached 55.2 per cent

Australian actors: Kerry Armstrong, Eric Bana, Jacinda Barrett, Ray Barrett, Cate Blanchett, Bryan Brown, Tom Burlinson, Rose Byrne, Toni Collette, Abbie Cornish, Judy Davis, Portia De Rossi, Jason Donovan, Colin Friels, Mel Gibson (born in New York), Rachel Griffiths, John Hargreaves, Chris Haywood, Paul Hogan, Nicholas Hope, Barry Humphries, Bill Hunter, Hugh Jackman, Norman Kaye, Graham Kennedy, Bill Kerr, Nicole Kidman, Anthony LaPaglia, Heath Ledger, Sophie Lee, Craig McLachlan, Julian McMahon, Kylie Minogue, Radha Mitchell, Helen Morse, Frances O'Connor, Barry Otto, Guy Pearce, Susie Porter, Richard Roxburgh, Geoffrey Rush, Yahoo Serious (born Greg Pead), Noah Taylor, Rod Taylor, Jack Thompson, Naomi Watts (born in England), David Wenham, Hugo Weaving, Peta Wilson

Australian composers: Percy Grainger, John Williams (also an accomplished guitarist), Malcolm Williamson

Australian novelists: Elias Canetti, Peter Carey, Miles (Stella) Franklin, Helen Garner, Xavier Herbert, Thomas Keneally, David Malouf, Colleen McCullough, Frank Moorhouse, Randolph Stow, P(amela) L(yndon) Travers, Patrick White (born in London), Tim Winton, Markus Zusak

Australian playwrights: Robert Amos, Richard Beynon, Thomas Louis Esson, Oriel Gray, Dorothy Hewett, Jack Hibberd, Ray Lawler, Barry Oakley, Hal Porter, John Romeril, Alan Seymour, Patrick White (born in London), David Williamson

Australian outlaws: Ben Hall, Ned Kelly

Australian painters: Sir William Dobell, Rolf Harris, Sir Sidney Nolan, Tom William Roberts, Charles Wheeler

Australian princess: Mary Donaldson (a former estate agent from Hobart) aka Her Royal Highness Crown Princess Mary Elizabeth

Australian singers: Delta Goodrem, Michael Hutchence, Natalie Imbruglia, Olivia Newton-John, Ronald Belford 'Bon' Scott (lead vocalist of AC/DC)

Australian statesmen: Edmund Barton (first prime minister, from 1901 to 1903), Alfred Deakin, Andrew Fisher, Malcolm Fraser, Bob Hawke, Sir Harold Holt, John Howard, Billy Hughes, Paul Keating, Sir Robert Menzies, Gough Whitlam

Austria: republic in central Europe

    capital: Vienna

    currency: euro; formerly: Austrian schilling

language: German

religion: Roman Catholic

villages of note: Fucking, Windpassing (famous for their name, rather than any geographic distinction)

Austrian and famous: Klaus Maria Brandauer, Alfred Brendel, Anton Bruckner, Christian Doppler (physicist), Falco (real name: Johann Hölzel), Sigmund Freud, Kurt Gödel (mathematician and philosopher), Peter Handke (dramatist and poet), Michael Haneke, Joseph Haydn, Adolf Hitler, Franz Kafka, Natascha Kampusch (ten-year-old girl held captive beneath a garage for eight years), Herbert von Karajan, Gustav Klimt, Oskar Kokoschka (painter, poet and playwright), Hedy Lamarr, Niki Lauda, Gustav Mahler, Marie Antoinette, Wolfgang Amadeus Mozart, Ferdinand Porsche (designer of the Volkswagen), Max Reinhardt, Joseph Roth (novelist), Maximilian Schell, Arthur Schnitzler, Romy Schneider, Arnold Schoenberg, Franz Schubert, Arnold Schwarzenegger (later took up American citizenship), Rudolf Steiner, Johann Strauss the Elder, Johann Strauss the Younger, Josef Von Sternberg (filmmaker), Erich Von Stroheim (actor and filmmaker), Kurt Waldheim, Oskar Werner, Simon Wiesenthal, Ludwig Wittgenstein, Fred Zinnemann, Stefan Zweig (playwright and novelist)

Austrian composers: Alban Berg, Anton Bruckner, Karl Czerny, Joseph Haydn, Gustav Mahler, Wolfgang Amadeus Mozart, Arvo Pärt (born in Estonia), Arnold Schoenberg, Franz Schubert, Johann Strauss the Elder, Johann Strauss the Younger, Anton Von Webern

Austrian emperor: Kaiser

Austrian painters: Gustav Klimt, Egon Schiele

Austrian princess: Marie Antoinette

Austro-Prussian War: 1866

author, adjective: auctorial

authors, patron saints of: Francis de Sales, John the Apostle, Lucy of Syracuse

authors, young: Katie Chadd, seven (*The Snail Who Lost His Shell*), Daisy Ashford, nine (*The Young Visiters*; 1860s, Caitlin Moran, 13 (*The Chronicles of Narmo*), Mary Shelley, 19 (*Frankenstein*)

autistic character: Raymond Babbitt (played by Dustin Hoffman in *Rain Man*)

autobiography: "Probably the most respectable form of lying" – Humphrey Carpenter

autobiography in the English language, first: by the religious fanatic Margery Kemp, who dictated her life story (*The Boke of Margery Kempe*) to a priest between 1431 and 1438

auto-nod: a movement of the head intended to show interest

Avengers, The: cult, fantastical and macabre British TV series featuring Patrick Macnee as John Steed, a bowler-hatted secret agent with cane (a character inspired by Ralph Richardson's Charles Hammond from the 1939 spy film *Q Planes*). Steed first appeared in the ABC melodrama *Police Surgeon* (1960), starring Ian Hendry, but evolved into a vehicle for the debonair Macnee when Hendry dropped out. Steed had three female accomplices in 161 episodes and the series spawned a spin-off, *The New Avengers* (1976–1977), also with Macnee, and a feature-length movie (1998) with Ralph Fiennes as Steed, Uma Thurman as Emma Peel and Sean Connery as the villainous Sir August de Wynter

created by Sydney Newman

broadcast: 7 January 1961–21 May 1969

cast: Patrick Macnee (John Wickham Gascone Berresford Steed), Honor Blackman (Dr Catherine 'Cathy' Gale), Diana Rigg (Emma Peel), Linda Thorson (Tara King), Ian Hendry (Dr David Keel)

aviation, patron saint of: Joseph of Cupertino

aviation entrepreneurs: Richard Branson, Stelios Haji-Ioannou, Sir Freddie Laker

aviators: Henry H. Arnold, Floyd Bennett, Louis Blériot, Richard Evelyn Byrd, Amelia Earhart, Howard Hughes, W.E. Johns, Amy Johnson (the first woman to fly solo from England to Australia), Charles Lindbergh, James Mollison (married to Amy Johnson), Wiley Post, Charles Rolls, Orville and Wilbur Wright
- see pilots, fighter pilots

aviators, patron saint of: Thérèse of Lisieux

avocado: fruit eaten as a vegetable, originating in Central America. Also known as an alligator pear

avocado sauce: guacamole

award ceremonies, fact: in 2000 there were a total of 564 showbiz awards' ceremonies, at which 4,025 trophies were handed out

awards: Academy Award, Adult Video News Awards, Alfred B. Nobel Prize, American Music Awards, BAFTA, Booker Prize, CFDA (Council of Fashion Designers of America), César (French Oscar), Clio, Emmy, Felix (European Oscar), Genie (Canadian Oscar), Golden Globe (film and TV), Golden Kite (presented by the Society of Children's Book Writers), Grammy, Mercury Music Prize, National Association for the Advancement of Colored People Awards, National Book Award, Newbery Medal (presented by the Association for Library Services to Children), Oscar, People's Choice Awards, Pulitzer Prize, Screen Actors Guild Awards, Tony, Whitbread

axe: invented by Daedalus of Athens in 1240 BC (according to legend)

AZ: postcode for Arizona

A-Z of London atlas: originally compiled by Phyllis Pearsall

Azerbaijan: republic in north-west Asia
    capital: Baku
    currency: manat
    language: Azerbaijani
    religion: Shiite Muslim

Aztec emperor: Moctezuma (aka Montezuma) II

B

Baader-Meinhof Gang: Andreas Baader, Gudrun Ennslin, Ulrike Meinhof

baboon: drill, gelada, hamadryas, mandrill, sphinx

baboon, collective noun: rumpus, troop

baboon, female: babuina

baboon, young: infant

baboon god: Khonsu (Egyptian mythology)

baby, adjective: infantile

baby killers: Bruno Hauptmann (executed for the murder of the baby boy of Charles Lindbergh), Herod, Louise Woodward
- see child killers

Babylonian king: Belshazzar

Babylonian lovers: Pyramus and Thisbe

bachelors, patron saint of: Luke the Apostle

back, adjective: dorsal, lumbar, notal, tergal

back parts: loin, sacral dimples, scapula, spine, trapezius

back scratching during sex: amychesis

backpacker: Peter Falconio (murdered by Bradley Murdoch in July of 2001 in Australia)

backward sensation, moving: vection illusion (created when one is stationary but another vehicle is moving)

bacteria, adjective: bacteroid

bacteria, collective noun: culture

bacteria, fact: human bacteria fights off other, potentially harmful bacteria

bacteria, study of: bacteriology

bacteriologists: Emil von Behring, Jules Jean Baptiste Vincent Bordet, Charles Calmette, Paul Ehrlich, Christiaan Eijkman, Sir Alexander Fleming, Hans Gram, Sir William B. Leishman, Hideyo Noguchi, Louis Pasteur, Sir Ronald Ross

bacteriology, father of: Louis Pasteuir

bacterium, plural: bacteria

bad breath, agents: alcohol, antidepressants, antihistamines, coffee, fish, mouthwash (amazingly), tobacco

bad breath, antidotes: chewing gum, cinnamon, cloves, dark green vegetables, eucalyptus, lemon, mint, parsley, water (and plenty of it)

badger, adjective: meline, mustelid

badger, collective noun: cete

badger, fact: the mammal is the largest non-human carnivore in Britain

badger, famous: Badger (from *Wind in the Willows*), Bill Badger (friend of Rupert Bear), Cornelius (from the film *Once Upon a Forest*), Frances (from the series of children's books by Frances Hoban), Gloria (from the series of children's books by Frances Hoban), Josiah (pet belonging to Theodore Roosevelt)

badger, female: sow

badger, male: boar

badger, young: cub, kit

badminton missile: shuttlecock

bag: duffel bag, Gladstone bag, holdall, knapsack, mussuck (leather bag for carrying water), pannier, papoose (bag for carrying a baby on the back), pocketbook, portmanteau, rucksack, satchel, tote bag, valise, vanity bag
- see handbags

bagpipe: first appeared 51 AD

bagpipe drone: bourdon, skirl

bagpipe lament: pibroch, piobaireachd

bagpipe player, famous: John D. Burgess

Bahamas: nation comprising a group of more than 700 Caribbean islands
   capital: Nassau
   currency: Bahamian dollar
   language: English
   fact: while the Bahamas constitute over 700 coral islands, only twenty of them are inhabited

Bahrain: independent sheikdom in the Persian Gulf comprising several islands
   capital: Manama (on the largest island)
   currency: Bahrain dinar
   language: Arabic
   religion: Muslim

bait for fish: chum (usually made of chopped fish)

baker, collective noun: tabernacle

bakers, patron saint of: Elizabeth of Hungary and Nicholas

baking, adjective: panary

Balaclava, Battle of: 25 October 1854 (unsuccessful Russian offensive on the British base)

bald and famous: Errol Brown, Yul Brynner, Winston Churchill (almost), Cecil B. DeMille, Vin Diesel, Duncan Goodhew (swimmer), Richard Fairbrass (of Right Said Fred), William Haigh, Isaac Hayes, Nick Hornby, Huffty (lesbian TV presenter), Henri-Desire Landru (serial killer nicknamed 'Bluebeard'), Moby, Benito Mussolini, Sinead O'Connor (sometimes), Telly Savalas, Michael Stipe, Erich von Stroheim, David Walliams, Irvine Welsh, Bruce Willis

balding: follicularly challenged (pc)

baldness: acomia, alopecia, phalacrosis

baldness, adjective: calvous

ballerinas – see ballet dancers

ballet companies, world's 10 best: 1) L'Opera Ballet (Paris); 2) Ballet of the Marinsky Theatre (aka the Kirov) (St Petersburg); 3) Royal Danish Ballet (Copenhagen); 4) Royal Ballet Company (London); 5) The Birmingham Royal Ballet (Birmingham, UK); 6) New York City Ballet; 7) American Ballet Theater (New York); 8) Australian Ballet (Melbourne); 9) National Ballet of Canada (Toronto); 10) Houston Ballet Foundation. *And not forgetting*: Ballet Frankfurt, Bolshoi (Moscow), Joffrey Ballet of Chicago, National Ballet of China (Beijing), Pacific Northwest Ballet (Seattle), San Francisco Ballet

ballet critic: Clement Crisp

ballet dancers: Carlos Acosta, Altynai Asylmuratova, Mikhail Baryshnikov, Pierre Beauchamp, Deborah Bull, Darcey Bussell, Maria Camargo, Michael Clark, Alina Cojocaru, Adam Cooper, Jonathan Cope, Dame Margot Fonteyn, Dame Beryl Grey, Sylvie Guillem, Rosella Hightower, Sir Kenneth Macmillan, Natalia Makarova, Dame Alicia Markova, Bronislava Nijinska, Vaslav Nijinsky, Rudolf Nureyev, Anna Pavlova, Rupert Pennefather, Maya Plisetskaya, Dame Marie Rambert, Tamara Rojo, Marie Sallé, Moira Shearer, Alina Somova, Rasta Thomas (teenage Kirov sensation), Galina Ulanova, Dame Ninette de Valois, Diana Vishneva (Kirov ballerina), Sarah Wildor

ballet impresario: Sergei Diaghilev

ballet moves: arabesque, assemblé, cambre, enlèvement, entrechat, gargouillade, glissade, jeté, pirouette, plie, saute

ballet rail: barre

ballet teachers: Pierre Beauchamp, Carlo Blasis, Rosella Hightower, Christian Johansson, Kirsten Ralov, Vera Volkova

ballet terms: attitude, en pointe, fermé, fouetté, pas de deux, soutenu

Ballo in maschero, Un: opera by by Giuseppe Verdi first produced in Rome 17 February 1859

balloon: first appeared in 1670

balloon flight, manned; first: November 1783, in which Pilatre de Rozier and the Marquis d'Arlandes were carried seven miles at a height of 3,000 feet

balloon flight, first to circle the world: *Breitling Orbiter 3*, piloted by Brian Jones of Britain and Bertrand Piccard of Switzerland, who completed their trip in 19 days in March of 1999

balloon, hot air: invented by Joseph and Jacques Montgolfier in 1783

balloons, fear of: globophobia

ball-point pen: devised in 1938 by the Hungarian sculptor and hypnotist László Bíró

ball-shaped: conglobate

balloonists: Jean-Pierre Blanchard, Richard Branson, Jacques Charles, Phileas Fogg, John Jeffries, Jacques and Joseph Montgolfier, Auguste Piccard, Jean Felix Piccard

Baltimore, birthplace of: John Wilkes Booth, Charles S. Dutton, Philip Glass, Billie Holiday, Barry Levinson, Babe Ruth, Upton Sinclair (novelist), Sisqo, Anne Tyler, John Waters, Edward Witten (theoretical physicist)

Baltimore, river: Patapsco

Bambi (1942 film), famous lines: Bambi: "What happened, Mother? Why did we all run?" Bambi's mother: "Man was in the forest."; Bambi: "Mother! Where are you, Mother? Mother!"; Great Prince of the Forest: "Your mother can't be with you any more."

bamboo sticks, combat with: kendo

banana, fact: first imported to Britain (from the Canaries) in 1882; regular trade of bananas to Britain started from 1901

banana, fact: the fruit's vulnerability stems from the fact that it is a genetically decrepit mutant - today's banana is the descendant of rare seedless mutants propagated by Stone Age man. Since there is no sexual reproduction involved, these seedless bananas are all virtual clones of one another

banana disease: Black Sigatoka, a fungal disease that is laying waste crops from the Amazon to Uganda

banana-like fruit: plantain

bandit queens: Phoolan Devi, Belle Starr

bandleaders: Count Basie, Dave Brubeck, Hoagy Carmichael, Chick Corea, Billy Cotton, Miles Davis, Jimmy Dorsey, Tommy Dorsey, Eddy Duchin, Duke Ellington, Benny Goodman, Lionel Hampton, Woody Herman, Stan Kenton, Glenn Miller, Charles Mingus, Jelly Roll Morton, Don Redman, Artie Shaw, John Philip Sousa, Sun Ra, Jack Teagarden, Bobby Vinton, Lawrence Welk, Paul Whiteman

Bangkok: Good Time City

Bangkok: "City of angels by tradition, city of sin by lurid reputation, city of horrendous traffic by common consent" - Andrew Harvey

Bangladesh: republic in southern Asia, formerly known as East Bengal (until 1947) and East Pakistan (until 1970)

    capital: Dhaka

    currency: taka

    language: Bangla (Bengali)

    religions: Sunni Muslim (85%), Hindu (14%)

Bangladeshi president: Ziaur Rahman (1977–1981)

banjo players: Béla Fleck, Taj Mahal

bank: "A bank is a place that will lend you money if you can prove that you don't need it" - Bob Hope

bank, connected words: ATM, bank draft, certified cheque, clearing house, debit, deposit, joint account, money order, overdraft, safety deposit box, standing order, teller, vault, withdrawal

bank, Queen's: Coutts & Co.

bank, world's largest: Citigroup

bank clerk: Joseph K (from Kafka's *The Trial*)

bank note, fact: notes in Britain were individually 'signed' until the 1850s

bank note, parts of: serial number, thread mark, watermark

bank robbers: Clyde Barrow, Christopher Clarkson (arrested in 2005 after spending 30 years on the run), Thomas Crown, John Dillinger, Charles 'Pretty Boy' Floyd, Jesse James, Jacques Mesrine, Bonnie Parker, Cole Younger

bankers: Robert Barclay, Roberto Calvi (found hanged under Blackfriars Bridge, London, in 1982), Sir Fred Goodwin, Amadeo Giannini, Edward Harkness, Nick Leeson (rogue trader who brought down Barings' bank), J. P. Morgan, Robin Leigh-Pemberton, James Loeb, Medici family, Mayer Amschel Rothschild - see economists, financiers

bankers, collective noun: wunch

bankers, patron saint of: Matthew

bankrupt and famous: Kim Basinger, Peter Bogdanovich, Gary Coleman, Gabriele D'Annunzio, Thomas Jefferson, MC Hammer, Burt Reynolds, Debbie Reynolds, Sir Walter Scott, Mike Tyson, Oscar Wilde

banks: Abbey National, Alliance & Leicester, Barclays, Barings, Bradford & Bingley, Citigroup, Coutts & Co., CSFB, Drummonds, Halifax, HSBC, Lloyds TSB, Midland, NatWest, Royal Bank of Scotland, Santander, UBS, Woolwich

banquet, adjective: Lucullan

Bantu warrior, collective noun: impi

baptismal water: laver

Barbados: independent state in the Caribbean, a former British colony
   capital: Bridgetown
   currency: Barbados dollar
   language: English and Bajan (Barbadian English dialect)
   religion: Anglican (70%), Methodist (9%), Roman Catholic (4%)
   birthplace of: Minnie Driver (actress/singer), Rihanna

barbed wire: patented in 1867 by Lucien B. Smith, in the US; first manufactured in 1874 by Joseph Glidden, in the US

barbers: Figaro, Sweeney Todd

barber, collective noun: babble

The Barber of Seville: opera by Gioacchino Rossini first produced in Rome in 1816

Barbie: doll created by Ruth Handler, launched in 1959

Barcelona: Catalan capital
   birthplace of: Daniel Brühl (actor), José Carreras, Joan Miró
   cathedral: the Sagrada Familia (designed by Antonio Gaudí) site of the 1992 Olympic Games

Bard, the: nickname for William Shakespeare

barefoot: discalced (said of a nun or friar)

barefoot divas: Abebe Bikila (Ethiopian runner), Zola Budd, Cesária Évora, Peter Jackson, Diane Keaton, Beatrix Kiddo (from the 2003 film *Kill Bill*), Kate Moss, Nicole Richie, Sandie Shaw, Joss Stone

baritones: Sir Thomas Allen, Peter Dawson, Simon Keenlyside, Aldo Protti, Harold Williams

bark (of the canine variety), adjective: latrant

bark (of the tree variety), adjective: cortical

barley, adjective: hordeaceous

barman, collective noun: promise

barnacle, adjective: balanid

barometer: invented in 1643 by Evanglelista Torricelli, in Italy

baron, mode of verbal address: Your Lordship

baroness, mode of verbal address: Your Ladyship

barracuda, adjective: percesocine

barracuda, collective noun: battery

barrel maker: hooper

barrel organ: invented circa 1800 by Giovanni Barberi

barrel repairer: hooper

barrel-shaped: dolioform

barrier of spikes: cheval-de-frise

barristers: Clive Anderson, Tony Blair, Cherie Booth (later Blair), Sir William Garrow, Dame Brenda Hale, John Mortimer, Sir Robert Morton (from *The Winslow Boy*), Geoffrey Robertson (Amnesty International's 'pet barrister'), Cornelia Sorabji

baseball, fact: the game was first recorded in 1744 as 'basteball'

baseball bat: Louisville Slugger

baseball club, first established: The Knickerbocker Club, on 13 September 1845

baseball game, first, professional: played in 1846 in Hoboken, New Jersey

baseball players: Hank Aaron, Grover Alexander, Johnny Lee Bench, Vida Blue, Barry Bonds, Roger Clemens, Ty Cobb, Dizzy Dean, Joe DiMaggio, Lou Gehrig, Catfish Hunter, Reggie Jackson, Ben Johnson, Sandy Koufax, Connie Mack, Mickey Mantle, Jackie Robinson, Pete Rose, Babe Ruth (real name: George Herman Ruth)

BASIC: Beginner's All-Purpose Symbolic Linstruction Code

basket: chip, coop (for catching fish), corf (for holding fish alive in the water), crate, creel, dillybag, gabion, hamper, linen basket, lobster pot, pannier, punnet (to hold fruit or vegetables), seed-lip, skep, trug, work-basket, w.p.b. (waste-paper basket)

basketball: invented by Dr James Naismith in 1891

basketball moves: draw a foul, dribble, feed, give and go, jam, jump shoot, pick and roll, pivot, pullup, reverse lay-up, run and gun, slam dunk, stuff, trap

basketball coach: Adolph Rupp

basketball players: Kareem Abdul-Jabbar, Kobe Bryant, Wilt 'the Stilt' Chamberlain (the first man to perfect the 'slam dunk'), Alan Iverson, LeBron James, Earvin 'Magic' Johnson, Michael Jordan, Kevin McHale, Cheryl Miller (the first woman to dunk a ball in regulation play), Steve Nash, Michael Olowkandi, Shaquille O'Neal, Dennis Rodman, Yao Ming

basketball player, slang: hoopster

bass, collective noun: shoal

bass-baritone: Bryn Terfel

bassoon player: fagottist

bastards, famous – see illegitimate and famous

Basutoland: former name for Lesotho (until 1966)

bat, adjective: pteropine, vespertilian, vespertilionid, vespertilionine

bat, collective noun: cloud

bat, largest: kalong, a fruit bat

bat, sound: ping

bat, young: pup

bath, adjective: balneal

bathing, adjective: balneal

Batman: The Caped Crusader, Dark Knight, Bruce Wayne; Robin: The Boy Wonder, Dick Grayson; together: the Dynamic Duo

Batman played by: Lewis Wilson (1943), Robert Lowery (1949), Adam West (1966–1968), Michael Keaton (1989, 1992), Val Kilmer (1995), George Clooney (1997) and Christian Bale (2005–2008)

Battersea Power Station: iconic structure on the south side of the river Thames in London, designed by Sir Giles Gilbert Scott. The station was originally erected in 1933, combining the first turbine hall and two of its distinctive chimneys. In 1953 a second turbine hall and two more chimneys were added. Then, in 1982, the station was closed, fuelling much talk about its future. Various wild theories were bounced around, with official planning for an indoor theme park secured in 1986. However, after funding fell through, Parkview acquired the site in 1993 and further designs were drawn up and various repairs embarked upon. The station's standing as a favourite London landmark was boosted with its appearance on the cover of the 1977 Pink Floyd album *Animals*

battle, god of: Odin (Norse mythology)

Battle of Agincourt: 25 October 1415 (the Hundred Years' War)

Battle of Alma River: 20 September 1854 (when the Russians were defeated by British, French, and Ottoman forces)

Battle of El Alamein, first: 1–27 July 1942 (World War II)

Battle of El Alamein, second: 23 October-4 November 1942 (World War II)

Battle of Amiens: 8–11 August 1918 (World War I)

Battle of Antietam: 17 September 1862 (American Civil War)

Battle of Arras: 9 April-16 May 1917 (World War I)

Battle of Atlanta: 22 July 1864 (American Civil War)

Battle of Austerlitz: 2 December 1805 (War of the Third Coalition)

Battle of Balaclava: 25 October 1854 (Crimea War)

Battle of Bannockburn: 23–24 June 1314 (the Wars of Scottish Independence)

Battle of Blenheim: 13 August 1704 (War of the Spanish Succession)

Battle of Borodino: 7 September 1812 (French invasion of Russia)

Battle of Bosworth Field: 22 August 1485 (the Wars of the Roses)

Battle of Britain: 10 July-31 October 1940 (World War II)

Battle of Bull Run, first: 21 July 1861 (American Civil War)

Battle of Bull Run, second: 28–30 August 1862 (American Civil War)

Battle of Cannae: 2 August 216 BC (Second Punic War – Roman losses estimated at 48,000–50,000, making this the bloodiest battle of ancient times)

Battle of Culloden: 16 April 1746 (when Hanoverian forces defeated the Jacobite Highlanders)

Battle of Dresden: 26–27 August 1813 (War of the Sixth Coalition)

Battle of Dunkirk: 26 May-4 June 1940 (World War II)

Battle of Edgehill: 23 October 1642 (English Civil War)

Battle of El Alamein: 23 October–5 November 1942

Battle of Flodden Field: 9 September 1513 (War of the League of Cambrai)

Battle of Gettysburg: 1–3 July 1863 (American Civil War)

Battle of Hastings: 14 October 1066 (Norman Conquest)

Battle of Ipsus: 301 BC (Wars of the Diadochi)

Battle of Issus: 5 November 333 BC (Wars of Alexander the Great)

Battle of Iwo Jima: 16 February-26 March 1945 (World War II)

Battle of Jutland: 31 May-1 June 1916 (an inconclusive conflict involving the British and German navies)

Battle of Kursk: 4 July–23 August 1943 (biggest tank battle of all time)

Battle of Lepanto: 7 October 1571 (defeat of the Ottoman fleet by the Holy League)

Battle of Leyte Gulf: 23–26 October 1944 (World War II, involving 218 Allied warships and 64 Japanese warships in the Philippines)

Battle of Little Bighorn: 25–26 June 1876 (Custer's last stand against the Sioux and Cheyenne)

Battle of Lundy's Lane: 25 July 1812 (the bloodiest ever fought in Canada)

Battle of Marston Moor: 2 July 1644 (when the Royalists were defeated by Cromwell)

Battle of Naseby: 14 June 1645 (when the Royalists were defeated by Cromwell)

Battle of Petersburg: 15 June 1864–25 March 1865 (American Civil War)

Battle of Rorke's Drift: 22–23 January 1879 (Anglo-Zulu War)

Battle of Shiloh: 6-7 April 1862 (American Civil War)

Battle of Solway Moss: 24 November 1542 (the Anglo-Scottish Wars)

Battle of Stalingrad: 21 August 1942–2 February 1943 (World War II, with a death toll estimated at 1,109,000)

Battle of Stamford Bridge: 25 September 1066 (Harold II defeats Norse invaders)

Battle of Stirling Bridge: 11 September 1297 (the Wars of Scottish Independence)

Battle of the Alamo: 23 February-6 March 1836 (the Texan War of Independence)

Battle of the Boyne: 1690 (when James II's Catholic forces were defeated by William II)

Battle of the Bulge: 16 December 1944–25 January 1945 (World War II)

Battle of the Somme: June-November 1916; March 1918 (World War I)

Battle of Thermopylae: 11 August 480 BC (the Persian Wars)

Battle of Trafalgar: 21 October 1805 (the Napoleonic Wars, in which 47,000 sailors participated)

Battle of Verdun: 21 February-19 December 1916 (fought between France and Germany)

Battle of Vicksburg: 18 May-4 July 1863 (American Civil War)

Battle of Waterloo: 18 June 1815 (War of the Seventh Coalition)

Battle of Ypres: 19 October-22 November 1914, 22 April-15 May 1915, 31 July-November 6 1917, 28 September-2 October 1918 (all World War I)

battle of words: logomachy

battlefields: Passchendaele (Belgium), the Somme, Verdun, Ypres (West Belgium)

bauble: gewgaw

bayonet, collective noun: grove

Baywatch, TV series produced by NBC which was cancelled after its first season, but then became an international hit in syndication
  created by: Michael Berk, Douglas Schwartz and Gregory J. Bonann
  broadcast: 22 September 1989–14 May 2001
  cast: David Hasselhoff (Mitch Buchannon), Parker Stevenson (Craig Pomeroy), Shawn Weatherly (Jill Riley), Billy Warlock (Eddie Kramer), Erika Eleniak (Shauni McClain), Alexandra Paul (Lt. Stephanie Holden), Pamela Anderson (C.J. Parker), Nicole Eggert (Summer Quinn), Susan Anton (Jackie Quinn), Yasmine Bleeth (Caroline Holden, Stephanie's younger sister), Gena Lee Nolin (Neely Capshaw)

BBC: British Broadcasting Corporation

BBC, first broadcast: 26 August, 1936, made by Leslie Mitchell from Alexandra Palace

BBC, nicknames: Auntie, the Beeb

beach, adjective: littoral

Beach Boys, The: sunny Californian pop group formed in Hawthorne, near Los Angeles, in 1961; original members included the brothers Brian Wilson,

Carl Wilson and Dennis Wilson, their cousin Mike Love, and David Marks. Marks was replaced by Al Jardine in 1963 and Bruce Johnston joined the band in April of 1965

beadle: Mr Bumble (from *Oliver Twist*)

beak, shaped like a hook (adjective): hamirostrate

bean: baked bean, black-eyed pea, broad bean, chickpea, French bean, haricot, kidney bean, lentil, lima bean, mangetout, runner bean, snow pea, soybean

bean, adjective: leguminous

Beano, The: classic children's comic first published by D.C. Thomson of Dundee, Scotland, on 30 July 1938

bear, adjective: ursine, arctoid

bear, collective noun: sloth, sleuth

bear, famous: Aloysius, Baloo (from *The Jungle Book*), Bart, Br'er Bear, Bruin, Care Bears, Corduroy, Fozzie, Paddington, Rupert, Sooty, SuperTed, Teddy (from *Mr Bean*), Tessie Bear (from *Noddy*), Winnie the Pooh, Yogi Bear - see teddy bears

bear, female: sow

bear, killing of: ursicide

bear, largest: Kodiak

bear, male: boar

bear, sound: growl

bear, young: cub

bear nymph: Callisto

bear-like: arctoid

beard: beaver, burnsides, chinstrap, full, Garibaldi, goatee, imperial, royale, soul patch, stubble, Van Dyke, Verdi, whiskers

beard, aversion to: pogonophobia

beard, overgrowth of: pogoniasis

beard book: pogonology

beard growth in women: pogoniasis

beard lover: pogonophile

bearded, adjective: barbigerous

beatbox, human: Jason Singh

beaten, fear of being: rhabdophobia

Beat Generation, father of: Kenneth Rexroth

Beat poets: Allen Ginsberg, Jack Kerouac

Beatles, The: legendary pop group formed in Liverpool in 1958, when they were known as The Quarrymen. Later, they – John Lennon, Paul McCartney and George Harrison – changed the group's name to Johnny and The Moondogs, then to The Rainbows and next to The Silver Beatles (with Stu Sutcliffe as bass guitarist). In 1960 Pete Best joined the group on drums. In 1962 Sutcliffe died and Ringo Starr (real name: Richard Starkey) replaced Pete Best, when the group changed its name again, this time to The Beatles. The group disbanded 10 April 1970

Beatles' assassin: Mark David Chapman who, clutching a copy of J.D. Salinger's *Catcher in the Rye*, shot John Lennon dead in New York on 8 December 1980

Beatles' manager (between 1962 and 1967): Brian Epstein

Beatles' producer: George Martin

Beau, the: nickname for the Duke of Wellington

Beaufort scale (as devised by Francis Beaufort in 1805): 0) calm; 1) light air; 2) light breeze; 3) gentle breeze; 4) moderate breeze; 5) fresh breeze; 6) strong breeze; 7) moderate gale; 8) fresh gale; 9) strong gale; 10) whole gale; 11) storm; 12) hurricane

beauties: Cleopatra (albeit much disputed), Helen of Troy, Audrey Hepburn, Grace Kelly
- see pin-up girls; sex symbols, female; supermodels, etc

beautiful: attractive, babelicious, bonny, comely, cosmetically enhanced, cosmetically well aranged, dishy, fair of face, foxy, gorgeous, photogenic, pretty, pulchritudinous, ravishing, statuesque, traffic-stopping

beautiful women, dislike of: dyscallignia

beauty: "The problem with beauty is that it's like being born rich and getting poorer" – Joan Collins

beauty, collective noun: bevy

beauty, goddess of: Aphrodite (Greek mythology), Freya (Norse), Venus (Roman)

beauty, love of: philocaly

beauty, lover of: aesthete (usually to an exaggerated degree)

beaver, collective noun: colony, lodge

beaver, habitat: lodge

beaver, young: kit, kitten

Bechuanaland: former name for Botswana (until 1966)

bed, abnormal desire for lying in: clinomania (i.e. 'bed rest')

bed bugs, killing of: cimicide

Bedfordshire, administrative centre: Bedford

bedtime, fear of: clinophobia

bee, adjective: apian, apiarian

bee, collective noun: swarm

bee, habitat: apiary, hive

bee, sound: buzz

bee, young: larva

bees, fear of: apiophobia

bees, obsession with: apimania

bees, study of: melittology

bee-keeping: apiculture

bee-keeping, adjective: apiarian

Bee Gees: UK vocal trio formed in Brisbane in 1967; comprised of the brothers Barry, Robin and Maurice Gibb

Beeb, The: nickname for the BBC

beech tree fruit: beechmast

beehive (one usually made of straw): skep

beer: ale, amber fluid (Australian slang), amber nectar (Australian slang), apple fritter (CRS for bitter), beevos (American campus slang), bitter, brew, brewski, ciscos (Latino slang), cold coffee, coldie (Australian slang), dog's head (American), draught, grog (Australian slang), lager, monkey piss (slang for weak beer), oh my dear (CRS), piss (Australian slang), sauce, kvas (weak)

beer brands: Abbot Ale, Adnams, Amstel light (from Amsterdam), Anchor Bitter, Ara bier, Badger Best, Bass, Beamish, Becks, Blackadder, Boddingtons (draught bitter), Brakspear, Bud Light, Budwar, Budweiser, Carling (formerly known as Carling Black Label), Carlsberg, Castle Lager, Castlemaine, Charrington, Courage, Courage Best, Courage Directors, Dogfish Head World Wide Stout, Dorset IPA, Eagle, Everards Tiger Best, Flowers IPA, Foster's, Four X, Les Frères de la Bière ('Brother's Beer' - a blend of Kent hops, Pas de Calais and £40,000 of taxpayers' money), Fuller's, Greene King, Greene King IPA, Grolsch, Guinness, Harveys, Heineken, Hoffbrau lager, Holsten, John

Marston's Pedigree (draught bitter), John Smith's, Kirin, Kronenberg, Lapin,
London Pride, Lowenbrau, Michelob, Miller, Mitchell, Molsen, Murphy's,
Newquay Steam lager, Nicholson's, Nicholson's Best, Oatmeal Stout,
Pedigree, Peroni, Phuket, Pils, Pilsner, Red Stripe, Rolling Rock, Ruddles,
Ruddles County, Schlitz, Singha, Stella Artois, Tanglefoot, Tennent's Extra,
Tennent's Pilsner, Tetley, Theakston, Theakston XB, Thwaites Best Mild, Tiger,
Tsing Tao, Vice Beer, Wadworth, Wadworth 6X, Webster's, Wells Bombadier
Best, Worthington Best, XXXX, Young's, Young's Special, Zythum (of ancient
Egypt)

beer, adjective: cervisial

beer, patron saint of (unofficially): Gambrinus

beer, strongest in world: Dogfish Head World Wide Stout

beer, weak: kvas (Russian)

beer, world's top consumer of: Czech Republic

beer gut: liquid grain storage facility (pc)

Beethoven's symphonies, nicknames for: No. 3: 'Eroica', No. 6: 'Pastoral', No. 8:
'The Little Symphony'; No. 9: 'Choral Symphony'

beetle, adjective: coleopteral, coleopterous, coleopteroid

beetle, largest: goliath

beetle, number of species: 370,000

beetle, young: grub

beetle amulet: scarab

beetroot soup: borstsch

beggar: Lazarus

beheaded and famous – see decapitated and famous

Beijing, birthplace of: Jet Li

Beijing; Tiananmen Square massacre: 3-4 June 1989 (in which 5,000 were killed
and 10,000 injured)

being, science of: ontology

Belarus: republic in eastern Europe
  capital: Minsk
  currency: Belarussian rouble
  language: Belarussian, Russian
  nickname: White Russia
  religion: Christian, Roman Catholic, Russian Orthodox

belch: burp, eruct, expectorate (verb)

Belfast, birthplace of: Kenneth Branagh, St John Ervine (playwright), James
Galway, Gary Moore, Van Morrison, Stephen Rea (actor)

Belgian and famous: Father Abraham (creator of The Smurfs), Leo Baekeland
(inventor of Bakelite), Jacques Brel (composer and singer), Cécile De France
(actress), James Ensor (painter and engraver), Marie Gillain (actress), Johnny
Hallyday, Hergé (aka George Prosper Remi, creator of *Tintin*), Jackie Ickx
(racing driver), Georges Lemaître (astrophysicist and cosmologist), Lio (singer;
real name: Wanda Ribeiro de Vasconcelos), Lucky Luke, René Magritte (artist),
Eddy Merckx (cyclist), Amélie Nothomb (writer), Hercule Poirot, Django
Reinhardt (guitarist), Adolphe Sax (inventor of the saxophone), Georges
Simenon (novelist), the Smurfs, Tintin, Jean-Claude Van Damme, Herman
Van Rompuy (first permanent president of the European Council), Henri
Vieuxtemps (violinist), Eugène Ysaÿe (violinist)

Belgian health resort: Spa

Belgium: federal kingdom in north-west Europe
  capital: Brussels (see)

currency: euro; formerly the Belgian franc
language: Flemish (in the North), Wallonia (in the South)
ports: Antwerp, Ostend, Zeebrugge
religion: Roman Catholic
Belgrade, river: Danube
Belize: state in Central America, formerly known as British Honduras
    capital: Belmopan
    currence: Belize dollar
    language: English (official), Carib, Spanish
    mountain range: Maya Mountains
    religion: Roman Catholic (60%), Protestant (35%)
bell, adjective: campanular
bell, collective noun: change
bell ringer: campanologist, carillonneur
bells, ringing of: tintinnabulation
bells, set of: carillon
bell-shaped: campaniform, campanulate
Belle of the Nineties (1934 film), famous line: Ruby Carter (Mae West): "It's better to be looked over than overlooked."
belly, adjective: alvine (obsolete)
belly, divination by: gastromancy
belly, endowed with a big one: abdominous
belly button: navel, omphalos
belly-worshiper (as in a glutton): gastrolater
belt for storing cartridges (military): bandoleer
Ben & Jerry's: ice cream company founded by Long Island hippies Ben Cohen and Jerry Greenfield in a Vermont petrol station in 1978
benefactor: Ruth Lilly (who donated more than $100 million to the American literary journal *Poetry*, even though it had rejected her poetic submissions for decades)
- see philanthropists
Bengali nationalist: Ziaur Rahman
Benin, People's Republic of: republic in West Africa; formerly known as Dahomey
    capital: Cotonou (official), Porto Novo
    currency: CFA franc
    language: French (official), Fon (47%)
    religion: animist (65%), Christian (17%), Muslim (13%)
Beninois and famous: Djimon Hounsou (actor), Angélique Kidjo (singer)
bent at a sharp angle: geniculate
Berkshire, administrative centre: Reading
Berlin: capital of Germany
Berlin, birthplace of: Frank Auerbach, Marlene Dietrich, Sir Clement Freud, Lucian Freud, Walter Gropius (architect), Frederick Loewe (composer, songwriter), Mike Nichols (filmmaker), Leni Riefenstahl (documentarian)
Berlin, history: East and West Berlin formally united in 1990
Berlin architect: Karl Friedrich Schinkel (who built Berlin's finest and most grandiose buildings of the 18th century)
Berlin parliamentary building: Reichstag (burned down in 1933; new design by Sir Norman Foster)
Berlin rivers: Havel, Spree
Berlin Wall: built in 1961
Berlin Wall demolition: commenced 9 November 1989

berries: arbutus (fruit of the strawberry tree), bilberry, blackberry, blackcurrant, blueberry, boysenberry, buffalo berry, Cape gooseberry, chickoo (aka naseberry), cloudberry, cranberry, dwarf Cape gooseberry (aka ground cherry), elderberry, goji, gooseberry, grape, ground cherry, hawthorn, honey berry (related to the raspberry), huckleberry (aka bilberry), loganberry, mulberry, naseberry, peppercorn, phenomenal berry, raspberry, red currant, salmonberry, sapodilla (aka naseberry), strawberry, tangleberry, veitchberry (very similar to the loganberry), white currant, wild strawberry, strawberry tomato (aka ground cherry), whortleberry (aka bilberry), worcesterberry (an American version of the gooseberry)

berry, adjective: baccate

best boy: chief electrician's assistant on a film set

bestseller: "There's many a bestseller that could have been prevented by a good teacher" - Flannery O'Connor

Beverly Hills 90210, Fox TV series set in and around West Beverly High School, dealing predominantly with alcohol, drugs and sex
  broadcast: 4 October 1990–17 May 2000
  cast: Jason Priestley (Brandon Walsh), Shannen Doherty (Brenda Walsh), Carol Potter (Cindy Walsh), James Eckhouse (Jim Walsh), Jennie Garth (Kelly Taylor), Luke Perry (Dylan McKay), Tori Spelling (Donna Martin), Christine Elise (Emily Valentine), Grant Show (Jake Hanson), Cory Tyler (Herbert), Kathleen Robertson (Clare Arnold), Rebecca Gayheart (Antonia Marchette)

Bewitched: popular American TV sitcom about an all-American housewife who also happens to be a witch; adapted to the big-screen in 2005 with Nicole Kidman as a witch who's cast as Samantha in an updated series
  created by Sol Saks for ABC TV
  broadcast: 17 September 1964–25 March 1972
  cast: Elizabeth Montgomery (Samantha Stephens/Serena), Dick York (1964–69) and Dick Sargent (1969–72) (Darrin Stephens), Agnes Moorehead (Endora), David White (Larry Tate), Alice Pearce (1964–66) and Sandra Gould (1966–72) (Gladys Kravitz), George Tobias (Abner Kravitz), Maurice Evans (Maurice), Alice Ghostley (Esmeralda)

Beyond the Fringe: satirical revue which began life at the 1960 Edinurgh Festival and featured Alan Bennett, Peter Cook, Jonathan Miller and Dudley Moore

Bhutan: kingdom in central Asia
  capital: Thimbu
  currency: ngultrum
  language: Dzongkha (official), Sharchop, Bumthap, Nepali, English
  nickname: Land of the Thunder Dragon (Druk Yul), The Last Shangri-La
  religion: Lamaistic Buddhist (state religion), Hindu (25%)

Bible, The (Christian): comprising the Old Testament (39 books) and the New Testament (27 books)

Bible, The; appendix to the Old Testament (but not included in the Hebrew canon): Apocrypha

Bible, The; nickname: The Good Book

Bible, The; types of: Authorised Version, Bishops', Coverdale's, Cranmer's, Douai, Geneva, Gideon, Great, Gutenberg, King James's, Matthew's, Matthew Parker's, Mazarin, New English, Revised Standard Version, Revised Version, Taverner's, Tyndale's, Wyclif's

bicycle: invented in 1840 by Kirkpatrick MacMillan

bicycle, formerly known as: velocipede

bicycle, parts: binder bolt, brake lever, brake pad, cable guide, chain, chain ring, chain stay, crank, crank bolt, crossbar, derailleur, down tube, fork, frame, freewheel sprocket, gear, gear cable, gearshift, handlebar, handlebar grip, head tube, hub, inner tube, pannier, pedal, presta valve, pulley bolt, saddle, saddle clamp, seat post, seat stay, seat tube, spider, spoke, spoke guard, straddle wire, tension pulley, toe clip, toe strap, tyre, wheel rim

bifocal lens: invented in 1780 by Benjamin Franklin

Big Apple: nickname for New York

Big Bang: theory that the universe exploded into existence 13.7 billion years ago, proposed (in 1945) by the Belgian astrophysicist and cosmologist Georges Lemaître

big-bellied: ventricose

Big Ben: nickname for the clock on St Stephen's Tower (aka the Clock Tower), Houses of Parliament, London

Big Bird: eight-foot, two-inch canary created by Jim Henson (and first manhandled by Frank Oz and then by Carroll Spinney) – see Sesame Street

Big Easy, the: nickname for New Orleans

Big Issue, The: British magazine championing the cause of and sold by homeless people, founded in September 1991 by John Bird and Gordon Roddick

Big Sleep, The (1946 film), famous lines: Philip Marlowe (Humphrey Bogart): "She tried to sit on my lap while I was standing up"; Philip Marlowe: "I don't mind if you don't like my manners. I don't like them myself. They're pretty bad. I grieve over them long winter evenings"; Philip Marlowe: "You've got a touch of class, but, uh, I don't know how…. how far you can go." Vivian Sherwood Rutledge (Lauren Bacall): "A lot depends on who's in the saddle"; Vivian (after Marlow kisses her): "I liked that. I'd like more."

Big Yin, the: nickname for Billy Connolly

bigamy: "Bigamy is having one wife too many. Monogamy is the same" - Oscar Wilde

biggest living thing in the world – see largest living thing in the world

bikini: microkini, monokini, string, tanga (very skimpy), tankini, two-piece

bile, adjective: cholic

bile, lack of: acholia

bile, producing a flow of: cholagogic

billionaire, first: John D. Rockefeller

billionaires: Roman Abramovich, Karl Albrecht, Theo Albrecht, Paul Allen, Prince Alwaleed Bin Talal Alsaud, Mukesh Ambani, Boris Berezovsky (Russian exile), Silvio Berlusconi, Mohammad Bin Laden, Björgólfur Thor Björgólfsson, Eli Broad (building tycoon), Warren Buffett, Sir James Dyson, King Fahd, John Fredriksen, Bill Gates, Jean Paul Getty, Sir James Goldsmith, Sir Philip and Lady Cristina Green, Gerald Grosvenor, Gopi Hinduja, Sri Hinduja, Sheila Johnson, David Khalili, George Lucas, Forrest Mars Jr., John Mars, Lakshmi Mittal (steel magnate), Li Ka-shing, Sean Mulryan (property tycoon), Rupert Murdoch, Kerry Packer, Jim Ratcliffe, Hans, Jorn and Kirsten Rausing, Sumner Redstone, David and Simon Reuben, J.K. Rowling, Sheikh of Abu Dhabi, Jeff Skoll, Carlos Slim, Martha Stewart, Sultan of Brunei, Thaksin Shinawatra (deposed Thai prime minister), Sir Allen Stanford, Alice Walton, Helen Walton, Jim Walton, John Walton, S. Robson Walton, Bruce Wayne, Oprah Winfrey (the first black billionairess), Mark Zuckerberg (founder of Facebook)

billionairess, first black female: Sheila Johnson

biochemists: Sir Edward Abraham, George Wells Beadle, Sune Bergström, Melvin Calvin, Ernst Chain, Stanley Cohen, Carl Cori, Gerty Cori, Gerhard Domagk, Sir Frederick Hopkins, Sir Hans Adolf Krebs, Leonor Michaelis, Severo Ochoa, Max Perutz, Frederick Sanger, Lester Smith, Alexander R. Todd, Otto Heinrich Warburg, James Watson

biographers: Peter Ackroyd, James Boswell, John Buchan, James MacGregor Burns, Humphrey Carpenter, John Debrett, Albert Goldman, Anthony Holden, Michael Holroyd, Roy Jenkins, Samuel Johnson, Kitty Kelley, John Gibson Lockhart, Andrew Morton, Cornelius Nepos, Plutarch, Hilary Spurling, Leslie Stephen, Lytton Strachey, Claire Tomalin, Giorgio Vasari, A.N. Wilson, Stefan Zweig

biography: "Biography is merely nosiness dressed up as literature" - Nigel Jones (biographer)

biography, types of: demonography (a biography that defiles its subject), hagiography (a biography that idolises its subject), hatchet job, pathography (a biography that focuses on the negative elements of its subject)

biologists: Karl Ernst von Baer, George Wells Beadle, Sidney Brenner, Rachel Carson, Francis Crick, Paul and Anne Ehrlich, Stephen Jay Gould, J.B.S. Haldane, Michinomiya Hirohito, Sir Julian Huxley, Jacques Loeb, Lynn Margulis, John Maynard Smith, Peter Medawar, Zhores Medvedev, Gregor Mendel, Stanley Miller, Jacques Monod, Sir Richard Owen, Gregory Pincus, J. Craig Venter, Baron Solly Zuckerman

biophysicists: Alan Hodgkin, Andrew Huxley

bird, adjective: avian, volucrine

bird, collective noun: congregation, flock, dissimulation, volery

bird, famous: Big Bird (see)

bird, fastest: peregrine falcon

bird, habitat: aviary, nest

bird, largest: ostrich

bird, most common in Britain: wren

bird, mythical: phoenix, roc

bird, sound: song, tweet, twitter

bird, vocal organ: syrinx

bird, young: chick, hatchling

bird artist: John James Audubon

bird catcher: Papageno (from *The Magic Flute*)

bird of prey, adjective: raptorial

bird painters: John James Audubon, Roger Tory Peterson, Sir Peter Scott, Charles Tunnicliffe

birds, fear of: ornithophobia

birds, rare, in Britain: bittern, citrine wagtail, snipe

birds' beak: neb

birds' eggs, study of: oology

birds' egg collector: oologist

birds of prey: buzzard, caracara, cormorant, eagle, falcon, harrier, hawk, kite, lammergeier (or lammergeyer), marabou, merlin, osprey, owl, raptor, shrike, skua, vulture

birds' tail: uropygium

Birmingham, UK; birthplace of: Jasper Carrott, David Edgar (dramatist), Trevor Eve, Tony Garnett (TV producer), Tony Hancock, Jamelia, Ozzy Osbourne, Martin Shaw, The Streets, Julie Walters, Steve Winwood

Birmingham, UK; groups: Black Sabbath, The Charlatans, Dexy's Midnight Runners, Duran Duran, Electric Light Orchestra, Fine Young Cannibals, Guillemots, Judas Priest, The Moody Blues, Musical Youth, Ocean Colour Scene, Pop Will Eat Itself, Spencer Davis Group, The Streets (aka Mike Skinner), Traffic, UB40, Wizzard

Birmingham native: Brummie

birth, adjective: natal

birth, study of: obstetrics

birth doctor: obstetrician

birth control: "My favoured method of birth control is leaving the lights on" - Joan Rivers

birth control advocates: Emma Goldman, Marie Stopes

birth rate, in Britain: one baby born every 52 seconds

birth rate, lowest in world: Spain (1.2 per family)

bisexuals: Joan Baez, Josephine Baker, Tallulah Bankhead, Sandra Bernhard (arguably), Leonard Bernstein, Paul Bowles, Marlon Brando, Lord Byron, Dora Carrington, Bruce Chatwin, Montgomery Clift, Colette, Ani DiFranco (American folk singer), Errol Flynn, André Gide, Cary Grant (rumoured), Alec Guinness (arrested while cottaging in 1948), Hadrian, Billie Holiday (occasionally), Simon Hughes (Lib Dem politician), Frida Kahlo, Danny Kaye, Alfred Kinsey, Lindsay Lohan, Rebecca Loos, W. Somerset Maugham, Harold Nicolson, Laurence Olivier, Cole Porter, Tyrone Power, Michael Redgrave, Tony Richardson, Vita Sackville-West, Randolph Scott, William Shakespeare (if the sonnets he wrote to a male lover are to be correctly interpreted), Oscar Wilde, Walt Whitman, Leonard Woolf, Virginia Woolf

bishop, adjective: episcopal

bishop, collective noun: bench, episcopacy

bishop, killing of: episcopicide

bishop, mode of verbal address: Your Lordship

bishops: Jacob Amman (whose followers founded the Amish sect), Dr David Hope (Bishop of London), Richard Trench, Desmond Tutu, Roderick Wright (former Roman Catholic Bishop of Argyll and the Isles, disgraced for running off with a divorcee, confessing to having a 15-year-old son and selling his story to the tabloids)
- see Archbishops of Canterbury

bishop, gay, the world's first: Gene Robinson; consecrated in November 2003 in New Hampshire, USA

bishop, gay, British: Canon Jeffrey John, proposed Suffragan Bishop of Reading (Britain's first openly homosexual Anglican bishop, but who turned down the post 6 July 2003

bishop's-cap (flowering plant): mitrewort

bishop's ceremonial vestment: cope

bishop's chair: faldstool

bishop's staff: crosier

Bislama: language spoken in the republic of Vanuatu

bison, adjective: bisontine

bison, collective noun: herd

Black Adder, The: BBC comedy series set during the Middle Ages, Elizabethan England, The First World War, etc, written by Richard Curtis, Ben Elton and Rowan Atkinson

broadcast: 15 June 1983–2 November 1989 (further 'specials' were filmed up to 1999)

cast: Rowan Atkinson (Black Adder/Edmund Blackadder/E. Blackadder Esq., etc), Tony Robinson (Baldrick), Miranda Richardson (Queen Elizabeth I), Stephen Fry (Lord Melchett/General Sir Anthony Cecil Hogmanay Melchett), Hugh Laurie (Prince Regent, etc), Tim McInnerny, Brian Blessed, Miriam Margolyes

black earth: fertile soil known more formally as chernozem

Black Eyed Peas: alternative rap group formed in 1996 in Los Angeles; comprised of Taboo, Will.I.Am, Apl de Ap and Fergie (real name: Stacy Ann Ferguson)

black magic: necromancy

black man: African-American, brother, darkie, ghetto pimp, golliwog, juba (American), jungle bunny, Kaffir (deeply offensive, applied to black South Africans), Mandingo, monkey, negro, nigger, nignog, person of colour, sooty, spade, Uncle Tom, wog

blacks, first in Britain: 1962, first peer: Lord (Learie) Constantine of Maraval and Nelson, West Indian cricketer; 1973, first TV reporter: ITN's Trevor McDonald; 1975, first Mayor: Randolph Beresford, of Hammersmith and Fulham; 1978, first footballer to play for England: Viv Anderson; 1982, first headmaster: Carlton Duncan, of George Dixon Secondary School in Birmingham; 1987, first MPs: Bernie Grant, Diane Abbott and Paul Boateng; 1988, first QC: John Roberts; 1991, first trade union leader: Bill Morris, of the Transport and General Workers Union; 2002, first Cabinet minister: Paul Boateng

Black Panther leader: Huey P. Newton

Black Panther movement, slogan: 'Power to the People'

Black Sabbath: heavy metal band from Birmingham, UK, formed in 1967; comprised of Tony Iommi (guitar), Bill Ward (drums), Ozzy Osbourne (real name: John Osbourne; vocals), Geezer Butler (real name: Terence Butler; bass); formerly known as Earth.

black slang: booty (female body), Boss Charley (white man, especially one in charge), dime (ten-year prison sentence), dip (a hat), Dr Thomas (a middle-class black aspiring to white status), duster (buttocks), fly (smart), hammer (beautiful black girl), phat (excellent, hot), Sylvester (white man), tree-suit (coffin), zazzle (sexual desire)

black velvet: drink comprised of equal parts of stout and champagne

black vernacular: Ebonics

blackbird, adjective: icterine

blackcurrant liqueur: cassis

blackmailer: Uriah Heep (from *David Copperfield*)

Blackpool, fact: the Lancashire town allegedy has more hotels and bed and breakfast facilities than all of Portugal

blacksmiths: Brontes (Greek mythology), Joe Gargery (from *Great Expectations*)

blacksmiths, patron saint of: Dunstan

blackthorn fruit: sloe

bladder, adjective: vesical

bladder; sexual arousal derived from a full bladder: omorashi

bladder doctor: urologist

blank verse, earliest English drama written in: Thomas Norton and Thomas Sackville's *The Tragedie of Gorboduc* (1560)

blankets: first manufactured in 1337 (in Bristol, England)

bleeding, sexual arousal derived from the sight of: hematolagnia

Blenheim Palace: stately home in Woodstock, Oxfordshire, designed by Sir John Vanbrugh with parkland and formal gardens landscaped by 'Capability' Brown. The house was a gift from Queen Anne to John Churchill, the first Duke of Marlborough, in gratitude for his victory over the French near the small village of Blenheim (or Blindheim). Construction started in 1705 but, in 1714, the Marlboroughs had to cough up £500,000 themselves to complete the project

blind, patron saint of the: Lucy

blind, politically correct terms: optically challenged, visually inconvenienced

blind, teacher of: Louis Braille

blind and famous: Amadou and Mariam (West African jazz duo), Johann Sebastian Bach, Blind Harry (Scottish poet), David Blunkett (Home Secretary), Andrea Bocelli (opera singer), Jorge Luis Borges, Louis Braille, Clarence Carter (singer), Mary Cassatt (partially), Ray Charles, Bruce Chatwin (temporarily), Enrico Dandolo, Daredevil, Honoré Daumier, Frederick Delius, José Feliciano, Sir John Fielding (magistrate), Galileo Galilei, Francisco Goya (at the end of his life), George Frideric Handel, James Holman (travel writer), Homer, Isaac, Derek Jarman (in his last days), James Joyce, Helen Keller, Fritz Lang, Amyas Leigh (from *Westward Ho!*), Sir John Mills (in his later years), Ronnie Milsap (Country singer), John Milton, Claude Monet (suffered from cataracts, resulting from his muddier compositions later in life), Moondog, John Newton (in his later years), Oedipus, Polyphemus (cyclops blinded by Odysseus), Joseph Pulitzer, Joshua Reynolds, Edward Rochester (from *Jane Eyre*), Joaquin Rodrigo, Samson (blinded by the Philistines), Art Tatum (jazz pianist), Norman Taurog (film director), James Thurber, Tiresias, Tommy (%The Who), Sue Townsend, Doc Watson (Country guitarist), Stevie Wonder, Zatoichi

Blind Date: British TV game show-cum-dating service hosted by Cilla Black.

    broadcast: 30 November 1985–31 May 2003 on London Weekend Television

blind spot: scotoma

bling bling: diamonds, jewelry and other forms of ostentation (coined by New Orleans rap family Cash Money Millionaires)

blinking, constant condition of: blepharospasm

blister: vesicle

blonde, types of: ash, dumb, platinum, strawberry

blondes: bombshell blonde, brassy blonde, cool blonde, dangerous blonde, society blonde, strawberry blonde, sunny blonde

blood, adjective: haemal, sanguineous

blood, artificial: invented in 1966 by Leland C. Clark and Frank Gollan

blood, fear of: haematophobia, haemophobia, haemaphobia

blood, stain with: imbrue (rare)

blood, study of: haematology

blood circulation, discovered by: William Harvey (in 1628), although some sources cite the 13th century Arab physician Ibn al-Nafis al-Quarashi

blood clot: crassamentum

blood deficiency: anaemia

blood doctor: haematologist

blood of the gods: ichor

blood poisoning: pyaemia, sepsis, septicaemia

blood staunching: haemostasis
blood vomiting: haematemesis
blood-boosting drug: EPO
blood-clotting agent: platelet
blood-letting: phlebotomy
blood-related: parentelic (adjective)
bloody scene (as in a massacre): aceldama
Bloomsbury Group, members of: Clive Bell, Vanessa Bell, Dora Carrington, E.M. Forster, Roger Fry, Duncan Grant, John Maynard Keynes, Desmond MacCarthy, Frances Partridge, Lytton Strachey, Leonard Sidney Woolf, Virginia Woolf
blowfish: fugu
blow job: fellatio
Blue: teen-friendly R&B/dance quartet formed in London in 2000; comprised of Duncan James, Anthony Costa, Simon Webbe and Lee Ryan
Blue Peter, TV magazine show for school-aged children, devised by John Hunter Blair.
    first broadcast on the BBC 16 October 1958
    presenters include: Christopher Trace, Leila Williams, Valerie Singleton, Peter Purves, John Noakes, Richard Bacon (who was fired after admitting that he took cocaine), Matt Baker, Katy Hill, Konnie Huq, John Leslie, Stuart Miles, Simon Thomas, Anthea Turner
    canine mascot: Petra (from 1962 to 1977)
bluebird, adjective: turdine
blues, empress of: Bessie Smith
blues, father of the: W.C. Handy
blues singers: Blues Brothers, Big Bill Broonzy, J.J. Cale, Ray Charles, Albert Collins, Billie Holiday, John Lee Hooker, Elmore James, Blind Lemon Jefferson, Robert Johnson, Janis Joplin, Louis Jordan, B.B. King, Gladys Knight, Leadbelly (aka Huddie Ledbetter), Memphis Slim, Ma Rainey, Bonnie Raitt, Bessie Smith, Irma Thomas, T-Bone Walker, Dinah Washington, Muddy Waters
blur in printing: mackle (noun)
blushing, dread of: ereuthophobia
BMA: British Medical Association
boa constrictor, adjective: boid
boar, collective noun: pack, singular, sounder
boar, female: sow
boar, male: boar
boar, slaughter of: apricide
boar, young: piglet
board games: backgammon, chess, Cluedo, draughts, Golden Balls, Ludo, mah-jong, Monopoly, Othello, Pictionary, Scrabble, snakes and ladders, Trivial Pursuit, Twister
boastful and famous: Niobe (whose children were slaughtered by Apollo and Artemis to punish her pride)
boasting: braggadocio (noun)
boasting, act of: jactation (rare but evocative)
boat, adjective: navicular
boat, killed by: Kirsty Maccoll
boat, movement of: pitch, roll, yaw
boat, parts of: outboard motor
boat-shaped: cymbiform, scaphoid
bobcat, male: tom

bobcat, female: lioness

Bodleian Library: Oxford library originally founded by Humphrey, the Duke of Gloucester, in the fifteenth century. Re-established in 1602 by the scholar Thomas Bodley, after whom it is now named

body: "Every body is a mask of our inner beauty" – Ewen Brownrigg

body (distinct from its soul): soma

body clock: circadian rhythm

body function, study of: physiology

body movement, adjective: gestic, gestical

body movement, study of: kinesiology

body odour, fear of: bromidrosiphobia, osphresiophobia

body part, admiration for: agastopia

body tissue, science of: histology

body snatchers: William Burke, William Hare

bodyguards: Frank Farmer (played by Kevin Costner in the 1992 film *The Bodyguard*), Trevor Rees-Jones (who survived the car crash in which Princess Diana died)

Boer leader: Louis Botha

Boer War: 1899–1902

Boer-Zulu War: 1838–1839

Bohème, La: opera by Giacomo Puccini first produced in Turin in 1896

boil, adjective: furunculoid

Bolivia: republic in South America; formerly known as Upper Peru (until 1825)
    capital: La Paz (administrative), Sucre (judicial)
    currency: boliviano
    language: Spanish, Aymara, Quechua
    religion: Roman Catholic

Bolsheviks: Sergey Kirov, Vladimir Ilyich Lenin

bomb: aerial, atom, boobytrap, bouncing Betty, Claymore mine, cluster, depth charge, directional mine, doodlebug, H-bomb, incendiary, landmine, laser-gided, mine, Molotov cocktail, mortar, neutron, nuclear, nuclear warhead, TV-guided, V-1, water

Bombay, birthplace of: Rajiv Gandhi, Anish Kapoor, Rudyard Kipling, Zubin Mehta, Rohinton Mistry, Juliet Prowse, Salman Rushdie, T.H. White (British writer)

Bombay, fact: In 1998, benches in some of Bombay's parks were removed to prevent courting couples from sitting on them

Bombay, Hindi name: Mumbai

bombers (people): Saajid Badat (shoe bomber), David Copeland (dubbed 'the London nailbomber'), Tom Ferebee (bombardier aboard the Enola Gay), Guy Gibson (led the 1943 'dambusters' raid on the Möhne and Eder dams), Richard Colvin Reid (dubbed the 'shoe bomber'), Verloc (from Joseph Conrad's *The Secret Agent*)

Bonanza: long-running Western TV series set in and around Virginia City, Nevada, featuring the Cartwrights, an industrious, upstanding family who owned the 600,000-acre Ponderosa ranch
    created by David Dortort
    broadcast: 12 September 1959–16 January 1973
    cast: Lorne Greene (Ben Cartwright), Pernell Roberts (Adam Cartwright), Dan Blocker (Eric 'Hoss' Cartwright), David Canary (Candy Canaday), Lou Frizzell (Dusty Rhoades), Michael Landon (Joseph 'Little Joe' Francis Cartwright), Tim Matheson (Griff King), Bing Russell (Deputy Clem Foster), Ray Teal (Sheriff Roy Coffee), Mitch Vogel (Jamie Hunter-Cartwright), Victor Sen Yung (Hop Sing)

Bond, James: first appeared in print in *Casino Royale* (1953)
> **first played by** Barry Nelson in the live CBS TV production of *Casino Royale* (1954)
> **first played on radio by** Bob Holness on the radio in 1956
> **first played on film by** Sean Connery in *Dr No* (1962); and subsequently by George Lazenby, Roger Moore, Timothy Dalton, Pierce Brosnan and Daniel Craig
> **favourite drink:** vodka martini (very dry, shaken not stirred)
> **author:** Ian Fleming (in 2007, Fleming's estate disclosed that Sebastian Faulks had been approved to write a new James Bond novel – *Devil May Care* – to mark the centenary of Fleming's birth)
> **gun:** Walther PPK
> **name** borrowed from the American ornithologist whose principle work was *Birds of the West Indies* (1936)

bondage, dread of: merinthophobia
bondage paraphernalia: adhesive tape, ball gag, bar gag, body harness, bridle, cage, chains, collar, crucifix, leather cuffs, dildo gag, gag, handcuffs, head harness, hood, lacing, mittens, mouth cover, muzzle, padlocks, rape rack, ropes, shackles, speculum, spreader bar, stocks, straightjacket, stuffer, three-legged bloomers
bone, adjective: osteal, osteoid
bone disease: osteoporosis, rickets
bone doctor: orthopaedist
bones, number in human body: 206
bones, study of: osteology
Bony: nickname for Napoleon Bonaparte
bony outgrowth: osteophyte
Boobs from Brazil, the: nickname for Gisele Bündchen
book: airport novel, beach reading, bestseller, blockbuster, bonkbuster, doorstop, edition, hardback, novel, novella, page-turner, paperback, penny-dreadful, potboiler, publication, pulp fiction, tome
> - see literary genres

book burner: biblioclast
book collecting, desire for: bibliomania
book editor: Maxwell Perkins
book festivals: Edinburgh, Frankfurt, Hay-on-Wye, Lincoln, New Orleans, Oxford, Toronto
book hater: bibliophobe
book lover: bibliophile
book of fabric samples: swatch
book parts: flyleaf, title page, prelims, front matter, contents, prologue, epilogue, index, endpaper, recto, verso, spine
book printed before 1501: incunabulum
book prizes: Costa (formerly Whitbread), Man Booker, National Book Award, Newbery Medal, Pulitzer Prize for Fiction
book production: bibliogenesis
book town: Hay-on-Wye
book types – see literary genres
book thief: biblioklept
book-binding, art of: bibliopegy
Booker Prize (from 1980):
> **1980:** Rites of Passage, by William Golding
> **1981:** Midnight's Children, by Salman Rushdie
> **1982:** Schindler's Ark, by Thomas Keneally

1983: Life and Times of Michael K, by J.M. Coetzee
1984: Hotel Du Lac, by Anita Brookner
1985: The Bone People, by Keri Hulme
1986: The Old Devils, by Kingsley Amis
1987: Moon Tiger, by Penelope Lively
1988: Oscar and Lucinda, by Peter Carey
1989: The Remains of the Day, by Kazuo Ishiguro
1990: Possession: A Romance, by A.S. Byatt
1991: The Famished Road, by Ben Okri
1992: The English Patient, by Michael Ondaatje
　　　　 Sacred Hunger, by Barry Unsworth (a tie)
1993: Paddy Clarke Ha Ha Ha, by Roddy Doyle
1994: How Late It Was, How Late, by James Kelman
1995: The Ghost Road, by Pat Barker
1996: Last Orders, by Graham Swift
1997: The God of Small Things, by Arundhati Roy
1998: Amsterdam, by Ian McEwan
1999: Disgrace, by J.M. Coetzee
2000: The Blind Assassin, by Margaret Atwood
2001: True History of the Kelly Gang, by Peter Carey
2002: Life of Pi, by Yann Martel
2003: Vernon God Little, by D.B.C. Pierre (real name: Peter Finlay)
2004: The Line of Beauty, by Alan Hollinghurst
2005: The Sea, by John Banville
2006: The Inheritance of Loss, by Kiran Desai
2007: The Gathering, by Anne Enright
2008: The White Tiger, by Aravind Adiga
2009: Wolf Hall, by Hilary Mantel
2010: The Finkler Question, by Howard Jacobson
books, banned: *Lady Chatterley's Lover, Lolita*, Aristophanes' *Lysistrata* (banned in 1967 by the Greek junta), *My Life and Loves* (Frank Harris's autobiography, in four volumes), *Shanghai Baby, Tropic of Cancer, Ulysses* (banned in Britain for 14 years), *The Well of Loneliness* (a pioneering lesbian novel by Radclyffe Hall)
books, collection of: bibliotheca
books, controversial: *Lady Chatterley's Lover, Mein Kampf, My Life and Loves, Plateforme* (by Michel Houellebecq), *The Protocols of the Elders of Zion, Rage and Pride* (by Oriana Fallaci), *The Satanic Verses, The Story of O, The Well of Loneliness, Wicked Bible* (1631 edition which contains the misprint "thou shalt commit adultery")
books, destruction of: biblioclasm
books, fear of: bibliophobia
books, making of: bibliopoesy
books, seller of rare volumes of: bibliopole
bookmakers: Ladbrokes, William Hill
bookseller: bibliopole
bookseller, famous: John Smith
bookshops: Barnes & Noble, Blackwells, Books Etc, Borders, Dillons, Foyle's, Hatchards, Waterstone's
bookshop, biggest in the world: Barnes & Noble in Union Square, New York
bookshops, fact: bookshops are visited by less than 40% of the British population
boot: balmoral, beetle-crusher, bovver boot, buskin, Chelsea boot, desert boot, DMs, Doc Martens, finnesko, Hessian boot, jackboot, kinky boot, larrigan, monkey boot, napoleon, Russian boot, stogy, veldskoen, wellington boot

bootlegger: Jack 'Legs' Diamond
boredom: "The desire for desires"- Leo Tolstoy
boring, politically correct term: charm-free, differently interesting
Bosnia-Herzegovina: country in south-western Europe
    capital: Sarajevo
    currency: marka; formerly: dinar
    international peacekeeping force: SFOR
    language: Serbo-Croation (variation of
    religion: Sunni Muslim, Serbian Orthodox, Roman Catholic
boss-eyed: strabismal, strabismic
Boston, birthplace of: Ralph Waldo Emerson, Benjamin Franklin, Jack Lemmon,
    Leonard Nimoy, Edgar Allan Poe, Donna Summer, Uma Thurman
Boston airport: Logan
Boston groups: Aerosmith, Boston, The Cars, The Folk Implosion, The Gigolo
    Aunts, The Lemonheads, Letters to Cleo, The Magnetic Fields, The Mighty
    Mighty Bosstones, New Edition, New Kids On the Block, Overcast, Pixies
Boston river: Charles
botanists: Sir Joseph Banks (accompanied Captain Cook to Australia), Sabin
    Berthelot, Emma Braun, Robert Brown, George Carver, Arthur Cronquist,
    George Forrest, George Gardner, Sir Joseph Dalton Hooker, Carolus Linnaeus,
    Gregor Mendel, Robert Morison, Karl von Nägeli, Roscoe Pound, Wilhelm
    Schimper, Sir Hans Sloane, Armen Takhtajan, Eugenius Warming
Botox manufacturer: Allergan
Botswana: republic in southern Africa
    capital: Gaborone
    currency: pula
    language: English (official), Setswana
    religion: indigenous beliefs (85%), Christian (15%)
bottom – see buttocks
Bottomley, Virginia: anagram for "I'm an evil Tory bigot"
Boudicca's tribe: Iceni
bound and gagged, fear of being: merinthophobia
bounders – see rakes, famous
bounty hunters: Kola Bomm (from the *Zarn* books), Duane 'Dog' Chapman
    (reputedly the world's leading tracker), Domino Harvey (daughter of the actor
    Laurence Harvey), Tom Horn
bow, god of the: Ullr (Norse mythology)
bow stroke (on a cello, violin, etc): colpo
bow-shaped: arcate, arcuate
boxer: arm puncher, babyweight, bantamweight, champion, cruiserweight, dukester,
    featherweight, glass jaw, granite chin, heavyweight, light heavyweight,
    lightweight, middleweight, prizefighter, pro, pugilist, slugger, welterweight
boxers: Muhammad Ali, Max Baer, Nigel Benn, Jim J. Braddock, Frank Bruno,
    Joe Bugner, Joe Calzaghe, Primo Carnera, Georges Carpentier, Henry Cooper,
    James L. Corbett (aka 'Gentleman Jim'), Tom Cribb (bare knuckle champion
    of Britain, 1809–22), Oscar De La Hoya ('Golden Boy' of American boxing, a
    featherweight/ welterweight former Olympic gold-medal winner, twice accused
    of rape), Jack Dempsey, Chris Eubank, Bob Fitzsimmons, George Foreman,
    Julius Francis, Joe Frazier, Rocky Graziano, Emile Griffith (welterweight
    champion whose assault on Benny Paret in the ring led to the latter's death),
    Marvin Hagler, 'Prince' Naseem Hamed, Ricky Hatton, David Haye, Thomas

'Tommy' Hearns (aka 'Hit Man'), Larry Holmes, Evander Holyfield, Jack Johnson, Colin Jones, Roy Jones Jr, Amir Khan, Daisy Lang (nicknamed 'The Lady' in Germany), Art Lasky, Sugar Ray Leonard, Lennox Lewis, Sonny Liston, Joe Louis, Rocky Marciano, Floyd Mayweather, Oliver McCall, Barry McGuigan, Michael Moorer, James Murray, Manny Pacquiao, Floyd Patterson, Hasim Rahman, Sugar Ray Robinson, Max Schmeling, Leon Spinks, Michael Spinks, Tom Spring, Gary Stretch, John L. Sullivan (first heavyweight champion), Gene Tunney, Mike Tyson, Howard Winstone, Tim Witherspoon

boxers; formerly: Hume Cronyn, Bob Hope, Dean Martin, Robert Mitchum, Anthony Quinn, Oliver Reed (of the fairground variety), Robert Ryan, Ray Winstone

boxing, adjective: fistic, pugilistic

boxing attendant: cornerman, second

boxing commentator: Harry Carpenter

boxing managers: Joe Gould, Jackie Kallen (played by Meg Ryan in the film *Against the Ropes*)

boxing promoter: Don King

boxing terms: bagged fight, below the belt, bob and weave, bolo punch, bout, clinch, cold cock, combination, cross punch, dance, double up, drop one's guard, feint, go the distance, haymaker (a heavy punch), heel hook, jab, kidney punch, knockdown, knockout, low blow, mandatory eight count, mouse (a black eye), neutral corner, one-two punch, over and under, overhand punch, pull a punch, put away, rabbit punch, roll with a punch, round, roundhouse, shadow box, shaking off the cobwebs, slugfest, south of the border, stick (to jab), sucker punch (a surprise punch), Sunday punch, take out, technical draw, technical knockout, telegraphing a punch, throwing in the towel, TKO (technical knockout), under and over, uppercut

boxing trainer: handler

boy: BMOC, cat, chap, dude, frat boy, frat-jock, guy, hotshot, jock, kid, lad, nerd, street urchin

boy, collective noun: blush

boy bands: Backstreet Boys, Blue, Boyzone, Boyz II Men, Busted, Color Me Badd, East 17, Hanson, The Hoosiers, JLS, Jonas Brothers, McFly, The Monkees, 'N Sync, New Kids on the Block, Plain White Ts, Scouting for Girls, Take That, Westlife

Boy Scouts: founded in 1908 by Lord Robert Baden-Powell

Boy Scouts, patron saint of: George

Boyzone: Irish pop band prefabricated in Dublin in 1993; comprised of Ronan Keating (lead vocals), Stephen Gately (died: 10 October 2009), Keith Duffy, Shane Lynch and Mikey Graham. The actor Colin Farrell auditioned to join the band but was turned down

BPI: British Phonographic Industry

bra: originally known as a strophium in ancient Rome, the modern bra was invented by Herminie Cadolle in 1889. The word brassiere is French for "child's vest"

bra makes: Playtex, Triumph, Wonderbra

Bradford, birthplace of: Sir Edward Appleton (physicist), John Braine (novelist), Frederick Delius, Gareth Gates, David Hockney, Samuel Lister (inventor and industrialist), Albert Pierrepoint (hangman), J.B. Priestley, Peter Sutcliffe, Timothy West

Bradford riots: 9-10 June 1995

brain: "If the human brain were simple enough to understand, we'd be too simple to understand it" - Victor Lewis-Smith

brain: encephalon (technical term)
brain, adjective: encephalic
brain, base of: medulla oblongata
brain, inflammation of: encephalitis
brain, outer covering: dura mater
brand names, top ten twenty in the world: 1) Coca-Cola (brand value: 70,453);
    2) Microsoft; 3) IBM; 4) General Electric; 5) Intel; 6) Nokia; 7) Disney; 8)
    McDonald's; 9) Marlboro; 10) Mercedes; 11) Toyota; 12) Hewlett-Packard;
    13) Citibank; 14) Ford; 15) American Express; 16) Gilette; 17) Cisco;
    18) Honda; 19) BMW; 20) Sony (brand value: 13,153)
brandy: aqua vitae, Benedictine, calvados, cognac, Courvoisier, dop (cheap), eau-
    de-vie, frog's wine (slang), grappa, Hennessy, kirsch, Kirschwasser (made from
    cherries), marc, Martell, Pomace brandy, Presidente, pulque, Rémy Martin,
    slivovitz, VSOP
brandy, archaic name for: aqua vitae
brandy glass: snifter
brass, adjective: aeneous, aerose
brass instrument (musical): euphonium, flugelhorn, French horn, horn, ophicleide,
    saxhorn, sousaphone, trombone, trumpet, tuba, Wagner tuba
brass tarnish: verdigris
brassicas: broccoli, Brussels sprouts, cauliflower, kale, kohlrabi, spring greens
brat, collective noun: passel
Brazil: republic in South America
    capital: Brasília
    currency: real
    language: Portuguese (official); 120 native languages
    religion: Roman Catholic (89%), various Indian faiths
    fact: Brazil is the only country in the world named after a tree
    football, fact: Brazil is the five-time winner of the World Cup
Brazilian architect: Oscar Niemeyer
Brazilian Bombshell: nickname for Carmen Miranda
Brazilian footballers: Carlos Alberto Torres, Garrincha, Jairzinho, Pelé, Roberto
    Rivelino, Ronaldo, Socrates, Zico
Brazilian music: MPB, i.e. musica popular brasileira (the all-purpose term used by
    Brazilians to describe their pop music)
Brazilian novelist: Paulo Coelho
Brazilian racing drivers: Emerson Fittipaldi, Nelson Piquet
Brazilian singers: Céu, Cibelle, Astrud Gilberto, Bebel Gilberto
Brazilian supermodels: Gisele Bündchen, Fabiane Nunes, Caroline Ribeiro,
    Fernanda Tavares
Brazilian victim: Jean Charles de Menezes (shot dead by London police in the
    wake of the 7 July 2005 bombings)
bread: bagel, bap, barmbrack, barracouta, baton, Belgian, Belgain roll, black bread,
    bloomer, brick, bridge roll, bun, challah, chapatti, cholla, ciabatta, cob, coburg,
    collas, cornbread, cottage, crust, Danish, dodger (slang), doorstep, fancy milk,
    fancy rumpy, farmhouse, focaccia, French bread, French toast, fruit loaf, granary,
    heel, Hovis, loaf, long Vienna, matzo, milk loaf, nan, panada, paratha, pitta, plait,
    pone, poppadom, pumpernickel, roll, roti, rusk, rye, sandwich, scone, second,
    soda bread, sourdough, split long, split tin, spoon-bread, tea-bread, three-decker,
    tin, toast, top cottage, Turog bread, twist, Vienna, wheatsheaf, wholegrain,
    Wonderbread, Wonderloaf

Bread: American soft rock group formed in Los Angeles in 1968; comprised of David Gates (songwriter, vocals, guitar, keyboards), James Griffin (vocals, guitar), Robb Royer (vocals, keyboards) and Mike Botts (drummer). Disbanded in 1977

bread, adjective: panary

bread, blessed: eulogia (handed out to members of the congregation after the liturgy)

bread, for dipping into soup (a piece): sippet

breakfast, adjective: jentacular

breakfast cereals: All-Bran, Alpen, Bran Flakes, Cheerios, Coco Pops, Coco Snaps, Common Sense, Cornflakes, Corn Pops, Crunchy Nut Cornflakes, Frosties, Fruit 'n' Fibre, Golden Grahams, Grape Nuts, Harvest Crunch, Honey Nut Loops, Lucky Charms, Malties, muesli, Perfect Balance, Puffed Wheat, Raisin Wheats, Rice Krispies, Rice Pops, Shredded Wheat, Shreddies, Snow Flakes, Special K, Sugar Puffs, Sultana Bran, Sweetie Puffs, Toppas, Trix, Weetabix, Weeta Flakes, Weetos

    infant breakfast cereals: Foodle, Fush, Hello-Bito, Krinkle, Malt-Ho, Oatsina, Try-a-Bite

breast, adjective: mammary

breast, parts of: areola, Montgomery's glands (named after the obstetrician William Fetherston Montgomery, who identified them), nipple

breast, fact: one in two hundred women is born with a third breast, often a 'blind breast' without a nipple (according to Desmond Morris)

breast cancer, fact: one in nine women suffer from breast cancer

breast cancer, fact: only two per cent of all breast cancer cases are genetic

breast feeding: thelasis

breast formation in men: gynaecomastia

breast lift (surgical operation): mastopexy

breast-endowed: mammiferous

breast-shaped: mastoid

breasts: beauts, bee stings, boobs, bosoms, Bristol Cities (CRS), Bristols, cans, cantaloupes, dairy farm, flapjacks, flops tetitas, fried eggs, front bumpers, fun bags, gazungas, gib teesurbs (19th century slang, referring to particularly large breasts), globes, grapefruits, grapes, hooters, jubbies, jugs, kajoobies, knockers, lollies, mamas, melons, milk bottles, milkers, mosquito bites (particularly small ones), tatas, tits, wallopies, watermelons

breasts; average bust size: 36C (increased from the previous average of 34B)

breasts; endowed with large ones: macromastic

breasts; endowed with very small ones: micromastic

breasts, lack of: amastia

breasts, sexual arousal derived from: mazophilia

breasts, sexual arousal derived from the caressing of: erotomastia

breasts for birthday girl: Jenna Franklin, 15, from Warsop Vale in Nottinghamshire, who asked for and received breast implants for her 16th birthday

breastbone: sternum

breath, foul-smelling: bromopnea, halitosis

breath, shortness of: anhelation, dyspnea

breathe fluid into the lungs: aspirate (especially after vomiting, etc)

breathe on (particularly when introducing the Holy Spirit): insufflate

breathing (restoration of), adjective: anapnoic

breathing, laboured: dyspnoea

breathing, study of: pulmonology

breathing, temporary cessation of: apnoea

breathing aperture: nostril, spiracle (in insects, whales, etc)
breathing disorders: apnoea, asthma, cystic fibrosis, dyspnoea, pleurisy
breezes, fear of: aurophobia
brewers: Sir Benjamin Guinness, Edward Guinness
brewers, patron saints of: Augustine of Hippo and Luke the Apostle
brewer, collective noun: feast
bricks, artist displaying: Carl Andre
bridge: air, Bailey, bascule, cantilever, floating, foot, gangway, humpback, pontoon, suspension, swing, toll, tower
bridge, other side of: transpontine (adjective)
bridge authority (as in an expert of the game): Ely Culbertson
bridge players: Ely Culbertson, Omar Sharif
bridges, famous: Akashi-Kaikyo Bridge (Japan), Bridge of Sighs (Venice), Brooklyn Bridge (New York), Golden Gate Bridge (San Francisco), Great Belt Bridge (Denmark), Oresund Bridge (a ten-mile road and rail link connecting Sweden to mainland Europe via Copenhagen and Malmoe), Rialto Bridge (Venice), Tower Bridge (London), Tsing Ma suspension bridge in Hong Kong (a 4,475 ft road/rail bridge, a $920m joint British-Japanese venture)
bridges, fear of: gephyrophobia
Bridgewater Four: Michael Hickey, his cousin Vincent Hickey, James Robinson and Patrick Molloy (who died in prison in 1981), convicted of the murder of newspaper boy Carl Bridgewater in 1978; released at the end of February 1997 after the Crown decided not to contest their appeal (the Four had always protested their innocence)
Brief History of Time, A: bestselling book on science by Stephen Hawking
  original publisher: Transworld; paperback: Bantam
  world sales: over eight million
  British sales: 750,000 copies (hardback)
  final line: "For then we would know the mind of God"
brighten by cleaning: esclarish (verb)
Brighton, birthplace of: Chesney Allen, Aubrey Beardsley, Simon Cowell, Fatboy Slim (real name: Norman Cook), Eric Gill, Nigel Kennedy, The Levellers (folk-rock band), Max Miller, Steve Ovett (athlete), Sir Martin Ryle (astronomer)
Brighton bomb attack: 12 October 1984. The Grand Hotel, hosting the Conservative conference, was bombed by Patrick Magee, killing five
Bristol, birthplace of: Banksy, Julie Burchill, Thomas Chatterton (poet), Russ Conway, Tom Cribb, Lee Evans, Cary Grant, Damien Hirst, Nik Kershaw, Peter Nichols, Robert Southey (poet), Edward Teach (aka Blackbeard), Tricky
Bristol, fact: rated the friendliest town in Britain in a 2002 survey
Bristol groups: Day One, Massive Attack, Portishead, Straw, The Third Eye Foundation, Tricky
bristles, adjective: setaceous, setiferous, setose
Britain; slang: Fogland (Australian)
Britannia: royal yacht which served 43 years in the Royal Navy service, making 697 overseas visits. It was withdrawn from service in November 1997
British composers: Sir Malcolm Arnold, Sir Arnold Bax, Sir Henry Bishop, Sir Arthur Bliss, Frank Bridge, Benjamin Britten, William Byrd, William Cornyshe, Sir Noël Coward, Frederick Delius, John Dunstable, Sir Edward Elgar, John Foulds, Peter Fricker, Iain Hamilton, George Frideric Handel (born in Saxony), Josef Holbrooke, Gustav Holst, John Ireland, Constant Lambert, Thomas Linley, Elisabeth Lutyens, Peter Maxwell Davis, Ivor

Novello, Michael Nyman, John Ogdon, Sir Charles Hubert Parry, Henry
Purcell, Alan Rawsthorne, Edmund Rubbra, Kaikhosru Sorabji, Sir Arthur
Sullivan, John Taverner, Sir Michael Tippett, Ralph Vaughan Williams, Sir
William Walton, Sir Henry Wood
British Film Institute: established in 1933
British footballers: Jimmy Armfield, Alan Ball, Michael Ballack, Gordon Banks,
Cliff Bastin, David Beckham, George Best, Sir Trevor Brooking, Sir Matt
Busby, Sol Campbell, Sir Bobby Charlton, Jack Charlton, Brian Clough, Ashley
Cole, Joe Cole, Peter Crouch, Kenny Dalglish, Dixie Dean, George Eastham,
Michael Essien (from Ghana), Rio Ferdinand, Robbie Fowler, Trevor Francis,
Paul Gascoigne, Steven Gerrard, George Graham, Ryan Giggs, Jimmy Greaves,
John Greig, Jimmy Hill, Sir Jeff Hurst, Alex James, Vinnie Jones (played for
Wimbledon, Leeds United, Chelsea, Queen's Park Rangers), Roy Keane, Kevin
Keegan, Frank Lampard, Gary Lineker, Sir Stanley Matthews, Robert McColl,
James McFadden, Billy McNeill, Bobby Moore, Peter Osgood, Michael Owen,
Alf Ramsey, Micah Richards, Wayne Rooney, David Seaman (Arsenal and
England goalkeeper), Bill Shankly, Alan Shearer, Nobby Stiles, John Terry,
Vivian Woodward, Billy Wright, Ian Wright, Shaun Wright-Phillips
British generals: Oliver Cromwell, J.F.C Fuller, Charles Gordon, Henry V, William
Howe, Herbert Kitchener, Duke of Marlborough, George Monck, Bill Slim,
Duke of Wellington, Garnet Wolseley, Duke of York
- see soldiers
British Honduras: former name for Belize (until 1973)
British painters: Frank Auerbach (born in Berlin), Peter Blake, William Blake,
Ford Madox Brown (born in Calais), John Constable, Richard Dadd, Henry
Fuseli (born in Zurich), Thomas Gainsborough, Spencer Gore, Nicholas
Hilliard, William Hogarth, Augustus John, Leon Kossoff, Sir Edwin Landseer,
Wyndham Lewis, John Martin, Sir John Everett Millais, Ben Nicholson,
Samuel Palmer, Sir Edward Poynter, Sir Joshua Reynolds, Bridget Riley,
George Romney, Dante Gabriel Rossetti, Walter Sickert, George Stubbs,
Sir James Thornhill, Joseph Mallord William Turner, Joseph Wright of Derby
- see Pre-Raphaelites
British playwrights: Sir Alan Ayckbourn, J.M. Barrie, Sir Francis Beaumont, Aphra
Behn, Alan Bennett, Arnold Bennett, Alan Bleasdale, Edward Bond, Howard
Brenton, George Chapman, Caryl Churchill, William Congreve, Ray Cooney,
Sir Noël Coward, Thomas Dekker, Shelagh Delaney, John Drinkwater, John
Dryden, David Edgar, T.S. Eliot (born in Missouri), Sir George Etherege, John
Fletcher, John Ford, Michael Frayn, John Galsworthy, John Godber, Harley
Granville-Barker, Simon Gray, Robert Greene, Trevor Griffiths, Christopher
Hampton, David Hare, Richard Harris, Ronald Harwood, Thomas Heywood,
Thomas Holcroft, Ben Johnson, Sarah Kane, Thomas Kyd, Frederick Lonsdale,
Patrick Marber, Christopher Marlowe, John Marston, David Mercer, Thomas
Middleton, John Mortimer, Thomas Nashe, Peter Nichols, Joe Orton, John
Osborne, Thomas Otway, Joe Penhall, Sir Arthur Wing Pinero, Harold Pinter,
Alan Plater, Stephen Poliakoff, Sir Terence Rattigan, Jack Rosenthal, Thomas
Sackville, Anthony Shaffer, Sir Peter Shaffer, William Shakespeare, R.C.
Sherriff, James Shirley, Sir Tom Stoppard (born in Czechoslovakia), David
Storey, Cyril Tourneur, Sir Peter Ustinov, John Webster, Timberlake
Wertenbaker, Arnold Wesker, William Wycherley
British Telecom slogans: 'It's For Yoo-Hoo!'; 'It's Good To Talk'
Brixton riots: 11 April 1981, 13 December 1995

broadcasters: Alistair Cooke, Chris Evans, Sir Clement Freud, Emma Freud, Sir David Frost, Gloria Hunniford, Clive James, William Joyce (aka Lord Haw-Haw), Ludovic Kennedy, David Kossoff, Magnus Magnusson, Sir Jonathan Miller, Edward R. Murrow, Jeremy Paxman, Roy Plomley, Libby Purves, Jon Snow, Ed Sullivan, Studs Terkel, Mark Tully, Jeremy Paxman, Ruby Wax, Huw Wheldon, Alan Whicker, Terry Wogan, Alan Yentob
- see disc jockeys, radio presenters, TV newscasters, TV presenters, etc

Broadwater Farm riot: 6 October 1985; victim: PC Keith Blakelock; instigator: Winston Silcott

Broadway, nickname: the Great White Way

Brontës: Anne (aka Acton Bell), Charlotte (aka Currer Bell) and Emily Jane (Ellis Bell)

Bronx Bull: nickname for the boxer Jake LaMotta

bronze tarnish: verdigris

Brooklyn, birthplace of: Woody Allen, David Blaine, Mel Brooks, Al Capone, Neil Diamond, Jimmy Durante, Malcolm Forbes, George Gershwin, Ira Gershwin, Jackie Gleason, Rita Hayworth, Lena Horne, Michael Jordan, Danny Kaye, Larry King, Lenny Kravitz, Ralph Lauren, Bernard Malamud, Barry Manilow, Mary Tyler Moore, Eddie Murphy, Lou Reed, Joan Rivers, Mickey Rooney, Adam Sandler, Jerry Seinfeld, Tupac Shakur, Al Sharpton, Bugsy Siegel, Barbara Stanwyck, Barbra Streisand, Mike Tyson, Mae West

Brooklyn cuisine: Belgian waffles

Brookside, twice-weekly TV serial set on a Liverpudlian housing estate
    created by Phil Redmond
    broadcast: 2 November 1982–4 November 2003 (on Channel Four)
    cast: Rob Spendlove (Roger Huntington), Amanda Burton (Heather Huntington), Simon O'Brien (Damon Grant), Paul Usher (Barry Grant), Shelagh O'Hara (Karen Grant), Sue Johnston (Sheila Grant), Ricky Tomlinson (Bobby Grant), Katrin Cartlidge (Lucy Collins), Nigel Crowley (Gordon Collins), Jim Wiggins (Paul Collins), Doreen Sloane (Anabelle Collins), Daniel Webb (Gavin Taylor), Alexandra Pigg (Petra Taylor), Bryan Murray (Trevor Jordache), Sandra Maitland (Mandy Jordache), Anna Friel (Beth Jordache), Claire Sweeney (Lindsey Corkhill)

brothel, adjective: lupanarian

brother, adjective: fraternal

brothers, famous – see siblings, twins

brotherly love, adjective: philadelphian

brow, adjective: superciliary

bruise: contusion

Brunei: sultanate in north-west Borneo
    capital: Bandar Seri Begawan
    currency: Brunei dollar
    language: Malay, English
    religion: Muslim

Bruno: nickname for Bruce Willis

Brussels: "the briefcase capital of Europe"
    birthplace of: Jan Brueghel the Elder, Audrey Hepburn, Agnes Varda (filmmaker)
    buildings: Palais de Justice (the largest building constructed in the 19th century)
    statue: Mannekin-Pis (statue of a little boy urinating, originally sculpted by Jerome Duquesnoy but now replaced by a copy)

BSE: bovine spongiform encephalopathy; human variety: Creutzfeldt-Jakob disease (CJD)

BTW: by the way

buccaneers – see pirates

bucket wheel: noria

Buckingham Palace: royal household in the heart of London occupying 60 acres, with nearly 40 acres of garden. Built in 1702–1705 for the Duke of Buckingham – and named Buckingham House - the building was acquired by George IV in 1819 and completely overhauled by John Nash. As the construction work continued, Nash was dismissed in 1830, the king died the same year, while the monarch's brother, King William IV, died seven years after that. The architect Edward Blore completed the structure in 1847 (after removing the Marble Arch from the forecourt and placing it at the top of Park Lane) and Queen Victoria moved in. The famous classical façade – designed by Sir Aston Webb - was added in 1913. Today, the palace boasts 240 bedrooms, 19 state rooms and 78 bathrooms

Buckinghamshire, administrative centre: Aylesbury

Buck's Fizz: cocktail of champagne (or sparkling white wine) and orange juice

Budapest, nickname: the Pearl of the Danube

> **attraction:** the thermal baths (gushing at a rate of 70m gallons a day, up to 80° C)
>
> **birthplace of:** Zsa Zsa Gabor, Harry Houdini, Arthur Koestler, István Szabó (filmmaker)
>
> **river:** Danube

Buddha's teachings: the Four Noble Truths

Buddhism: founded by Siddhartha Gautama in the 6th century BC

Buddhist laws (the Eightfold Path): Right Understanding, Right Thought, Right Speech, Right Action, Right Livelihood, Right Effort, Right Mindfulness, Right Concentration

Buddhist divisions: Theravada Buddhism, Mahayana Buddhism, Vajrayana Buddhism (aka Tantric Buddhism)

Buddhist state of bliss and purity: nirvana

Buddhist temple, largest in the world: Borobudur in Central Java, Indonesia, built 750–842 AD

Buddhists, famous: Orlando Bloom, Neve Campbell, Jim Carrey, Leonard Cohen, Dalai Lama, Rupert Everett, Richard Gere, Philip Glass, Goldie Hawn, Courtney Love, Janet McTeer, Thich Quang-Duc, Charlie Sheen, Koo Stark, Patrick Swayze, Uma Thurman

Buenos Aires, birthplace of: Hector Babenco (filmmaker), Daniel Barenboim, Jorge Luis Borges, Leopoldo Galtieri, Olivia Hussey (actress), Fernando Lamas (actor), Juan Domingo Perón, Manuel Puig, Lalo Schifrin (composer), Guillermo Vilas

> **opera house:** Colon Theatro
>
> **presidential palace:** Casa Rosada
>
> **river:** Río de la Plata (aka the River Plate)

buffalo, collective noun: herd, obstinacy

buffalo, female: cow

buffalo, male: bull

buffalo butter: ghee

buffalo cheese: mozzarella

buffalo hunter: Buffalo Bill (aka William Cody)

Buffy The Vampire Slayer: phenomenally successful TV series about The Chosen One, Buffy Summers, a Valley Girl dedicated to ridding the world of vampires and the forces of evil
> **broadcast:** 10 March 1997–20 May 2003
> **created by** Joss Whedon, based on the 1992 film of the same name (in which Buffy was played by Kristy Swanson)
> **cast:** Sarah Michelle Geller (Buffy Summers), Nicholas Brendon (Alexander 'Xander' Harris), Alyson Hannigan (Willow Rosenberg), Charisma Carpenter (Cordelia Chase), Anthony Head (Rupert Giles), David Boreanaz (Angel/Angelus), Seth Green (Daniel 'Oz' Osbourne), James Marsters (Spike/William the Bloody), Marc Blucas (Riley Finn), Emma Caulfield (Anya Christin Emmanuella Jenkins/Anyanka), Michelle Trachtenberg (Dawn Summers), Amber Benson (Tara Maclay), Kristine Sutherland (Joyce Summers)

bugle belt: baldric
bugle call (to attack): warison
bugle call (to retire): first post, last post
bugle call (to wake): reveille
building, adjective: tectonic
building, tallest in world: the 162-storey Burj Dubai (2,716ft; completed in 2010);
> **second tallest building in the world:** the 101-storey Taipei 101, in Taipei, Taiwan (1,667ft; completed in 2004);
> **third tallest:** the 101-storey World Financial Center in Shanghai, China (1,614ft; completed in 2008)

building, tallest in Europe: Commerzbank Zentrale, in Frankfurt (850ft; completed in 1997)
building, tallest in the United Kingdom: Canada Tower, Canary Wharf, London (800ft; completed in 1991; designed by Cesar Pelli)
building society, biggest in the world: Nationwide
Bulgaria: republic in south-eastern Europe
> **capital:** Sofia
> **currency:** lev
> **language:** Bulgarian
> **religion:** Christian (Bulgarian Orthodox)

Bulgarian and famous: Elias Canetti (writer), Christo (artist), Georgi Dimitrov (politician), Anna Tomowa-Sintow, Ivan Vazov (poet)
bulge, adjective: bulbous, tumescent
bulimics: Paula Abdul, Russell Brand, Kelly Clarkson, David Coulthard, Princess Diana, Jane Fonda, Uri Geller, Elton John, John Prescott, Joan Rivers
bull, adjective: taurine
bull, castrated: steer
bull, collective noun: herd
bull, penis of: pizzle
bull, sound: bellow
bull, young: calf
bull-bodied man: Minotaur (Greek mythology)
bullet: blank, cartridge, dumdum, pellet, plastic bullet, rubber bullet, slug, tracer
bullet, explosive: first conceived by Leonardo Da Vinci in 1495
bullet belt: bandolier
bullet groove: cannelure
bulletproof vest: flak jacket, Kevlar vest
bullfight: corrida, tauromachy (archaic term)
bullfighter: matador, picador (mounted), torero

bullfighters, famous: El Cordobés (real name: Manuel Benítez), Julián Lopez (a star at 16, nicknamed "El Juli"), Manolete (real name: Manuel Sánchez), Enrique Ponce, Christina Sánchez

bullfighter's constable: algauzile

bullfighter's dart: banderilla

bullfighter's team: cuadrilla

bullfinch, collective noun: bellowing

bullock, collective noun: drove

bully: Harry Flashman

bulls, famous: Ferdinand, Little White Bull (from the Tommy Steele song)

bum crack: natal cleft

bumblebee, adjective: bombid

bundle, adjective: fascicular, fasciculate

burden, adjective: onerous

burglars: James Aitken (aka John the Painter), Arsene Lupin, A.J. Raffles

burglar killer: Tony Martin (who was jailed 'for life' for defending his home)

burglary, fact: burglary in the US fell by half between 1973 and 1992

burial, adjective: funerary

buried alive, fear of being: taphephobia

buried treasure book: Masquerade, by Kit Williams (which, within a children's story, hid clues to the location of a golden hare)

Burkina-Faso, formerly known as Upper Volta (until 1984)

   capital: Ouagadougou

   currency: African franc

   language: French (official), Mossi

   nickname: Land of the Upright Men

   religion: animist (with a sizeable Muslim minority)

Burkina-Faso filmmaker: Idrissa Ouedraogo

Burma: republic in South-East Asia officially known (since 1989) as the Union of Myanmar

   capital: Pyinmana (aka Nay Pyi Taw or Naypyidaw Myodaw); formerly: Yangon (also known as Rangoon)

   language: Burmese

   religion: Buddhist

   fact: world capital of snake-bite fatalities (an annual average of 1,400)

   birthplace of: Saki (the British writer, born Hector Hugh Munro)

   guerrilla group fighting the military regime: God's Army (once led by the ten-year-old twins Johnny and Luther Htoo – until they surrendered to Thai police in January 2001)

Burmese diplomat: U Thant

Burmese pro-democracy leader: Aung San Suu Kyi

burp: eructation

burrow, adjective: cunicular

Burundi: republic in East Central Africa; formerly known as Urundi (until 1962)

   capital: Bujumbura

   currency: Burundi franc

   language: Kirundi, French

   religion: Christian

bus: double-decker, minibus, Routemaster (traditional London double-decker, which graced the capital's streets for 50 years before being scrapped in December 2005), trolley

bus passenger: Rosa Parks (who, on 1 December 1955, refused to give up her seat to a white man and was consequently arrested, her trial leading to the abolition of transport segregation in the US)

bushbaby: galago

bushrangers: Ben Hall, Ned Kelly

business executives: Armand Hammer, Sir Terry Leahy, Robert McNamara, Sun Myung Moon, Mary Tyler Moore, Akio Morita, Yoko Ono, Sir John Rose, Sir Stuart Rose, Sir Alan Sugar, Thomas J. Watson
- see tycoons

bustard, adjective: otidine

butcher, collective noun: goring

butchers, patron saint of: Luke

butlers: Benson, Harold Brown (accused by police of stealing from Princess Diana), Paul Burrell (% Princess Diana), Hobson (played by John Gielgud in *Arthur*), Angus Hudson (played by Gordon Jackson in TV's *Upstairs, Downstairs*), Jeeves, Lurch (played by Ted Cassidy in TV's *The Addams Family*), Merriman (from *The Importance of Being Earnest*), Parker (from *Lady Windermere's Fan*), Alfred Pennyworth (% Batman), Stevens (played by Anthony Hopkins in *The Remains of the Day*)

butler, collective noun: sneer

butter: Alpine, Anchor, Dairy Valley, Danish, galam, Kerrygold, Lurpack, President, shea

butter, clarified: ghee

butter, melted: beurre noir

butter, rhyming slang: Danny Rucker (US), Dan Tucker (obsolete), lay me in the gutter

butterflies, British: blue, brimstone, brown, common blue, copper, dark green fritillary, fritillary, green hairstreak, green-veined white, grizzled skipper, marbled white, orange-tip, painted lady, skipper, small copper, small heath, small skipper, small tortoiseshell, vanessid, wall brown, white, white admiral

butterfly, adjective: lepidopteran, lepidopterous, pieridine, pierine

butterfly, collective noun: flutter

butterfly, fact: the insect uses its back feet to taste

butterfly, young: caterpillar

butterfly bush: buddleia

butterfly collector: lepidopterist

buttock, adjective: natal

buttock muscle: gluteus

buttock soreness: pygalgia

buttocks: aristotle, arse, ass, bottom, bubblebutt, bum, buns, butt, cheeks, derrière, duster (black slang), fern, frances, ghetto butt (a large behind), heinie, kun (Farsi), nates, Queen Mum (CRS for 'bum'), rear, rump, seat, sitter, tail, tush

buttocks, adjective: gluteal, natiform, pygal

buttocks, arousal derived from: pygophilia

buttocks, crack: natal cleft; gluteal fold (at which point the buttock meets the upper thigh)

buttocks, endowed with particularly beautiful ones: callipygian

buttocks, endowed with particularly hairy ones: dasypygal

buttons, fear of: koumpounophobia

buxom: busty, curvy, pneumatic, well-stacked, zaftig

buzzard, adjective: cathartine

buzzard, collective noun: wake
buzzard, young: chick
Byrds, The: influential US Country-folk/pop bank formed in Los Angeles in 1964;
    comprised of Roger McGuinn (guitar, vocals), Chris Hillman (bass), Gene
    Clark (vocals, tambourine), David Crosby (born: David Van Cortland; vocals,
    guitar) and Michael Clarke (drums). The group disbanded in 1973
Byzantium: former name for Istanbul

C

CA: postcode for California
cab drivers – see taxi drivers
cabaret singer, fictional: Sally Bowles
cabbages and brassicas;
    cabbages: pak-choi, pe-tsai, red cabbage, roundhead, Savoy, white cabbage
    brassicas: broccoli, Brussels sprouts, cauliflower, kale, kohlrabi, spring greens
cabbage soup: shchi
cabinetmakers: André Charles Boulle, Thomas Chippendale, George Hepplewhite,
    Jean Paul Riesener
cads – see rakes, famous
CADET: Can't Add, Doesn't Even Try
Cadillac: cattle train (black slang)
Cadiz, the sacking of: 1587 (in which Sir Francis Drake destroyed much of Philip
    II's Armada)
Caenozoic periods: Eocene (70 million years ago), Oligocene (34 million to
    23 million years ago), Miocene (25 million years ago), Pliocene (five to
    one million years ago), Pleistocene (11,550 years ago)
Caesar's first expedition to Britain: 55 BC
cake: angel cake, Battenburg, birthday cake, Black Forest, cheesecake, corn cake,
    cupcake, fruitcake, galette, gateau, Genoa, jellyroll, Linzer torte, Madeira,
    pound cake, rum baba, simnel, sponge cake, stollen, Swiss roll, teacake, torte,
    upside-down cake
calculus: invented by either Gottfried Wilhelm Leibnitz in 1674 or Sir Isaac
    Newton around the same time (the matter has still to be resolved)
Calcutta, birthplace of: William Makepeace Thackeray, Vikram Seth
    river: Hooghly (branch of the Ganges)
calf (of the bovine variety), adjective: vituline
calf (of the leg), adjective: sural
California, 31st state (1850), Golden State
    capital: Sacramento
    birthplace of: Jennifer Aniston, Belinda Carlisle, Mia Farrow, William Randolph
        Hearst, Jack London, Marilyn Monroe, Richard M. Nixon, Jimmy Osmond,
        Gwyneth Paltrow, Pete Sampras, John Steinbeck, Adlai Stevenson, Tiger
        Woods
    motto: 'Eureka' ('I have found it')
    state bird: California valley quail
    state flower: golden poppy
    state tree: California redwood
    tourist attractions: Yosemite Valley, Lake Tahoe, Napa Valley
    fact: in June of 2003 the state is declared 'bust,' with a $26 billion defecit
Caligula's horse: Incitatus
calming: ataractic

Calvin Kleins jeans, slogan: 'You know what comes between me and my Calvins? Nothing!'

Cambodia: country in South-East Asia
    capital: Phnom Penh
    currency: riel
    language: Khmer, French
    religion: Theravāda Buddhist

Cambodian leader: Pol Pot

Cambridge, adjective: Cantabrian or Cantabrigian

Cambridge Five: a spy ring that passed British secrets to the Russians during the Second World and on into the Cold War. Although the fifth member of the unit has not been officially identified, it is generally held that it was Victor Rothschild. The other four, Kim Philby, Donald Duart Maclean, Guy Burgess and Anthony Blunt, were all recruited at Trinity College in Cambridge, England, while serving as members of the Cambridge Apostles, a secret debating society

Cambridge University: "As far as I'm concerned, the real advantage of having gone to Cambridge is that you never have to attempt or even think about coping with not having gone there" – Stephen Fry

Cambridgeshire, administrative centre: Cambridge

Camden Town Group: organisation of English artists who thrived during the early twentieth century, including Harold Gilman, Charles Ginner, Spencer Gore and Walter Sickert

camel: Arabian, Bactrian, dromedary, oont (Anglo-Indian dialect), tylopod

camel, adjective: cameline

camel, collective noun: flock

camel, male: bull

camel, female: cow

camel, sound: groan, grunt

camel, young: calf, colt

camel driver: cameleer

camera makes: Canon, Kodak, Leica, Minolta, Nikon, Olympus, Pentax, Polaroid, Sony

Cameroon: a republic in West Africa
    capital: Yaoundé
    currency: African franc
    language: French and English (both official
    nickname: the Hinge of Africa
    religion: Christian, Muslim, animist

campaign for the abolition of piped music: Pipe Down

campaign for the abolition of smoking: Ash (Action on Smoking and Health)

campaigners: Erin Brockovich, Michael Foot, Lord Longford, Bertrand Russell, Mary Whitehouse
    - see activists

Campania, ancient language of: Oscan

Cams: acronym for Complementary or alternative medicines

Canada: "One of the great constitutional swamps of the Western world" - Mark Steyn, *The Spectator*

Canada: country in North America, formerly known as New France; the second largest country in the world
    capital: Ottawa
    currency: Canadian dollar

language: English, French
religion: Christian
highest point: Mount Logan
nickname: The Great White North
patron saints of: Anne, Joseph
Canada, number of words unique to: 10,000 (like 'skookum' for 'strong')
Canadian, nickname: Canuck
Canadian and famous: Pamela Anderson, Margaret Atwood, Dan Aykroyd, Saul
  Bellow, Genevieve Bujold, Raymond Burr, James Cameron, Neve Campbell,
  John Candy, Jim Carrey, Leonard Cohen, Douglas Coupland, David Cronenberg,
  Marie Dressler, Deanna Durbin, Atom Egoyan (film director), Linda
  Evangelista, Gil Evans (jazz pianist), Michael J. Fox, Bonnie Fuller ('queen of
  the newsstand'), Frank Gehry (architect), Phil Hartman, Margot Kidder, Stephen
  Butler Leacock (humorist), Amanda Marshall (singer-songwriter), Yann Martel,
  Louis-Joseph de Montcalm (soldier), L.M. Montgomery (author of *Anne of
  Green Gables*), Rick Moranis, Carrie-Anne Moss, Alice Munro (writer), Mike
  Myers, Leslie Nielsen, Michael Ondaatje, Ellen Page, Matthew Perry, Mary
  Pickford, Christopher Plummer, Keanu Reeves, Ryan Reynolds, Seth Rogen,
  Mack Sennett, William Shatner, Howard Shore (composer), Norma Shearer,
  Martin Short, Jeffrey Skoll, Donald Sutherland, Vanity, Jacques Villeneuve,
  Fay Wray, Neil Young
Canadian disc jockey: Pierre Brassard (who quizzed the British Queen on radio)
Canadian singers: Bryan Adams, Paul Anka, Natalie Appleton, Nicole Appleton,
  Michael Bublé, Celine Dion, Deanna Durbin, Nelly Furtado, Dan Hill, Terry
  Jacks, France Joli, Diana Krall, k.d. lang, Daniel Lanois, Avril Lavigne, Gordon
  Lightfoot, Sarah McLachlan, Joni Mitchell, Alanis Morissette, Anne Murray,
  Robbie Robertson, Shania Twain, Vanity, Martha Wainwright, Rufus Wainwright,
  Neil Young
canary, famous: Big Bird (see)
Canary Islands, birthplace of: Javier Bardem, Manolo Blahnik (shoe designer)
cancer: "We think of it as a death form, but perhaps we should think of it as
  another form of life, with its own appetites, feeding off us as we feed off other
  animals, fish, vegetables" – Simon Gray
cancer, fact: by the year 2020 one in two British people will develop cancer at some
  point in their lives
cancer, fear of: carcinomatophobia
cancer, preventive chemicals: lignans, isoflavanoids, sinigrin (found in Brussel
  sprouts)
cancer, preventive mineral: selenium (found in Brazil nuts, kidneys, mushrooms,
  spinach)
cancer, preventive sweet: PrevaCan
cancer, treatment pioneer: Sir Richard Doll
cancer doctor: oncologist
candelabrum: menorah (Jewish)
candelabrum, famous: Lumiere (from Disney's *Beauty and the Beast*)
candidate, collective noun: slate
candle maker/seller: chandler
candlestick: candelabrum, flambeau, girandole, menorah, sconce
candlestick stand: torchère
cane toad, fact: was introduced into Australia from South America in 1932 in an
  "ill-fated attempt" to combat a plague of grey-backed beetles

canine tooth, adjective: caniniform

cannabis: blow, Bob, draw, ganja, gear, grass, hash, hashish, marijuana, pot, puff, skunk, weed

cannabis cigarette: spliff

cannibal, adjective: anthropophagous

cannibals, famous: Idi Amin Dada (allegedly), Sawney Beane (15th century Scottish carnivore who, with his wife, children and grandchildren, was said to have killed and eaten over 1,000 people), Gabriele d'Annunzio (Italian writer and military leader who claimed to have eaten a roasted baby), Albert Fish (a house painter from New York City who cooked and ate children, preferably with carrots and onions), Edmund Kemper (6'9" American psycho who confessed to the murder of six co-eds and to a catalogue of decapitation, necrophilia and cannibalism), Lewis Keseberg (the American pioneer who, in 1846, was accused of eating six of his fellow travellers), Leatherface (protagonist of the 1974 film *The Texas Chain Saw Massacre*), Hannibal Lecter (creation of Thomas Harris), Arnim Meiwes (the German who, in 2001, videotaped the murder, dissection and consumption of Bernd Jürgen Brandes, allegedly at the latter's behest), Alferd Packer (the only person in US history to be convicted of cannibalism), Ratu Udre Udre (19th century Fijian chief who allegedly consumed up to 999 people)

cannibalism: anthropophagy

cannon: invented by Archimedes in the 2nd century BC

canoeist: Richard Fox
   - see rowers

canon, mode of verbal address: Canon _____

Canterbury, first archbishop of: Augustine
   - see Archbishops of Canterbury

cantor: Johann Sebastian Bach

Cape Verde: a republic off the coast of West Africa
   capital: Praia
   currency: Cape Verdean escudo
   language: Portuguese (official)
   religion: Christian (Roman Catholic), animist minority

Caped Crusader: nickname for Batman

capital punishment: judicial killing

capital punishment, USA: 38 out of 50 states still enforce the death penalty (those states that don't: Alaska, Hawaii, Iowa, Maine, Massachusetts, Michigan, Minnesota, North Dakota, Rhode Island, Vermont, West Virginia and Wisconsin - as well as the District of Columbia)

capitalism: "Under capitalism, man exploits man, while under communism it's the other way round" - old Czech joke

captains – see sea captains

Captain Pugwash characters: Captain Pugwash, Cut-Throat Jake, Tom the Cabin Boy, Barnabas and Willy. The characters Master Bates, Roger the Cabin Boy and Seaman Staines never appeared in the TV series (which was aired by the BBC between 1958 and 1967) as reported in the *Sunday Correspondent* and *The Guardian*. The series' creator John Ryan successfully won a retraction from *The Guardian* (and damages and legal fees) after the newspaper had propagated the urban myth in the 13 September 1991 edition of the *Young Guardian*.

car: boy racer, clunker, gas guzzler, jalopy, jam jar (CRS), motor, wheels

car, collective noun: fleet

car, top-selling (of all-time, anywhere): Toyota Corolla (1966)

car crash, killed in: Dodi Al-Fayed, Ian Bannen (actor), Marc Bolan, Albert Camus, Eddie Cochran, James Dean (in a Porsche), Princess Diana, Alexander Dubček, Grace Kelly, Mary Jo Kopechne (on Chappaquiddick Island, Massachusetts), Ernie Kovacs, Lisa Lopes, Linda Lovelace, Jayne Mansfield, Tom Mix, F.W. Murnau, Helmut Newton, Alan J. Pakula (filmmaker), General George S. Patton, Jackson Pollock, Steve Prefontaine, Bessie Smith, David Smith (American sculptor)

car designers: Herbert Austin, Harley Earl, Alfredo Ferrari, William Morris, Ferdinand Porsche

car fatality, first: Bridget Driscoll, who was killed in London in 1896 by a Roger-Benz driving at 4pmh

car manufacturers: Karl Benz, David Buick, Walter Chrysler, Gottlieb Daimler, John DeLorean, Enzo Ferrari, Henry Ford, Sir Edward Holden, Soichiro Honda, Charles Rolls, Sir Henry Royce, Ratan Tata, Kiichiro Toyoda

car salesman: Arthur Daley (from TV's *Minder*)

car theft control: the 'Minder,' an implanted electronic device the size of a cigarette packet that tracks vehicles remotely and can slow them down to 15mph

car types: banger, beetle, bubble car, convertible, coupé, dragster, estate, four-by-four, hatchback, hot rod, Humvee, jeep, landrover, limousine, model T, people carrier, saloon, sedan, sports car, station wagon

cars, famous: The Beast (Barack Obama's presidential Cadillac), Chitty Chitty Bang Bang, The Fast Lady, Genevieve, The Gnome-Mobile, Herbie the Love Bug, The Yellow Rolls-Royce

caraway seed liqueur: kümmel

carbon, adjective: carbonic

card, collective noun: hand, flush, suit, trick

card games: baccarat, beggar-my-neighbour, bezique, blackjack, Boston, brag, bridge, canasta, coon-can, cribbage, écarté, euchre, fan-tan, faro, gin rummy, grab, happy families, imperial, klaberjass, lansquenet, loo, Michigan, muggins, Napoleon, Newmarket, old maid, ombre, patience, Pelmanism, pinochle, piquet, poker, pontoon, Pope Joan, primero, quadrille, rummy, skat, skin, snap, solitaire, solo whist, vint, whist

card game authority: Edmond Hoyle

Cardiff, birthplace of: Charlotte Church, Roald Dahl, Dame Tanni Grey-Thompson, Ioan Gruffudd, Cerys Matthews, Ivor Novello, Griff Rhys Jones

Cardiff river: Taff

cardinals: Basil Hume, Stephen Langton, Henry Manning, Jules Mazarin, Reginald Pole, Armand Richelieu, Jaime L. Sin, Nicholas Wiseman, Thomas Wolsey

cardinal, fact: state bird of Illinois, Indiana, Kentucky, North Carolina, Ohio, Virginia and West Virginia

cardinal's hat: red hat, scarlet hat

cardiologist: Paul Dudley White

career, adjective: professional

caribou, female: doe

caribou, male: stag

caribou, young: fawn

caricaturists: Sir Max Beerbohm, George Cruikshank, Honoré Daumier, André Gill, James Gillray, Al Hirschfeld, E.T.W. Hoffmann, Thomas Rowlandson, Gerald Scarfe, Ralph Steadman

Carlsberg, slogan: 'Probably the best lager in the world'

Carmen: opera by Georges Bizet first produced in Paris in 1875; based on the 1847 novel by Prosper Mérimée

carnival, biggest in Europe: Notting Hill

carnival, biggest in the world: Mardi Gras, in Rio de Janeiro

Carnival of Animals, The: musical composition for two pianos and an orchestra written by Camille Saint-Saëns in 1886

carnivals: Aruba, Mardi Gras, Notting Hill, Rio de Janeiro, Trinidad, Venice

carp (fish): bream, crucian, dace, golden orfe, goldfish, ide, koi, minnow, mirror carp, orfe, roach, tench

carp (fish), adjective: cyprinoid

carpenter: chippie, wood butcher

carpenters: Adam Bede, Harrison Ford, James Hargreaves (who invented the spinning-jenny), Jesus, Joseph, John Meard, Denmark Vesey

carpenters, patron saint of: Joseph

carpet: Ardabil, Axminster, Brussels, Kidderminster, kilim, Persian, prayer mat, Savonnerie, sitringee, Turkish, Turkoman, Wilton

carriages, fear of: amakaphobia

carrot: root vegetable cultivated by the Dutch in the Middle Ages

carrot, white: white satin

carrots, cooked with: à la Croissy

Carry On Cleo (1964 film), famous line: Julius Caesar (Kenneth Williams): "Infamy! Infamy! They've all got it in for me!"

cart: carriole, dray, float, hackery (often pulled by a bullock), ralli car, surrey, tumbril

Carthaginian soldier: Hannibal

cartographers: John Bartholomew, Martin Behaim, Sebastian Cabot, Samuel de Champlain, Juan de la Cosa, Henry Gannett, Eduard Imhof, Eusebio Francisco Kino, Gerardus Mercator, Abraham Ortelius, Erwin Josephus Raisz, John Smith, John Speed, Martin Waldseemüller

cartoon, first animated on film: *Humorous Phases of Funny Faces* (1906; USA)

cartoonists: Charles Addams, Brad Anderson (*Marmaduke*), Tex Avery, Lynda Barry, Henry M. Bateman (Australian-born cartoonist who specialised in scenes of embarrassment), Leo Baxendale, Sir Max Beerbohm, Berkeley Breathed, Mel Calman, Al Capp, Caran d'Ache (Moscow-born, French pioneer of the comic strip), Daniel Clowes (famous for the semi-annual comic magazine *Eightball* and the graphic novels *Ghost World*, *Caricature*, *David Boring*, etc), George Cruikshank, Robert Crumb, Jim Davis (*Garfield*), Otto Dix, George du Maurier, Jules Feiffer, Lyonel Feininger, Michael ffolkes (born Brian Davis), Max Fleischer, Carl Ronald Giles, James Gillray (1757–1815), Alex Graham (creater of *Fred Basset*), Matt Groening, Hergé (aka George Prosper Remi, creator of *Tintin*), Al Hirschfeld, Daniel Johnston, Chuck Jones, Hank Ketcham, Osbert Lancaster, Gary Larson, Stan Lee, Sir David Low (political cartoonist), Donald McGill (renowned as the king of seaside smut), Gary Panter, Matt Pritchett (grandson of V.S. Pritchett and brother of gag writer Georgia Pritchett), Heath Robinson (famous for his satirical designs of elaborate machinery), Willie Rushton, Gerald Scarfe, Ronald Searle, David Shrigley, Jerry Siegel (with Joseph Shuster, creator of *Superman*), Shel Silverstein, Saul Steinberg, Norman Thelwell, James Thurber, Bill Tidy, Garry Trudeau (creator of *Doonesbury*), Bill Watterson (*Calvin and Hobbes*)

carving, adjective: glyptic (especially on precious stones)

carving, prehistoric: petroglyph

Casablanca (1942 film), famous lines: Rick Blaine (Humphrey Bogart): "Of all the gin joints in all the towns in all the world, she walks into mine"; Ilsa Lund

(Ingrid Bergman): "Play it, Sam. Play *As Time Goes By*"; Rick Blaine: "Here's looking at you, kid"; Ilsa Lund: "What about us?" Rick Blaine: "We'll always have Paris"; Rick Blaine, to Captain Renault: "Louis, I think this is the beginning of a beautiful friendship"

case: attaché case, briefcase, carpet bag, duffle bag, étui, Gladstone bag, handbag, suitcase

case, in law: deposition, lawsuit, pro bono publico, settlement, suit, testimony

cash machine: ATM, automated teller machine, cash dispenser, hole in the wall, Link machine

cashew nut, adjective: anacardic

cask: barrel, butt, firkin, hogshead, kilderkin, puncheon, tun, vat

cask stopper: bung, peg, spigot

cask-maker: cooper

castaway: Robinson Crusoe

Castlemaine XXXX lager, slogan: 'Australians wouldn't give a XXXX for anything else'

castles: Airth, Alnwick (used as the location for Hogwarts in the *Harry Potter* films), Angers, Arundel, Balmoral, Bamburgh, Barnard, Belvoir, Berkeley, Blarney, Bolingbroke, Bran (briefly the home of Vlad the Impaler and consequently dubbed 'Dracula's Castle'), Broughton, Bungay, Campbell, Cardiff, Cardross, Chirk, Christiansborg, Colditz, Conwy, Corfe, Craigievar, Culzean, Deal, Dover, Drogo (the last castle to be built in England), Dublin, Dunbar, Dunheved, Dunstanburgh, Dunster, Edinburgh, Glamis, Herstmonceux, Hever, Hillsborough (actually a Georgian mansion), Howard, Hohenschwangau, Kenilworth, Leeds, Malahide, Montezuma, Muncaster, Neuschwanstein (fairy-tale castle in the Bavarian Alps), Norris, Norwich, Nottingham, Odescalchi (Italy), Penrhyn, Pontefract (formerly known as Pomfret), Rothesay, Scarborough, Spilberk, Spis, Stirling, Stokesay, Terabil, Turnberry, Urquhart, Warwick, Windsor

castle, fictional: Gormenghast (% Mervyn Peake)

castle wall: bailey

castrated animal: spado

castration: atestus (removal of the testicles), deballing, doctoring, ederacinism (in which the sexual organs are torn out by the roots), emasculation, fixing, gelding, orchiectomy (surgical), penectomy (penis only), shave (removal of the penis *and* testicles)

castrato: Farinelli (born Carlo Broschi)

cat: Abyssinian, alley cat, Angora, Burmese, calico, chinchilla, Korat, Manx, moggie, Persian, piebald, purebred, Rex, sealpoint, Siamese, tabby, Tonkinese, tortoiseshell
- see cat, wild

cat, abnormal interest in: ailuromania

cat, adjective: feline

cat, collective noun: clowder, glaring (less common)

cat, fact: the average domestic cat spends 10,950 hours of its life purring

cat, fear of: aelurophobia, ailourophobia

cat, female: queen

cat, genetically modified: hypoallergenic cat (a genetically adapted feline whose skin will not secrete the protein that triggers most cat allergies)

cat, killing of: felicide

cat, male: tom

cat, sound: caterwaul, mew, meow, miaow, purr, spit

cat, wild: bobcat, bushcat, catamountain, catus, cheetah, cougar, jaguar, leopard, liger, lion, lynx, margay, mountain lion, ocelot, panther, puma, serval, tiger, tiglon, wildcat

cat, young: kitten

cat food: Authority, Choosy, Felix, Go Cat, Gourmet, Katkins, Kitekat, Nature's Recipe, Nutro, Paws, Sheba, Sophistacat, Whiskas

cat hater: ailurophobe

cat lover: ailurophile

cat-headed goddess: Bastet (Egyptian mythology)

cats, famous: Arthur (spokescat for Spillers Pet Food, in particular Kattomeat), Bagpuss, Bastet (Egyptian mythology), Beerbohm (beloved mouse-catcher at the Globe Theatre in London), Brobdingnagian Cat (from *Gulliver's Travels*), Bustopher Jones (from T.S. Eliot's *Old Possum's Book of Practical Cats*), Cat Gut, The Cat in the Hat, The Cheshire Cat, Cool Cat, Duchess (from *The Aristocats*), Faron (from *Peanuts*), Felix the Cat, Fritz the Cat, Garfield (the cartoon drawn by Jim Davis), Graymalkin/Grimalkin (from *Macbeth*), Grizabella (from T.S. Eliot's *Old Possum's Book of Practical Cats*), Growltiger (from T.S. Eliot's *Old Possum's Book of Practical Cats*), Humphrey (resident of No. 10 Downing Street), Mr Jinx, Krazy Kat (cartoon character), Lady Jane (from Dickens' *Bleak House*), Macavity (from T.S. Eliot's *Old Possum's Book of Practical Cats*), Mittins (Beatrix Potter character), Mog the Forgetful Cat, Moppet (Beatrix Potter character), Mr Mistoffelees (from T.S. Eliot's *Old Possum's Book of Practical Cats*), Mrs Ribby (Beatrix Potter character), Mungojerrie (from T.S. Eliot's *Old Possum's Book of Practical Cats*), Munkustrap (from T.S. Eliot's *Old Possum's Book of Practical Cats*), Old Deuteronomy (from T.S. Eliot's *Old Possum's Book of Practical Cats*), Ollie (comic strip), Pasht (Egyptian mythology), Pepper (silent movie star), Percy (Beatrix Potter character), Puff (from the *Dick and Jane* books), Puss-in-Boots, Ra/Re (Egyptian mythology), The Rum Tug Tugger (from T.S. Eliot's *Old Possum's Book of Practical Cats*), Rumpleteazer (from T.S. Eliot's *Old Possum's Book of Practical Cats*), Salem (from TV's *Sabrina the Teenaged Witch*), Scat (from *The Aristocats*), Sergeant Tibbs (from Walt Disney's *101 Dalmatians*), Sillabub (from the musical *Cats*), Simpkin (Beatrix Potter), Skimbleshanks (from T.S. Eliot's *Old Possum's Book of Practical Cats*), Snagglepuss (cartoon character), Snaggletooth (cartoon character), Sylvester, Tabitha Twitchit (Beatrix Potter), Thomas O'Malley (from Disney's *The Aristocats*), Thomasina (Paul Gallico), Tibbald (Persian folklore), Tom Kitten (Beatrix Potter), Tom (nemesis of Jerry), Top Cat (cartoon character), Webster (P.G. Wodehouse creation)

cats, murder rate: it is estimated that between 92 million and 275 million wild animals are killed in the UK every year by cats

cataleptic: Silas Marner

catapults, ancient: ballista (used for hurling large stones), mangonel (used for hurling large stones and fiery missiles), onager (popular with the Romans)

caterpillar: cankerworm, looper, measuring worm, palmer, palmer-worm, silkworm, span-worm, webworm, woolly-bear

caterpillar, collective noun: army

caterpillar leg: proleg

catfish, adjective: silurid

cathedrals, British: Aberdeen (St Machar's), Arundel, Bangor, Birmingham, Blackburn (Cathedral Church of St Mary the Virgin), Bradford, Brecon,

Brentwood (Cathedral Parish of St Mary and St Helen), Bristol, Bury St
Edmunds, Canterbury, Cardiff, Carlisle, Chelmsford, Chester, Chichester,
Coventry, Derby, Dundee, Dunkeld, Durham, Edinburgh, Elgin, Ely, Exeter
(St Peter's), Glasgow, Gloucester, Guilford, Hereford, Inverness, Kirkwall,
Lancaster, Leeds, Leicester, Lichfield, Lincoln, Liverpool, Llandaff,
Manchester, Middlesborough, Millport, Motherwell, Newcastle, Newport,
Northampton, Norwich, Nottingham, Oban (St. Columba's), Oxford, Paisley,
Perth, Peterborough, Plymouth, Portsmouth, Ripon, Rochester, Salford, St
Alban's, St Andrews, St Asaph, St Davids, St Paul's (London), Salisbury,
Sheffield, Shrewsbury, Southwark (London), Southwell, Swansea, Truro,
Wakefield, Wells, Westminster (London), Winchester, Worcester, Wrexham
(St Mary's), York Minster

cathedrals, French: Amiens Bayeux, Chartres, Notre Dame

cathedral, largest in the world: St John of the Divine in New York City

cathedral, oldest in America: Catedral Santa María La Menor, in Santo Domingo,
Dominican Republic

cathedral, oldest in Britain: Canterbury

Catherine the Great: nickname for Empress Catherine II of Russia

Catholics, number in world: 1.1 billion

cattle, adjective: bovine

cattle, collective noun: herd

Caucasian, derogatory term: honky, ofay

Caucasian, politically correct term: melanin impoverished, person of non-colour

cause, science of: aetiology

cautionary tales: *Accidents and Remarkable Events, Cautionary Tales for Children,
Dangerous Sports, Flowers of Instruction, Original Poems for Infant Minds,
Struwwelpeter, Tales Uniting Instruction with Amusement*

Cavalier poets: Thomas Carew, Robert Herrick, Richard Lovelace, John Suckling
- see English poets, poets, etc

cave, adjective: spelaean, speluncar

cave, deepest in the world: Réseau Jean Bernard in France

cave dweller: troglodyte

cave expert: speleologist

cave explorer: speleologist, spelunker

cave paintings: Ajanta (India), Altamira (southern France), Bédeilhac (the
Pyrenees), Lascaux (southern France)

caves, study of: speleology

caviar: beluga, oscietra, sevruga

caviar producers: lumpfish, paddlefish, sturgeon (a large, shark-like fish)

caviar substitute: Avruga (made from the roe of the common herring)

cavity in mouth, adjective: buccal

CBE: Commander of the Order of the British Empire

CCTV: close circuit television

CCTV, fact: ten per cent of the world's 30 million CCTV cameras are in Britain; the
average UK citizen is caught on camera 300 times a day

CD: compact disc

CD: first marketed in 1983 (in Europe)

celebrity: "A person who works hard all his life to become known, then wears dark
glasses to avoid being recognised" - Fred Allen; "I *plummeted* to stardom...and
it's a little like drinking strained orange juice. Being a celebrity removes the
pulp from life.. You lose a lot of the nutrients" - Dustin Hoffman; "Celebrity is

a mask that eats into the face'" - John Updike; "In the future, everyone will be world famous for 15 minutes" – Andy Warhol, Stockholm, 1968; "Celebrity is about swapping a load of good friends for a load of acquaintances" - Irvine Welsh

cellists: Sir John Barbirolli, Pablo Casals, Jacqueline du Pré, Steven Isserlis, Maria Kliegel, Julian Lloyd Webber, Gregor Piatigorsky, Mstislav Rostropovich, Guilhermina Suggia, Paul Tortelier, Yo-Yo Ma

cello: Davidoff

cello makers: Andrea Amati, Giovanni Battista Guadagnini, Giuseppe Guadagnini

cells (of animals and plants), science of: cytology

celluloid: cellulose-based material from which film stock is made

Celtic priest: Druid

censors: Robin Duval, James Ferman, Will Hays, Andreas Whittam Smith, John Trevelyan

censorship: DA-Notice (previously known as a D-Notice)

centenarians, fact: in 1951 there were only 271 people aged more than 100 in Britain; in 1971 there were 1,185; in 1997 there were 8,000

Centigrade: temperature scale devised by Anders Celsius in 1741

Central African Federation – see Federation of Rhodesia and Nyasaland

Central African Republic: land-locked country in central Africa; formerly known as Ubangi-Shari (until 1958)
>   **capital:** Bangui
>   **currency:** African franc
>   **language:** French (official), Sango
>   **religion:** Christian, animist

centre of attention: cynosure

CEO: Chief Executive Officer

ceramic designers: Grayson Perry, Adelaide Robineau

cereals - see breakfast cereals

Ceylon: former name for Sri Lanka

CFA: Communauté Financière Africaine (African Financial Community)

Chad: republic in north-central Africa
>   **capital:** Ndjamena
>   **currency:** African franc
>   **language:** Arabic (official), French
>   **native:** Chadian
>   **nickname:** The Dead Heart of Africa
>   **religion:** Muslim; also Christian, animist

Chadian dictator: Hissene Habre

chaff, adjective: paleaceous

chain, adjective: catenary, catenoid, catenular, catenulate, concatenate

chain mail coat: habergeon, hauberk

chair: American Windsor, armchair, Boston rocker, button-back, cain chair, Carver, chair-bed, chaise longue, Chippendale, commode, deckchair, easy chair, electric, faldstool (for a bishop), jampan (type of sedan), ladder-back, Morris chair, Philadelphia, recliner, rocking chair, rush seat, sedan, sling-back, William and Mary banister back, Windsor, Windsor rocker

chalk, adjective: cretaceous

chamber, adjective: cameral

champagne: "In victory you deserve Champagne; in defeat you need it" – Napoleon Bonaparte

champagne: Charles de Fere Brut Reserve, Charles de Fere Brut Rose, Laurent Perrier Brut, Mercier Brut, Perrier Jouet Brut, Perrier Jouet Fleur de Champagne, Piper Sonoma Brut, California, Tattinger Brut Reserve, Tattinger Brut Reserve Rose Champagne, Piper SonomaBrut, California, Tattinger Brut Reserve, Tattinger Brut Reserve Rose

champagne, fact: the UK imports more champagne than any other country in the world (34.5 million bottles a year)

champagnes, luxury: Bollinger R.D., Chasteau de Irroy, Diamant Bleu, Dom Perignon, Dom Ruinart, Mercier Reserve de l'Empereur, Roederer Cristal, Taittinger Comtes de Champagne

chance, adjective: aleatoric, aleatory

change loyalties, principles, sides, etc: tergiversate

chaos, goddess of: Eris (Greek)

Chappaquiddick car crash: 18 July 1969, in which Senator Edward Kennedy drove his car off Dike Bridge. His passenger, Mary Jo Kopechne, died in the accident

character; second most important in a play or novel: deuteragonist

chariot: quadriga

chariot god: Helios (Greek)

charities: Age Concern (an alliance of over 400 charities), Barnardos, Brake (road safety), Cancer UK (largest charity in Britain, a merger of Imperial Cancer and Cancer Research), Centrepoint (for homeless young people), Christian Aid, Crimestoppers, Crisis (for the homeless), Dorcas Society, Help the Aged, Kidscape, The Leprosy Mission, Make Trade Fair, Marie Curie Cancer Care, Mind (mental health), The National Aids Trust, The National Society for the Prevention of Cruelty to Children (NSPCC), Oxfam (the UK's second-largest charity, with an annual turnover of £200 milion and with 600,000 members), Prince's Trust, The Samaritans, Save the Children, Scope, Shelter, SSAFA (Soldiers', Sailors' and Airmen's Families Association), The Spastics' Society (Scope), UNICEF (United Nations Children's Fund), The Victoria Society

charities, patron saint of: Vincent de Paul

charity, adjective: eleemosynary

Charles, Prince; favourite words (in order of preference): extraordinary, ghastly, appalling, absolutely, wonderful, dreadful, horrid, stark staring mad, amazing, awful

Charles the Great: nickname for Charlemagne

Charleston, South Carolina: site of the opening battle of the American Civil War (marked by the Fort Sumter National Monument)

Charlie's Angels: light-hearted, one-hour crime show on ABC TV featuring three visually alluring police academy graduates. Over the seasons (and a total of 115 episodes), the graduates changed faces (and bra size) but all worked as private detectives for Charles Townsend Associates. In 2000 the series was adapted for the big screen with Cameron Diaz, Drew Barrymore and Lucy Liu as the angelic trio, followed in 2003 by a sequel, *Charlie's Angels: Full Throttle*

    created by: Ben Roberts

    broadcast: 22 September 1976–19 August 1981

    cast: Kate Jackson (Sabrina Duncan), Farrah Fawcett-Majors (Jill Munroe), Jaclyn Smith (Kelly Garrett), David Doyle (John Munroe), John Forsythe (the voice of Charlie Townsend), Cheryl Ladd (Kris Munroe), Shelley Hack (Tiffany Welles), Tanya Roberts (Julie Rogers)

charm: "The ability to be truly interested in other people" – Richard Avedon; "An art developed by men to spare them the risks of the fight" - Leanda de Lisle

chastity: "Of all sexual aberrations, chastity is the strangest" - Anatole France

chastity, patron saint of: Agnes of Rome

chat show hosts – see talk show hosts

Chattanooga, battles of: 7 June-8 June 1862, 21 August 1863, 23 November-25 November 1863

chattering classes: term coined in the 1980s (by the journalist Frank Johnson) to describe intellectually precocious and socially outspoken Lefties

chauffeurs: Henri Paul (who was driving the Mercedes that killed Princess Diana and Dodi Fayed in Paris), Aloysius Parker (from *Thunderbirds*), Thomas Watkins (from TV's *Upstairs, Downstairs*)

cheap: bargain-basement, cut-rate, dirt-cheap, el cheapo, low-budget, low-cost, steal

cheapest cities in the world: Asuncion (in Paraguay); Montevideo (in Uruguay); and Santo Domingo (in the Dominican Republic)

Chechnya: constituent republic of South Russia; aka Chechen Republic
    capital: Grozny
    currency: Russian rouble
    language: Russian, Chechen
    religion: Sunni Muslim

cheek, adjective: buccal, malar

cheek (protruding), adjective: buccate

cheek, plastic surgery of: genyplasty

cheekbone, adjective: malar

cheers!: cin cin! (Italian), kampai! (Japanese), l'chaim! (Hebrew, Yiddish), na zdrowie! (Polish), prosit! (Dutch), salud! (Spanish), salute! (Italian), santé! (French), selamat! (Malay), skål! (Danish, Swedish), vivas! (Portuguese)

Cheers: NBC TV sitcom set in a bar in downtown Boston
    created by Glen Charles, Les Charles and James Burrows
    broadcast: 30 September 1982–20 May 1993
    cast: Ted Danson (Sam 'Mayday' Malone), Shelley Long (Diane Chambers), Nicholas Colasanto (Coach Ernie Pantusso), Rhea Perlman (Carla Tortelli), George Wendt (Norm Peterson), John Ratzenberger (Cliff Clavin), Kelsey Grammer (Dr Frasier Crane), Woody Harrelson (Woody Boyd), Bebe Neuwirth (Dr Lilith Sternin), Kirstie Alley (Rebecca Howe), Tom Skerritt (Evan Drake), Roger Rees (Robin Colcord), Jay Thomas (Eddie LeBec)

cheese: "Milk's leap towards immortality" – Clifton Fadiman

cheese: Allerdale, Asiago d'Allevio, Asiago Grasso di Monte, Baby Bel, Bavarian Blue, Bel Paese, Bergkase, Bleu d'Auvergne, Bleu d'Aveyron, Bleu de Bresse, Bleu de Corse, Bleu de Gex, Bleu de Laqueuille, Blue Castello, blue Cheshire, blue Lymeswold, blue Shropshire, blue Stilton, Blue Swaledale, brie, brie de meaux, Caciocavallo, Camembert, cantal, Chamois d'Or, Chaumes, cheddar (including Canadian, English, farmhouse, Scottish, Somerset, etc), Cheshire, chèvre, chèvre blanc, Cilowen organic, cottage cheese, cream cheese, Danish Blue, Danish Mycella, Danish Svenbo, Daylesford Organic, Dolcelatte, Doux de Montagne, Dutch Gouda, Edam, Emmental, farmhouse cheddar, feta, Fourme d'Ambert, fromage blanc, fromage frais, gammelost, goat Camembert, goat's log, Gorgonzola, Gouda, Gruyère, halloumi, Havarti, Innes button natural, Jarlsberg, Kefalotyri, Limburger, Lymeswold, manchego, mascarpone, Monterey Jack, mousetrap, mozzarella, Mycella, Neufchatel, Norwegian Jarlsberg, Oxford blue, Parmesan, pecorino, Pecorino Pepato, Pecorino Romano, Pecorino Sardo, petit Suisse, Pipo Crem', Port Salut, pot cheese, Provolone, quark, ricotta, Romano, Roquefort, roule garlic, sage Derby, Sapsago, Sbrinz, smoked Emmental, St Paulin, Strathdon blue, Swiss Emmental, Swiss Gruyère, Taleggio, Vacherin, Vacherin Fribourgeois, Wensleydale, white Lymeswold

cheese, adjective: caseous

cheese, British: Allerdale, Appleby's Cheshire, Blue Swaledale, Caerphilly, Cheshire, Cilowen organic, Colston Bassett stilton, Daylesford Organic, Derby, Derbyshire, double Gloucester, Innes button natural, Kirkham's Lancashire, Lancashire, Leicester, Montgomery's cheddar, Oxford blue, Red Leicester, Sage Derby, Shropshire Blue, Somerset brie, Somerset organie brie, Sparkenhoe Red Leicester, Stilton, stinking bishop, Strathdon blue

cheese, to become like: caseate

cheese exhibition: Nantwich Cheese Show (Britain's leading cheese competition)

cheese wheel (small): truckle

cheetah, young: cub

cheetah conservationist: Laurie Marker

chef's hat: toque

chefs: Ferran Adrià, Raymond Blanc, Heston Blumenthal (invented bacon and egg ice-cream), Michel Bourdain, Marie-Antoine Carême, Antonio Carluccio, Robert Carrier, Julia Child, Auguste Escoffier, Hugh Fearnley-Whittingstall, Keith Floyd, Sir Clement Freud, Conrad Gallagher, Sophie Grigson, Ken Hom (wok master), Loyd Grossman (from TV's *Masterchef*), Ainsley Harriott, Madhur Jaffrey, Graham Kerr (aka 'The Galloping Gourmet'), Peter Kromberg, Nico Ladenis, Anton Mosimann, Jean-Christophe Novelli, Jamie Oliver, Gordon Ramsay, Gary Rhodes, Claudia Roden, Albert Roux, Zena Skinner (1950s' TV cook), Delia Smith, Eliza Smith, Alexis Soyer (known as the first celebrity chef), Rick Stein, Marco Pierre White, Antony Worrall Thompson - see cooks, cookery writers, food writers

chemical weapons: A-232 (a binary nerve agent developed by the Russians that is so lethal that a microscopic amount can kill), agent orange, anthrax, botulinum, nerve gas, ricin

chemists: Richard Abegg, Sir Frederick Abel, Sir William Abney, John Anderson, Francis William Aston, Amedeo Avogadro, Konrad Bloch, Jesse Boot, Robert Boyle, Robert Bunsen (inventor of the Bunsen burner), Wallace Carothers, Frank Cotton, Charles Coulson, Sir William Crookes, Sir James Dewar (invented the forerunner to the vaccum flask), Otto Diels, Johann Döbereiner, Jean Baptiste Dumas, Manfred Eigen, Michael Faraday, Joseph Gay-Lussac, Josiah Willard Gibbs, Fritz Haber, Otto Hahn, Jean-Baptiste van Helmont, Cyril Hinshelwood, George H. Hitchings Jr., Dorothy Hodgkin, Robert Hooke, Frédéric Joliot-Curie, Irène Joliot-Curie, Sir Harold Kroto, Irving Langmuir, Primo Levi, William Lipscomb, James Lovelock, John Macadam, Dmitri Mendeleyev, Thomas Midgley Jr, Ludwig Mond, Walther Nernst, Nicéphore Niepce, Alfred Nobel, Louis Pasteur, Linus Pauling, Jean Felix Piccard, Sir William Ramsay, Theodore Richards, Sir Robert Robinson, Sir Henry Roscoe, Christian Schönbein, Leo Sternbach, Arne Tiselius, Alexander Todd, Harold Urey, Alfred Werner, Richard Willstätter, Georg Wittig, Friedrich Wöhler

cherry, wild: gean, mazard

cherry brandy: kirsch

cherry liqueur: maraschino, ratafia (although not exclusively cherry)

cherry plum: myrobalan

cherry-coloured: cerise

cherubs, in painting: amoretto, putto
Cheshire, administrative centre: Chester
chess: game descended directly from the Indian chaturanga, played thirteen
    centuries ago
chess, adjective: scacchic
chess, parallel games: chaturanga, Chinese chess, Japanese Shogi
chess champions: Alexander Alekhine, Mikhail Botvinnik, José Raúl Capablanca,
    Pedro Damiano, Louis Charles de la Bourdonnais, Pierre Charles de Saint-
    Amant, Max Euwe, Bobby Fischer, Gioachino Greco, David Howell (at eight,
    the youngest person ever to beat a chess grandmaster - in August 1999), Anatoli
    Karpov, Garry Kasparov, Paul Keres, Victor Korchnoi, Alexandra Kosteniuk,
    Vladimir Kramnik, Emanuel Lasker, Ruy Lopez, Luis Ramirez de Lucena,
    Alexander McDonnell, Luke McShane (a champion at the age of ten), Paul
    Morphy, Tigran Petrosian, François-André Danican Philidor, Giulio Polerio,
    Nigel Short, Vasili Smyslov, Boris Spassky, Howard Staunton, Wilhelm Steinlitz,
    Mikhail Tal
chess computer: Deep Blue (c/o IBM)
chess pieces: bishop, king, knight, pawn, queen, rook (standard); archbishop,
    chancellor, empress, grasshopper, nightrider (unorthodox)
chess tournament, annual venue: Linares in Spain
chessboard column: file
chest, adjective: pectoral
chest pain: angina
chestnut, adjective: castanean, castanian
chew: manducate, masticate
chewing gum: patented in 1869 by the American William F. Semple
Chicago, birthplace of: Patricia Arquette, Raymond Chandler, John Cusack,
    Bruce Dern, Walt Disney, James T. Farrell (novelist), Harrison Ford, Benny
    Goodman, Ernest Hemingway, John Hughes, Richard Kiley, Ken Olin, Fritz
    Pollard (footballer), Sidney Sheldon, Gary Sinise, Gloria Swanson, Ruby Wax,
    Raquel Welch
Chicago airport: O'Hare
Chicago building: the 110-storey Willis Tower (formerly known as the Sears Tower)
Chicago nickname: Second City, Windy City
Chicago river: Chicago
Chicago subway: CTA (Chicago Transit Authority) - nicknamed 'the El'
Chicago tourist attraction: Chicago Museum of Science and Industry
Chicago fire: 8–10 October 1871
chicken, adjective: gallinaceous
chicken, castrated: capon
chicken, collective noun: brood, clutch, peep
chickens, fact: there are more chickens in the world than humans
chicken, famous: Chicken Little, Ginger (from the film *Chicken Run*), Rocky (from
    the film *Chicken Run*)
chickens, fear of: alektorophobia
chicken, female: hen
chicken, male: cock, rooster
chicken, sound: cackle, peep
chicken, young: chick, chicken
chicken house: coop, pen
chicken's posterior: curpin

chickenpox: varicella

child: ankle biter, bambino, brat, kid, nipper, rug rat, sprog, stripling, tot, tyke

child: "A child's place is in the wrong" - Rachel Sylvester, *The Daily Express*

child abuse, fact: British children are less likely to be killed by accident or abuse than those in any other country except Sweden (according to a Unicef report)

child abuse organisation: Accuracy About Abuse

child killers: Paul Bernardo, Herod of Judaea, Karla Homolka, Peter Kurten (immortalised in the 1931 film *M*), Dennis Rader (aka 'the BTK killer'), Gilles de Rais (murdered and mutilated more than 50 children), Robert Thompson, Jon Venables, Frederick West
- see baby killers

child prodigies of art: Marla Olmstead, Kieron Williamson, Stephen Wiltshire

child stars: Baby Le Roy, Freddie Bartholemew, Linda Blair, Abigail Breslin, Jackie Coogan, Jackie Cooper, Macaulay Culkin, Bobby Driscoll, Dakota Fanning, Jodie Foster, Mark Lester, Roddy McDowall, Hayley Mills, Margaret O'Brien, Tatum O'Neal, Anna Paquin, Mary Pickford, Mickey Rooney, Brooke Shields, Shirley Temple, Mara Wilson, Natalie Wood

childbirth, adjective: obstetric

childbirth, goddess of: Eileithyia (Greek), Heket (Egyptian), Juno (Roman)

childbirth, fear of: tocophobia

childbirth, patron saints of: Gerard Majella and Raymond Nonnatus

childbirth, prolonged: dystocia

childbirth doctor: obstetrician

childbirth specialists: Sheila Kitzinger, Dr Benjamin Spock

childhood: "I had a wonderful childhood, which is tough, because it's hard to adjust to a miserable adulthood" - Larry David; "The credit balance of the novelist" - Graham Greene

childless: nulliparous

childless woman: nullipara

children, family average in Britain: 1.2; formerly: 2.4

children, hatred of: misopaedia (especially of one's own offspring)

children, killing of: infanticide

children, naked pictures and figures of in art: putti

children, patron saint of: Nicholas

children, study of (in medicine): paediatrics

children, without: nulliparous (adjective)

children's characters: Barney, Basil Brush, The BFG, Big Bird, Bill & Ben the Flowerpot Men, Budgie the Little Helicopter, Clifford the Big Red Dog, Donald Duck, Goofy, Heidi, Humpty Dumpty, Kermit, Mickey Mouse, Miss Piggy, Mr Blobby, Sonic the Hedgehog, Noddy, Paddington Bear, Roland Rat, Scooby Doo, Sooty & Sweep, Henry Sugar, Tom Thumb, Winnie the Pooh, Willy Wonka
- see fairy tale characters

Children's Crusade: 1212

children's doctor: paediatrician

children's writers: Aesop, Hans Christian Andersen, Robert Ballantyne, J.M. Barrie, Enid Blyton, Christianna Brand, Frances Hodgson Burnett, Eric Carle, Lewis Carroll, Sharon Creech, Roald Dahl, Julia Donaldson, Mary Elliott, Elizabeth Enright, Anne Fine, Kenneth Grahame, Kate Greenaway, Jacob Ludwig and Wilhelm Carl Grimm, Daniel Handler (aka Lemony Snicket), Roger Hargreaves (creator of the Mr Men books), Shirley Hughes, W.E. Johns, Dick King-Smith, C.S. Lewis, Hugh Lofting, George Macdonald, William

Mayne, Geraldine McCaughrean, A.A. Milne, L.M. Montgomery, Michael
Morpurgo, E(dith) Nesbit, Mary Norton, Michelle Paver, Carmen Posadas,
Beatrix Potter, Philip Pullman, Frank Richards (creator of 'Billy Bunter'),
Michael Rosen, J.K. Rowling, Louis Sachar, Maurice Sendak, Dr Seuss,
Darren Shan, Shel Silverstein, R.L. Stine, Jeremy Strong, G.P. Taylor, P(amela)
L(yndon) Travers, Chris Van Allsburg, Tracey West, Jacqueline Wilson,
Diane Wynne Jones

Chile: republic in South America
  capital: Santiago
  currency: peso
  language: Spanish
  religion: Roman Catholic
  fact: where 47 per cent of women expect to be sexually attacked
  fact: a bill to implement divorce was passed for the first time in March 2004

Chilean and famous: Isabel Allende (novelist), Alejandro Amenábar (filmmaker
  who now works in Spain), Tom Araya (singer), Claudio Arrau (pianist), Patricia
  Demick (boxer), Ariel Dorfman (novelist and playwright), Ricardo Lagos
  Escobar (president), Patricio Guzmán (documentarian), Víctor Jara (folk
  musician), Alejandro Jodorowsky (filmmaker), Pablo Neruda (poet), Augusto
  Pinochet Ugarte (dictator), Raúl Ruiz (filmmaker), Leonor Varela (actress)

Chilean conservation park: Pumalin (developed by Douglas Tompkins)

chilli, hottest: datil, habanero, Scotch Bonnett

chimpanzee, adjective: simiid

chimpanzee, collective noun: cartload

chimpanzee, famous: Bonzo (film character), Bubbles (companion to Michael
  Jackson), Cheeta (companion to Tarzan), Darwin (from *The Wild Thornberries*),
  Ham (simiid astronaut), Mojo Jojo (from *The Powerpuff Girls*), Oliver (the
  'missing link')

chimpanzee, sound: hoot, scream

chimpanzee, young: infant

chimpanzee conservationist: Jane Goodall

chin: Andy McGinn (CRS), button, China chin, glass chin, glass jaw

chin, adjective: rimate

chin, projecting: prognathous (adjective)

chin, saggy mass beneath: buccula

chin, types of: chinless, double-chinned, glass-jawed, lantern-jawed, weak-chinned

china: bone china, crockery, Dresden china, Minton, porcelain
  - see porcelain

China, People's Republic of: republic in East Asia
  capital: Beijing
  currency: yuan
  language: Mandarin, Cantonese; official spoken language: Putongua ("standard
    speech"; sometimes known to Westerners as Mandarin, it is the dialect of
    North China. This dialect was declared the common language at the
    National Conference on Reform of the Chinese Written Language in 1955)
  religion: nonreligious majority, Buddhist and Taoist minorities
  fact: the country now has 90 cities with populations of more than one million
    citizens each
  rivers: Si Kiang, Yangtze, Yellow
  seven ancient kingdoms: Han, Qi, Qin, Qu, Wei, Yan, Zhao
  Tiananmen Square massacre: June 3-4, 1989 (5,000 killed, 10,000 injured)

China, fear of: Sinophobia

China's last emperor: Xuantong (Hsüan-t'ung), regal name of Pu Yi (1906–1967)

Chinese, adjective (prefix): Sino-

Chinese astronaut (aka taikonaut): Yang Liwei (who entered space on 15 October 2003)

Chinese cabbage: napa, pak-choi

Chinese cloth: nankeen

Chinese crackdown on crime, name of: Strike Hard

Chinese Cultural Revolution: launched 16 May 1966

Chinese eddo (type of edible root): taro

Chinese emperor, first: Shi Huangdi (aka Ying Zheng), whose burial site measures 35 square miles and was guarded by around 1,000 terracotta soldiers

Chinese executions, fact: an estimated 6,500 executions were carried out in 1999

Chinese film directors: Chen Kaige, King Hu, Huang Jianxin, John Woo, Zhang Yimou

Chinese game: mah-jong

Chinese idol: Lei Feng

Chinese journalist: Shi Tao (jailed for ten years after her e-mails had been intercepted from Yahoo!)

Chinese leaders: Chiang Kai-shek, Deng Xiao Ping, Hua Guo Feng, Mao Tse-tung, Zhou Enlai

Chinese manners, culture, art, etc: chinoiserie

Chinese novelists: Ba Jin, Eileen Chang, Iris Chang (born in Princeton, New Jersey), Ma Jian, Anchee Min, Amy Tan (born in Oakland, California), Wang Meng, Zhou Wei Hui (whose *Shanghai Baby* was banned by the authorities)

Chinese philosophers: Confucius, Feng Youlan, Laozi

Chinese playwright: Cao Yu

Chinese prisons, fact: about three million Chinese are in prison at any one time

Chinese puzzle: tangram

Chinese rivers: Yangtze, Yellow River

Chinese sleuth: Charlie Chan

Chinese soldier: Zhu De

Chinese villain: Fu Manchu

chipmunk, adjective: sciurine

chipmunk, famous: Alvin (from the TV cartoon)

chisel-shaped: scalpriform

chivalrous combat: wuxia (Chinese term)

chocolate centres: amaretto truffle, calypso coffee, caramel, cherry, coconut, cognac truffle, double espresso, Irish cream truffle, marizpan, orange, peppermint, whiskey truffle

chocolate consuming nations, top: USA (654,000 tonnes), followed by Germany, the UK, France and Japan

chocolate discoloration: bloom (the white that appears on old or refrigerated chocolate)

chocolate manufacturers: Cadbury Schweppes, Hershey, Lindt, Mars, Nestlé, Thorntons, Willy Wonka

choirboy: Anthony Way

choirboys, patron saint of: Dominic Savio

choking, fear of: pnigerophobia

cholera, fear of: cholerophobia

Chop Sticks: simple, irritating waltz composed for piano by the eleven-year-old British girl Euphemia Allen in the mid 1870s. The piece was published under the pseudonym of Arthur de Lulli in 1877

chopsticks, fear of using: consecotaleophobia

Choral Symphony: Beethoven's nickname for his *Symphony No. 9*, first performed in 1824

choreographers: Sir Frederick Ashton, George Balanchine, Mikhail Baryshnikov, Pina Bausch, Michael Bennett, Busby Berkeley, Matthew Bourne, Trisha Brown, Christopher Bruce, Rosemary Butcher, Enrico Cecchetti, Michael Clark, Merce Cunningham, Laura Dean, Anton Dolin, Isadora Duncan, Katherine Dunham, Michel Fokine, William Forsythe, Bob Fosse, Martha Graham, Sir Robert Helpmann, Doris Humphrey, Lev Ivanov, Gene Kelly, Michael Kidd, Gillian Lynne, Sir Kenneth Macmillan, Wayne McGregor, Mark Morris, John Neumeier, Alwin Nikolais, Hermes Pan, Steve Paxton, Jules Perrot, Arlene Phillips, Pearl Primus, Jerome Robbins, Ruth Saint Denis, Ted Shawn, Wayne Sleep, Glen Tetley, Twyla Tharp, Ninette de Valois, Onna White

chorus girls: Gaiety Girls, Pan's People, Legs and Co., The Rockettes, Tiller Girls

chough (bird), collective noun: chattering

Christ – see Jesus, other names for

Christ, statue of in state of death: mortorio

Christian church, adjective: ecclesiastical

Christian Science: religious system founded by Mary Baker Eddy in 1866

Christie's: the world's oldest fine arts auctioneers, founded in London on 5 December 1766

Christmas: Crimble, Noël, Xmas, Yule, Yuletide

Christmas, fact: the festival was first celebrated in the year 356 AD

Christmas card: "For a combination of bogus sentiment and graphic tat, mixed with some nasty clutter and wanton waste of resources, it's hard to think of anything more deadly" – Stephen Bayley

Christmas card: established in 1843 by Sir Henry Cole when he commissioned John Calcott Horsley to illustrate his festive correspondence

Christmas characters: Father Christmas (see), The Grinch, Santa Claus, Ebenezer Scrooge, Snowman

Christmas trees: Blue spruce, Fraser fir, Noble fir, Noble & Nord, Nordman fir, Norway spruce, Scots pine

Christmas weight gain, average: 5lbs, allowing for the average 6,000 calories consumed on Christmas Day

chromosomes, study of: cytogenetics

Chukotka: a federal subject of Russia (full title: Chukotka Autonomous Okrug)
    capital: Anadyr
    radio station: Blizzard FM
    fact: four times the size of Great Britain, Chukotka's population is 69,000, only slightly larger than the capacity of Stamford Bridge
    fact: alcoholism among the natives is 60% (and this a conservative estimate)

church, adjective: ecclesiastical

church, fact: attended by 40% of Americans every Sunday

church, fact: attended by 7% of Britons every Sunday
    - see parish churches

church, largest in the world: the Basilica of Our Lady of Peace in Yamoussoukro, the Ivory Coast (although the religious structure Angkor Wat in Cambodia is bigger)

church council: synod
church courtyard: parvis
churches, fear of: ecclesiaphobia
CIA: Central Intelligence Agency
CIA headquarters: Langley, Virginia
cicada, sound: singing
cider: Bellwether, Blackthorn, Cornish Scrumpy, Magners, Merrydown, Strongbow
cigar: cheroot, Cuban, Garcia y Vega, Hamlet, Manila, panatella, stogy, Tampa Nugget
cigars (top of the range): Churchill, Cohiba, Davidoff, Diamond Crown, Don Melo Centenario, Fuente Fuente OpusX, Graycliff, Hamlet, Havana, Macanudo, Montecristo, Nat Sherman, Padron, Robusto
cigarette card collector: cartophilist
cigarette of the media: Marlboro lights
cigarette stub: skag
cigarettes: Basic, Benson and Hedges, Camel, Capri, Chesterfields, Embassy, Kent, Lambert and Butler, Marlboro, Misty Lights, Newport Lights, Pall Mall, Regal, Rothman's, Silk Cut, Special Lights, Tru Blu, Virginia Slims. Safeway brand: Kingston and Virginia Star; Sainsbury's brand: Statesman; Tesco brand: Benington
cigarettes, French: Boyard, Disc Bleu, Gitanes, Gauloise
Cincinnati, birthplace of: Doris Day, Charles Manson, Tyrone Power, Roy Rogers, Pete Rose, Steven Spielberg, William H. Taft (27th president of the US), Ted Turner
Cincinnati, former mayor: Jerry Springer
Cincinnati river: Ohio
cinematographic effects: cut, dissolve, fade-in, fade-out, iris effect, natural wipe, optical wipe, pan, ripple dissolve, washout, whip-pan, zoom
Cipango: mythical name for Japan
circle, adjective: circular, cycloid
circumcision: peritomy
circuses: Barnum & Bailey, Billy Smart's, Cottle & Austen, Cirque du Soleil, Culpepper & Merriweather, Ringling Brothers
cities, fact: cities occupy two per cent of the world's surface, yet use more than 75 per cent of its resources
citrus fruit: citron, clementine, grapefruit, kumquat, lemanderin, lemon, lime, orange, pomelo, rangpur, satsuma, tangelo, tangerine, ugli
citrus fruit, largest: pomelo
city: conurbation, megalopolis, metropolis
city, adjective: civic, urban
civic planners: Baron Georges-Eugène Haussmann (remodelled Paris), John Nash, Karl Friedrich Schinkel (remodelled Berlin)
Civil Partnership Act: legislation passed in Britain on 5 December 2005 allowing same-sex couples to register their relationships. Under the law, homosexual partners have the same rights as married couples regarding benefits, housing, employment and tax
- see homosexual marriage, first
civil rights activist: Winnie Mandela
- see activists, political activists
civil rights icons: Rosa Parks, Emmett Till
civil rights leader: Jesse Jackson

civil servants, patron saint of: Thomas More

clam, collective noun: bed

clam, young: larva

clank-knapper (archaic): petty thief

clapperclaw (obsolete): one who fights unarmed

claqueur: someone paid to applaud at public events and performances

clairvoyants: Jeremiah Horrocks, David Mandell (predicted – and drew pictures of – the Concorde crash and the events of September 11), Nostradamus (aka Michel de Notredame), Madame Vasso (real name: Vissiliki Kortesis)

clarinet players: Woody Allen, Acker Bilk, Buddy DeFranco, Eric Dolphy, Benny Goodman, Emma Johnson, Artie Shaw, Lester Young

Clash, The: UK punk band formed in London, 1976; comprised of Joe Strummer (guitar/vocals; real name: John Mellors; died: December 2002), Mick Jones (guitar), Paul Simonon (bass) and Nicky 'Topper' Headon (drums). Disbanded in 1986

classical music, roughly arranged as: abstract, impressionistic and descriptive

classical composers, female: Hildegard of Bingen (1098–1179), Euphemia Allen (who, in the mid 1870s, composed the piano waltz *Chop Sticks*), Elisabeth Lutyens (1906–1983), Elizabeth Maconchy (1907–1994), Grazyna Bacewicz (1909–1969), Sofia Gubaidulina (b.1931), Kaija Saariaho (b. 1954), Judith Weir (b.1954)

classical composers, ten of the best: J.S. Bach, Beethoven, Brahms, Chopin, Handel, Haydn, Liszt, Mahler, Mozart, Tchaikovsky

   - see American composers, Austrian composers, Czech composers, English composers, French composers, German composers, Italian composers, Spanish composers, Russian composers

classification, science of: taxonomy

claws, without: adactylous (adjective)

clay, adjective: bolar

clay, made of: figulate, figuline (adjective)

clay pigeon launcher: trap

cleaning aids (for the human body): flannel, loofah, nailbrush, pumice stone, soap, sponge, washcloth

cleaning products: Ariel, Brasso, Brillo pads, Harpic, Johnson wax, Lux flakes, Lux liquid, Omo, Persil, Pledge, Skip, Vim

   - see washing powders

cleavage, impressive: bathycolpian (adjective)

cleft palate surgery: staphylorrhaphy

clergy, adjective: ecclesiastic, ecclesiastical

clergy, patron saint of: Gabriel of Our Lady of Sorrows

clergymen: Reverend W. Awdry (creator of Thomas the Tank Engine), Edmund Cartwright, John Cotton, John Keble, Martin Luther, Thomas Malthus, Jonathan Swift

   - see priests

clergymen, directory of: Crockford's Clerical Directory

clerics – see priests

Cleveland, birthplace of: Halle Berry, Drew Carey, Eric Carmen, Tracy Chapman, Wes Craven (filmmaker), Dorothy Dandridge, Phil Donahue, Harlan Ellison (writer), Screamin' Jay Hawkins, Hal Holbrook, Don King, Henry Mancini, Burgess Meredith, Paul Newman, Harvey Pekar, Debra Winger

Cleveland, UK, administrative centre: Middlesbrough

clever: bright, fly, highbrow, on the ball, savvy, sharp as a tack, smart, smart as a whip

cliché: banality, bromide, chestnut, platitude

cliché: "Avoid clichés like the plague" - Sam Goldwyn

cliché user: poll parrot

cliffs, obsession with: cremnomania

climate study (of the geological past): palaeoclimatology

climatologists: Heinrich Dove, George Symons

climbing, adjective: scansorial

climbing boots: crampon, kletterschuh

clitoral circumcision: infibulation

clitoris: button, clit, clitty, little man in the boat, spare tongue

clitoris, removal of to prevent sexual intercourse: infibulation

clitoris, surgical removal of: clitoridectomy

clockmaker: horologist

clockmaker, famous: Thomas Tompion
    - see watchmakers, famous

clog, Japanese: geta

cloister, adjective: caustral

cloned cat, first: CopyCat (in 2001)

cloned dog, first: Snuppy (in 2005)

cloned sheep, first: Dolly (in 1996)

cloning, first animal: Dolly the Sheep (created by British Professor Ian Wilmut, with the cooperation of the Roslin Institute in Edinburgh)

cloning, pioneer in human: Dr Severino Antinori (aka Dr Volcano)

closed spaces, dread of: claustrophobia

Close Encounters of the Third Kind (1977 film), tagline: "We are not alone"

closing words of a manuscript: explicit

cloth merchant: draper

clothing: apparel, clobber, duds, garments, raiment (archaic), threads, togs

clothing, fact: evolved approximately 72,000 years ago

cloud: altocumulus, altostratus, cirrocumulus, cirrostratus, cirrus, cumulonimbi, cumulus, mare's tail, mushroom cloud, nimbostratus, nimbus, rain cloud, storm cloud, stratocirrus, stratocumulus, stratus, thundercloud

cloud, adjective: nebular, nebulous, nepheloid

cloud precipitation: virga

clouds, fear of: nephophobia

clouds, study of: nephology

clowns: Bozo, Coco, Grock, Joseph Grimaldi, Jack (from the *Dick and Jane* books), Emmett Kelly, Ronald McDonald, Pepito, Nicolai Poliakoff (aka Coco), Slava Polunin, Alfredo Rastelli, Tommy the Clown (who, in 2002, inspired a new dance craze in Los Angeles which, literally, evolved from clowning; real name: Tommy Johnson), Touchstone
    - see fools, silent film comedians

clowns, fear of: coulrophobia

clown fish, famous: Marlin (from *Finding Nemo*, voiced by Albert Brooks), Nemo (from *Finding Nemo*)

club foot: cyllosis, talipes

clubfooted and famous: Lord Byron, Dudley Moore

club-shaped: clavate

clubs - see gentlemen's clubs

clumsy, politically correct term: uniquely coordinated

CO: postcode for Colorado

coal, adjective: carboniferous

coast, adjective: littoral

cobbler, collective noun: cutting, drunkship

cobra, collective noun: quiver

cobra goddesses: Meretseger (Egyptian mythology), Wadjet (Egyptian)

Coca Cola: invented in 1886 by the chemist John Pemberton

cocaine: blow, Bob Marley, Charlie, chippy, freeze, gianluca, dust, golden girl (high grade), jam, joy powder, naughty salt, nose candy, snow, zip

cocaine: "Cocaine is God's way of saying you're making too much money" - Robin Williams

cocaine users in the US, number of: 3.5 million

cock: Chanticleer (of fable)

cock, sound: crow

cock's long neck feather: hackle

cock-fighting: alectryomachy

cockroach, adjective: blattoid

cockroach, collective noun: intrusion

cockroach, famous: Archy (from Don Marquis' newspaper column)

cockroach, young: larva

cocktails: Alexander, Americano, B-52, Bacardi, black Cossack, black Russian, bloody Mary, Brandy Alexander, brandy sour, Buck's Fizz, champagne cocktail, daiquirí, gimlet, gin and tonic, gin sour, Godfather, grog, hairy navel, Harvey wallbanger, Irish coffee, John Collins, julep, kamikaze, Long Island iced tea, Manhattan, margarita, martini, Mickey Slim, mint julep, orgasm, Piña Colada, pink gin, Planter's punch, punch, rum and Coke, rusty nail, salty dog, screwdriver, sex on the beach, sidecar, Singapore sling, sloe comfortable screw, stinger, tequila sunrise, Tom Collins, Uncle Vanya, velvet hammer, vodka martini, whiskey sour, white lady, white Russian, white spider, zombie

coconut fibre: coir

coconut kernel: copra

cod, adjective: gadoid

cod, young: scrod

coffee: Américano, Arbuckle's (Old West), beans, café Américano, Cafe Hag, caffe alto (weak coffee), caffeine, caffelatte (milky coffee), Camp (chicory & coffee essence), cappuccino, cappuccino forte, coarse grinds, coffee arabica, coffee robusta, coffee liberica, corretto (coffee with liqueur), Costa Rican roasted beans, Costa Rican unroasted beans, dandelion coffee, decaffeinated, doppio (two espressos in one cup), Douwe Egberts, espresso, fine grinds, Folgers, frappuccino, full roast beans, Hag (decaffeinated coffee), high roast beans, instant, instant freeze-dried, jamoka (Old West), java (American, informal), Kenco, latté, latté macchiato (milk with a spot of coffee), light roast beans, lungo (weak coffee), Maxwell House, medium grinds, medium-light roast, Melitta, Moka (Mocha coffee), Nescafé, Red Mountain, ristretto (strong coffee), Robusta (from Congo, India and Indonesia), Roots

coffee bars: Aroma, Caffè Nero, Coffee Republic, Costa Coffee, Starbucks

coffee, fact: first recorded in 1000 AD, when it was used medicinally; not until the 16th century, in Arabia and Persia, was it drunk as a social beverage

coffee, instant: first produced on a commercial scale by Nestlé in 1937

coffee, slang: battery acid, Everton toffee (obsolete), java (American)

coffee liqueur: tia maria

coffee-importing countries, top-ten: 1) United States; 2) Germany; 3) Japan; 4) France; 5) Italy; 6) Spain; 7) Canada; 8) United Kingdom; 9) Poland; 10) the Netherlands

coffin, types of: Cottswold, Norfolk, Oxford, Sherwood

coffin support: bier, catafalque

cognac: Courvoisier, Grand Marnier, Hennessy, Martell, Remy Martin

coin: angel (old English), as (Roman), bezant (Byzantine), cent, centavo, centime, copper (bronze), crown (British), denarius (Roman), dime, double eagle (American), doubloon (Spanish), drachma (Greek), ducat, eagle (American), farthing, fen (Chinese), florin, groat, groschen (Austrian), guilder (gold), guinea (gold), half-crown, halfpenny, half-sovereign (gold), krugerrand (South African), lepton (Greek), louis (French), mite (Flemish), moidore (Portuguese), nickel (American), noble (English), obol (Greek), paisa, penny, peseta, pfennig, piastre, picayune (small coin of miniscule value), pistole (gold), quarter, real, schilling (Austrian), sequin (Venetian), sesterce (Roman), shekel, shilling (British), sixpence, solidus (Roman), sou (French), sovereign (gold), spur royal, stater (Greek), stiver, thaler (German), threepenny bit

coin, adjective: nummary

coin, back side of: reverse

coin, facing side of: obverse

coin collecting: numismatics, numismatology

coin collector: numismatist

coin disc: flan, planchet

coin design: incuse

coin edge: milling

coin inscription: legend

coin money: specie (as opposed to paper money)

coin waste (left over bits during manufacture): scissel

coin-shaped: nummiform, nummular

coins, cylindrical packet of: rouleau

cold: euphemism for an unidentified viral respiratory disease

cold, dread of: cheimaphobia

cold in the head: coryza

cold remedies: a) wash your hands frequently; b) consume extra vitamin A; c) take hot foods and liquids, hot chicken soup with extra garlic being particularly effective; d) add chilli powder, turmeric and cayenne to your food; e) cut down on your dairy intake; f) drink a glass of alcohol a day (any more than a glass will destroy the vitamin C in your body); g) don't use a cloth hanky; h) don't lie around in bed - light exercise and fresh air are more likely to lead to a swift recovery

cold sore: herpes labialis

cold-blooded: poikilothermic

coldest place on earth: Plateau Station, Antarctica (average temperature: -56.7 C)

Coldplay: UK rock band formed in London in 1998; comprised of Chris Martin (vocals, keyboards), Will Champion (drums), Guy Berryman (bass) and Johnny Buckland (guitar)

collage artists: Brion Gysin, Richard Hamilton, Robert Motherwell, Sir Eduardo Paolozzi

collarbone: clavicle

collarbone, adjective: clavicular
cologne: Allure, Amen, Animale, Brut, Bugs Bunny, Bvlgari, By, Byblos, Caesars,
    Calvin Klein, Camera, Captain, Casmir, Casual, Catalyst, Cerruti Image, Chaz,
    Chemistry, Chic, Dolce & Gabbana, English Leather, Extreme, Face a Face,
    Fahrenheit, Gentleman, Givenchy Cologne for Men, Grey Flannel, Happy,
    Iceberg, Iron, Jaguar, Jaguar Pure Instinct, Jordan, KL Homme, Lacoste,
    Lagerfeld, Live Jazz, Mariella Burani, Metal Jeans, Michael Jordan, Nemo,
    Nicole Miller, Obsession, One Man Show, Opium, Oxygene, paco rabanne,
    Passion, Paul Smith, Perry, Pheromone, Pierre Cardin, Pleasures, Poison, Polo,
    Preferred Stock, Quartz, Raw Vanilla, Romance, Safari, Salvador, Samba,
    Samourai (c/o Alain Delon), Sandalwood, Sculpture, Sexual, Silver Mountain
    Water, Spark, Swiss Army, Tarzan, Ted, Tiffany, Tuscany, Ultraviolet, Van Cleef,
    Vendetta, Vera Wang, Versus, Very Sexy, Wall Street, Witness, X-Centric,
    Xeryus, XXXL, Yang, Zanzibar
Colombia: republic in South America
    capital: Bogotá
    currency: peso
    language: Spanish
    religion: Roman Catholic
    guerrilla groups: ELN, Farc (strictly Marxist)
    fact: Colombia is the world leader in kidnapping, with one abduction occuring
        every four hours
Colombian and famous: Fernando Botero (painter), Pablo Escobar (drug baron),
    John Leguizamo (actor), Gabriel García Márquez, Shakira
Colombian statesmen: Andres Pastrana, Ernesto Samper, César Gaviria Trujillo,
    Álvaro Uribe
Colorado, 38th state (1876), Centennial State
    capital: Denver
    birthplace of: Tim Allen, Lon Chaney, Jack Dempsey (boxer), Douglas
        Fairbanks Snr, John Kerry, Ken Kesey
    motto: 'Nil Sine Numine' ('Nothing without Providence')
    state bird: lark bunting
    state flower: Rocky Mountain columbine
    state tree: bluce spruce
    tourist attractions: Rocky Mountain National Park, Garden of the Gods, Mesa
        Verde National Park
    fact: Colorado is the US state with the highest altitude
    fact: the town of Nederland celebrates the unusual holiday of 'Dead Guy Day'
colour, adjective: tinctorial
colour, aversion to: chromatophobia
colour blind: dyschromatoptic
colour blindness: achromatopsia, acritochromacy
colour blindness, fact: a condition suffered by 8% of British males
colt, collective noun: rag
Columbine massacre: on 20 April 1999, twelve students and one teacher were shot
    dead at Columbine High School in Littleton, a suburb of Denver, Colorado; the
    killers - Eric Harris and Dylan Klebold - belonged to the Trenchcoat Mafia and
    struck out on Hitler's birthday. They later killed themselves that same day
column band (in architecture): cincture
columnists, random list of: Julie Burchill, Nigel Dempster, Jeane Dixon, Maureen
    Dowd, Helen Fielding, Thomas Friedman, Christopher Hitchens, Sir Simon

Jenkins, Ann Landers, Bernard Levin, Lynda Lee-Potter (real name: Lynda Higginson), Ed Sullivan

coma victim: Terry Wallis of Big Flat, Arkansas, who was left unconscious in a 1984 car crash and came round 19 years later. At the time of the accident he was 19 and newly married with a baby. He woke up on 12 June 2003 believing that Ronald Reagan was still president

comb-shaped: pectinate

comedian: "They all laughed when I said I wanted to be a comedian. They're not laughing now" – Bob Monkhouse

comedians: Bud Abbott, Dave Allen, Fred Allen, Arthur Askey, Rowan Atkinson, David Baddiel, Bill Bailey, Sacha Baron Cohen, Julian Barrett, Stanley Baxter, Jack Benny, Jo Brand, Russell Brand, Fanny Brice, Mel Brooks, Lenny Bruce, Ed Byrne, Sid Caesar, Jimmy Carr, Jasper Carrott, Frank Carson, Cedric the Entertainer, Chevy Chase, Charlie Chester, Jimmy Clitheroe, Billy Connolly, Peter Cook, Tommy Cooper, Lou Costello, Billy Crystal, Jim Davidson, Les Dawson, Jack Dee, Ken Dodd, Charlie Drake, Jimmy Durante, Jenny Éclair, Jimmy Edwards, Ben Elton, Dick Emery, Harry Enfield, Lee Evans, Kenny Everett, Marty Feldman, Tina Fey, Sid Field, Noel Fielding, Al Franken, Dawn French, Stephen Frost, Rikki Fulton, Ricky Gervais, Whoopi Goldberg, Larry Grayson, Tony Hancock, Tommy Handley, Jeremy Hardy, Lenny Henry, Bill Hicks, Charlie Higson, Benny Hill, Harry Hill, Bob Hope, Frankie Howerd, Sean Hughes, John Inman, Eddie Izzard, Sidney James, Phill Jupitus, Peter Kay, Paul Kaye, Dan Leno, Jimmy Logan, Lee Mack, Bill Maher, Bernard Manning, Steve Martin, Francesca Martinez (22-year-old, cerebral palsic winner of the Open Mic award, August 2000), Jackie Mason, Michael McIntyre, Dennis Miller, Max Miller, Spike Milligan, Bob Monkhouse, Eric Morecambe, Eddie Murphy, Bob Newhart, Rob Newman, Ross Noble, Graham Norton, Dara O'Briain, Emo Philips, Richard Pryor, Ted Ray, Vic Reeves, Joan Rivers, Chris Rock, Jennifer Saunders, Alexei Sayle, Harry Secombe, Jerry Seinfeld, Peter Sellers, Garry Shandling, John Shuttleworth, Frank Skinner, Mark Steel, Jon Stewart, Jimmy Tarbuck, Catherine Tate, Lily Tomlin, Tommy Trinder, Johnny Vegas, Max Wall, Ruby Wax, Paul Whitehouse, Kenneth Williams, Robin Williams, Victoria Wood, Harry Worth

comedians, patron saint of: Vitus

comedy: burlesque, farce, humour, lampoon, laugh-fest, parody, romp, satire, sitcom, slapstick, spoof

comedy: "Comedy is tragedy that happens to other people" - Angela Carter; "We participate in tragedy. At comedy we only look" – Aldous Huxley; "Pain plus time equals comedy" - Mike Myers; "Comedy is only tragedy gone wrong" - Peter Ustinov

comedy, adjective: thalian

comedy, muse of: Thalia

comedy double-acts: Abbott and Costello (William 'Bud' Abbott and Lou Costello), Ant and Dec (Ant McPartlin and Declan Donnelly), Beavis & Butthead, Cannon and Ball (Tommy Cannon and Bobby Ball), Cheech and Chong (Cheech Marin and Tommy Chong), Peter Cook and Dudley Moore, Flanders and Swann (Michael Flanders and Donald Swann), French and Saunders (Dawn French and Jennifer Saunders), Fry and Laurie (Stephen Fry and Hugh Laurie), Hale and Pace (Gareth Hale and Norman Pace), Hinge and Bracket (Dr Evadne Hinge and Dame Hilda Bracket), Laurel and Hardy (Stan Laurel and Oliver Hardy), Lewis and Martin (Jerry Lewis and Dean Martin), Little and Large (Syd Little and Eddie Large), (Eric) Morecambe and (Ernie) Wise, (David) Mitchell and (Robert) Webb, Mortimer and Reeves (Bob Mortimer and Vic Reeves), the Two Ronnies (Barker and Corbett), Rowan and Martin (Dan Rowan and Dick Martin), Wallace and Gromit, Mike and Bernie Winters, Wood and Walters (Victoria Wood and Julie Walters)

Comedy Store: stand-up comedy venue in London, opened 19 May 1979

comet: Hale-Bopp

comets, dread of: cometophobia

Comfort fabric conditioner slogan: 'Softness is a thing called Comfort'

comic book artists: Will Eisner, Frank Miller, Art Spiegelman - see comic strip artists

comic book publishers: DC Comics (see), DC Thomson, Image and Flypaper Press, IPC, Marvel Comics (see)

comic book writer: Harvey Kurtzmann

comic books' first gay superheroes: Apollo and Midnighter in *The Authority* (DC Comics)

comic duos – see comedy double-acts

comic strip artists: Robert Crumb, Jack Davis, Will Eisner, Chester Gould, Frank Miller, Moebius (aka Gir), Alan Moore, Alex Raymond (creator of *Flash Gordon*), Gilbert Shelton, Joe Shuster, Bill Sienkiewicz, Osamu Tezuka, Roy Wilson, Wallace Wood

comic strip creators: Gilbert and Jaime Hernandez, Bob Kane, Stan Lee, Dave Sim

comic strip heroines: Aya (from *Middle East Heroes*), Barbarella, Batgirl, The Black Canary, Modesty Blaise, Catwoman, Carol Day, Marla Drake (aka Miss Fury), Elektra, Miss Fury (aka Marla Drake), Hellcat, The Invisible Woman, Jalila (from *Middle East Heroes*), Jane (from *The Daily Mirror*), Tiffany Jones, Lois Lane, Lady Luck, Liberty Belle, Ms Marvel, Miss Masque, Moon Girl, Phantom Lady, Red Sonja, Rocket Girl, The Scarlet Witch, Storm, Supergirl, Valkyrie, The Wasp, Wonder Woman

comics, classic: *Battle, The Beano, Bunty, Buster, Commando, The Dandy, The Eagle, Girls' Crystal, June, Mandy, Princess Tina, The Rover, Schoolfriend, Smash!, Topper, Valiant, The Victor, War Picture Library, Warlord, Whizzer and Chips, Whoopee!*

Comical Ali: nickname for Mohammed Saeed al-Sahhaf

commercial: advert, advertisement, message, a short break

commercial, first on British television: SR toothpaste (22/9/55)

committee: "A body that keeps minutes and wastes hours" (anon.)

common language (adopted by speakers whose own tongue is different): lingua franca

commoner: Mary Donaldson (the Australian who married Crown Prince Frederik of Denmark in May 2004)

communications regulator, UK: Ofcom (Office of Communications)

Communion cup: chalice

Communion plate: paten

communism: "Communism doesn't work because people like to own stuff" – Frank Zappa

communist hunter: Senator Joseph McCarthy

communist leaders: Yuri Andropov, Enrico Berlinguer, Leonid Brezhnev, Fidel Castro, Nicolae Ceauşescu, Konstantin Chernenko, Deng Xiaoping, Wladyslaw Gomulka, Ho Chi Minh, Erich Honecker, Enver Hoxha, Gustáv Husák, János

Kádár, Nikita Khrushchev, Kim Jong-il, Vladimir Lenin, Mao Tse-tung, Georges Marchais, Antonín Novotný, Pol Pot, Joseph Stalin, Josip Broz Tito, Walter Ulbricht, Georgy Zhukov

communist theorists: Friedrich Engels, Karl Marx, Leon Trotsky

Comoros: island republic off the north-west coast of Madagascar
    capital: Moroni
    currency: African franc
    language: Comorian, French, Arabic, Swahili
    religion: Muslim

composers – see American composers, Austrian composers, Czech composers, English composers, French composers, German composers, Italian composers, Spanish composers, Russian composers

comprehension: "You do not really understand something unless you can explain it to your grandmother" - Albert Einstein

compromise (noun): via media

computer: "To err is human, but to really foul things up you need a computer" – Paul Ehrlich; "I think there is a world market for, maybe, five computers" – Thomas Watson, chairman of IBM, 1943

computer designer: Seymour Cray

computer hacker: cyberpunk, Christopher Pile ('the Black Baron')
    - see viruses

computer scientist: Herman Hollerith

computers, patron saint of: Isidore of Seville

computer-speak, verbs: access, click, crash, delete, download, hack into, interface, log off, log on, poke, surf the Net, upgrade

con artists – see conmen

conceit: "Conceit is the finest armour a man can wear" - Jerome K. Jerome

concentration camps: Auschwitz-Birkenau, Dachau, Buchenwald, Flossenbürg, Maidanek, Mauthausen, Ravensbrück, Zeitz

concentration camp for women: Sachsenhausen

conceptual artists: Joseph Beuys, John Cage, Christo, Martin Creed, Marcel Duchamp, Tracey Emin, Damien Hirst, Sarah Lucas, Yoko Ono
    - see installation artists

concert promoter: Harvey Goldsmith

Concorde, maiden flight: 9 April 1969
    first commercial flight: 22 January 1976 (from France to Rio de Janeiro)
    average journey time: 3 hours, 40mins (a record crossing between London and New York took 2 hours, 53mins)
    number of aircraft built: 20 (at a cost of £55 million each)
    top speed: 1,345mph, twice the speed of sound
    the end: crashed near Paris in 2000, killing 113, and was withdrawn from service

condom: Durex, frogskin (Australian slang), Jiffy, the Performa (intended to help men combat premature ejaculation, being coated on the inside with benzocaine, a local anaesthetic), Trojan, wise monkey

conductors: Claudio Abbado, Ernest Ansermet, Vladimir Ashkenazy, Sir John Barbirolli, Daniel Barenboim, Sir Thomas Beecham, Leonard Bernstein, Richard Bonynge, Pierre Boulez, Sir Adrian Boult, Frank Bridge, Riccardo Chailly, Sir Andrew Davis, Sir Colin Davis, Antal Doráti, Sir Edward Downes, Gustavo Dudamel, Sir Mark Elder, Georges Enesco, Wilhelm Furtwängler, Sir John Eliot Gardiner, Valery Gergiev, Jane Glover, Sir Charles Groves,

Bernard Haitink, Sir Charles Hallé, Nikolaus Harnoncourt, Sir George Henschel, Mariss Jansons, Herbert von Karajan, Rudolf Kempe, Otto Klemperer, James Levine, Sir Charles Mackerras, Bruno Maderna, Sir Neville Marriner, Zubin Mehta, Willem Mengelberg, Sir Roger Norrington, André Previn, Sir Simon Rattle, Sir Malcolm Sargent, Arnold Schoenberg, Leonard Slatkin, Sir Georg Solti (naturalised British), Leopold Antoni Stanislaw Stokowski, Johann Strauss the Elder, Johann Strauss the Younger, Yuri Temirkanov, Arturo Toscanini, Bruno Walter, Sir David Willcocks, Sir Henry Wood

cone, adjective: conic

congestion charge: traffic fee introduced in Singapore since the 1970s and in Norwegian cities since the 1990s; introduced in Durham since October 2002, and in central London since 17 February 2003

Congo: former name for the Democratic Republic of the Congo

Congo, Democratic Republic of: republic in south-central Africa formerly known as Zaïre (1971–97), Congo-Kinshasa (1960–71), Belgian Congo (1908–60), Congo Free State (1885–1908)
   capital: Kinshasa
   currency: Congolese franc
   language: French
   religion: Christian majority, animist
   birthplace of: Mbilia Bel (singer)

Congo, People's Republic of: republic in West Central Africa, also known as Congo-Brazzaville
   formerly known as Middle Congo (until 1958)
   capital: Brazzaville
   currency: franc
   language: French
   religion: Christian majority

Congressional Medal of Honor: the highest US military decoration, introduced by Congress in 1861 for the navy and in 1862 for the army. Since 1942 the medal has been awarded only for situations in combat

coniferous forest: taiga

conjecture, adjective: stochastic

conman terms: bait, flat (victim), mark, roper, sharp, shield

conmen: Frank Abagnale Jr (played by Leonardo DiCaprio in *Catch Me If You Can*), Giacomo Casanova, Arthur Daley (from TV's *Minder*), John DeLorean, Peter Foster (involved with Cherie Blair), Harold Hill (from *The Music Man*), Neville Heath, Clifford Irving (who wrote an authorised 'autobiography' of Howard Hughes), Henri Désiré Landru, Marcel Petiot, D.B.C. Pierre

Connecticut, fifth state (1788); Constitution State, Nutmeg State
   capital: Hartford
   birthplace of: Phineas T. Barnum, George W. Bush, Glenn Close, Samuel Colt (inventor of the revolver), Katharine Hepburn, Stephenie Meyer, Meg Ryan, Dr Benjamin Spock, Harriet Beecher Stowe (author of *Uncle Tom's Cabin*), Noah Webster (lexicographer)
   motto: 'Qui Transtulit Sustinet' ('He who transplanted still sustains')
   nickname for a citizen of Connecticut: Nutmegger
   state bird: robin
   state flower: mountain laurel
   state tree: white oak

tourist attractions: Mark Twain House, Peabody Museum, P.T. Barnum Museum

fact: Connecticut had the first written constitution in the United States

conquerors: Alexander the Great, Attila the Hun, Julius Caesar, Francisco Hernández de Córdoba, Genghis Khan, Adolf Hitler, Napoleon Bonaparte, Shi Huangdi (aka Ying Zheng), Tamerlane, William I of England

conscience: "The inner voice that warns us someone may be looking" – H.L. Mencken

consciousness: "Human consciousness is an immaterial property beyond the current explanations of science" - David Chalmers, *The Conscious Mind*

conservation groups: Friends of the Earth, Greenpeace, National Wildlife Federation

conservationists: John Aspinall, Gerald Durrell, Gavin Maxwell, Max Nicholson, Sir Peter Scott, Douglas Tompkins, Orlando and Claudio Villas Boas - see eco-warriors

consistency: "The hobgoblin of a small mind" - Winston Churchill

consonants: alveolar, aspirate, fricative, guttural, labial, plosive, spirant, stop

conspirators: Cassius, Robert Catesby, Guy Fawkes, Abu Hamza, Titus Oates, Claus Schenk Graf von Stauffenberg

constable – see policemen

Constantinople: former name for Istanbul

Constantinople, fall of: 29 May 1453

constellations, adjective: sidereal

constipated: costive

constipation: dyschezia (usually due to rectal interference)

constipation medicine: dejector, laxative

construction, adjective: tectonic

consultant: "Someone who borrows your watch then tells you the time" - anonymous

contact lenses: Acuvue, Boots Integra, Focus

contact lenses, the first US president to wear: Ronald Reagan

contagion, fear of: tapinophobia

contraceptive pills: Femodene, Femodene ED, Marvelon, Mercilon, Minulet, Triadene, Tri-Minulet (all risk-related, re deep-vein thrombosis)

constipation, fear of: coprostasophobia

constipation, severe: copremesis (so severe, in fact, that one vomits one's own faeces)

contagious diseases, study of: epidemiology

contamination, fear of: molysmophobia

conversation: blether (Scot.), chin-wag, jive

conversationalist: deipnosophist

convicts, escaped: George Blake, Giacomo Casanova, Henri Charrière (escaped from Devil's Island and recorded his adventures in the 1970 best-selling memoir *Papillon*), Edmond Dantès (from *The Count of Monte Cristo*), John Dillinger, Abel Magwitch (from *Great Expectations*)

convoluted: anfractuous

cook: chef, jeppo, pot slinger, sous-chef, stew builder

cook, collective noun: hastiness

cook's hat: toque

cooker: Aga, cooker, microwave, oven, range, slow cooker, stove

cookery: haute cuisine

cookery, adjective: cordon bleu (de luxe), culinary

cookery books, influential: *Apicius* (the only surviving culinary text from the Roman Empire), *Larousse Gastronomique* (first published 1938)

cookery writers: Eliza Acton, Mrs Isabella Beeton, Curnonsky, Elizabeth David, Alexandre Dumas, Auguste Escoffier, Jane Grigson, Madhur Jaffrey, Nigella Lawson, Gillian McKeith, Marguerite Patten, Nigel Slater, Delia Smith
    - see food writers

cooking, adjective: culinary

cooks: Eliza Acton, Marcel Boulestin (first proponent on British TV), Robert Carrier, Fanny Cradock, Elizabeth David, Keith Floyd, Alexis Soyer
    - see chefs

coot: pelick (USA)

coot, collective noun: cover

coot, young: hatchling

Copenhagen, aka København (meaning "merchant's port")
    opera house: Royal Theatre
    Oresund Bridge: a ten-mile construction connecting Denmark to Malmoe in Sweden (opened in July 2000)
    palace: Frederiksberg Palace
    statue: Little Mermaid, sculpted by Edvard Erichsen and unveiled in 1913

copper, adjective: cupreous, cupric

copper tarnish: verdigris

cops, fictitious – see policemen, fictitious

copulate: ball, bang, boink, bonk, bump, dip your wick, discuss Uganda, do the nasty, flutter, fornicate (outside of marriage), frig, fuck, fug, gee, grind, honk, hump, jounce (of a man), lay, lock loins, make love, park the pink Cadillac, pestle (of a man), poke (of a man), pomp (South African,) quiff, roger, roll in the hay, schtup, score, screw, service, shaft, shag, skeet (black slang), sleep with, swive (archaic)

copulation: beef injection, coitus, cowp (Scot.), fornication, hanky panky (euphemistic), horizontal mambo, humpy-pumpy, pile-driving (coarse), poop-noddy (quaint), rumpy-pumpy, Russian duck (Cockney Rhyming Slang), scortation (obscure), sculduddery (ancient Scottish), sexual intercourse

coral, adjective: coralline

Cordobés, El: nickname for the matador Manuel Benítez

cork, adjective: subereous

Cork, the Republic of Ireland: birthplace of Michael Collins, Roy Keane, Danny La Rue, Cillian Murphy (actor), Fiona Shaw (actress)
    headquarters of Murphy's breweries

cormorant, adjective: phalacrocoracine

cormorant, collective noun: gulp

corn dealer: corn chandler

cornea, inflammation of: keratitis

cornea, plastic surgery of: keratoplasty

cornet players: Nathaniel 'Nat' Adderley, Bix Beiderbecke

Cornish words (used in the English language): bludgeon, puffin

Cornwall, administrative centre: Truro

Coronation of Queen Elizabeth II: 2 June 1953

Coronation Street, long-running TV soap set in a working-class street in the North of England and at the local pub, the Rovers Return; originally called *Florizel Street*

first broadcast: 9 December 1960 in twice-weekly, half-hour instalments
created by Tony Warren
original cast: Peter Adamson (Len Fairclough), Margot Bryant (Minnie
Caldwell), Violet Carson (Ena Sharples), Jack Howarth (Albert Tatlock),
Arthur Leslie (Jack Walker), Pat Phoenix (Elsie Tanner), William Roache
(Ken Barlow), Doris Speed (Annie Walker); followed by: Bryan Mosley
(Alf Roberts), Arthur Lowe (Leonard Swindley), Kenneth Cope (Jed
Stone), Eileen Derbyshire (Emily Nugent), Bernard Youens (Stan Ogden),
Jean Alexander (Hilda Ogden), Anne Kirkbridge (Deirdre Langton), Betty
Driver (Betty Turpin), Julie Goodyear (Bet Lynch), Thelma Barlow (Mavis
Riley/Wilton), Geoffrey Hughes (Eddie Yeats), Sally Whittaker (Sally
Webster), Ian McKellen (Mel Hutchwright), Ben Kingsley (Ron Jenkins)
corporate raiders: Gordon Gekko (played by Michael Douglas in the 1987 film
Wall Street), T. Boone Pickens Jr
corpse: body, cold meat, dead meat, fly bait, goner, stiff, worm chow
corpse, politically correct term: non-living person
corpse, post-mortem examination of: autopsy
corpse lover: necrophiliac
corpses, fear of: necrophobia
corpses, sexual attraction to: necrophilia
corset maker: corsetière
Corsica: French-owned island in the Mediterranean
  capital: Ajaccio
Così fan tutte: opera by Wolfgang Amadeus Mozart first produced in Vienna in
1790
cosmetic alteration: Botox, breast enlargement, breast reduction, facelift,
liposuction, nose job
cosmetic firms: Elizabeth Arden, Cacharel, Chanel, Clarins, Christian Dior, Estée
Lauder, Fragonard, Lancôme, Max Factor, Revlon, Yves Saint-Laurent
cosmetic queens: Elizabeth Arden, Estée Lauder, Helena Rubinstein
cosmetic surgery, most popular operations: 1) liposuction; 2) breast enlargement; 3)
eyelid surgery; 4) nose job; 5) breast reduction
cosmic harmony, goddess of: Maat (Egyptian mythology)
cosmologists: Stephen Hawking, Georges Lemaître
cosmologist, collective noun: galaxy
cosmonaut: Valentina Tereshkova (first woman in space)
  - see astronauts
cosmos, adjective: cosmic
Cossack dance: kozachoc
costume designers: James Acheson, Theoni V. Aldredge, Colleen Atwood, Sir Cecil
Beaton, Jenny Beavan, Milena Canonero, Edith Head, Ellen Mirojnick, Ruth
Myers, Anthony Powell, Sandy Powell, Ann Roth, Albert Wolsky
Costa Rica: republic in Central America
  capital: San José
  currency: colón
  language: Spanish
  religion: Roman Catholic
Côte d'Ivoire: republic in West Africa formerly known as the Ivory Coast (until
1986)
  capital: Yamoussoukro (administrative), Abidjan (legislative)
  currency: African franc

language: French
religion: Muslim (majority), animist, atheist, Roman Catholic
Côte d'Ivoire, birthplace of: Didier Drogba
cougar, female: lionness
cougar, male: tom
cougar, young: kitten
council member, collective noun: intrigue
council tax rebel: Sylvia Hardy (who, in 2005, was jailed for refusing to pay her tax increase)
counts: Basie, Bezuhov, Dracula, Fosco, of Monte Cristo, Plessis-Praslin, Stroganoff, Friedrich von Bülow
countess, mode of verbal address: Your Ladyship
countries, number of in the world: 193 (recognised by the UN), excluding Taiwan and Vatican City
countries with the largest border: 1) China; 2) Russia; 3) Brazil
country, largest: 1) Russia; followed by: 2) Canada; 3) USA; 4) China; 5) Brazil; 6) Australia; 7) India; 8) Argentina; 9) Kazakhstan; 10) Sudan
country, literacy rate, lowest: 1) Burkina Faso; 2) Eritrea; 3) Sierra Leone; 4) Benin; 5) = Guinea and Somalia
country, newest: Kosovo (officially became an independent nation 17 February 2008); second newest country: Montenegro (3 June 2006); third newest country: East Timor (since 20 May 2002)
country, smallest: Vatican City; followed by: 2) Monaco; 3) Nauru; 4) Tuvalu; 5) San Marino
Country singers: Clint Black, Boxcar Willie, Garth Brooks, Glen Campbell, Mary Chapin Carpenter, Carlene Carter, Johnny Cash, Rosanne Cash, Patsy Cline, Eddie Cochran, John Denver, Dixie Chicks, Steve Earle, Everly Brothers, Tennessee Ernie Ford, Janie Fricke, Bobbie Gentry, Vince Gill, Merle Haggard, Faith Hill, Emmylou Harris, Waylon Jennings, Toby Keith, Kris Kristofferson, k.d. lang, Brenda Lee, Loretta Lynn, Don McLean, Roger Miller, Ronnie Milsap, Willie Nelson, Dolly Parton, Elvis Presley, Marvin Rainwater, Bonnie Raitt, Jim Reeves, Charlie Rich, Marty Robbins, Jimmie Rodgers, Kenny Rogers, Linda Ronstadt, Ricky Skaggs, George Strait, Taylor Swift, Randy Travis, Tanya Tucker, Conway Twitty, Slim Whitman, Hank Williams, Lucinda Williams, Tammy Wynette, Dwight Yoakam
countryside: daisyville (American slang)
countryside, adjective: bucolic, rural, rustic; campestral (re open countryside)
countryside, to depart to: rusticate
Courage Tavern beer, slogan: 'It's what your right arm's for'
court cry for order: oyez
courtesans: Camille, Marie Duplessis, Kitty Fisher, Marguerite Gautier, Lola Montez, Nana (c/o Émile Zola), Olympia (as painted by Manet), Harriette Wilson
couture, designers - see fashion designers
cow: Angus, Ayrshire, Brown Swiss, Dexter, Dutch Belted, Friesian, Guernsey, Hereford, Holstein-Friesian, Illawarra, Jersey, Milking Shorthorn, Wagyu (pampered cow whose beef is the most expensive in the world – the animals are fed top-quality food, drink beer and receive regular skin treatments and massages)
cow, adjective: vaccine

cow, collective noun: herd, kine (archaic)

cow, famous: Audhumla (the cow that nourished Ymir), Ermintrude (from *The Magic Roundabout*), Norman (the calf in the film *City Slickers*)

cow, sound: low, moo

cow, young: calf

cow barn: byre

cow goddess: Hathor (Egyptian mythology)

cowards: Sir John Falstaff, Harry Feversham (although he goes on to disprove his cowardice), Lord Jim, Caspar Milquetoast (cartoon character)

cowboys: Bronco Billy Anderson, Gene Autry, Billy the Kid (aka William Bonney), William Boyd (aka Hopalong Cassidy), Kit Carson (aka Christopher Houston), Butch Cassidy (aka Robert Leroy Parker), Hopalong Cassidy, Buffalo Bill (aka William Frederick Cody), Billy Clanton, Ike Clanton, 'Old Man' Clanton, Phineas Clanton, William F. Cody (aka Buffalo Bill), Gary Cooper, Eddie Dean, Wyatt Earp, Clint Eastwood, William S. Hart, Wild Bill Hickok (aka James Buter), Terence Hill (Italian film star), Doc Holliday (aka John Henry), Tom Horn, Frank James, Jesse James, Buck Jones, Alan Ladd, the Lone Ranger, Harry Longbaugh (aka the Sundance Kid), Ken Maynard, Tim 'Colonel' McCoy, Joel McCrea, Tom Mix, Audie Murphy, Roy Rogers, Will Rogers, Randolph Scott, Bob Steele, the Sundance Kid (aka Harry Longbaugh), Tom Tyler, Lee Van Cleef, John Wayne, Lee 'Lasses' White, Yosemite Sam, Cole Younger, James Younger, John Younger, Robert Younger

cowgirls: Calamity Jane, Annie Oakley, Belle Starr

coyote, collective noun: band, pack, shift

coyote, famous: Wile E. Coyote

coyote, female: bitch

coyote, male: dog

coyote, young: pup

crab, adjective: cancroid, carcinomorphic

crab, famous: Sebastian (from Disney's *The Little Mermaid*)

crab, female: hen

crab-shaped: cancriform

crab claw: chela

crab movement: scuttle, sidle

cracks in a painting (or in its varnish): craquelure

cradle, adjective: cunabular

craftsman, adjective: artisanal

Craiglockhart inmates: Wilfred Owen, Siegfried Sassoon

crane, adjective: grallatorial, gruine

crane, collective noun: herd, sedge, sledge

crane, young: hatchling

crayon: first made in 1748, by L'Oriot

CRB: Criminal Records Bureau

Cream: pioneering UK rock group formed in London in June of 1966; comprised of Eric Clapton (lead guitar), Jack Bruce (bass) and Peter 'Ginger' Baker (drums). Cream disbanded in 1968 but we reunited in 1993 and 2005

cream cheese: Kraft, mascarpone, Philadelphia

creation, goddess of: Hathor (Egyptian mythology)

creatures: amphisbaena, basilisk, behemoth, brownie, bunyip, centaur, chimera, cockatrice, dementor (from *Harry Potter*), demon, dragon, elf, ent (from *The Lord of the Rings*), fell beast (from *The Lord of the Rings*), gnome, goblin,

gorgon, gremlin, griffin, harpy, hippogriff, hippogryph, imp, jabberwock, kobold (in German mythology), kraken, lamia, leprechaun, leviathan, manticore, mermaid, mûmakil (from *The Lord of the Rings*), orc (from *The Lord of the Rings*), phoenix, ringwraith (from *The Lord of the Rings*), salamander, snark, sphinx, sprite, succubus, troll, unicorn, vampire, Womble
- see dragons, giants

cremation, adjective: crematory

crescent-shaped: lunate

Crete, fact: this Greek island was the location for the world's very first flush toilet

cricket: "The English are not a very spiritual people, so they invented cricket to give them some idea of eternity" – George Bernard Shaw; "Cricket civilizes people and creates good gentlemen. I want everyone to play cricket in Zimbabwe; I want ours to be a nation of gentlemen" – Robert Mugabe (of all people); "Personally, I have always looked on cricket as organised loafing" – William Temple

cricket, fact: the rules of which were drawn up by the second Duke of Richmond in 1727

cricket (insect), famous: Jiminy Cricket (from *Pinocchio*)

cricket almanack: Wisden

cricket bowling method: googly

cricket commentators: Richie Benaud, Henry Blofeld, Geoffrey Boycott

cricket stump crosspiece: bail

cricket umpire: Darrell Hair (who accused Pakistan of cheating at the 2006 Oval Test match)

cricketers: Wasim Akram, Curtly Ambrose, Les Ames, Wasim Bari, Sydney Barnes, Ken Barrington, Bishan Singh Bedi, Sir Alec Bedser, Richie Benaud, Allan Border, Sir Ian Botham, Geoffrey Boycott, Sir Donald Bradman, Ali Brown (Surrey Cricket Club's opening batsman who hit the highest score in the history of limited-overs cricket anywhere in the world), Denis Compton, Lord (Learie) Constantine of Maraval and Nelson, Colin Cowdrey (aka Baron Cowdrey of Tonbridge), Hansie Cronje (captain of South Africa's team who accepted money from an Indian bookmaker), Basil D'Oliviera, Godfrey Evans, Andrew 'Freddie' Flintoff, Mike Gatting, Sunil Gavaskar, Graham Gooch, Murray Goodwin, David Gower, William Gilbert Grace, Jack Gregory, Tony Greig, Sir Richard Hadlee, Wally Hammond, Desmond Haynes, Rachel Heyhoe-Flint, Sir Jack Hobbs, Sir Len Hutton, Kapil Dev, Imran Khan, Brian Lara, Harold Larwood, Tony Lewis, Dennis Lillee, Raymond Lindwall, Sir Clive Lloyd, Devon Malcolm, Glenn McGrath, A.D. Nourse, Kevin Pietersen, Derek Randall, K.S. Ranjitsinhji, Wilfred Rhodes, Barry Richards, Sir Vivian Richards, Jack Russell, Sir Gary Sobers, Alec Stewart (accused of accepting £5,000 from an Indian bookmaker in return for giving information about match conditions during England's 1993 tour of India and Sri Lanka), Herbert Sutcliffe, Maurice Tate, Claire Taylor, Sachin Tendulkar, Fred Trueman, Phil Tufnell, Michael Vaughan, Sir Clyde Walcott, Shane Warne, John Wisden, Frank Woolley, Bob Woolmer, Frank Worrell

crime, fact: in 2006 less than one per cent of all crimes in Britain resulted in a custodial sentence

crime, national association for ex-offenders: Unlock

crime rate, fact: in 1921 there were 103,000 recorded crimes in England and Wales; in 2002, there were 5.5 million

crime writers: Eric Ambler, Lawrence Block, James M. Cain, Raymond Chandler, Agatha Christie, Wilkie Collins, Sir Arthur Conan Doyle, Patricia Cornwell,

John Creasey, Colin Dexter, James Ellroy, Karin Fossum, Erle Stanley Gardner, Elizabeth George, Tess Gerritsen, Michael Gilbert, Dashiell Hammett, Patricia Highsmith, George V. Higgins, Reginald Hill, P.D. James, Stieg Larsson, Dennis Lehane, Elmore Leonard, Ross Macdonald, Henning Mankell, Ngaio Marsh, Ed McBain, Walter Mosley, Sara Paretsky, T. Jefferson Parker, James Patterson, George Pelecanos, Edgar Allan Poe, Ellery Queen (pseudonym of Frederick Dannay and Manfred Lee), Ian Rankin, Ruth Rendell, Dorothy L. Sayers, Georges Simenon, Mickey Spillane, Jim Thompson, Edgar Wallace, Joseph Wambaugh, Donald E. Westlake
- see detective writers, thriller writers, etc

crime-mapping system: Compstat (a computer system that measures urban crime)

Crimean War: 1853–1856

criminals: Ronnie Biggs (member of a gang that held up the Glasgow-to-London mail train in 1963, stealing £2 million), Al Capone, Moriarty (nemesis of Sherlock Holmes)
- see bank robbers, gangsters, serial killers, train robbers, etc

crisis, adjective: climacteric

critics: "People who know the way but can't drive the car" - Kenneth Tynan; "They search for ages for the wrong word which, to give them credit, they eventually find" - Peter Ustinov

critics: Kenneth Allsop, Charles Baudelaire, Arnold Bennett, Thomas De Quincey, John Drinkwater, William Gifford, Harley Granville-Barker, Robert Graves, Friedrich Grimm, Jeremiah, Samuel Johnson, H.L. Mencken, William Rossetti, Dame Edith Sitwell, Sir Leslie Stephen, Xenophanes
- see art critics, film critics, literary critics, theatre critics, etc

critcism: animadversion

Croatia: republic in South-East Europe
    capital: Zagreb
    currency: kuna
    language: Croatian
    nickname: Our Beautiful
    religion: Roman Catholic
    birthplace of: Marco Polo

crocodile: false gharial, gharial, mugger, saltwater crocodile

crocodile, adjective: crocodilian

crocodile, collective noun: bask, float

crocodile hunter: Steve Irwin

crocodile-headed god: Sobek (Egyptian mythology)

croissant: pastry roll invented in Vienna in 1683

Cromwell's head – the head of Oliver Cromwell, Lord Protector of the British Commonwealth: buried in 1960 within the ante-chapel of Sidney Sussex College, Cambridge

crooners: Charles Aznavour, Tony Bennett, Silvio Berlusconi (formerly), Pat Boone, Michael Bublé, Nat King Cole, Harry Connick Jr, Bing Crosby, Jamie Cullum, Vic Damone, Bobby Darin, Neil Diamond, Vince Hill, Michael Holliday, Frank Ifield, Sir Elton John, John Legend, Barry Manilow, Dean Martin, Al Martino, Guy Mitchell, Matt Monro, Alberto Podestá, Neil Sedaka, Frank Sinatra, Mel Tormé, Frankie Vaughn, Slim Whitman, Andy Williams, Will Young

crop-circle maker: Paul Obee

crops, god of: Frey (Norse mythology)

crops, science of: agronomy

cross: ankh, Celtic, crucifix, Greek, Latin, Lorraine, Maltese, papal, patriarchal, Saint Andrew's, Saint Anthony, swastika
cross-shaped: cruciform
crossbow: arbalest
crossbow bolt: quarrel
crossbow virtuoso: William Tell
crossword compiler: cruciverbalist
crotch-staring, prone to: krukolibidinous
crow, adjective: corvid, corvine
crow, collective noun: murder
crow, collective noun (in flight): cawroboree
crow, sound: caw
crow, young: chick, hatchling
crowds, fear of: enochlophobia, ochlophobia
crowds, sexual arousal derived from: ochlophilia
crown, adjective: calvarial
CRS: Cockney Rhyming Slang
Crusades, The: 1095–1291
Crusades opponent: Saladin
crustacean, adjective: carcinomorphic
cry-babies: Halle Berry, David Beckham, Sébastien Chabal, Roger Federer, Paul Gascoigne, Tom Hanks, Harold Macmillan, Napoleon Bonaparte, Gwyneth Paltrow, Matthew Pinsent, Paula Radcliffe, Cristiano Ronaldo, Britney Spears, John Terry, Justin Timberlake, Michael Vaughan
crying, adjective: lachrymal
crying, prone to: larmoyant
cryptologist: Sophie Neveu (from *The Da Vinci Code*)
crystals, aversion to: chrystallophobia
crystallographers: Rosalind Franklin, Dorothy Hodgkin
CSA: Child Support Agency
CT: postcode for Connecticut; computerised tomography (as in a CT scan)
Cuba: republic in the Caribbean
    capital: Havana
    currency: peso
    language: Spanish
    religion: nonreligious majority
Cuban and famous: Reinaldo Arenas (poet), Desi Arnaz, Fidel Castro, Celia Cruz, Gloria Estefan, Ibrahim Ferrer, Andy Garcia, Eduardo Sanchez
Cuban prison: Guantanamo Bay (under US control)
cubes: Necker cube, Rubik's Cube, Soma cube
Cubism: abstract art movement that evolved in Paris in 1908
Cubists: Georges Braque, Paul Cézanne, Tamara de Lempicka, Marcel Duchamp, Lyonel Feininger, Juan Gris, Fernand Léger, Emilio Pettoruti, Pablo Picasso
cuckolds: Agamemnon, Prince Andrew, Prince Charles, Sir Clifford Chatterley, January (from Chaucer's *The Merchant's Tale*), Harold Macmillan, Menelaus, George Tesman (from *Hedda Gabler*), Adam Verver (from Henry James' *The Golden Bowl*)
cuckold, female: cuckquean
cuckold, tolerant: wittol
cuckolds, patron saint of: Monica
cuckoo, adjective: cuculine, cuculoid

cuckoo-spit: spit-like froth found on plants, exuded from the anus of froghopper larvae

cucumber: bêche-de-mer, gherkin, holothurian, pickle

cucumber-shaped: cucumiform

cud-chewing animal: ruminant

cults: Branch Davidians, Children of God (now known as The Family International), Church of the Sub-Genius (formed in 1978), The Family International, Lord's Resistance Army, Rastafarianism, Fundamentalist Church of Jesus Christ of Latter-Day Saints, Unification Church

cult leaders: Shoko Asahara (leader of the Aum Supreme Truth, which carried out a gas attack on the Tokyo underground in 1995), David Berg (founder of the Children of God), L. Ron Hubbard, Warren Jeffs, Reverend Jim Jones, Joseph Kibweteere (of Uganda's Movement for the Restoration of the Ten Commandments of God, in which, in March of 2000, 500 members died in an apparent mass suicide, locked inside the movement's church when it was set ablaze with all the doors and windows boarded up from inside), David Koresh, Jeffrey Lundgren (Mormon splinter group), Maharishi Mahesh Yogi (one time friend of The Beatles), Rev. Sun Moon

cultural commentators: Vance Packard, Theodor Roszack, Susan Sontag

cultural critic: Christopher Lasch

cultural theorist: Marshall McLuhan

culture: "Culture is not a stately mansion which we file around in respectful silence, but a loud, multi-storey leisure complex" - Richard Lloyd Parry, in *The Sunday Times*

Cumbria, administrative centre: Carlisle

cunnilingus: Aussie kiss (a French kiss 'down under'), carpet-munching, cunt-lapping, eating at the Y, eating out, face job, fish dinner, giving face, muff diving, pearl diving, yodelling in the canyon

cup bearer of the gods: Ganymede

cup-like: calicular

cup-shaped: calathiform, cyathiform

cur, collective noun: cowardice

cure, adjective: sanative

cure-all: elixir, nostrum (usually mythological), panacea

curiosity: "He who asks is a fool for five minutes, but he who does not ask remains a fool forever" - Chinese proverb; "More often than not, curiosity is mere vanity. We only want to know something in order to talk about it" – Blaise Pascal

curlew, collective noun: herd

curries (potency measured in scovilles): korma (600 scovilles), bhoona (5,000 scovilles), madras (30,000 scovilles), vindaloo (100,000 scovilles), tindaloo (150,000 scovilles), phal (200,00 scovilles)

curry measurement of potency: scoville

curved line, adjective for: curvilinear, curvilineal

cushion, adjective: pulvillar

custard: "Custard is a detestable substance produced by a malevolent conspiracy between the hen, the cow and the cook" - Ambrose Bierce

Custer's Last Stand: 25–26 June 1876 (in which General George Armstrong Custer died at the hands of the Sioux and Cheyenne Indians at Little Bighorn in Montana)

cutlery, unused (after a meal): sunbeam (Australian)

cutlery bender: Uri Geller

cutting edge, adjective: morsal
cv: curriculum vitae (Latin for 'course of life')
cybernetics, founder of: Norbert Wiener
cyborg: term coined in 1960 by Manfred Clynes and Nathan Kline, doctors from the
 Rockland State Hospital in Orangeburg, New York; the word is a contraction of
 'cybernetic organism'
cyborgs: Bionic Woman, Cybermen, RoboCop, Six Million Dollar Man, The
 Terminator, Terminator T-800, T-X (from *Terminator 3: Rise of the Machines*),
 Jason Voorhees
cyclists: Jacques Anquetil, Lance Armstrong (Texan who, in July of 1999, won the
 Tour de France just three years after being given a 40% chance of recovering
 from testicular cancer – he then won it a further five consecutive times), Gino
 Bartalli, Chris Boardman, Louison Bobet, Mark Cavendish, Fausto Coppi,
 Charly Gaul, Raphael Geminiani (aka 'le Grand fusil'), Reg Harris, Barry
 Hoban, Sir Chris Hoy, Ferdi Kubler, Eddie Merckx (aka 'the Cannibal'), David
 Millar, Graeme Obree, Sir Hubert Opperman, Brian Robinson, Rebecca
 Romero, Tom Simpson, Marshall 'Major' Taylor (in 1899 he became the first
 world champion), Jan Ullrich
cynic: "A blackguard whose faulty vision sees things as they are, not as they ought
 to be" – Ambrose Bierce; "An injured romantic" – Ewen Brownrigg
Cyprus: island in the East Mediterranean
  capital: Nicosia
  currency: Cypriot pound and Turkish new lira
  language: Greek and Turkish
  religion: Greek Orthodox and Muslim
Czech and famous: Karel Čapek, Alexander Dubček, Milos Forman, Jan Hammer
 (composer and musician), Jaroslav Hašek (writer), Václav Havel, Eva
 Herzigova, Bohumil Hrabal (writer), Erich Wolfgang Korngold, Milan Kundera
 (novelist), František Kupka (painter), Ivan Lendl (tennis champ), Thomas
 Masaryk (statesman), Jiří Menzel (film director), Martina Navratilova, Paulina
 Porizkova, Josef Skvorecký (novelist; settled in Canada)
Czech composers: Antonin Dvořák, Leoš Janáček, Bohuslav Martinů, Bedřich
 Smetana
Czechoslovakia: former socialist republic now divided into the Czech Republic and
 Slovakia
Czech Republic: country in Central Europe
  capital: Prague
  currency: koruna
  language: Czech
  nickname: Bohemia and Moravia
  religion: Christian

D

DA: District Attorney
Dabda: acronym for "denial, anger, bargain, depression and acceptance," the five
 stages of coping with death as conceived by Elisabeth Kübler-Ross
Dadaists: Jean Arp, Hugo Ball, Jean Dubuffet, Marcel Duchamp, Max Ernst,
 Francis Picabia, Man Ray

Dad's Army: TV sitcom set during the early years of the Second World War and featuring members of the British Home Guard created and written by Jimmy Perry and David Croft
   broadcast: 31 July 1968–13 November 1977 on BBC1 (and filmed in 1971)
   cast: Arthur Lowe (Captain George Mainwaring), John Le Mesurier (Sgt. Arthur Wilson), Clive Dunn (Lance Cpl. Jack Jones), John Laurie (Private Jock Frazer), Ian Lavender (Private Frank Pike), Arnold Ridley (Private Charles Godfrey), James Beck (Private Joe Walker), Bill Pertwee (Warden William Hodges), Frank Williams (Rev. Timothy Farthing), Liz Fraser (Mrs Pike)
dagger handle: haft
dagger symbol: daggern, obelus
Dahomey: former name for the People's Republic of Benin (until 1975)
daily: circadian, diurnal, quotidian
Daily Express, The: daily British newspaper founded in 1900
Daily Sketch, The: tabloid British newspaper founded in 1909 (and folded in 1971)
Daily Mail, The: daily British newspaper founded in 1896
Daily Star, The: daily British tabloid newspaper founded in 1888
Daily Telegraph, The: daily British newspaper and the first to be issued in London for a penny; founded in 1855 by Joseph Levy, who also served as the publication's first editor
Dalai Lama, real name: Tenzin Gyatso
Dallas: prime-time American soap opera chronicling the personal and commercial adventures of the oil-rich Ewing family on their South Fork ranch. There was also a TV film (1986) and in 2006 a theatrical feature with John Travolta, Jennifer Lopez and Shirley MacLaine was announced and then abandoned
   created by David Jacobs for Lorimar Productions
   broadcast: 2 April 1978–3 May 1991
   cast: Barbara Bel Geddes (Eleanor 'Miss Ellie' Ewing) – briefly replaced by Donna Reed in 1984, Jim Davis (John 'Jock' Ewing), Larry Hagman (John 'J.R.' Ross Ewing), Linda Gray (Sue Ellen), Patrick Duffy (Bobby Ewing), Victoria Principal (Pamela Ewing), Ken Kercheval (Cliff Barnes), David Wayne (Willard 'Digger' Barnes), Charlene Tilton (Lucy Ewing), Steve Kanaly (Ray Krebbs), Mary Crosby (Kristin), Susan Howard (Donna Culver), Jared Martin (Dusty Farlow), Howard Keel (Clayton Farlow), Audrey Landers (Afton Cooper), Priscilla Beaulieu Presley (Jenna Wade), Jennilee Harrison (Jamie Ewing)
dam, first: Egypt, 300 BC; the first hydraulically operated dam was constructed in 1300 BC in the Orontes Valley in Syria
Dambusters' RAF wing-commander: Guy Gibson
dames of the theatre: Judith Anderson, Julie Andrews, Peggy Ashcroft, Eileen Atkins, Lilian Braithwaite, Gladys Cooper, Cicely Courtneidge, Judi Dench, Edith Evans, Gracie Fields, Wendy Hiller, Thora Hird, Celia Johnson, Madge Kendal, Helen Mirren, Anna Neagle, Joan Plowright, Diana Rigg, Flora Robson, Margaret Rutherford, Maggie Smith, Elizabeth Taylor, Marie Tempest, Ellen Terry, Sybil Thorndike, Dorothy Tutin, Irene Vanbrugh, May Whitty
damp, fear of: hygrophobia
dance: ballet, ballroom, barn dance, beguine, belly dance, black bottom, bolero, boogie, bossa nova, bourrée, breakdance, cachucha, cakewalk (1890's-1920's, originating among black Southerners), cancan, carioca, cha cha, chaconne, charleston, clowning (popular in South Central Los Angeles), conga, cotillion,

country dance, country two-step, csardas, cumbia, East Coast swing, écossaise, excuse-me, fandango, farruca, flamenco, foxtrot, gavotte, go-go, gopak, habanera (slow Cuban dance), hay, Highland fling, hokey-cokey, hornpipe, hula, jig, jitterbug, jive, Kathakali, kazachok, krumping (popular in South Central Los Angeles), lambada, limbo, line dance, mambo, mazurka, merengue, minuet, morris dance, musette, one-step, pas de deux, pas seul (solo), paso doble, passacaglia, passepied, pavane, polka, pogo, polonaise, quickstep, ragtime, reel, rigadoon, rumba, salsa, saltarello, samba, saraband, shimmy, siciliano, square dance, strathspey, swing, syrtaki, tango, tarantella, tea dance, turkey trot, twist, veleta, waltz, zapateado (flamenco), zydeco

dance, adjective: Terpsichorean

dance, muse of: Terpsichore

dance, verb: cut a rug, hoof it, shake one's skirt, trip the light fantastic

dance critic: Clement Crisp

dance with masks: masquerade

dancers, famous: Fred Astaire, Michael Bennett, Fernando Bujones, Cyd Charisse, Joaquin Cortes (flamenco sensation), Merce Cunningham, Laura Dean, Anton Dolin, Sir Anthony Dowell, Isadora Duncan, Katherine Dunham, Michael Flatley (formerly of Riverdance), Savion Glover, Erick Hawkins, Gregory Hines, Doris Humphrey, Tai Jiminez, Gene Kelly, Mata Hari, Wayne McGregor, Meredith Monk, Lola Montez, Jules Perrot, Desmond Richardson, Jerome Robbins, Ginger Rogers, Ruth Saint Denis, Marie Sallé, Salome, Ted Shawn, Dame Antoinette Sibley, Ninette de Valois, Violette Verdy – see ballet dancers

dancers, patron saint of: Vitus

dancing, adjective: saltatorial

dandy: James Aitken (aka John the Painter), Adam Ant, Count Bezuhov, Manolo Blahnik, Sir Percy Blakeney (aka the Scarlet Pimpernel), Beau Brummell, Brandon Flowers, King George IV of England, Griswold Lorillard (who christened the dinner jacket when, in 1896, he wore one to a ball at a country club in Tuxedo Park, New York), Richard Nash (aka Beau Nash), the Scarlet Pimpernel, Robert Louis Stevenson, Oscar Wilde

Dandy, The: classic children's comic first published by D.C. Thomson of Dundee, Scotland, on 4 December 1937

Danish and famous: Hans Christian Andersen, Bille August (filmmaker), Vitus Bering (navigator), Karen Blixen (aka Isak Dinesen) (novelist), Niels Bohr (physicist), Victor Borge (pianist), Tycho Brahe (astronomer), King Canute, Helena Christensen (model), Sophus Claussen (poet), Isak Dinesen (aka Karen Blixen), Carl Theodor Dreyer (filmmaker), John Dreyer (astronomer), Hamlet (tragic prince), Vilhelm Hammershøi (painter), Jean Hersholt (actor), Søren Kierkegaard (existentialist philosopher), Carl Nielsen (composer and conductor), Connie Nielsen (actress), Douglas Sirk (filmmaker later naturalised as an American), Gunnar Axel Thorson (marine ecologist), Bertel Thorvaldsen (sculptor), Lars Ulrich (drummer with Metallica), Thomas Vinterberg (filmmaker), Lars von Trier (filmmaker)

Danish composer: Carl Nielsen

Danish king: Canute (also known as Cnut)

Dapper Don: nickname for John Gotti

Dark Horse Comics titles: Blade of the Immortal, Flaming Carrot, Fray, Groo the Wanderer, Hellboy, Madman, The Mask, Mysterymen, Sin City, SpyBoy, Usagi Yojimbo

darkness, god of: Erebus (Greek mythology)
darkness, fear of: achulophobia, nyctophobia
dart, tail of: flight
dart champions: Ray Barneveld, Eric Bristow, Andy Fordham ('The Viking'), Trina Gulliver, John Lowe, Phil Taylor
Da Schnozz: nickname for Jimmy Durante
dash, curved (~): swung dash
date rape drug: GHB (gamma hydroxybutyrate), Liquid E, Liquid X, Rohypnol, Xanax
daughter, adjective: filial
dawn, dread of: eosophobia
dawn, goddess of: Eos (Greek), Aurora (Roman)
dawn, prior to (adjective): antelucan
Dawson's Creek: TV series, a teenage drama set in Capeside, a small suburb of Boston
    broadcast: 20 January 1998–14 May 2003
    created by Kevin Williamson
    cast: James Van Der Beek (Dawson Leery), Katie Holmes (Josephine 'Joey' Potter), Michelle Williams (Jennifer 'Jen' Lindley), Joshua Jackson (Pacey Witter), Kerr Smith (Jack McPhee), Mary Beth Peil (Evelyn 'Grams' Ryan), Mary-Margaret Humes (Gail Leery), Monica Keena (Abby Morgan), Leann Hunley (Tamara Jacobs)
daughter, murder of: filicide
day, adjective: diurnal
day, god of: Jupiter (Roman mythology)
Day at the Races, A (1937 film), famous lines: Flo (Esther Muir): "I've never been so insulted in my life." Dr Hackenbush (Groucho Marx): "Well, it's early yet"; Dr Hackenbush, to Mrs Upjohn: "Emily, I have a little confession to make. I really am a horse doctor. But marry me and I'll never look at any other horse" [last line]
Day of Atonement: Yom Kippur
day of judgement: dies irae
Day of the Dead: Mexican festival celebrated 1-2 November
daydreamers: Billy Liar, Walter Mitty
daydreaming of a sexual nature: emeronaria
daylight, fear of: phengophobia
daytime sleeping: diurnation
DBN: Distressed British National (Foreign Office term)
DC Comics titles: The Authority, Batman, Catwoman, Jonah Hex, Superman, Wonder Woman
D-Day: 6 June 1944
D-Day beaches: Juno, Omaha, Utah, Sword, Gold
DE: postcode for Delaware
DEA: Drug Enforcement Administration
deacons, patron saint of: Stephen
dead: belly-up, bit the dust, checked out, deceased, departed, flatlined, gone for a burton, kaput, kicked the bucket, nonviable (pc), passed away, pushing up the daisies, six feet under, terminally inconvenienced (pc), toes-up
dead, god of the: Mors (Roman), Odin (Norse), Thanatos (Greek), Upuaut (Egyptian)
dead, goddess of the: Hathor (Egyptian mythology), Hel (Norse)
dead, politically correct term: terminally inconvenienced

dead, the worship of: necrolatry

dead person, returned: revenant

deadlines: "I love deadlines. I like the whooshing sound they make as they fly by" – Douglas Adams

deadly nightshade: belladonna, dwale

deadly sins: pride, covetousness (or greed), lust, envy, gluttony, anger and sloth

deaf: aurally inconvenienced (pc), Mutt and Jeff (RS)

deaf and famous (partially or completely): Ludwig Van Beethoven, Halle Berry, Georges Clemenceau (French prime minster), Thomas Edison, Lou Ferrigno, Dame Evelyn Glennie (percussionist), Francisco Goya, Howard Hughes, Holly Hunter, Helen Keller, Philip Larkin, Rush Limbaugh, Rob Lowe, David Mamet, Marlee Matlin, George Melly, Bedrich Smetana, Erastus Smith, Louise Stern (writer), Margaret Sullavan (in her later years), Eric Sykes, Tommy (c/o The Who), Pete Townshend

deafness, patron saint of: Francis de Sales

dean, collective noun: decanter, decorum

DEAR: Diamonds, Emeralds, Amethysts, and Rubies

death: "Death is the greatest kick of all. That's why they save it for last" - Carlos Castaneda; "Life does not cease to be funny when people die any more than it ceases to be serious when people laugh" - George Bernard Shaw

death, adjective: fatal, mortal

death, fact: in the 20th century, 191 million people lost their lives in war

death, fact: in the United Kingdom, one person dies every day from Aids

death, fact: in the United Kingdom, 300 people a day die from smoking-related illness

death, fact: violence is now the leading cause of death among people aged 15 to 44, according to the World Health Organisation

death, fear of: necrophobia

death, god of: Odin (Norse mythology)

death, goddess of: Hecate (Greek), Libitina (Roman), Hel (Norse), Ran (Norse)

death, patron saints of: Joseph, Michael, Gabriel and Raphael

death, study of: thanatology

death penalty – see capital punishment

death penalty; Texan politician who campaigned for children over 11 to be subject to capital punishment: Jim Pitts

death tolls: fewer than 400,000 Americans died in all the wars of the 20th century

    D-Day: 6 June 1944, 8,600 Allied soldiers killed

    Hiroshima: 6 August 1945: 140,000 killed

    Indian Ocean tsunami: 26 December 2004: 140,000 killed

    Pearl Harbour: 7 December 1941: 2,400 killed

    Waterloo: on the last day of battle, on 18 June 1815, 61,000 soldiers killed

deaths from overdose – see overdose, accidental death from

deaths from aeroplane accident – see plane crash, killed in

Debrett's Peerage of England, Scotland and Ireland: Classification of the British peerage first published by John Almon in 1769 as *The New Peerage*. In 1802, John Debrett took over the editorship and the volume continued publication until the late 1980s, more than 150 years after Debrett's death

debt avoider: scofflaw

decapitated and famous: Madame du Barry, Kenneth Bigley, Anne Boleyn, King Charles I of England, Marcus Cicero, Oliver Cromwell (after his death),

Thomas Cromwell, Georges Danton, Lord Guilford Dudley, John Dudley 1st Duke of Northumberland, Ganesha, Lady Jane Grey, Holofernes (Assyrian general), Catherine Howard, Apostle James, John the Baptist, William Laud, King Louis XVI, Jayne Mansfield, Marie Antoinette, Mary Queen of Scots, Medusa, Mimir, Mishima Yukio, Sir Thomas More, Vic Morrow (by a helicopter's rotar blades), Apostle Paul, Sir Walter Raleigh, Maximilien Robespierre, Shiva (Hindu mythology), Edward Teach (aka Blackbeard), William Wallace

decathlete: Daley Thompson

decaying matter, fear of: septophobia

decisions, fear of making: decidophobia

deck, highest on a ship: poop

deck, lowest on a ship: orlop

Deep Throat: pseudonym adopted by Mark Felt to leak secrets about the Nixon administration to journalists Carl Bernstein and Bob Woodward. Felt, an assistant director of the FBI, hid behind his nom de guerre for thirty years until, aged 91, he revealed his true identity in June of 2005

deep-freezing bodies, practice of (in the hope that they can be resurrected in the future): cryonics

deep-sea diving vessel, manned: bathyscaphe

deep-sea observation vessel: bathysphere

deep-vein thrombosis (aka DVT): economy-class syndrome

deer, adjective: cervine

deer, collective noun: herd

deer, eviscerate: gralloch (verb)

deer, fact: according to the RSPCA, the animal is involved in around 1,500 road traffic accidents in the UK every year

deer, famous: Bambi

deer, female: doe

deer, male: buck, stag

deer, sound: bell (of a male in the rutting season)

deer, tail: scut

deer, young: fawn, yearling

deer meat: venison

deer offal: umbles

defeat, fear of: kakorrhiaphobia

defecation, involuntary: copracrasia

deformity, fear of: dysmorphophobia, teratophobia

deformity, fear of inheriting: patriophobia

degree: BA, diploma, doctorate, MA, magnum cum laude, Masters, PhD

Delaware, 1st state (1788), Diamond State, First State
    capital: Dover
    birthplace of: Ryan Phillippe (actor), Howard Pyle (illustrator and writer), Elisabeth Shue (actress)
    motto: 'Liberty and Independence'
    state bird: blue hen chicken
    state flower: beach blossom
    state tree: American holly
    tourist attraction: Fort Christina Monument, the site of the founding of New Sweden
    fact: Delaware is the very first state in the United States

democracy: "Democracy must be more than two wolves and a sheep voting on what to have for dinner" - James Bovard; "It's not the voting that's democracy; it's the counting" – Tom Stoppard

Democratic Republic of the Congo: republic in south-central Africa; formerly known as Congo Free State (until 1908), Belgian Congo (until 1960), Congo-Kinshasa (until 1971), Zaïre (until 1997)
  capital: Kinshasa
  currency: Congolese franc
  language: French
  religion: Christian (majority), animist

demons, fear of: demonophobia

demons, study of: demonology

demons, worship of: demonolatry

Denmark: kingdom in northern Europe
  birthplace of: Carlsberg
  capital: Copenhagen
  currency: krone
  language: Danish
  religion: Christian, Lutheran
  fact: happiest nation in Europe (according to a 1999 survey)
  factoid: where, reportedly, as many as 100 convicted criminals have paid
      impersonators to stand in for them in prison
  - see Danish and famous

denouncer: Jeremiah

dental procedure, without drilling: photo-activated disinfection

dentist, collective noun: drill (joc.)

dentists, famous: Thomas Bell (also a distinguished naturalist), William Guy, Ben Harper (played by Robert Lindsay in TV's *My Family*), Doc Holliday, John Smith

dentists, fact: there are 30,500 dentists registered in the UK by the General Dental Council

dentists, patron saint of: Apollonia

Denver, birthplace of: Tim Allen, India.Arie (soul singer), Douglas Fairbanks Snr, David Fincher (filmmaker), John Kerry, Antoinette Perry (theatre director), Dean Reed (singer), Jill Sobule (singer-songwriter), Jack Swigert (astronaut)

department stores: Army & Navy Stores, Belk, Bergdorf Goodman, Bloomingdale's, British Home Stores, Debenhams, Dickins & Jones, Fortnum & Mason, Harrods, Harvey Nichols, J.C. Penney, John Lewis, Kmart, Liberty, Macy's, Selfridges, Wal-Mart, Woolworth

depression: "The real problem with depression is that you see only a portion of the world all too clearly and are blind to the rest" – Will Cohu

depth, fear of: bathophobia

depth measurement (of water, the sea, etc): bathymetry

Derbyshire, administrative centre: Matlock

desert, adjective: eremic (particularly regarding sandy deserts)

desert, largest in the world: Sahara, North Africa (second largest: Australian)

Desert Fox: nickname for Erwin Rommel

Desert Island Discs: radio programme created by Roy Plomley in 1942, accompanied by Eric Coates' theme *By the Sleepy Lagoon*. Each week a guest celebrity chooses eight records that he or she would take to a desert island, along with one luxury item. The first guest was the comedian Vic Oliver (who appeared on 29 January 1942), and the first guest to appear more than once was the actress Valerie Hobson. On his death in 1985, Plomley was replaced by Michael Parkinson for two years and then by Sue Lawley, who was replaced in 2006 by Kirsty Young

desert wind: simoom

deserts: Arabian (southwest Asia), Atacama (Chile and Peru), Australian, Gibson (Australia), Gobi (central Asia), Great Sandy (Australia), Great Victoria (Australia), Kalahari (Botswana, Namibia and South Africa), Libyan, Mojave (USA), Namib (southwest Africa), Sahara (North Africa), Simpson (Australia), Somali (Somalia), Sonoran (USA and Mexico), Takla Makan (China), Thar (Pakistan and northen India), Turkestan (Central Asia)

deserts, study of: eremology

designers: Laura Ashley, Stephen Bayley, Coco Chanel, Sir Terence Conran, Erté (real name: Romain de Tirtoff), Ken Grange, Hans Gugelot, Charles Harper, Thomas Heatherwick, Barbara Hulanicki, Alec Issigonis, Raymond Loewy, Eliot Noyes, Dieter Rams, Ettore Sottsass
- see fashion designers

desire, adjective: amatory, amorous

Desperate Housewives: caustic, enormously popular ABC TV soap opera satirising the forbidden lives of the modern American hausfrau
    first broadcast: 3 October 2004 (pilot) created by Marc Cherry
    cast: Teri Hatcher (Susan Mayer), Felicity Huffman (Lynette Scavo), Marcia Cross (Bree Van De Kamp), Eva Longoria (Gabrielle Solis), Nicollette Sheridan (Edie Britt), Brenda Strong (Mary Alice Young), James Denton (Mike Delfino), Steven Culp (Rex Van De Kamp)

desperation: anagram for "a rope ends it"

despots – see dictators

dessert: baklava, banoffi, bomba Sofia (ice cream bombe with black cherries and cherry brandy), bread-and-butter pudding, crème brulée, crêpes Suzette, crumble, meringue, millefeuilles (multi-layered cream slice made from puff pastry), pavlova, pera Elena (pears and vanilla ice cream with chocolate sauce), rice pudding, semolina, spotted dick, tart, tiramisu, trifle, zabaglione (egg flip with white wine and marsala)
- see puddings

destiny: "A tyrant's authority for crime and a fool's excuse for failure" – Ambrose Bierce

destiny, goddess of: Norn (comprising Urdr, Verdandi and Skuldr, i.e. Fate, Being and Necessity, or Past, Present and Future) (Norse mythology)

Destiny's Child: US pop group formed in Houston, Texas, in 1990; comprised of: Beyoncé Knowles, Kelly Rowland and Michelle Williams; previous members include LeToya Luckett, LaTavia Roberson, Farrah Franklin

destroy completely: extirpate

destruction, god of: Ares (Greek), Mars (Roman)

detectives: Charles F. Field, Allan Pinkerton, Jack Slipper (aka 'Slipper of the Yard'), François Vidocq

detectives in fiction: Tom Barnaby, Tony Baretta, Boston Blackie, Father Brown, Inspector Bucket (from *Bleak House*), Cadfael, Albert Campion (amateur), Nick Carter, Charlie Chan, Nick Charles, Nora Charles, Inspector Clouseau, Lieutenant Columbo, Sergeant Richard Cuff (from Wilkie Collins' *The Moonstone*), Adam Dalgliesh, Lt. Frank Drebin (from *The Naked Gun*), Nancy Drew, Auguste Dupin (fiction's first detective), 'the Falcon,' Jessica Fletcher,

Joe Friday, Jack Frost, Mike Hammer, Sherlock Holmes, Lone Wolf (aka Michael Lanyard), Thomas Lynley, Jules Maigret, Philip Marlowe, Miss Jane Marple, Inspector Morse, Mr Moto, Porfiry Petrovich (from *Crime and Punishment*), Hercule Poirot, Inspector John Rebus, Eddie Shoestring, Dr Mark Sloan (from TV's *Diagnosis Murder*), Sam Spade, Dick Tracy, Lord Peter Wimsey, Mr Wong

detective agencies: Control Risks, Kroll

detective story, first: Edgar Allan Poe's *Murders in the Rue Morgue* (1841)

detective writers: John Carr, Raymond Chandler, Agatha Christie, Sir Arthur Conan Doyle, John Creasey, James Ellroy, Dashiell Hammett, Georgette Heyer, P.D. James, Dame Ngaio Marsh, Val McDermid, Ian Rankin, Ruth Rendell, Dorothy L. Sayers, Georges Simenon, Mickey Spillane - see crime writers, thriller writers, etc

detention camps: Abu Ghraib, Guantanamo Bay

Detroit: 'automobile capital of the world'

Detroit, birthplace of: Jerry Bruckheimer (film producer), Alice Cooper, Henry Ford II, Aretha Franklin, Berry Gordy Jr, Neil LaBute, Charles Lindbergh, Suzi Quatro, Smokey Robinson, Sugar Ray Robinson, Tom Selleck, Betty Shabazz, Lily Tomlin, The White Stripes

Detroit, elopers' retreat: Hotel Yorba (the subject of a song by The White Stripes)

Detroit river: Detroit

Devil, the - see Satan

Devil, the; adjective: diabolic

devils, fear of: demonophobia

Devon, administrative centre: Exeter

dew, adjective: rorulent (as in "covered with dew")

dew, goddess of: Tefnut (Egyptian mythology)

diagram, tree-shaped: cladogram, dendrogram

dialect expert: Alexander John Ellis

diamond: carbonado (used for drills, etc)

diamond, adjective: diamantine

diamond company: De Beers

diamond pattern (on pullovers, socks, etc): argyle

diamond-cutting capital of the world: Antwerp

diamond-shaped pane of glass: quarry

Diana, Princess of Wales (1961–1997), original name: Lady Diana Frances Spencer
    charities: Centrepoint (for homeless young people), English National Ballet, Great Ormond Street Hospital for Children, The Leprosy Mission, The National Aids Trust, The Royal Marsden Hospital
    bodyguard (who survived her fatal car crash): Trevor Rees-Jones
    driver (held responsible for her death): Henri Paul
    lovers: Dodi Fayed, James Gilbey, James Hewitt, Hasnat Khan

dialects, British: according to the language expert Mario Pei, there are thirty dialects in England and Wales, nine in Scotland and three in Ireland

diaphragm, adjective: phrenic

diarists: Walter Bagehot, Fanny Burney, Alastair Campbell, Alan Clark, Chips Channon, Richard Crossman, Nigel Dempster, John Evelyn, Anne Frank, André Gide, Charles Greville, Bridget Jones, James Lees-Milne, Adrian Mole, Harold Nicolson, Samuel Pepys, Samuel Sewall, Dorothy Wordsworth

diarrhoea: collywobbles, Montezuma's revenge

diarrhoea, adjective: diarrhoeal, diarrhoeic

diarrhoea in farm animals: scour

Dick Barton – Special Agent! (1946–1951), the BBC's first daily radio serial
 created by Norman Collins and written by Edward J. Mason and Geoffrey Webb
  cast: Noel Johnson (Dick Barton, 1946–49), Duncan Carse (Dick Barton,
   1949–50), Gordon Davies (Dick Barton, 1951), Alex McCrindle (Jock),
   John Mann (Snowey White)

dictators: Sani Abacha (of Nigeria), Idi Amin Dada, Hafez al-Assad, Jean-Bertrand
 Aristide (of Haiti), Mustafa Kemal Atatürk, Siad Barre (of Somalia), Omar al-
 Bashir (Sudan), Fulgencio Batista, Jean-Bédel Bokassa (of the Central African
 Republic), Habib Bourguiba, Julius Caesar, Fidel Castro, Nicolae Ceausescu,
 Porfirio Díaz, José Eduardo dos Santos (of Angola), François 'Papa Doc'
 Duvalier, General Francisco Franco, führer, Ernesto Geisel (of Brazil), Gelon
 of Syracuse, Hissene Habre, Adolf Hitler, Enver Hoxha (Albania), Saddam
 Hussein, Joseph Kabila (of the Congo), Kim-Il Sung, Kim Jong- il, Vladimir
 Ilyich Lenin, Mao Tse-tung, Robert Mugabe, Benito Mussolini, Saparmyrat
 Niyazov (of Turkmenistan, who banned ballet in his country, renamed January
 after himself and ordered the construction of the world's largest shoe), Manuel
 Antonio Noriega, Muhammad Reza Pahlavi (aka the Shah of Iran), Papa Doc
 (popular name for François Duvalier), Juan Perón, Józef Pilsudski, Augusto
 Pinochet Ugarte, Miguel Primo de Rivera, Juan Manuel de Rosas (Argentina),
 António de Oliveira Salazar, Joseph Stalin, Lucius Sulla, Charles Taylor (of
 Liberia), Than Shwe (of Burma), Marshal Josip Broz Tito, Sékou Touré,
 General Rafael Leonidas Trujillo Molina

didgeridoo player: Rolf Harris

die: bite the dust, buy the farm, call off all bets, cash in one's chips, croak, expire,
 go the way of all flesh, go west, kick the bucket, meet Mr Jordan, meet one's
 Maker, pass away, sprout wings, strike out

diesel engine: invented by Rudolf Diesel in 1892

diets: Atkins, Corti Slim, Dash, F Plan, Flush, Gi, Grapefruit, Hayes, Hollywood,
 Ketogenic, Mediterranean, South Beach, Warrior, XYZ, Zone

diet, adjective: dietary

diet, science of: sitology

diet guru: Dr Robert Atkins

dieticians, patron saint of: Martha

dieting device: AromaTrim (you sniff it and lose your appetite)

differential calculus, inventor of: Pierre de Fermat

digestion, adjective: peptic

digestive system, study of: gastroenterology

dime novelists: Ned Buntline (real name: Edward Zane Carroll Judson), Richard
 Allen

dining, art of: aristology

dinner, adjective: prandial

dinosaur: ankylosaur, apatosaur, brachiosaur, carnotaur, dilophosaur, euoplocephalid,
 gigantosaurus, hadrosaur, hesperonychus, hypsilophodontid, iguanodon, maiasaur,
 microceratop, othnielia, oviraptor, pachyrhinosaur, procompsognathid, pterosaur,
 spinosaurus, stegosaurus, styracosaur, T-rex, triceratop, tyrannosaur, velociraptor

dinosaur, biggest predatory: spinosaurus

diplomacy: "Diplomacy is letting someone else have your way" - Lester Pearson
 (former Canadian prime minister)

diplomats: Kofi Annan, John Bigelow, Otto von Bismarck, Hans Blix, Sir Thomas
 Bodley, Anatoli Dobrynin, Marnix Gijsen, George Kennan, Henry Kissinger,

Bernard Kouchner, Ferdinand de Lesseps, Paul Nitze, Javier Pérez de Cuéllar, Matthew Prior, Porfirio Rubirosa, Raoul Wallenberg, Sir Francis Younghusband
Dire Straits; UK rock band formed in Deptford, South London, in 1977; comprised of Mark Knopfler (vocals, guitar), brother David Knopfler (rhythm guitar), John Illsey (bass) and Pick Withers (drums). Disbanded in 1995
dirt, fear of: mysophobia
Dirty Digger: nickname for Rupert Murdoch
Dirty Harry (1971 film), famous line: Insp. Harry Callahan (Clint Eastwood): "I know what you're thinking. Did he fire six shots or only five? Well, to tell you the truth, in all this excitement, I've kind of lost track myself. But being as this is a .44 Magnum, the most powerful handgun in the world, and would blow your head clean off, you've got to ask yourself one question: 'Do I feel lucky?' Well, do you, punk?"
disabled and famous: Christy Brown, Max Cleland, Stephen Hawking, Ron Kovic, Alison Lapper (artist), Hilary Lister (who, paralysed from the neck down, sailed across the English Channel in August 2005), Christopher Reeve, Franklin D. Roosevelt, Ramon Sampedro (Spanish writer), George Wallace
- see amputees, paraplegics, etc
disappeared and famous: Mehdi Ben Barka (Moroccan statesman who, in 1965, vanished after being taken into custody by French police), Steve Fossett (adventurer who vanished in a small plane on 3 September 2007, declared legally dead 15 February 2008), Jesus de Galindez (exiled Spanish politician and FBI informer, in New York, 1956), Jimmy Hoffa (Teamster leader who vanished in 1975), Harold Holt (Australian prime minister, 17 December of 1967, disappeared while swimming near his holiday home in Portsea), Lord Lucan (on the evening of 7 November 1974, having incurred massive gambling debts and, apparently, after murdering his family's nanny Sandra Rivett), Richey James Edwards (guitarist with the Manic Street Preachers, vanished 1 February 1995 after he checked out of his London hotel; two weeks later his abandoned car was found near the Severn Bridge), John Stonehouse (Labour MP who left his wife and daughter to pursue a new life in Australia under the alias of John Markham)
disasters:
Bam earthquake (26 December 2003), killed 30,000 people in Iran;
BP oil leak in the Gulf of Mexico, the biggest oil spill in United States history (2010);
Bradford (1985), fire at Yorkshire football stadium, 53 killed;
Burma (2008), cyclone Nargis, killed up to 127,990;
Chernobyl (1986), nuclear accident 60 miles from Kiev;
Estonia (1994), ferry capsized in Baltic Sea, over 900 killed;
Exxon Valdez (1989), oil spill in Prince William Sound, Alaska, 10,080,000 gallons lost;
Haiti earthquake (12 January 2010), killed 222,570 people;
Indian Ocean tsunami (December 26, 2004), killed approximately 300,000;
King's Cross (18 November, 1987), fire at London underground station, 30 killed;
Kobe earthquake (17 January, 1995), more than 5,500 killed;
Krakatau (1883), volcanic eruption on Indonesian island causing a tidal wave that killed 36,000 in nearby Java and Sumatra;
Lockerbie (1988), Pan Am Boeing 747 crash in Scotland, 270 killed;
London bombings (7 July, 2005), terrorist attack in which 56 died (including the four bombers);
Los Angeles earthquake (1994), measured 6.7 on the Richter scale, killed 57 and caused $20 billion worth of damage;
Madrid train bombings (2004), terrorist attack in which 191 people died and 1,800 were injured;

Pompeii (79 AD), Vesuvius erupts over Naples Bay, with lava engulfing three cities;
Russian earthquake (1995), devastated the town of Neftegorsk on Russia's far
    eastern island of Sakhalin, 1,632 killed;
Taiwan earthquake (20 September 1999), over 2,000 killed;
Three Mile Island (1979), nuclear meltdown in Middletown, Pennsylvania;
Titanic (14 April, 1912), shipwreck of British ocean liner which hit an iceberg
    in the North Atlantic, 1,503 killed, while an estimated 712 survived;
Turkey earthquake (August 1999), over 18,000 killed;
World Trade Centre (11 September 2001), terrorist attack in which 2,974 died;
Zeebrugge (1987), British ferry capsized off Belgium coast; 188 killed
- see hurricanes

disapproving: dyslogistic

disc jockeys: Gerry Anderson, Danny Baker, Simon Bates, Jeremy Beadle, Rodney
    Bingenheimer, Tony Blackburn, Kurtis Blow (real name: Curtis Walker), Edith
    Bowman, Bruno Brookes, Ken Bruce, Nicky Campbell, Dave Cash, Terry
    Christian, Sarah Cox, Gary Davies, Noel Edmonds, Chris Evans, Kenny Everett,
    Neil Fox, Alan Freed, Alan Freeman, Emma Freud, Petey Greene, Bob Harris,
    David Jacobs, Duncan Johnson, Margaret Jones, Andy Kershaw, Janice Long,
    Zane Lowe, Simon Mayo, Scott Mills, Chris Moyles, Colin Murray, Pete Murray,
    Annie Nightingale, Michael Parkinson, Dave Pearce, Andy Peebles, John Peel,
    Gilles Peterson, Peter Powell, Mark Radcliffe, Anna Raeburn, Mike Raven, Mike
    Read, Jonathan Ross, Sybil Ruscoe, Sir Jimmy Savile, Keith Skues, Mike Smith,
    Ed Stewart, David Symonds, Chris Tarrant, Pete Tong, Dave Lee Travis, Johnny
    Vaughan, Jo Whiley, Sir Terry Wogan, Steve Wright, Sir Jimmy Young
    - see broadcasters

discord, Greek goddess of: Eris

disease, fear of: nosophobia

disease, fear of inheriting: patriophobia

disease, in cattle: bovine spongiform encephalopathy, BSE, CJD, Creutzfeld-Jakob
    Disease, foot and mouth, mad cows' disease

disease, medical branch of: nosology

disease, study of cause of: etiology

disease, systematic description of: nosography

disease of unknown origin: idiopathy

diseased origins, science of: etiology

disembowel: eviscerate

dish, most widely ordered in British restaurants: chicken tikka masala (11 million
    diners apparently ask for it every year)

Disney, Walt (1901–1966); first film seen: a silent version of *Snow White*

Disneyland: theme park opened 17 July, 1955, in Anaheim, Orange County,
    California, near the junction of the Santa Ana Freeway (I-5) and Harbor
    Boulevard. In order to realise his dream of an "entertainment kingdom," Walt
    Disney bought a 160-acre orange grove, cut down the trees, removed fifteen
    houses from the plot and in the space of twelve months constructed his "magical
    park." While the kingdom had a wobbly start – opening day was marred by 110-
    degree temperatures, molten tarmac, a plumbers' strike and a flood of counterfeit
    tickets – Disneyland had seen 50,000,000 visitors in its first decade. In 1971 Walt
    Disney World opened in Orlando, Florida, in 1983 Tokyo Disneyland was
    unveiled in Urayasu, Japan, and in 1992 Europe saw its very own Disneyland
    Paris. Hong Kong Disneyland was launched in September of 2005

disorder, fear of: ataxiophobia
dispute, adjective: eristic
divers: Jacques Cousteau, Greg Louganis
divination, adjective: mantic
divination by dripping blood: dririmancy
divination by entrails: epatoscomancy, extispiciomancy
divination by fire: pyromancy
divination by handwriting: graphomancy, graphtomancy
divination by salt: halomancy
divination by tea leaves: foliomancy
divination by the belly: gastromancy
divination by the stars: sideromancy
divination by the use of passages from the Bible: bibliomancy
divine and human, adjective: theanthropic
divine human (ie Christ), adjective: theandric
diviners – see soothsayers
divorce: "Getting married is just the first step toward getting divorced" - Zsa Zsa
    Gabor; "Divorce - from the Latin word meaning to rip out a man's genitals
    through his wallet" – Robin Williams
divorce, fact: 50% of all marriages in the US end in divorce
divorce, fact: 40% of all marriages in the UK end in divorce (the highest rate in Europe)
divorce capital of the United States: Reno
divorcees, royal: Princess Anne (aka the Princess Royal), Henry VIII, Camilla
    Parker Bowles, Wallis Simpson
Dixie Chicks, The: Country music trio formed in Dallas in 1989; originally
    comprised of the sisters Martie Erwin and Emily Erwin, and the singers Laura
    Lynch and Robin Lynn Macy. Then, after various changes in personnel, and
    with Martie and Emily taking up their married names of Martie Maguire and
    Emily Robison, the Chicks hit the big time in 1995 with the employ of new
    lead singer Natalie Maines. With Maines on board, the group's fourth album,
    Wide Open Spaces, became the top-selling album in history produced by a
    Country group. However, on the eve of America's invasion of Iraq in March of
    2003, Maines upset many fans by declaring, "we're ashamed the president of
    the United States is from Texas"
Dixon of Dock Green: 367-part TV police series set in the fictitious neighbourhood
    of Dock Green in London's East End
    created by Ted Willis, from the 1949 film *The Blue Lamp*
    broadcast: 9 July 1955–1 May 1976 on BBC
    cast: Jack Warner (PC George Dixon, later Sgt. Dixon), Arthur Rigby (Sgt.
        Flint), Peter Byrne (Andy Crawford), Billie Whitelaw (Mary Dixon),
        Moira Mannion (Sgt. Grace Millard)
DJs – see disc jockeys
Djibouti: republic in East Africa
    capital: Djibouti
    currency: Djibouti franc
    language: Arabic, French
    religion: Muslim
DLG: Dark Latin Groove
DMZ: demilitarised zone
DNA: deoxyribonucleic acid, genetic map discovered by James D. Watson, Francis
    Crick and Maurice Wilkins

DNS (in computing): domain name server

doctor: doc, Keith and Proctor (American Rhyming Slang), medic, physician, quack, sawbones

doctor, collective noun: dose

doctor, fact: In Britain, on average 45 million people consult their GP seven times a year

doctor of cancer: oncologist

doctor of children: paediatrician

doctor of reproduction: obstetrician

doctor of rheumatic disease: rheumatologist

doctor of the bladder: urologist

doctor of the blood: haematologist

doctor of the bones: orthopaedist

doctor of the bottom (anus, rectum, etc): proctologist

doctor of the ear: otologist

doctor of the eye: ophthalmologist

doctor of the foot: chiropodist, podiatrist

doctor of the heart: cardiologist

doctor of the kidneys: nephrologist

doctor of the lungs: pulmonologist

doctor of the nervous system: neurologist

doctor of the skin: dermatologist

doctor of the spine: orthopaedist

doctor of the stomach and intestines: gastroenterologist

doctor of women's conditions: gynaecologist

doctors, famous: John Addenbrooke (notable benefactor), Alfred Adler, Elizabeth Anderson (the first female English doctor), Martin Arrowsmith (from the novel by Sinclair Lewis), Edward Bach (who developed remedies from flowers), Peter Benton, Caligari, Cameron, Ben Casey, Elizabeth Corday, Hawley Crippen, Dolittle, Charlie Fairhead, Faustus, Alan Finlay, Mark Greene, Gaston Grimsdyke, William Harvey (discovered the nature of the blood's circulation), Gregory House (from TV's *House*), Imhotep, Jekyll, Samuel Johnson, Hilary Jones, James Kildare, Bernard Kouchner, Mabuse, William Marsden, Josef Mengele, Sir Jonathan Miller, Marcel Petiot (serial killer), Phibes, Michaela 'Mike' Quinn, Doug Ross (from TV's *ER*), Jack Shepherd (from TV's *Lost*), Harold Shipman (serial killer), Mark Sloan (from TV's *Diagnosis: Murder*), Samuel Smiles, Simon Sparrow, Spock, Sam Strachan (from TV's *Holby City*), Strangelove, Frederick Treves, Adam Truman (from TV's *Casualty*), Michael A. Upton, John Watson, Who, Zhivago
- see physicians, surgeons

doctors, fear of visiting: iatrophobia

doctors, number in Britain: 36,000 (compared to 49,000 complementary medicine practitioners)

doctor's oath: The Hippocratic oath

doctor's forced resignation: struck off

Doctor Who: cult BBC TV series about an eccentric, time-travelling trouble shooter played by eleven different actors since November 1963. The Doctor is a member of a humanoid race known as the Time Lords (from the planet Gallifrey) and travels through time and space in the Tardis, a structure that resembles an old London telephone box. His most notable enemies have included the Cybermen, Daleks, Davros, Mechanoids, Movellans, Nestenes and the Silurians. The series has inspired countless books, conventions, fan clubs, comics, two films starring Peter Cushing and a TV special featuring Paul McGann

created by Sydney Newman and Donald Wilson
cast: William Hartnell, Richard Hurndall, Patrick Troughton, Jon Pertwee,
Tom Baker, Peter Davison, Colin Baker, Sylvester McCoy, Christopher
Eccleston, David Tennant and Matt Smith (Dr Who), William Russell
(Ian Chesterton), Jacqueline Hill (Barbara Wright), Peter Purves (Steven
Taylor), Louise Jameson (Leela), Frazer Hines (Jamie McCrimmon),
Elizabeth Sladen (Sarah Jane Smith), Katy Manning (Jo Grant), Sophie
Aldred (Ace)
documentary, TV, average UK cost: £100,000-£125,000
documentary filmmakers: Nick Broomfield, Ken Burns, Emile De Antonio, Robert
J. Flaherty, John Grierson, Patricio Guzmán, Humphrey Jennings, Barbara
Kopple, Albert and David Maysles, Ross McElwee, Michael Moore, Errol
Morris, D.A. Pennebaker, Leni Riefenstahl, Frederick Wiseman, Terry Zwigoff
dodo, adjective: didine
dog: bowwow, doggy, Fido, flea hotel, four-legged friend, hound, man's best friend,
mutt, pooch, pup
dog, adjective: canine
dog, collective noun: pack
dog, fear of: cynophobia
dog, female: bitch
dog, killer: akita (Japanese hunting dog), Alsatian, Doberman pinscher, dogo
Argentino, fila Brasileiro, German shepherd, mastiff, pit bull, Rottweiler, tosa
dog, male: dog
dog, obsession with: cynomania
dog, sound: bark, growl, howl, snarl, woof, yelp
dog, young: pup, puppy, whelp
dog authority: Charles Cruft
dog breeds: Afghan hound, Airedale terrier, Akita Inu, Alsatian, basset hound,
beagle, bichon frise, bloodhound, Border collie, border terrier, borzoi, Boston
terrier, boxer, Brittany spaniel, bull terrier, bulldog, cairn terrier, Chihuahua,
chow-chow, clumber spaniel, cocker spaniel, collie, corgi, dachshund,
Dalmatian, deerhound, dingo, Doberman pinscher, dogo Argentino, elkhound,
English foxhound, English mastiff, English setter, English springer spaniel, field
spaniel, fila Brasileiro, fox terrier, German shepherd (aka Alsatian), golden
retriever, Gordon setter, Great Dane, greyhound, griffon, harrier, husky, Irish
setter, Irish terrier, Irish water spaniel, Irish wolfhound, Jack Russell terrier,
kelpie, Kerry blue terrier, King Charles spaniel, Labradoodle, Labrador,
Labrador retriever, malamute, Maltese, Manchester terrier, mastiff,
Newfoundland, Norwich terrier, Old English sheepdog, otterhound, papillon,
Pekingese, pointer, Pomeranian, poodle, Portuguese cattle dog, Portuguese water
dog, pug, puggle, Pyrenean mountain dog, Rhodesian ridgeback, Rottweiler,
Saluki, schnauzer, Scottish terrier, Sealyham terrier, setter, shar pei, sheepdog,
Shetland sheepdog, shih-tzu, Skye terrier, spaniel, spitz, springer spaniel,
Staffordshire bull terrier, St Bernard, Sussex spaniel, Swiss mountain dog,
Tasmanian dog, terrier, Tibetan mastiff, Tibetan spaniel, Tibetan terrier, tosa,
vizsla, water spaniel, Weimaraner, Welsh Border collie, Welsh corgi, Welsh
hound, Welsh terrier, West Highland white terrier, whippet, Yorkshire terrier
dog disorder (in which an individual believes himself to be canine): cynanthropy
dog food: Bonio, Chappie, Pal, Pedigree Chum, Royal Canin, Winalot
Dog Star: sirius
Dog Star, adjective: canicular

dog trainers: Cesar Millan, Barbara Woodhouse
dog-headed man: cynocephalus
dogs, famous: Alpha (TV's *Bewitched*), Andy (from Peanuts), Anubis (Egyptian mythology), Argus (Greek Mythology), Asta (from *The Thin Man* films), Augie Doggie (cartoon character), Balto (cartoon), Barney (George W. Bush's Scottish terrier), Barry (altruistic St Bernard), Beethoven (movie character), Belka (space dog, passenger on *Sputnik 5*), Belle (from Peanuts), Belvedere (comic strip character), Benji, Betty Boop (cartoon character), Bluebell (from *Animal Farm*), Brian (from TV's *Family Guy*), Buck (from *Call of the Wild*), Bullseye (from *Oliver Twist*), Cerberus (three-headed dog of Greek mythology), Charley (John Steinbeck's travelling companion), Clifford (cartoon character), Copper (from Disney's *The Fox and the Hound*), Cujo (psychotic St Bernard from the Stephen King story), Cynthia (from TV's *Green Acres*), Dawg (comic strip character), Deputy Dawg (cartoon character), Digby (the Biggest Dog in the World), Dippy Dawg (Disney cartoon), Dogmatix (Asterix canine), Dougal (from *The Magic Roundabout*), Droopy (Tex Avery creation), Fred Basset (comic strip character), Gnasher (from Hank Ketcham's *Dennis the Menace*), Goober (cartoon character), Goofy (Disney character), Greyfriars Bobby (Skye terrier), Gromit (Claymation character), Henry (Clement Freud's dog), Hobo (from TV's *The Littlest Hobo*), Howard Huge (comic strip character), Huckleberry Hound (cartoon character), Jock (from Disney's *Lady and the Tramp*), Lady (from Disney's *Lady and the Tramp*), Laika (aka Limonchik/Malyshka, the first Earth-born creature in space, courtesy of the Russian satellite *Sputnik 2*), Lassie, Lucky (from Disney's *101 Dalmatians*), Luke (Fatty Arbuckle's pet in the Mack Sennett comedies), Marmaduke (comic strip character), Max (The Grinch's dog), Missis (from Dodie Smith's *The Hundred and One Dalmatians*), Montmorency (from Jerome K. Jerome's *Three Men in a Boat*), Nana (from *Peter Pan*), Napoleon (comic strip character), Nipper (Jack Russell that listened to His Master's Voice – HMV emblem), Old Yeller, Omisto (Japanese mythology), Patch (from Disney's *101 Dalmatians*), Perdita (from Disney's *101 Dalmatians*), Petra (original mascot of TV's *Blue Peter*), Pilot (from *Jane Eyre*), Pluto (Disney character), Pongo (from Disney's *101 Dalmatians*), Porthos (canine companion of J.M. Barrie and the inspiration for *Peter Pan*'s Nana), Rowlf (Muppet), Sadie (real-life sniffer dog who saved the lives of many British soldiers in Afghanistan), Sam (eponymous Labrador retriever of the CBS TV show), Savage Sam (son of Old Yeller), Sandy (from *Little Orphan Annie*), Scamp (from Disney's *Lady and the Tramp*), Scooby Doo, Shep (from TV's *Blue Peter*), Skippy (productive terrier who appeared in many films, including *The Thin Man* series, as Asta), Slinky (from *Toy Story*), Snoopy, Snowy (Tintin's fox terrier), Snuppy (first cloned dog), Sweep (Sooty's friend), Toby (from the Punch & Judy show), Toto (from *The Wizard of Oz*), Tramp (from Disney's *Lady and the Tramp*), White Fang (half-wolf, half-huskie), Wishbone dogs, history of: cynology
dollar, fact: for which there are 293 ways to make change
doll, Russian: babushka, Marusia
dolls, American: Barbie, Cali Girl Barbie, Ken (Barbie's boyfriend), Samantha Parkington
dolls: Blaine (surfer dude from Australia), Bratz, Gonk
dolls, fear of: paediophobia
dolls, love of: paediomania
dolphin, adjective: delphine, delphinoid
dolphin, collective noun: pod

dolphin, fact: in a two-hour period, an average dolphin sheds its entire outer layer of skin (such skin-shedding is designed to reduce friction and to enable dolphins to reach much greater speeds)

dolphin, famous: Flipper

dolphin, sound: click

dolphin authority: Janet Mann

domesticity, goddess of: Hestia (Greek mythology)

Dominica: republic in the eastern Caribbean
>   **capital:** Roseau
>   **currency:** East Caribbean dollar
>   **language:** English
>   **religion:** Roman Catholic

Dominican Republic: republic in the Caribbean
>   **capital:** Santo Domingo
>   **currency:** peso
>   **language:** Spanish
>   **religion:** Roman Catholic
>   **dictator:** General Rafael Leonidas Trujillo Molina (ruling from 1930 to 1938 and again from 1943 to 1952, being one of the tightest dictatorships in the world)

don, collective noun: obscuration

Don Camillo: an unconventional priest, played in several films by the French actor Fernandel (from 1952) and on television by Mario Adorf (1980)

donkey: ass, burro (used as a pack animal), cuddy, moke (UK), neddy, yeknod (slang)

donkey, adjective: asinine

donkey, collective noun: drove

donkey, female: jenny

donkey, male: jackass

donkey, sound: bray, hee-haw

donkey, young: foal, mule (in collaboration with a female horse)

donkey and horse offspring: hinny

donkey worship: onolatry

donkeys, famous: Donkey (from *Shrek*), Eeyore (c/o A.A. Milne)

Don Quixote's squire: Sancho Panza

donut, alternative spelling: doughnut

donut brands: Cuzin's Duzin, Donut Connection, Daylight Donuts, Dunkin' Donuts, Entenmann's, Krispy Kreme

doomsayer: Jeremiah

Doors, The: US rock band formed in Los Angeles in 1965; comprised of Jim Morrison (vocalist; died: 3 July 1971 in Paris), Ray Manzarek (piano, organ), Robby Kreiger (guitar), Doug Labahn (bass) and John Densmore (drums). Morrison named the band after Aldous Huxley's book about experimenting with drugs, *The Doors of Perception*

door, Japanese (of the sliding kind): shoji

dormitory: anagram for "dirty room"

dormouse, adjective: myoxine

Dorset, administrative centre: Dorchester

Dorset, fact: it is the happiest county to live in in England

DOS: disk operating system

DoT: Department of Transport
dotcom pioneers: Brent Hoberman, Martha Lane Fox
double chin: choller
double entendre: "A woman walks into a pub and asks for a double entendre.
    So the barman gives her one" (joke)
double vision: diplopia
double-acts in comedy – see comedy double-acts
doubter: Thomas (the Apostle)
doughnut-shaped: toroidal
dove, adjective: columbiform, columbine
dove, collective noun: dole, dule
dove, sound: coo
dove, young: squab
drafts, dread of: aerophobia, pneumatophobia
drag racer: Shirley Muldowney
dragons: Drago (from the film *Dragonheart*), Fafnir (slain by Sigurd), George the
    Friendly Dragon (author: E.T. Matthews), Grendel (slain by Beowulf), Peist
    (Irish dragon imprisoned by St Patrick), Pocket Dragons, Puff, puk, Python
    (killed by Apollo), wivern, wyvern
dragon, adjective: draconic
dragon's jewel (said to be found inside a dragon's head): draconite
dragon slayers: Beowulf, St George, Marduk, St Michael, Sigurd, Yahweh
drag queen: "A gay man with way too much fashion sense for one gender" -
    Wesley Snipes in *To Wong Foo, Thanks For Everything, Julie Newmar* (1995)
drag queens: Dame Edna Everage (Barry Humphries), Eddie Izzard, Edward
    Kynaston, Danny La Rue (Daniel Patrick Carroll), Dennis Rodman, RuPaul
    (RuPaul Andre Charles), Lily Savage (Paul O'Grady)
dragonfly, adjective: libellulid
dragonfly, nickname: devil's darning needle
drama (of the stage), adjective: thespian
drama, founder of: Thespis
draper: Alfred Polly (from H.G. Wells' *The History of Mr Polly*)
draughts, fear of: anemophobia
dream specialist: oneirologist
dreamers: Billy Fisher (from the musical *Billy*), Billy Liar (aka Billy Fisher),
    Walter Mitty
dreaming, fact: the average human spends six years in a lifetime dreaming
dreams, adjective: oneiric
dreams, fear of: oneirophobia
dreams, god of: Morpheus (Greek)
dreams, interpretation of: oneiromancy
dreams, study of: oneirology
dreams and memories, the condition of confusing: paramnesia
Dresden bombing: 13 February 1945 (when 25,000 people died)
dressing gown: kimono, negligée, peignoir
drink: bevvy (Scot.), booze, draught, liquid cheer, potation, quencher, snifter, tipple
drink, adjective: sorbile, potatory
drink, aversion to: potophobia
drink, spiked with a narcotic or laxative: Mickey Finn
drink measure: optic (fitted to the neck of an inverted bottle)

drinkable: potable, sorbile

drinking, a postponement of (as in a vow to stay off the booze for a certain period): cagg

drinking, adjective: bibitory, potatory

drinking, aversion to: dipsophobia

drinking, fact: number of binge drinkers in Britain: 200,000

drinking bout: compotation

drinks: aperitif, babycham, beer (see), brandy (see), Dubonnet, fine, fruit juice (see), gin (see), liqueur (see), port, soda, soft, spirit, vermouth, whisky, wine (see)

drivers, patron saint of: Fiacre

driving, facts: 20% of accidents on British motorways are caused by drivers falling asleep

DRM: digital rights management

Dr No (1962 film), famous line: James Bond (Sean Connery, introducing himself to fellow gambler Sylvia Trench): "Bond. James Bond"

drooping, adjective: nutant

drop, the last in the glass: heeltap

dropsy: oedema

drowned and famous: George Washington Adams (lawyer), Alcyone, Jeff Buckley, Ann Cargill (opera singer), Hart Crane (poet), Rudolf Diesel, W.S. Gilbert, Harold Holt (Australian prime minister), Icarus, Brian Jones, Claude Jutra, Herbert Kitchener, Leander, Ludwig II, Robert Maxwell, Josef Mengele, Protagoras, Roy Raymond (founder of Victoria's Secret), Orville Redenbacher, Percy Bysshe Shelley, Aulus Vitellius (Roman emperor), Matthew Webb (in the rapids below Niagara Falls), Dennis Wilson (Beach Boy), Natalie Wood, Virginia Woolf, Wozzeck

drowning as execution: noyade

drowning, goddess of: Ran (Norse mythology)

drug: "A drug is a chemical which, when injected into a laboratory animal, will produce a scientific paper" – Professor William Paton

drugs, medicinal: Alka-Seltzer (fast relief from headache with upset stomach), amytal (a barbiturate), aspirin, barbiturate, Paracetamol, Rennie (fast efective relief from acid indigestion and heartburn), sedative, Tylenol benzocaine (a local anaesthetic), clomipramine (anti-depressant with yawning-related orgasmic side effect), corticosteroids, Dutasteride (for restoring hair to bald men), GHB (date rape drug), ibogaine (antidote to addiction), ibuprophen, Lithium Carbonate (treatment for manic depression), Lustral (anti-depressant), Prozac (anti-depressant), Ritalin (a behaviour modification drug, taken by 12% of American children aged between two and four), Rohypnol (sedative and date rape pill), steroids, Succinylcholine (a paralytic), venlafaxine (anti-depressant), Zoloft (anti-depressant known as Lustral in UK)

drugs, recreational: amphetamines, angel dust, blow, Bob, boo, boy, cannabis (see), cocaine (see), crack, crank, dope, ecstasy, fantasy, gear, GHB, girl, grass, hallucinogen, hashish, heroin (see), hop, Liquid E, Liquid X, ludes, marijuana, mescaline, mojo, nose candy, phantasia, pot, psilocybin, puff, shit, snow, speed, spliff, weed, yaba (a concentrated crystal form of methamphetamione, a form of speed popular in Thailand, also known as ice and glass and, by the Thais, 'crazy medicine')

drugs, champion for the legalisation of cannabis in Britain: Labour MP Clare Short

drugs manufacturer: Jesse Boot (opened his first chemist's shop in 1877 in Nottingham)

drugs, book of: pharmacopoeia
drugs, budget of US federal government to fight problem: $19.2 billion annually
drugs, fact: percentage of British children under 13 to have tried illegal drugs: 10%
drugs, fact: the business of illegal drugs generates $400 billion per annum, roughly
    8% of all international trade
drugs, fear of: pharmacophobia
drugs, science of: pharmacology
drug addiction: chemical inconvenience (pc), habit, hooked on, substance abuse
drug overdose, died from – see overdose, accidental death from
drug tsars: Pablo Escobar, Frank Lucas
drug users: Lester Bangs, Tallulah Bankhead, Syd Barrett, Jean-Michel Basquiat,
    John Belushi, John Berryman, Russell Brand, Lenny Bruce, William S.
    Burroughs, Johnny Cash, Carlos Castaneda, Ray Charles, Eric Clapton, Miles
    Davis, Thomas De Quincey, Pete Doherty, Robert Downey Jr., Bob Dylan,
    Jeanne Eagels, Rainer Werner Fassbinder, Marvin Gaye, Jimi Hendrix, Michael
    Herr, Billie Holiday, John C. Holmes, Sherlock Holmes, Dennis Hopper, Aldous
    Huxley, Samuel L. Jackson, Brian Jones, Janis Joplin, Jack Kerouac, Calvin
    Klein, Timothy Leary, Charles Manson, Bob Marley, O.D.B. (American rapper),
    Charlie Parker, Edith Piaf, Elvis Presley, Mark Renton (played by Ewan
    McGregor in *Trainspotting*), Little Richard, Sly Stone, Hunter S. Thompson,
    Donatella Versace, Sid Vicious, Hank Williams, Robin Williams, Brian Wilson
    (composed *Pet Sounds* and *Smile* while under the influence of LSD)
drug users' magazine: *Mainline Lady* (funded by the Dutch Health Ministry)
drums – see percussion instruments
drummers: Animal (from *The Muppet Show*), John Bonham (of Led Zeppelin),
    Billy Cobham, Phil Collins, Jack DeJohnette, Nicky 'Topper' Headon (of The
    Clash), Gene Krupa, Keith Moon (of The Who), Paul Motian, Sandy Nelson,
    Buddy Rich, Max Roach, Phil Rudd, Sheila E, Ringo Starr, Charlie Watts
drunk: "Drunk is feeling sophisticated when you can't say it" - anonymous
drunk (adjective): aled up, alkied, all in, arseholed, basted, blotto, boohonged, bung
    (Scottish slang), clobbered, crapulent, crunk (teenage slang), elephant's trunk
    (CRS), full as a goog (Australian slang), hammered, happy, honking, hosed,
    John Bull, kaschnickered, lame, liquored up (old-fashioned), mellow (slightly),
    mizzled, mortalled (21st century Cockney), out of one's skull, paralytic, pissed,
    plastered, pot-shot, potsick, rat arsed, ripped, shaved, shickered (Australian), shit-
    face, skunked, soaked, soused, sozzled, squiffy (slightly), stewed, stiff, stoned
    (dated), stotious (Irish), tipsy, tired and emotional, under the table, woozled
drunkard: dipso, dipsomaniac, elbow bender, piss artist, soak, souse, toper, tosspot,
    winebibber
DSMAC: Digital Scene Matching Area Correlation
Dublin: headquarters of Guinness (brewers of stout)
Dublin, birthplace of: Bertie Ahern, Maria Aitken (actress), Eamonn Andrews,
    Francis Bacon (painter), Thomas Barnardo, Samuel Beckett, Brendan Behan,
    George Berkeley, Bono, The Boomtown Rats, Elizabeth Bowen, Edmund
    Burke, Robert Castlereagh, Michael Collins, Roddy Doyle, The Dubliners,
    Brenda Fricker, Michael Gambon, Bob Geldof, Brendan Gleeson, Hothouse
    Flowers, James Joyce, Thomas Moore, Dame Iris Murdoch, Graham Norton,
    Sinéad O'Connor, George Bernard Shaw, Thin Lizzy, U2, Oscar Wilde
Dublin river: Liffey
Dubya: nickname for George W. Bush
duchess, mode of verbal address: Your Grace

duck, adjective: anatine

duck, collective noun: flock (in air), paddling (in water), raft (while idle in water), safe, team

duck, fact: until proved otherwise in September of 2003, a duck's quack was believed to be unable to produce an echo

duck, female: duck

duck, male: drake

duck, sound: quack

duck, young: duckling

ducks, famous: Daffy Duck, Donald Duck, Jemima Puddle-Duck (c/o Beatrix Potter), Orville, the Ugly Duckling (who actually turns out to be a swan)

Duck Soup (1933 film), famous lines: Rufus T. Firefly (Groucho Marx), to Mrs Teasdale: "Well, that covers a lot of ground. Say, you cover a lot of ground yourself. You better beat it. I hear they're going to tear you down and put up an office building where you're standing. You can leave in a taxi. If you can't leave in a taxi you can leave in a huff. If that's too soon, you can leave in a minute and a huff"; Mrs Teasdale (Margaret Dumont): "Oh, your Excellency!" Rufus T. Firefly: "You're not so bad yourself"; Rufus T. Firefly, to Vera Marcal: "I could dance with you till the cows come home. On second thoughts, I'd rather dance with the cows till you came home"; Rufus T. Firefly, to the Minister of Finance: "Why, a four-year-old could understand this report. Run out and find me a four-year-old child. I can't make head or tail out of it"

duct shaped: vasiform

DUI: Driving Under the Influence (of alcohol or drugs)

Duke, the: nickname for John Wayne

duke, mode of verbal address: Your Grace

dumb and famous: Helen Keller, Tommy (c/o The Who)

Dunblane Massacre: on 13 March 1996, at the Dunblane Primary School in Scotland, Thomas Hamilton killed 16 schoolchildren and their teacher (Mrs Gwen Mayor) and then shot himself

Dundee nickname: City of Discovery

dung, adjective: fimetic, stercoraceous

dung, fear of: coprophobia

dung, feeding on: coprophagous, scatophagous

dung, growing on: coprophilous

dung-fuelled power station: £7 million plant in Holsworthy, Devon

dung beetle, god depicted as: Khepri (Egyptian mythology)

dungeon, secret: oubliette

Dunkirk, evacuation of: 27 May-2 June, 1940

Durham, administrative centre: Durham

Durham river: Wear

dust, aversion to: amathophobia

dust, love of: amathomania

dustman: Alfred P. Doolittle (from *Pygmalion* and *My Fair Lady*)

Dutch and famous: Pope Adrian VI, Willem Barents (explorer), Anton Corbijn (photographer), Johan Cruyff (footballer), Jan De Bont (filmmaker), Desiderius Erasmus, Anne Frank (diarist), Ruud Gullit (footballer), Rutger Hauer (actor), Audrey Hepburn, Jeroen Krabbé (actor/director), Mata Hari, Famke Janssen

(actress), Ruud van Nistelrooy (footballer), Johanna ter Steege (actress), Peter Stuyvesant, Monique van der Ven (actress), Theo Van Gogh, Vincent Van Gogh, Paul Verhoeven (filmmaker), William of Orange
- see Dutch painters, Dutch writers

Dutch artist: Maurits Escher (who delighted in creating woodcuts and lithographs that defied perspective)

Dutch Guiana: former name for Suriname

Dutch painters: Karel Appel, Hieronymus Bosch, Pieter Claesz, Gerrit Dou, Frans Hals, Pieter de Hooch, Piet Mondrian, Rembrandt, Jan Steen, Gerard Terborch, Hendrik Terbrugghen, Vincent Van Gogh, Johannes Vermeer

Dutch Wars of Independence: 1568–1648

Dutch writers: Ferdinand Bordewijk, Eduard Dekker (aka Multatuli), Geert Groote, Pieter Corneliszoon Hooft, Willem Frederik Hermans, Constantijn Huygens, Harry Mulisch, Gerard Reve, Joost van den Vondel

duty, adjective: deontic

DVD, first film in the format title to sell over a million copies: *The Matrix*

DVT: deep-vein thrombosis

dwarf, adjective: nanoid

dwarf god: Bes (Egyptian mythology)

dwarf king: Alberich (in German legend)

dwarf planet: Pluto

dwarfs: Andvari, Bes (the Egyptian god of music and pleasure), Peter Dinklage (actor), Gimli (from *The Lord of the Rings*), Daniel Quilp (from *The Old Curiosity Shop*), Tokoloshe (Zulu mythology), troll

Dwarfs, The Seven (as featured in Disney's *Snow White and the Seven Dwarfs*): Bashful, Doc, Dopey, Grumpy, Happy, Sleepy and Sneezy

DWI: driving while impaired

dyeing, adjective: tinctorial

dying: "The truth is that we are all terminally ill. Once we recognise that, we can enjoy the life we have left" - Elisabeth Kübler-Ross; "I want to die like my father, peacefully in his sleep, not screaming in terror like his passengers" - Bob Monkhouse

dying, five stages of (as conceived by Elisabeth Kübler-Ross): denial, anger, bargain, depression, acceptance

dynamite: invented by Alfred Nobel in 1866 and patented in 1867

Dynasty, prime-time TV serial modelled on *Dallas* (see), about the fortunes and misfortunes of a Denver family in the oil business
 created by Richard and Esther Shapiro
 broadcast: 12 January 1981–11 May 1989
 cast: John Forsythe (Blake Carrington), Linda Evans (Krystle Jennings), Pamela Sue Martin and later Emma Samms (Fallon Carrington), Al Corley and later Jack Coleman (Steven Carrington), John James (Jeff Colby), Lloyd Bochner (Cecil Colby), Bo Hopkins (Matthew Blaisdel), Pamela Bellwood (Claudia Blaisdel), Joan Collins (Alexis Carrington), James Farentino (Dr Nick Toscanni), Heather Locklear (Sammy Jo Dean), Kathleen Beller (Kirby Anders), Michael Nader (Dex Dexter), Diahann Carroll (Dominique Deveraux), Catherine Oxenberg (Amanda Bedford Carrington), Rock Hudson (Daniel Reece), Christopher Cazenove (Ben Carrington), Kate O'Mara (Cassandra 'Caress' Morrell), Stephanie Beacham (Sable Colby) The show produced a spin-off, *The Colbys*, broadcast 20 November 1985–26 March 1987

dyslexic and famous: Muhammad Ali, Hans Christian Andersen, Fred Astaire, Harry Belafonte, Alexander Graham Bell, Richard Branson, George Burns, Cher, Agatha Christie, Winston Churchill, Tom Cruise, Walt Disney, Thomas Edison, Albert Einstein, Michael Faraday, Gustave Flaubert, Harrison Ford, Henry Ford, Danny Glover, Whoopi Goldberg, Duncan Goodhew, Susan Hampshire, Michael Heseltine, Eddie Izzard, Magic Johnson, John F. Kennedy, Nigel Kennedy, Keira Knightley, John Lennon, General George Patton, River Phoenix, Pablo Picasso, Sir Steve Redgrave, Oliver Reed, Keanu Reeves, Beryl Reid, Guy Ritchie, Nelson Rockefeller, Jackie Stewart, James Stirling (architect), Billy Bob Thornton, Ted Turner, Andy Warhol, George Washington, Marco Pierre White, F.W. Woolworth, W.B. Yeats

E

eagle, adjective: aquiline
eagle, collective noun: convocation
eagle, nest: eyrie
eagle, sound: scream
Eagle, The: British comic first published 14 April 1950 by Hulton Press
eagle, young: eaglet, eyas
eagle spirit: Thunderbird (in North American Indian mythology)
Eagles, The: US rock group formed in Los Angeles in 1971; disbanded in 1982 and reformed in 1994; comprising Don Henley (vocals, drums), Glenn Frey (vocals, guitar), Bernie Leadon (vocals, guitar, banjo, mandolin) and Randy Meisner (vocals, bass). In 1974 Don Felder joined the band as a session guitarist. When Leadon left for a solo career in 1975 and was replaced by Joe Walsh. In 1977 Meisner was succeeded by Timothy B. Schmit
Ealing Studios: West London film studio which, founded in 1902, can lay claim to being the oldest in the world. The studio closed as a production company in 1957, but was bought by the BBC two years later and became a fertile ground for television production. In 2000 Ealing was acquired by Uri Fruchtmann, Barnaby Thompson, Harry Handelsman and John Kao and witnessed a renewed vigour in the making of theatrical features
ear, adjective: aural, auricular
ear, external projection of: auricle or pinna
ear, inflammation of: otitis
ear, instrument for examining: otoscope
ear, parts of: ampulla, anvil, auditory canal, auditory nerve, auricle (pinna), cochlea, ear ossicle, endolymph, Eustachian tube, external auditory meatus, hammer, incus (or anvil), inner ear, lobe, the malleus (or hammer handle), middle ear, outer ear, oval window, perilymph, pinna, round window, sacculus, stapes (or stirrup), stirrup, tympanic membrane, tympanum
ear, study of: otology
ear discharge: otorrha, otorrhea
ear diseases, study of: otolaryngology
ear doctor: otologist
ear infections: acute mastoiditis, herpes zoster of the ear, infectious myringitis, otitis externa, otitis media, serous otitis media, vestibular neuronitis
ear inflammation: otitis
ear job: otoplasty (surgical correction of protruding ears)
ear muscle: auricularis (that which wiggles the outer ear)

ear ringing: tinnitus
ear wax: cerumen
ear wax, excessive secretion of: ceruminosis
earache: otalgia
earache, patron saint of: Polycarp
eardrum: tympanic membrane
eardrum tube (for draining): grommet
earl, mode of verbal address: Your Lordship
Earth: third planet from the sun
earth (or land), adjective: terrigenous
earth (or soil), adjective: telluric
Earth, adjective: terrestrial
Earth, god of: Keb (Egyptian mythology)
Earth, goddess of: Gaea (Greek), Tellus (Roman)
Earth, statistics:
    equatorial circumference: 24,902.4 miles
    polar circumference: 24,860.2 miles
    equatorial diameter: 7,926.42 miles
    polar diameter: 7,899.83 miles
    total surface area: 196,950,000 square miles
    temperature, highest: 136° F (in Al Aziziyah, Libya)
    temperature, lowest: -128.6° F (at Vostok Station, Antarctica)
Earth, Wind and Fire: flamboyant, mystical R&B band formed in Chicago in
    1969. Group members have included Maurice White (vocals, drums), Philip
    Bailey (vocals), Verdine White (bass), Larry Dunn (keyboards), Johnny Graham
    (guitar), Al McKay (guitar), Andre Woolfolk (reeds, Phoenix horns), Ralph
    Johnson (drums) and Freddie White (drums). Maurice, Verdine and Freddie
    White are brothers
earth eating: geophagous (adjective)
earth pig: aardvark
earth's crust: lithosphere
earth's surface, science of: physiography
Earthly Powers (1980 novel by Anthony Burgess); opening line: "It was the
    afternoon of my eighty-first birthday, and I was in bed with my catamite when
    Ali announced that the archbishop had come to see me"
earthquake: quake, seismic wave, shaker, tremor
earthquake, adjective: anaseismic, seismic
earthquakes, god of: Poseidon (Greek mythology)
earthquakes, patron saint of: Francis Borgia
earthquakes, prone to (adjective): malloseismic
earthquakes, study of: seismology
earthquake faults: blind thrust fault, hidden fault, San Andreas (750 miles long)
earthquake scale: Richter, moment-magnitude
earthquakes, famous (in order of strength): Chile (22 May 1960), killed more than
    2,000; Prince William Sound, Alaska (28 March 1964), killed 125; Sumatra-
    Andaman Islands (26 December 2004), in which 224,495 lost their lives;
    Kamchatka, Russia (4 November 1952), no lives lost; Cascadia Subduction
    Zone, including northern California, Oregon, Washington and southern British
    Columbia (26 January 1700); off the coast of Ecuador (31 January 1906); Chile
    (27 February 2010), killed more than 723 people; Northern Sumatra, Indonesia
    (28 March 2005); New Madrid, Missouri (December 1811); Michoacan, Mexico
    (19 September 1985); San Francisco (18 April 1906); Loma Prieta, California

(18 October 1989); Kobe, Japan (16 January 1995), killed 5,500; San Fernando, California (9 February 1971), 65 killed; Northridge, Los Angeles (17 January 1994), killed 60; Turkey (17 August 1999), killed over 18,000; Taiwan (20 September 1999), killed over 2,000; Bam, Iran (26 December 2003), 30,000 killed
- see disasters

earthworm, adjective: lumbricoid

earthworm, fact: the invertebrate has ten hearts

earthworm, habitat: earth

East Bengal: former name for Bangladesh (until 1947)

East Germany: former republic in central Europe, officially known as the German Democratic Republic; reunited with West Germany in 1990

East Pakistan: former name for Bangladesh (from 1947 to 1970)

East Timor: country in the Indian Ocean that officially became an independent nation 20 May 2002; formally known as the Democratic Republic of Timor-Leste
    capital: Dili
    currency: US dollar; formerly: Indonesian Rupiah (IDR)
    language: Tetum and Portuguese (both official); also Indonesian and English
    religion: Roman Catholic; also Muslim, Protestant

East Wind god: Eurus (Greek mythology)

EastEnders: enormously popular BBC television soap set in and around Albert Square in the London borough of Walford, E20
    first broadcast: 1 February 1985
    created by Julia Smith and Tony Holland
    local pub: The Queen Vic
    cast: Anna Wing (Lou Beale), Peter Dean (Pete Beale), Gillian Taylforth (Kathy Beale/Mitchell), Adam Woodyatt (Ian Beale), Wendy Richard (Pauline Fowler), Bill Treacher (Arthur Fowler), David Scarboro and Todd Carty (both Mark Fowler), Susan Tully (Michelle Fowler), Leslie Grantham ('Dirty' Den Watts), Anita Dobson (Angie Watts), John Altman (Nick Cotton), June Brown (Dot Cotton), Tony Caunter (Roy Evans), Michelle Collins (Cindy), Letitia Dean (Sharon Mitchell), Craig Fairbrass (Dan Sullivan), Perry Fenwick (Billy Mitchell), Dean Gafney (Robbie Jackson), Carol Harrison (Louise Raymond), Jane How (Jan Hammond), Louise Jameson (Rosa di Marco), Martin Kemp (Steve Owen), Ross Kemp (Grant Mitchell), Martine McCutcheon (Tiffany), Tamzin Outhwaite (Melanie Healy/Owen), Sid Owen (Ricky Butcher), Mike Reid (Frank Butcher), Barbara Windsor (Peggy Mitchell/Butcher), Daniella Westbrook (Sam Mitchell), Shane Richie (Alfie Moon), Leslie Schofield (Jeff Healy), Nicola Stapleton (Mandy Salter), Dudley Sutton (Wilfred Atkins), Rudolph Walker (Patrick Trueman)

Easter, adjective: paschal

Easter Island: volcanic island in the Pacific, 2,300 miles west of South America and 1,400 miles east of Pitcairn Island, its nearest neighbour. It was discovered by the Dutch in 1722 and is now officially a part of Chile. The island is also known as the End of the Land, the Navel of the World and Rapa Nui

Easter Island statue: moai (all 1,000 of them)

eau de Cologne: alcohol-based scent invented around 1850 by Johann Maria Farina of Cologne, Germany – see scent

eavesdropper on sexual sounds: ecouteur

easy: easy-peasy, falling off a log, no problem, no sweat, nothing to it

easy thing: no-brainer, picnic, piece of cake, piece of piss (Australian), pushover, slam-dunk, soft touch, turkey shoot, walk in the park

easyJet: budget airline founded by Stelios Haji-Ioannou in 1995

eat without appetite: pingle

eating, adjective: edacious, gastronomic

eating, dread of: phagophobia

eating, fond of: coenaculous

eating, study of: gastronomy

eating rapidly, the act of: tachyphagia

eau de toilette: Aramis, Cerruti 1881, Cool Water (Davidoff), Eden, Jazz (Prestige - Yves Saint Laurent), Joop!, Loulou, Miss Dior, New West (for him), Obsession, Zino

   - see cologne

eBay: founded in San Jose on 4 September, 1995, by Pierre Omidyar. Jeff Skoll joined the company in 1996 as its first president and full-time employee.

echidna: spiny anteater

echidna, famous: Knuckles (from the *Sonic the Hedgehog* video game)

echidna, young: puggle

echo, adjective: catacoustic

echo free: anechoic (adjective)

eco-protesters: Ben Hartley, Swampy (aka Daniel Hooper)

eco-warriors: Kofi Annan, Sir Richard Branson, Rachel Carson, Al Gore, Woody Harrelson, Sir Nicholas Stern, Sting, Douglas Tompkins (who bought nearly one million acres of rainforest in Chile)

   - see conservationists

ecologists: Daniel Cohn-Bendit, René Dubos, Charles Elton, Buckminster Fuller, Edward Goldsmith, John Robert Lewis, James Lovelock, Wangari Maathai, David McTaggart, Eugene Odum, Jonathon Porritt, Ernst Schumacher

   - see environmentalists

ecology, patron saint of: Francis of Assisi

economic historian: Walt Rostow

economic theorist: Karl Marx

economist: "If you laid all the economists end to end, they still wouldn't reach a conclusion" - George Bernard Shaw

economists: Abel Agenbegyan, Jeremy Bentham, Gerard Debreu, Hernando de Soto, Irving Fisher, Milton Friedman, J.K. Galbraith, André Gorz, Alan Greenspan, Friedrich von Hayek, Hesiod, Ellen Johnson-Sirleaf, John Maynard Keynes, James Lovelock, Thomas Malthus, James Meade, Gunnar Myrdal, Arthur Okun, Vilfredo Pareto, Johann Rodbertus, Paul Samuelson, Thomas Sargent, Amartya Sen, Ernst Schumacher, Arthur Seldon, Adam Smith (author of *The Wealth of Nations*), Solon, Thomas Sowell, Sir Nicholas Stern, Sir Alan Walters, Sidney Webb, Max Weber, Barbara Wootton, Tatyana Zaslavskaya

economy: plutonomy

Ecstasy: disco biscuit, methylenedioxymethamphetamine

ecstasy, god of: Bacchus (Greek and Roman mythology)

Ecuador: republic in South America

    capital: Quito

    currency: sucre

    language: Spanish

    religion: Roman Catholic

    birthplace of: Sir Frederick Ashton

fact: according to a recent survey, ingrained lateness costs the country $2.5b
  a year
Eden Project: the largest conservatory in the world
  location: near St Austell in Cornwall
  opened: May 2000
  roofing material: Ethylene Tetrafluoroethylene
edible substance: esculent
Edinburgh: "A little part of Scotland that remains forever English" (anon.)
Edinburgh, birthplace of: Robert Ballantyne, Alexander Graham Bell, Tony Blair,
  James Boswell, Sean Connery, Sir Arthur Conan Doyle, Iain Glen (actor), Kenneth
  Grahame, Field Marshal Douglas Haig, David Hume, Shirley Manson (lead singer
  of Garbage), James Clerk Maxwell, John Napier, The Proclaimers, Finley Quaye,
  David Roberts (painter), Sir Walter Scott, Richard Norman Shaw (architect),
  Alastair Sim, Dame Muriel Spark, Robert Louis Stevenson, Irvine Welsh
editing, in film: "The only film craft that is entirely indigenous to the cinema and
  which has some bearing on every other facet of the art" - Edward Dmytryk
editor: blue penciler, ed, red penciler, third eye
editor, first woman of a British national newspaper: Rosie Boycott, who took over
  the reins of *The Independent* in 1998
editors, patron saint of: John Bosco (aka Giovanni Melchior Bosco)
education: "If you think education is expensive, try ignorance" - Derek Bok; "If
  you're planning for one year, plant rice. If you're planning for ten years, plant
  trees. If you're planning for 100 years, educate people" - old Chinese proverb;
  "The brief interval between ignorance and arrogance" - adage quoted by Louis
  Quesnel; "That which reveals to the wise, and conceals from the stupid, the vast
  limits of their knowledge" – Mark Twain; "Education is all that is left behind
  when you have forgotten what you have learnt" – the governess of Alexander
  Waugh
education, adjective: pedagogical
education, patron saint of: John Chrysostom
education primer: Cliffs Notes
educational body, UK: Ofsted (Office for Standards in Education)
educational entertainment: edutainment
educationists: Felix Adler, Mary McLeod Bethune, Louis Braille, Ritchie Calder,
  John Dewey, Maria Grey, Sir William Hadow, Dr Kurt Hahn, Motoko Hani,
  Sheila Kitzinger, Anne Macy, Horace Mann, Maria Montessori, Elizabeth
  Palmer Peabody, Patrick Pearse, Jean-Jacques Rousseau, Rudolf Steiner, Harry
  Sullivan, Henry Symonds, Carey Thomas, Booker T. Washington, Barbara
  Wootton
eel, collective noun: swarm
eel, cooked: spitchcock
eel, young: elver
eel dish: anguille (poached in herb sauce)
eel-shaped: anguilliform
efficiency in the workplace, study of: ergonomics
effort: "Trying is the first step toward failure" - Homer Simpson
egg, collective noun: clutch
egg, famous: Humpty Dumpty
egg, white of: albumen
egg, yellow of: yolk
egg yolk, adjective: vitelline

egg-shaped: oval, ovate, oviform, ovoid

eggplant: aubergine, brinjal (Indian)

egotism: "Usually just a case of mistaken nonentity" - Barbara Stanwyck

egotist: "A person me-deep in conversation" (anon.); "A person of low taste, more interested in himself than me" - Ambrose Bierce

egotistical, fear of being: autophobia

egret plume: aigrette

Egypt: republic in north-eastern Africa; officially known as the Arab Republic of Egypt
  capital: Cairo
  currency: pound
  language: Arabic
  religion: Muslim (Sunni majority)

Egyptian and famous: Alaa Al Aswany (writer), Youssef Chahine (filmmaker), Cleopatra (although, strictly speaking, she was Greek), Amr Diab (singer), Dinah (belly dancer), Mohamed Al-Fayed, Hatshepsut (pharaoh), Zahi Hawass (Egyptologist), Umm Kulthum (singer, aka Oum Kalsoum), Naguib Mahfouz (novelist), Hosni Mubarak (president), Gamal Abdel Nasser (president), Nyarlathotep (fictitious character), Ptolemy, Anwar Sadat (president), Omar Sharif (actor and bridge player), Tutankhamen

Egyptian astronomer: Ptolemy

Egyptian boat: fellucca

Egyptian deities: Amen-Ra (of the sun), Anubis (of the dead, cemeteries and burial rituals), Apis (an earthly form of Ptah, depicted as a bull), Apophis (snake god of the underworld and enemy of the sun), Aten (sun god), Atum (creator of gods), Bastet (lion-headed goddess), Bes (depicted as a deformed dwarf, offered protection of women in childbirth), Geb (of fertility), Hapy (of the Nile flood), Hathor (a sky goddess and protector of cemeteries), Heket (goddess of childbirth and fertility), Horus (sky god and sun god), Isis (of fertility), Khepri (a form of the sun god Ra), Khnum (guardian of the source of the Nile), Khonsu (moon god and god of war, often portrayed as a baboon or with a falcon's head), Maat (goddess of cosmic harmony), Meretseger (cobra goddess), Min (god of sexual activity and fertility), Montu (god of war), Mut (sky goddess and goddess of war), Nefertum (god of rebirth), Neith (goddess of war), Nekhbet (goddess of Upper Egypt), Nephthys (funerary goddess), Nun (of water), Nut (sky goddess), Osiris (of the underworld), Ptah (of creation and the arts), Ra (sun god), Renpet (goddess of youth), Sekhmet (goddess of war), Seshat (goddess of recording and writing), Set/Seth (god of evil), Shu (god of air), Sobek (crocodile water god), Sokar (god of the dead), Sothis (herald of the New Year and the Nile flood), Tawaret (protector of women in childbirth), Tefnut (goddess of rain), Thoth (god of magic and wisdom), Upuaut (god of the dead), Wadjet (goddess of Lower Egypt), Wepwawet (a guide of the dead), Wosret (goddess of Thebes), Yah (of the moon)

Egyptian kings: Ptolemy, Tutankhamen (aka King Tut)

Egyptian peasant: fellah

Egyptian picture-writing: hieroglyphs

Egyptian queens: Cleopatra, Nefertiti

Egyptian ruler, ancient: Pharaoh

Egyptian sultan: Saladin

Egyptian symbol of life: ankh

Egyptian viceroy: khedive

Egyptian writing: hieroglyphics

Egyptologists: Howard Carter, Zahi Hawass, Karl Lepsius, Sir Gaston Maspero, George A. Reisner

Eiffel Tower: 1,007ft high structure in the centre of Paris, France; erected 1887–1889; designed by Gustave Eiffel (1832–1923). There are 1,080 steps to the second platform, the third platform only reachable by lift

eight, adjective: octamerous

eight, fear of: octophobia

eight, group of: octad, octave, octet, ogdoad

eight-faced solid figure: octahedron

eight-lined stanza: ottava rima

eight-sided figure with eight angles: octagon

eight-yearly: octennial

eighteenth century, adjective: settecento

eighty-year-old (and upwards to 89): octogenarian

Eightfold Path (Buddhist laws): Right Understanding, Right Thought, Right Speech, Right Action, Right Livelihood, Right Effort, Right Mindfulness, Right Concentration

elbow: cubitus

elbow, adjective: cubital

elbow bone: olecranon

elections: "The problem is, whoever you vote for, the government always gets in" - anonymous

election campaign: hustings

elections and voting, study of: psephology

electric advertisement, first: used for Bovril in Piccadilly Circus, in 1890

electric chair: conceived of by Harold P. Brown and first put into use 6 August 1890 at Auburn Prison in New York when the convicted murderer William Kemmler took several minutes to die

electric sign, first: used in 1882, in Berlin, London and New York

electric toothbrush: first manufactured in 1961

electronic acquisition of private details via fraudelent means: phishing

electrical engineer: Fred Terman

electrical engineer, collective noun: grid

electricity: first established as a phenomenon in 1600 by the physician William Gilbert

electricity, fear of: elektrophobia

electromagnet: invented by William Sturgeon in 1824

electromagnetic induction: discovered by Michael Faraday in 1831

electronic engineer: Sir Clive Sinclair

electrophysiologist: Willem Einthoven

Elektra: opera by Richard Strauss first produced in Dresden in 1909

element, heaviest: uranium (the naturally occuring element with the highest atomic weight)

element, heaviest synthetic: ununoctium

element, lightest: hydrogen

elephant: African bush dweller, African forest dweller (with rounder ears and smaller tusks than its bush-dwelling counterpart - aka loxodonta cyclotis), Asian elephant, pachyderm

elephant, adjective: elephantine, elephantoid, pachydermic

elephant, collective noun: parade, herd

elephant, country with most: Tanzania, which hosts 73,459 African elephants
elephant, extinct: mammoth, mastodon
elephant, female: cow
elephant, male: bull
elephant, young: calf
elephant driver: mahout
elephant goad or stick: ankus
elephant god: Ganesa, Ganesha
Elephant Man: nickname for John Merrick
elephant seat: houdah, howdah
elephant sound: trumpet
elephant seal, collective noun: pod
elephant seal, young: weaner, yearling
elephant-headed god: Ganesa
elephants, famous: Abul-Abbas (Charlemagne's), Babar, Celeste, Dumbo, Elmer
    the Patchwork Elephant, Colonel Hathi (from *The Jungle Book*), Horton
    (% Dr Seuss), Jumbo (P.T. Barnum's), Nellie, Saggy Baggy, Edward Trunk
    (friend of Rupert Bear)
elevator: first constructed in 236 BC, by Archimedes
eleven plus two: anagram for "twelve plus one"
eleven years, adjective: undecennary
eleven-sided plane figure: hendecagon
eleventh year, adjective: undecennial
elf – see creatures
elf, famous: Dobby (from *Harry Potter*)
elf, German: kobold
elf, Irish: leprechaun
elk: moose
elk, adjective: cervine
elk, collective noun: gang
elk, young: calf
El Salvador: republic in Central America
    capital: San Salvador
    currency: colón
    language: Spanish
    religion: Roman Catholic
    - see Salvadorian
ELO: Electric Light Orchestra
eloquence, muse of: Polyhymnia
Elysium flower: asphodel (alternately identified as a lily or narcissus)
email pioneer: Ray Tomlinson
embarrassment: "Embarrassment is the one ailment that lessens with age" -
    Craig Brown
emblem of publisher on a book: colophon
embroidery frame: tambour
embryo, rudimentary: blastula
embryologists: Hwang Woo-Suk, Dr Ian Wilmut
empie, adjective: imperial
Emerald City: fictitious capital of the Land of Oz as featured in the books of
    L. Frank Baum
emotions, study of: pathognomy

emperor, adjective: imperial
emperor of Germany: Kaiser
emperor of Japan: Mikado
emperor of Russia: Tsar
Empire State Building: New York monolith which, completed in May of 1931, has
    inspired Hollywood and tourists alike. Designed by the architectural firm of
    Shreve, Lamb & Harmon Associates, it was the tallest building in the world
    until surpassed by the first tower of the World Trade Centre in 1972. Situated
    at 350 Fifth Avenue between 33rd and 34th Streets (the site of the old Waldorf-
    Astoria Hotel), the building consists of 102 floors, 6,400 windows, ten million
    bricks and stands at 1,250 feet. Bizarrely, it was initially used as a mooring for
    airships, but the high winds that threatened to sweep personnel into the wide
    blue yonder quickly put a stop to that
empress, Russian: Alexandra (wife of Nicholas II), Catherine the Great
Empress of Soul: nickname for Gladys Knight
emptiness, fear of: kenophobia
emu, adjective: ratite, struthious
emu, collective noun: mob
emu, famous: Emu (glove puppet c/o of Rod Hull)
emu, young: chick, hatchling
EMU: Economic and Monetary Union (of Europe)
encore (in music): altra volta
encyclopaedia, on-line: Wikipedia
Encyclopaedia Britannica, first edition: 1768
encyclopaedists: David Brewster, Ephraim Chambers, Denis Diderot, Pierre
    Larousse
enema, to administer: clyster (verb)
enemas, sexual arousal derived from: klismaphilia
enemies: "Friends may come and go, but enemies accumulate" - Thomas Jones;
    "If you don't have enemies, you don't have character" – Paul Newman
enemy, adjective: inimical
energy unit: erg, joule
engineers: Archimedes, Sir Ove Arup, Cecil Balmond, Henry Bessemer, Kenneth
    Bigley (captured and beheaded by Islamist militants in Iraq), Thomas Brassey,
    Wernher von Braun, Isambard Kingdom Brunel, Sir Marc Isambard Brunel,
    Christopher Cockerell, Gottlieb Daimler, Abraham Darby III, Rudolf Diesel,
    Sir James Dyson, Gustave Eiffel, James Francis, Robert Fulton, Dennis Gabor,
    Peter Goldmark, John Holland, Godfrey Hounsfield, Arthur Kennelly, Leonardo
    Da Vinci, William Metford, John Milne, James Nasmyth, George Pullman, Sir
    John Rennie, Sir Henry Royce, Sir Clive Sinclair, George Stephenson, Robert
    Stephenson, William Symington, Thomas Telford, Richard Trevithick, Sir
    Barnes Wallis, Sir Robert Watson-Watt, James Watt, Sir Frank Whittle
    - see inventors, railway engineers, etc
engineers, patron saints of: Patrick and Ferdinand III
England: Blighty, "This scepter'd isle" (Richard II)
England, patron saints of: Augustine of Canterbury, Cuthbert, George and Gregory
    the Great
English Channel, first man to swim: Captain Matthew Webb, in August 1875
    (in 21 hours, 45 minutes)
English Channel, first woman to swim: Gertrude Ederle, in 1926
English composers – see British composers

English counties: Bedfordshire, Berkshire, Bristol, Buckinghamshire, Cambridgeshire, Cheshire, Cleveland, Cornwall, Cumbria, Derbyshire, Devon, Dorset, Durham, East Sussex, Essex, Gloucestershire, Greater London, Greater Manchester, Hampshire, Herefordshire, Hertfordshire, Humberside, Isle of Wight, Kent, Lancashire, Leicestershire, Lincolnshire, Merseyside, Norfolk, Northamptonshire, Northumberland, North Yorkshire, Nottinghamshire, Oxfordshire, Rutland, Shropshire, Somerset, South Yorkshire, Staffordshire, Suffolk, Surrey, Tyne and Wear, Warwickshire, West Midlands, West Sussex, West Yorkshire, Wiltshire, Worcestershire

English Civil War: 1642–1646 (Charles I vs. Cromwell)

English language experts: Bill Bryson, Robert Claiborne, Paul Dickson, Willard Espy, Samuel Johnson, Richard Lederer, Sir James Murray, Mario Pei, Henry Sweet
- see language experts, linguistic authorities, lexicographers

English painters – see British painters

English poets: Simon Armitage, Matthew Arnold, W.H. Auden, Pam Ayres, George Barker, Sir John Betjeman, William Blake, Rupert Brooke, Robert Browning, Lord Byron, T.P. Cameron Wilson, Lewis Carroll, Geoffrey Chaucer, G.K. Chesterton, John Clare, Samuel Taylor Coleridge, Wendy Cope, Cecil Day-Lewis, Walter de la Mare, John Donne, Michael Drayton, John Dryden, Carol Ann Duffy, Edward Fitzgerald, John Gay, John Gower, Robert Graves, Thomas Gray, Thomas Hardy, Sir A.P. Herbert, Robert Herrick, Geoffrey Hill, Thomas Hood, Ted Hughes, Leigh Hunt, John Keats, Rudyard Kipling, William Langland, Philip Larkin, Edward Lear, Thomas Lodge, Christopher Marlowe, John Masefield, Roger McGough, Ian McMillan, Spike Milligan, John Milton, Sir Andrew Motion, Wilfred Owen, Thomas Love Peacock, Alexander Pope, Matthew Prior, Sir Walter Raleigh, Isaac Rosenberg, Christina Rossetti, Dante Gabriel Rossetti, Thomas Sackville, Vita Sackville-West, William Shakespeare, Percy Bysshe Shelley, Dame Edith Sitwell, Christopher Smart, Stevie Smith, Sir Stephen Spender, Edmund Spenser, Lytton Strachey, Francis Thompson, Dorothy Wordsworth, William Wordsworth, Sir Thomas Wyatt, Edward Young, Benjamin Zephaniah

English pope: Adrian IV (originally Nicolas Breakspear), 1100–1159; elected pope in 1154

engravers: Stefano Della Bella, Thomas Bewick, William Blake, Gustave Doré, Albrecht Dürer, James Ensor, Eric Gill, Stanley Hayter, William Hogarth, John Martin, Emil Nolde, Felix Vallotton

engravers, patron saints of: John the Apostle and Thiemo

engraving, adjective: glyptic (especially on precious stones)

enjoyment region of the brain: dorsal striatum

Enron: US corporation set up in July of 1985 as a natural gas pipeline company. By the early months of the 21st century, Enron had become the seventh largest company in the United States, while in August 2000 its stock reached an all-time high of $90. However, in October of 2001, Enron shredded one ton of its documents and in November its shares plunged below $1. On 2 December 2001, the company filed for Chapter 11 bankruptcy protection and a criminal investigation ensued. In July of 2004, founder Kenneth L. Lay was indicted on eleven criminal counts of fraud and deception and was arrested by the FBI. In the event, Enron's top executives walked away with over one billion dollars while its investors and employees lost everything. On 4 July 2006, Lay suffered a massive heart attack while on holiday and died the following day. Jeffrey

Skilling, the Chief Executive and Chief Operating Officer of Enron, was sentenced to 292 months imprisonment in October 2006

entertainment as education: edutainment

enthusiasm: "Enthusiasm, ever the deadly foe of accuracy" – Lord Redesdale

entomologist: Sir Vincent Wigglesworth

entrails inspector (for interpreting omens): haruspex

entrepreneurs: Chris Anderson, Richard Branson, George Cadbury, Prince Charles, Simon Cowell, Sir James Dyson, Kim Fowley, Matt Furey, Yoram Globus, Menahem Golan, Sir James Goldsmith, Berry Gordy Jr., Stelio Haji-Ioannou (the man behind easyJet and easyCinema), Howard Hughes, Steve Jobs, Ray Kroc, Sir Freddie Laker, Ferdinand Lesseps, Rupert Murdoch, George Peabody, Anita Roddick, Joseph Rowntree, Samuel Ryder, Kawasaki Shozo, Sir Clive Sinclair, Martha Stewart, Sir Alan Sugar, Ted Turner, Madame C.J. Walker (real name: Sarah Breedlove), Simon Woodroffe, Frank Woolworth, Steve Wozniak
- see billionaires, business executives, tycoons, etc

environment, science of: ecology

environmental organisations: The Countryside Agency, EcoNet, Friends of the Earth, Greenpeace, Rainforest Action Network, United Nations Educational, Scientific and Cultural Organisation (UNESCO), World Wide Fund for Nature (WWF)

environmentalists: David Buckland, John Burroughs, Rachel Carson, Jaques-Yves Cousteau, John Denver, Zac Goldsmith, Al Gore, Julia Butterfly Hill, Steve Irwin, Tony Juniper, John Muir, Jonathon Porritt (former director of Friends of the Earth), Anita Roddick, Theodore Roosevelt, Pete Seeger, Sir Nicholas Stern, Sting, Henry Thoreau, Douglas Tompkins (who purchased nearly one million acres of Chilean rainforest)
- see eco-protesters, eco-warriors, ecologists

environmentalists, patron saints of: Francis of Assisi and Kateri Tekakwitha

epic poetry, muse of: Calliope

epidemics, patron saints of: Lucy of Syracuse and Roch

epidemiologists: Richard Doll, Donald Henderson

epilepsy, mild form of: petit mal

epilepsy, patron saints of: John Chrysostom, Dymphna, Vitus and Willibrord

epilepsy, serious form of: grand mal

epileptics: Alexander the Great, Richard Burton (the film star), Lord Byron, Julius Caesar, Charles Dickens, Fyodor Dostoevsky, Anne Fadiman (New York writer), Gustave Flaubert, Fritz Haarmann (mass murderer), Georg Friederich Händel, Prince Myshkin (from Dostoevsky's *The Idiot*), Napoleon Bonaparte, Pyotr Tchaikovsky

eponyms: Baroque (after the Italian painter Federigo Barocci), beef stroganoff (after Count Paul Stroganoff), Belisha beacon (after Leslie Hore-Belisha, the minister of transport who introduced the road signs in the 1930s), biro (after László Bíró, its inventor), bloomers (popularised by the pioneering feminist Amelia J. Bloomer), bowdlerize (after the Shakespearean expurgator Thomas Bowdler), boycott (after the exploitative land agent Charles C. Boycott), braggadocio (after Braggadochio, a braggart in Spenser's *Faerie Queene*), braille (after its inventor, Louis Braille), Bunsen burner (after its inventor, R. W. Bunsen), burnsides (pattern of facial hair named after General A.E. Burnside), cardigan (named after the 7th Earl of Cardigan), clarence (horse-drawn carriage named after the Duke of Clarence), condom (after the inventor Dr Condom), dunce (after the Scottish theologian John Duns Scotus), eggs Benedict (after its inventor, E.C.

Benedict), epicure (after the Greek philosopher Epicurus), Fahrenheit (after the German physicist Gabriel Daniel Fahrenheit), guillotine (after the French physician, Joseph Ignace Guillotin), gypsy (originally thought to have come from Egypt), hansom cab (after Joseph Hansom), hooker (allegedly after General Joseph Hooker, who supplied professional women for his troops), hooligan (after the 19th century hooligan Patrick Hooligan), Huntington's chorea (after the neurologist George Huntington), jacuzzi (after Roy Jacuzzi), jeremiad (from the prophet Jeremiah), Kalashnikov (the rifle *and* the vodka, after the Russian designer), klaxon (after the company that first manufactured the horn), Macadamia nut (in honour of the Australian chemist John Macadam), mansard (after the French architect François Mansart), mayonnaise (after Mago, Hannibal's brother), Melba toast (in honour of the Australian opera singer Dame Nellie Melba), morphine (after Morpheus, the god of sleep and dreams), munchkin (from *The Wonderful Wizard of Oz*), nicotine (after Jean Nicot, who introduced tobacco to the French court), praline (after the chef who worked for Count Plessis-Praslin), quisling (after the Nazi collaborator Vidkun Quisling), sandwich (after the fourth earl of Sandwich, who liked to eat food trapped between two pieces of bread), serendipity (after Serendip, the medieval name for Sri Lanka), shrapnel (after General H. Shrapnel), stetson (after the American hat-maker John B. Stetson), tantalise (after the frustrated Greek king Tantalus), volt (after Alessandro Volta)

equality, adjective: egalitarian

equator, adjective: equatorial

Equatorial Guinea: republic in West Africa
    capital: Malabo
    currency: African franc
    language: Spanish, French
    religion: Roman Catholic

equestrians and equestriennes: Princess Anne, David Broome, Colonel Piero d'Inzeo, Lucinda Green, Harry Llewellyn, Richard Meade, Cian O'Connor, Zara Phillips, Billy Smart Jr, Harvey Smith, Pat Smythe, Mark Todd, Hans Günter Winkler

equestrians, patron saints of: Anne, George and Martin of Tours

equinox, adjective: equinoctial

Equity, full name: British Actors' Equity Association (membership: 36,000)

ER: long-running NBC TV medical drama set in and around Cook County General Hospital, Chicago
    first broadcast: 19 September 1994
    created by Michael Crichton
    cast: Anthony Edwards (Dr Mark Greene), George Clooney (Dr Douglas Ross), Eriq La Salle (Dr Peter Benton), Julianna Margulies (Nurse Carol Hathaway), Sherry Stringfield (Dr Susan Lewis), Laura Innes (Dr Kerry Weaver), Maria Bello (Dr Anna Del Amico), Noah Wyle (John Carter), Michael Michele (Dr Cleo Finch), Alex Kingston (Dr Elizabeth Corday), Paul McCrane (Dr Robert Romano), Goran Visnjic (Dr Luka Kovac), John Aylward (Donald Anspaugh), Jorjan Fox (Maggie Doyle), Gloria Reuben (Jeanie Boulet), Mekhi Phifer (Dr Gregory Pratt), Maura Tierney (Dr. Abby Lockhart) Parminder K. Nagra (Neela Rasgotra)

era, adjective: eral

erectile organ, pertaining to: balanic (relating to either the clitoris or penis)

erection: bone, boner, cunt stretcher, hard-on, horn, Irish toothache, lead in one's pencil, rise, rod-on, stiffy, touch-on, woody

erection, adjective: orthostatic, phallic
erection, fear of: medorthophobia
erection failure, dread of: medomalacuphobia
Eritrea: country in north-eastern Africa
    capital: Asmara
    currency: nakfa
    language: Arabic, English, Afar
    religion: Muslim, Christian
    recent history: gained independence from Ethiopia in 1993
ERM: Exchange Rate Mechanism
Eroica Symphony: composition by Ludwig Van Beethoven which was premiered on
    7 April 1805 in Vienna. Beethoven had originally titled his work *The Bonaparte*
    Symphony, but changed the name after Napoleon had the gall to proclaim
    himself emperor. Officially, it is Beethoven's *Symphony No. 3*
escapees: Natascha Kampusch, Richard Kimble (played by David Janssen in the
    1963–1967 TV series *The Fugitive* and by Harrison Ford in the 1993 film of
    the same name), Matthew Scott (a 19-year-old student from London who
    successfully evaded his Colombian kidnappers in September of 2003)
    - see also abductees, kidnapping victims
escapologists: Criss Angel, David Blaine, Harry Houdini, James Randi
Eskimo: Aleut (Alaskan), Inuit (Canadian), Inupat (Alaskan), Yupik (Alaskan)
Eskimo boat: kayak, umiak (Inuit word for "woman's boat")
Eskimo dog: malamute
Eskimo house: igloo
Eskimology, father of: Knud Johan Victor Rasmussen
esoteric knowledge: gnosis
essayists: Joseph Addison, Al Alvarez, Francis Bacon, Walter Bagehot, James
    Baldwin, Elizabeth Bowen, Randolph Bourne, Samuel Butler, Thomas Carlyle,
    Josep Carner, G.K. Chesterton, Seamus Deane, Thomas De Quincey, Havelock
    Ellis, Ralph Waldo Emerson, E.M. Forster, Robert Graves, William Hazlitt,
    Leigh Hunt, Aldous Huxley, Clive James, D.H. Lawrence, Thomas Malthus,
    Czeslaw Milosz, Charles Montague, Michel Montaigne, George Orwell, Walter
    Pater, Plutarch, V.S. Pritchett, John Ruskin, Adam Smith, Sir Richard Steele,
    William Makepeace Thackeray, John Updike, E.B.White, Oscar Wilde,
    Xenophon, Stefan Zweig
Essex, administrative centre: Chelmsford
estate agent: Jonathan Harker (from Bram Stoker's *Dracula*)
Estonia: republic in north-eastern Europe
    capital: Tallinn
    currency: kroon
    language: Estonian
    religion: Christian
    recent history: independence declared in 1991
Estonian and famous: Louis I. Kahn (architect), Paul Keres (chess player), Carmen
    Kass (supermodel), Jaan Kross (novelist), Arvo Pärt (composer)
ETA: estimated time of arrival
etchers: Robert Austin, Gustave Doré, Francisco Goya, Augustus John, Paul Klee,
    Samuel Palmer, William Strang, George Stubbs, James McNeill Whistler,
    Anders Leonhard Zorn
ethanal: acetaldehyde
Ethiopia: state in north-eastern Africa

capital: Addis Ababa
currency: birr
language: Amharic
religion: Christian
Ethiopian baboon: gelada
Ethiopian Jew: Falasha
Ethiopian leaders: Haile Selassie, Meles Zenawi, Mengistu Haile Mariam
Ethiopian ruler: Negus
ethnologists: Richard Dawkins, Ella Deloria, Fritz Graebner
ethologists: Richard Dawkins, Konrad Lorenz, Desmond Morris, Vero Wynne-Edwards
etiquette authority: Emily Post
Eton College: the most prestigious public school in Britain, founded as a grammar school in 1440 by Henry VI. Nineteen British prime ministers were educated there
Etonians: Jonathan Aitken, Michael Bentine, James Bond, Jeremy Brett, David Cameron, Christopher Cazenove, Mark Darcy (from *Bridget Jones's Diary*), Sir Alec Douglas-Home, Sir William Douglas-Home, Sir Anthony Eden, Henry Fielding, Sir Ranulph Fiennes, Ian Fleming, Sebastian Flyte (c/o *Brideshead Revisited*), Bamber Gascoigne, William Gladstone, Sir James Goldsmith, Peter Hannay, Prince Harry, Michael Holroyd, Captain James Hook, Hugh Hudson (filmmaker), Aldous Huxley, Sir Julian Huxley, Boris Johnson, Sir Ludovic Kennedy, John Maynard Keynes (economist), Hugh Laurie, Lord Lucan, Humphrey Lyttelton, Harold Macmillan, Patrick Macnee, Daniel Massey, George Orwell, Sir Matthew Pinsent, William Pitt, Anthony Powell, Allan Quatermain, Percy Bysshe Shelley, Julian Slade, John Steed, Sir Jocelyn Stevens, Sir Robert Walpole, Arthur Wellesley, 1st Duke of Wellington, Prince William, Lord Peter Wimsey, Bertie Wooster
E.T. The ExtraTerrestrial (1982 film), famous line, E.T.: "E.T. Phone home."
EU: European Union
Eucharist: Communion, Holy Communion, Lord's Supper, Mass
Eucharist cup: chalice
Eucharist plate: paten
Eucharist presentation of bread and wine: oblation
Eucharist priest: celebrant
Eucharist vessel: chalice, ciborium, flagon, pyx (containing the consecrated bread)
Eucharist vestment: chasuble, tunicle
Eugene Onegin: opera by Pyotr Tchaikovsky first produced in Moscow in 1879
eunuchs: Zai Lun (who invented paper back in 104 AD), Zheng He (Chinese admiral who allegedly discovered America 72 years before Christopher Columbus)
Europe, largest countries in: 1) Russia; 2) Ukraine; 3) France; 4) Spain (including its offshore islands); 5) Sweden; 6) Germany; 7) Finland; 8) Norway; 9) Poland; 10) Italy
Europe, patron saints of: Benedict, Bridget of Sweden and Teresa Benedicta of the Cross
Europe, poorest nation: Moldova
European Union, new member states as of 30 April 2004: Czech Republic, Estonia, Greek Cyprus, Hungary, Latvia, Lithuania, Malta, Poland, Slovakia, Slovenia
European Union, official anthem: Beethoven's *Ode to Joy*

Eurovision Song Contest: critically reviled pop competition started in 1956
    First winner (1956): Switzerland's Lys Assia with *Refrain*
    First British winner (1967): Sandie Shaw with *Puppet On a String*
    fact: in 2003, and for the first time in its 48-year-old history, Britain finished
        last, with Jemini's *Cry Baby*
euthanasia, champions of: Diane Pretty, Ramón Sampedro, Kelly Taylor
euthanasia, the first country to introduce legislation for: Holland (since 1984)
euthanasia, the first US state to introduce legislation for: Oregon (since 1997)
euthanasia clinic: Dignitas, outside Zurich, in Switzerland, founded in 1998 by
    Ludwig Minelli
evangelist: anagram for "evil's agent"
evangelists: Philip Bliss, Bill Bright, Frank Buchman, Paul Crouch, Jerry Falwell,
    Marjoe Gortner, Billy Graham, Franklin Graham, Billy James Hargis, T.D.
    Jakes, Denise Mathews (formerly the singer known as Vanity), Aimee Semple
    McPherson, Dwight L. Moody, Joel Osteen, Oral Roberts, Pat Robertson,
    Robert Schuller, Billy Sunday, Jimmy Swaggart, Rick Warren, John Wesley
evangelists, patron saint of: Paul the Apostle
evening, adjective: vespertine
Evening Post: first British evening newspaper, founded in 1706
everyone: *tout le monde*
everything, fear of: pantophobia
evidence, sworn: deposition
evidence, types of: accumulative, admissible, circumstantial, cumulative, deposition,
    external, forensic, hard, inadmissible, inconclusive, internal, King's, negative,
    presumptive, Queen's, state's, uncorroborated
evil, god of: Loki (Norse mythology), Set/Seth (Egyptian)
Evita: nickname for Eva Duarte de Perón
evolutionary theorists: Charles Darwin, Richard Dawkins, Jean-Baptiste Lamarck,
    Herbert Spencer, Alfred Russel Wallace
ewe, to copulate with: blissom
ewe, young: theave
exaggeration: "An exaggeration is a truth which has lost its temper" – Kahlil Gibran
exaggerator: mythomane, mythomaniac
excellent: admirable, ace, A-1, awesome, bonzer (Australian slang), consummate,
    cool, copasetic, corking, creditable, delicious, dope, dynamite, estimable, gilt-
    edged, incomparable, inimitable, irreproachable, jim-dandy, killer, knockout,
    kopasetic, nang (modern teenage slang), peerless, phat, ripper (Australian
    slang), ripping, something else, superior, superlative, talented, wonderful
excess: "Excess on occasion is exhilarating. It prevents moderation from acquiring
    the deadening effect of habit" – W. Somerset Maugham
exchange, adjective: catalactic
exclamation mark: "Exclamation marks are the equivalent of laughing at your own
    jokes" - E.M. Forster
excrement: egesta
excrement authority: Gillian McKeith
excrement, adjective: stercoraceous
excrement, fear of: coprophobia
excrement, fossilized: coprolite
excrement, hardened ball of: coprolith
excrement, lover of: coprophiliac
excrement, sexual gratification from handling or smelling of: coprolagnia

excrement, sexual gratification from thinking about: coprophilia

excrement, study of: scatology

excrement, to splatter with: beray, bescumber

excrement-eating (adjective): coprophagous

execution, adjective: patibulary

execution by drowning: noyade

executioners: Jack Ketch (hopelessly inefficient English executioner who began his dreadful career in 1663 and whose name became synonymous with executioners for the next two hundred years), Albert Pierrepoint (phenomenally efficient English hangman, responsible for the executions of Derek Bentley, Ruth Ellis, Timothy John Evans and Lord Haw-Haw)

executive toys: Newton's cradle (the one with the row of suspended steel balls), perpetual pendulum, pin art

exercise: "The only exercise I take is walking behind the coffins of friends who took exercise" – Peter O'Toole

exercise equipment: barbell, bench, dumbbell, exercise bike, mat, recumbent bike, rowing machine, skipping rope, stabilising ball, stepper, Swiss ball, treadmill, weights

exercise gurus: Charles Atlas, Billy Blanks, Jane Fonda, Matt Furey, Michael King (Pilates), Jack LaLanne, Tony Little, Diana Moran (aka 'the Green Goddess'), Joseph Hubertus Pilates (1880-born founder of Pilates), Susan Powter, Richard Simmons

exercise machines: Bowflex, Cybex, Nautilus, Soloflex, StairMaster

exercise techniques: aerobics, callisthenics, cross training, isometrics, Pilates (whose eight principals are Concentration, Breath, Centering, Control, Precision, Flowing Movement, Isolation and Routine), resistance training, Tai Chi (providing energy through breathing and posture), yoga

exhaustion, fear of: kopophobia

exiles: Adelaide, Pope Alexander III, Isabel Allende, Thomas Arundel, Aung San Suu Kyi, Thomas à Becket, Henry Bolingbroke, Fidel Castro, Charles II, El Cid, Dalai Lama, Dante Alighieri, Charles De Gaulle, Fyodor Dostoevsky, Edward IV, Francisco Goya, Haile Selassie I, Henry IV, James II, Stanley Kubrick, Louis XVIII, Ludwig II, Napoleon Bonaparte, Daniel Ortega, Juan Perón, Sergei Rachmaninoff, John Reed, Andrei Sakharov, Joseph Stalin, Leon Trotsky

exiles, patron saints of: Adelaide, Clotilde and Elizabeth of Hungary

existentialists: Edward Albee, Woody Allen, Michelangelo Antonioni, Simone de Beauvoir, Samuel Beckett, Ingmar Bergman, Robert Bresson, Albert Camus, Philip K. Dick, Fyodor Dostoevsky, Marguerite Duras, Ralph Ellison, Jean-Luc Godard, Jean Genet, Andre Gide, Martin Heidegger, Werner Herzog, Hermann Hesse, Henrik Ibsen, Eugène Ionesco, Franz Kafka, Jack Kerouac, Søren Kierkegaard, R.D. Laing, Yukio Mishima, Harold Pinter, Rainer Maria Rilke, Alain Robbe-Grillet, Jean-Paul Sartre, François Truffaut, Luchino Visconti, Colin Wilson

exorcists: John Constantine, Father Lankester Merrin (from *The Exorcist*), Dr Pinch (from *The Comedy of Errors*)

expectant mothers, patron saints of: Anne, Elizabeth, Joseph and Ulric

expensive cities, least: 1) Asuncion (in Paraguay); 2) Montevideo (in Uruguay); 3) Santo Domingo (in the Dominican Republic)

experience: "Experience is a good school. But the fees are high" – Jewish saying

experience, derived from: empirical (adjective)

expert: "A person who has made all the mistakes that can be made in a very narrow field" – Niels Bohr

explorers: Afonso de Albuquerque, Roald Amundsen (the first man to reach the South Pole), Tom Avery, William Baffin, Willem Barents, Heinrich Barth, Vitus Bering, Sir Richard Burton, Richard Evelyn Byrd, John Cabot, Professor Challenger (from Conan Doyle's *The Lost World*), Samuel de Champlain, William Clark, Christopher Columbus, Captain James Cook, Jacques Cousteau, William Dampier, Sir Francis Drake, Erik the Red, Leif Ericson, João Fernandes (Lavrador), Sir Ranulph Fiennes, Sir John Franklin, Simon Fraser, John Charles Frémont, Sir Martin Frobisher, Vasco da Gama, Sir Humphrey Gilbert, Sir George Grey, Wally Herbert, Thor Heyerdahl, Sir Edmund Hillary (the first to reach the summit of Mount Everest), Henry Hudson, Alexander von Humboldt, René La Salle, Meriwether Lewis, David Livingstone, Sir Alexander Mackenzie, Ferdinand Magellan, George Mallory, Fridtjof Nansen, Tenzing Norgay (who, with Sir Edmund Hillary, was the first man to reach the summit of Mount Everest), Mungo Park, William Parry, Robert Peary, Marco Polo, Pytheas, Sir Walter Raleigh, Gerhard Rohlfs, Sir James Clark Ross, Robert Falcon Scott (played on film by John Mills), Sir Ernest Shackleton, John Smith, John Hanning Speke, Sir Henry Stanley, Freya Stark, Georg Steller, Abel Tasman, Wilfred Thesiger, David Thompson, George Vancouver, Amerigo Vespucci, Sir Hugh Willoughby, Sir Francis Younghusband, Zheng He (Chinese eunuch admiral who discovered America 72 years before Christopher Columbus, according to Gavin Menzies, a former British submarine commander)
- see navigators

explosive: charge, detonator, plastic explosive, plunger detonator, receiver bomb, semtex (plastic explosive)
- see bombs

exports, from UK: 1) electrical machinery; 2) mechanical machinery; 3) road vehicles; 4) scientific and photographic equipment; 5) petroleum and petroleum products

Expressionist painters: Max Beckmann, James Ensor, Edvard Munch, Emil Nolde, Oskar Kokoschka, Leon Kossoff, Georges Rouault, Chaim Soutine, Vincent Van Gogh

extinct organisms, ecology of: palaeoecology

extraterrestrial life, study of: exobiology

extremeties, adjective: acroteric

eye, adjective: ocular

eye, endowed with only one: monoptic

eye, largest: belongs to the giant squid, known to exceed 15 inches in diameter

eye, light-reflecting (as in cats, etc): tapetum

eye, Oriental fold: epicanthus, epicanthic fold

eye, parts of: aqueous humour, canthus, conjunctiva, cornea, crow's-foot, eye socket, eyeball, eyebrow, eyelash, eyelid, fovea, hyaloid membrane, iris, lens, leucoma, optic nerve, orbit, pupil, rod, sclera, uvea

eye, protruding, adjective: exophthalmic

eye, study of: ophthalmology

eye disease doctor: ophthalmologist (formerly known as an oculist)

eye disease: glaucoma

eye disorders: astigmatism, blepharitis, cataracts, colour blindness, conjunctivitis, dry eye, iritis (inflammation of the iris), lippitude (bleariness or soreness of), macular degeneration, myopia, night-blindness (aka nyctalopia), presbyopia (loss of focus), red eye, retinal detachment, scleritis, snowblindness

eye lens, adjective: lenticular

eye membrane (in some amphibians, birds, etc): nictitating membrane

eye movement (such as in a sudden change of focus): saccade

eye movement, adjective: oculomotor

eye muscles, study of abnormalities of: phorometry

eye opening (the act of), fear of: optophobia

eye problems, patron saint of: Lucy

eye shadow: surma (in India)

eye-moistening: hygrophthalmic (adjective)

eyeball, abnormal protrusion of: exophthalmos

eyeball-licking (for sexual arousal): oculolinctus

eyebrows: supercilium

eyebrows, adjective: superciliary

eyebrows, overhanging: beetle-browed (adjective)

eyelash, adjective: ciliary

eyelid: blephar, palpebra

eyelid, adjective: blepharal, ciliary, palpebral

eyelid, drooping of: ptosis

eyelid surgery: blepharoplasty

eyelids, disease of: blefora (which makes the eyelids swell - Michael Caine had it), blepharitis

eyes, fear of: ommatophobia

eyes, protruding (adjective): exophthalmic

eyes, sexual arousal derived from: oculophilia

eyes, study of: ophthalmology

eyesight specialist: optometrist

eyesight test (utilizing rows of letters): Snellen test

eyestrain: asthenopia

eyewash: collyrium

F

fabric: acetate, alpaca, angora, Balbriggan, Bedford cord, beige, bouclé, brilliantine, brocade, brushed fabric, bunting, byssus, calico, cambric, camel-hair, cavalry twill, challis, charmeuse, check, chenille, chiffon, chino, chintz, cilice, ciré, cloqué, cloth, cord, corduroy, cotton, crash, crêpe, cretonne, crimplene, crinoline, damask, denim, diamanté, diaper, dimity, Dralon, drill, drugget, duck, dupion, elastic, fibreglass, fishnet, flannel, flannelette, fleece, folkweave, gauze, gazar, gingham, glass cloth, glass fibre, Gore-Tex, grenadine, grogram, grosgrain, haircloth, heather mixture, holland, honeycomb, hopsack, HPA 1000 (bullet proof), huckaback, jacquard, kapok, khaki, kincob, lace, lamé, lawn, leathercloth, leno, linen, linsey-woolsey, lint, lock-knit, lurex, lustre, lutestring, Lycra, madras, marabou, marl, marocain, marquisette, material, matting, mohair, moire, mousseline, mungo, muslin, nainsook, nankeen, needlecord, net, netting, ninon, numdah, nylon, oilcloth, organdie, organza, panne, parramatta, peau-de-soie, percale, pilot cloth, piqué, plaid, polycotton, polyester, polypropylene, pongee, poplin, print, prunella, rayon, rep, ripstop, sackcloth, samite, satin, seersucker, sendal, serge, silk, spandex, surat, taffeta, tricot, tussah, twill, velour, velvet, whipcord, wincey, worsted, zephyr

fabric dealer: draper
fabric roll: bolt
face, adjective: facial, prosopic
face, possessing a large one: megaprosopous
face, possessing a long and narrow one (such as in the portraits of El Greco and
    Amedeo Modigliani): dolichoprosopic
face, possessing a long one: dolichofacial
face blindness: prosopagnosia
face transplant, first: performed during a 15-hour operation on 27 November 2005
    in Amiens, Picardy, France, on Isabelle Dinoire
Facebook: social networking website founded by Mark Zuckerberg in 2004
facial contortion: gurning
facial dyslexia: prosopagnosia
facial expressions: deadpan, grimace, long-faced, phiz, po-faced, poker-faced,
    stone-faced
fads – see Nineteen Fifties, Nineteen Sixties, etc
fado singers: Mariza, Amália Rodrigues
faeces – see excrement
faeces, fear of: coprophobia
Fahrenheit: temperature scale devised by Gabriel Daniel Fahrenheit in 1717
failure: "Success has many parents, but failure is an orphan" (anon); "Failure is not
    falling down. Failure is falling down and not getting up again to continue with
    life's race" – Richard Nixon; "I run into people all the time who are paralyzed by
    the fact that they might fail. To me, there's no failure. This is all an exploration" -
    John Sayles; "Trying is the first step toward failure" – Homer Simpson
    - see loser
failure, fear of: kakorrhiaphobia
fairies: Cottingley fairies, Queen Mab, Puck (from *A Midsummer Night's Dream*),
    Tinker Bell
fairy godmothers, good witches, etc: Clarence, Glinda (from *The Wizard of Oz*),
    guardian angel, Mary Poppins, Samantha Stephens (from TV's *Bewitched*),
    Tinker Bell
    - see witches
fairy king: Oberon (from *A Midsummer Night's Dream*)
fairy painters: Cicely Mary Barker, Richard Dadd, Brian Froud, Ida Rentoul
    Outhwaite, Arthur Rackham
fairy queens: Mab, Titania (from *A Midsummer Night's Dream*)
fairy tale characters: Aladdin, Cinderella, Goldilocks, the Little Mermaid, Mother
    Goose, Pinocchio, Prince Charming, Puss-in-Boots, Rapunzel, Rumpelstiltskin,
    Shrek, Sleeping Beauty, Snow White, Tom Thumb, Dick Whittington (albeit
    based on a real character)
fairy tale creatures – see creatures
faith: "Faith may be defined briefly as an illogical belief in the occurrence of the
    improbable" – H.L. Mencken
faith, adjective: pistic
faith, science of: pisteology
faith healers; estimated number in Britain: 20,000
faith systems: Baha'i, Buddhism, Christianity, Confucianism, Hinduism, Islam,
    Jainism, Judaism, Kabbalah, Kwanza, New Age, Shintoism, Sikhism, Taoism,
    spiritualism, Voudou, Zoroastrianism
falcon, adjective: raptorial (an adjective describing all birds of prey)
falcon, collective noun: cast

falcon, male: tercel, tiercel
falcon god: Horus (Egyptian mythology)
falcon leash: lune
falcon-headed god: Horus (Egyptian mythology), Khonsu (Egyptian mythology), Montu (Egyptian mythology)
Falklands' war: 2 April-14 June 1982
Falklands' war survivor: Simon Weston
Falklands' war, survivors' fact: since the war, 264 Falklands' veterans have committed suicide, nine more than were killed in the war
falling, fear of: basophobia
fame: "Fame and talent divorced a long time ago. Now fame just sleeps around with the media" (anon.); "The higher the baboon goes up the tree, the more we see of its arse" – Simon Hughes MP; "Fame was once seen as recognition of your accomplishments in the world. Now it just means being recognised" - Mick Hume; "Fame is the sum of all the misunderstandings which collect about a name" - Rainer Maria Rilke; "In this day and age, if you're not a public freak, people assume you're a private one" - Kevin Spacey; "In the future, everyone will be world famous for 15 minutes" - Andy Warhol, Stockholm, 1968
family: "Happiness is having a large, caring, close-knit family in another city" - George Bernard Shaw
family, goddess of: Hestia (Greek mythology), Vesta (Roman)
Famous Five, the: George (Georgina) Kirrin, Dick (Richard) Kirrin, Julian Kirrin, Anne Kirrin and Timmy their mongrel dog (the intrepid protagonists of Enid Blyton's series of novels for children – 21 in all)
fan-shaped: flabellate, rhipidate
fantasists: Billy Fisher (from the musical *Billy*), Billy Liar (aka Billy Fisher), Walter Mitty
farceurs: John Chapman, Ray Cooney, Georges Feydeau, Jean-Baptiste Molière, Brian Rix
farmers: Gaston Dominici, Bathsheba Everdene (from *Far from the Madding Crowd*), Tony Martin, Oliver Wendell Douglas (from TV's *Green Acres*)
farmers, number in England and Wales: 180,000
farmers, patron saint of: Isidore the Farmer
farter, professional: Joseph Pujol (aka Le Pétomane)
farting, prone to: bdolotic [pronounced 'doll-uh-tik']
farting, prone to uncontrollable bouts of: meteorism
farting, that which relieves: carminative
farting, uncontrollable tendency for: meteorism
Fascists: Gabriele d'Annunzio, William Joyce, Diana Mitford, Unity Mitford, Oswald Mosley, Benito Mussolini, Ezra Pound
fashion: "What you adopt when you don't know who you are" – Quentin Crisp
fashions – see Nineteen Fifties, Nineteen Sixties, etc
fashion buff: fashion victim, fashionista
fashion designers: Miguel Adrover, Giorgio Armani, Laura Ashley, Pierre Balmain, Sir Cecil Beaton, Rose Bertin (Minister of Fashion to Marie Antoinette), Pierre Cardin, Oleg Cassini, Roberto Cavalli, Nino Cerruti, Hussein Chalayan, Coco Chanel, Jasper Conran, André Courrèges, Christian Dior, Randolph Duke, Alber Elbaz, Erté (real name: Romain de Tirtoff), Gianfranco Ferre, Alberta Ferretti, Tom Ford, Bella Freud, John Galliano, Eric Gaskins, Jean Paul Gaultier, Guccio Gucci, Roy Halston Frowick, Katharine Hamnett, Scott Henshall, Tommy Hilfiger, Marc Jacobs, Betsey Johnson, Rei Kawakubo, Kenzo (Takada), Calvin

Klein, Christian Lacroix, Karl Lagerfeld, Ralph Lauren, Herve Leger, Claire McCardell, Stella McCartney, Alexander McQueen, Issey Miyake, Isaac Mizrahi, Edward Molyneux, Franco Moschino, Roland Mouret, Jean Muir, Bruce Oldfield, Rifat Ozbek, Phoebe Philo, Miuccia Prada, Emilio Pucci, Mary Quant, Nina Ricci, Narciso Rodriguez, Sonia Rykiel, Yves Saint-Laurent, Elsa Schiaparelli, Samantha Shaw, Sir Paul Smith, Vivienne Tam, Matteo Thun, Pauline Trigère, Richard Tyler, Valentino (Garavani), Carmen Marc Valvo, Gloria Vanderbilt, Dries Van Noten, Atelier Versace, Gianni Versace, Vera Wang, Vivienne Westwood, Charles Frederick Worth ('father of haute couture'), Ermenegildo Zegna

fashion houses: Alessandro de Benedetti, Burberry, Gucci, Iceberg, Missoni, La Perla, Ralph Lauren, Rimmel, Rocco Barocco, Versace, Yves St Laurent, Valentino

fashion leader: Beau Brummell

fashion photographers: Richard Avedon, David Bailey, Guy Bourdin, Terence Donovan, Brian Duffy, Patrick Lichfield, Helmut Newton
- see photographers

fashion weeks: London (September), Milan (September), New York (September), Paris (July)

fashionable society: beau monde, glitterati

fasts: Ember days, Lent, Ramadan, Yom Kippur

fast food outlets: Burger King, Domino's Pizza, Dunkin' Donuts, Hardee's, Kentucky Fried Chicken, Krispy Kreme, McDonald's, Nando's, Pizza Hut, Subway, Taco Bell, Wendy's, Wimpy

fast musical tempos: allegretto, allegro, prestissimo, presto, vivace, vivacissimo, vivo

fasting month: Ramadan
- see fasts

fat: beefy, big, big-boned, bloated, chubby, chunky, corpulent, *embonpoint*, Falstaffian, fleshy, full-bodied, large, obese, overweight, plump, portly, stout, tubby, ventricose, voluptuous, well-upholstered

fat, adjective: adipose, lipoid

fat, fear of being: adipophobia

fat and famous: Queen Anne (of England), Fatty Arbuckle, Jo Brand, Marlon Brando (in his later years), Mr Bumble (from *Oliver Twist*), Billy Bunter, G.K. Chesterton, Winston Churchill, Alexandre Dumas, Vernon Dursley (from Harry Potter), Sir John Falstaff, Fat Albert, Gustave Flaubert, Count Isidor Ottavio Baldassare Fosco (from Wilkie Collins' *The Woman in White*), Dawn French, King George IV of England, Oliver Hardy, King Henry VIII of England, Alfred Hitchcock, Judge Holden (from Cormac McCarthy's *Blood Meridian*), Charles Laughton, King Louis XVIII, Luciano Pavarotti, Piggy (from *Lord of the Flies*), John Prescott, Ignatius J. Reilly (from *A Confederacy of Dunces*), Santa Claus, Two-Ton Tessie, Peter Ustinov, Queen Victoria, Harvey Weinstein, Orson Welles, Oprah Winfrey (sometimes)

fat person: baby elephant, butterball, fatty, hippo, lard arse, lard-ass, pot-guts, puff guts, thunder thighs, two-ton Tessie

fat-producing hormone: leptin (which turns off the hunger switch in the brain)

fatalities, fact: on average six Britons die a year in airline crashes, 33 drown in the bath, 616 die falling down stairs and 31,486 die from lung cancer

fate, goddesses of: the Moirae (Clotho, Lachesis and Atropos) (Greek), the Parcae (Nona, Decima and Morta) (Roman)

Fatha: nickname for the jazz pianist Earl Hines
father: da, dad, daddy, daddio, old man, padre, papa, paterfamilias, pops
father: "A father is only as happy as his saddest child" - Quincy Jones
father, adjective: paternal
father, murder of: patricide
father, old: Kohath (who, according to the Book of Exodus, fathered a child at 130)
Father Christmas: Kriss Kringle, Saint Nicholas, Santa, Santa Claus
Father of haute couture: Charles Frederick Worth
Father of history: Herodotus
Father of Lies: Satan
Father of nuclear physics: Ernest Rutherford
Father's Day: third Sunday in June
fathers, patron saint of: Joseph
fatigue, fear of: kopophobia, ponophobia
faun: Mr Tumnus (from *The Lion, The Witch and the Wardrobe*)
Faust: opera by Charles Gounod first produced in Paris in 1859
Fawlty Towers: classic, hugely popular TV sitcom set in a run-down Torquay hotel
    created by John Cleese and Connie Booth
    broadcast: 19 September 1975–25 October 1979 on BBC2
    cast: John Cleese (Basil Fawlty), Prunella Scales (Sybil Fawlty), Connie Booth
        (Polly), Andrew Sachs (Manuel), Ballard Berkeley (Major Gowen)
FBI: Federal Bureau of Investigation; formed in 1908
FBI, slogan: 'Fidelity, Bravery, Integrity'
FBI agent: Fed, G-man
FBI director: J. Edgar Hoover
FBW: full bikini wax, as in a 'Hollywood' or 'Sphynx' shave of the genital area
fear, fear of: phobophobia
feasts: Agape (early Christian), Assumption (Roman Catholic), Candlemas
    (Christian), Corpus Christi (Catholic), movable feast, Passover (Jewish),
    Pentecost, potlatch (Chinook), Purim (Jewish), Succoth (Jewish), wayzgoose
    (held by a printing house)
feather, adjective: pinnate
feathers, fear of: pteronophobia
feather vane: vexillum
feather-legged (as of birds): braccate
feather-shaped: penniform
Federation of Rhodesia and Nyasaland: a federal group of states incorporating
    Northern Rhodesia, Southern Rhodesia and Nyasaland, in existence between
    1953 and 1963. Sometimes referred to as the Central African Federation
    capital: Salisbury (now Harare)
    currency: pound sterling
    language: English
    prime minister: Sir Roy Welensky (1956–1963)
feel-good chemicals: dopamine, serotonin
feet, adjective: podalic
feet, average use of per day: four hours' worth
feet, doctor of: chiropodist, podiatrist
feet, possessing long ones: dolichopodous (adjective)
feet, someone endowed with large ones: macropod
feet, specialised for walking: gressorial, gressorious (adjectives)
feet, study of: podiatry, chiropody

fellatio: French art, French culture
female, adjective: gynaecic
female artsists – see painters, female
female descent, adjective: matrilineal
female leaders: Cory Aquino (The Philippines), Gloria Macapagal-Arroyo (The
    Philippines), Michelle Bachelet (Chile), Sirimavo Bandaranaike (Ceylon),
    Violeta Barrios de Chamorro (Nicaragua), Benazir Bhuto (Pakistan), Boudicca
    (the Iceni), Gro Harlem Brundtland (Norway), Kim Campbell (Canada),
    Catherine the Great (Russia), Dame Eugenia Charles (Dominica), Helen Clark
    (New Zealand), Cleopatra (Egypt), Edith Cresson (France), Luisa Diogo
    (Mozambique), Elisabeth Domitien (Central African Republic), Cristina
    Fernández (Argentina), Vigdís Finnbogadóttir (Iceland), Indira Gandhi (India),
    Julia Gillard (Australia), Tarja Halonen (Finland), Han Myeong Sook (South
    Korea), Ellen Johnson-Sirleaf (Liberia), Cristina Fernández de Kirchner
    (Argentina), Chandrika Bandaranaike Kumaratunga (Sri Lanka), Megawati
    Sukarnoputri (Indonesia), Golda Meir (Israel), Angela Merkel (Germany),
    Pratibha Patil (India), Isabelita Perón (Argentina), Maria de Lourdes Pintasilgo
    (Portugal), Mary Robinson (Ireland), Jenny Shipley (New Zealand), Jóhanna
    Sigurðardóttir (Iceland), Portia Simpson-Miller (Jamaica), Hatshepsut (ancient
    Egypt), Margaret Thatcher (United Kingdom), Yulia Tymoshenko (Ukraine),
    Vaira Vike-Freiberga (Latvia), Khaleda Zia (Bangladesh)
female reproductive organs, study of: gynaecology
feminine names, males with: Hilary Benn (Labour MP), Alice Cooper, Shirley
    Crabtree (aka Big Daddy), Jesse James, Dr Hilary Jones, Marilyn Manson,
    Marion Morrison (John Wayne), Mandy Patinkin (actor), Sir Carol Reed, Lynn
    Stallmaster (casting director), Jocelyn Stevens, Evelyn Waugh, Jackie Wilson,
    Winnie the Pooh
feminists: Dame Margery Ashby, Simone de Beauvoir, Amelia J. Bloomer (whose
    predilection for wearing loose trousers gathered at the knee resulted in the
    garment being named after her), Barbara Bodichon, Rosie Boycott (co-founder
    of *Spare Rib* magazine), Nancy Chodorow, Emily Davison, Dorothy Dinnerstein,
    Marguerite Durand, Andrea Dworkin, Nora Ephron, Dame Millicent Fawcett,
    Shulamith Firestone, Nancy Friday, Betty Friedan, Charlotte Perkins Gilman,
    Emma Goldman, Germaine Greer, Gisèle Halimi, Harriet Harman, Katharine
    Hepburn, He Xiangning, Shere Hite, Frida Kahlo, Naomi Klein, Julia Kristeva,
    Catherine Macaulay, Lee Miller, Kate Millett, Juliet Mitchell, Mary Muller,
    Margarita Nelken, Margaret Oliphant, Camille Paglia, Christabel Pankhurst,
    Emmeline Pankhurst, Jeannette Rankin, Eleanor Rathbone, Ruth Rohde, Dora
    Russell, George Sand, Rosika Schwimmer, Hannah Sheehy-Skeffington, Dale
    Spender, Gloria Steinem, Lucy Stone, Lady Jessie Street, Carey Thomas,
    Natasha Walter, Ellen Willis, Naomi Wolf, Mary Wollstonecraft, Virginia Woolf
feminist icon: Lee Miller
feminist publication: *Spare Rib* (co-founded by Rosie Boycott)
femmes fatale: Carmen, Célimène (from Molière's *The Misanthrope*), Delilah,
    Tamara Drewe, Gilda (from the 1946 film of the same name), Holly Golightly,
    Helen Grayle (c/o *Farewell My Lovely*), Christine Keeler, Manon Lescaut (c/o
    Abbe Prevost), Pandora, Mandy Rice-Davies, Milady de Winter (from *The
    Three Musketeers*)
fence (recipient of stolen goods): Fagin
fence frame (usually made of twigs, stakes, split rods, etc): wattle
fencer's breast-shield: plastron

fencing, Japanese: kendo (using bamboo swords)
fencing thrust: fleche, passado
fermentation, adjective: zymotic
fermentation, study of: zymology
ferns, British: black spleenwort, bracken, hard fern, hartstongue fern, lady fern, maidenhair spleenwort, male fern, polypody, royal fern, rustyback, sea spleenwort, wall-rue
fern-shaped: filiciform
ferret, adjective: musteline
ferret, collective noun: business, fesnyng
ferret, male: jack
ferret, female: jill
ferries: Brittany Ferries, P&O European Ferries, Speed-Ferries, Stena Sealink
ferries, capsized: Estonia (in the Baltic, September 1994), Marchioness (on the River Thames, 20 August 1989), al-Salam 98 (in the Red Sea, February 2006)
ferryman of the river Styx: Charon
fertility, god of: Frey (Norse mythology), Geb (Egyptian), Min (Egyptian), Priapus (Greek)
fertility, goddess of: Astarte (Phoenician), Heket (Egyptian), Ishtar (Babylonian), Rhea (Greek), Ops (Roman), Tellus or Terra Mater (Roman)
festivals: All Saints' Day, Bacchanalia (Roman), Beltane (Celtic), carnival, Christmas, Diwali (Hindu), Easter, Eid (Muslim), encaenia, Epiphany, fête, fête champêtre, fête galante, fiesta, Greater Bairam (Muslim), Hanukkah (Jewish), Hocktide (British), Holy Cross Day, Holy Rood Day, Lammas *harvest festival), Lesser Bairam (Muslim), May Day, Passover (Jewish), Pentecost, Pesach (Passover), pongal (Tamil), Purim (Jewish), saint's day, Samhain (Celtic), Saturnalia (Roman), septcentenary, Succoth (Jewish), symposium, Twelfth Day, Visitation, Yule (Christmas)
fever: pyrexia
fever, adjective: febrile, pyretic
fever, causing: febricant
fever, reducing: febrifuge
fever, without: afebrile (adjective)
fever chill: algidity
fibula, adjective: peroneal
fiddlers: Nero, Bob Wills (creator of Western swing) - see violinists
Fidelio: opera by Ludwig Van Beethoven (his only one) first produced in Vienna in 1805
field, adjective: campestral
Field of Dreams (1989 film), famous line: The Voice: "If you build it, he will come"
fields, god of: Pan (Greek), Faunus (Roman), Silvanus (Roman)
fifty-year-old: quinquagenarian
fifty pound note, illustrated notable thereon: the bank gatekeeper John Houblon
fig, adjective: caricous
fig-shaped: ficiform
fight: brannigan, brawl, rumble, scrap, shindy, spat, swedge (Scot.)
fighter pilots: Douglas Bader, James Bigglesworth (aka Biggles), William Bishop, Baron Manfred von Richthofen (aka 'the Red Baron'), Bruno Stachel (as played by George Peppard in *The Blue Max*)

fighting, adjective: bellicose

figure skaters – see ice skaters

figurines, make of: Lladró (from Spain)

Fiji: independent republic in the south-west Pacific (consisting of 844 islands)
    capital: Suva
    currency: dollar
    language: English
    religion: Christian, Hindu

film, first: *La Sortie des ouvriers de l'usine Lumière* (*Workers Leaving the Lumière Factory*) (1895)
    first British film: *The Soldier's Courtship* (1896)
    first Western: Edison's *Cripple Creek Bar-Room Scene* (1899)
    first film with sound: *Don Juan* (1926)
    first all-talking film: *The Lights of New York* (1928)
    first British all-talking film: *Blackmail* (1928)

film, adjective: filmic

film buff: cineaste

film composers: John Barry, Elmer Bernstein, Philip Glass, Jerry Goldsmith, Bernard Herrmann, James Horner, Maurice Jarre, Jan A.P. Kaczmarerk, Erich Wolfgang Korngold, Francis Lai, Michel Legrand, Henry Mancini, Ennio Morricone, Alfred Newman, Alex North, Michael Nyman, Nino Rota, Miklos Rozsa, Lalo Schifrin, Howard Shore, Dmitri Shostakovich, Alan Silvestri, Max Steiner, Mikis Theodorakis, Dimitri Tiomkin, Vangelis, William Walton, Franz Waxman, John Williams, Hans Zimmer

film critics: James Agee, Lindsay Anderson, David Ansen, Peter Bogdanovich, Jay Cocks, Richard Corliss, Judith Crist, David Denby, Roger Ebert, Víctor Erice, Nino Frank, Philip French, Jean-Luc Godard, Graham Greene, Penelope Houston, Stephen Hunter, Pauline Kael, Harry Knowles, Jeffrey Lyons, Derek Malcolm, Leonard Maltin, David Manning (fictitious critic dreamed up by two executives at Sony Pictures to help plug their films on posters), Todd McCarthy, George Melly, Barry Norman, George Perry, Dilys Powell, Rex Reed, Richard Roeper, Jonathan Ross, Andrew Sarris, Richard Schickel, Paul Schrader, Gene Shalit, Joel Siegel, Gene Siskel, F. Maurice Speed, Bertrand Tavernier, David Thomson, Bertrand Tavernier, Peter Travers, François Truffaut, Kenneth Turan, Alexander Walker

film directing: "Like trying to do a painting through binoculars from three blocks away with forty people holding the brush" - David Fincher

film directors – see Chinese film directors, French film directors, German film directors, Italian film directors, Japanese film directors, Spanish film directors

filmmaking terms: arc shot, angle of view, blocking, cineaste, depth of focus, dissolve, dubbing, editor, establishing shot, exposure, fade, freeze-frame, genre, high-angle shot, insert shot, jump-cut, kinestasis (the use of photographs to tell a story), low-angle shot, master shot, matte shot, McGuffin, montage, multiple-image shot, newsreel, New Wave, obscured frame, outtake, pixilation, reaction shot, reverse-angle shot, ripple dissolve, rough cut, running gag, score, screenplay, shock cuts (fast editing), Spielberg zoom, split-screen process, travelling matte, underexposure, voice-over, washout, wipe, zoom shot

film noir: term coined by the French critic Nino Frank in 1946

film tycoons: Louis B. Mayer, Michael Eisner, Samuel Goldwyn, Howard Hughes, Sherry Lansing, J. Arthur Rank, Steven Spielberg, Bob Weinstein, Harvey Weinstein, Darryl F. Zanuck, Adolph Zukor

Financial Times, The: business-orientated national British newspaper founded in 1888
financiers: Conrad Black, Ivan Boesky, Jean-Baptiste Colbert, Sir Thomas Gresham, Baron Georges-Eugène Haussmann, Kirk Kerkorian, James Lick, Bernie Madoff, Andrew W. Mellon, Mike Milken, J. P. Morgan, Mayer Rothschild, George Soros, Sir Allen Stanford
  - see bankers, economists
finch, adjective: fringilline
finch, collective noun: charm
finch, young: chick, hatchling
FINE (pronounced "fine"): freaked out, insecure, neurotic and emotional
finger: index finger (or forefinger or pointer finger), little finger (or pinky), middle finger (or long finger), ring finger, thumb
finger, adjective: digital
fingers, the act of counting on: dactylonomy
fingers, without: adactylous (adjective)
fingering during foreplay: contrectation
fingernail, adjective: onychoid, ungual
fingernail biting, the habit of: onychophagy
fingernail tear: agnail (a piece of torn skin at the root of a fingernail)
fingerprints, study of: dermatoglyphics
Finland: republic in northern Europe
  capital: Helsinki
  currency: euro; formerly: markka
  language: Finnish, Swedish
  religion: Christian, Lutheran
  national tipple: Koskenkorva
  fact: Finland has one sauna for every two citizens
Finnish and famous: Alvar Aalto (architect), Wäinö Aaltonen (sculptor), Albert Edelfelt (painter), Mika Hakkinen (racing driver), Renny Harlin (film director), Tove Jansson (writer and illustrator), Aki Kaurismaki (film director), Linda Lampenius (violinist), Eino Leino (poet and novelist), Paavo Nurmi (athlete), Kimi Räikkönen (racing driver), Eero Saarinen (architect), Jean Sibelius (composer), Artturi Virtanen (biochemist), Georg Henrik von Wright (philosopher)
Finnish-Russian war: 1939–1940
fir trees – see Christmas trees
fir tree, adjective: abietic
fire, adjective: fiery, igneous
fire, fear of: pyrophobia
fire, god of: Agni (Hindu), Hephaestus (Greek), Kagutschi (Japanese), Vulcan (Roman)
fire, killed by: Miss Havisham, Dame Barbara Hepworth, Joan of Arc, Steve Marriott (of the Small Faces and Humble Pie), Matilda (c/o Hilaire Belloc), Ronnie Scott
fire, obsession with: empresiomania, pyromania
fire extinguisher: invented in 1816 by Captain George Manby
firearm: blunderbuss, culverin, musket, pistol
  - see guns
firearms and munition inventors: John Browning, Antonie Chassepot, Samuel Colt, Sir William Congreve, Uziel Gal, Richard Gatling, Mikhail Kalashnikov, Alfred Krupp, Peter Mauser, Henry Shrapnel, Horace Smith, Daniel Wesson, O.F. Winchester

Fire of Chicago: October 8–10 1871

Fire of London: 2-5 September 1666 (death toll: eight)

firefly, adjective: lampyrid

firemen: Red Adair, Peter Burgess (Australian volunteer with the rural fire service who, in June of 2002, was jailed for two years after admitting to starting 25 fires in New South Wales), Fireman Sam

fireworks, adjective: pyrotechnic

firing squad, states in the USA which still use: Idaho, Oklahoma

First Amendment: guarantee of free speech

First Ladies: Barbara Bush, Laura Bush, Hillary Rodham Clinton, Mamie Eisenhower, Betty Ford, Rachel Jackson, Martha Jefferson, Jackie Kennedy (Onassis), Pat Nixon, Michelle Obama, Nancy Reagan, Eleanor Roosevelt, Martha Washington, Edith Wilson

first words of medieval manuscript: incipit

First World War: 28 July 1914–11 November 1918

fish: "The only food that is considered spoilt once it smells like what it is" – P.J. O'Rourke

fish, adjective: ichthyic, ichthyoid, piscatory, piscatorial, piscine

fish, alternative spelling: ghoti ('gh' as in enou*gh*, 'o' as in wom*e*n and 'ti' as in na*ti*on – devised by George Bernard Shaw)

fish, collective noun: school, shoal

fish, eating of: ichthyophagy

fish, eviscerate: gut (verb)

fish, fastest: sailfish

fish, fear of: ichthyophobia

fish, largest: whale shark

fish, plural: fish

fish, poisonous (if not prepared correctly before consumption): blowfish (or fugu)

fish, raw (in Japanese cuisine): sashimi

fish, rhyming slang: Lillian Gish

fish, study of: ichthyology

fish, worship of: ichthyolatry

fish, young: fry

fish and chip shop: chippie

fish basket: corf, creel

fish gelatin: isinglass

fish hook, weighted (to stay under water): drail

fish poisoning: ichthyism, ichthyotoxism

fish seller: Fanny (Marcel Pagnol heroine)

fish semen: milt

fish soup: bouillabaisse, kakavía, suquet

fish stew: bouillabaisse, kakavía, matelote, suquet

fish-eating: piscivorous (adjective)

fish-shaped: ichthyomorphic

fisherman's attendant: gillie (or ghillie)

fisherman's basket: creel

fishermen: Captain Ahab, Pascal Cognard (fly fishing champion), Peter Grimes, J.R. Hartley (the fictitious author of *Fly Fishing*), Brian Leadbetter (fly fishing champion), the Old Man and the Sea (c/o Ernest Hemingway), Saint Peter, Simon, Izaak Walton

fishing, adjective: halieutic, piscatory, piscatorial

fishing, art of: halieutics

fishing aids: fly, jig, lure, plug, rod, spoon

fishmonger: ichthyopolist

fitness gurus: Jane Fonda, Michael King (Pilates), Jack La Lanne ('the Godfather of Fitness'), Diana Moran ('the Green Goddess'), Joseph Hubertus Pilates, Jerome Rodale (who died of a heart attack while appearing on *The Dick Cavett Show*), Richard Simmons

five, adjective: quinary

Five Pillars of Wisdom (in the Islam faith): Shahada (faith); Salah (prayer); Zakat (charity); Hajj (pilgrimage to Mecca); Saum (the recognition of Ramadam, the month of fasting)

five senses: feeling, hearing, seeing, smelling and tasting

five wits: common sense, imagination, fantasy, estimation and memory

five yearly: quinquennial

five-hundredth anniversary: quincentenary

five years' long: quinquennial

five-year period: lustrum, pentad

FL: postcode for Florida

flag, adjective: vexillary

flags, study of: vexillology

FLAK: Fondest, Love and Kisses

flame-coloured: flammeous

flame-less, adjective: aphlogistic

flamenco dancers: Joaquín Cortés, El Farruco (real name: Antonio Montoya Flores), Farruquito (real name: Juan Montoya)

flamenco guitarist: Paco de Lucia

flamingo, adjective: phoenicopteroid

flamingo, collective noun: stand

flamingo, young: chick

Flanders, king of: Gambrinus

flashback in film, first use of: in *The Yiddisher Boy* (1908)

flasher, fact: a flasher is typically caught after 70 to 80 'offences'

flashes, fear of: selaphobia

flatfish, largest: halibut

Flatiron Building: unusual edifice in Manhattan, New York, designed by Daniel Burnham. The erection, which was originally called the Fuller Building, was completed in 1902 and has been a curiosity ever since due to its flat, triangular shape. Indeed, the atypical structure is prone to creating wind currents at ground level, initially requiring the conscription of police officers to prevent male onlookers from peering at the wind-blown skirts of female passers-by

flatmates of yore (celebrities who – often prior to stardom – used to room together): Ben Affleck and Matt Damon; Wes Anderson and Owen Wilson; Judd Apatow and Adam Sandler; Tony Blair and Lord (Charles) Falconer; Ian Botham and Viv Richards; Michael Caine and Terence Stamp; Henry Fonda and James Stewart; Nick Frost and Simon Pegg; Mel Gibson and Geoffrey Rush; Al Gore and Tommy Lee Jones; Cary Grant and Randolph Scott; Ioan Gruffud and Matthew Rhys (actors); Gene Hackman and Dustin Hoffman; Daryl Hannah and Rachel Ward; Thomas Kyd and Christopher Marlowe

flattery: encomia

flatterer: encomiast
flatulence – see farting
flatulence aiding: carminative
flautists: Sharon Bezaly, Theobald Boehm, Frederick the Great of Prussia, James Galway
flavour, adjective: saporific
flay: excoriate
flea, adjective: pulicine
flea, fact: the insect can jump 350 times its body length (the equivalent of a man leaping the span of a football field)
flea-infested: pulicose
Fledermaus, Die: operetta by Johann Strauss the Younger first produced in Vienna in 1874
Fleetwood Mac: UK blues-rock-pop band formed in 1967 in London; comprised of Mick Fleetwood (drums), John McVie (bass) and Christine McVie (piano), and at various other junctures: Peter Green (guitar), Lindsey Buckingham (vocals, guitar), Stevie Nicks (vocals), Jeremy Spencer (guitar), Christine Perfect (keyboards, vocals), Danny Kirwan (guitar) and Bob Welch (guitar)
Flemish novelist: Hendrik Conscience
Flemish painters: Jan Brueghel, Pieter Brueghel, Frans Hals, Quentin Matsys, Hans Memling, Sir Peter Paul Rubens, Sir Anthony Van Dyck, Jan van Eyck
flesh, adjective: carnal, creatic, sarcoid
flesh, anatomy of: sarcology
flesh-coloured: incarnadine, sarcoline
flight, adjective: volar
Flight of the Bumble-Bee, The: orchestral interlude from the 1900 opera *The Legend of Tsar Saltan* by Nikolai Rimsky-Korsakov
flock, adjective: gregal
flocks, god of: Pan (Greek mythology), Silvanus (Roman)
flogging, fear of: mastigophobia
flood, adjective: clysmian, diluvian
flood, fear of: antlophobia
Florence, birthplace of: Dante Alighieri, Giovanni Boccaccio, Sandro Botticelli, Catherine de Médicis, Donatello, Oriana Fallaci, Jean Baptiste Lully, Niccolò Machiavelli, Florence Nightingale, Andrea del Sarto, Paolo Uccello, Franco Zeffirelli
Florence, places of interest: The Duomo (church), Uffizi gallery
Florence river: Arno
Florida, 27th state (1845), Sunshine State
    capital: Tallahassee
    state bird: mockingbird
    state flower: orange blossom
    state tree: sabal palm
    motto: 'In God we trust'
    birthplace of: The Backstreet Boys, Patricia Cornwell, Faye Dunaway, Debbie Harry, Carl Hiaasen, James Weldon Johnson (writer), Lynyrd Skynyrd, Jim Morrison, Tom Petty, Sidney Poitier, Janet Reno, Wesley Snipes, Mel Tillis
    tourist attractions: Disneyworld, EPCOT, Everglades National Park, Spaceport USA
    fact: there are more lakes in Florida than in any other state

flower: "A flower is just a weed that got lucky" - adage quoted by A.A. Gill

flower, adjective: anthoid, floral

flower arranging, Japanese style: ikebana

flower girl: Eliza Doolittle

Flower Pot Men: Bill and Ben

flower preservative: Liquid Love (a floral version of Viagra, according to scientists)

flower stalk: pedicel, peduncle

flower-bearing: anthophorous

flowers: abelia, acacia, agapanthus, anemone, aster, azalea, begonia, buddleia, busy lizzie, camellia, campanula,carnation, chrysanthemum, cosmos, crocus, cyclamen, dahlia, daisy, delphinium, flax, forget-me-not, foxglove, freesia, fuchsia, gentian, geranium, hollyhock, honeysuckle, hydrangea, hypericum, iris, jonquil, larkspur, lily, lobelia, lupin, Micheaelmas daisy, narcissus, nasturtium, oxlip, pansy, peony, petunia, phlox, polyanthus, poppy, primrose, primula, rose, snapdragon, stock, sweet pea, sweet William, syringa, tulip, viola, violet

flowers, cultivation of: floriculture

flowers, fear of: anthophobia

flowers, goddess of: Chloris (Greeky mythology), Flora (Roman)

flowers, obsession for: anthomania, florimania

flowers, sexual arousal derived from smelling of: antholagnia

flu: influenza

fluid abstinence: adipsia

fluid intoxication (not just alcohol): polydipsia

flutes, fear of: aulophobia

fly, collective noun: business, swarm

fly, sound: buzz

fly, young: maggot

flying, ability for: volitant, volitorial (adjective)

flying machine: aerodyne (that which is heavier than air), aerostat (that which is lighter than air)

foamy: spumescent

foetus, killing of: aborticide, feticide, foeticide

fog, fear of: homichlophobia

foghorn: first demonstrated by Captain J.N. Taylor in London in May of 1844

folic acid: discovered in 1941

folk music gathering: hootenanny

folk music uniform: beard, knitted pullover, paisley waistcoat, pastel colours

folk singers: Joan Baez, Battlefield Band, Oscar Brand, Carter family, The Chieftains, Judy Collins, Billy Connolly, Ani di Franco, Lonnie Donegan, Donovan, Bob Dylan, Charlie Dore, Fairport Convention, Arlo Guthrie, Woody Guthrie, Tim Hardin, Burl Ives, Bert Jansch, Victor Jara, Kingston Trio, Seth Lakeman, Leadbelly (aka Huddie Ledbetter), Gordon Lightfoot, Lindisfarne, Kate and Anna McGarrigle, Phil Ochs, Beth Orton, Pentangle, Tom Robinson, Kate Rusby, Pete Seeger, Simon and Garfunkel, The Spinners, Steeleye Span, Al Stewart, Dave Van Ronk, Loudon Wainwright, The Weavers

folklorists: Jacob and Wilhem Grimm, Alan Lomax, Iona Opie, Peter Opie

folly: "There is a limit to wisdom; but there is no limit to folly" - Turkman proverb

fondling, pathological desire for: contrectation

food: "There is no love more sincere than the love of food" – George Bernard Shaw

food, adjective: alimentary, cibarious

food, aversion to: sitophobia

food, most widely ordered dish in British restaurants: chicken tikka masala (reportedly, 11 million diners ask for it every year)

food, obsession for: acoria, phagomania

food, partially digested: chyme

food of the gods: ambrosia

food packaging tycoon: Hans Rausing

food poisoning: botulism, campylobacter, E coli 0157, ergotism, salmonella

food writers: Mary Berry, Quentin Crewe, Curnonsky (born Maurice Edmond Sailland), Elizabeth David, Patience Gray, Simon Hopkinson, Ruth Reich, Egon Ronay
- see cookery writers

foods that lessen the appetite: chillies, coffee, garlic, red peppers, tea

fools: Feste (from *Twelfth Night*), Lavache (from *All's Well That Ends Well*), Touchstone (from *As You Like It*), Trinculo (from *The Tempest*), Yorick (lamented by Hamlet)
- see clowns

foot, adjective: pedal, pedate

foot, upper surface of: acropodium

foot; person endowed with a large pair: macropod

foot and mouth epidemics, years in Britain: 1967–1968; 2001 (which started at Burnside Farm, Heddon-on-the-Wall, Northumberland, in February)

foot deformity: club foot, cyllosis, talipes

foot doctor: chiropodist, podiatrist

foot massage to relieve tension and to treat ills: reflexology

foot-bath: pediluvium

foot-shaped: pediform

football, tabletop game: Subbuteo (made by Hasbro)

football disaster: Hillsborough (15th April, 1989), when 96 people were crushed to death

football coaches: Sven-Göran Eriksson, George Halas (Chicago Bears), Stuart Pearce, Terry Venables

football managers: Jimmy Armfield, Ron Atkinson, Sir Matt Busby, Fabio Capello, Brian Clough, Sir Alex Ferguson, George Graham, Ron Greenwood, Helenio Herrera, Glenn Hoddle, Sir Stanley Matthews, Billy McNeill, José Mourinho, Sir Alf Ramsey, Sir Bobby Robson, Bill Shankly, Arsène Wenger

footballers: Carlos Alberto Torres (Brazil), Roberto Baggio (Italy), Franz Beckenbauer (West Germany), Andreas Brehme (West Germany), Paul Breitner (West Germany), Eric Cantona (France), Johan Cruyff (Holland), Alfredo Di Stefano (Argentina/Spain), Didier Drogba (Côte d'Ivoire), Eusébio da Silva Ferreira (Portugal), Giacinto Facchetti (Italy), Luis Figo (Portuguese), Just Fontaine (France), Garrincha (Brazil; born: Manuel dos Santos), David Ginola (France), Ruud Gullit (Holland), Thierry Henry (France), Jairzinho (Brazil), Pat Jennings (Ireland), Miroslav Klose (Germany), Ruud Krol (Holland), Diego Maradona (Argentina), Lothar Matthaus (West Germany), Lionel Messi (Argentina), Gerd Müller (Germany), Johan Neeskens (Holland), Ruud van Nistelrooy (Holland), Daniel Passarella (Argentina), Pelé (Brazil), Michel Platini (France), Ferenc Puskas (Hungary), Helmut Rahn (Germany), Roberto Rivelino (Brazil), Ronaldo (Brazil), Cristiano Ronaldo (Portugal), Gaetano Scirea (Italy), Andriy Shevchenko (Ukraine), Socrates (Brazil), Patrick Vieira (France), Berti Vogts (West Germany), Lev Yashin (Soviet Union), Zico (Brazil; born: Arthur Coimbra), Zinedine Zidane (France), Dino Zoff (Italy)
- see American footballers, British footballers, goalkeepers

football, slang: footie, pigskin (the ball), soccer
fop: Beau Brummell
- see dandy
forces' sweetheart: Dame Vera Lynn
forearm, adjective: antibrachial, cubital
forearms, possessing long ones (adjective): dolichocercic
forehead, adjective: metopic
forehead mark/spot: tilak or 'third eye'
foreign languages, aversion to: xenoglossophobia
Foreign Legion, hero of: Beau Geste
foreign place name, word for: exonym (as in Cologne for Koln and Florence for Firenze)
foreigners, hatred of: xenophobia
forensic entomology: the application of insect biology to the investigation of crime
forensic entomologist: Zakaria Erzinçlioğlu (who describes himself as a "maggotologist")
forensic pathologist: Kay Scarpetta
foreskin: prepuce
foreskin, tip of: akroposthion
foreskin constriction: phimosis
forest, adjective: sylvan
forge, of a blacksmith: stithy
forgers: Clarence Hatry, Gerd Heidemann (Hitler's 20 diaries), Tom Keating (painter), Han van Meegeren (painter), Robert Thwaites (painter), Thomas Wainewright (painter), Thomas Wise (bibliophile)
forgetfulness, river of: Lethe (Greek mythology)
forgiveness: "The weak can never forgive. Forgiveness is the attribute of the strong" – Mahatma Gandhi; "Forgive your enemies, but never forget their names" John F. Kennedy; "Always forgive your enemies: nothing annoys them so much" – Oscar Wilde
Formosa: former name for the Asian country Taiwan
Formula One champions – see racing drivers
Forrest Gump (1994 film), famous lines: Forrest Gump (Tom Hanks): "My momma always said, life was like a box of chocolates. You never know what you're gonna get." Forrest Gump: "Momma says stupid is as stupid does."
Forsyte Saga, The: classic 26-part series based on John Galsworthy's literary cycle, focusing on a London family from the 1870s to the 1920s
    created by Donald Wilson
    broadcast: 7 January 1967–1 July 1967 on BBC2
    cast: Kenneth More (Jolyon Forsyte), Eric Porter (Soames Forsyte), Nyree Dawn Porter (Irene Heron/ Forsyte), Susan Hampshire (Fleur), Margaret Tyzack (Winifred), June Barry (June), Michael York (Jolly). The series was remade by London Weekend Television in 2002 with Damian Lewis (Soames), Gina McKee (Irene), Ioan Gruffudd (Phillip Bosinney), Amanda Ooms (Helène), Corin Redgrave (old Jolyon) and Rupert Graves (young Jolyon)
fortune teller, famous: Maurice Woodruff
- see mediums, mystics
fortune teller, female: spaewife
fortune teller's tool: crystal ball
forty days' long: quadragesimal (adjective)

forty-year-old: quadragenarian
fossil expert: Chris Stringer
fossilised dung: coprolite
fossilised footprint: ichnite
foul language: coprolalia
fountain nymph: naiad
fountain pen: conceived by Robert Thomson (1822–1873), but successfully patented by the American insurance broker Lewis E. Waterman in 1884
four, adjective: quaternary
four years' long: quadrennial (adjective)
four-footed: tetrapous
four-sided plane figure: quadrangle
four-sided solid figure: tetrahedron
four-winged: tetrapteran
four-year period: quadrennium
fowl, domestic, adjective: gallinaceous
fowl, eviscerate: draw (verb)
fox, adjective: vulpine
fox, collective noun: skulk, leash
fox, fact: the British fox population reached a record-breaking 600,000 in 2002, 13% of which – 78,000 – live in Britain's cities
fox, famous: Basil Brush, Brer Fox, Reynard (of fable), Tod (from Disney's *The Fox and the Hound*)
fox, female: vixen
fox, habitat: earth
fox, male: dog, vix
fox, sound: bark, yelp
fox, young: cub, kit, pup
fox, young; adjective: vulpecular
fox-killing: vulpicide
fraction of a second: attosecond (ten million billionth of), nanosecond (one thousand-millionth of)
France: republic in western Europe
    adjective: Gallic
    capital: Paris
    currency: euro; formerly: franc
    language: French
    nickname: The Hexagon
    patron saint: Dionysius (Denis) of Paris
    religion: Roman Catholic
    rivers: Garonne, Loire, Rhine, Rhône, Seine
Franciscan Order: founded by Saint Francis of Assisi in 1210
Franco-Prussian War: 1870–1871
Frankfurt, ballet company: Ballet Frankfurt
Frankfurt, birthplace of: Anne Frank, Erich Fromm, Johann Goethe, Heinrich Hoffmann, Martin Lawrence (comedian), Henri Nestlé, Marcel Ophüls (filmmaker), Mayer Rothschild, Dr Ruth Westheimer, Hans Zimmer (film composer)
Frankfurt river: Main
Frankfurt sausage: Frankfurter Wurst
Frankfurt School: school of philosophy founded by Theodor Adorno and Herbert Marcuse in 1923, based on the principles of Marx and Freud

Frankish leaders: Charlemagne (aka 'Charles the Great'), Charles Martel
Frasier: perennial sitcom set in Seattle in which Kelsey Grammer recreated his role
of the flustered psychiatrist Frasier Crane from *Cheers* (see)
broadcast: 16 September 1993–13 May 2004
cast: Kelsey Grammer (Frasier Crane), John Mahoney (Martin Crane), David
Hyde Pierce (Niles Crane), Jane Leeves (Daphne Moon), Mercedes Ruehl
(Kate Costas), Peri Gilpin (Roz Doyle), Eddie (Moose, a Jack Rusell terrier)
fraternal twins, technical term: dizygotic twins (see identical twins)
fraternities: Beta Sigma Phi, Freemasons, Phi Kappa Sigma, Pi Kappa Alpha
fraudulent acquisition of private details via electronic communication: phishing
freckles: ephelides
freckle of old age: lentigo (plural: lentigines)
free runners (or 'parkours'): David Belle, Sebastien Foucan
freedom: "The only man who is really free is the one who can turn down an
invitation to dinner without giving an excuse" - Jules Renard
freedom, fear of: eleutherophobia
freedom fighter: Mahadev Desai
- see activists, political activists
freezing, fear of: cryophobia
French composers: Georges Auric, Jean Barraqué, Hector Berlioz, Georges Bizet,
Pierre Boulez, François Couperin, Achille-Claude Debussy, Léo Delibes, Paul
Dukas, Henri Duparc, Gabriel Fauré, Charles Gounod, Jacques Ibert, Jean
Baptiste Lully, Jules Massenet, Olivier Messiaen, Jean Philippe Rameau,
Maurice Ravel, Camille Saint-Saëns, Erik Satie, Jean Sibelius, Edgard Varèse
French film directors: Jean-Jacques Annaud, Jacques Audiard, Jacques Becker,
Jean-Jacques Beineix, Claude Berri, Luc Besson, Bertrand Blier, Robert
Bresson, Marcel Carné, Claude Chabrol, René Clair, René Clement, Henri-
Georges Clouzot, Jean Cocteau, Philippe de Broca, Jacques Demy, Jacques
Deray, Julien Duvivier, Jean-Luc Godard, Jean-Pierre Jeunet, Patrice Leconte,
Claude Lelouche, Louis Malle, Jean-Pierre Melville, François Ozon, Jean
Renoir, Alain Resnais, Jacques Rivette, Alain Robbe-Grillet, Eric Rohmer,
Claude Sautet, Coline Serreau, Jacques Tati, Bertrand Tavernier, André
Téchiné, François Truffaut, Roger Vadim, Agnès Varda, Jean Vigo, Claude Zidi
French flag: Oriflamme (in the Middle Ages), tricolore
French novelists: Alain-Fournier, Honoré de Balzac, Henri Barbusse, Simone de
Beauvoir, François-René de Chateaubriand, Colette, Sophie Cottin, Alexandre
Dumas, Marguerite Duras, André Gide, Edmond de Goncourt, Jules de
Goncourt, Michel Houellebecq, Victor Hugo, Alphonse Karr, Gaston Leroux,
Guy de Maupassant, Prosper Mérimée, Georges Perec, Raymond Queneau,
Alain Robbe-Grillet, Françoise Sagan, George Sand, Nathalie Sarraute, Jean-
Paul Sartre, Claude Simon, Stendhal, Jules Verne
French painters: Jean Arp, Count Balthasar Balthus, Jules Bastien-Lepage, Pierre
Bonnard, François Boucher, Georges Braque, Bernard Buffet, Paul Cézanne,
Marc Chagall, Philippe de Champaigne, Jean-Baptiste Chardin, Jean Clouet,
Jean Baptiste Camille Corot, Gustave Courbet, Honoré Daumier, Jacques-Louis
David, Edgar Degas, Eugène Delacroix, Gustave Doré, Raoul Dufy, Jean-
Honoré Fragonard, Paul Gauguin, Théodore Géricault, Baron Antoine-Jean
Gros, Jean Auguste Dominique Ingres, Wassily Kandinsky (born in Moscow),
Georges de La Tour, Claude Lorrain, Édouard Manet, Henri Matisse, Jean-
François Millet, Claude Monet, Camille Pissarro, Nicolas Poussin, Pierre-

Auguste Renoir, Georges Rouault, Henri Rousseau, Georges Seurat, Alfred
Sisley, Chaim Soutine, Henri-Marie-Raymond de Toulouse-Lautrec, Maurice
Utrillo, Felix Vallotton, Joseph Vien, Édouard Vuillard, Antoine Watteau
- see impressionist painters

French playwrights: Athur Adamov, Jean Anouilh, Marcel Aymé, Jean-Louis
Barrault, Pierre Caron de Beaumarchais, Henri Becque, Georges Bernanos,
Eugène Brieux, Albert Camus, Paul Claudel, Jean Cocteau, Pierre Corneille,
Savinien Cyrano de Bergerac, Alexander Dumas, Charles Favart, Georges
Feydeau, Jean Genet, Henri Ghéon, André Gide, Jean Giraudoux, Victor Hugo,
Eugène Ionesco, Eugène Labiche, Henri-René Lenormand, Gabriel Marcel,
Pierre de Marivaux, François Mauriac, Jean-Baptiste Molière, Henry de
Montherlant, Alfred de Musset, André Obey, Marcel Pagnol, Georges de
Porto-Riche, Jean Racine, Jules Romains, Edmond Rostand, Armand Salacrou,
George Sand, Victorien Sardou, Jean-Paul Sartre, Francis Veber, Roger Vitrac,
Voltaire, Emile Zola

French poets: Guillaume Apollinaire, Charles Baudelaire, Hilaire Belloc, André
Breton, Jean Cocteau, Victor Hugo, Jean de Meung, Jean Racine, Arthur
Rimbaud, Paul Verlaine, François Villon

French presidents: Jacques Chirac, Charles de Gaulle, Alexandre Millerand,
François Mitterrand, Napoleon III of France, Georges Pompidou, Nicolas
Sarkozy

French prime ministers: Jacques Chirac, Georges Clemenceau, Charles de
Gaulle, Lionel Jospin, Alain Juppé, Pierre Laval, Philippe Pétain, Georges
Pompidou

French sculptors: Aristide Maillol, Auguste Rodin, François Rude

French singers: Charles Aznavour, Gilbert Bécaud, Georges Brassens, Patrick
Bruel, Maurice Chevalier, Dalida (born Yolanda Gigliotti), Natalie Dessay,
Sacha Distel, Jacques Dutronc, Serge Gainsbourg, Juliette Gréco, Françoise
Hardy, Patricia Kaas, Jacques Lantier, Vicky Léandros, Mireille Mathieu,
Mireille (born Mireille Hartuch), Eddy Mitchell, Yves Montand, Vanessa
Paradis, Edith Piaf, Serge Reggiani, Alain Souchon, Charles Trenet

French Somaliland: former name for Djibouti

French songs: *Boum, Je t'aime...moi non plus, La mer, La vie en rose*

French Sudan: former name for Mali (from 1898 to 1959)

French Revolution: 1789–1792

French writer: Catherine Millet

fresh water, adjective: limnetic

fresh water life, study of: limnobiology

Friday the thirteenth, fear of: friggatriskaidekaphobia, paraskevidekatriaphobia

friars – see monks

friends: "You don't make friends, you earn them" – anonymous; "You can make
new friends, but you can't make old friends" – Martin Amis; "Friends are God's
apology for relations" - old maxim

Friends: phenomenally popular TV sitcom on NBC featuring six friends who live
together in New York City and hang out at the Central Perk Cafe
created by David Crane and Marta Kauffman
broadcast: 22 September 1994–6 May 2004
cast: Jennifer Aniston (Rachel Karen Green), Courteney Cox (Monica Geller),
    Lisa Kudrow (Phoebe Buffay/Ursula Buffay), Matt LeBlanc (Joey Frances
    Tribbiani), Matthew Perry (Chandler Bing), David Schwimmer (Ross
    Geller), Tom Selleck (Dr Richard Burke), Elliott Gould (Jack Geller)

friend, killing of: amicicide

friend of the people: demophile

friendship: "The greatest act of friendship that a woman can perform for another is to put on weight" – Sarah Sands

frigid: heterosexually celibate (PC)

fringe, adjective: fimbrial

frisking device: Geiger counter

frog, adjective: batrachian, ranine

frog, collective noun: army

frog, sound: croak

frog, young: fry, polliwog (US dialect), pollywog (US dialect), tadpole

frog-goddess: Heket (Egyptian mythology)

frogs, famous: Kermit, Mr Jeremy Fisher (Beatrix Potter)

frogs, fear of: ranidaphobia

frond-shaped: frondiform

front-wheel drive: invented in 1769 by Nicholas Joseph Cugnot

frontiersmen: Jim Bowie, Davy Crockett, Tom Jeffords, John Smith

frontierswoman: Calamity Jane (originally Martha Jane Burke)

Frost Report, The: satirical BBC TV series of sketches, music and monologues, and one of the last such comedy shows to be broadcast live

    broadcast: 10 March 1966–29 June 1967

    produced by James Gilbert

    written by Graham Chapman, John Cleese, Marty Feldman, Willis Hall, Eric Idle, Antony Jay, Terry Jones, John Law, Frank Muir, Dennis Norden, David Nobbs, Michael Palin, Peter Tinniswood and Keith Waterhouse

    regular cast members: David Frost, John Cleese, Ronnie Barker, Ronnie Corbett, Sheila Steafel and Nicky Henson, with music provided by Tom Lehrer and Julie Felix

frozen foods: first commercialised in 1924 by Clarence Birdseye

fruit, adjective: fructiform

fruit, goddess of: Pomona (Roman mythology)

fruit, non-yielding: acarpous (adjective)

fruit, study of: carpology

fruit eating: carpophagous

fruit expert: pomologist

fruit growing: pomiculture

fruit growing, science of: pomology

fruit juice drinks: Bulmer's Orangina, Capri-Sun mountain cooler, Capri-Sun orange, Capri Sun tropical orange, Del Monte lemonade burst, Del Monte orange burst, Five Alive Mediterranean, Five Alive mixed citrus, Five Alive tropical, Jurassic juice (orange), Kia-Ora whole orange, Libby's apple C, Libby's Orange C, Libby's Um Bongo, Ocean Spray Cranberry Classic, Ocean Spray Cranberry & Raspberry, Ocean Spray Cranberry & Blackcurrant, Ribena blackcurrant, Ribena orange & apricot, Ribena raspberry, Ribena strawberry, Robinson's orange, Rowntree fruit juice, Smoothie

fruit preserved in syrup: compote

fruit trees, goddess of: Pomona (Roman mythology)

FSB: Russian Federal Security Bureau

FUBAR: fucked up beyond all recognition

FUBIS: Fuck you buddy, I'm shipping out

fuck; first used in print: in the 1475 poem *Flen flyys* (albeit used in code)

fuck; first uttered in a mainstream feature film: Joseph Strick's *Ulysses* (1967)

fugitives: Ronald Biggs, Osama bin Laden, Michelangelo da Caravaggio, Richard Hannay (from *The Thirty-Nine Steps*), Dr Richard Kimble (from ABC TV's *The Fugitive*)

Führer, the: Adolf Hitler
fumigants (in agriculture), first used: 1920
funeral, adjective: funerary, funereal
funeral directors: Basil Bulstrode (from TV's *That's Your Funeral*), Herman Munster
funeral procession: cortège
funeral rights: exequies
funeral rights, goddess of: Libitina (Roman)
fungi, disease caused by: mycosis
fungi, study of: mycology
fur, aversion to: doraphobia
fur trader: Jedediah Smith
furniture: armoire, bed, bureau, cabinet, canapé, canterbury, chair (see), chaise
     longue, chesterfield, couch, credence table, credenza, cupboard, Davenport
     (US), desk, divan, dressing table, dumbwaiter, escritoire, lazy Susan (US),
     lowboy, rolltop desk, settee, sideboard, sofa, table (see), tallboy, tête-à-tête,
     triclinium, Welsh dresser, whatnot (a portable stand with shelves)
furniture designers: Robert and James Adam, Harry Bertoia, Marcel Lajos Breuer,
     André Charles Boulle, Thomas Chippendale, Charles Le Corbusier, Charles
     Eames, Ray Eames (née Kaiser), Charles Lock Eastlake, Norman Bel Geddes,
     George Hepplewhite, Thomas Hope, Filippo Juvarra, David Linley, George
     Logan, Charles Rennie Mackintosh, William Morris, Duncan Phyfe, Augustus
     Welby Northmore Pugin, Gerrit Thomas Rietveld, Eero Saarinen, Thomas
     Sheraton, Henri Clemens van de Velde
furniture styles: Adam, Chippendale, colonial, Empire, Hepplewhite, Jacobean,
     Queen-Anne, reproduction, Sheraton
FWD: four wheel drive

G

G7 member countries: Canada, France, Germany, Italy, Japan, United Kingdom
     and United States
G8 member countries: Canada, France, Germany, Italy, Japan, Russia, United
     Kingdom and United States
GA: postcode for Georgia
Gabon: republic in west-central Africa
     capital: Libreville
     currency: African franc
     language: French
     religion: Christian, animist
gaiety, aversion to: cherophobia
gall bladder, adjective: cholecystic
Galloping Gourmet: nickname for the TV chef Graham Kerr
gallows, adjective: patibulary
Gambia, The: republic in West Africa
     capital: Banjul
     currency: dalasi
     language: English
     religion: Muslim
     fact: The Gambia is the smallest country in Africa
gamblers: Nick Arnstein (from *Funny Girl*), Giacomo Casanova, Fyodor
     Dostoevsky, King George IV of England, Wild Bill Hickok (aka James Buter),

Doc Holliday, Barry Lyndon (from the novel by Thackeray), Sky Masterson (from *Guys and Dolls*), Bret Maverick (from TV's *Maverick*), Richard 'Beau' Nash, Frank 'Lefty' Rosenthal

gambler, collective noun: talent

gamblers, patron saints of: Bernardine of Siena and Camillus de Lellis

gambling in the US; first outlawed in: Nevada (but made legal again in 1931)

gambling, types of: baccarat, bingo, blackjack, craps, one-armed bandit, poker, roulette, slot machines

gamekeeper: Oliver Mellors (from *Lady Chatterley's Lover*)

Gang of Four: founders of the Social Democratic Party in Britain, namely Shirley Williams, William Rodgers, Roy Jenkins, and David Owen

gangsta rap acts: Ant Banks, Big Punisher, B-Legit, Bone Thugs-N-Harmony, Boogie Down Productions, Brotha Lynch Hung, Capone-N-Noreaga, Compton's Most Wanted, Dr Dre, Eazy-E, Geto Boys, Ice Cube, Ice-T, Master P, The Notorious B.I.G., N.W.A., Snoop Dogg, 2Pac
- see rap/hip-hop artists

gangsters: Albert Anastasia, Kate 'Ma' Barker, Clyde Barrow, Al Capone, Frank Costello, Jack 'Legs' Diamond, John Dillinger, Charles 'Pretty Boy' Floyd, John Gotti, Henry Hill, Reggie Kray, Ronnie Kray, Louis Lepke, Frank Lucas, Charles 'Lucky' Luciano, Bugs Moran, Dominic Noonan, Bonnie Parker, Bugsy Siegel

gap between the teeth: diastema

gap-toothed and famous: Lynn Barber, Jane Birkin, Ernest Borgnine (actor), Jilly Cooper, Angela Davis, Laurence Fishburne (actor), Gareth Gates, Eddy Grant, Lewis Hamilton, Ainsley Harriott, Michael Howard, Lauren Hutton, John Inman, David Letterman, Humphrey Lyttelton, Madonna, Chris Martin, David Mellor, Eddie Murphy, Vanessa Paradis, Anneka Rice, Condoleezza Rice, Ronaldo, Omar Sharif, Oliver Stone (filmmaker), Jimmy Tarbuck, Terry-Thomas, Frederick West (serial killer), the Wife of Bath (c/o Chaucer)

garage music acts: ? & the Mysterians, The Barbarians, Blues Magoos, The Chocolate Watchband, The Electric Prunes, The Kingsmen, Love, Lovestation, Mis-Teeq, Pleasure Seekers, Paul Revere & the Raiders, The Seeds, Shadows of Knight, The Sonics, 13th Floor Elevators, The Trashmen, The White Stripes, Yeah Yeah Yeahs

garden, adjective: hortensial, hortensian

garden designers: Lancelot Brown (aka Capability Brown), Gertrude Jekyll, André Le Nôtre, George London, Joseph Paxton

garden structure: gazebo

garden-fresh (cookery term): affriole

gardeners: Rachel de Thame, Charlie Dimmock, Monty Don, Bunny Guinness, Mr McHenry (from *The Magic Roundabout*), Tim Smit (head of Cornwall's Eden project), Joe Swift, Percy Thrower, Alan Titchmarsh, Ali Ward

gardeners, patron saints of: Adelard, Agnes of Rome and Fiacre

gardens, famous: Eden, Great Dixter, the Hanging Gardens of Babylon, Jardin du Luxembourg (in Paris), the Lyceum (where Aristotle taught), Tuileries (in Paris)

garlic, adjective: alliaceous

garlic, aversion to: scorodophobia

gas: chlorofluorocarbon, choke-damp, CS gas, effluvium, ether, flatulence, hydrochlorofluorocarbon, methane, natural, nerve, sarin, tear gas

gas, adjective: gaseous

gas lighting, domestic: devised in 1792 by William Murdoch in Cornwall, using bladders of coal gas

gas lighting, domestic: first installed on a permanent basis by Samuel Clegg in
 1811, at 101, The Strand, in London

gas lighting, on the street: first installed experimentally in 1807 in London, along
 Pall Mall, then on a permanent basis in September of 1813, also in London,
 along Downing Street, Bridge Street, Great George Street and Millbank

gas lighting, workplace: devised in 1795 by William Murdoch, using jets connected
 to bladders of coal gas at the James Watt factory in Old Cumnock, Ayrshire

gas mask: invented by Sir Robert Davis in 1915

gas warfare: gases such as tear gas, chlorine gas and phosgene (lung irritants), and
 mustard gas (causing burns), were first used in World War I to break the trench
 warfare stalemate

gate, rear: postern

gay icons: Cher, Dorothy (from *The Wizard of Oz*), Jodie Foster, Judy Garland,
 Deborah Harry, Madonna, Ethel Merman, Bette Midler, Liza Minnelli, Kylie
 Minogue, Rachel Stevens, Barbra Streisand, Rufus Wainwright, Sigourney
 Weaver

Gaza Strip: disputed coastal territory (administered by the Palestinian National
 Authority since 1994) lying between Israel and Egypt

GCSE: General Certificate of Secondary Education

GE: General Electric

geese, patron saint of: Martin of Tours

gem engraver or polisher: lapidary

generals – see British generals, Roman generals, etc; soldiers

generality (of speech), adjective: phatic

Generation X: term coined by Douglas Coupland in his 1991 novel of the same
 name

Genesis: UK rock band formed in 1967; previously known as Garden Wall;
 comprised of Peter Gabriel (vocals), Tony Banks (keyboards), Michael
 Rutherford (guitar, bass and vocals), Anthony Phillips (guitar) and Chris
 Stewart (drums). Stewart, whose parents felt he should focus on his further
 education, was replaced on drums by John Silver, and then by John Mayhew
 and then by Phil Collins. Anthony Phillips was later replaced by Steve Hackett
 on guitar. Other members have included Chester Thompson (on drums) and
 Daryl Stuermer (on bass). The band went on hiatus in 1999 but reformed in
 2007 for a world tour with Collins, Banks, Rutherford, Stuermer and Thompson

genetic engineering pioneer: Dr Ian Wilmut

genetic science project: the Human Genome Project

genetics, fact: there are more than 4,000 hereditary diseases caused by defects in
 single genes

geneticists: George Wells Beadle, Francis Collins, J.B.S. Haldane, Sir Henry Harris,
 Sir Alec Jeffreys, Edward Tatum, Sir David Weatherall, Sewall Wright

genital, licker of: lecheur

genital warts: condylomata acuminata

genital wig: merkin

genitals, female: minge (slang)

genius: "Genius is childhood recaptured at will" – Charles Baudelaire; "Genius
 only thrives in the dark. Like celery" - Aldous Huxley

Gentleman Jim: nickname for the boxer James L. Corbett

gentlemen's clubs: Albemarle, Arts, Aspinall's, Athenaeum, Boodle's, Brooks's,
 Chelsea Arts, East India, Garrick, Hurlingham, Reform, Savile, White's (all in
 London)

geographers: Peter Haggett, Sir Halford Mackinder
geologists: Stephen Jay Gould, Sir Charles Lyell, Henry Sorby, Abraham Gottlob
  Werner, Josiah Whitney
geometricians: Archimedes, Euclid, Pythagoras
Georgia: republic in north-west Asia
  capital: Tbilisi
  currency: lari
  language: Georgian
  religion: Christian, Muslim
Georgia, 4th state (1788), Empire State of the South, Peach State
  capital: Atlanta
  birthplace of: Erskine Caldwell, Jimmy Carter, Ray Charles, Ty Cobb, Laurence
    Fishburne, Oliver Hardy, Hulk Hogan, Holly Hunter, Jasper Johns, Martin
    Luther King, Gladys Knight, Little Richard, Margaret Mitchell (novelist),
    Flannery O'Connor, Julia Roberts, Michael Stipe, Alice Walker, Joanne
    Woodward
  motto: 'Wisdom, justice and moderation'
  state bird: brown thrasher
  state flower: cherokee rose
  state tree: live oak
  tourist attractions: State Capitol, Stone Mountain Park, Mount State Park,
    Six Flags over Georgia, Underground Atlanta
  fact: Georgia is the first place in the world to serve a Coca-Cola (in 1887)
gerbil, adjective: cricetine
gerbil, famous: Edam (comic book character)
German: Jerry (derog.), Kraut (derog.)
German air force: Luftwaffe
German and famous: Johann Sebastian Bach, Boris Becker, Ludwig van
  Beethoven, Pope Benedict XVI, Willy Brandt, Gottlieb Daimler, Rudolf Diesel,
  Marlene Dietrich, Albrecht Dürer, Friedrich Engels (philosopher), Rainer
  Werner Fassbinder, Carl Friedrich Gauss (mathematician, astronomer and
  physicist), Johann Goethe, Steffi Graf, Günter Grass, Georg Hegel, Werner
  Herzog, Hans Holbein, Klaus Kinski, Kraftwerk, Hardy Kruger, Karl Marx,
  Max Planck (physicist), Ferdinand Porsche, Erich Remarque (novelist), Ludwig
  Renn (novelist), Karl Rundstedt (soldier), Friedrich Schiller, Gerhard Schroder,
  Michael Schumacher, Ernst Stadler (poet), Wim Wenders, Katerina Witt
  (ice skater)
  - see German composers, German film directors, German novelists, German
    painters, German playwrights, Nazis
German composers: Johann Sebastian Bach, Ludwig van Beethoven, Georg Benda,
  Johannes Brahms, Max Bruch, Christoph Willibald Gluck, Hans Werner Henze,
  Paul Hindemith, Engelbert Humperdinck, Johann Kuhnau, Felix Mendelssohn,
  Giacomo Meyerbeer, Jacques Offenbach, Carl Orff, Johann Pachelbel, Robert
  Schumann, Louis Spohr, Karlheinz Stockhausen, Richard Strauss, Richard
  Wagner, Kurt Weill
German film directors: Percy Adlon, Wolfgang Becker, Doris Dörrie, Roland
  Emmerich, Rainer Werner Fassbinder, Marc Forster, Werner Herzog, Oliver
  Hirschbiegel, Agnieszka Holland, Fritz Lang, Caroline Link, Ernst Lubitsch,
  F.W. Murnau, Wolfgang Petersen, Edgar Reitz, Leni Riefenstahl, Volker
  Schlöndorff, Robert Schwentke, Tom Tykwer, Margarethe Von Trotta, Wim
  Wenders

German measles: rubella
German novelists: Michael Ende, Theodor Fontane, Günter Grass, Erich Kästner, Heinrich Mann, Thomas Mann, Erich Maria Remarque, Christoph Martin Wieland, Christa Wolf
German painters: Lucas Cranach the Elder, Otto Dix, Albrecht Dürer, Max Ernst, Caspar David Friedrich, Matthias Grünewald, Hans Holbein the Elder, Hans Holbein the Younger, Max Liebermann, Franz Marc, Anton Mengs, Gabriele Münter, Emil Nolde
German people, adjective: Teutonic
German playwrights: Bertolt Brecht, Georg Büchner, Johann Goethe, Gerhart Hauptmann, Friedrich Hebbel, Georg Kaiser, Heinrich von Kleist, Johann Schiller, Ernst Toller, Frank Wedekind
German words used in the English language: abseil, angst, apfelstrudel, autobahn, blitzkrieg, chorale, dachshund, delicatessen, diktat, doppelgänger, edelweiss, ersatz, frankfurter, führer, glockenspiel, hausfrau, hinterland, kaiser, kaput, kindergarten, kirsch, kitsch, Lebensraum, lederhosen, leitmotif, lied, panzer, putsch, poltergeist, pretzel, quark, realpolitik, schadenfreude, schnitzel, stein, Sturm und Drang, umlaut, wanderlust, Wiener schnitzel, wunderkind, zeitgeist
Germany, Federal Republic of: country in central Europe
    capital: Berlin
    currency: euro; formerly Deutschmark
    language: German
    religion: Christian, Protestant
    government seat: Bonn
    rivers: Danube, Elbe, Neisse, Oder, Rhine, Weser
    - see Nazis; neo-Nazi party
Gestapo (acronym): Geheime Staats Polizei (German secret police)
Ghana: republic in West Africa
    capital: Accra
    currency: cedi
    language: English; Twi, Ga, Ewe
    religion: Christian, Muslim, animist
Ghanaian cloth: kente
Ghanaian diplomat: Kofi Annan
Ghanaian president: Kwame Nkrumah (in office: 1957–1960)
GHB: gamma hydroxybutyrate (date rape drug also known as Liquid E and Liquid X)
Gherkin, The: nickname for the 30 St Mary Axe building in the City of London designed by Sir Norman Foster and Ken Shuttleworth. The building is also known as The Swiss Re Tower
ghetto, first: that which was established in 1516 in the Jewish quarter of Venice
ghost: duppy, ghoul, juba (American negro), phantom, spectre, spirit, spook, wraith
ghost story writer: Montague Rhodes James
ghost, returned from the dead: revenant
ghosts: Banquo, the Canterville Ghost (from the Oscar Wilde story), Casper, Elvira Condomine (from Noël Coward's *Blithe Spirit*), Hamlet's father (the king of Denmark), Jacob Marley, Moaning Myrtle (from *Harry Potter*), Nearly Headless Nick (from *Harry Potter*), Sam Wheat (played by Patrick Swayze in *Ghost*)
ghosts, belief in: eidolism
ghosts, fact: The British Tourist Association publishes a list of 82 haunted inns and hotels

ghosts, fact: eighty per cent of ghosts are sighted between 3pm and 4pm

ghosts, fear of: phasmophobia

ghosts, three distinct types: poltergeist, "imprint" ghost, haunting

ghostwriters: Andrew Crofts ("the king of British ghostwriters" – *The Daily Telegraph*), Dougal Douglas (from Muriel Spark's *The Ballad of Peckham Rye*)

giants: Alifanfaron (from *Don Quixote*), Anak (Old Testament), Antæus (Greek mythology), Argus (Greek mythology), Atlas (Greek mythology), Balan, Bellerus, BFG (Big Friendly Giant), Blunderbore, Briareus (Greek mythology), Brontes (Greek mythology), Colbronde (Danish), Cormoran (Cornish), Cottys (Greek mythology), Cyclops (Greek mythology), Despair (from *Pilgrim's Progress*), Enceladus (Greek mythology), Ephialtes (Greek mythology), Ferragus, Sir Fierabras, Gargantua, Gog, Goliath, Rubeus Hagrid (c/o *Harry Potter*), Irus (Greek mythology), Jolly Green Giant, Lurch (from *The Addams Family*), Magog, Mimir (Norse mythology), Morgante, Herman Munster (from TV's *The Munsters*), Oceanus, Og (Old Testament), Orgoglio, Orion (Greek mythology), Pallas (Greek mythology), Pantagruel, Polyphemus (Greek mythology), Titan, troll, Typhœus (Greek mythology), Ymir (Scandinavian mythology)

giants, tribes of: Anakim, Cyclops, Nephilim, Rephaim

GIB: good in bed

gibbon, adjective: hylobatine

Gibraltar: ceded to Britain in perpetuity under the 1713 Treaty of Utrecht

Gilbert & Sullivan: writers of operettas; from 1871 the duo produced 14 comic operas together

gin: Beefeater, frog's wine (slang), Gordon's, London, Plymouth, Seagram's Extra Dry, Tanqueray

giraffe, adjective: artiodactylous

giraffe, collective noun: corps, herd

giraffe, famous: Jeb

giraffe, female: cow

giraffe, male: bull

giraffe, sound: bleat, grunt

giraffe, young: calf

girl: angel, Aphrodite, arm candy, babe, beanie (Anglo-Jamaican slang), belle, Betty, bimbette, bint (derog.), bird, bitch, bonny hinny (Geordie compliment), burner (very sexy), cat, chick, colleen (Irish), crumpet, cupcake, cutie, deuce (not so attractive), dime (attractive), dish, dog, doll, dorkarella, dreamboat, filly, floozy, fox, glamazon, hinny (Geordie), honey, hottie, hussy, knockout, ladette, lass, Lolita, matron, minx, moll, nymphet, ocean pearl (CRS), petticoat, princess, scrubber, sexpot, siren, skirt, sylph, temptress, vamp, Venus, vixen, wench, wren (attractive version)

- see woman

girl groups: Alisha's Attic, All Saints, Andrews Sisters, Atomic Kitten, Bananarama, Crystals, Destiny's Child, Dixie Chicks, Girls Aloud, Martha and the Vandellas, Marvelettes, Mis-Teeq, Nolans, Pointer Sisters, Ronettes, Salt-n-Pepa, Shangri-Las, Shirelles, Spice Girls, Sugababes, Supremes, T.A.T.u., Vandellas, Weather Girls, Wilson Phillips

Girl Guides: founded in 1910 by Lord Robert Baden-Powell

girls, fear of (especially young girls): parthenophobia

girls, patron saint of: Agnes of Rome and Maria Goretti

girls' schools, UK; top of the line: Badminton School (Bristol), Benenden School (Cranbrook, Kent), Cheltenham Ladies' College (Gloucestershire), Edgbaston

High School for Girls Birmingham, Roedean School (Brighton), St Leonard's
    School (St Andrews, Fife)
Giselle: ballet composed by Adolphe Adam, first produced in 1841 in Paris
glacial crack: crevasse
glacial deposit: drift
glacial hill: drumlin
glacial tower: serac
gladiators, famous: Maximus Decimus Meridius (played by Russell Crowe in
    Gladiator), Publius Ostorius, Spartacus
gladiator with net: retiarius
glance: oeillade (from the French)
gland: adrenal, endocrine gland, ovary, pancreas, parathyroid, pituitary, tear gland,
    testis, thyroid, uterus (but not the lymph gland, which is not a gland)
gland, adjective: adenoid
gland-shaped: adeniform
glands, inflammation of: adenitis
glands, study of: adenology
glandular fever: mononucleosis
Glasgow, birthplace of: Stanley Baxter, Gordon Brown, Gerard Butler, Menzies
    Campbell, Robert Carlyle, Billy Connolly, Kenny Dalglish, Donovan, Sheena
    Easton, Rikki Fulton (comedian), Iain Hamilton (composer), R.D. Laing, Lulu,
    Alistair MacLean (novelist), John Martyn (singer), James McAvoy, Allan
    Pinkerton, Eddi Reader, Jimmy Somerville, Nigel Tranter (historian)
Glasgow groups: Average White Band, Aztec Camera, Belle & Sebastian, The Blue
    Nile, Deacon Blue, Del Amitri, Dogs Die in Hot Cars, Franz Ferdinand, Midge
    Ure, Mogwai, Orange Juice, Simple Minds. Snow Patrol, Texas, Travis, Wet
    Wet Wet
    - see Scottish groups
glass, adjective: vitreous, vitric
glass, diamond-shaped pane: quarry
glass, fear of: crystallopbobia
glass, volcanic: obsidian
glass agent: glazier
glass engravers: Laurence Whistler, Simon Whistler
glass tile used in mosaics: tessera
glassware, crystal: Swarovski
glassware, frosted: Lalique
glassware, heat resistant: Pyrex
glassware designers: Émile Gallé, René Lalique
Glastonbury: Annual music festival held over a three-day period in Glastonbury,
    rural Somerset. Officially known as the Glastonbury Festival of Contemporary
    Performing Arts – and locally as the Pilton Festival – the event was set up by
    Andrew Kerr, the Methodist dairy farmer Michael Eavis and Arabella Churchill
    (granddaughter of Sir Winston), and first unfolded over the weekend of 19–20
    September, 1970. The first acts to perform there included T. Rex, Amazing
    Blondel, Quintessence, Sam Apple Pie and Steamhammer.
global warming, fact: in 1200, Europe was two degrees warmer than it is now, with
    vineyards as far north as Northumberland; in the latter part of the 16th century,
    during the 'Little Ice Age,' storms increased by 85%
Gloucestershire, administrative centre: Gloucester
glove maker: glover

glove puppets – see hand puppets, puppets

glow-worm, adjective: lampyrid

glue (rubber-based): invented in 1850

glue (synthetic, epoxide resin-based): invented in 1958

glue, adjective: glutinous

glue ear: otitis media

glutton: bellygod, chowhound, cormorant, gastrolater, gormandizer, gourmand, gundygut, pig, tenterbelly, trencherman

gluttons, famous: Billy Bunter, Mr Creosote (played by Terry Jones in *Monty Python's The Meaning of Life*)

GMD: Guided Missile Destroyer

gnat, collective noun: cloud, horde

gnat, killing of: culicicide, culicide

goalkeepers: Gordon Banks, Fabien Barthez, Iker Casillas, Renat Dasaev, Robert Green (who famously coerced a ball into his own goal while playing against the United States in the 2010 World Cup), Bruce Grobelaar, David James, Oliver Kahn, Sepp Maier, Bayern Munich, Peter Schmeichel, David Seaman, Ricardo Zamora

goat: angora, ibex, markhor (North Indian), mountain goat, Rocky Mountain goat, Spanish ibex

goat, adjective: caprine, hircine

goat, collective noun: tribe, trip

goat, female: nanny

goat, male: billy

goat, smell of: caprylic (adjective)

goat, young: kid

goat hair: angora, mohair

goat leather: chamois, morocco

goat murdered on orders of the British Ministry of Agriculture: Misty (of Dumfries)

goat-legged god: Pan

goats, famous: Misty, Zlateh (from Isaac Bashevis Singer's *Zlateh the Goat*)

Go-Between, The (1953 novel by L.P. Hartley); opening line: "The past is a foreign country: they do things differently there"

God: Abba, Allah, Almighty, Deity, Dominus, Father, Jehovah, the Lord, Man Upstairs, Monad, Our Lord, the Supreme Being, Yahweh

god, belief in: deism (based on reason rather than personal interaction)

god, belief in: theism (based on personal interaction)

god, fear of: theophobia

god, government of: thearchy

god, juice of: ichor

god, manifestation of: theophany

God, Son of: Jesus Christ, David Icke (self-proclaimed)

god in human form: numen

god with elephant head: Ganesa

God's work: "Not only does God play dice, but He sometimes throws them where they cannot be seen" - Stephen Hawking

gods, home of: Asgard (Norse mythology), Olympus (Greek mythology)

gods, queen of: Hera (Greek mythology), Juno (Roman mythology)

gold: figure denoting one million units in record sales - see platinum

gold, adjective: aureate, auric

gold-coloured: aureate

GoldenEye (1995 James Bond film), famous line: M (Judi Dench) to James Bond (Pierce Brosnan): "I think you're a sexist, misogynist dinosaur. A relic of the Cold War, whose boyish charms, though wasted on me, obviously appealed to the young lady I sent out to evaluate you"

goldfinch, collective noun: charm

goldfish, adjective: cyprinid

goldfish, collective noun: troubling

goldsmiths: Benvenuto Cellini, Johannes Gutenberg, Nicholas Hilliard, Charles Tiffany, Andrea del Verrocchio

goldsmiths, patron saint of: Dunstan

goldsmith's crucible: cruset

golf clubs: baffy (a No.5 wood), blade (a type of putter), brassie (No.2 wood), iron (any club with a metal head), mashie (No. 5 iron), mashie iron (No.4 iron), mashie niblick (No. 7 iron), midiron (No. 2 iron), mid mashie (No.3 iron), putter (No.10 iron), spade mashie (No.6 iron), spoon (No.3 wood)

golf terms: divot, fairway, gentleman's game, green, handicap, rough, tee, whiff (to miss the ball completely)

golf courses, countries with most per ground area: 1) Singapore; 2) UK (accounting for 10% of the world's golf courses)

golf events: Masters, Ryder Cup, St Andrews Trophy, US Open

golfers: Tommy Armour, Severiano Ballesteros, Patty Berg, James Braid, Michael Campbell, David Carter, Darren Clarke, Sir Henry Cotton, Fred Couples, John Daly ("the Gazza of golf"), Laura Davies, Sir Nick Faldo, Raymond Floyd, Jim Furyk, Bernard Gallacher, Walter Hagen, Todd Hamilton, Pádraig Harrington, Ben Hogan, Tony Jacklin, Bobby Jones, Nancy Lopez, Sandy Lyle, Carl Mason, Phil Mickelson, Colin Montgomerie, Jack Nicklaus, Greg Norman, Se Ri Pak, Arnold Palmer, Jesper Parnevik, Gary Player, Nick Price, Gene Sarazen, Vijay Singh, Sam Snead, Annika Sorenstam (the first woman for 58 years to participate in a men's professional tour event – i.e. the Bank of America Colonial Tournament in Fort Worth, Texas, in May 2003), Lee Trevino, Jean Van de Velde, Harry Vardon, Tom Watson, Lee Westwood, Eldrick 'Tiger' Woods, Ian Woosnam

Gondoliers, The: operetta by W.S. Gilbert and Arthur Sullivan, first produced in 1889 in London

gondolier's song: barcarolle

Gone With the Wind (1939 film), famous lines: Rhett Butler (Clark Gable): "Frankly, my dear, I don't give a damn"; Scarlett O'Hara (Vivien Leigh): "I'll go home and I'll think of some way to get him back. After all, tomorrow is another day" [last line]

gong: established in Indonesia by the 9th century; reached Europe by at least the 18th century

gong, centre piece: boss

gong, Chinese: tam-tam

gong, drumstick: knobbed or padded beater

gong player for the J. Arthur Rank Organisation: from 1935 until 1947: British heavyweight boxing champion Bombardier Billy Wells (known as "Beautiful Billy"); 1947–1955: wrestler and stuntman Phil Nieman; 1955–2001: amateur champion wrestler Ken Richmond (the sound of the gong being struck was actually supplied by the world famous percussionist James Blades)

gonorrhoea: the clap

Gonzo journalists: Jon Ronson, P.J. O'Rourke, Hunter S. Thompson
good: accomplished, brilliant, consummate, cool, dope, excellent, exceptional, exemplary, first-rate, phat, righteous, stunning, sweet
good, adjective: boniform
Good Book, The: nickname for The Bible
Good Food Guide, The: founded by Raymond Postgate
Good Life, The: TV sitcom set in Surbiton in which Tom Good gives up his job as a draughtsman to live off the land (i.e. his small back garden). Known as *The Good Neighbors* in the US
  created and written by John Esmonde and Bob Larbey
  broadcast: 4 April 1975–10 June 1978 on the BBC
  cast: Richard Briers (Tom Good), Felicity Kendall (Barbara Good), Paul Eddington (Jerry Leadbeatter), Penelope Keith (Margot Leadbeatter), Reginald Marsh (Sir Andrew), Moyra Fraser (Felicity)
good Samaritan: Amélie Poulain (from the film *Amélie*)
  - see philanthropists
Good Time Charlie: nickname for King Charles II
goodbye: adieu (French), adiós (Spanish), arrivederci (Italian), auf wiedensehen (German), au revoir (French), ciao (Italian), do svidaniia (Russian), do widzenia (Polish), ¡hasta la vista! (Spanish), pip! pip! (old-fashioned), sayonara (Japanese), selamat tinggal (Malay), shalom (Hebrew), zayt gezunt (Yiddish), zai jian (Mandarin)
Google: founded in 1998 by Stanford University students Larry Page and Sergey Brin (as a graduate project)
Goons, The, members: Michael Bentine, Spike Milligan, Harry Secombe, Peter Sellers
Goon Show, The: radio comedy show transmitted on the BBC's Home Service, first broadcast in May of 1951 under the title *Crazy People*. The title was switched to *The Goon Show* (dreamed up by Spike Milligan) in June of 1952. An anarchic and surreal compendium of sketches, the enterprise constantly courted controversy, with Peter Sellers' impersonation of Winston Churchill banned in 1954
goose, adjective: anserine
goose, collective noun: gaggle, skein (in flight), wedge (when flying in a 'V' formation)
goose, famous: Gussy (from *Charlotte's Web*)
goose, female: goose
goose, male: gander
goose, young: gosling
Gordonstoun: public school in the north of Scotland founded in 1933 by Dr Kurt Hahn
Gordonstoun pupils: Prince Andrew, William Boyd, Prince Charles, Lara Croft, Prince Edward, Prince Philip, Zara Phillips, Suzanne Turley (originally refused admission by social workers)
Gorgons: Euryale, Medusa, Stheno
gorilla: eastern lowland gorilla, mountain gorilla, silverback, western lowland gorilla
gorilla, adjective: pongid
gorilla, famous: Binti Jua (famous for saving a human boy), Colo (first gorilla born in captivity), Gorilla Stan (from TV's *The Zone*), King Kong, Koko (famous for communicating in sign language)
gorilla conservationist: Dian Fossey (killed by poachers in 1985)
goshawk, male: tiercel

gospel singers: Yolanda Adams, Professor Alex Bradford, Rev. James Cleveland, Edwin Hawkins Singers, Mahalia Jackson, The Staple Singers
gossip queens: Nigel Dempster, Bonnie Fuller, Sheila Graham, Hedda Hopper, J.J. Hunsecker (as played by Burt Lancaster in *Sweet Smell of Success*), Louella Parsons, Liz Smith, Walter Winchell
Gothic painter: Matthias Grünewald
Gothic queen: Tamora
goty: acronym for getting older, thinking young (member of social group)
gout: podagra (especially of the big toe)
governesses: Jane Eyre, Maria (from *The Sound of Music*)
governess, collective noun: galaxy
governor general, mode of verbal address: Your Excellency
government by angels: angelocracy
government by athletes: athletocracy
government by best men: aristarchy
government by bishops: episcopacy
government by children: paedarchy
government by demons: demonocracy
government by gods: thearchy, theocracy
government by old men: gerontocracy
government by one person: autocracy, monocracy
government by priests: hierocracy
government by prostitutes: pornocracy
government by the few: oligarchy
government by the military: stratocracy
government by the nobility: aristocracy
government by the people: democracy
government by the poor: ptochocracy
government by the rich: plutocracy
government by the workers: ergatocracy
government by two independent authorities: diarchy
government by women: matriarchy
governor, adjective: gubernatorial
GPS: Global Positioning Satellite/System
Graces: Aglaia, Euphrosyne, Thalia
graffiti artists: Banksy, Jean-Michel Basquiat, Keith Haring, The Invader (anonymous artist known for his 'Space Invader' mosaics), 'the Plug'
grain-eating: granivorous
grammarian: Lindley Murray
grammarian, collective noun: conjunction
gramophone: invented in 1887 by Emil Berliner
Grand Canyon: spectacular gorge on the Colorado River in northern Arizona, which plunges to over one mile in depth and at its widest point is 18 miles across
grand slam, first person to win: Donald Budge
grandmother, young: metrona
grandparents, patron saint of: Anne and Joachim
grape, adjective: uvic, uval, uva
grape grower: viniculturist
grape skin: epicarp, exocarp
grape vine disease: phylloxera
grape-shaped: aciniform

grapes, shaped like a cluster of; adjective: botryoid(al)
graphic artist: Jamie Reid
graphics designers: Saul Bass, Neville Brody, Eric Gill
grass, adjective: graminaceous, poaceous
grass, artificial: Astroturf
grass-eating: graminivorous
grasshopper, adjective: acridid
grasshopper, famous: Hopper (from the 1998 film *A Bug's Life*)
grasshopper, sound: chirp, pitter, stridulation
grasshopper, young: pup
gratitude: "Gratitude is merely the secret hope of further favours" - François de la Rochefoucauld
graves, fear of: taphophobia
grave robbers: William Burke, William Hare
gravedigger: Robert 'Old Scarlett' (who buried both Catherine of Aragon and Mary, Queen of Scots)
gravediggers, patron saint of: Anthony the Abbot
gravity, aversion to: barophobia
gravity, opposite of: cosmological repulsion
gravity theorist: Sir Isaac Newton
Great Fire of London: 1666; death toll: eight
Great Lakes: Erie, Huron, Michigan, Ontario, Superior
Great Profile, the: nickname for John Barrymore
Great Stone Face: nickname for Buster Keaton
Great Train Robbery: spectacular robbery carried out on 8 August, 1963, at Bridego Railway Bridge, Ledburn, in Buckinghamshire, England, where £2.6 million was stolen. The 15-member gang, led by Bruce Reynolds, included Ronnie Biggs, Charlie Wilson, Jimmy Hussey, John Wheater, Brian Field, Jimmy White, Tommy Wisbey, Gordon Goody and Buster Edwards. No guns were used in the hold-up, although the train's driver, Jack Mills, was hit over the head with iron bars and was forced to retire. Thirteen of the thieves were caught and imprisoned, although Reynolds, Biggs and Wilson all later escaped. The stolen money was never recovered
great white shark, largest ever documented: 21ft long (caught off Cuba)
great white shark, number of teeth: 3,000
Great White Way, the: nickname for Broadway
Greece, adjective: Hellenic
Greece: republic in south-eastern Europe
    capital: Athens
    currency: euro; formerly: drachma
    language: Greek
    nickname: Hellas
    religion: Eastern Greek Orthodox
Greece, lover of: philhellene
Greek alphabet: alpha (a); beta (b); gamma (g); delta (d); epsilon (e); zeta (z); eta (h); theta (th); iota (i); kappa (k); lambda (l); mu (m); nu (n); xi (x); omicron (o); pi (p); rho (r); sigma (s); tau (t); upsilon (u); phi (ph); chi (ch); psi (ps); omega (o)
Greek and famous: Spiro Agnew (son of a Greek immigrant), Theo Angelopoulos (filmmaker), Jennifer Aniston (of Greek descent), Archimedes, Aristophanes, Aristotle, Michael Cacoyannis (filmmaker), Cleänthes, Cleopatra, King

Constantine, Michael Dukakis (the son of Greek immigrants), Olympia Dukakis
(the daughter of Greek immigrants), Euclid, Euripides, Hipparchus, Homer,
Nikos Kazantzakis (novelist and poet), Vicky Leandros (singer), Melina
Mercouri, George Michael (of Greek descent), Nana Mouskouri, Stavros
Niarchos (ship owner), Aristotle Onassis, Georgios Papadopoulos, Andreas
Papandreou, Irene Papas, Parmenides of Elea, Prince Philip the Duke of
Edinburgh (of Greek extraction), Plato, Plutarch, Protagoras, Pythagoras, Demis
Roussos, Telly Savalas (of Greek extraction, real name: Aristotle Savalas),
Socrates, Sophocles, Mikis Theodorakis, Thespis, Timon of Athens, Vangelis,
Yanni (musician and pianist), Zeno of Citium, Zeno of Elea, Zeno of Sidon
Greek composers: Mikis Theodorakis, Vangelis, Yannis Xenakis
Greek dance: syrtaki
Greek dramatists: Aeschylus, Aristophanes, Euripides, Sophocles
Greek historians: Herodotus, Plutarch, Xenophon
Greek maidens: Hesperides
Greek philosophers: Aristotle, Epicurus, Plato, Plutarch, Protagoras, Pythagoras,
  Socrates, Thales of Miletus, Zeno of Citium, Zeno of Elea
Greek poets: Alcaeus, Antimachus, Archilochus, Eratosthenes, Hesiod, Homer,
  Ibycus, Pindar, Sappho, Simonides of Ceos, Thespis
Greek restaurant: taverna
Greek vampire: stringes
Greek vase: amphora
Greek warriors: Achilles, Agamemnon, Ajax, Hector, Jason, Paris, Perseus
Green Goddess: nickname for Diana Moran
Greenland: world's largest island, lying off the north-east coast of North America
  and situated largely within the Arctic Circle; a former Danish colony granted
  full self-government in 1981
Greenland, capital: Nuuk (formerly known as Godthaab – until 1979)
Greenland, language: Greenlandic
greenness: virescence
Greenpeace: environmental organisation founded in Canada in 1971
Greenpeace ship: Rainbow Warrior
greeting with a friendly knock of the fist: spud
Grenada: island state in the Caribbean
    capital: St George's
    currency: East Caribbean dollar
    language: English
    religion: Christian
Grenada invasion: 1983
Grenoble: the economic and intellectual capital of the French Alps
Grenoble, birthplace of: Henri Stendhal
Grenoble tourist attractions: Musée de la Résistance et de la Déportation, Musée
  de Peinture et de Sculpture, Palais de Justice
Greyfriars School pupil: Billy Bunter
greyhound, collective noun: leash
greyhound, sound: roo
greying hair (prematurely): poliosis
grief: "Happiness is beneficial for the body but it is grief that develops the powers
  of the mind" - Marcel Proust
grinding of teeth: bruxism
grooms, patron saints of: Louis of France and Nicholas

grooved (round the edge, such as coin): contorniate (adjective)
grooved wheel (as in a pulley-block): sheave
ground, growing on: geogenous (adjective)
ground, level: campestral (adjective)
groundhog: woodchuck
grouse, adjective: gallinaceous, tetraonine
grouse, collective noun: drumming
grouse, sound: drum
grouse, young: cheeper, chick
grunge groups: Alice in Chains, Babes in Toyland, Bastard, Cosmic Psychos
     (Australian), Helmet, Hole, Membranes (British), Nirvana, Pearl Jam,
     Soundgarden, Stone Temple Pilots
GCSE: General Certificate of Secondary Education
Guardian, The: newspaper (originally known as *The Manchester Guardian*),
     founded by John Edward Taylor in 1821 and first published on 5 May
Guatemala: republic in Central America
     capital: Guatemala City
     currency: quetzal
     language: Spanish
     religion: Roman Catholic
Guernica: market town in Spain that suffered the first onslaught of saturation
     bombing on European soil. For three hours on 26 April 1937, German and
     Italian planes bombed the Basque town, killing 1,645 people and destroying
     most of the buildings. Pablo Picasso commemorated the tragedy with his
     famous painting (1937) of the same name
guerrillas: Ernesto 'Che' Guevara, Abimael Guzman (of the Shining Path)
guerrilla group: The Shining Path (led by Abimael Guzman)
guillotine: contraption designed for beheading, championed by the French physician
     Joseph Ignace Guillotin and largely based on the Yorkshire device the Halifax
     Gibbet. The guillotine was first set up on 11 April 1792 in France. It was last
     used at the Baumettes Prison in Marseilles on 10 September 1977 (on the
     murderer Hamida Djandoubi)
Guinea: republic in West Africa
     capital: Conakry
     currency: African franc
     language: French
     religion: Muslim, animist
Guinea-Bissau: republic in West Africa
     capital: Bissau
     currency: peso
     language: Portuguese, Cape Verde creole
     religion: animist, Muslim
guinea fowl, sound: cry
guinea fowl, young: keet
guinea pig: cavy
guinea pig, sound: squeak, whistle
Guinness Book of World Records: co-founded in 1955 by the twin brothers Norris
     and Ross McWhirter
Guinness chief executive, disgraced: Ernest Saunders
guitar: invented in 1850
guitar, number of strings: six

guitar picker: fingerpick (a plectrum attached to the finger), plectrum

guitar types: acoustic, Airline, bottleneck, classical, Dobro resonator, electric,
Fender jazz bass, Fender Stratocaster, Gibson, Gibson Les Paul, Gibson LS,
Godin, Martin D.35, Montgomery Ward Airline, Rickenbacker (vintage rock 'n'
roll), slide guitar, Spanish guitar, steel string, Stratocaster, Taylor, Washburn
twelve-string

guitar-like instruments: balalaika, banjo, gittern, samisen, ukulele, vihuela, viola
da mano

guitarists: Howard Alden, Chet Atkins, Jeff Beck, Adrian Belew, Ritchie Blackmore,
Julian Bream, Big Bill Broonzy, Kenny Burrell, J.J. Cale, Charlie Christian, Eric
Clapton, Eddie Cochran, Allen Collins, Ry Cooder, Paco de Lucia (flamenco),
Bo Diddley, Duane Eddy, José Feliciano, Jerry Garcia, Buddy Guy, Jimi
Hendrix, Elmore James, Lonnie Johnson, Robert Johnson, Barney Kessel,
Albert King, B.B. King, Eddie Lang, John McLaughlin, Jimmy Page, Paco Peña
(flamenco), Joe Perry (of Aerosmith), Bonnie Raitt, Vini Reilly, Django
Reinhardt, Randy Rhodes, Carlos Santana, Andrés Segovia, Eddie Van Halen,
Muddy Waters, Hank Williams Jr., John Williams, Frank Zappa

gulag: Magadan (the most brutal of the Siberian labour camps)

Gulf War: 2 August 1990–28 February 1991 (when the ceasefire came just 43 days
after the start of the allied air campaign)

gull, adjective: laroid

gullet: oesophagus

Gulliver's Travels: seminal satire by Jonathan Swift, first published in 1726.
The narrative of travels is divided into four parts, taking place in the islands
of Lilliput (where the inhabitants are six inches high), Brobdingnag (where
the natives are as tall as steeples) and the flying island of Laputa and its
neighbouring continent and capital Lagado. In the third part, the narrator, the
surgeon Lemuel Gulliver, also visits Glubbdubrib, the Island of Sorcerers, and
meets up with the immortal and unhappy race of Struldbrugs. The last part
finds Gulliver in the land of the Houyhnhnms, a country inhabited by level-
headed horses and the disgusting human-like Yahoos. It was this chapter in
particular that caused outrage among Swift's literary contemporaries.

gum (of the mouth): gingiva (technical term)

gums, adjective: gingival, uletic

gums, study of: periodontics

gum inflammation: gingivitis, periodontitis

gun: ack-ack, air rifle, AK47, archy, assault rifle, automatic, BB gun, Beretta,
blaster (sci-fi term), blunderbuss, breech-loader, Bren gun, broomhandle,
Browning, canon, Colt, Colt Lightning, Colt Peacemaker, Colt Python, double-
barrelled gun, field gun, Five-SeveN (with 20 times the range and penetrating
power of the most powerful militaty pistols in use), flintlock, .44 Magnum
(favoured by Dirty Harry), front loader, Glock, harquebus, Heckler & Koch
USP, howitzer, Lewis gun, Luger, Mauser, MP5 (assault rifle), musket, petronel
(16th century), piece, pistol, pom-pom, pump-action shotgun, repeater, revolver,
rifle, SA80 rifle (the unreliable type used by the British army which jammed in
Sierra Leone), semi-automatic, shotgun, six-shooter, Smith and Wesson, SPG
(self-propelled gun), Sten gun, submachine gun, taser (which fires electric
darts), tommy-gun, Thompson, tranquilliser gun, Uzi, Walther PPK (as used by
James Bond), Winchester

gunfighters: Butch Cassidy (aka Robert Leroy Parker), Billy Clanton, Ike Clanton,
'Old Man' Clanton, Phineas Clanton, Wyatt Earp, Bob Ford (cousin and

assassin of Jesse James), Pat Garrett, Wild Bill Hickok (aka James Buter),
Doc Holliday (aka John Henry), Frank James, Jesse James, Calamity Jane,
Harry Longbaugh (aka the Sundance Kid), Annie Oakley, Cole Younger,
James Younger, John Younger, Robert Younger
– see cowboys

gunfire facts: in 1993, 14,000 Americans were killed by gunfire in 1997, 21,259
Americans were killed by gunfire in 1998, somebody in the US was killed by
gunfire every 18 minutes
    average annual figures for death by gunfire in the US: 11,127
    average annual figures for death by gunfire in the UK: 68
    average annual figures for death by gunfire in Canada: 165

gunners, patron saint of: Barbara

Gunpowder Plot: 5 November 1605, devised by Robert Catesby and Guy Fawkes

Guns N' Roses: US rock band formed in Los Angeles in 1985; comprised of Axl
Rose (vocals; real name: William Bailey), Izzy Stradlin (guitar; real name:
Jeff Isabelle), Michael 'Duff' McKagan (bass), Slash (guitar; real name: Saul
Hudson) and Steven Adler (drums)

gunslingers – see cowboys, gunfighters

gunsmith – see firearms and munition inventors

gurus: Deepak Chopra, Dev, Maharishi Mahesh Yogi, Bhagwan Rajneesh, Sai Baba

gushing: scaturient

gut, adjective: visceral

Guyana: republic in north-east South America; formerly known as British Guiana
(until 1966)
    capital: Georgetown
    currency: dollar
    language: English
    religion: Christian, Hindu

GWB: general well-being

gymnasiums: The Curzons Gym, The Fitness Exchange, Fitness First, Gold's Gym,
Holmes Place, LA Fitness

gymnasium, Greek or Roman: palaestra

gymnasium equipment: barbell, dumbbell, exercise bike, Nautilus, stabilising ball,
Swiss ball, stairmaster, treadmaster, treadmill

gymnasts: Dmitri Bilozerchev, Olga Bitcherova, Svetlana Boginskaya, Nadia
Comaneci, Olga Korbut, Yuri Korolev, Mary Lou Retton, Peter Sumi, Marco
Torrès, Ludmila Turischeva

gypsies: Carmen, Esméralda (c/o *The Hunchback of Notre Dame*), Heathcliff

gypsy, PC term: Romany

H

H-shaped: zygal

hacker: black hat, grey hat, script kiddie, white hat

hackers (aka cyber armies), fact: hackers have been trained to disable foreign
electricity grids, transport networks, emergency services, etc, by the governments
of China, Taiwan, Singapore and South Korea

hackers, famous: Matthew Bevan, Gary McKinnon (accused in May 2006 of
accessing 97 US government computers), Christopher Pile ('the Black Baron')

hacking tools: exploit, root kit, trojan horse, vulnerability scanner

haddock, young: scrod

haematologist: Donnall Thomas
haemorrhoids, patron saint of: Fiacre
haemorrhoids, troubled by: cresty (adjective)
Haig whisky, slogan: 'Don't Be Vague – Ask For Haig'
hair: pez (black slang), righteous moss, thatch, wig
hair, adjective: capillary, crinal, trichoid
hair, aversion to: chaetophobia, trichopathophobia
hair, covered with: pilose (adjective)
hair, premature greying of: poliosis
hair, study of: trichology
hair, to remove: depilate
hair accessories: bobby pin, brush, comb, hair dryer, hair extension, hairgrip, hairpin, kirby grip
hair pulling: trichotillomania
hairdresser: barber, crimper, hair bender, stylist
hairdresser, adjective: tonsorial
hairdressers, famous: Madame du Barry, Nicky Clarke, Beverly Cobella, Daniel Galvin, Anthony Mascolo, Jon Peters, Vidal Sassoon, Trevor Sorbie, Charles Worthington
hairdressers: Blades, Eclipse Hair & Beauty, Essensuals, Hebe Hair Salon, Jeffery & Michael, Regis, Sanrizz, Supercuts, Toni & Guy, Trumper's, Vidal Sassoon, Worthington Charles
hairdressers, patron saint of: Martin de Porres
hairdressing, adjective: tonsorial
hairs, average number lost on the human head every 24 hours: 65
hairstyles: abstract, Afro, Afro puffs, American Indian, Argentine ducktail, bangs, beehive, bob, braids, bun, buzz cut, chignon, comb-over, conk, contour, corn rows, crew cut, crimps, Croydon facelift, curtains, dreadlocks, duck's arse, elephant trunk, Eton crop, executive contour, flat-top, flop, fringe, jheri curl (a loose curl popularised by blacks in the 1980s), kiss curl, Mohican, mullet, pageboy, perm, pompadour, ponytail, quiff, Rastafarian, samurai-cut, scalp lock (as in Mohican), shingle, vanguard, widow's peak
hairy: crinose, hirsute
Haiti: republic occupying the west side of the Caribbean island of Hispaniola (the world's first black republic)
	capital: Port-au-Prince
	currency: gourde
	language: French and Haitian creole
	religion: Roman Catholic, voodoo
Haitian dictators: Jean-Bertrand Aristide, François 'Papa Doc' Duvalier, Toussaint Louverture
Haitian-born rapper: Wyclef Jean
Hallowe'en: the eve of All Saints' Day, celebrated on 31 October
hallucinatory drug: LSD, methylenedioxymethamphetamine
Hamburg, birthplace of: Johannes Brahms, Karl Lagerfeld, Felix Mendelssohn, Helmut Schmidt, Douglas Sirk
Hamburg river: Elbe
Hamlet: The Melancholy Dane, Prince Amled, Prince of Denmark, Prince of Jutland
Hamlet cigar slogan: 'Happiness Is A Cigar Called Hamlet'
hammer: beetle, claw hammer, gavel, jackhammer, mallet, plexor, sledgehammer, steam hammer, tenderizer, tilt-hammer

hammer handle: helve

hammer head: face (striking end), peen (curved or wedge-shaped end)

hammer used by an auctioneer or judge: gavel

hammer used to test reflexes: plessor, plexor

hammer-shaped: malleiform

Hampshire, administrative centre: Winchester

hamster, famous: Ben (comic book character), Bruce (comic book character), Chuck (comic book character), Clint (comic book character), Jackie (comic book character)

hamstrings, adjective: popliteal

Hancock's Half Hour: classic TV comedy series featuring the dour and demonstrative histrionics of Tony Hancock, evolved from a 1954 radio show
    broadcast: 7 July 1956–30 June 1961 on BBC scripted by Alan Simpson and Ray Galton
    cast: Tony Hancock, Bill Kerr, Sidney James, Patricia Hayes, Irene Handl, Valentine Dyall, Hermione Baddeley, Warren Mitchell, Kenneth Williams, Hattie Jacques

HAND: Have A Nice Day

hand, adjective: chiral, manual, palmate (especially with the fingers spread out)

hand cleaner: Swarfega

hand parts: fingers, knuckles, palm, purlicue (space between extended thumb and index finger), thumb

hand puppets: Basil Brush, Emu, Judy, Kermit, Lamb Chop, Punch, Sooty, Sweep

handbags: Balenciaga Classique, Balenciaga Lariat, Bayswater, Celine, Chloé Paddington, Dior, Fendi, Gucci, Hermès Birkin, Hermès Kelly, Helmut Lang, Miu Miu, Prada, Roxanne, Tod's, Louis Vuitton

handbook: enchiridion

Handel's Messiah: oratorio by George Frideric Handel, first performed in 1742 in Dublin

Handel's Water Music: orchestral suite written by George Frideric Handel to accompany a 1717 ceremonial party for King George I on the river Thames

handle, adjective: ansate

handsome and famous: Adonis – see sex symbols, male

handwriting: chirography

handwriting, adjective: calligraphic, calligraphical

handwriting, art of: calligraphy

handwriting, bad: cacography

handwriting, divination by: graphomancy, graphtomancy

handwriting, study of: graphology

hanging, UK; last people hanged in Britain: Gwynne Evans and Peter Allen, on 13 August, 1964

hanging, USA: the last person hanged in the USA was Billy Bailey, executed in Delaware on 25 January 1996

hanging, USA; fact: states that still conduct hanging as capital punishment: New Hampshire, Washington

hangmen: William Calcraft (Britain's chief hangman between 1829 and 1874), Albert Pierrepoint (the fastest hangman in Britain, whose victims included Derek Bentley, Ruth Ellis, Timothy John Evans and Lord Haw-Haw)

hangover cure: Antipokhmelin (aka RU-21)

Hanoi Jane: nickname for Jane Fonda

happiest nations: 1) Australia; 2) USA; 3) Venezuela; 4) Kuwait; 5) India; happiest nations in Europe: 1) Denmark; 2) United Kingdom

happiness: "The secret of happiness is a good digestion and a bad memory" - Ingrid Bergman; "Happiness is not getting what you want; it is wanting what you have" – Andrew Clark; "In every life there is tragedy. It is the one promise that life always fulfils. Thus, happiness is a gift. The trick is not to expect it but to delight in it when it comes" – Charles Dickens, *Nicholas Nickleby*; "Happiness is not something you experience; it's something you remember" - Oscar Levant; "Ask yourself whether you are happy and you cease to be so" - John Stuart Mill; "Happiness is a way station between too much and too little" - Channing Pollock; "A man is happy as long as he chooses to be happy - and nothing can stop him" - Alexander Solzhenitsyn; "If only we'd stop trying to be happy, we'd have a pretty good time" – Edith Wharton

happiness, somebody addicted to the state of: habromaniac

happiness chemical: seratonin (found naturally in the body as well as in mushrooms, fruit, etc)

happiness hormone: dopamine

happiness, loathing of: cherophobia

happiness region of the brain: dorsal striatum

'Happy Birthday To You': four-line ditty written as a classroom greeting on June 27, 1859, by two Louisville schoolteachers, Mildred J. Hill (an authority on Negro spirituals) and Dr. Patty Smith Hill (professor emeritus of education at Columbia University). The song was first published in 1893, was copyrighted in 1935 and then renewed in 1963. In 1988, Birch Tree Group Ltd. sold the rights to Warner Communications (along with all other assets) for an estimated $25 million (for considerably more than a song). In the 1980s, it was believed to generate about $1 million in annual royalties. With 'Auld Lang Syne' (see) and 'For He's a Jolly Good Fellow,' it is one of the three most popular songs in the English language and continues to bring in approximately two million dollars in licensing revenue every year

hardback, collective noun: library

hare: jack rabbit, mara

hare, adjective: leporid, leporine

hare, collective noun: down, husk

hare, famous: the March Hare (from *Alice's Adventures in Wonderland*)

hare, female: doe

hare, habitat: down, form

hare, male: buck

hare, sound: squeak

hare tail: scut

harmonica: invented by C.F.L. Buschmann in 1821

harmonica players: Larry Adler, Van Morrison, Willie Mae 'Big Mama' Thornton

harp, neck of: harmonic curve

harp makers: Aoyama, Lyon & Healy, Salvi

harp-like musical instrument: kora

Harper's Monthly Magazine: American periodical founded in June of 1850

harpists: Catrin Finch, Joanna Newsom, Jemima Phillips, Julia Thornton

harpist, collective noun: melody

harpoon spike: fluke

harpsichord: cembalo

harpsichordists: Johann Kuhnau, Wanda Landowska

hartebeest, female: cow
hartebeest, male: bull
Harvard: founded in 1636 in Cambridge, Massachusetts
harvest festival: crop-over (West Indian), Lammas Day, Pentecost
Hastings, fact: suicide capital of England (albeit briefly eclipsed in 2007 by the
    village of Gnosall in South Staffordshire)
hat: Akubra (Australian stetson), balibuntal (type of straw hat), balmoral, baseball
    cap, beanie, bearskin, beaver, billycock, boater, bowler hat, busby, calpack, cap,
    chapeau-bras, cloche, coolie hat, deerstalker, Derby, Dolly Varden, fedora, fez,
    glengarry (Scottish), hard hat, helmet, Homburg, leghorn, nor'wester, panama,
    petasus (as worn by Hermes), picture hat, pillbox, pixie hat, pork-pie, red hat
    (worn by a cardinal), scarlet hat (worn by a cardinal), shako (military), shovel
    hat (worn by clergymen), silk hat, skimmer (straw hat), slouch hat, sombrero
    (Mexican), sou'wester, stetson, stovepipe, straw hat, tarboosh, tarpaulin (worn
    by a sailor), ten-gallon hat (worn by a cowboy), terai, titfer (CRS), tin hat
    (military), top hat, topi, topper, toque, tricorne, trilby, turban, velour (made of
    felt), wideawake
hat, Cockney rhyming slang: bladder of fat, titfer (as in, "tit for tat")
hat designers: Louis Mariette, Philip Treacy
hat plume: osprey
hates, pet: dropping the toilet roll into the pan, funny ringtones, laziness, other
    people's burglar alarms, mobile phones (on trains, in cinemas, restaurants, etc),
    packets that explode when you open them, wasted time
hatred: "Love turns, with a little indulgence, to indifference or disgust: hatred alone
    is immortal." William Hazlitt
hatred, Greek goddess of: Eris
hatred of men: misandry
hatred of women: misogyny
Havana, birthplace of: Celia Cruz, Gloria Estefan, Andy Garcia
Hawaii, 50th state (1959), The Aloha State, The Big Island (formerly known as the
    Sandwich Islands)
    birthplace of: Jack Johnson, Nicole Kidman, Bette Midler, Barack Obama, Kelly
        Preston (actress)
    capital: Honolulu
    motto: 'The life of the land is perpetuated in righteousness'
    state bird: nene (Hawaiian goose)
    state flower: hibiscus
    state tree: kukui (candlenut)
    tourist attractions: Hawaii Volcanoes, Haleakala National Parks, Waikiki Beach
    fact: Hawaii is the only North American state that is not in North America
    fact: Hawaii is the only state that grows coffee
Hawaii Five-O: enduring TV crime series set in America's 50th state and in
    particular on the beat of Hawaii's special investigative unit. The show's
    percussive theme tune – which Morton Stevens took eleven minutes to
    compose – has become one of the most recognisable TV themes of all time
    created by: Leonard Freeman
    broadcast: 26 September 1968–26 April 1980
    cast: Jack Lord (Steve McGarrett), James MacArthur (Danny 'Dano' Williams),
        Kam Fong (Chin Ho Kelly), Zulu (Kono), Richard Denning (Governor
        Keith Jameson), Maggi Parker (May), Peggy Ryan (Jenny Sherman),
        Sharon Farrell (Lori Wilson)

Hawaiian dance: hula
Hawaiian dress: muu-muu (brightly coloured and loose-fitting)
Hawaiian greeting: Aloha
Hawaiian song: *Aloha Oe* (*Farewell to Thee*), composed by Queen Liliuokalani in 1878
hawk, adjective: accipitrine
hawk, collective noun: cast, kettle
hawk, male: tercel, tiercel
hawk, sound: scream
hawk, young: eyas
hawk's tether: jess
hawk-headed god: Sokar (Egyptian mythology)
hay fever: pollinosis
hay turner (machine): tedder
HDC: home detention curfew
HDV: high-definition video
HE: High Explosive
head, adjective: cephalic
head, slang: attic, coconut, conk, dome, noggin, noodle, packy (West Indian), pate, potato, pumpkin
head, back of: occiput; pertaining to the back of the head: occipital
head, front of, pertaining to: procephalic
head types; medium-headed: mesaticephalic
  round-headed: retuse
  small-headed: microcephalic
head lice, fact: seven out of 10 schoolchildren in the UK harbour the parasite
headache: cephalalgia (technical term), migraine (severe), sick headache, splitting headache
headaches, patron saint of: Teresa of Avila
headline, type of (in publishing): bank, banner, bikini head, binder line, circus makeup, drophead, eyebrow, jump head, overline, ribbon, rocket head, screamer, skyline head, subhead
headmaster, adjective: archididascalian
healing, god of: Apollo (Greek and Roman), Asclepius (Greek), Aesculapius (Roman)
healing, goddess of: Eir (Norse)
health, goddess of: Hygeia (Greek mythology)
health-giving: salubrious
hearing, adjective: acoustic, audile, audio, aural, auricular
hearing, study of: audiology
hearing impaired celebrities - see deaf and famous
hearing with one ear: monaural (adjective)
heart, adjective: cardiac
heart, gap in: patent foramen ovale
heart, study of: cardiology
heart disease, fear of: cardiophobia
heart doctor: cardiologist
heart membrane (the sac enclosing the organ): pericardium
heart patients, patron saint of: John of God
heart transplant: first performed successfully in December 1967 by Dr Christiaan Barnard

heart transplant, first patient: Louis Washkansky (who, unfortunately, died 18 days later from pneumonia)

heart-shaped: cordiform

heartbeat, rapid: tachycardia

hearth, goddess of: Hestia (Greek), Vesta (Roman)

heat, absorbing: endothermic

heat, adjective: calorific, thermal

heat, dread of: thermophobia

heat, giving off: exothermic (adjective)

heat, science of: thermotics

heat, without: athermic (adjective)

heat application (in medicine): diathermy

Heathrow: selected as London's principal airport in 1943

    first planes used: Lancastrians

    first scheduled flight to: Sydney, Australia

    London Underground connection: opened in 1977

Heaven: Canaan, Eden, Fiddler's Green (for sailors), Paradise, Pearly Gates, Valhalla

Heaven, adjective: celestial

Heaven, fear of: ouranophobia

heavens, science of: astronomy

heavy metal bands: AC/DC, Black Sabbath, Blind Guardian, Danzig, Deep Purple, Def Leppard, Guns n' Roses, HammerFall, Helloween, Iron Maiden, Judas Priest, Kiss, Led Zeppelin, Linkin Park, Megadeth, Mercyful Fate, Metallica, Mötley Crüe, Motorhead, Queensryche, Scorpions, Skid Row, Slayer, Testament, Twisted Sister, Van Halen, Venom, W.A.S.P.

Hebrew prayer box: phylactery

Hebrew words: Adam's apple, behemoth, cherub, chutzpah, Jehovah, jubilee, kosher, rabbi, sabbath, Satan, seraph, shibboleth

hedgehog, adjective: erinaceous

hedgehog, collective noun: array, prickle (joc.)

hedgehog, famous: Mrs Tiggy-Winkle (Beatrix Potter), Sonic the Hedgehog

hedgehog, nickname: urchin

hedgehog, young: piglet

heel, adjective: calcaneal, calcarine

heel bone: calcaneum

height, average of American male: 5ft 10in

height, average of British male: 5ft 5in (in 1900); 5ft 9in (in 1970); 5ft 10in (in 1996), 5ft 10$^{1}/_{2}$in (2004)

height, average of Dutch male: over six foot

heights, fear of: acrophobia

Heineken lager, slogan: 'Heineken refreshes the parts other beers cannot reach'

heiresses: Patty Hearst, Paris Hilton, Jemima Khan, Dame Shirley Porter, Sunny von Bülow

helicopter: Apache, autogiro, Black Hawk, Chinook, chopper, egg-beater (US slang), Iroquois, Little Bird (attack helicopter), Lynx, Medevac (US army), Merlin Mark 1 (anti-submarine), Sea Cobra, Sea Knight, Sea Sprite, Sea Stallion, Sikorsky, whirlybird

hell: Annwyn (Welsh mythology), Gehenna (Jewish), Hades (Greek mythology), Naraka (in Buddhism), netherworld, Sheol (Jewish), Tartarus, underworld

hell, adjective: avernal, Hadean, infernal, Tartarean

hell, doctrine of: tartarology

hell, dread of: stygiophobia
helmet: balaclava, bearskin, busby, casque, crash helmet, headpiece, pickelhaube
      (spiked), pith helmet, sallet, schapska, skid-lid (slang for crash helmet), sola
      topi, tin hat, topi
helmet, adjective: galeate
helmet face-guard: beaver
helmet plumage: panache
hen, collective noun: brood
Henry VIII, chief minister of: Thomas Cromwell
Henry VIII's musical compositions: *Greensleeves* (allegedly), *Passtyme with Good
      Cumpanye* (a song for three voices) and two masses (lost to posterity)
Henry VIII's six wives: Catherine of Aragon (divorced), Anne Boleyn (beheaded),
      Jane Seymour (died 12 days after giving birth to Edward VI), Anne of Cleves
      (divorced), Catherine Howard (beheaded) and Catherine Parr (survived)
Herald Tribune, The International, newspaper founded 4 October 1887
heraldic colour: tincture
heraldic image: charge
heraldry, adjective: armorial
herbs: angelica, anise, basil, bay leaf, bergamot, borage, camomile, chervil, chicory,
      chives, comfrey, coriander, coriander salantro, coriander santro, dill, dittany,
      fennel, fenugreek, lavender, lemon mint, lovage, marjoram, mint, oregano,
      parsley, peppermint, pot-herb, rosemary, rue, saffron, sage, savory, sesame,
      sorrel, spearmint, sweet cicely, tarragon, thyme, winter savory
herbs, bundle of: bouquet garni
herbs, fact: there are approximately 1,800 herbs recorded
herbalists: Cadfael, Paracelsus
heredity, adjective: genetic
heredity, aversion to: patroiophobia
Herefordshire, administrative centre: Hereford
heretics: Giordano Bruno, Thomas Cranmer, Joan of Arc, Hugh Latimer, Pelagius,
      Nicholas Ridley, William Tyndale, Mary Ward
hermit: eremite
hermit, adjective: eremitic
hernias, study of: herniology
hero: "Most heroes are created by incompetence at high level" – Richard Morrison
heroin: aitch, angel, Aunt Hazel, beast, the big H, blue magic, boy, brother,
      Cadillac, China white, Chinese red, chiva, dynamite, ferry dust, Harry, gear,
      hop, horse, joy powder, junk, Lady H, lemonade, Mexican mud, noise, onick
      (Elizabethan slang), Persian brown, polvo, rock candy, scag, schmeck, skag,
      smeck, snow, sugar, tru blu, white lady, the witch
heroin, fact: the drug was outlawed in Britain in 1971
heroin, tools required for application: flame (candle or lighter), spoon, syringe,
      tourniquet
heroin, world's main supplier: Afghanistan (accounting for more than 93% of the
      total global output)
heroin casualty: Rachel Whitear (21-year-old whose corpse – with a needle still in
      the arm – was photographed and widely published as a warning to other young
      heroin users)
      - see overdose, accidental death from
heron, adjective: grallatorial
heron, collective noun: sedge, serge, siege

herring: alewife (related), anchovy, brisling (small), buckling (smoked), kipper (cured), pilchard, red herring (smoked), shotten herring (spawned), sild (young)

herring, adjective: clupeoid

herring, collective noun: shoal

herring, young: brit, sild

herring-shaped: harengiform

Hertfordshire, administrative centre: Hertford

HI: postcode for Hawaii

hiccoughs/hiccups: singultus

hide (animal skin), aversion to: doraphobia

Hi-De-Hi!: camp BBC sitcom set in and around the chaos of the fictitious Maplin's Holiday Camp at Crimpton-on-Sea
    created by Jimmy Perry and David Croft
    broadcast: 26 February 1981–30 January 1988
    cast: Simon Cadell (Jeffrey Fairbrother), Paul Shane (Ted Bovis), Ruth Madoc (Gladys Pugh), Jeffrey Holland (Spike Dixon), Leslie Dwyer (Mr Partridge), Su Pollard (Peggy Ollerenshaw), David Griffin (Squadron Leader Clive Dempster DFC)

high jumper: Dick Fosbury
    - see show jumpers

highwaymen: James Aitken (aka John the Painter), Claude Duval, Robert King, Macheath (from *The Beggar's Opera*), Dick Turpin

Hindi words: bungalow, cummerbund, gymkhana, pundit, samosa, shampoo, tandoori, yoga Hindu book of teachings: Bhagavad-Gita

Hindu castes: Brahman (highest), Kshatriya (including the military), Vaisya (comprising the farmers and merchants), Sudra (lowest)

Hindu festival: Diwali

Hindu loincloth: dhoti

Hindu philosophers: Shankaracharya, Swami Vivekananda

Hindu queen: ranee

Hindu sage: maharishi

Hindu shirt: kurta

Hindu trader: banyan

Hindu tunic: kurta

hip, adjective: sciatic

hip bone: ilium, innominate bone

hip joint: coxa

hip-hop: urban subculture embracing rap, breakdancing and graffiti art

hip-hop stars – see rap/hip-hop artists

hippopotamus, collective noun: bloat, pod

hippopotamus, fact: many experts maintain that the hippo is the world's second largest land animal (in contention with the white rhino)

hippopotamus, fact: some hippos have been known to run as fast as 30mph

hippopotamus, fact: the nearest living relative of the hippo is the whale

hippopotamus, fact: the skin exudes a substance that acts as both an antibiotic and sunscreen

hippopotamus, fact: the skin of the average hippo weighs one ton

hippopotamus, female: cow

hippopotamus, male: bull

hippopotamus, sound: bray, snort

hippopotamus, young: calf

hippopotamus goddess: Ipy, Taweret (both from Egyptian mythology)

Hiroshima, bombing of: 6 August 1945 (140,000 killed)

Hispaniola: Caribbean island comprising Haiti in the west and the Dominician Republic in the east

historians: Peter Ackroyd, Henry Adams, Max Arthur, Francis Bacon, Juliet Barker, Charles Beard, Mary Beard, Carl Becker, Saint Bede, Antony Beevor, Hilaire Belloc, Geoffrey Bolton, Fernand Braudel, James MacGregor Burns, Callisthenes of Olynthus, Thomas Carlyle, G.K. Chesterton, Sir Winston Churchill, Alan Clark, Sir Julian Corbett, Joaquín Costa, Dio Cassius, Sir Robert Ensor, Esmond de Beer, Orlando Figes, Michel Foucault, Samuel Gardiner, Edward Gibbon, Saxo Grammaticus, John Hammond, Marcus Lee Hansen, Sir Max Hastings, Herodotus, Christopher Hill, Eric Hobsbawm, M.H. Holcroft, Homer, W.H. Hoskins, Anthony Howard, David Hume, David Irving (disgraced in April 2000), C.L.R. James, Emmanuel Le Roy Ladurie, Henry Lodge, Catharine Macaulay, Thomas Macaulay, Roy Medvedev, Gavin Menzies, James/Jan Morris, Samuel Morison, Cornelius Nepos, Ulrich Phillips, Pliny the Elder, Plutarch, Procopius, Peter Radford, Andrew Roberts, Alfred Rowse, Steven Runciman, Simon Schama, Arthur Schlesinger, David Starkey, John Stow, Abbot Suger, Sir Ronald Syme, Tacitus, R.H. Tawney, A.J.P. Taylor, Studs Terkel, E.P. Thompson, Thucydides, Alexis de Tocqueville, Arnold Toynbee, Nigel Tranter, Barbara W. Tuchman, Erich von Däniken, Max Weber, Dame Veronica Wedgwood, H.G. Wells, Xenophon

historical novelists: Peter Ackroyd, William Ainsworth, Pat Barker, Bernard Cornwell, Alexandre Dumas, George Macdonald Fraser, Ken Follett, Georgette Heyer, Patrick O'Brian, Mary Renault, Sir Walter Scott, Mary Stewart, Leon Uris

history: "An anthology of mistakes" - anonymous; "People are trapped in history, and history is trapped in them" - James Baldwin; "History is one bloody thing after another" – Herbert Butterfield; "History is not what you thought. It is what you remember. All other history defeats itself" - from *1066 and All That*

history, muse of: Clio

Hitler's favourite filmmaker: Leni Riefenstahl

Hitler's favourite food (at least, in the last weeks of his life): chocolate cake

HIV: human immunodeficiency virus (computer analysis of the spread of HIV-1 suggests that it began in Africa some time in the 1930s)

HIV, identified by: Dr Robert Gallo

HLF: Heritage Lottery Fund

H.M.S. Pinafore: operetta by W.S. Gilbert and Arthur Sullivan, first produced in 1878 in London in

Hobbit: nickname for the humanoid species *Homo floresiensis*, a hairy, metre-tall people who once lived on the island of Flores, 370 miles east of Bali. With extended arms and lengthy fingers, the Hobbit was remarkable for the pendulous breasts of the female (which, apparently, she slung over her shoulder). According to locals, the last time that they were sighted on the island was in the 19th century, shortly before the arrival of Dutch colonists

hobos: Woody Guthrie, Jack London, Harry Partch (later a successful composer)

hockey mom: Sarah Palin

hockey start: bully-off

hog, adjective: suilline

hog, collective noun: drift, parcel, passel

holiday, adjective: ferial (rare)

Holland, estimated number of brothels: 2,000

Holland, fact: around 100 well organised criminal groups are currently active there

Hollywood: Sodom-by-the Sea, Tinseltown

Hollywood: "You can take all the sincerity of Hollywood, put it in a flea's naval, and still have room left over for three caraway seeds and an agent's heart" - Fred Allen; "I once heard someone say that Hollywood is like a beautiful woman with the clap" – Bruce Willis

Hollywood Madam: nickname for Heidi Fleiss

Holmes, Sherlock: modelled on Dr Joseph Bell
    – see Sherlock Holmes

holography pioneer: Dennis Gabor

Holy Grail, guardian of: the Fisher King

Holy See – see Vatican City

holy war: jihad

holy water, vessel of: stoup

homage, adjective: reverential

home: "Home is where one starts from" - T.S. Eliot

home, abnormal desire to stay at: oikomania

home, Cockney rhyming slang: gates of Rome

home, fear of: domatophobia, ecophobia

home, love of: ecomania

home, powerful desire to return to: nostomania

Home & Country: journal of the Federation of Women's Institutes founded in 1919

homeless, fact: an estimated 2,000 people sleep rough in Britain each night

homeless, patron saint of: Benedict Joseph Labre

homeless charity: Crisis

homes of the famous: Buckingham Palace (Queen Elizabeth II), Camp David (US president), Chartwell (Winston Churchill), Down House (Charles Darwin), Élysée Palace (French president), Fairlane (Henry Ford), Graceland (Elvis Presley), Iranistan (P.T. Barnum), Monticello (Thomas Jefferson), Mount Vernon (George Washington), Neverland (Michael Jackson), No.10 Downing Street (British Prime Minister), 50 Wimpole Street (Elizabeth Barrett Browning), 221B Baker Street (Sherlock Holmes), Pickfair (Douglas Fairbanks and Mary Pickford), San Simeon (William Randolph Hearst), White House (US president), Xanadu (Charles Foster Kane)

homesickness: philopatridomania

homophobe (especially one who interferes in the gay world): carlotta

homosexual: angel (male who tends to support and indulge his more effeminate partner), arse bandit, auntie, banana, bear (a particularly masculine one), chicken hawk, chicken queen, faggot, fagola, fairy, friend of Dorothy, haricot (Aus.), Hollywood hustler (US slang), honey-bum (passive type), lamb (young homosexual boy), lavender, lesbian, maneater, maricon (Mexican slang), Marmite driller, mincer, Nancy, nancy-boy, pansy, poof, poofter, powder puff, queen, queer, rump ranger, sailor, sister, skin-diver, twink (young and available), uranist, woofter, woolly woofter

homosexuals, famous (selected, naturally): Peter Ackroyd (novelist), Edward Albee, Peter Allen, Pedro Almodóvar, Hans Christian Andersen, Lindsay Anderson, Kenneth Anger, Sir Frederick Ashton, W. H. Auden, Francis Bacon, James Baldwin, Samuel Barber, Michael Barrymore, Sir Cecil Beaton, Alan Bennett, Dirk Bogarde, Benjamin Britten, Derren Brown, Lord John Browne of Madingley, Guy Burgess, Raymond Burr, William S. Burroughs, John Cage, Simon Callow, Truman Capote, Richard Chamberlain, Graham Chapman,

Julian Clary, Jean Cocteau, Aaron Copland, Noël Coward, Quentin Crisp,
George Cukor, Jeffrey Dahmer, Divine, Marcel Duchamp, Edward II, Brian
Epstein, Kenny Everett, Rupert Everett, Rainer Werner Fassbinder, E.M. Forster,
Stephen Fry, David Geffen, Jean Genet, John Gielgud, Peter Greenaway, Lorenz
Hart, Nigel Hawthorne, Terrence Higgins, David Hockney, Frankie Howerd, Tab
Hunter, Christopher Isherwood, Sir Derek Jacobi, Sir Elton John, Karl Lagerfeld,
T.E. Lawrence, David Laws, Liberace, Federico García Lorca, Matt Lucas,
Peter Mandelson, Robert Mapplethorpe, Jean Marais, Christopher Marlowe,
Armistead Maupin, Sir Ian McKellen, Freddie Mercury, George Michael,
Harvey Milk, Graham Norton, Joe Orton, John Osborne, Wilfred Owen, Cole
Porter, Robert Reed (actor best known for playing Mike Brady on TV), Howard
E. Rollins Jr, Siegfried Sassoon, John Schlesinger, Franz Schubert (allegedly),
Sir Antony Sher, Chris Smith (politician), Socrates, Jimmy Somerville, Stephen
Sondheim, Yves St Laurent, David Starkey, Michael Stipe, Lytton Strachey,
Peter Tatchell, Pyotr Tchaikovsky, Gore Vidal, Jann Wenner, James Whale,
Oscar Wilde, Kenneth Williams, Will Young
- see bisexuals and lesbians
homosexual comic book, first: *The Authority* (DC Comics), featuring Apollo and
Midnighter
homosexual couple, first married in UK: Grainne Close and Shannon Sickles
(united 19 December 2005)
homosexual marriage, first: 31 March, 2001, when two lesbian brides and six
homosexual grooms were officially joined in matrimony at a ceremony in
The Netherlands to mark the institution of same-sex marriage
homosexual terms: angel, gym bunny, meanwhile, newbie, OGT (obviously gay trait)
homosexuality: "The love that dared not speak its name has become the love that
simply won't shut up" - Matthew Parris, *The Sunday Times*
homosexuality in males: uranism
homosexuality, fear of: uranophobia
homosexuality, hatred of: homophobia
Honduras: republic in Central America
  capital: Tegucigalpa
  currency: lempira
  language: Spanish (official), English, various Indian languages
  religion: Roman Catholic
honey, adjective: mellaginous
honey bear: kinkajou
honey-coloured: melichrous
honey-eating: meliphagous
honeycomb cell: alveolus
Hong Kong: semi-autonomous outpost of China, a British colony until 1997
  official title: The Special Administrative Region of the People's Republic
    of China
  administrative centre: Victoria
  language: Cantonese
  post colonial leader: Tung Chee-hwa
  birthplace of: Jackie Chan, Chow Yun-Fat, Romola Garai (actress), Sally
    Phillips (actress/comedian)
  bridge: Tsing Ma (suspension bridge linking urban HK with its new airport on
    reclaimed land north of Lantau Island - see bridges)
hood, adjective: capistrate

hooded: capistrate
hood-shaped: cucullate
hoof, adjective: ungual
hoofed mammal: ungulate
hook, adjective: hamate, uncinate
hook-like: unciform
hook-shaped: ancistroid, hamiform
hopeless causes, patron saint of: Jude
hormones, study of: endocrinology
horn, adjective: corneous, keratinous
horn of plenty: cornucopia
horn players: Aubrey Brain, Dennis Brain
hornet, collective noun: bike, nest
hornet, young: larva
horror characters: Count Dracula, Frankenstein's Monster, Fu Manchu, Matthew
    Hopkins (the Witchfinder General), Freddy Krueger, Mr Hyde, Michael Myers,
    Dr Phibes, Pinhead, Jason Voorhees, The Wolf Man
horse: appaloosa, Arab, broodmare, caballo, Cleveland Bay, Clydesdale, cob, colt,
    dobbin, draught, filly, foal, gelding, hack, Hunter, Irish draught, jennet, mare,
    mount, mustang, nag, orlov trotter, palfrey, palomino, Percheron, pinto, piebald,
    Przewalski, Shetland (orig. Scotland; 10hh), Shire, skewbald, stallion, steed,
    Suffolk, Suffolk Punch, thoroughbred
horse, adjective: equine
horse, Cockney rhyming slang: bottle of sauce
horse, collective noun: harras, ramuda, string, team
horse, female: mare
horse, male: stallion
horse, movement of: canter, gallop, pace, tantivy, trot, walk
horse, sound: neigh, whinny
horse, untamed: buckjumper (Australian)
horse, young: colt (male), filly (female), foal
Horse & Hound: equestrian magazine founded in 1884
horse ankle: fetlock
horse artists: Edgar Degas, Michael Lyne, Alfred Munnings, George Stubbs,
    Norman Thelwell
horse attendant: ostler
horse comb: curry-comb
horse leap: gambade
horse market: Tattersall's of London
horse parts: byental, cannon-bone, chestnut, coronet, crest, croup, fetlock, flank,
    forelock, gaskin, haunch, hock, hoof, mane, muzzle, pastern, poll, shannon-
    bone, stifle, withers
horse sculptor: Philip Blacker
horse thieves: Ned Kelly, Belle Starr, Hank Vaughan
horse's penis: byental
horses, famous: Arion (c/o Hercules), Babieca (c/o El Cid), Balios (Greek
    mythology), Black Agnes (c/o Mary, Queen of Scots), Black Beauty, Black Bess
    (c/o Dick Turpin), Blackie (c/o Chief Sitting Bull), Borak (c/o Mohammed),
    Bucephalus (c/o Alexander the Great), Champion (c/o Gene Autry), Cincinnati
    (c/o General Ulysses S. Grant), Copenhagen (c/o Duke of Wellington), Flicka,
    Fritz (c/o William S. Hart), Fury, Hercules (c/o Steptoe and Son), Hippocampus

(c/o Neptune), Incitatus (c/o Caligula), Ivan (bed companion for Catherine the Great), Kantaka (c/o Buddha), Lamri (c/o King Arthur), Magnolia (c/o George Washington), Marengo (c/o Napoleon), Mr Ed, Pegasus, Phantom (c/o Zorro), Roan Barbary (c/o Richard II), Rocinante (c/o Don Quixote), Rosabelle (c/o Mary, Queen of Scots), Sand, Scout (c/o Tonto), Shadowfax (c/o Gandalf), Silver (c/o The Lone Ranger), Sleipnir (c/o Odin), Smoky (the Cowhorse), Sorrel (c/o William III), Spirit (Stallion of the Cimarron), Tony (c/o Tom Mix), Topper (c/o Hopalong Cassidy), Tornado (c/o Zorro), Toytown (c/o Zara Phillips), Traveler (c/o General Robert E. Lee), Trigger (c/o Roy Rogers), Uffington White Horse (carved into the Berkshire Downs), Vic (c/o General George Armstrong Custer), White Flash (c/o Tex Ritter), White Surrey (c/o Richard III), Xanthus (c/o Achilles)
   – see racehorses
horses, fear of: hippophobia
horses, god of: Poseidon (Greek myth)
horses, obsession with: hippomania
horses, patron saint of: Martin of Tours
Horse Feathers (1932 film), famous lines: Professor Wagstaff (Groucho Marx): "I'm ashamed to be your father. You're a disgrace to our family name of Wagstaff, if such a thing is possible"; Professor Wagstaff: "Barovelli, you've got the brain of a four-year-old boy, and I bet he was glad to get rid of it"; Barovelli: "There's a man outside with a big black moustache." Professor Wagstaff: "Tell him I've got one."
horse riders – see equestrians and equestriennes
horse riding, adjective: equestrian
horse-loving: philhippic
horsehair fabric: crinoline
horseradish: root introduced to Britain from the Middle East in the 15th century
horseradish, Japanese: wasabi
horseshoe: first used in the 4th and 5th centuries
hospitals: Cedars-Sinai Medical Center (Los Angeles), Cook County General Hospital (Chicago), Great Ormond Street Hospital for Sick Children (London), Moorfields Eye Hospital (London), Motion Picture & Television Hospital (Woodland Hills, California), Mount Sinai Medical Centre (Miami)
hospital, first: Baghdad, established in 809 AD
hospitals, patron saints of: Camillus de Lellis and John of God
hospital for teaching, first: Baghdad, established in 978 AD
hostages, famous: Terry Anderson (American), Brian Keenan (teacher from Belfast held in Beirut by the Islamic Jihad), John McCarthy (the UK's longest-held captive in Beirut, where he was imprisoned for 1,943 days), Frank Reed, Yvonne Ridley (journalist held hostage by the Taliban in Afghanistan, 2001, who later converted to Islam), Matthew Scott (held by Colombian kidnappers), Tom Sutherland, Terry Waite
   - see abductees, escapees and kidnapping victims
hostage rescues - see sieges
hot-air balloonists - see balloonists
hotel, first to offer central heating and private 'facilities' for every room: The Goring, Victoria, London
hotel, seven-star (the only one in the world): Burj Al Arab in Dubai
hoteliers: Robert Bigelow, Basil Fawlty, Mohamed Al-Fayed, Charles Forte, Conrad Hilton, Howard Hughes, Sol Kerzner, J. Willard Marriott, César Ritz, Kemmons Wilson

hotels, London's best: Beaufort (SW3), Berkeley (SW1), Blakes (SW7), Capital Hotel (SW3), Claridge's (W1), Connaught (W1), Dorchester (W1), Dukes Hotel (SW1), Four Seasons Inn On the Park (W1), Gore (SW7), Halcyon (W11), Halkin Hotel (SW1), Hazlitt's (W1), Hyde Park (SW1), Lanesborough (SW1), Langham Hilton (W1), Ritz (W1), Savoy (WC2), Stafford (SW1)

hotels, world's best: Burj Al Arab (Dubai), The Carlyle (New York), Hotel Cipriani (Venice), Claridge's (London), Hotel De Crillon (Paris), Grand Hyatt (Hong Kong), Mandarin Oriental (Hong Kong), The Oriental (Bangkok), The Regent (Hong Kong), The Regent (Sydney), Hotel Seiyo (Tokyo)

hound, collective noun: cry, mute, pack

hound, young: pup

hour, adjective: horal, horary (archaic)

house: adobe, bungalow, cabin, chalet, chateau, cottage, dacha, gîte, igloo, manor, manse, mansion, palace, pied-à-terre, pile, prefab, semi-detached, tepee, terraced, wigwam, yurt

house, largest in Britain: Knole, a stately home near Sevenoaks in Kent

House of Lords: "The House of Lords is like Heaven. You want to get there some day, but not while there is any life in you" - Lord Denning

Houses of Parliament, Westminster, London SW1: designed by Sir Charles Barry and Augustus Pugin (the latter adding the Gothic look), with building commencing in 1837. Construction was completed ten years later in 1847, with the Clock Tower completed in 1858

housefly, adjective: cyclorrhaphous

housekeepers: Mrs Danvers (from *Rebecca*), Nelly Dean (from *Wuthering Heights*), Mrs Alice Fairfax (from *Jane Eyre*), Mrs Grose (from *The Turn of the Screw*), Mrs Hudson (for Sherlock Holmes), Clara Peggotty (from *David Copperfield*), Mrs Pipchin (from *Dombey and Son*), Virginia 'Pepper' Potts (from Marvel Comics' *Iron Man*)

housewives: Mrs Isabella Beeton, Janet Chisholm (who was a spy in her spare time), Dame Edna Everage, Mrs Miniver, Lydia E. Pinkham, Shirley Valentine, Mary Whitehouse

housewives, patron saints of: Ann, Joachim, Martha and Zita

housework: "I hate housework. You make the beds, do the dishes and six months later you have to start all over again" - Joan Rivers

housing development: council estate, high-rise estate, housing estate, projects, sink

housing project; first tower block construction: L'Uunité d'Haibitation in Marseilles, designed by Charles Le Corbusier and completed in 1952

Houston, birthplace of: Red Adair, Yolanda Adams, Wes Anderson (filmmaker), Destiny's Child, Hilary Duff, Jennifer Garner, Howard Hughes, Billy Preston, Anna Nicole Smith

hovercraft: invented in 1910 by Toivo Kaario

Hovis theme tune: second movement from Dvorak's *Symphony No. 9, Opus 95, 'From the New World'*, popularised as the song *'Goin' Home'*

HP Sauce: 'Houses of Parliament' sauce

HPA: Health Protection Agency

HRT: hormone replacement therapy

H-shaped: zygal

HSS: high speed steel

HTML: hyper-text markup language (on web pages)

hug, easy or pleasant to: evancalous

Hull, birthplace of: Ian Carmichael, Tom Courtenay, Everything But the Girl, The Housemartins, Amy Johnson, Maureen Lipman, Edward Milne (astrophysicist), The Paddingtons, Stevie Smith, James Ward (philosopher), William Wilberforce
Hull rivers: Hull, Humber
hum loudly: bombilate
human beatbox: Jason Singh
human behaviour, science of: psychology
human beings, fear of: anthropophobia
human customs, science of: anthropology
human remains, science of: archaeology
human rights activist - see activists, political activists
humanists: Roger Ascham, Sebastian Brant, Étienne Dolet, Desiderius Erasmus, William Tyndale, Laurentius Valla
humanitarians: Bono, John Rockefeller, Eleanor Roosevelt, Mother Teresa, Terry Waite
Humberside, administrative centre: Hull
humidity, adjective: hygrothermal
hummingbird, adjective: trochiline
hummingbird, collective noun: charm
hummingbird, sound: click, whir
hummingbird, young: chick
humour: "Humour is an affirmation of dignity, a declaration of man's superiority to all that befalls him" - novelist Romain Gary; "The expression of our existential disappointment" - Howard Jacobson; "Humour is emotional chaos remembered in tranquility" - James Thurber
humour, researcher of: gelatologist
humour, types of: black comedy, burlesque, caricature, double entendre, farce, gallows humour, joke, lavatorial, mimicry, parody, riddle, saracasm, satire, schadenfreude, slapstick, whimsy, wit
Hun: Attila
hunchbacks, famous: Igor, Jean de Florette, Quasimodo, Richard III (Shakespeare's version), Riff Raff (from *The Rocky Horror Show*)
hunchback, adjective: gibbous
hunchback, condition of: kyphosis
hundred years, adjective: centenary
hundredth: centesimal
hundredth anniversary: centenary
hundred-year-old: centenarian
Hundred Years' War: 1337–1453
Hungarian and famous: Béla Bartók, László Benedek (filmmaker), Michael Curtiz, Joe Eszterhas (screenwriter), Eva Gabor, Zsa Zsa Gabor, Peter Carl Goldmark (inventor), Harry Houdini, Zoltan Karpathy (the 'dreadful' Hungarian from *My Fair Lady*), Alexander Korda, Zoltán Kodály (composer), Arthur Koestler, László Kovács (cinematographer), Ferencz Lehár (composer), Györgi Ligeti (composer), Franz Liszt, Joseph Pulitzer, Egon Ronay, Ernő Rubik, István Szabó (filmmaker), Istvan Szechenyi (soldier and reformer), Vilmos Zsigmond (cinematographer), Adolph Zukor (founder of Paramount Pictures)
Hungary: republic in central Europe (Hungarian name: Magyarország)
   capital: Budapest

currency: forint
language: Hungarian
religion: Christian
rivers: Danube, Dráva, Tisza
fact: boasts the world's first *official* UFO landing site
patron saints of: Gerard and Stephen
hunger striker: Bobby Sands
Hungerford Massacre: 19 August 1987, when Michael Ryan took the lives of 16 people in the town of Hungerford, Berkshire
hungover: chippy (19th century slang)
hungry, excessively: famished, gutfoundered, ravenous, starving
hunt, god of: Ull (Norse mythology)
hunt, goddess of: Artemis (Greek), Diana (Roman)
hunter, collective noun: blast
hunters: Captain Ahab, Atalanta, John Huston, Baron Munchhausen, Nimrod (Biblical), Orion (Greek mythology)
hunters, patron saints of: Hubert and Eustachius
hunting, adjective: venatic, venatical
hunts: Beaufort Hunt, Middleton Hunt, Quorn
hurdler: Jesse Owens
hurricanes, major, USA: Rita (2005), Katrina (2005), Charley (2004), Frances (2004), Ivan (2004), Isabel (2003), Floyd (1999), Pauline (1997), Andrew (1992), Betsy (1965)
husband, adjective: marital
husband, killing of: mariticide, viricide
hydrometer: instrument for measuring the density of liquids, in all probability devised by Leonardo Da Vinci
hyena, adjective: hyenine
hyena, collective noun: cackle
hyena, famous: Shenzi (from Disney's *The Lion King*)
hyena, sound: giggle, laugh
hymen: membrane which encloses the entrance to the vagina and is found in humans, horses, hyenas, lemurs, moles, mole-rats and whales (but not, incidentally, in monkeys or apes)
hymns: *Abide With Me, All Things Bright and Beautiful, Amazing Grace, Ave Maria, Ave Verum, He Who Would Valiant Be, I Vow To Thee My Country, Jerusalem, Let All the World in Every Corner Sing, Mine Eyes Have Seen the Glory of the Coming of the Lord, Morning Has Broken, Onward Christian Soldiers, O Valiant Heart, Praise My Soul the King of Heaven*
hymn writers: Philip Bliss, Thomas Ken, Henry Francis Lyte, John Newton, Isaac Watts, Charles Wesley, William Williams Pantycelyn
hypnosis, adjective: hypnoid
hypnotic drug: thiopentone
hypnotists: László Bíró (who also invented the ball-point pen), James Braid, Derren Brown, Dr Caligari, Émile Coué, Sigmund Freud, Jafar (from Disney's *Aladdin*), Paul McKenna, Dr Franz Mesmer, Grigori Rasputin, Svengali (from George du Maurier's 1894 novel *Trilby*)
hypochondriac: Argan (from Molière's *Le Malade Imaginaire*)
hypocrite: Seth Pecksniff (from Dickens' *Martin Chuzzlewit*)

I

IA: postcode for Iowa
ice, fear of: cryophobia, kristallophobia
ice coating: verglas
ice cream: Baskin-Robbins, Ben & Jerry's, Häagen-Dazs, Lyons Maid, Neapolitan,
    spumoni, Wall's
ice cream consuming nations per capita, top: New Zealand (followed by the
    United States, Canada, Australia, Belgium and Sweden)
ice games: curling, ice hockey
ice hockey kick-off: face-off
ice hockey missile: puck
ice hockey players: Ken Dryden (goaltender), Wayne Gretsky, Gordie Howe,
    Maurice Richard
ice rink machine: Zamboni (used to resurface the ice)
ice skaters: Oksana Baiul, Robin Cousins, John Curry, Christopher Dean, Tonya
    Harding (also a film star), Sonja Henie, Lynn-Holly Johnson, Nancy Kerrigan
    (also advertising ambassador of Campbell's soup, Disney, Reebok and Revlon),
    Irina Rodnina, Jayne Torvill, Katerina Witt
ice skaters, patron saint of: Lydwina of Schiedam
ice skating moves: arabesque, arabian, axel, Bielmann spin, camel, Choctaw,
    crossfoot spin, deathdrop, death spiral, double axel, figure eight, flying camel,
    flying sit spin, flying spin, freestyle, Grafstrom spiral, hydrant lift, inside axel,
    jump, Lutz, overhead lift, pair sit spin, pivot, Russian split, Salchow, serpentine,
    sit spin, spin, split, spread eagle, stag
ice slide: glissade
Iceland: island republic in the North Atlantic
    capital: Reykjavik
    currency: króna (subdivided into 100 aurar)
    language: Icelandic
    religion: Evangelical Lutheran
    nickname: Land of the Midnight Sun
    parliament: Althing (the oldest in the world)
    pop groups: Bellatrix, Hjaltalin, Mezzoforte (jazz-funk), Sigur Rós, The
        Sugarcubes
    fact: the country boasts the greatest number of Miss Worlds per capita
    fact: birth and death records stretch back to the Viking era
Icelandic and famous: Vladimir Ashkenazy, Björk, Bobby Fischer (granted
    citizenship in 2005), Jóhannes Kjarval (painter), Magnus Magnusson
ICU: intensive care unit
ID: postcode for Idaho
Idaho, 43rd state (1890), Gem State
    capital: Boise
    motto: 'Esto Perpetua' ('It is perpetual')
    state bird: mountain bluebird
    state flower: syringa
    state tree: white pine
    birthplace of: Gutzon Borglum (sculptor), Sarah Palin, Ezra Pound, Lana
        Turner
    fact: the first electricity generated from atomic energy was produced in Idaho
        (in 1951)

fact: the state still uses the firing squad as a mode of capital punishment
tourist attractions: Craters of the Moon, Crystal Falls Cave, Hells Canyon (the deepest gorge in North America), Sun Valley, World Center for Birds of Prey
Ideal Home: glossy magazine founded in 1920
idealism, school of; founder: George Berkeley
ideas, fear of: ideophobia
identical twins, technical term: monozygotic twins (see fraternal twins)
idiot: dill (Australian slang), dipstick, doofus, dork, fool, goofball, klutz, lamebrain, lob, loser, moron, muttonhead, nimshi, numbskull, pumpkin head, putz, schlemiel, schlepper, schmo, schmuck, soap (Australian), twerp, yutz (Yiddish)
idle: otiose
idleness: "There's no fun in doing nothing when you have nothing to do. Idleness, like kisses, to be sweet must be stolen" - Jerome K. Jerome
idler: cumberwordle (archaic), flâneur
idler, famous: Oblomov
igneous rock, adjective: trappean
ignorance: "People who know the least know it loudest" - Ernst Anderson
iguana, collective noun: mess
Ike: nickname for Dwight D. Eisenhower
Ikea: global furniture store founded by Ingvar Kamprad in 1943
IL: postcode for Illinois
Il Duce: nickname for Benito Mussolini
Île-de-France: former name for Mauritius (until 1810)
Ilium: Latin name for ancient Troy
illegitimate and famous: Florentino Ariza (from *Love in the Time of Cholera*), Sarah Bernhardt, Giovanni Boccaccio, Cesare Borgia, Lucrezia Borgia, Willy Brandt, Giacomo Casanova, Fidel Castro, Eric Clapton, Marie Corelli (novelist), Bobby Darin, Walt Disney (urban legend), Tracey Emin, Desiderius Erasmus, 50 Cent (aka Curtis Jackson), Josef Fritzl, Heathcliff, Hercules, Etta James, Steve Jobs, Leonardo Da Vinci, Jack London, Sophia Loren, Ramsay MacDonald, Marilyn Monroe, Eva Perón, Sir Carol Reed, Adèle Rochester (from *Jane Eyre*), George Sand, David Warner (actor), William the Conqueror, Paula Yates
Illinois, 21st state (1818), The Prairie State
   capital: Springfield
   motto: 'State sovereignty – national union'
   state bird: cardinal (a state bird it shares with Indiana, Kentucky, North Carolina, Ohio, Virginia and West Virginia)
   state flower: violet
   state tree: white oak
   birthplace of: Joshua Bell, Jack Benny, William Borah (Republican politician), Ray Bradbury, Jimmy Connors, Miles Davis, Walt Disney, Wyatt Earp, Benny Goodman, Ernest Hemingway, Charlton Heston, Wild Bill Hickok, Doris Humphrey (choreographer), Howard Keel, Ray Kroc, Bill Murray, Richard Pryor, Ronald Reagan, Sam Shepard
   tourist attractions: the Springfield home and tomb of Abraham Lincoln, Mormon settlement at Nauvoo, Starved Rock State Park
illiterate: alternatively schooled (PC)
illness, dread of: nosemaphobia
I Love Lucy: iconic TV sitcom, the first to be filmed before a live audience
   broadcast: 15 October 1951–6 May 1957 on CBS TV

cast: Lucille Ball (Lucy Ricardo), Desi Arnaz (Ricky Ricardo), William
    Frawley (Fred Mertz), Vivian Vance (Ethel Mertz)

illusionists: David Blaine, Jonathan Creek (title protagonist of the BBC TV series),
    David Copperfield, Harry Houdini

Illustrated London News, The: biannual magazine founded in 1842

illustrators: Djuna Barnes, Aubrey Beardsley, Thomas Bewick, Quentin Blake,
    Randolph Caldecott, Eric Carle, George Cruikshank, Gustave Doré, George
    du Maurier, Edmund Dulac, Will Eisner, Charles Dana Gibson, Edward
    Gorey, Kate Greenaway, Frank Hampson, David Jones, Paul Nash, Kay
    Nielsen, Sidney Paget, Maxfield Parrish, Mervyn Peake, Phiz (real name:
    Hablot K(night) Browne), Beatrix Potter, Arthur Rackham, Charles Robinson,
    Heath Robinson, Norman Rockwell, Ronald Searle, Maurice Sendak, Dr Seuss,
    E.H. Shepard, Ralph Steadman, Sir John Tenniel, Florence Upton, Alberto
    Vargas

IM: image messaging

imaginary friends: God, Harvey

IMF: International Monetary Fund

IMHO: in my humble opinion

immigrants, patron saint of: Frances Xavier Cabrini

immigrant trafficker: coyote (slang)

immortality: "I don't want to achieve immortality through my work. I want to
    achieve it by not dying" - Woody Allen; "The blazing evidence of immortality
    is our dissatisfaction with any other solution" - Ralph Waldo Emerson; "The
    key to immortality is first living a life worth remembering" - St Augustine

immune system, study of: immunology

immunologists: Paul Ehrlich, Jacques Miller

I'm No Angel (1933 film), famous lines: Tira (Mae West): "Beulah! Peel me a
    grape." Tira: "It's not the men in my life, but the life in my men." Tira: "When
    I'm good, I'm very, very good. But when I'm bad, I'm better." Tira: "I've been
    things and seen places."

impala, female: ewe

impala, male: ram

imperfection, fear of: atelophobia

impersonator of Queen Elizabeth II: Jeanette Charles

impersonators – see impressionists

implant: transponder (cyborg-friendly)

impossible causes, patron saints of: Frances Xavier Cabrini and Rita of Cascia

impostors: Arthur Orton (aka the Tichborne Claimant), Perkin Warbeck

impotence: acratia

impotence pill: Cialis (which allows men to achieve an erection up to 24 hours
    after ingestion), Tadalafil, Viagra

impotent person: spado

impresarios: Max Bialystock (from Mel Brooks' *The Producers*), Allan Carr,
    Richard D'Oyly Carte, Bernard Delfont, Sergei Diaghilev, Georges Edwardes,
    Lew Grade, Norman Granz, Oscar Hammerstein, Philip Henslowe, Sol Hurok,
    Bill Kenwright, Andrew Lloyd Webber, Cameron Mackintosh, Malcolm
    McLaren, Sir Brian McMaster, Max Reinhardt, John Ringling, Johann Peter
    Salomon, Robert Stigwood, Lucia Elizabeth Vestris, Florenz Ziegfeld

impressionists: Ronni Ancona, Rory Bremner, Faith Brown, Phil Cornwell, Tina
    Fey, Frank Gorshin, Alistair McGowan, John Sessions, Mike Yarwood

Impressionist painters: Frédéric Bazille, Eugène Boudin, Mary Cassatt, Edgar

Degas, Édouard Manet, Claude Monet, Berthe Morisot, Camille Pisssarro, Pierre-Auguste Renoir, Alfred Sisley, Walter Sickert

IN: postcode for Indiana

Incan city: Machu Picchu

incense burning: thurification

incestuous and famous: Princess Berenice of Judea, Anne Boleyn (as accused by Henry VIII), Cesare Borgia, Lucrezia Borgia, Giacomo Casanova, Cleopatra (married to at least one of her brothers), Cronus, Moll Flanders, Freya, Freyr, Hera, Herod Antipas, Herodias, Isis, Jocasta, Oedipus, Osiris, Ptolemy II (married his sister), Rhea, Sigmund (in Norse mythology), Uranus, Voltaire (who had a fling with his niece), Zeus

income: "I'm living so far beyond my income that we may almost be said to be living apart" – e.e. cummings

Independent, The: British newspaper founded in 1986

Independent on Sunday: British newspaper founded in 1990

India: republic in sothern Asia

    capital: New Delhi

    currency: rupee

    language: Hindi, English, Assamese, Bengali, Gujarati, Kannada, Kashmiri, Malayalam, Marathi, Oriya, Punjabi, Sanskrit, Sindhi, Tamil, Telugu, Urdu – among 22 'national' languages, alongside as many as 240 dialects and 1,726 'mother tongues'

    religion: Hindu (majority), Muslim

    birthplace of: Ali Bongo, Julie Christie, Gerald Durrell, Lawrence Durrell, Engelbert Humperdinck, M.M. Kaye, Rudyard Kipling, Vivien Leigh, Margaret Lockwood, Spike Milligan, Merle Oberon, Juliet Prowse, Michael Radford (filmmaker), Cliff Richard, Peter Sarstedt, William Makepeace Thackeray, Googie Withers

    controversial novels: *The Satanic Verses*; *Surviving Men: the Smart Woman's Guide to Staying On Top*

    fact: India is supposedly the fifth happiest nation in the world

    fact: India is the country with the most daily newspapers (over 2,000)

    literacy: a third of men and two thirds of women still cannot read or write

India, patron saint of: Our Lady of the Assumption

India caste system: Brahmans (earthly gods), the Kshatriyas (the warrior caste), the Vaisyas (farmers and merchants), the Sudras (laborers, born to be servants to the other three castes, especially the Brahman), the Harijans (or untouchables)

Indian and famous: Indira Gandhi, Mahatma Gandhi, Rajiv Gandhi, Shashi Kapoor, Jawaharlal Nehru, Vikram Seth, Ravi Shankar, Shilpa Shetty

Indian bandits: Phoolan Devi, Koose Muniswamy Veerappan (aka the 'Jungle Cat', who allegedly murdered more than 120 people)

Indian film: Bollywood blockbuster, Bombay talkie, Hindi film, masala movie

Indian film directors: Deepa Mehta, Mira Nair, Satyajit Ray

Indian god, with elephant head: Ganesa

Indian goddess of destruction: Kali

Indian independence leader: Mahatma Mohandas Gandhi

Indian jacket: banyan

Indian loincloth: dhoti

Indian mausoleum: Taj Mahal (see)

Indian musical instruments: sarangi, sitar, tabla

Indian philosopher: Gotama

Indian public crier (calling Muslims to prayer): muezzin
Indian scout – see Native American Indian scout
Indian shirt: kurta
Indian singer: Lata Mangeshkar
Indian spot on forehead: tilak, 'third eye'
Indian turban: puggaree
Indian writers: C. Subramania Bharati, Vikram Chandra, Deepak Chopra,
    Mahadev Desai, Amitav Ghosh, Hari Kunzru (part British), Rohinton Mistry,
    R.K. Narayan, Arundhati Roy, Salman Rushdie, Vikram Seth
Indiana, 19th state (1816), Hoosier State
    capital: Indianapolis
    motto: 'Crossroads of America'
    native: Hoosier
    state bird: cardinal (a state bird it shares with Illinois, Kentucky, North
        Carolina, Ohio, Virginia and West Virginia)
    state flower: peony
    state tree: tulip poplar
    tourist attractions: Wyandotte Cave, Indiana Dunes, Hoosier National Forest
    birthplace of: Hoagy Carmichael, James Dean, Theodore Dreiser (novelist),
        Jimmy Hoffa, Janet Jackson, Michael Jackson, Jim Jones, Greg Kinnear,
        David Letterman, Steve McQueen, John Mellencamp, Jane Pauley, Cole
        Porter, Dan Quayle, Twyla Tharp, Kurt Vonnegut Jr, Lew Wallace, Wilbur
        Wright
    fact: the first state to implement co-education
    fact: the US state with the highest incident of syphilis
Indianapolis, birthplace of: John Dillinger, Brendan Fraser, David Letterman,
    Dan Quayle, Kurt Vonnegut Jr
Indianapolis river: White River
indifferent person: pococurante (someone prone to apathy)
indigestion: dyspepsia
Indonesia: republic in south-eastern Asia
    capital: Jakarta
    currency: rupiah
    language: Bahasa Indonesia
    religion: Muslim
Indonesian leaders: Thojib N.J. Suharto, Achmed Sukarno
Indonesian War of Independence: 1945–1949
industrialists: Sir Richard Arkwright, William Armstrong, Clarence Birdseye,
    Andrew Carnegie, Gottlieb Daimler, John Deere, Eleuthère Irénée Du Pont de
    Nemours, Pierre Samuel Du Pont, George Eastman, Henry Ford, John Paul
    Getty, Meyer Guggenheim, Howard Hughes, Henry Kaiser, Alfred Krupp,
    Samuel Lister, Lakshmi Mittal, Alfred Mond, Alfred Nobel, Robert Owen,
    George Pullman, John D. Rockefeller, Oscar Schindler, Henry Seebohm, Ernst
    Werner von Siemens, Tony Stark (aka 'Iron Man'), Sir Alan Sugar
industry, goddess of: Athena (Greek mythology)
infants' talk: lallation
infection, fear of: molysmophobia, tapinophobia
infertility, patron saints of: Rita of Cascia and Philomena
infidelity: apistia (of the marital kind)
infinity: "Only two things are infinite, the universe and human stupidity, and I'm
    not sure about the former" - Albert Einstein
infinity, fear of: apeirophobia

influenza, fact: on average, in an average winter flu is responsible for 12,000 deaths in the UK

ingrowing nail: acronyx

initials, adjective: acrologic

injections, fear of: trypanophobia

injury, fear of: traumatophobia

injustice, dread of: dikephobia

ink cartridge: invented by M. Perrand in 1927 and patented in 1935

ink-blot test: Rorschach test

inmates, famous – see jailed and famous

innocent: prelapsarian (prior to the Fall of Man)

inoculation, fear of: trypanophobia

Inquisitor-General: Tomás de Torquemada

insanity: "The definition of insanity is doing the same thing over and over again and expecting different results" - Oscar Wilde; "I quite agree that all men of genius are insane, but you forget that all sane people are idiots" - Oscar Wilde

insanity, fear of: lyssophobia

insane, patron saint of the: Dympna

insane and famous: Abdul Alhazred (from the works of H.P. Lovecraft), Titus Andronicus, Clara Bow, John Clare (poet), Richard Dadd (painter of fairies, no less), Georges Feydeau (in the last years of his life), Samuel Johnson (partially), Lady Caroline Lamb, Constance (from Shakespeare's *King John*), George III, Hamlet (debatably), Adele Hugo, Margery Kempe, Lady Caroline Lamb, King Lear, Ludwig II (Bavarian king), Lycurgus, Lady Macbeth, Malvolio, Ophelia, Ezra Pound, Augustus Pugin (architect), Bertha Rochester (from *Jane Eyre*), John Ruskin, Marquis de Sade, Robert Schumann, Christopher Smart (poet), Bedrich Smetana, Vincent Van Gogh, Jan Vermeer

insane, patron saint of: Dymphna

insect, adjective: entomic

insect, collective noun: swarm

insect, excrement: frass

insect, fact: there are 1,400,000 identified (and named) species of insect in the world

insect, fastest: dragonfly

insect, largest: stick insect

insect, smallest: the feather-winged beetle (which grows to just 0.01 inch)

insect, young: larva, nit, nymph

insect-eating: entomophagous (adjective)

insects, fear of: entomophobia

insects, obsession with: entomomania

insects, study of: entomology

insect's head plate: clypeus

inside traders: Ivan Boesky, Gordon Gekko (from Oliver Stone's *Wall Street*), Nick Leeson, Jeffrey Skilling, Martha Stewart

insomnia, adjective: agrypnotic

inspiration, god of: Odin (Norse mythology)

installation artists: Joseph Beuys, Dan Flavin, Sarah Lucas, Kurt Schwitters

instant, adjective: liminal

instant coffee: first produced on a commercial scale in 1937 (by Nestlé)

insults: "It takes him an hour and a half to watch *60 Minutes*" (said of politician David C. Treen by Louisiana governor Edwin Edwards); "His men would follow him anywhere, but only out of morbid curiosity" (from an employee performance evaluation); "I've had a wonderful time, but this wasn't it" - Groucho Marx

intellect, adjective: noetic

intellectual: "A man who takes more words than necessary to tell more than he knows" - Dwight Eisenhower

intelligences, as defined by Dr. Howard Gardner: visual/spatial intelligence, musical intelligence, verbal/linguistic intelligence, logical/mathematical intelligence, interpersonal intelligence, intrapersonal intelligence, bodily/kinesthetic intelligence, naturalistic intelligence, naturalist intelligence, and existentialist intelligence

interior designers: Carl Larsson, Elsie de Wolfe

internal examination of the body by camera (in surgery): endoscopy

internal organs, adjective: visceral

International Herald Tribune, The: newspaper founded 4 October, 1887, by James Gordon Bennett, Jr

Internet: global computer network (aka the Infopike and the World Wide Web), invented by the British scientist Sir Tim Berners-Lee

Internet, fact: 86.5 per cent of all web pages are in the English language

Internet, fact: 95 of the top 100 sites are invariably pornographic

Internet, fact: 40% of UK home Internet users look at porn sites

Internet, fact: the top ten most popular sites are almost always pornographic

Internet, patron saint of: Isidore of Seville

Internet address: URL (Universal Resource Locator)

Internet film critic: Harry Knowles (of the Ain't It Cool News website)

Internet virtuosi: digerati

Internet users: the Internet is used mostly by Americans, then the Japanese, then the Chinese

interval, adjective: intervallic

interviewers: Clive Anderson, Johnny Carson, Sir Robin Day, Sir David Frost, Russell Harty, Jay Leno, David Letterman, Sir Michael Parkinson, Jeremy Paxman, Dan Rather, Jonathan Ross, Tomás de Torquemada, Brian Walden, Barbara Walters
- see talk show hosts

intestinal rumbling: borborygmus

intestines, adjective: alvine (rare), enteric

intestines, study of: entrology

invaders – see conquerors

invalids, patron saint of: Roch

inventions, fact: an invention belongs to the inventor for 20 years and, beginning in year two, he must pay huge annual renewal fees to protect his patent globally

inventions, fact: 54% of the world's most important inventions over the past 100 years were British, 25% American and 5% Japanese

inventors: Archimedes, Sir Richard Arkwright, William Armstrong, John Logie Baird, Alexander Graham Bell, Sir Tim Berners-Lee, Johann Bodmer, John Browning, Chester Carlson, Edmund Cartwright, Jacques Charles, Samuel Colt, Thomas Crapper, Gottlieb Daimler, Sir Humphry Davy, Lee De Forest, John Deere, Rudolf Diesel, John Boyd Dunlop, George Eastman, Thomas A. Edison, Michael Faraday, James Francis, Benjamin Franklin, Rube Goldberg, Peter Carl Goldmark, Charles Goodyear, James Hargreaves, Elwood Haynes, William Hewlett, Ted Hoff, Herman Hollerith, Robert Hooke, Frank Hornby, Edwin Land, Leonardo Da Vinci, Samuel Lister, James Lovelock, Kirkpatrick Macmillan, Guglielmo Marconi, William Metford, Elisha Otis, David Packard, George Pullman, Ernő Rubik, Ernst Werner von Siemens, Sir Clive Sinclair,

William Symington, Alessandro Volta, Sir Barnes Wallis, James Watt, Sir Frank
Whittle, Zai Lun (the eunuch who invented paper from tree bark and rags)
inventors, fictitious: Phileas Fogg, Caractacus Potts (from *Chitty Chitty Bang
Bang*), Wallace (Claymation character)
investigative reporters: Carl Bernstein, Seymour Hersh (who exposed the My Lai
massacre, among other things), Bob Woodward
- see journalists, etc
investment: "Buy land. They aren't making it any more" - Mark Twain
Iolanthe: operetta by W.S. Gilbert and Arthur Sullivan, first produced in London
and New York (simultaneously) in 1882
Iowa, 29th state (1846), Hawkeye State
    capital: Des Moines
    motto: 'Our liberties we prize and our rights we will maintain'
    state bird: Eastern goldfinch
    state flower: wild rose
    state tree: oak
    tourist attractions: Herbert Hoover birthplace and library, Effigy Mounds
        National Monument, Amana Colonies
    birthplace of: Bill Bryson, Buffalo Bill (aka William F. Cody), Johnny Carson,
        Herbert Hoover, Ashton Kutcher, Glenn Miller, John Wayne, Andy
        Williams, Elijah Wood, Grant Wood
    fact: Des Moines was the location of the world's first McDonald's fast-food
        restautant
iPod: conceived and marketed in 2001, designed by Apple Computer
IQ, average (in the UK): 100
IRA leaders: Gerry Adams, Martin McGuinness, Seamus Twomey
IRA victims: Louis Mountbatten, Tory MPs Ian Gow and Airey Neave (killed by
car bombs)
Iran: republic in south-west Asia; formerly known as Persia (until 1935)
    capital: Tehran
    currency: rial
    language: Farsi
    religion: Muslim
    birthplace of: Doris Lessing
    volunteer Islamic militia: Basij
Iran-Iraq Gulf War: 1980–1988
Iranian filmmakers: Abbas Kiarostami, Majid Majidi
Iranian shah: Mohammad Reza Pahlavi (overthrown in 1979)
Iranian spiritual leader: Ayatollah Khomeinei
Iraq: republic in south-west Asia (the territory of modern Iraq is roughly equivalent
to that of ancient Mesopotamia)
    capital: Baghdad
    currency: dinar
    language: Arabic, Kurdish
    religion: Muslim
Iraqi architect: Zaha Hadid
Iraqi cleric: Moqtada al-Sadr
Iraqi invasion of Kuwait: launched 2 August 1990
Iraqi president: Saddam Hussein (1979–2003)
Iraqi prime minister: Iyad Allawi (after the fall of Saddam Hussein)
Iraqi prison: Abu Ghraib (famous for its abuse of detainees by the Americans)

Iraqi terrorist: Abu Musab al-Zarqawi
Ireland, Republic of: republic occupying much of the island of Ireland; aka Eire,
    the Emerald Isle, Erin (poetic name for), Hibernia (ancient name for)
    capital: Dublin (see)
    currency: euro, formerly the punt
    language: Irish Gaelic, English
    religion: Roman Catholic
    patron saints of: Brigid of Kildare, Patrick and Columba
Ireland, adjective: Hibernian
iris examination: iridology
Irish nationalists: Brendan Behan, Michael Collins, Éamon de Valera, John Devoy,
    Thomas MacDonagh, Patrick Pearse
Irish playwrights: Samuel Beckett, Brendan Behan, Maeve Binchy, St John Ervine,
    Brian Friel, Oliver Goldsmith, Donagh MacDonagh, Conor McPherson, Dame
    Iris Murdoch, Arthur Murphy, Sean O'Casey, George Bernard Shaw, Richard
    Sheridan, Sir Richard Steele, J.M. Synge, Oscar Wilde, W.B. Yeats
Irish rebellion (aka Easter Rising): 24 April-30 April 1916
Irish writers: John and Michael Banim, Samuel Beckett, Brendan Behan, Maeve
    Binchy, Elizabeth Bowen, Erskine Childers, Seamus Deane, J.P. Donleavy,
    Roddy Doyle, St John Ervine, Frank Harris, Seamus Heaney, James Joyce,
    Molly Keane, Mary Lavin, Sheridan Le Fanu, Sir Shane Leslie, Charles Lever,
    Frank McCourt, George Moore, Dame Iris Murdoch, Edna O'Brien, Flann
    O'Brien, Sean O'Faolain, Liam O'Flaherty, Patrick Pearse, Edith Somerville
Irishman: bogtrotter (derog.), Mick, Mikey (US slang), Paddy
Irishman, adjective: Hibernian
iron, adjective: ferric, ferrous, ferreous
Iron Chancellor: nickname for Otto von Bismarck
Iron Duke: nickname for Duke of Wellington
Iron Lady: nickname for Ellen Johnson-Sirleaf (Liberian politician), Margaret
    Thatcher
Iron Maiden: UK heavy metal rock group formed in London in 1976; comprised
    of Steve Harris (bass), Dave Murray (lead guitar), Paul Di'anno (vocals) and
    Doug Sampson (drums)
ironmongers, patron saint of: Sebastian
Ironside: nickname for Oliver Cromwell
irony: "Irony is the hygiene of the mind" - Elizabeth Bibesco
IRS: Internal Revenue Service
ISA: individual savings account
ISBN: international standard book number
ISDN: intergrated services digital network
Islam, founder of: Mohammed
Islam, orthodox; the two branches of: Shiah and Sunni
Islamic leader: Omar Abdel-Rahman (responsible for the World Trade Centre
    bombing of 1993)
Islamic militant group: Jemaah Islamiah (JI)
Islamic public crier (calling Muslims to prayer): muezzin
Islamic robe, required to be worn by woman: burqa, chador, chuddah, chuddar
island, adjective: insular
island, world's most populous: Java
islands, world's largest: 1) Greenland; 2) New Guinea; 3) Borneo; 4) Madagascar;
    5) Baffin Island; 6) Sumatra; 7) Honshu; 8) Great Britain; 9) Victoria Island;
    10) Ellesmere Island

Isle of Man: island in the British Isles, independent of the United Kingdom
(although a Crown property)
    capital: Douglas
    currency: British pound, Manx pound
    language: English, Manx (now almost extinct)
    religion: Anglican, Roman Catholic, Methodist, Baptist, Presbyterian, Society
        of Friends
Isle of Wight: island (and county) in the English Channel
Isle of Wight, administrative centre: Newport
ISP: Internet service provider
Israel: republic in south-west Asia established in 1948
    capital and largest city: Jerusalem
    currency: shekel
    language: Hebrew and Arabic (both official); also Yiddish
    religion: Judaism
    nicknames: Holy Land, Land of Milk and Honey
Israel, first king of: Saul
Israeli and famous: Daniel Barenboim, Sharon Bezaly (flautist), Eli Cohen
    (spy), Dana International (singer), Moshe Dayan, Alber Elbaz (fashion
    designer), Uri Geller, Yoram Globus (film tycoon), Menahem Golan (film
    tycoon), Moshe Katsav (president charged with rape), Golda Meir, Amos
    Oz (novelist), Itzhak Perlman, Yitzhak Rabin, Ariel Sharon, King Solomon,
    Chaim Topol
Israeli intelligence agency: Mossad
Israeli president, first: Chaim Azriel Weizmann (1949–1952)
Istanbul: Turkish city formerly known as Byzantium and then Constantinople
    (330–1926)
    birthplace of: Tchéky Karyo (actor), Eliza Kazan
    river: Golden Horn
    strait: Bosphorus
    tourist attractions: Aya Sofya mosque, Topkapi Palace of the Sultans
        (complete with a 400-room harem), Sultan Ahmet mosque
    fact: the only city in the world to have been the capital of both Christian and
        Islamic empires
    fact: the city straddles two continents, Europe and Asia
Italian: dago, dingbat, eytie, ghinny, gibroney, ginzo, greaseball, guinzo, meatball,
    pizza man, spic, wop
Italian actors: Roberto Benigni, Rossano Brazzi, Claudia Cardinale, Walter Chiari,
    Vittorio Gassman, Terence Hill, Gina Lollobrigida, Sophia Loren, Anna
    Magnani, Silvana Mangano, Giulietta Masina, Marcello Mastroianni, Isa
    Miranda, Franco Nero, Alberto Sordi, Ugo Tognazzi, Totò, Rudolph Valentino,
    Alida Valli, Monica Vitti, Gian Maria Volonté, Lina Wertmüller
Italian art of the fourteenth century: trecento
Italian art of the fifteenth century: quattrocento
Italian art of the sixteenth century: cinquecento
Italian art of the seventeenth century: seicento
Italian composers: Luciano Berio, Arcangelo Corelli, Gaetano Donizetti,
    Baldassaro Galuppi, Bruno Maderna, Pietro Mascagni, Claudio Monteverdi,
    Giacomo Puccini, Ottorino Respighi, Gioacchino Rossini, Alessandro Scarlatti,
    Domenico Scarlatti, Giovanni Sgambati, Giuseppe Verdi, Antonio Vivaldi

Italian film directors: Gianni Amelio, Michelango Antonioni, Dario Argento, Marco Bellocchio, Roberto Benigni, Bernardo Bertolucci, Liliana Cavani, Vittorio De Sica, Federico Fellini, Marco Ferreri, Sergio Leone, Mario Monicelli, Nanni Moretti, Ermanno Olmi, Pier Paolo Pasolini, Elio Petri, Gillo Pontecorvo, Francesco Rosi, Roberto Rossellini, Ettore Scola, Paolo and Vittorio Taviani, Giuseppe Tornatore, Luchino Visconti

Italian Job, The (1969 film), famous lines: Charlie Croker (Michael Caine): "You're only supposed to blow the bloody doors off!" (after a van is blown to smithereens); Charlie: "Hang on a minute, lads, I've got a great idea... er..." [last line]

Italian novelists: Giovanni Boccaccio, Italo Calvino, Gabriele d'Annunzio, Umberto Eco, Giuseppe Tomasi di Lampedusa, Alessandro Manzoni, Pier Paolo Pasolini, Luigi Pirandello, Leonardo Sciascia, Italo Svevo, Giovanni Verga

Italian painters: Andrea del Sarto, Fra Angelico, Pietro Annigoni, Antonello da Messina, Giuseppe Arcimboldo, Jacopo Bassano, Giovanni Bellini, Gian Lorenzo Bernini, Sandro Botticelli, Agnolo Bronzino, Canaletto, Michelangelo da Caravaggio, Vittore Carpaccio, Agostino Carracci, Giorgio de Chirico, Antonio da Correggio, Duccio (di Buoninsegna), Orazio Gentileschi, Giorgione, Giotto (di Bondone), Leonardo da Vinci, Pietro Lorenzetti, Filippino Lippi, Fra Filippino Lippi, Lorenzo Lotto, Andrea Mantegna, Simone Martini, Masaccio, Michelangelo Buonarroti, Amedeo Modigliani, Piero della Francesca, Salvator Rosa, Raphael Santi, Giovanni Battista Tiepolo, Tintoretto, Titian, Paolo Uccello, Paolo Veronese

Italian playwrights: Dario Fo, Giuseppe Giacosa, Carlo Goldoni, Luigi Pirandello

Italian racing driver: Alberto Ascari

Italian restaurant: trattoria

Italian scooter: Vespa

Italian singers: Andrea Bocelli, Carla Bruni, Enrico Caruso, Luciano Pavarotti

Italian soldier: Giuseppe Garibaldi

Italian statesmen: Giuliano Amato, Giulio Andreotti, Silvio Berlusconi, Bettino Craxi, Aldo Moro, Benito Mussolini, Giorgio Napolitano, Romano Prodi

Italian words (used in the English language): a cappella, adagio, al dente, al fresco, allegro, alto, andante, antipasto, aria, arpeggio, ballerina, basso profundo, belvedere (summer house), biretta (three-pointed hat), bordello, bravura, brio, cadenza, cameo, cannelloni, cantata, cappuccino, casino, castrato, cavatina, chiaroscuro, coda, cognoscenti, concerto, confetti, contralto, crescendo, dilettante, ditto, diva, divertimento, espresso, falsetto, fantasia, fata morgana, finale, fiasco, fresco, furore, ghetto, gondola, grappa, gusto, imbroglio, imprimatura, incognito, inferno, intermezzo, largo (a slow, dignified tempo), lasagna, lava, libretto, literati, macaroni, madonna, maestro, manifesto, mascara, mezzo soprano, minestrone, monsignore, mozzarella, novella, oratorio, padrone, pasta, pergola, pianissimo, piano, piazza, pizza, portico, presto, prima donna, prosciutto, putto, ravioli, regatta, replica, risotto, salami, scampi, scenario, simpatico, sirocco (a hot wind), solo, sonata, soprano, sotto voce, spaghetti, staccato, stiletto, stanza, stucco, tempo, terra cotta, terrazzo, timpani, torso, trattoria, trio, tutti frutti, vendetta, virtuoso, vista, zabaglione

Italy: republic in southern Europe, known as "the boot country," "a paradise of exiles" (according to Shelley) and "a paradise for horses, hell for women" (c/o Robert Burton)
  capital: Rome
  currency: euro; formerly: lira
  language: Italian

religion: Roman Catholic
mountain range: Apennines
patron saints of: Francis of Assisi, Bernardine of Siena and Catherine of Siena
rivers: Adige, Arno, Po, Rubicon, Tiber
itching, fear of: acarophobia
ITV, first broadcast: 22 September 1955: a variety show and drama excerpts linked
    by Robert Morley (upstaged by Grace Archer's death – by fire – in BBC Radio's
    The Archers)
ITV, first commercial on: SR toothpaste
IVF: in vitro fertilisation
Ivory Coast: republic in West Africa known as Côte d'Ivoire since 1986 (see)
Ivy League schools: Brown University, Columbia University, Cornell University,
    Dartmouth College, Harvard University, Princeton University, University of
    Pennsylvania, Yale University
IYKWIMAITYD: if you know what I mean and I think you do

J

jackal-headed gods: Anubis, Wepwawet (both Egyptian mythology)
jacket: anorak, banyan, Barbour, blazer, blouson, bolero, bomber jacket, bush
    jacket, cagoule, dinner jacket, dolman, donkey jacket, doublet, Eton jacket,
    Pacamac, parka, puffa
jack rabbit, collective noun: husk
Jacksons, The: US pop group formed in 1965; comprised of Jackie (real name:
    Sigmund Esco Jackson), Tito (real name: Toriano Adryll Jackson), Marlon
    Jackson, Jermaine Jackson and Michael Jackson
Jack the Ripper suspects: Prince Albert Victor, Joseph Barnett, Alfred Napier
    Blanchard, W.H. Bury, Lewis Carroll, David Cohen, Dr. T. Neill Cream,
    Frederick Deeming, Montague John Druitt, Sir William Gull, George
    Hutchinson, James Kenneth Stephen, Severin Antoniovich Klosowski (aka
    George Chapman), Aaron Kosminski, Jacob Levy, James Maybrick, Michael
    Ostrog, Dr Alexander Pedachenko (aka Count Luiskovo), Walter Sickert,
    Robert Donston Stephenson (aka Dr Roslyn D'Onston), Francis Thompson,
    Francis Tumblety, Nicholas Vassily
Jack the Ripper victims: Mary Ann Nichols (killed 31 August, 1888), Annie
    Chapman (killed 8 September, 1888), Elizabeth Stride (29 September, 1888),
    Catherine Eddowes (killed 29 September, 1888), Marie Jeanette Kelly (killed 9
    November, 1888)
Jacobean playwrights: Francis Beaumont, John Fletcher, Ben Jonson, Thomas
    Middleton, William Rowley, John Webster
Jacobites: Alan Breck (from Stevenson's *Kidnapped*), King James II of England,
    Charles Edward Stuart, James Edward Stuart
Jacobite Rebellion: 1715–1716
jailed and famous: Jonathan Aitken, Fatty Arbuckle, Jeffrey Archer, Ares, Joan
    Baez, Hastings Banda, Banksy, Bartleby (from Melville's *The Piazza Tales*),
    Brendan Behan, Chuck Berry, George Best, Ronald Biggs, Ivan Boesky, Lord
    Brockett, Bobby Brown, Divine Brown, James Brown, Lenny Bruce,
    Michelangelo da Caravaggio, Giacomo Casanova, Fidel Castro, Miguel de
    Cervantes, Lindy Chamberlain, Ray Charles, Eldridge Cleaver, Alex Comfort,
    Thomas Cromwell, Richard Dadd, Moshe Dayan, Daniel Defoe, Guillaume

Depardieu, Johnny Depp, Denis Diderot, Pete Doherty, William Dorrit (from Dickens' *Little Dorrit*), Robert Downey Jr, Queen Elizabeth I, Moll Flanders, Heidi Fleiss, Larry Flynt, Margot Fonteyn, Stephen Fry, Klaus Fuchs, Mahatma Mohandas Gandhi, Marcus Garvey, Jean Genet, Sir John Gielgud, Gary Glitter (real name: Paul Gadd), Danny Glover, Charles Goodyear, Gunther von Hagens, Naseem Hamed, Lady Emma Hamilton, Václav Havel, Patty Hearst, Paris Hilton, Alger Hiss, Adolf Hitler, Ho Chi Minh, James Hoffa, Abbie Hoffman, Billie Holiday, Leigh Hunt, David Irving, Jesse Jackson, Dr John, Ben Johnson (playwright), Jack Johnson (boxer), Brian Jones, Garry Kasparov, Stacy Keach, Jomo Kenyatta, Imran Khan, King of Ruritania (the Prisoner of Zenda), Leadbelly (aka Huddie Ledbetter; blues singer), Timothy Leary, Primo Levi, G. Gordon Liddy, Lindsay Lohan, Jack London, Malcolm X, Nelson Mandela, Charles Manson, Christopher Marlowe, John McCarthy, John McVicar, Robert Mitchum, Sun Myung Moon, Sir Thomas More, Jawaharlal Nehru, Richard Neville, Ivor Novello, O.D.B., Joe Orton, Thomas Paine, Jafar Panahi (Iranian filmmaker), Emmeline Pankhurst, Giancarlo Parretti (head of MGM-Pathé), Sean Penn, Juan Perón, Marco Polo, Porgy (from *Porgy and Bess*), Richard Pryor, Sir Walter Raleigh, Keith Richards, Bertrand Russell, Anwar Sadat, Marquis de Sade, Martin Sheen, O.J. Simpson, Christian Slater, Jimmy Smits, Aleksandr Solzhenitsyn, Benjamin Spock, Joseph Stalin, Martha Stewart, Mikis Theodorakis, Sir Michael Tippett, Ricky Tomlinson, Leon Trotsky, Mike Tyson, Vince Vaughn, Paul Verlaine (poet), Voltaire, Mark Wahlberg, Terry Waite, Edmund Waller, Sir William Waller, Mary Ward, Mae West, Oscar Wilde, John Wilkes, Hank Williams, Abdullahi Yusuf Ahmed
- see convicts, escaped

Jamaica: island state in the Caribbean
   capital: Kingston
   currency: Jamaican dollar
   language: English, Jamaican creole
   religion: Protestant (70%), Rastafarian
   resort: Montego Bay
   fact: where tourists are three times less likely to be murdered than in
      Washington DC
Jamaican and famous: Usain Bolt (sprinter), Ken Boothe, Desmond Dekker,
   Marcus Garvey (activist), Lorna Goodison (poet), Grace Jones, Bob Marley,
   Sean Paul, Lee 'Scratch' Perry (recording engineer), Mary Seacole (nurse)
James Bond – see Bond, James
JAP: Jewish American Princess
Japan: empire in eastern Asia
   capital: Tokyo
   currency: yen
   language: Japanese
   religion: Shinto, Buddhist, Christian
   nickname: Land of the Rising Sun
   mythical name: Cipango
   bowing fact: the average Japanese businessman will bow 200 times a day
   mountains: Japan Alps, Mount Fuji, Mount Aso
   patron saints: Francis Xavier and Peter Baptist and Companions
Japanese art of paper folding: origami
Japanese art of paper folding and cutting: kirigami

Japanese artist: Hokusai
Japanese battle-cry: banzai!
Japanese Buddhist teacher: bonze
Japanese clog: geta
Japanese composers: Ryuichi Sakamoto, Toru Takemitsu
Japanese crime syndicate: yakuza
Japanese cuisine: miso (soup made from a red bean paste), sashimi (raw fish),
    sukiyaki (dish comprised of sliced meat fried with vegetables and sauce),
    sushi (small circles of rice cooked with seaweed, covered with various foods),
    tempura (pieces of fish, shrimps and vegetables, dipped in batter and deep
    fried), wasabi (horseradish paste)
Japanese door (sliding): shoji
Japanese emperor: mikado, tenno
Japanese emperors: Akihito, Hirohito
Japanese fashion designers: Rei Kawakubo, Kenzo (Takada)
Japanese fencing: kendo (using bamboo swords)
Japanese film directors: Kon Ichikawa, Shōhei Imamura, Takeshi Kitano, Masaki
    Kobayashi, Akira Kurosawa, Takashi Miike, Kenji Mizoguchi, Hideo Nakata,
    Nagisa Oshima, Yasujiro Ozu, Hiroshi Teshigahara
Japanese floor covering (a rush-covered straw mat): tatami
Japanese flower arranging: ikebana
Japanese generals: Hideki Tojo, Tomoyuki Yamashita
Japanese leaders: Prince Konoe Fumimaro (1937–1939, 1940–1941), Sato Eisaku
    (1964–1972), Yamamoto Gombe (1913–1914; 1923–1924), Mitsumasa Yonai
    (1940), Yoshida Shigeru (1946–1947; 1948–1954)
Japanese martial art: aikido, ju-jitsu, karate
Japanese mattress: futon
Japanese musical instruments: kane (bell), koto (zither), shamisen (an ancient
    three-stringed instrument), taiko (drum)
Japanese photographer: Nobuyoshi Araki
Japanese poet: Hagiwara Sakutaro
Japanese porcelain: Arita
Japanese priest: bonze
Japanese restaurants: kaiten (conveyor belt selection), Nobu, Wagamama, Yo! Sushi
Japanese sash: obi
Japanese seaweed: kombu
Japanese silk painting: kakemono
Japanese sliding screen door: shoji
Japanese swordsman: samurai
Japanese theatre forms: Bugaku, Bunraku (puppetry), gigaku (earliest known type
    of Japanese theatrical entertainment), Kabuki, manzai (stand-up comedy), Noh,
    sangaku (typical acts of which include tightrope walking, juggling and sword
    swallowing)
Japanese writers: Dazai Osamu, Shusaku Endo, Kazuo Ishiguro, Yasunari
    Kawabata, Tayama Katai, Natsuo Kirino, Yukio Mishima, Haruki Murakami,
    Ryū Murakami, Mori Ogai, Natsume Soseki, Banana Yoshimoto
jaundice, adjective: icteric, icterical, icteroid
jaw, adjective: gnathal, gnathic, malar, maxillary
jawbone: mandible (lower jaw), maxilla (upper jaw)
jaws, without: agnathous (adjective)
Jaws 2 (1978 film), tagline: "Just when you thought it was safe to go back into the
    water..."

jay, collective noun: chatter

jazz composers: Duke Ellington, Charles Mingus, Thelonious Monk, Jelly Roll Morton, Sun Ra

jazz dances: black bottom, boogie-woogie, Charleston, jitterbug, jive
- see dance

jazz critic: Philip Larkin

Jazz Singer, The (1927 film), famous line [the first in cinema history]: Jakie Rabinowitz (Al Jolson): "Wait a minute, wait a minute, you ain't heard nothin' yet. Wait a minute, I tell ya. You ain't heard nothin'! You wanna hear *Toot, Toot, Tootsie*? All right, hold on, hold on"

jealous and famous: Daffy Duck, Green-Eyed Monster, Hera, Howard Hughes, Othello, Tiberius

jealousy: "Jealousy is all the fun you think they had" - Erica Jong

jealousy, aversion to: zelophobia

jeans: Bobson, Calvin Kleins, denims, Diesel, 501, 516, Gap, "hysterectomy pants," James, Lee, Levi's, red tab, Seven, silver tab, stretch denim jeans, Value (Tesco brand), Wrangler

Jedi knight: Obi-Wan Kenobi

Jehovah's Witnesses: founded in 1872 by Charles Taze Russell (aka The Bible Students' Association)

Jehovah's Witnesses, famous: George Benson, Naomi Campbell, Dwight D. Eisenhower (originally), Geri Halliwell, Ja Rule (originally), Michael Jackson (lapsed), Hank Marvin, Prince (real name: Prince Rogers Nelson), Patti Smith, Mickey Spillane, Serena Williams, Venus Williams

jelly: confiture, Jello-O, nervous pudding, preserve

jellyfish, adjective: discophoran

jellyfish, collective noun: fluther, smack, smuck, smuth

jellyfish, young: ephyra

jelly-like: colloid

Jerry Maguire (1996 film), famous lines: Rod Tidwell [Cuba Gooding Jr]: "Show me the money!"; Jerry Maguire [Tom Cruise], to Dorothy: "I'm lookin' for my wife. Wait. OK... OK... OK. If this is where it has to happen, then this is where it has to happen. I'm not letting you get rid of me. How about that? This used to be my specialty, you know. I was good in a living room. They'd send me in there, and I'd do it alone. And now I just... But tonight, our little project, our company had a very big night – a very, *very* big night. But it wasn't complete, wasn't nearly close to being in the same vicinity as complete, because I couldn't share it with you. I couldn't hear your voice, or laugh about it with you. I miss my... I miss my wife. We live in a cynical world – a cynical world – and we work in a business of tough competitors. I love you. You – complete me. I just had..." Dorothy [Renée Zellweger], interrupting: "Shut up. Just shut up. You had me at 'hello'"

Jerusalem, birthplace of: Natalie Portman (actress), Yitzhak Rabin, King Solomon
wall: Wailing Wall

jesters: Feste (from *Twelfth Night*), The Fool (from *King Lear*), Touchstone (from *As You Like It*), Trinculo (from *The Tempest*), Yorick
- see fools

jester's hat: coxcomb

Jesus, born: c.6 BC

Jesus, died: c.30 AD

Jesus' disciples: the twelve apostles (Simon, Andrew, James, John, Philip, Bartholomew, Thomas, Matthew, James, Thaddaeus, Simon the Zealot, Judas Iscariot, Matthias)

Jesus' father: God, Joseph
Jesus' home: Nazareth
Jesus' mother: Mary
Jesus, other names for: the Carpenter, Chi-Rho (Greek symbol for), Christ, the
     Chosen One, Dominus, Immanuel, King of the Jews, Lamb of God, the
     Magician of Nazareth, the Messiah, Prince of Peace, the Redeemer, the Saviour,
     Son of David, Son of God, Son of Man
Jesus, language of: Aramaic
Jesus, tribe of: Judah
jet lag: dysrhythmia
jet propulsion, father of: Sir Frank Whittle
Jew: Ashkenazi, clip (male only), fifteen and two (CRS), goose, kike, Moch,
     mockie, refusenik, Sabbatarian, Sephardi, Yehudi (USA slang), Yemenite, Yid
Jew, fictitious: Barabas (from Christopher Marlowe's *The Jew of Malta*), Fagin,
     Shylock
Jew, saver of: Frank Foley, Oscar Schindler
Jew of Malta: Barabas
jewel robbery, biggest in history: £65 million haul from the Antwerp Diamond
     Centre in 2003
jewel thieves: the Baron (aka John Mannering), Boston Blackie, Fay Cheyney, Joan
     Hannington (known as Britain's only female jewel thief), Lone Wolf (c/o Louis
     Joseph Vance), Porfirio Rubirosa
     - see thieves
jewellers, famous: René Lalique, Charles Tiffany
jewellers: Asprey & Garrard (the Queen's jewellers), Bulgari, Cartier, Leslie Davis,
     De Beers, Ernest Jones, H. Samuel, H. Stern, Tiffany & Co.
jewellers, London centre of: Hatton Garden
jewellers, patron saints of: Dunstan, Eligius
jewellers' magnifying glass: loupe
jewellery designers: Paloma Picasso, Simon Wilson
Jewish accessories: ephod, menorah, mezuzah, phylactery, tallith, tefillin, yarmulke
Jewish bread: challah (baked to celebrate the sabbath)
Jewish cult: Kabbalah
Jewish fast: Day of Atonement, Yom Kippur
Jewish law: contained in the Torah
Jewish Pentecost: Shavuoth
Jewish religion: Judaism
Jewish teacher: rabbi
Jewish usurer: Shylock
JFDI: just frigging do it
JI: Jemaah Islamiah (Islamic militant group)
jigsaw puzzle: first recorded in 1763
JIT: just in time
J.Lo: nickname for Jennifer Lopez
jockeys (of the horseracing variety): Frank Buckle, Willie Carson, Steve Cauthen,
     Frankie Dettori, Jacko Doyasbère, Richard Dunwoody, Pat Eddery, Kieren
     Fallon, George Fordham, Dick Francis, Richard Johnson, Michael Kinane,
     Julie Krone, Tony McCoy, Isaac Murphy, Tom Oliver, John Osborne, Lester
     Piggott, John 'Red' Pollard, Sir Gordon Richards, Jem Robinson, Peter
     Scudamore, Willie Shoemaker, Willie Simms, George Stevens, Ron Turcotte,
     Jimmy 'Wink' Winkfield

jockey's outfit: silks

Johannesburg: South African city dubbed 'the murder capital of the world'
    birthplace of: Allan Cormack (physicist), Sidney James, Mike Lubowitz
        (keyboard player with the pop group Manfred Mann), Miriam Makeba,
        Gary Player (golfer), Janet Suzman (actress)

joints, study of: arthrology, rheumatology

jokes, morbid impulse to tell: moria

jokers: Pierre Brassard (Canadian disc jockey who quizzed the British Queen on
    radio), Samantha Marson (21-year-old British student who was arrested at
    Miami airport after joking she had a bomb in her bag)
    - see clowns, comedians, pranksters

Jordan: kingdom in south-west Asia occupying the Biblical regions of Moab,
    Gilead and Edom; formerly known as Trans-Jordan
    capital: Amman
    currency: dinar
    language: Arabic
    religion: Muslim (Sunni)
    patron saint: John the Baptist

journalism: "A brothel which is easy to enter but impossible to escape" - Michael
    Ignatieff, paraphrasing Tolstoy

journalist: columnist, freeloader, hack, paparrazi, reporter, straggler

journalists: "People with nothing to say and who know how to say it" - Karl Kraus

journalists: George Alagiah, Thomas Barnes, Martin Bashir, James Gordon
    Bennett, Jeffrey Bernard, Carl Bernstein, Helen Gurley Brown, Michael Buerk,
    Wilfred Burchett, James Cameron, Georges Clemenceau, William Cobbett,
    W.F. Deedes, John Delane, Joan Didion, Harold Evans, Oriana Fallaci, Theodor
    Fontane, Paul Foot, Bonnie Fuller, Martha Gellhorn, Andrew Gilligan, Sheilah
    Graham, Horace Greeley, Sir Hugh Greene, Friedrich Grimm, Veronica Guerin,
    Motoko Hani, William Hazlitt, Michael Herr, Seymour Hersh, Anthony
    Howard, John Humphrys, Ryszard Kapuscinski, Ludovic Kennedy, Rudyard
    Kipling, Bernard Levin, Rod Liddle, Magnus Magnusson, Andrew Marr, Henry
    Mayhew, H.L. Mencken, Judith Miller (imprisoned for refusing to name her
    sources), Malcolm Muggeridge, Edward R. Murrow, Richard Neville, Flann
    O'Brien, P.J. O'Rourke, George Orwell, Dorothy Parker, Jane Pauley, Daniel
    Pearl (who was kidnapped and murdered in Karachi, Pakistan), John Pilger,
    Anna Politkovskaya (allegedly shot dead for criticising the political regime of
    Vladimir Putin), Libby Purves, James Redpath, John Reed, Jon Ronson, Jean
    Rook, Damon Runyon, George Sala, Sydney Schanberg, Jonathan Schell,
    Leonardo Sciascia, John Sergeant, Shi Tao (jailed for ten years after her e-mails
    had been intercepted from Yahoo!), I.F. Stone, Dorothy Thompson, Hunter S.
    Thompson, Philip Toynbee, Craig Unger, Alan Whicker, Katharine Whitehorn,
    A.N. Wilson, Tom Wolfe, Bob Woodward
    - see critics, film critics, literary critics, rock journalists, war correspondents, etc

journalists, patron saint of: Francis de Sales

journalists, rogue: Jayson Blair (invented stories for *The New York Times*), Stephen
    Glass (invented stories for *The New Republican*), Jack Kelley (invented stories
    for *USA Today*)

journey, adjective: viatic

jousting, fact: the state sport of Maryland

joy; enjoying the happiness of others: macarism

Judaea, king of: Herod

judge, mode of verbal address: Your Lordship

judges: Michael Argyle (*Oz* magazine trial), Roy Bean, Robert Braxfield, Constance Briscoe, Sir Joseph Cantley (Jeremy Thorpe trial), Henry Fielding, Dame Brenda Hale, Oliver Wendell Holmes (known as 'the great dissenter'), Sir John Holt, George Jeffreys (of the Bloody Assizes), Lance Ito (O.J. Simpson trial), Johannes van der Linden, Rodney Melville (Michael Jackson trial), Sandra Day O'Connor, Judith Sheindlin (aka Judge Judy, as seen on TV), Dame Janet Smith (entrusted with the Harold Shipman enquiry), Sir Peter Smith (*The Da Vinci Code* plagiarism trial), Lord Justice Stuart-Smith (Hillsborough enquiry), Earl Warren, Hiller Zobel (Louise Woodward trial)

judges, patron saint of: John of Capistrano

judo champions: Neil Adams, Ingrid Berghmans, Shozo Fujii

judo outfit: judogi

juggler's club: Indian club

jumping, adjective: saltatorial

jumping animals, adjective: saltigrade

jungle cities: Angkor Wat (in Cambodia), Iquitos (in Peru)

jungle inhabitants: Mowgli, Tarzan

Juno: planet discovered in 1804 by Karl Ludwig Harding

Jupiter, adjective: Jovian

jurists: David Dudley Field, Viscount Hailsham, Earl Warren

juror, corrupt: ambodexter

jury: "A jury consists of 12 persons chosen to decide who has the better lawyer" – Robert Frost

jury trial: first introduced in Britain in 1215

Just a Minute: radio panel game in which guests are required to talk on any given subject for one minute "without repetition, deviation or hesitation"

    devised by Ian Messiter (who came up with the idea on the top of a number 13 bus)

    first broadcast: 22 December 1967 on Radio 4 regular panellists originally included Clement Freud, Peter Jones, Derek Nimmo and Kenneth Williams, with the chair taken by Nicholas Parsons (after Jimmy Edwards turned it down)

    signature tune: Chopin's *The Minute Waltz*

justice, adjective: judicial

justice, aversion to: dikephobia

justice, god of: Forseti (Norse mythology)

justice, goddess of: Themis (Greek mythology)

juvenile delinquents, patron saint of: Dominic Savio

K

kaleidoscope: ancient Greek devise 'reinvented' by Sir David Brewster in 1816

Kampuchea: former name for Cambodia (1975–1981)

kangaroo, adjective: macropodine

kangaroo, collective noun: mob, troop

kangaroo, famous: Kanga (from *Winnie the Pooh*), Dinny Kangaroo (cartoon), Roo (from *Winnie the Pooh*), Skippy

kangaroo, fact: oddly, the marsupial is not known to break wind

kangaroo, female: flyer

kangaroo, killing of: macropocide

kangaroo, male: boomer

kangaroo, young: joey
Kansas, 34th state (1861), Sunflower State
    capital: Topeka
    birthplace of: Fatty Arbuckle, Annette Bening, Amelia Earhart, William Inge
        (playwright/novelist), Buster Keaton, Gordon Parks (filmmaker)
    state bird: Western meadowlark
    state flower: sunflower
    state tree: cottonwood
    motto: 'Ad Astra per Aspera' ('To the stars through difficulties')
    tourist attractions: Eisenhower Center, Bonner Springs, Fort Scott & Fort
        Larned
Kansas City, Missouri: location of the world's first purpose-built shopping centre,
    with parking for 5,500 cars
Kansas City, Missouri, birthplace of: Robert Altman, Burt Bacharach, Eminem
Kattomeat spokescat: Arthur
Kazakhstan: republic in central Asia
    capital: Astana (since 1997)
    currency: tenge
    language: Kazakh, Russian
    religion: atheist, Muslim, Christian
    fact: the humble apple originated here
Kent, administrative centre: Maidstone
Kentucky, 15th state (1792), Bluegrass State
    capital: Frankfort
    birthplace of: Muhammad Ali, Jim Bowie, Kit Carson, George Clooney,
        Johnny Depp, Irene Dunne, Abraham Lincoln, Joan Osborne, Diane
        Sawyer (broadcaster), Hunter S. Thompson, Gus Van Sant (filmmaker)
    state bird: cardinal (a state bird it shares with Illinois, Indiana, North Carolina,
        Ohio Virginia and West Virginia)
    state flower: goldenrod
    state tree: coffee tree
    motto: 'United we stand, divided we fall'
    tourist attractions: Kentucky Derby, Mammoth Cave National Park, Lincoln's
        birthplace at Hodgenville
Kentucky Fried Chicken, slogan: 'It's Finger Lickin' Good'
Kenya: republic in eastern Africa which gained its independence from Britain in
    1963
    capital: Nairobi
    currency: shilling
    language: Swahili, English
    religion: Christian (majority), animist
    thirty ethnic groups belonging to four linguistic families - Bantu, Nilotic,
        Paranilotic, and Cushitic. The largest ethnic groups are the Bantu-speaking
        Kikuyu, Luhya, and Kamba; the Nilotic-speaking Luo; and the Paranilotic-
        speaking Kalenjin; also the Pokot (220,000-strong)
Kenyan mountain: Mount Kenya
Kenyan writer: Ngugi wa Thiong'o
ketamine: Special K
Kew Gardens: Royal Botanic Gardens in Kew, London, developed by King George
    III and landscaped by Capability Brown. Consisting of 300 acres, the royal
    estate was appointed with pavilions and temples designed by Sir William

Chambers, whose most famous structure remains the 163-foot tall Chinese Pagoda. In 1841 the gardens were made public and today feature over 50,000 species of plant collected from around the world, as well as housing seven million preserved plant specimens

key: Allen, Chubb, master key, skeleton key, Yale

key to understanding: Rosetta Stone

keyboard layout: qwerty (standard English version)

KGB, successor to: Russian Federal Security Service

Khartoum, hero of: General Charles Gordon

Khmer Empire: former name for Cambodia

kickboxing: mo thai

kicking, adjective: calcitrant

kidnappers: Donald DeFreeze, Josef Fritzl, Bruno Hauptmann, Wolfgang Priklopil

kidnapping victims: Kenneth Bigley, Barbara Blandish (from the James Hadley Chase novel *No Orchids For Miss Blandish*), Lorna Doone, John Paul Getty Jr., Patricia Hearst, Alan Johnston (BBC journalist held captive in Gaza for 114 days), Brian Keenan, Pierre Laporte (Canadian politician), Madeleine McCann, John McCarthy, Aldo Moro, Daniel Pearl (American journalist murdered in Karachi, Pakistan), Hanns-Martin Schleyer, Matthew Scott, Elizabeth Smart, Faye Turney (Royal Navy Leading Seaman kidnapped by the Iranian Revolutionary Guard in March 2007)
- see also abductees, escapees

kidneys, adjective: renal

kidneys, study of: nephrology

kidney-shaped: reniform

kidney disease, patron saint of: Benedict

kidney fat (on oxen, sheep, etc): suet

kill: assassinate, bump off, butcher, cap, grease, ice, knock off, liquidate, neutralize, polish off, pop, put out to sleep, render nonviable (PC), rub out, smoke, snuff, terminate with extreme prejudice, top, whack

killers – see assassins, murderers and murderesses and killers, female

killers, female: Countess Elizabeth Báthory (who delighted in bathing in the blood of her victims), Lizzie Borden, Judy Goodyear (née Buenoano), Sabrina Butler, Faye Copeland, Ruth Ellis, Lafonda Foster, Yvette Gay, Myra Hindley, Deidre Hunt, Maria Isa, Debra Jean Milke, Blanche Taylor Moore, Violette Nozière, Marilyn Plantz, Tina Powell, Karla Faye Tucker, Maxine Walker, Aileen Wuornos
- see murderesses

Killers, The; alternative pop/rock American band, formed in Las Vegas in 2002; comprised of Brandon Flowers (vocals, keyboards), Dave Keuning (guitar, vocals), Mark Stoermer (bass guitar, vocals) and Ronnie Vannucci Jr. (percussion, drums)

kilt: "A skirt sometimes worn by Scotsmen in America and Americans in Scotland" – Ambrose Bierce

king, murder of: regicide, parricide (which also applies to the murder of a parent or close relitive)

king who abdicated: Edward VIII

King's Cross, London, nickname: the Bronx of Britain

king's staff: sceptre

kingdom, adjective: regnal

Kingfish, the: nickname for the American politician Huey P. Long

Kingmaker, the: nickname for Richard Neville, the Earl of Warwick (1428–1471)

Kings, Three Wise: Caspar, Melchior and Balthasar

Kinks, The: ground-breaking, quintessentially English pop group, formed in London in 1964, disbanded in 1996; comprised of Ray Davies (vocals, guitar), his brother Dave Davies (guitar), Peter Quaife (bass) and Mick Avory (drums). Rod Stewart was a founder member (when the band was known as The Ray Davies Quartet)

Kiribati: independent republic in the West Pacific
    capital: Bairiki port on South Tarawa
    currency: Australian dollar
    language: English, I-Kiribati (Gilbertese)
    religion: Christian

kiss: "A kiss is an application on the top floor for a job in the basement" – artwork at the Spectrum Art Exhibition; "A particular contact between the mucus membranes of the lips of the two people concerned, held in high sexual esteem among many nations in spite of the fact that the parts involved do not form part of the sexual apparatus but constitute the entrance to the digestive tract" - Sigmund Freud

kiss: air kiss, Eskimo kiss, French kiss, grace before meat, lip-lock, lip service (joc.), osculation (joc.), Park Avenue Grunt (air kiss), smooch, snog, suck face, swap spit

KISS: keep it simple, stupid

kissing, adjective: oscular

kissing, hatred of: philematophobia

kissing, science of: philematology

kissing with tongue: cataglottism

kitchen, adjective: culinary

kitchen garden: potager

Kit Kat: first produced in 1935 (when it was known as Chocolate Crisp, changing its name to Kit Kat in 1937)

kitten, collective noun: kindle

Kiwis, famous – see New Zealand

knee: genu (technical term)

knee, adjective: genual

knee, area behind; adjective: popliteal

knees, fear of: genuphobia

knee-shaped: genuform

kneecap: patella, rotula

kneecap, adjective: rotuliform

kneeling, adjective: genuflectory

knife: blade, bowie, butter knife, carving knife, dirk (worn with a kilt), flick nife, frogsticker (US slang for pocket knife), kukri (used by Gurkhas), lancet (used in surgery), machete, palette knife, panga (East African), parang (Malayan), pig-sticker, pocket knife, scalpel, skean (Gaelic), skean-dhu (worn with a kilt), Stanley knife, Swiss army knife, switchblade, utility knife (American for Stanley knife)

knife handle: haft

knighthoods, declined by: David Bowie, Joseph Conrad, Albert Finney, Lucian Freud, Charles Holden (architect), Aldous Huxley, Neil MacGregor, Harold Pinter, Anthony Powell, Paul Scofield. And Doris Lessing and Vanessa Redgrave rejected offers to be made a dame

knights: Galahad, Gawain, Geraint, Ivanhoe, Lancelot, Perceval, Don Quixote,
     Prince Valiant
knights, American: George Bush, Douglas Fairbanks Jr, Ronald Reagan, Steven
     Spielberg
knights, theatrical: Richard Attenborough, Alan Ayckbourn, Felix Aylmer, Stanley
     Baker, Alan Bates, Dirk Bogarde, Michael Caine, Lewis Casson, Charles
     Chaplin, John Clements, Sean Connery, Tom Courtenay, Noël Coward, Richard
     Eyre, Johnston Forbes-Robertson, Michael Gambon, John Gielgud, Alec
     Guinness, Peter Hall, Cedric Hardwicke, David Hare, Rex Harrison, Nigel
     Hawthorne, Ian Holm, Anthony Hopkins, Michael Hordern, Nicholas Hytner,
     Henry Irving, Derek Jacobi, David Jason, Ben Kingsley, David Lean,
     Christopher Lee, Andrew Lloyd Webber, Henry Lytton, Cameron Mackintosh,
     Ian McKellen, Bernard Miles, John Mills, Roger Moore, Kenneth More,
     Laurence Olivier, Alan Parker, Arthur Wing Pinero, Sidney Poitier, David
     Puttnam, Michael Redgrave, Carol Reed, Ralph Richardson, Ridley Scott,
     Peter Shaffer, Antony Sher, Donald Sinden, C. Aubrey Smith, Robert Stephens,
     Patrick Stewart, Tom Stoppard, Herbert Beerbohm Tree, Peter Ustinov, Norman
     Wisdom, Donald Wolfit
knights of pop music: Bono (honorary), Bob Geldof (honorary), Mick Jagger,
     Elton John, Tom Jones, Paul McCartney, Cliff Richard
knot: bowline, carrick bend, clove hitch, Gordian's, granny knot, half hitch, hitch,
     overhand knot, porter's knot, reef knot, running knot, sheepshank, slip-knot,
     surgeon's knot, timber hitch, true-love knot, Turk's head, wale-knot
knot, adjective: nodal, nodose
know-alls: Stephen Fry, Proteus
knowledge, adjective: epistemic
knowledge, theory of: epistemology
knuckle rub of the head: noogie
Korean War: June 1950-July 1953
Kosovo: independent republic, formerly a part of Yugoslavia; declared its
     independence from Serbia on 17 February 2008
     capital: Priština
     currency: euro (formerly Serbian dinar)
     language: Albanian, Serbian, English, Turkish
     religion: Muslim and Eastern Orthodox
Kraftwerk: influential techno band formed in 1969 in Düsseldorf, Germany;
     comprised of: Ralf Hütter, Florian Schneider, Wolfgang Flur (electronic
     percssion) and Klaus Roeder (electric violin). Flur was replaced by Karl Bartos
     in 1975
KS: postcode for Kansas
Kuala Lumpur, nickname: The Big Durian
Kuala Lumpur building (once the tallest in the world): The 88-storey Petronas
     Twin Towers (1,483ft) on the outskirts of Kuala Lumpur
Ku Klux Klan member: Edgar Killen (convicted of manslaughter in 2005, aged 80)
Kung Fu: stylised Western TV series featuring Kwai Chang Caine, a man trained to be
     a Shaolin monk but forced by circumstance to repeatedly practise the martial arts
     created by Ed Spielman
     developed by Herman Miller (who also co-produced)
     broadcast: 1 October 1972–26 April 1975
     cast: David Carradine (Kwai Chang Caine), Keye Luke (Master Po), Philip
     Ahn (Master Kan)

interesting fact: in the TV movie, *Kung Fu: The Movie*, the young Caine was played by Brandon Lee. Brandon's father, Bruce Lee, had been earlier rejected for the lead in the series

kung fu stars: Bruce Lee, Leung Siu Lung, Yuen Qui
  - see martial arts stars

Kuwait: state on the north-west coast of the Persian Gulf
  capital: Kuwait
  currency: dinar
  language: Arabic
  religion: Muslim

Kuwait invasion (by Iraq): 2 August 1990
  - see Gulf War

Kwanzaa: seven-day cultural celebration for people of African descent, established in 1966. Observed from 26 December to 1 January, Kwanzaa complies with Seven Principles pertaining to family and community

KY: postcode for Kentucky

Kyrgyzstan: republic in central Asia that gained its independence from Russia on 31 August 1991
  capital: Bishkek
  currency: som
  language: Kirghiz, Russian
  religion: atheist, Muslim

L

LA: postcode for Louisiana

labia: beef curtains, piss flaps

Labradors, famous: Buddy (canine companion to Bill Clinton), Sadie (who saved the lives of dozens of soldiers in Afghanistan by discovering an unexploded bomb)

lacemakers, patron saint of: Luke the Apostle

ladder, adjective: scalar, scalariform

ladder assault (especially against a fortification): escalade

Lady Chatterley's Lover (1928 novel by D.H. Lawrence), opening line: "Ours is essentially a tragic age, so we refuse to take it tragically"

Lady Ella: nickname for Ella Fitzgerald

Lady of the Lake: Viviane (in Arthurian legend)

Lady with the Lamp: nickname for Florence Nightingale

ladykiller: Bluebeard
  - see serial killers, womanisers, etc

lake, adjective: lacustrine

lake, deepest in the world: Baykal in southern Siberia

lake, highest in the world: Lhagba Pool in Tibet

lake, largest in England: Windermere

lake, largest in Europe: Ladoga (Russia)

lake, largest in North America: Lake Superior (Canada/USA)

lake, largest in the UK: Lough Neagh (Northern Ireland)

lake, largest in the USA: Lake Michigan (Illinois/Indiana/Michigan/Wisconsin)

lake, largest in the world: Caspian Sea (Iran/USSR); second largest: Superior (Canada/USA)

lake, largest in Western Europe: Vänern (Sweden)

lake, lowest in the world: Dead Sea (Israel/Jordan)
lake, navigable, highest in the world: Lake Titicaca in the Andes
lakes, fear of: limnophobia
lakes, study of: limnology (particularly of fresh water lakes)
Lake District writers: Samuel Taylor Coleridge, Thomas De Quincey, Beatrix
    Potter, John Ruskin, Robert Southey, William Wordsworth
La Lollo: nickname for Gina Lollobrigida
lambs, famous: Lamb Chop, Larry the Lamb (from the BBC's *Children's Hour*),
    Louise (introduced on BBC TV's *For the Children*)
lamentation, songs of: keen (Irish), threnody
lampoon acted out in public: pasquinade
Lancashire, administrative centre: Preston
land, adjective: agrarian, terrestrial, terrigenous
land animal, largest in the world: African elephant
Land of the Free: nickname for Thailand
Land of the Thousand Lakes: nickname for Finland
landfill sites, fact: responsible for one third of all ground-water pollution incidents
landing craft: Daihatsu 14M (Japanese), Higgins boat, LCVP, LEM, lunar
    excursion module
landladies: Mrs Pipchin (from *Dombey and Son*), Mistress Quickly (of the Boar's
    Head Tavern, from *The Merry Wives of Windsor*)
landlords: Al Murray, Rupert Rigsby (played by Leonard Rossiter in TV's *Rising
    Damp*)
landscape architects/gardeners: Lancelot Brown (aka Capability Brown), Gertrude
    Jekyll, Sir Geoffrey Jellicoe, André Le Nôtre, George London, Frederick Law
    Olmstead, Joseph Paxton
landscape painters: Pieter Bruegel, Antonio Canaletto, Frederic Church, Thomas
    Cole, John Constable, Jean Baptiste Camille Corot, Caspar David Friedrich,
    Thomas Gainsborough, Ambrogio Lorenzetti, Piet Mondrian, Samuel Palmer,
    Camille Pisssarro, Salvator Rosa, Théodore Rousseau, Jacob van Ruïsdael,
    J.M.W. Turner, Jan Vermeer, Claude-Joseph Vernet, Richard Wilson
language employing the most letters: Cambodian
language employing the most words: English (490,000, plus another 300,000
    technical terms)
    - see vocabulary
language experts: Bill Bryson, Alexander John Ellis, H.W. Fowler, Samuel
    Johnson, H.L. Mencken, Lynne Truss
    - see linguistic authorities, lexicographers
language, adjective: lingual, linguistic
language, artificial: Denglish (an English corruption of Deutsch), doublespeak,
    Esperanto, Franglais (an English corruption of French), jargon, mumbo-jumbo,
    newspeak
language, common (adopted by speakers whose own tongue is different): lingua
    franca
language, fact: roughly two dozen languages disappear every year
language, science of: linguistics, philology
language, speaker of several: polyglot
language, study of: glottology
language shared by different peoples: koine
language-associated region of the brain: Wernicke's area
languages, number in the world: 2,796 (according to the Académie Française)

languages, speaker of all: pantoglot
Laos: republic in south-eastern Asia
    capital: Vientiane
    currency: kip
    language: Lao
Laos religion: Buddhist, various tribal beliefs
lap, adjective: gremial
lap dancing establishments: For Your Eyes Only, Spearmint Rhino
LAPD: Los Angeles Police Department
lapwing (bird), collective noun: deceit, desert
largest living thing in the world: the *Armilla ostoyae*, or honey mushroom, in
    Oregon. At 3.5 miles across and a metre deep, it covers an area as big as 1,665
    football fields
lark, collective noun: ascension, bevy, exaltation
lark, young: chick
larynx, adjective: laryngeal
larynx, inflammation of: laryngitis
laser (acronym): Light Amplification by Stimulated Emission of Radiation
Last of the Summer Wine: British TV sitcom set in the South Yorkshire
    countryside and featuring the adventures of three elderly male friends, created
    as a submission for the BBC's *Comedy Playhouse*
    written by Roy Clarke
    broadcast: 12 November 1973– 29 August 2010 on BBC1
    cast: Bill Owen (Compo Seminite), Peter Sallis (Norman Clegg), Michael Bates
        (Blamire), Brian Wilde (Foggy Dewhurst), Michael Aldridge (Seymour
        Utterthwaite), Thora Hird (Aunt Edie, Seymour's sister), Kathy Staff (Mrs
        Batty), Jean Alexander (Auntie Wainwright)
last words of a manuscript: explicit
Las Vegas, birthplace of: André Agassi, The Killers
Las Vegas, nickname: The Neon City
Las Vegas casino, most famous: Caesar's Palace
Las Vegas chapels: Graceland Wedding Chapel (complete with Elvis impersonator),
    The Little Church of the West (venue for the marriages of Bob Geldof and
    Paula Yates, Noel Gallagher and Meg Mathews, Richard Gere and Cindy
    Crawford, Zsa Zsa Gabor, Judy Garland, Mickey Rooney, Telly Savalas, Johnny
    Halliday, Dudley Moore, Billy Bob Thornton and Angelina Jolie, and Chris
    Evans and Billie Piper), A Little White Chapel (venue for the marriages of Joan
    Collins, Michael Jordan, etc)
Las Vegas hotels: Caesar's Palace, California, Circus Circus, El Rancho Vegas (first
    resort hotel, opened in 1941), Flamingo (opened in 1946 by Benjamin 'Bugsy'
    Siegel), Excalibur (Arthurian-themed), Hard Rock Hotel, The Luxor (boasting the
    largest atrium in the world), MGM Grand (biggest hotel in the USA; 5,005 rooms;
    cost: $1b), Mirage (complete with belching volcano), Riviera, Sheraton Desert
    Inn, The Treasure Island, Tropicana (complete with swim-up gaming tables)
Las Vegas museum: Liberace Museum
Las Vegas thoroughfares: The Strip; Charleston Boulevard, Desert Inn Road,
    Flamingo Road, Las Vegas Boulevard, Maryland Parkway, Oran K. Gragson
    Expressway, Paradise Road, Sahara Avenue, Tropicana Avenue, Twain Avenue
Las Vegas weddings, fact: an average 80,000 services are performed annually
late: temporally challenged (PC)
late bloomer: opsimath
Latin Lover, the: nickname for Rudolph Valentino

Latin terms: ad infinitum, ad nauseam, annus mirabilis, ante meridiem, bona fide, camera obscura, compos mentis, et cetera, habeas corpus, id est, in flagrante delicto, ipso facto, non sequitur, per diem, per se, prima facie, pro rata, quid pro quo, tabula rasa, vox populi

lattice, adjective: clathrate

Latvia: republic in north-eastern Europe that gained its independence from Russia in 1991

  capital: Riga
  currency: lats
  language: Latvian
  religion: atheist, Christian

Latvia, birthplace of: Mark Rothko

laugh, collective noun: barrel

laughing: riant

laughter, adjective: gelastic

laughter, easily prone to: ridibund (adjective)

laughter, one who does not engage in: agelast (noun)

laughter, study of: gelotology

laundry, fact: in Victorian England clothes were washed in lye or urine (a natural bleach)

laurel nymph: Daphne

law, adjective: jural, legal

law, science of: jurisprudence, nomology

law enforcers: Judge Roy Bean, Wyatt Earp, Tony Martin (Norfolk farmer who shot the 16- year-old Fred Barrass dead after the latter broke into his home, 'Bleak House')
  - see judges

lawgiver: Moses

lawmakers: Draco, Solon

lawn bowls, terms: jack (target), wood (the ball)

lawn bowls champ: Griff Sanders (British player who received a nationwide ban for excessive swearing on the green)

lawyer: attorney, contract fielder, pettifogger (derog.), shark, solicitor

lawyer, adjective: leguleian

lawyers: George Washington Adams, James Anderson, Francis Bacon, F. Lee Bailey, Peter Benenson, Marcia Clark (O.J. Simpson prosecutor), Hillary Rodham Clinton, William Cobbett, Johnny Cochran (O.J. Simpson defender), Christopher Darden (O.J. Simpson prosecutor), Clarence Darrow, John Dean, Alan Dershowitz (Claus von Bullow case), John Foster Dulles, Ezra (from the Bible), Edward Fitzgerald (who defended Derek Bentley, the last man to be hanged in Britain), John Grisham, Anita Hill (who accused Clarence Thomas of sexual harassment), Andrew Jackson, Anthony Julius (represented Princess Diana), Abraham Lincoln, Sol Linowitz, Nelson Mandela, Thomas Mesereau (Michael Jackson defender), John Mortimer, Ralph Nader, Thomas Norton, Daniel Petrocelli (O.J. Simpson prosecutor), Barry Scheck (O.J. Simpson prosecutor, Louise Woodward defender), Clive Stafford Smith (devoted to fighting the American death penalty), Cornelia Sorabji, Cyrus Vance, Jacques Vergés (professional and private associate of Pol Pot, Slobodan Milosevic, Carlos the Jackal and Klaus Barbie), Daniel Webster, Sarah Weddington (helped to legalise abortion in the US), Mabel Willenbrandt
  - see barristers

lawyers, fictitious: Gomez Addams (from *The Addams Family*), Sydney Carton (from Dickens' *A Tale of Two Cities*), Atticus Finch (from *To Kill a Mockingbird*), Billy Flynn (from *Chicago*), Tom Hagen (from *The Godfather*), Perry Mason, Ben Matlock, Ally McBeal, Anthony Petrocelli (from the 1974–76 TV series *Petrocelli*), Horace Rumpole, Mr Tulkinghorn (from Charles Dickens' *Bleak House*)
- see barristers

lawyers, number in the USA: 800,000

lawyers, patron saints of: Thomas More and Raymond of Penyafort

LCD: liquid-crystal display

lead (metallic element), adjective: plumbeous, plumbic, plumbous

lead poisoning: plumbism

Leadbelly: nickname for the folk musician Huddie William Ledbetter

leaf, adjective: phylline

leaf-eating: frondivorous, phyllophagous

leaf-shaped: phylliform

leaf stalk: petiole

leaflet, adjective: foliolate

leap, adjective: saltant, saltatorial, saltatory

leap year, adjective: bissextile

learner, late in life: opsimath

learning while asleep: hypnopaedia

leather, adjective: coriaceous, leathern (archaic)

leaves, without: aphyllous (adjective)

Lebanon: republic in western Asia
  capital: Beirut
  currency: Lebanese pound
  language: Arabic (official), French, English
  religion: Muslim, Christian
  birthplace of: Mika, Keanu Reeves
  nickname: Pearl of the Mediterranean

LED: light-emitting diode

Led Zeppelin: blues and folk-based heavy metal UK group formed in London in 1968; comprised of: Jimmy Page (guitar), John Paul Jones (keyboards), Robert Plant (vocals) and John Bonham (drums); previously known as The New Yardbirds. The group officially disbanded in 1980 after the death of Bonham, but reunited for a spectacular gig in London on 10 December 2007

leech, adjective: hirudinal, hirudine, hirudinoid

Leeds, adjective: Leodensian

Leeds, birthplace of: Alan Bennett, Barbara Taylor Bradford, Barry Cryer, John Atkinson Grimshaw (painter), Malcolm McDowell, Chris Moyles, Jeremy Paxman, Corinne Bailey Rae, Arthur Ransome, Vic Reeves, Rhianna (full name: Rhianna Kenny), Sir Jimmy Savile, Arthur Scargill, Keith Waterhouse, Marco Pierre White, Tom Wilkinson (actor)

Leeds groups: Bedlam Ago Go, Chumbawamba, Embrace, Gang of Four, Kaiser Chiefs, The Music, Overseer, Scritti Politti, Sisters of Mercy, Spacehog

Leeds river: Aire

left, adjective: sinistral

left-hand page of a book or magazine: verso (compare recto)

left-handed: sinistral (compare dextral)

left-handed and famous: Alexander the Great, Dan Aykroyd, Lord Baden-Powell, Sacha Baron Cohen, Drew Barrymore, Osama bin Laden, Boston Strangler, Matthew Broderick, Julius Caesar, Fidel Castro, Charlie Chaplin, Charlemagne, Prince Charles, Bill Clinton, Phil Collins, Robert De Niro, John Dillinger, Charlie Dimmock, Eminem, Gerald Ford, Benjamin Franklin, James A. Garfield, Jean-Paul Gaultier, Germaine Greer, Herbert A. Hoover, Natalie Imbruglia, Jack the Ripper, Angelina Jolie, Nicole Kidman, Spike Lee, Leonardo Da Vinci, John McCain, Paul McCartney, Napoleon Bonaparte, Barack Obama, Sarah Jessica Parker, Pablo Picasso, Gordon Ramsay, Keanu Reeves, Julia Roberts, Greg Rusedski, Ayrton Senna, Bart Simpson, Harry S. Truman, Queen Victoria, Prince William, Bruce Willis, Owen Wilson
left-handedness: mancinism
leg, adjective: crural
leg, inflammation of: phlebitis
leg bones: femur, fibula, patella, tibia
leg pain: sciatica
leg stabbing (with knife, broken bottle, etc): juking
legs, sexual arousal derived from: crurophilia
legs; possessing long ones: dolichocnemic
legal rights, adjective: jural
Leicester Square, London; statues: Charlie Chaplin, William Hogarth, John Hunter, Sir Isaac Newton, Sir Joshua Reynolds, William Shakespeare
Leicestershire, administrative centre: Leicester
lemming, adjective: microtine
lemming, fact: the female Norway lemming can start breeding as young as 15 days of age
lemon, adjective: citric
lemon-coloured: citrine, citreous
length of 1,000 metres (approx. 0.62 miles): kilometre
length of 1,760 yards (approx. 1.609 kilometres): mile
length of approximately nine inches: span
length of approximately 39.4 inches: metre
length of approximately 45 inches: ell (obsolete)
length of approximately 1.1 kilometre (0.66 mile): verst (Russian measurement)
length of one-twelfth of a foot (2.54 cm): inch
length of three feet (0.9144 metre): yard
length of twelve inches: foot (30.48 cm)
Leningrad: former name for St Petersburg (1937–1991)
lens, adjective: lenticular
lens-shaped: lentoid
leopard: pard (poetic)
leopard, adjective: pardine
leopard, collective noun: leap
leopard, female: leopardess
leopard, male: leopard
leopard, young: cub
Lepanto, battle of: 7 October 1571 (defeat of the Ottoman fleet by the Holy League)
leprosy, adjective: lepric
leprosy, fear of: leprophobia
lesbian: dyke, fairy lady, finger artist, Jasper (black slang), tribade (the one who takes the male role)

lesbian, former: hasbian
lesbians, famous: Joan Armatrading, Tallulah Bankhead, Sarah Bernhardt, Enid
  Blyton, Chastity Bono, Julie Burchill, Saffron Burrows (actress), Rhona
  Cameron, Tracy Chapman, Patricia Cornwell, Joan Crawford, Ellen DeGeneres,
  Marlene Dietrich, Portia de Rossi (actress), Carol Ann Duffy, Melissa
  Etheridge, Jodie Foster, Samantha Fox, Anne Heche (formerly), Angelina Jolie
  (part-time), Billie Jean King, k.d. lang, Kelly McGillis, Martina Navratilova,
  Sinead O'Connor, Rosie O'Donnell, Camille Paglia, Alex Parks, Vita Sackville-
  West, Fiona Shaw, Valerie Singleton, Ione Skye, Gertrude Stein, Alice B.
  Toklas, Lily Tomlin, Sophie Ward, Rachel Williams, Jeanette Winterson
  - see bisexuals
lesbianism: sapphism
Lesotho: kingdom in southern Africa; formerly known as Basutoland (until 1966)
  capital: Maseru
  currency: loti
  language: Sesotho, English
  religion: Christian
Les Six: avante-garde group of musicians comprised of Darius Milhaud, Francis
  Poulenc, Arthur Honegger, Louis Durey, Germaine Tailleferre and Georges
  Auric. The group was dubbed 'Les Six' in 1920 by the critic Henri Collet,
  with Jean Cocteau acting as their spokesman
letter, adjective: epistolary
letters, silent: twenty-four of the twenty-six letters in the English alphabet are silent
  in some words (for instance, the 'b' in debt, the 'x' in Sioux and the 'z' in
  rendezvous). The sole exception are the letters 'j' and 'v'
lettuce: batavia, frisby (with crinkly edges), iceberg, little gem, lollo biondo
  (light green, frilly leafed, with a delicate texture and mild flavour), lollo rosso
  (fruity flavoured), mizuna (with an attractive light green serrated leaf, mustard
  flavoured), oak leaf (nutty flavoured), red batavia (curly headed in colour from
  deep red to green, robust with a mild flavour), red oak leaf, rocket (salad herb
  with fiddle-shaped leaves, with a distinctive flavour), roquette, Webb's wonder
lexicographers: Nathaniel Bailey, Robert Burchfield, Robert Cawdrey (whose
  A Table Alphabeticall, written in 1604, is recognised as the first English
  dictionary), Sir Thomas Elyot, H.W. Fowler, Jacob and Wilhem Grimm, Samuel
  Johnson, Pierre Larousse, Sir James Murray, Charles Onions, Eric Partridge,
  Paul Robert, Peter Roget, Sir William Smith, Richard Trench, Noah Webster
liars: Ananias (New Testament), Sir John Falstaff, Billy Fisher (from the musical
  Billy), Billy Liar (aka Billy Fisher), Richard M. Nixon, Pinocchio, Diego
  Rivera (Mexican painter), Sapphira (New Testament)
liberal: "A liberal is a man who leaves the room when a fight starts" - Dorothy
  Parker
Libération: Left-wing daily French newspaper founded in 1973 by Jean-Paul
  Sartre, Serge July and associates
Liberia: republic in West Africa
  capital: Monrovia
  currency: African dollar
  language: English
  religion: Christian, animist
  fact: the country was the first in non-Arabic black Africa to establish its
    independence, set up in 1847 by freed American slaves
Liberian footballer: George Weah

Liberian presidents: Ellen Johnson-Sirleaf (2006–), Charles Taylor (1997–2003), William R. Tolbert, Jr. (1971–1980)
libertine: Lothario
- see womanisers, etc
Liberty Bell, The: military march composed in 1893 by John Philip Sousa
libido, that which suppresses: anaphrodisiac
librarians: Daniel Boorstin, Jorge Luis Borges, Giacomo Casanova, Demetrius of Phalerum, Archibald MacLeish
librarians, patron saint of: Jerome
libraries: Bibliothèque Nationale (Paris), Bodleian (principal library of Oxford University), British Library (British Museum, London), Library of Congress (Washington DC), National Library of Canada (Ottawa)
library: bibliotheca
library, cataloguing system: Dewey Decimal Classification
library, earliest: the Nineveh library in Babylon
library, largest in world: Library of Congress, Washington DC (see)
library, most borrowed author from (UK): Jacqueline Wilson; formerly: Catherine Cookson
Library of Congress: the world's largest library, in Washington DC. After the library was burned down by the British in 1814, US president Thomas Jefferson donated 6,487 copies of his own books to re-establish the present institution. Today, the collection – housed on 64 acres – contains over 29 million books (and other printed materials) and comprises approximately 530 miles of bookshelves
librettists: Lionel Bart, Leslie Bricusse, Betty Comden, Howard Dietz, Dorothy Fields, Ira Gershwin, Sir W.S. Gilbert, Adolph Green, Arthur Laurents, Alan Jay Lerner, Sir Tim Rice, Julian Slade, Richard Stilgoe, P.G. Wodehouse
Libya: republic in north Africa
  capital: Tripoli
  currency: Libyan dinar
  language: Arabic
  religion: Sunni Muslim
lice, adjective: pedicular
lice, fear of: pediculophobia
lice infestation: pediculosis
licker of genitals: lecheur
lie: collar and tie (CRS), dissemble, equivocate, fib, porky, pork pie, soft-soap
lie, adjective: mendacious
lie, collective noun: pack, tissue
lie detector, portable: the Handy Truster Emotion Reader, which can be plugged into telephones and mobile phones
lie detector test: polygraph test
Liechtenstein: small principality in central Europe
  capital: Vaduz
  currency: Swiss franc
  language: German
  religion: Roman Catholic
  river: Rhine
life: "The chief danger in life is that you may take too many precautions" - Alfred Adler; "Life is meaningless, but it is wonderful. Where would we be without it?" - Ronnie Barker; "Life is not measured by the number of breaths we take,

but by the moments that take our breath away" - George Carlin; "The secret of
a happy and interesting life is to talk to everyone, everywhere" - Sir Sidney
Cockerell; "Life is an adventure in which all dreams are possible. The only
thing that can hold you back is fear or laziness. Coffins should contain only
dead bodies, not dead dreams" - John Irvin, *The World According to Garp*;
"Life is a comedy to those who think, a tragedy to those who feel" – Horace
Walpole; "Life shrinks or expands in proportion to one's courage" - Anais Nin;
"Every man dies, not every man really lives" - William Wallace; "One's real
life is so often the life that one does not lead" - Oscar Wilde

life, adjective: biotic
life, fond of: vitative (adjective)
life, science of: biology
life expectancy, countries with highest: 1) Japan; 2) Australia; 3) France; 4) Sweden; 5) Spain; 6) Italy; 7) Greece; 8) Switzerland; 9) Monaco; 10) Andora
life expectancy, average in EU for men: 73.9 years
life symbol: ankh
lifeless: azoic
lifestyle gurus: Carole Caplin, Eliza Smith, Martha Stewart
lift: first constructed in 236 BC, by Archimedes
light, adjective: luciform
light, aversion to: photophobia
light, god of: Apollo (Greek and Roman), Balder (Norse)
light, obsession with: photomania
light, without: aphotic
light bulb: first demonstrated by Thomas Edison in 1879
lighthouse authority, UK: Trinity House
lightning, fear of: astraphobia, astrapophobia
lightning, fact: a phenomenon that kills between three and six people a year in Britain
odds of being struck by lightning: 1 in 10,000,000
lily-shaped: crinoid
limbless: acolous
limbless people in Britain, number of: 65,000
lime, adjective: calcine
limestone, adjective: calcareous
Lincolnshire, administrative centre: Lincoln
linden tree, adjective: tileaceous
line, collective noun: pencil
linen fabrics: batiste, cambric, duck, flax, lawn, lint
lingerie: bloomers, bra, brassière, bustier, camisole, chemise, corset, drawers, garters, girdle, knickers, panties, petticoat, shift, slip, stays, suspenders, teddy
lingerie designer: Janet Reger
linguistic authorities: Benito Arias, Émile Benveniste, Leonard Bloomfield, Bill Bryson, Noam Chomsky, Robert Claiborne, David Crystal, Ella Deloria, Alexander John Ellis, John Rupert Firth, Roman Jakobson, Daniel Jones, Richard Lederer, Charles Kay Ogden, Mario Pei, Henry Sweet, Michael Ventris
lion, adjective: leonine
lion conservationists: George Adamson (murdered in 1989 by shifta bandits), Joy Adamson, Tony Fitzjohn, Beverly and Dereck Joubert
lion, collective noun: pride, sawt, sowse
lion, fact: nine out of ten lions will back off if you charge at them (according to George Adamson)

lions, famous: Aslan, Clarence the Cross-Eyed Lion, the Cowardy Lion, Elsa (reared by Joy Adamson), Kimba the White Lion (Japanese cartoon), Kitty Kat (from *The Addams Family*), Lenny the Lion (c/o Terry Hall), Leo the Lion (MGM mascot), Linus the Lionhearted (cartoon), Mufasa (from Disney's *The Lion King*), Nala (from Disney's *The Lion King*), Nemean Lion (killed by Hercules), Scar (from Disney's *The Lion King*), Simba (from Disney's *The Lion King*)
lion, female: lioness
lion, male: lion
lion, sound: growl, roar
lion, young: cub
Lion Heart, the: nickname for King Richard I of England
lion-bodied creatures of mythology: griffin, sphinx
lip ornament/pearcing: labret
lip reading: labiomancy
lips: apple pips (CRS), bee-stung, central lip depression (or philtral dimple), Cupid's bow, philtral ridge, philtrum (upper lip, divided into the philtral columns on the side and the philtral dimple in the middle), snuffle-trough (informal term for upper lip)
lips, adjective: labial
lips, thick: labrose (adjective)
lips, without: achilous (adjective)
lip ornament: labret
lips; edge of: vermilion border
liqueurs: chartreuse (green, brandy-based), Cointreau (from bitter oranges), Drambuie (whisky), Liqueur d'or (with gold flakes), Liqueur des Moines (aromatic plants and Cognac), sambuca (Italian, made from aniseed), Tia Maria (coffee-flavoured)
    alcohol blanc liqueurs: alisier (rowanberry), coing (quince), cumin (cummin), fraise (strawberries), framboise (raspberries), himbeergeist (German/Swiss raspberry brandy), houx (holly berry), kirsch (cherries), mirabelle (small golden plums), myrtille (bilberries), poire Williams (William pear), prunelle sauvage (sloe), quetsch (Switzen plum), slivovitz (Yugoslavian/Rumanian plum brandy), tutti frutti (mixture of fruits)
    chocolate liqueurs: Cacao mit Nuss (German), Cheri-Suisse (Swiss chocolate and cherry), creme de cacao, Royal Mint-Chocolate, Royal Orange-Chocolate, Sabra (Israeli chocolate and bitter orange), Vandermint (Dutch chocolate mint)
    digestive liqueurs: creme d'ananas (pineapple), creme de banane (banana), creme de menthe (mint), creme de roses (oil of rose petals), creme de violettes (petals of violets)
    nut liqueurs: Amaretto (almonds), creme de noisette (hazelnuts), creme de noix (walnuts), Creme de Noyaux (apricot pits), Creme mit Nuss (German, hazelnuts and chocolate), eau-de-noix (walnuts), Persico
    other liquers: anisette (liquorice, made from aniseed), kümmel (caraway seed), curaçao (orange peel), sloe (sloe gin)
liquid, curved surface of: meniscus
liquid-extracting instrument (in surgery): trocar
liquids in motion, adjective: hydraulic
liquorice man: Bertie Bassett
Lisbon, nickname: The White City
    capital of fado music

birthplace of: St Antony of Padua, Joaquim de Almeida (actor), Maria de
  Medeiros (actress and filmmaker), Fernando Pessoa (poet), Dame Paula
  Rego (artist), Amália Rodrigues (fado singer)
fact: Lisbon is the westernmost capital on mainland Europe
Lisbon river: Tagus
lispers, famous: Humphrey Bogart, Sir Winston Churchill, Daffy Duck, Chris
  Eubank, Al Gore, Peter Lorre, Frank Muir, Sylvester, Will Young
  - see stammerers, famous
listening (as in paying attention): audient
literary assistant: amanuensis
literary critics: Harold Bloom, Norman O. Brown, Sterling Brown, G.K. Chesterton,
  Edward Dowden, Leslie Fiedler, William Hazlitt, Christopher Hitchens, Sir
  Frank Kermode, Julia Kristeva, F.R. Leavis, Q.D. Leavis, Wyndham Lewis, John
  Gibson Lockhart, Georg Lukacs, Sir Desmond MacCarthy, F.O. Matthiessen,
  H.L. Mencken, Sir V.S. Pritchett, Sir Christopher Ricks, George Ripley, Charles
  Augustin Saint-Beuve, Michel Serres, George Bernard Shaw, George Steiner,
  Lionel Trilling, Theodore Watts-Dunton, Edmund Wilson
  - see journalists, film critics, rock critics
literary genres: airport thriller, antinovel, beach read, Bildungsroman, bodice-ripper,
  bonkbuster, celebrity biography, chicklit, detective novel, dime novel, doorstop,
  graphic novel, hagiography, hierology, horror, kid-lit, kidult, killerchiller, ladlit,
  literary fiction, metafiction, Mills & Boon, mystery, novelette, novella, penny
  dreadful, photonovel, potboiler, pulp fiction, romance, Romantic, roman-à-clef,
  roman-fleuve, science fiction, sexandshopping, three-decker, thriller, whodunnit,
  yellowback
literary theorists: Paul de Man, Jacques Derrida, Umberto Eco, Northrop Frye,
  Julia Kristeva, Edward Said
lithographers: Winslow Homer, David Roberts
Lithuania: republic in north-east Europe, an independent state from 1991
  capital: Vilnius
  currency: litas
  language: Lithuanian
  religion: Roman Catholic
  birthplace of: Laurence Harvey, Al Jolson, Hannibal Lecter, Jacques Lipchitz
    (sculptor)
  fact: as calibrated by the French National Geographical Institute, Lithuania is
    at the geographical centre of Europe
  fact: Lithuania is the last country in Europe to adopt Christianity
  fact: Lithuania is the world leader in suicide, where 42 in every 1,000 citizens
    kill themselves
litigation, mania for: processomania
Little Britain: hugely popular comedy TV show (evolved from BBC Radio 4)
  featuring writer-creators Matt Lucas and David Walliams as a wide range of
  characters, from the wheelchair-bound Andy Pipkin and chav Vicky Pollard to
  the unconvincing transvestite Emily Howard and gay Welshman Daffyd
  broadcast: 16 September 2003–31 December 2006
Little League: baseball for minors
Little Sparrow: nickname for Edith Piaf
liver, adjective: hepatic
liver, study of: hepatology
liver disease: alagille syndrome, cirrhosis, galactosemia, haemangioma,
  haemochromatosis, hepatitis, porphyria cutanea tarda, rotor syndrome,
  Wilson disease

liver spot: lentigo (plural: lentigines)

Liverpool, birthplace of: Arthur Askey, Dame Beryl Bainbridge, Cilla Black, Kim Cattrall, John Conway (mathematician), Ken Dodd, Billy Fury, William Gladstone, George Harrison, John Lennon, Sir Paul McCartney, Leonard Rossiter, Ringo Starr, George Stubbs (painter)

Liverpool airport: John Lennon Airport

Liverpool groups ('the Merseybeat'): Atomic Kitten, The Beatles, The Boo Radleys, The Christians, Dead or Alive, Echo & the Bunnymen, A Flock of Seagulls, Frankie Goes To Hollywood, Gerry and the Pacemakers, Lightning Seeds, The Merseybeats, The Searchers, The Spinners, The Swinging Blue Jeans, The Teardrop Explodes, The Zutons

Liverpool inhabitant: Liverpudlian, Scouse

Liverpool river: Mersey

Liverpool, adjective: Liverpudlian

lizard, adjective: lacertilian, saurian

lizard, largest in the world: Komodo monitor

llama, young: cria

Lloyd's bank, slogan: 'At the sign of the black horse'

LMC: lower middle class

lobe, adjective: lobate

lobster: decapod, langouste, Norway lobster

lobster, adjective: homarine

lobster, female: hen

lobster, male: cock

lobster, number of limbs: ten

lobster claw: chela, nipper

lobster dish: lobster thermidor

lobster fat: tomalley (eaten as a delicacy)

lobster roe: berry, coral (unfertilized)

lobster soup: bisque

lobster trap: creel

lobster's gills: dead man's fingers

location, misplacing of: anatopism

lock: bolt, central locking, Chubb, combination lock, deadlock, drawback lock, mortise, padlock, snib, time lock, Yale lock
- see keys

Lockerbie disaster: 21 December 1988, when a Pan Am 103 was blown up, killing 270

locksmith: Robert Barron

locksmiths, patron saint of: Dunstan

Lock, Stock and Two Smoking Barrels (1998 film), famous lines: Nick the Greek (Stephen Marcus): "I'll need a sample." Tom (Jason Flemyng): "Ah, no can do I'm afraid." Nick the Greek: "What's that? Some place near Kathmandu? Meet me halfway mate"; Eddy (Nick Moran): "They're armed." Soap (Dexter Fletcher): "Armed? Armed with what?" Eddy: "Feather duster, colourful language, what do you think? Guns, you tit!"; Rory Breaker (Vas Blackwood): "If you hold back anything, I'll kill ya. If you bend the truth or I think you're bending the truth, I'll kill ya. If you forget anything, I'll kill ya. In fact, you're gonna have to work very hard to stay alive, Nick. Now, do you understand everything I've said? Because if you don't, I'll kill ya"

locust, collective noun: plague, swarm

locust, sound: stridulation

locust, young: larva
logarithms: invented by the Scottish mathematician John Napier in 1614
logic impairing disorder: dyspraxia
logicians: Kurt Gödel, A.N. Whitehead, Ludwig Wittgenstein
Lohengrin: opera by Richard Wagner first produced in Weimar in 1850
loins, adjective: lumbar
loin pain: osphyalgia
LOL (text shorthand): laugh out loud, lots of love
London, A-Z atlas: originally compiled by Phyllis Pearsall
London: birthplace of: George Arliss, David Bowie, Sir Michael Caine, Charlie
  Chaplin, Geoffrey Chaucer, Daniel Day-Lewis, Daniel Defoe, Queen Elizabeth
  II, Sir Alfred Hitchcock, Angela Lansbury, Ida Lupino, John Nash, Henry
  Purcell, Jerry Springer, Kiefer Sutherland, Elizabeth Taylor, J.M.W. Turner,
  Peter Ustinov
London, old name: Londinium
London, tallest building: Canada Tower, in Canary Wharf
London Eye: 443 foot-high wheel that cost £35 million to construct, provides a 30-
  minute ride with up to 25-mile views in good weather; includes 32 'capsules'
  that can accommodate up to 25 people each
London Library: established by Thomas Carlyle in 1841 at 49 Pall Mall, when it
  comprised 2,500 books. Presidents of the Library have included Carlyle, Lord
  Alfred Tennyson, Leslie Stephen and Tom Stoppard
London Marathon: launched in 1981 by Chris Brasher and John Disley, the charity
  run starts at Blackheath and ends at Buckingham Palace
London streets, number of: 23,000
London tourist attractions: Buckingham Palace (see), Changing the Guard, Houses
  of Parliament, London Aquarium, London Dungeon, London Eye (see), Madame
  Tussaud's, Planetarium, Tower of London
loneliness, fear of: monophobia
long jumper: Jesse Owens
  - see athletes, runners, etc
long-lasting: diuturnal
long-legged: dolichocnemic
long-winded: aeolistic
longevity, patron saint of: Peter
longing: "No one really wants what they want" -John Bayley, husband of Iris Murdoch
looked at, dread of being: scopophobia
loony: Mickey Rooney (CRS)
loop-shaped: ansiform
looped edging: picot
loose women: Carmen, Emmanuelle, Moll Flanders, Fanny Hill
  - see prostitutes, strippers, women of ill repute, etc
Lord Justice of Appeal, mode of verbal address: Your Lordship
Lord Mayor, mode of verbal address: Your Lordship
Lord of the Rings: Fellowship of the Ring, The (2001 film), famous lines: Frodo
  (Elijah Wood): "You're late." Gandalf (Ian McKellen): "A wizard is never late,
  Frodo Baggins. Nor is he early. He arrives precisely when he means to";
  Gollum (Andy Serkis): "It came to me on my birthday... it is mine... my own...
  my... precioussss"
Lord Provost, mode of verbal address: Your Lordship

Lord's Prayer (especially in Latin): paternoster

L'Oréal slogan: 'Because you're worth it'

Los Angeles, full name: El Pueblo de Nuestra Senora la Reina de los Angeles de
   Porciumcula

Los Angeles, up-market neighbourhoods: Bel-Air, Beverly Hills, Brentwood, Santa
   Monica, Westwood, West Hollywood ('Gay City')

Los Angeles cinema: Grauman's Chinese Theatre

Los Angeles hotel: The Hotel Bel-Air (the best hotel in the world? - voted "most
   beloved hotel" by the American magazine *Gourmet*)

Los Angeles native: Angeleno

Los Angeles nickname: City of the Angels, LaLa Land

loser: "He has a knack for making strangers immediately" (anon.); "Show me a
   good loser and I'll show you a loser" - business saying

loser: deadbeat, goomer (American slang), nebbish, nerd, sad sack, schlemiel

lost cities: Atlantis, Machu Pichu (see), Vineta (the Atlantis of the North)

Louisiana, 18th state (1812), Pelican State
   capital: Baton Rouge
   motto: 'Union, justice and confidence'
   state bird: brown pelican
   state flower: magnolia
   state tree: bald cypress
   birthplace of: Louis Armstrong, Truman Capote, Fats Domino, Lillian
      Hellman, Mahalia Jackson, Dorothy Lamour, Jerry Lee Lewis, Huey Long,
      Wynton Marsalis, Jelly Roll Morton, Britney Spears
   tourist attractions: Aquarium of the Americas, Mardi Gras, French Quarter of
      New Orleans, Superdome
   fact: by law pupils in Louisiana must address their teachers "sir" or "ma'am"

Louisiana Purchase: area of land west of Mississippi (885,000 square miles) which
   Napoleon I sold to the US in 1803 for $15 million (or three cents per acre)

Lourdes visionary: Bernadette Soubirous

louse, adjective: pedicular

louse, collective noun: colony

louse, plural: lice

louse, young: nit

love: "Love is the delightful interval between meeting a beautiful girl and discovering
   she looks like a haddock" - John Barrymore; "A temporary insantiy curable
   by marriage" - Ambrose Bierce; "Friendship is a disinterested commerce
   between equals; love an abject intercourse between tyrants and slaves" - Oliver
   Goldsmith; "Love without irritation is just lust. Mind you, there's nothing wrong
   with lust..." - Walter Matthau in *Pete 'n' Tillie* (1972 film); "Age does not protect
   you from love, but to some extent love protects you from age" - Jeanne Moreau;
   "Love is the proper recognition that other people actually exist" - Iris Murdoch
   "Do you know what makes love so frightening? You don't own it. It owns you" -
   Gary Oldman in *Romeo is Bleeding* (1993 film); "If you can explain it, then it is
   not love" – Zhang Yimou

love, god of: Eros (Greek), Cupid (Roman), Kama (Hindu)

love, goddess of: Aphrodite (Greek), Freya (Norse), Ishtar (Babylonian), Venus (Roman)

love, sexual: amatory (adjective)

love and war, goddess of: Ishtar (Babylonian mythology)

love poetry, muse of: Erato

Love Story (1970 film), famous lines: Oliver Barrett IV (Ryan O'Neal): "What can you say about a 25-year-old girl who died? That she was beautiful and brilliant? That she loved Mozart and Bach, the Beatles, and me?' [opening line]; Oliver Barrett IV: "Love means never having to say you're sorry" [last line]

lover; an inadequate one: amatorculist

LSD: chocolate chips, lysergic acid diethylamide (technical term), the Mighty Quinn

LSO: London Symphony Orchestra

LTO: long-term occasional

LTR: living-together relationship

luck, adjective: aleatoric, aleatory

lucky person: the devil

luggage: Globetrotters, Louis Vuitton, Saratoga trunk, Quicksilver, Samsonite

luggage identification: tag and beacon technology

lumberjack: Paul Bunyan

lumberjack, politically correct term: tree butcher

lunch box, illustrated: the first lunch box to feature an image was in 1950 with a picture of Hopalong Cassidy. The publicity gimmick saw sales of the item jump from 50,000 units in 1949 to 600,000 units

luncheon voucher madam: Cynthia Payne

lung cancer, fact: on average 31,486 Britons die a year from lung cancer

lung disease: pleurisy

lung doctor: pulmonologist

lung membrane: pleura

lungs, adjective: pulmonary

lungs, study of: pulmonology

lust: concupiscence

lust, adjective: amorous

lute-like musical instruments: archlute, citole, liuqin, mandolin, pipa, ruan, sanxian, sitar, theorbo, yueqin

lute players: Julian Bream, Sting

Luxembourg: grand duchy in western Europe
    capital: Luxembourg
    currency: euro; formerly the Luxembourg franc
    language: French (official); also German and the local language of Letzeburgesch
    religion: Roman Catholic
    birthplace of: Edward Steichen (photographer)
    river: Moselle
    fact: claims to have more castles per square inch than any other country in the world
    fact: is the top alcohol-consuming nation in the world

lye: potassium hydroxide, sodium hydroxide

lying: "Lying isn't usually a failure of morality. It's almost always a failure of courage" – Tim Lott

lying down: recumbent

lymphatic system, study of: lymphology

lymphatic tumor: Burkitt's lymphoma

lyre, propelled by wind: aeolian harp

lyre-like instrument: psaltery

lyric misconstrued: mondegreen

lyrics, stolen: the lyrics to the U2 album *October*, which were stolen in 1981 in Portland, Oregon, and recovered 23 years later

lyricists: Leslie Bricusse, Lew Brown, Betty Comden, Hal David, Buddy De Sylva, Howard Dietz, Fred Ebb, Dorothy Fields, Ira Gershwin, Gerry Goffin, Adolph Green, Lorenz Hart, Gus Kahn, Alan Jay Lerner, Sir Tim Rice, Morrie Ryskind, Julian Slade, Stephen Sondheim, Richard Stilgoe, Bernie Taupin, P.G. Wodehouse
- see songwriters

M

MA: postcode for Massachusetts

macaroni, adjective: macaronic

macaw, adjective: psittacine

Macca: nickname for Paul McCartney

Macedonia: country in south-eastern Europe, declared independent in 1992; officially known as the Former Yugoslav Republic of Macedonia
    capital: Skopje
    currency: denar
    language: Macedonian
    religion: Christian, Muslim, atheist, Jewish

Macedonian generals: Antigonus, Nearchus

Macedonian kings: Alexander, Perseus, Philip

Macedonian queen: Olympias

machine, adjective: mechanical

machine gun: a weapon in use since the 15th century, in particular the French Ribaudequin Cannon or 'Volley Gun'. The mechanical machine gun first appeared around 1850, while the reyner gun was employed during the American Civil War (1861–65). The first continuous firing automatic machine gun was invented by Hiram S. Maxim in 1884

machinery, fear of: mechanophobia

Machu Pichu: lost city of the Incas rediscovered in 1911 by the American archaeologist Hiram Bingham

mackerel, adjective: scombrid

mad: crazy, ding-a-ling, emotionally different (PC), loco, loopy, unglued, unzipped

mad and famous – see insane and famous

mad cow disease, human form: vCJD

Mad magazine: satirical comic founded in 1952 by Harvey Kurtzman and William M. Gaines. Its full title was originally *Tales Calculated to Drive You Mad: Humor in a Jugular Vein*

Mad Men: cult, award-winning American TV series set in and around a 1960s' New York advertising agency
    first broadcast: 19 July 2007
    created by Matthew Weiner
    cast: Jon Hamm (Donald Francis 'Don' Draper), Elisabeth Moss (Margaret 'Peggy' Olson), Vincent Kartheiser (Peter Dyckman 'Pete' Campbell), January Jones (Elizabeth 'Betty' Draper Francis (née Hofstadt)), Christina Hendricks (Joan Harris (née Holloway)), John Slattery (Roger Sterling, Jr.)

Madagascar: island republic in the Indian Ocean, off the coast of Africa; formerly known as Malagasy Republic (until 1975)

capital: Antananarivo
currency: African franc
language: Malagasy, French
religion: animist, Christian
madams: Polly Adler, Heidi Fleiss, Xaviera Hollander, Margaret McDonald, Cynthia Payne (dubbed 'the luncheon voucher madam')
Madame Butterfly: opera by Giacomo Puccini first produced in Milan in 1904
Madame Tussaud's, average cost of a waxwork: £30,000
Madge: nickname for Madonna (the singer)
madness: "Madness is the exception in individuals but the rule in groups" – Friedrich Nietzsche
Madrid, birthplace of: Victoria Abril, Penélope Cruz, Placido Domingo, Enrique Iglesias, Julio Iglesias, Carmen Maura
Madrid bombing: 11 March 2004, in which ten bombs were detonated on four trains at the central stations of Atocha, El Pozo and Santa Eugenia, killing 191 people and injuring 1,500
Madrid bullring: the Ventas (largest and most prestigious)
Madrid galleries: The Prado, Centro de Arte Reina Sofia, Fundación Thyssen-Bornemisza
Madrid inhabitants: Madrileños
Mafia: La Cosa Nostra, la Eme (Mexican Mafia), The Mob, the Octopus (Cosa Nostra)
Mafia families: Corleonesi clan (Italy), the Gambinos, the Genovese (America's premier organisation)
Mafia figures: Albert Anastasia (aka 'the Mad Hatter'), Michael Corleone, Don Vito Corleone, John Gotti (the 'Dapper Don,' head of the Gambino family - jailed in 1992 for 14 murders), Lucky Luciano
Mafia members: capo, capo dei capi (boss of bosses), don, gangsters, hoodlums, mafiosi, mobsters; henchman, hitman
Mafioso, politically correct term: member of a career-offender cartel
Magi (the three wise men): Caspar, Melchior, Balthazar
magic, adjective: Chaldean, goetic, thaumaturgic
Magic Flute, The: opera by Wolfgang Amadeus Mozart first produced in Vienna in 1791
magic realist writers: Isabel Allende, Carlos Fuentes, Milan Kundera, Gabriel García Márquez, Haruki Murakami, Patrick Süskind, Virginia Woolf
magicians: Criss Angel, Keith Barry, David Blaine (who spent 62 hours encased in a block of ice in Times Square and starved himself for 44 days in a Perspex box suspended over the Thames in London), Ali Bongo (real name: William Wallace), Henry Bouton, Derren Brown, Lance Burton, Tommy Cooper, David Copperfield, Paul Daniels (partner: Debbie McGee), David Devant, Lee Grabel, Harry Houdini, Ricky Jay, Harry Kellar, John Nevil Maskelyne, Merlin, David Nixon, Penn and Teller, John Henry Pepper, Channing Pollock, James Randi, Siegfried and Roy, Howard Thurston, Orson Welles
magician's attendant: famulus
Magic Roundabout, The: children's television programme featuring puppets which became a cult with adults as well as very young children and spawned two big-screen off-shoots, *Dougal and the Blue Cat* (1970) and *The Magic Roundabout* (2004)
    created by the French author Serge Danot in 1965; English version re-written and voiced by Eric Thompson (father of the actress Emma Thompson).

Later episodes were discovered in 1991 and then dubbed into English by Nigel Planer

first broadcast on BBC1 in 1965–1975 and then again on Channel 4 in 1991

cast of characters: Brian (a snail), Dougal (a rather shaggy dog), Dylan (a live-wire rabbit), Ermintrude (a pink cow), Florence (a girl), Mr McHenry (the gardener) Zebedee (a bouncing character)

Magna Carta: historical charter signed in 1215 by King John

magnetic detector: patented in 1902, by Guglielmo Marconi

Magnificent Seven, The (as featured in the 1960 film): Yul Brynner (Chris), Steve McQueen (Vin), Charles Bronson (O'Reilly), Robert Vaughn (Lee), Brad Dexter (Harry Luck), James Coburn (Britt) and Horst Buccholz (Chico)

Magnum P.I.: light-hearted one-hour TV crime show set in Hawaii and featuring a private investigator

broadcast: 11 December 1980–1 May 1988

created by Donald P. Bellisario and Glen A. Larson

cast: Tom Selleck (Thomas Sullivan Magnum), John Hillerman (Jonathan Quayle Higgins III), Robin Masters (the voice of Orson Welles), Roger E. Mosley (T.C.), Larry Manetti (Orville 'Rick' Wright), Gillian Dobb (Agatha Chumley), Kwan Hi Lim (Tanaka), Kathleen Lloyd (Carol Baldwin), Elisha Cook Jr (Ice Pick)

magpie, adjective: corvoid

magpie, collective noun: tiding, tittering

magpie, sound: chatter

maharaja's widow or wife: maharanee

Maid of Orleans: nickname for Joan of Arc

maids: Rose Buck (from TV's *Upstairs, Downstairs*), Hazel Burke (of TV's *Hazel*), Ruby Finch (from TV's *Upstairs, Downstairs*), Marian, Sarah Moffat (from TV's *Upstairs, Downstairs*)

maids, patron saint of: Zita of Lucca

Mail On Sunday, The: British Sunday newspaper founded in 1982

Maine, 23rd state (1820), Pine Tree State

capital: Augusta

inhabitant's nickname: Down Easter

motto: 'Dirigo' ('I direct')

state bird: chickadee

state flower: white pine cone and tassel

state tree: white pine

birthplace of: John Ford (filmmaker), David E. Kelley (TV producer), Stephen King, Henry Wadsworth Longfellow

tourist attractions: Acadia National Park, Bar Harbor, Portland Art Museum

fact: the sun reaches Maine before any other state in the USA

Majorca, population: an estimated 300,000 Germans now live on the island permanently and Germans own 80% of the island's manor houses

malapropism, users of: Mrs Malaprop, Mistress Quickly

malaria, deaths by: Oliver Cromwell, David Livingstone, Amerigo Vespucci

malaria, fact: kills up to three million people a year (2.7 million in 2002)

Malawi: republic in eastern-central Africa; formerly known as Nyasaland (until 1964)

capital: Lilongwe

currency: kwacha

language: English and Chichewa (both official)

religion: Christian (75%) and Muslim (20%)

first prime minister: Hastings Banda (from 1963)

fact: one third of the country is water, including the lakes Malawi, Chilara and Malombe

Malaysia: federation in South-East Asia

    capital: Kuala Lumpur (formerly Putrajaya)

    currency: ringgit

    fact: it is the world's greatest exporter of semiconductors

    famous Malaysians: James Wan (horror director), Michelle Yeoh (film actress)

    language: Malay, English

    religion: Muslim

Maldives, Republic of: republic comprised of 1,087 coral islands in the Indian Ocean

    capital: Malé

    currency: rufiyaa

    language: Divehi

    religion: Muslim (Sunni)

male descent, adjective: patrilineal

male menopause: andropause (official name), change of life, hot flashes, mid-life crisis

male prostitutes: Rupert Everett, Jean Genet

Mali: landlocked republic in West Africa, formerly known as French Sudan (1898–1959)

    capital: Bamako

    currency: African franc

    language: French

    religion: Muslim, animist

Malian and famous: Amadou and Mariam (blind jazz duo), Toumani Diabate (musician), Salif Keita (singer), Oumou Sangare (iconic singer/diva), Tinariwen (band), Ali Farka Touré (guitarist and blues singer, known as the 'Bluesman of Africa')

mallard, collective noun: sord, sute

mallard, young: duckling

mallow, adjective: malvaceous

Malta: republic in the Mediterranean comprising the islands of Malta, Gozo and Comino, south of Sicily

    capital: Valletta

    currency: Maltese lira

    language: Maltese, English

    religion: Roman Catholic

    fact: divorce is still illegal

man, adjective: anthropoid

man/common man, adjective: demotic

man, collective noun: band

man, hatred of: misandry

Man Booker Prize – see Booker Prize

Man of a Thousand Faces: nickname for the actor Lon Chaney

Man of Steel: nickname for Superman

man-hater: Miss Havisham (from *Great Expectations*)

Manchester: city in north-west England, formerly nicknamed Cottonopolis

Manchester, adjective: Mancunian

Manchester, birthplace of: Tom Baker (actor), Danny Boyle (director), Anthony Burgess, Steve Coogan (comedian), Thomas De Quincey, Christopher

mariweegee, Mary and Johnnie, pot, spliff (cigarette), tuskie (a large cigarette), wisdom-weed, yen pop, zol

marijuana, fact: tried by 80 million Americans

marijuana butt: roach

marionettes: Andy Pandy, Pinocchio

marital problems, patron saint of: Rita of Cascia

market, adjective: nundinal

market day, adjective: nundinal

marks (in writing and printing): accent, accent acute, accent grave, apostrophe, asterisk, breve, caret, cedilla, circumflex, comma, diacritic, diaeresis, ellipsis, exclamation mark, macron, obelus, question mark, stet, tilde (ñ), umlaut

Marlboro theme tune: Elmer Bernstein's rousing theme from the 1960 Western *The Magnificent Seven*

marlin, adjective: istiophorid

Marlow, Berkshire, England: town where Mary Shelley wrote *Frankenstein* and Jerome K. Jerome wrote *Three Men in a Boat*

marmalade: conceived by James Keiller (1775–1839)

marmalade brands: Chivers Breakfast, Duerr's, Frank Cooper's, Golden Shred, MacKays, Robertson's, Silver Shred

marmoset, adjective: callithricid

marmot, adjective: sciurid

marquess, mode of verbal address: Your Lordship

marriage: "After a while marriage is a sibling relationship, marked by occasional, rather regrettable, episodes of incest" - Martin Amis; "Marriages are like tornadoes. There's all this blowing and sucking at the beginning; and at the end you lose your house" – James Caan; "Like a garden, marriage requires both rain and sunshine to make it grow stronger" – Ewen Brownrigg; "When there's no argument in a marriage, someone is the underdog" - Roy Castle's father; "My wife and I were happy for 20 years. Then we met" - Rodney Dangerfield; "Some marriages are made in Heaven, but so are lightning and thunder" - Clint Eastwood; "Marriage is like the army. Everybody complains but you'd be surprised how many re-enlist" – James Garner; "Marriage is either very easy or it's impossible. With Rita and I it's like we gave birth to each other" - Tom Hanks; "Marriage is like throwing yourself into a river when you only wanted a drink of water" - David Jason; "There's no such thing as a successful marriage. There are marriages that give up and marriages that keep on trying. That's the only difference" - Garrison Keillor; "Essentially, men want to be married to a pal with breasts" - Christopher Middleton; "Marriage is the alliance of two people, one of whom never remembers birthdays and the other who never forgets" - Ogden Nash; "The chains of marriage are so heavy that it often takes more than two to bear them" - La Rochefoucauld; "Marriage is like the question of asparagus eaten with vinaigrette or hollandaise – a matter of taste but of no importance" – Françoise Sagan; "Chains do not hold a marriage together. It is threads, hundreds of tiny threads which sew people together through the years. That is what makes a marriage last" - Simone Signoret; "All men make mistakes, but married men find out about them sooner" - Red Skelton; "The secret of a happy marriage is to share a roof but not a ceiling" – Leonard Woolf

marriage, adjective: conjugal, connubial, marital

marriage, fact: fifty per cent of all marriages in the US end in divorce

marriage, fear of: gamophobia

marriage, god of: Hymen (Greek and Roman mythology)

marriage, goddess of: Hera (Greek mythology), Juno (Roman)

marriage, unhappy: cagamosis

marriage between persons highly suitable for each other: nomogamosis

marriage broker: schatchen

marriage in space, first: between Yuri Malenchenko, a Russian air force colonel, and his earth-bound bride, Ekaterina Dmitriev, in August 2003. The ceremony was carried out via video link at the Johnson Space Centre in Houston

marriage in which one or both partners are quite advanced in age: opsigamy

Marriage of Figaro, The, comic opera by Wolfgang Amadeus Mozart first produced in Vienna in 1786

marriage outside one's own social group (or tribe): exogamy

marriage service: "Dearly beloved, we are gathered together here in the sight of God..." (see The Form of Solemnization of Matrimony in the book of Common Prayer)

marriage types: endogamy, morganatic (in which the man is socially superior to the woman), nomogamosis, opsigamy

marriage within the same tribe or community: endogamy

married women, patron saint of: Monica

Mars: aka the Red Planet

Mars, diameter: a little more than half that of Earth

Mars, distance from Earth: 119 million miles

Marseilles cuisine: bouillabaisse

marsh, adjective: helobious, paludal, paludine

Marshall Islands: republic made up of 34 coral islands in the western-central Pacific
    capital: Majuro
    currency: US dollar
    language: Marshallese, English
    religion: Roman Catholic

marten, collective noun: richness

martial arts: aikido, bo, capoeira, eskrima (Filipino), gatka (Sikh), hap ki do, jeet kune do, jujitsu, kali (Filipino), kali-eskrima-silat (a crude form of knife and stick fighting from Indonesia), karate, krav maga (contact combat), kung fu, lathi (Indian), muay Thai, shotokan (Japanese karate), tae kwon do (Korean art of self-defence), t'ai chi ch'uan, wing chun, wushu

martial arts, prime divisions: Wudan (for inner strength), Shaolin (for outer strength)

martial arts, slang: chop socky

martial arts choreographer: Yuen Wo Ping

martial arts stars: David Belle, Jackie Chan, Stephen Chow, Tony Jaa, Brandon Lee, Bruce Lee, Jet Li

martin (bird), adjective: hirundine

Martini: cocktail made of gin and French vermouth

Marvel Comic titles: Captain America, Daredevil, Elektra, Fantastic Four, Nick Fury, Incredible Hulk, Iron Man, Kick-Ass, The Punisher, Silver Surfer, Spider-Man, Thor, X-Men

martyrs: Saint Alban, Saint Boniface, Charles I ('the Martyred King'), Saint Christopher, Saint Edmund, King Edward of England, Che Guevara, Gunga Din, Joan of Arc, Hugh Latimer, Lawrence of Rome, Madame X, Harvey Milk, Jan Palach, Vibia Perpetua, Thich Quang-Duc, Nicholas Ridley, Oscar Romero, Bobby Sands, Stephen (first Christian martyr), Tolpuddle Martyrs, Saint Ursula, Saint Valentine, Saint Vitus, William Wallace

Marx Brothers: Chico (real name: Leonard), Groucho (real name: Julius Henry), Gummo (real name: Milton), Harpo (real name: Arthur) and Zeppo (real name: Herbert)

Marxists: Nikolai Bukharin, Carlos the Jackal, Maxim Gorky, Sergey Kirov, Vladimir Ilyich Lenin, Mao Tse-tung, Jean-Paul Sartre, Josip Broz Tito, Leon Trotsky, Virginia Woolf

Maryland, 7th state (1788), Old Line State, Free State, 'America in Miniature'
  capital: Annapolis
  state bird: Baltimore oriole
  state flower: black-eyed Susan
  state tree: white oak
  motto: 'Fatti Maschii, Parole Femine' ('Manly deeds, womanly words')
  birthplace of: Benjamin Banneker (astronomer), John Wilkes Booth, Eva Cassidy, Tom Clancy, Thomas Jane (actor), Barry Levinson (filmmaker), Jada-Pinkett-Smith (actress), Sisqo, John Waters (filmmaker)
  tourist attractions: Ocean City Beach, Fort McHenry, Antietam Battlefield

M*A*S*H: hugely popular TV series set in wartime Korea at the 4077th Mobile Army Surgical Hospital Unit; based on the 1970 film directed by Robert Altman (which in turn was adapted from the novel by Richard Hooker)
  broadcast: 17 September 1972–28 February 1983
  cast: Alan Alda (Captain Benjamin Franklin 'Hawkeye' Pierce), Wayne Rogers (Captain John F. X. 'Trapper John' McIntire), McLean Stevenson (Lt. Col. Henry Blake), Loretta Swit (Major Margaret 'Hot Lips' Houlihan), Larry Linville (Major Frank Burns), Harry Morgan (Colonel Sherman Potter), Mike Farrell (Captain B.J. Hunnicutt), David Ogden Stiers (Major Charles Emerson Winchester), Loudon Wainwright (Captain Calvin Spaulding), G.W. Bailey (Sergeant Luther Rizzo)

mask worn at a masquerade: domino mask

masked ball: masquerade

Masked Ball, A: an opera by Giuseppe Verdi first produced in Rome on 17 February 1859

mass, adjective: molar

Mass, cup used in: chalice
  - see Eucharist

mass murderers: Lavrenti Beria, Adolf Hitler, Thomas Midgley Jr (American chemist responsible for introducing lead into petrol and CFCs into refrigeration), Pol Pot, Joseph Stalin – see serial killers

Massachusetts, 6th state (1788), Old Colony
  capital: Boston
  motto: 'Ense Petit Placidam Sub Libertate Qietem' ('By the sword we seek peace, but peace only under liberty')
  state bird: chickadee
  state flower: mayflower
  state tree: American elm
  birthplace of: John Adams (second president), John Quincy Adams (sixth president), Leonard Bernstein, Calvin Coolidge (30th president), Cordelia's Dad (alternative folk quartet), Matt Damon, Nathaniel Hawthorne, John F. Kennedy (35th president), Matt LeBlanc, Conan O'Brien, Dr Seuss (full name: Theodor Seuss Geisel), Mark Wahlberg, Rob Zombie
  tourist attractions: Cape Cod, Plymouth Rock, Plymouth Plantation, Mayflower II, JFK Library, Museum of Fine Arts, Freedom Trail

massacres: Beslan (North Ossetia, Russia), Bolton (England), Columbine (see), Crow Creek (South Dakota), Custer's Last Stand (Montana), Dunblane

(Stirling, Scotland), Elphinstone's army (Afghanistan), Granada, Halabja poison gas attack (Iraq), Hungerford (Berkshire, England), Jamestown (Virginia), Kent State (Ohio), Khojaly (Azerbaijan), Laha (Indonesia), My Lai (South Vietnam), Qana (Lebanon), Rorke's Drift (Natal, South Africa), Sabra and Shatila (Lebanon), Saint Bartholomew's Day (Paris), Saint Brice's Day (England), Saint Valentine's Day (Chicago), Sand Creek (Colorado), September Massacres (France), Sharpville (South Africa), Tiananmen Square, Vukovar (Croatia), Wounded Knee (South Dakota)

massage, circular stroking technique in: effleurage

massage, rapid striking technique in: tapotement

Masters and Johnson: Dr William Masters and Dr Virginia Johnson (sex researchers)

masters of disguise: S. Emma E. Edmonds (nurse and spy in the American Civil War), Flambeau (from the *Father Brown* stories), Sherlock Holmes, Ethan Hunt (from *Mission: Impossible*), Mr Moto, Scarlet Pimpernel (aka Sir Percy Blakeney)

Master of Suspense: nickname given to Alfred Hitchcock

Mastersingers of Nuremberg, The, comic opera by Richard Wagner first produced in Munich in 1868

masturbate: beat off, beat one's dummy, beat one's hog, beat one's meat, jack off, jerk off, jill off (for women), puff the one-eyed dragon, pump cream, pump the monkey, pump the python, shank, slap the salami, spank (in the shower), wank, wank off, waz (for women)

masturbation: flying solo, gherkin jerking, hand jive, jerking off, onanism, pud wrestling, spanking the monkey, stroking the salami

masturbation, obsession with: chiromania

masturbator: chicken choker, diddler, hog flogger, jerk-off, peter-beater, pudpuller, wanker

matadors: El Cordobés (real name: Manuel Benítez), Joselito

match (of the lighting variety): Congreve, Cook's matches, fusee (for cigars and a pipe), lucifer (old-fashioned), safety match, Ship, Swan Vesta, vesuvian (old-fashioned)

Matchbox cars: co-founded by Leslie Smith, Rodney Smith and Jack Odell in 1953

matchmakers: Cupid, Dolly Levi (from Thornton Wilder's *The Matchmaker*), Emma Woodhouse (from Jane Austen's *Emma*)

materials – see fabric

materialism, culture of: affluenza

mathematician, slang: number-cruncher

mathematicians: Niels Abel, André-Marie Ampère, Apollonius of Perga, Kenneth Appel, Archimedes, Charles Babbage, Isaac Barrow, Friedrich Bessel, Henry Briggs, Girolamo Cardano, Lewis Carroll, Élie Cartan, John Horton Conway, Roger Cotes, René Descartes, Diophantus, Marcus du Sautoy, Eratosthenes, Euclid, Mitchell Feigenbaum, Pierre de Fermat, Klaus Fuchs, Galileo Galilei, Évariste Galois, Carl Friedrich Gauss, Kurt Gödel, Jacques Hadamard, Wolfgang Haken, Edmund Halley, Heron of Alexandria, David Hilbert, Hypatia of Alexandria, Carl Jacobi, William Thomson Kelvin, Roy Kerr, Pierre-Simon Laplace, Gottfried Leibniz, Marius Lie, Nikolai Lobachevski, Aleksandr Lyapunov, Benoit Mandelbrot, John Napier, John Forbes Nash Jr, John Von Neumann, Sir Isaac Newton, Richard Norwood, Omar Khayyám, Sir Roger Penrose, Grigori Perelman, Lev Semyonovich Pontryagin, Pythagoras, Bernhard Riemann, Bertrand Russell, Claude Shannon, James Sylvester, Alfred Tarski, René Thom, Alan Turing, Warren Weaver, Joseph Wedderburn, A.N. Whitehead, Norbert Wiener, Sewall Wright, Grigori Yakovlevich

mathematicians' prize: Fields Medal
maturity: "Age is a very high price to pay for maturity" – Tom Stoppard
Mauritania: republic in northern West Africa; officially known as the Islamic
Republic of Mauritania
capital: Nouakchott
currency: ouguiya
language: Arabic mainly, also Fulani, Soninke, Wolof and French
religion: Muslim
Mauritius: island state in the Indian Ocean, formerly known as Île-de-France (until
1810)
capital: Port Louis
currency: rupee
language: English, French creole
religion: Hindu (majority), Christian
mausoleum, famous: Taj Mahal
M/A/W: model/actress/waitress
Maxwell House coffee, slogan: 'Good To The Last Drop'
mayors: Marion Barry Jr (Washington DC, caught taking drugs while still in
office), Randolph Beresford (Hammersmith and Fulham, first black mayor in
Britain), Michael 'Mike' Bloomberg (New York), Sonny Bono (Palm Springs,
California), Willie Brown (San Francisco), Bill Campbell (Atlanta), Jacques
Chirac (Paris), Richard Daley (Chicago), Clint Eastwood (Carmel, California),
Rudolph 'Rudy' Giuliani (New York), Boris Johnson (London), Mel Lastman
(Toronto), John V. Lindsay (New York), Ken Livingstone (London), Betty
Loren-Maltese (Chicago), Paul Schell (Seattle), Jerry Springer (Cincinnati),
Jean Tiberi (Paris), Dick Whittington (London), Anthony Williams (Washington
DC), Andrew Young (Atlanta)
mayor, mode of verbal address: Your Worship
mayors, fact: more than 50 former US mayors were behind bars in 2002
MBE: Member of the Order of the British Empire
McDonald's: founded by Ray Kroc
first branch opened in Des Moines, Iowa, in 1955
first branch opened in Britain in 1974, in Woolwich
fact: has sold over 100 billion burgers, or 12 burgers for every human on the
planet
fact: one in eight Americans has worked for McDonald's at one stage in their
lives
fact: the store is visited by one in 200 people across the world every day
fact: on average, McDonald's opens 4.2 new branches somewhere in the world
daily
fact: a third of all cows reared in the US are destined for McDonald's
fact: eight per cent of America's entire potato crop is destined for McDonald's
world's busiest branch: Moscow's Pushkin Square
MD: postcode for Maryland
ME: postcode for Maine
ME: myalgic encephalomyelitis (Yuppie flu), aka chronic fatigue syndrome, from
which an estimated 150,000 people in the UK suffer
measurement, adjective: mensural
measurement of approximately 45 inches: ell (obsolete)
meat - see sausage
meat, adjective: creatic
meat, fear of: carnophobia

meat delicatessen: charcuterie

Mecca, pilgrim of: haji

medal collecting (also coins, bank notes, etc): numismatics, numismatology

media: paparazzi, stalkerazzi

media tycoons: Silvio Berlusconi, Conrad Black, Richard Branson, Barry Diller, Chris Evans, Alfred Harmsworth (later Lord Northcliffe), Robert L. Johnson, John Malone, Robert Maxwell, Rupert Murdoch, Kerry Packer, Sumner Redstone, Roy Thomson, Ted Turner

medicine, god of: Asclepius (Greek), Aesculapius (Roman)

medicines, book of: pharmacopoeia

medicines, list of: codex

Mediterranean islands: Amorgós, Anáfi, Ándros, Astipálaia, Corsica, Cyprus, Delos, Euboea, Formentera, Ibiza, Ios, Itháki, Kálimnos, Kárpathos, Kásos, Kastellórizon, Kéa, Kefallinía, Kérkira, Khálki, Khíos, Kíthnos, Kos, Léros, Lésvos, Levkás, Límnos, Lípsos, Majorca, Malta, Míkonos, Mílos, Minorca, Náxos, Nísiros, Páros, Pátmos, Rhodes, Sámos, Samothráki, Santoríni (aka Thera/Thíra), Sardinia, Sérifos, Sicily, Sífnos, Síkinos, Síros, Thásos, Thíra, Tílos, Tínos, Zákinthos

mediums: Derek Acorah, Madame Arcati (from Noël Coward's *Blithe Spirit*), Leslie Price, Doris Stokes

Medusa, slayer of: Perseus

meerkat, famous: Timon (from Disney's *The Lion King*)

Melbourne, birthplace of: Gillian Armstrong (filmmaker), Eric Bana, Cate Blanchett, Coral Browne, Jason Donovan, Flea, Malcolm Fraser, Percy Grainger, Germaine Greer, Rachel Griffiths, Barry Humphries, Kylie Minogue, Rupert Murdoch, Fred Schepisi (filmmaker), Gough Whitlam, David Williamson (playwright)

melody, adjective: ariose

melt: deliquesce

membership, UK organisations with biggest: 1) AA; 2) RAC; 3) National Trust

memories and dreams, the condition of confusing: paramnesia

memory, adjective: mnemonic

memory, goddess of: Mnemosyne (Greek mythology)

memory fabrication (a condition of the mind): paramnesia

memory jogger: mnemonic

memory loss: amnesia

Memphis, Ancient Egypt, founded by: Epaphus

Memphis, Tennessee, birthplace of: Kathy Bates (actress), Aretha Franklin, Morgan Freeman, George Hamilton, Ben Johnson (baseball star), Memphis Slim, Cybill Shepherd, Justin Timberlake

Memphis river: Mississippi

Memphis tourist attractions: Graceland, National Civil Rights Museum, Peabody Memphis (hotel famous for its ducks), Pyramid (a structure two-thirds the size of the Great Pyramid in Egypt, completed in 1991), Sun Studio

men, collective noun: band

men, fear of: androphobia

men, hatred of: misandry

men, love of: andromania

men and women: "Men and women are very different. There is no comparison in terms of anything. That whole thing of giving birth? That's a frame of mind that's impossible for a man to know. Getting a hard-on, that's something a woman will never understand. It has nothing to do with more or less or better or quality of mind, but it's like men have a better agent" - Christopher Walken

menstrual absence: amenorrhoea
menstrual discharge, the bad smell of: bromomenorrhea
menstruation: Aunt Flo (American slang) – see period
menstruation, painful: dysmenorrhoea
mental disorders, study of: psychiatry
mercenary: Gurkha, John Hawkwood
merchandising; the first film to benefit from merchandising mania: Jaws (1975)
merchants: Marco Polo, George Peabody, Shylock, Dick Whittington
merchant, collective noun: faith
merchants, patron saints of: Francis of Assisi and Nicholas
mermaids: Ariel (from Disney's *The Little Mermaid*), Mélusine (from the French
    folk tale), Miranda, Undine (from the story by La Motte Fouqué)
mermaid syndrome: sirenomelia (in which a child is born with its legs fused
    together)
Merry Widow, The: operetta by Ferencz Lehár first produced in Vienna in 1905
Merseysidse, administrative centre: Liverpool
Mesozoic periods: Triassic (225m years ago), Jurassic (180m), Cretaceous (135m)
messenger, collective noun: diligence
messenger of the Gods: Hermes (Greek mythology), Mercury (Roman mythology)
Mesopotamian city: Babylon
Messiah – see Handel's Messiah
Messiah: Jesus Christ (see Jesus)
metal, adjective: metallic
metal, heaviest: osmium
metal, lightest: lithium
metal bands – see heavy metal bands
Metallica: heavy metal rock band formed in San Francisco in 1981; comprised of
    Lars Ulrich (drums), James Hetfield (guitar, vocals), Cliff Burton (bass, died:
    1986), Jason Newsted (bass; from 1986) and Kirk Hammett (guitar). Original
    members: Dave Mustaine (guitar), Ron McGovney (bass) and Lloyd Grant
    (guitar)
metals, fear of: metallophobia
metal-working, god of: Hephaestus (Greek mythology), Vulcan (Roman)
metallurgist: Henry Sorby
metallurgist, collective noun: amalgamation
metaphysician: A.N. Whitehead
meteors, fear of: meteorophobia
meteorologists: James Glaisher, Erik Palmen, Reginald Sutcliffe
Methodism, founder of: John Wesley
metre, one-millionth of: micron
metronome: device invented in 1816 by Johann Maelzel, a friend of Beethoven's
Metropolitan Police Force: founded in 1829 by Sir Robert Peel
Mexican: bean eater, Chili, Cholo, taco-bender, taco-eater, taco-head, wetback (all
    derog.)
Mexican and famous: Lila Downs (singer), Carlos Fuentes (novelist), Gael García
    Bernal, Salma Hayek (actress), Pedro Infante (singer), Benito Juárez (national
    hero and president), Frida Kahlo (painter), Octavio Paz (poet), Anthony
    Quinn (actor), Antonio López de Santa Anna (soldier and statesman),
    El Santo (wrestler), Henryk Szeryng (violinist), Thalia Sodi (singer)
Mexican dog: chihuahua

Mexican festival: Day of the Dead (November 1)
Mexican film directors: Alfonso Arau, Alfonso Cuarón, Guillermo del Toro, Alejandro González Iñárritu
Mexican Mafia: la Eme
Mexican painters: Frida Kahlo, Diego Rivera, David Siqueiros (muralist), Rufino Tamayo
Mexican pop star: Thalia (whose sisters were kidnapped in 2002)
Mexican television personality: Paco Stanley (shot dead – four times in the head – in June of 1999)
Mexican War: 1846–1847 (between Mexico and the United States)
Mexico: republic in North America, officially known as United Mexican States
    capital: Mexico City
    currency: peso
    language: Spanish
    religion: Roman Catholic
    fact: on average at least 1,300 people are kidnapped every year
Mexico City, fact: the city is now 30 feet lower than it was in 1990
Mexico City, population: over 20,000,000
Mexico City, tourist attractions: The Anthropological Museum (built in the 1960s), the National Palace
MI: postcode for Michigan
Miami: The Magic City, Sin-City-sur-mer
Miami, birthplace of: Buster Rhymes, Patricia Cornwell, Deborah Harry, Sidney Poitier, Janet Reno, Ben Vereen
Miami, fact: two thirds of the city is now Hispanic, with whites making up less than 12%
Miami Vice: cult, self-consciously stylish TV series about a pair of fashion-vigilant, colour-coordinated undercover cops. The series, a calculated MTV-style franchise, made two-day stubble trendy and spawned a number one single with its theme composed by Czech instrumentalist Jan Hammer
    broadcast: 16 September 1984–26 July 1989
    created by Anthony Yerkovich and executive produced by Michael Mann
    cast: Don Johnson (Det. James 'Sonny' Crockett aka Sonny Burnett), Philip Michael Thomas (Det. Ricardo Tubbs), Edward James Olmos (Lt. Martin Castillo), Gregory Sierra (Lt. Lou Rodriguez), Saundra Santiago (Det. Gina Calabrese), Olivia Brown (Det. Trudy Joplin), Michael Talbott (Det. Stan Switek), John Diehl (Det. Larry Zito), Sheena Easton (Caitlin Davies). Guest stars included many names from the music industry, including James Brown, Leonard Cohen, Phil Collins, Miles Davis, Glenn Frey, Isaac Hayes, Ted Nugent and Vanity mice, famous – see mouse, famous
mice, fear of: murophobia, musophobia
Michigan, 26th state (1837), Great Lakes State, Wolverine State
    capital: Lansing
    state bird: robin
    state flower: apple blossom
    state tree: white pine
    motto: 'Si Quaeris Peninsulam Amoenam Circumspice' (If you seek a pleasant peninsula, look about you')
    birthplace of: Edna Ferber, Henry Ford, Bill Haley, Magic Johnson, John Kellogg, Will Kellogg, Ring Lardner, Charles Lindbergh, Madonna, Michael Moore, Smokey Robinson, Diana Ross, Steven Seagal, Tom

Selleck, Lily Tomlin, Stevie Wonder

tourist attractions: Henry Ford Museum, Hiawatha Falls

microbes, fear of: bacillophobia

microbiologists: John Enders, Sir Anthony Epstein, Alice Evans, Louis Pasteur, Anthony Pawson

microchip: invented by both Jack Kilby and Robert Noyce (separately) in 1959

Micronesia, Federated States of: island group in the West Pacific

    capital: Palikir

    currency: US dollar

    language: English, Micronesian

    religion: Christian

microphone: concept first conceived in 1667 by Robert Hozke

Microsoft: computer company co-founded in 1975 by Bill Gates and Paul Allen

microwave oven: invented in 1945 by the American physics engineer Percy Le Baron Spencer

microwave oven, debut: 1967, when the first domestic appliances were put on the market by Amana, a subsidiary of Raytheon

middle age: "Too old to be a toy boy and too young to be a sugar daddy" - Henry Magrill; "Middle age is when you've met so many people that every new person you meet reminds you of someone else" - Ogden Nash

midget, adjective: homuncular

MI5, first female head: Dame Stella Rimmington

MI5 traitor: David Shayler (who served a jail term for breaching the Official Secrets Act)

migraine, fact: a condition regularly suffered by 10 million Britons

Mikado, The: operetta by W.S. Gilbert and Arthur Sullivan, first produced in London in 1885

Milan: the murder capital of Italy

Milan opera house: La Scala

Milan river: Olona

mileage, instrument for measuring: mileometer, milometer, odometer

milf (acronym): Mother I'd like to fuck

militant groups – see terrorist organisations

military designer: Mikhail Kalashnikov

military in England, prior to 1066: fyrd

military leaders: Alexander the Great, Alexandre Berthier, Cesare Borgia, Louis Botha, Omar Bradley, Heinrich Brauchitsch, Charlemagne (aka 'Charles the Great'), Charles Martel, George Armstrong Custer, Moshe Dayan, Lt. General James Doolittle, Air Chief Marshal Sir Hugh Dowding, Dwight Eisenhower, El Cid (real name: Rodrigo Diaz de Vivar), Ferdinand Foch, Giuseppe Garibaldi, Genghis Khan, Charles Gordon, Field Marshal Douglas Haig, Vice-Admiral William F. 'Bull' Halsey, Hannibal, King Henry V, Sir Brian Horrocks, Kublai Khan, Bernard Law Montgomery, Napoleon Bonaparte, George Patton, Saladin, Myles Standish, Zhu De, Georgi Zhukov

military theorists: Carl von Clausewitz, John Fuller

milk, adjective: lacteal, lactic; of soured milk: clabrous

milk gone sour: bonnyclabber

milking cow: milch (noun)

milkmen: Ernie (the Fasted Milkman in the West; c/o Benny Hill), Tevye (from *Fiddler On the Roof*)

mill, adjective: molinary

mill watercourse: leat

millepede, adjective: arthropodal
Milton, John; word coined by: pandemonium
Milwaukee, birthplace of: Jeffrey Dahmer, Woody Herman (band leader), Alfred Lunt, Pat O'Brien (actor), Schlitz beer, Tom Snyder (newscaster), Spencer Tracy
Milwaukee, fact: where the world's first practical typewriter was designed (in 1867)
mime, muse of: Polyhymnia
mime artists: Colette (also a famous writer), Étienne Decroux, Lindsay Kemp, Marcel Marceau
mind, adjective: mental, phrenic (obsolete)
mind, fear of: psychophobia
mind, human: "The human mind, once stretched to a new idea, never goes back to its original dimensions" - Oliver Wendell Holmes
mind control expert: Derren Brown
mine entrance: adit
miner's pickaxe: mandrel
mineral spring, adjective: crenitic
mineral water: Abbey Well, Buxton, Evian, Highland Spring
mineralogy: oryctognosy
miners, patron saint of: Barbara
ministers – see priests
mink, adjective: mustelid
mink, young: kit
Minneapolis, birthplace of: Lew Ayres, Jean Paul Getty, Terry Gilliam, Prince, The Replacements, Charles Schulz, Soul Asylum, Vince Vaughn (actor), Jesse Ventura
Minnesota, 32nd state (1858), North Star State, Gopher State
   capital: St Paul
   state bird: common loon
   state flower: showy lady's-slipper (aka pink and white lady's-slipper)
   state tree: Norway pine (aka red pine)
   motto: 'L'Etoile du Nord' ('The star of the north')
   birthplace of: Eddie Cochran, Bob Dylan, F. Scott Fitzgerald, Judy Garland, John Paul Getty, Terry Gilliam, Garrison Keillor, Jessica Lange, Sinclair Lewis, E.G. Marshall, Eugene J. McCarthy, Breckin Meyer, Walter F. Mondale, Prince, Jane Russell, Winona Ryder, Charles Schulz, Seann William Scott (actor), Vince Vaughn (actor), Jesse Ventura
   tourist attractions: Minnehaha Falls, Voyageurs National Park
   fact: only canoes are permitted on most of the state's 1,000-plus lakes
minnow, adjective: cyprinid
Minstrel of Broadway: nickname for Al Jolson
mint, adjective: lamiaceous
mint liqueur: crème de menthe
Minute Waltz: nickname for Chopin's waltz in D flat major, opus 64, no. 1, written in 1847
miracle, adjective: thaumaturgic
miracle worker: thaumaturge
mirror: cheval glass (tall mirrow swung on a vertical frame)
Mirror, The: tabloid British newspaper founded in 1903
mirrors, fear of: catoptrophobia, eisoptrophobia

misanthropes: Alceste (from Molière's *The Misanthrope*), the Grinch, Mao Tse-tung, Ebenezer Scrooge

mischief, god of: Loki (Norse mythology)

misers: Barabas (from Christopher Marlowe's *The Jew of Malta*), Jack Benny, Fagin, Peggy Guggenheim, Harpagon (from Molière's *The Miser*), Lord Hertford, al Kindi (from Al Jahiz' *The Book of Misers*), Silas Marner, Ebenezer Scrooge

mishearing (of a word or phrase): mondegreen (coined by the American writer Sylvia Wright)

misnomers: blow job, Bombay duck, Buffalo Bill, catgut, centipede, chop sticks, Christian, hay fever, life sentence, pencil lead, rush hour, solar eclipse, VAT (Value Added Tax)

mispronunciation: cacology

missiles: ABM, ASM, bullet, ballistic missile, bolas, boomerang, brickbat, cannon ball, cruise missile, dart, drone, Exocet, guided missile, harpoon, heat-seeking missile, ICBM, IRBM, long-range missile, medium-range missile, Minuteman, MIRV, MRBM, Polaris, projectile, rocket, SAM (surface-to-air missile), scud, shot, SLBM, slug, spitball, torpedo, Trident, V-2, woomera (Aboriginal)

missiles, fear of: ballistophobia

missile launchers: ballista (used for hurling large stones), catapult, mangonel (used for hurling large stones and fiery projectiles), onager (popular with the Romans), slingshot
- see guns

missing and famous – see disappearances

missionaries: Gladys Aylward (as immortalised by Ingrid Bergman in *The Inn of the Sixth Happiness*), Saint Boniface, David Brainerd, Sarah Brown (from *Guys and Dolls*), Eli Jones, David Livingstone, Saint Paul, Albert Schweitzer, Mother Teresa (aka Teresa of Calcutta), Vivekananda, John Wesley

Mississippi, 20th state (1817), Magnolia State
  capital: Jackson
  state bird: mockingbird
  state flower: magnolia
  state tree: magnolia
  motto: 'Virtute et Armis' ('By valor and arms')
  birthplace of: Dana Andrews, Bo Diddley, William Faulkner, Shelby Foote, Jim Henson, James Earl Jones, B.B. King, Elvis Presley, Charley Pride, Muddy Waters, Eudora Welty, Tennessee Williams, Oprah Winfrey, Tammy Wynette
  tourist attractions: Vicksburg National Military Park and Cemetery, Natchez Trace

Mississippi River: begins 90 miles south of the Canadian border and heads 2,348 miles to the Gulf of Mexico. Includes more than 100 tributaries and takes in two Canadian provinces and 31 US States

Mississippi River, nickname: Old Man River

Missouri, 24th state (1821), Show Me State
  capital: Jefferson City
  state bird: bluebird
  state flower: hawthorn
  state tree: flowering dogwood
  motto: 'Salus Populi Suprema Lex Esto ('The welfare of the people shall be the supreme law')

birthplace of: Akon, Robert Altman, Burt Bacharach, Josephine Baker, General Omar Bradley, Calamity Jane, Dale Carnegie, Walter Cronkite, Sheryl Crow, T.S. Eliot, Eminem, Huckleberry Finn, Betty Grable, Langston Hughes (Negro poet), Jesse James, John Joseph Pershing, Ginger Rogers, Tom Sawyer, Harry S. Truman, Mark Twain, Dick Van Dyke

tourist attractions: Mark Twain Area, Pony Express Museum, Harry S. Truman Library

mistakes: "Fools learn from their mistakes; I prefer to learn from the mistakes of others" – Otto von Bismarck; "The greatest mistake you can make in life is to be continually fearing you will make one" - Elbert Hubbard; "Mistakes are the portals of discovery" – James Joyce; "The man who makes no mistakes does not usually make anything" - Edward John Phelps

mistletoe, adjective: loranthaceous

mistresses, famous (real or alleged): Faria Alam (c/o Sven-Göran Eriksson), Madame du Barry (c/o Louis XV of France), Eva Braun (c/o Adolf Hitler), Cleopatra (c/o Julius Caesar and Mark Antony), Annie Elizabeth Crook (c/o Prince 'Eddy' Albert, Duke of Clarence and Avondale), Edwina Currie (c/o Sir John Major), Delilah (c/o Samson), Nancy Dell'Olio (c/o Sven-Göran Eriksson), Antonia de Sancha (c/o David Mellor), Gennifer Flowers (c/o Bill Clinton), Nell Gwynn (c/o King Charles II), Emma Hamilton (c/o Lord Nelson), Christine Keeler (c/o John Profumo), Lady Caroline Lamb (c/o Lord Byron), Lillie Langtry (c/o the future King Edward VII), Monica Lewinsky (c/o Bill Clinton), Rebecca Loos (c/o David Beckham), Lola Montez (c/o King Ludwig I of Bavaria), Jane Morris (c/o Dante Gabriel Rossetti), Camilla Parker Bowles (c/o Prince Charles), Clara Petacci (c/o Benito Mussolini), Madame de Pompadour (c/o Louis XV of France), Kimberley Quinn (c/o David Blunkett), Frances Stevenson (c/o David Lloyd George), Tracey Temple (c/o John Prescott), Barbara Villiers (c/o King Charles II and the playwright William Wycherley), Petronella Wyatt (c/o Boris Johnson)

mite, adjective: acarid, acarine, acaroid

mites, study of: acarology

MMR: measles, mumps, rubella (triple vaccine)

MN: postcode for Minnesota

MO: postcode for Missouri

mob leader: demagogue

mobile artist: Alexander Calder

mockingbird: state bird of Arkansas, Florida, Mississippi, Tennessee and Texas

mockingbird, adjective: mimine

models – see supermodels

modelling agencies: Elite Model Management, Ford Agency

modern artists: Tracey Emin, Damien Hirst, Jenny Holzer, Anselm Kiefer, Edward Kienholz, Franz Kline, Jeff Koons, Barbara Kruger, Sol LeWitt, Steve McQueen, Kenneth Noland, Ad Reinhardt, Bridget Riley, Mark Rothko, David Salle, Andy Warhol

– see abstract painters, painters of the twentieth century, pop artists

Mohammed: Mustafa, the Prophet

Mohammed's daughter: Fatima

Mohammed's wife (his favourite): Aisha

moisture, aversion to: hygrophobia

moisture, goddess of: Tefnut (Egyptian mythology)

moisture absorbing: hygroscopic (adjective)

Moldova: republic in south-eastern Europe
    capital: Kishinev
    currency: leu
    language: Romanian
    religion: atheist, Christian
    fact: it is Europe's poorest nation
mole (animal), adjective: talpine, talpoid
mole (animal), collective noun: labour
mole (animal), habitat: fortress
mole (animal), young: pup
molecular biologists: Paul Berg, Michael Bishop, Francis Crick, Walter Gilbert, Brett Giroir, Cesar Milstein, James D. Watson, Maurice Wilkins
mollusc; living molluscs are generally classified into eight major groups: Tryblidia (neopilinids), Gastropoda (limpets, snails, whelks, slugs), Bivalvia (clams, mussels, oysters, scallops), Scaphopoda (tusk shells), Solenogastres (narrow-footed gliders), Cephalopoda (squid, cuttlefish, octopuses, nautiluses), Caudofoveata (mudmoles), and Placophora (chitons)
mollusc, adjective: malacological, molluscan
mollusc shells, collection and study of: conchology
molluscs, study of: malacology
Monaco: Mediterranean principality in south-west Europe occupying just 500 acres
    capital: Monaco-Ville
    currency: euro; formerly: franc
    language: French
    religion: Roman Catholic
Mona Lisa: 1503 portrait by Leonardo Da Vinci famous for its ambivalent smile and mysterious subject, said to be Lisa Gherardini (aka La Gioconda), the wife of a Florentine merchant. It's also the name of a 1950 song and a 1986 film starring Bob Hoskins
money: "Money isn't everything, but it sure does keep you in touch with your children" – anonymous; "Money is better than poverty, if only for financial reasons" - Woody Allen; "Money can't buy friends but you get a better class of enemy" - Spike Milligan; "Money doesn't make you happy. I now have $50 million, but I was just as happy when I had $48 million" – Arnold Schwarzenegger
money: bread, dingbat, do-re-mi, dough, feed, frog hair, gee, geech, grade (Elizabethan slang), gravy, green stamps, green stuff, hip gee, lettuce, lolly, lucre, the Mammon of Unrighteousness, mazuma, moolah, pesh
money, adjective: pecuniary
money, fear of: chrometophobia
money, slang: 10s/50p: half a bar; £5: half a cock; £10: cock and hen; £25: pony; £500/$500: monkey; £1000/$1000: grand
money, study of: chrematistics
moneylenders: Ralph Nickleby (from Dickens' *Nicholas Nickleby*), Quilp (from Dickens' *The Old Curiosity Shop*), Shylock (from *The Merchant of Venice*), Joshua Smallweed (from Dickens' *Bleak House*)
Mongol conquests: 1206–1405
Mongol conquerors: Genghis Khan, Kublai Khan, Tamerlane (aka Tamburlaine)
Mongolia: republic in eastern central Asia, formerly known as Outer Mongolia (until 1924) and as the Mongolian People's Republic (until 1992)
    capital: Ulan Bator
    currency: tugrik

language: Khalkha
religion: atheist
ruling party: The Mongolian People's Revolutionary Party (MPRP), led by
  Nambariin Enkhbayar
pop group: Lipstick
mongoose, adjective: viverrine
mongoose, famous: Riki-Tiki-Tavi (from the Rudyard Kipling story)
monk, adjective: monastic
monks: Fra Angelico (painter), St Antony of Padua, Roger Bacon, Saint Bede,
  Cadfael, Kwai Chang Caine (TV character), caloyer, the Dalai Lama, Brother
  Dominic (as played by Derek Nimmo in TV's *Oh, Brother!*), St Francis of
  Assisi, St Francis of Paola, Fra Filippo Lippi, John Lydgate, Edgar Mortara,
  Matthew Paris, Pelagius, François Rabelais, Grigori Rasputin, Andrei Rublev,
  St Sava, Tomás de Torquemada, Friar Tuck
Monkees, The: prefabricated pop group formed in Hollywood in 1965; comprised
  of Davy Jones (vocals), Mickey Dolenz (vocals, drums), Peter Tork (vocals,
  keyboards, bass, guitar) and Mike Nesmith (vocals, guitar). The group
  officially disbanded in 1970, although there have been several reunions
monkey, adjective: pithecoid, simian
monkey, collective noun: barrel, troup
monkey, sound: chatter, jibber
monkey, young: infant
Monkey Business (1931 film), famous line: Stowaway (Groucho Marx): "Oh,
  I realise it's a penny here and a penny there, but look at me: I worked myself
  up from nothing to a state of extreme poverty"
monkeys, famous: Able and Baker (the first animals sent into space by the USA),
  Abu (from Disney's *Aladdin*), Bandar-Log (from *The Jungle Book*), Cuddles
  (c/o Keith Harris), Curious George, Marcel (from TV's *Friends*), Mojo Jojo
  (from *The Powerpuff Girls*), Rafiki (from Disney's *The Lion King*), Sun
  Wukong (from *Journey to the West*), Zephir (from the Babar books)
monkey-god: Hanuman (Hindu mythology)
monster: bunyip (Australian), chimera, griffin, Hydra, orc, Snark (% Lewis Carroll)
  – see creatures
monsters, love of: teratism
Montana, 41st state (1889), Treasure State
  capital: Helena
  state bird: Western meadowlark
  state flower: bitterroot
  state tree: ponderosa pine
  motto: 'Oro y Plata' ('Gold and silver')
  birthplace of: Gary Cooper, Myrna Loy, Jeannette Rankin (feminist), Michelle
    Williams (actress)
  tourist attractions: Glacier National Park, Lewis and Clark Caverns State
    Park, Little Bighorn Battlefield National Monument
  fact: Montana is Spanish for 'mountain'
Montenegro: constituent republic of Yugoslavia, which gained independence from
  Serbia on 22 May 2006
  capital: Podgorica
  currency: euro; formerly the dinar
  language: Serbian (95%), Albanian
  religion: Orthodox (65%), Muslim (19%), Roman Catholic, Protestant
Montreal, birthplace of: Genevieve Bujold, Leonard Cohen, Claude Jutra, Oscar
  Peterson, William Shatner, Norma Shearer, Jeffrey Skoll, Pierre Trudeau

Montreal, fact: has one of the largest French-speaking populations of any city in
the world

Montreal rivers: Saint Lawrence and Ottawa

Monty Python's Flying Circus: absurd, surreal and manic satirical TV revue
written and performed by Graham Chapman, John Cleese, Terry Gilliam, Eric
Idle, Terry Jones and Michael Palin, interspersed with equally bizarre animated
sequences courtesy of Gilliam. Many of the show's sketches – the dead parrot,
Hell's Grannies and the Ministry of Silly Walks – have become classics in
themselves. The Monty Python enterprise went on to become a brand name,
producing movies, books, records and any number of unlikely off-shoots.
    produced by John Howard Davies and Ian MacNaughton, from an idea by
    Barry Took
    broadcast: 5 October 1969–5 December 1974 on BBC1

Monty Python and the Holy Grail (1975 film), selling line: "Makes *Ben-Hur* look
like an epic!"

moon, adjective: lunar, selenian, selenic

moon, god of: Tsuki-yumi (Japanese mythology)

moon, goddess of: Artemis, Selene (both Greek mythology), Diana and Luna (both
Roman)

moon, orbit nearest Earth: perigree

moon, orbit furthest from Earth: apogee

moon, study of: selenology

moon, types of: full moon, half moon, harvest moon, hunter's moon, new moon,
nimbus moon

moon, the twelve men who walked thereon: 1) Neil Armstrong (in July 1969);
    2) Edwin E. 'Buzz' Aldrin (in July 1969); 3) Pete Conrad (in November 1969);
    4) Alan L. Bean (in November 1969); 5) Alan B. Shepard (January/February
    1971); 6) Edgar D. Mitchell (January/February 1971); 7) David R. Scott
    (July/August 1971); 8) James B. Irwin (July/August 1971); 9) John W. Young
    (April 1972); 10) Charles M. Duke (April 1972); 11) Harrison Schmitt
    (December 1972); 12) Eugene Cernan (December 1972)

moon god: Khonsu (Egyptian mythology)

moon landing, first: 20 July 1969

moon tides: neap, spring

moor hen: gallinule

moose, adjective: cervine

moose, collective noun: herd

moose, famous: Bullwinkle, Thidwick the Big-Hearted Moose

moose, female: cow

moose, male: bull

moose, sound: bellow

moose, young: calf

morals, science of: ethics

moray eel, adjective: muraenoid

Mormonism: The Church of Jesus Christ of Latter-day Saints, founded by Joseph
Smith Jr

Mormons, famous: Amy Adams, Don Bluth (animator), Butch Cassidy, Brandon
Flowers, Katherine Heigl, Gladys Knight, Neil LaBute (playwright/film
director), Stephenie Meyer, the Osmonds, Mitt Romney, Brigham Young

morning, adjective: matutinal (often referring to the earlier part of the morning)
Morocco: kingdom in north-west Africa
    capital: Rabat
    currency: dirham
    language: Arabic (official), Berber, French
    religion: Muslim (Sunni)
Morse Code: sonic code devised by Samuel F. B. Morse and first used on 24 May
    1844 when Morse sent the message, "What hath God wrought?"
Morse Code, the: anagram for "here come dots"
mosaic, to create, inlay, etc: tessellate
mosaic tile: tessera
Moscow, birthplace of: Sergey Brin (co-founder of Google), Fyodor Dostoevsky,
    Lev Ivanov (choreographer), Wassily Kandinsky, Boris Pasternak, Alexander
    Pushkin, Irina Rodnina (figure skater)
Moscow ballet company: Bolshoi
Moscow centre: Red Square
Moscow film studio: Mosfilm
Moscow newspaper: *Pravda*
Moscow river: Moskva
Moslem – see Muslim
mosque complex, largest in the world: Shah Faisal Mosque, near Islamabad in
    Pakistan. The prayer hall alone can accommodate up to 100,000 people
mosque turret: minaret
mosquito, adjective: aedine
mosquito, collective noun: swarm
mosquito, killing of: culicicide, culicide
mosquito, lethal: Asian tiger mosquito
mosquito; malaria parasite carrier: anopheles
mosquito, slang: skeeter
mosquito, young: nymph
mosquito expert: culicidologist
moss, science of: bryology
moss root: rhizoid
moth, adjective: arctian, lepidopteran (also includes the butterfly family)
moth and butterfly collector: lepidopterist
mother: genetrix
mother: "A mother's place is in the wrong" – popular saying
mother, adjective: maternal
mother, murder of: matricide
mothers, patron saint of: Monica
Mother Earth: Gaia (Greek mythology), Terra (Roman mythology)
mother of one child, adjective: uniparous
mother-in-law: anagram for "woman Hitler"
mother-in-law, fear of: pentheraphobia
mother-of-pearl: nacre
mother-of-pearl, adjective: nacreous
mothers-from-hell: Joan Crawford, Mrs Dorsett (mother of Sybil Dorsett – see
    schizophrenics), Debbie Mathers-Briggs (according to her son, Eminem),
    Medea, Edina 'Eddy' Monsoon (from TV's *Absolutely Fabulous*), George Sand
motion, adjective: kinetic
motion, aversion to: kinesophobia
motivational speakers: Kriss Akabusi, Jack Canfield, Deepak Chopra

motorcyclists: Giacomo Agostini, Geoffrey E. Duke, Joey Dunlop, Mike Hailwood, Ewan McGregor, Steve McQueen, Valentino Rossi, Barry Sheene, John Surtees

motorists, patron saints of: Anthony the Great, Frances of Rome

motor racing drivers – see racing drivers

motor racing tycoon: Bernie Ecclestone

Motown: record company launched by Berry Gordy Jr in 1959

mountain, adjective: montane, mountainous

mountain, highest in England: Scafell Pike

mountain, highest in Europe: Elbruz, in the Caucasus mountains of Russia

mountain, highest in Great Britain: Ben Nevis (in Scotland)

mountain, highest in North America: Mount McKinley (in Alaska)

mountain, highest in Scotland: Ben Nevis

mountain, highest in the world: Mount Everest (Nepal/Tibet)

mountain, highest in Wales: Snowdon

mountain nymph: oread

mountains, science of: orography, orology

mountaineering, descend a cliff face by rope while: rappel

mountaineers: Rod Baber (the first climber to use a mobile phone from the summit of Mount Everest), Sir Chris Bonington, Jules Cartwright, Alison Hargreaves (the first woman to climb Everest without oxygen), Sir Edmund Hillary (with Norgay Tenzing, the first person to conquer Mount Everest), Robin Hodgkin, John Hunt, George Mallory, Sir Hugh Munro, Doug Scott, Junko Tabei, Norgay Tenzing (aka Sherpa Tenzing), Don Whillans, Edward Whymper (the first to scale Mount Chimborazo)

mountaineers, patron saint of: Bernard of Mont Joux

mountainous country, adjective: montane

Mount Everest, height: 29,118ft; first scaled by Edmund Hillary and the Sherpa Tenzing Norgay on 29 May 1953

Mount Rushmore: outcrop in South Dakota featuring the mountainous faces of the US presidents George Washington, Thomas Jefferson, Abraham Lincoln and Theodore Roosevelt, carved by Gutzon Borglum (completed in 1939)

mouse, adjective: murine, muriform, musine

mouse, collective noun: hoard, mischief

mouse, famous: Algernon, Fievel, Frederick (title character in the children's book), Gus (from Disney's *Cinderella*), Hashimoto (Japanese cartoon), Herman (TV cartoon), Hoppity Hooper (TV cartoon), Jerry (nemesis of Tom), Stuart Little, Mickey Mouse, Minnie Mouse, Speedy Gonzales, Mrs Tittlemouse (Beatrix Potter), Three Blind Mice, Topo Gigio

mouse, fear of: musophobia

mouse, plural: mice

mouse, sound: squeak, squeal

mouse, young: pinky

Mousetrap, The: play by Agatha Christie which opened in London on 25 November 1952

moustached heroine: Marian Halcombe (from Wilkie Collins' *The Woman in White*)

moustached painter, female: Frida Kahlo

mouth: chops, gob, kisser, pump up the knickers (Scot.), trap

mouth, adjective: buccal, cibarian, oral, stomatic

mouth, fact: there are eighty distinguishable species living in the average adult mouth

mouth, study of: oralogy, stomatology

mouth, when combined with cheeks, adjective: buccal

mouth inflammation: stomatitis

mouth organists: Larry Adler, Tommy Reilly

movement in humans, science of: kinesiology

movie critics – see film critics

movie tycoons – see film tycoons

moving backward sensation: vection illusion (created when one is stationary but another object or vehicle is moving)

Mozambique: republic in south-east Africa

    capital: Maputo

    currency: metical

    language: Portuguese

    religion: animist

    birthplace of: Mariza (fado singer)

    park: Great Limpopo Transfrontier Park

Mr, plural: Messrs

MRI: magnetic resonance imaging

MRSA: Methicillin-resistant Staphylococcus Aureus

Ms (term invented by Gloria Steinem), plural: Mses

MS: postcode for Mississippi

MSN: MicroSoft Network

MT: postcode for Montana

M25 motorway, outer London: completed in October of 1989

mucus, adjective: blennoid, muculent

mucus, the excessive secretion of: blennorrhea

mud, adjective: lutaceous

muddy: lutulent

mud-swallowing: limivorous (adjective)

Muhammad, traditions relating to: Hadith

mule, collective noun: barren, span

mule, famous: Francis the talking mule (voiced by Chill Wills in the Universal comedies, 1950–1956), Muffin (in partnership with Annette Mills, sister of John Mills)

mule, young: foal

multi-media artist: Laurie Anderson

multiple-personality subject: Shirley Ardell Mason (the model for Sybil Isabel Dorsett, the subject of Flora Rheta Schreiber's book *Sybil*)

multi-talented, adjective: pancratic

multiple intelligences – see intelligences

multiple sclerosis sufferers: Jacqueline du Pré, Bryan Forbes, Annette Funicello, Teri Garr, William Hartnell, Lena Horne, Ronnie Lane, Margaret Leighton, Richard Pryor, Montel Williams

multiplex, first in the world: Kansas City, Missouri (opened in 1963)

multiplex, first in the UK: Milton Keynes (opened in 1985)

multiplex with 16 or more screens: megaplex

Mumbai: Hindi name for Bombay (see)

mummy, with curse: The Princess of Amen-Ra

mumps: parotitis

Munich, birthplace of: Carl Orff, Walter Sickert, Richard Strauss

Munich hostage drama, aka Black September: on 5 September 1972, Arab guerrillas broke into the Israeli Olympic building and took nine athletes hostage. Just before midnight, at a military airport 25 miles from Munich, all the hostages were killed in a police ambush

Munich river: Isar

munition inventors – see firearms and munition inventors

Muppets: Kermit, Miss Piggy, Fozzie Bear, Animal, Beaker, The Birdman, Clifford, The Great Gonzo, Bunsen Honeydew, Rizzo the Rat, Sal Minella, Pepe the Prawn, Rowlf, Sam the Eagle, Statler, Dr Phil Van Neuter, Waldorf, etc

Muppie: Middle-aged Urban Professional

muralists: José Orozco, Diego Rivera, David Siqueiros

murder: "Kill a man and you are a murderer. Kill millions and you are a conqueror. Kill everyone and you are a god" - Jean Rostand

murder capital of the world: Johannesburg

murderer, first: Cain

murderers: Martin Bryant, Gaston Dominici (who reputedly butchered the British Drummond family in France, in 1952), Richard Elsey (killed Egyptian-born businessman Mohammed El-Sayed - in Bayswater - for a dare), Gary Gilmore, Thomas Hamilton (of Dunblane notoriety), Jack the Ripper, Nathan Leopold, Richard Loeb, Bradley Murdoch (Australian who killed British backpacker Peter Falconio in July of 2001), Donald Neilson (aka The Black Panther), James Petrolini (killed Egyptian-born businessman Mohammed El-Sayed - in Bayswater - for a dare), Christopher Scarver (killer of Jeffrey Dahmer), Perry Smith (killer chronicled in Truman Capote's *In Cold Blood*),
- see assassins, serial killers and killers, female

murderesses: Elizabeth Báthory, Elizabeth Brownrigg, Ruth Ellis, Barbara Graham (whom many believe was innocent of murdering an elderly woman during a burglary – but who was put to death anyway), Roxie Hart (from *Chicago*), Myra Hindley, Velma Kelly (from *Chicago*), Edith Jessie Thompson, Aileen Wuornos
- see female killers

muscle, adjective: myoid

muscle, largest in the human body: buttock

muscle, longest in the human body: sartorius

muscle, strongest in the human body: tongue

muscle degeneration: amyotrophy

muscle disease, study of: myology

muscle men: Charles Atlas, Geoff Capes, Lou Ferrigno, Hercules, Steve Reeves, Dwayne 'The Rock' Johnson, Arnold Schwarzenegger

muscle pain: myalgia

muscle types: flexor, extensor, multi-penniform (fan shaped), penniform, rhomboidal, strap-like (long and thin)

muscles, number of in the human body: 650

muscles, study of: myology, orthopaedics

muscles, without: amyous (adjective)

Muscles from Brussels, The: nickname for Jean-Claude Van Damme

muscles in the abdomen: cremaster, diaphragm, oblique

muscles in the arm: anconeus, biceps, biceps brachil, brachialis, coracobrachial, deltoid, infraspinatus, latissimus dorsi, palmaris

muscles in the calf: gastracnemius, soleus

muscles in the eye: ciliary, dilator of the eye, oblique

muscles in the eyelids: orbicularis oculi

muscles in the foot: abductor, abductor hallucis, achilles tendon, dorsal interossei, extensor digitorum, extensor hallucis, flexor digitorum, flexor hallucis, gastrocnemius

muscle in the forehead: corrugator

muscles in the hand: abductor pollicis, abductor pollicis brevis, abductor pollicis longus, extensor digitorum, extensor pollicis, flexor digitorum, flexor pollicis, interossei, lumbrical, palmaris

muscles in the jaw: buccinator, masseter, mylohyoid

muscles in the leg: achilles tendon, adductor, biceps femoris, extensors, flexors, gastracnemius, gemellus, gluteus maximus, gluteus medius, gluteus minimus, gracillis, hamstring, hiacus, peroneus brevis, peroneus longus, peroneus longus tendon, quadriceps femoris, sartorius, soleus, tendo-calcaneus (achilles tendon), tensor fasciae latae

muscles in the mouth: depressor, orbicularis oris

muscles in the neck: longus capitus, oblique

muscles in the nose: depressor of the nasal septum, dilator of the nose, nasalis

muscles in the pelvis: levator ani

muscles in the ribs: intercostal, oblique

muscles in the scalp: epicranial

muscles in the shoulder: levator scapulae

muscles in the skin: erector pili

muscles in the spine: iliocostal, longissimus

muscles in the thigh: adductor, adductor brevis, adductor magnus, flexors, gracilis, obturator, quadriceps femoris, sartorius, tensor fasciae latae

muscles in the throat: aryepiglottic, constrictor of pharynx

muscles in the tongue: chondroglossus, genioglossus, glosso palatine, lingual

muscles in the vocal chords: cricothyroid

muscles in the wrist: extensor carpi radialis, extensor carpi ulnaris, extensor carpi radialis, flexor carpi ulnaris

muscular spasm: clonus

muses: Calliope (of epic poetry), Clio (of history), Erato (love poetry), Euterpe (lyric poetry), Melpomene (of tragedy), Polyhymnia (of mime and sacred dance), Terpsichore (of dance), Thalia (of comedy), Urania (of astronomy)

museums: The British Museum, London; Egyptian Museum, Cairo; The Guggenheim, Bilbao, Spain; J. Paul Getty Museum, Los Angeles; Le Louvre, Paris; The Metropolitan Museum of Art, New York; Natural History Museum, London; The Prado, Madrid; Rijksmuseum, Amsterdam; Science Museum, London; The Smithsonian, Washington, D.C.; The State Hermitage, St. Petersburg; The Uffizi Gallery, Florence; The Vatican Museums, Vatican City, Italy

mushroom: chanterelle, field mushroom (v. common), garden mushroom (v. common), giant puffball, king boletus, morel, oyster mushroom, Périgord truffle, shaggy-mane, shitake, sulfur mushroom, truffle

mushroom, adjective: agaricoid

mushroom, collective noun: troop

mushroom, skin of: pellicle

mushroom-shaped: agariciform

music: a cappella, ambient, baroque, Bhangra, big band, blues, bluegrass, blues revival, bop, bossa nova, calypso, classical, crunk, downbeat, electric Chicago blues, death metal, disco, drum 'n' bass, dub, dubstep, easy listening, electric harmonica blues, electro, electronica, electropop, fado (Portuguese folk song), flamenco, folk, folk-rock, Fuji, funk, garage, glam rock, glitter, go-go, grime, grunge, high life, hi-life, honky-tonk, hip-hop, house, industrial, jazz, jit, juju, kadongo kamu (Ugandan), kaiso (based on the calypso of Trinidad), karaoke, Kraut rock, kwela, Latin continuum, Latin jazz, Latin pop, mambo, mento, metal, modern jazz, mum rock, muzak, nu-metal, punk, R&B, rai (Algerian), rap, reggae, rhythm and blues, rock, rock 'n' roll, salsa, samba, ska, skiffel (an amalgam of largely American styles – bluegrass, folk, blues - created by Lonnie Donegan), son, soul, swing, tango, tech-house, techno, trip-hop, tropical, tropicalismo, two-tone

music, dread of: musicophobia

music, god of: Apollo (Greek and Roman mythology), Bes (Egyptian)

music, goddess of: Bastet (Egyptian)

music, inability to perceive: amusia

music, muse of: Euterpe

music, parts of: air, passage, phrase, riff, rumble, strain, wave

music, study of: musicology

music critics: Adolphe Adam, Lester Bangs, Paul Bowles, Sir William Glock, E.T.W. Hoffmann, Greil Marcus, Edmund Rubbra, Camille Saint-Saëns, George Bernard Shaw

- see rock (music) journalists

Music Education Consortium: pressure group formed by Sir James Galway, Dame Evelyn Glennie, Michael Kamen and Julian Lloyd Webber

music executives: Simon Cowell, Kim Fowley, David Geffen, Berry Gordy Jr, Tony Wilson

- see record producers

music hall entertainers - see vaudevillians

music iconoclast: Boyd Rice

music impresarios: Simon Cowell, Frank Farian, Simon Fuller

music video, first: The Beatles' *I Feel Fine*, made in 1966

musical directions – see musical instructions

musical groups: duet, trio, quartet, quintet, sextet, septet, octet, nonet

musical instructions: accelerando, adagietto, adagio, adagissimo, ad libitum, affettuoso, affrettando, agilmente, agitato, allargando, allegramante, allegretto, allegro, allentando, altra volta, ancora, andante, ängstlich, animo, appassionato, attacca, Aufschwung, ballo, boca chiusa, bouche fermée, bravura, brusco, burlesco, calando, calcando, calmando, cedez, comodo, crescendo, da capo, decrescendo (aka diminuendo), delicato, delirio, diminuendo (aka decrescendo), dolce, dolente, doppio movimento, dramatico, eilend, élargissant, elegante, encore, facile, fastoso, festoso, feurig, fiero, forte, fortissimo, frettoloso, funerale, furioso, geheimnisvoll, Generalpause, grave, heftig, indeciso, innig, inquieto, lamentoso, larghetto, largo, legato, lettissimo, malinconico, mancando, marcato, mezza voce, mezzo forte, mezzo piano, millitare alla, ossia, parlato, pathetique, pianissimo, prestissimo, presto, ravvivando, ritardando, ritenuto, schleppend, sciolto, seconda volta, slancio con, sospirando, sotto voce, spiritoso, staccato, strisciando, tacet, teneramente, tonante, tranquillo, tre a, vide, vigoroso, vivo, volti subito, zoppa alla

musical instrument (stringed), adjective: fidicinal

musical instrument, inability to play: amusia

musical instruments, brass-wind: horn, trombone, trumpet, tuba

musical instruments, percussion: bass drum, celeste, cymbals, dulcimer, glockenspiel, side drum, timpani

musical instruments, rare: bouzouki (a Greek stringed instrument closely related to the mandolin), dhol (two-sided Armenian drum), duduk (Armenian wood instrument), gadulka (traditional Bulgarian fiddle with 3 melody strings and 11 sympathetic strings with bow), shamisen (an ancient three-stringed instrument from Japan)

musical instruments, string: cello, cittern, double-bass, gittern (obsolete), guitar, harp, lute, lyre, viola, violin, violoncello, zither

musical instruments, woodwind: bass clarinet, bass flute, basset-horn, bassoon, clarinet, cor anglais, double bassoon, flute, oboe, piccolo

musical terms: a cappella, acciaccato, accidentals, alto, aquarelle, arabesque, arpeggio, arrangement, aubade, bagatelle, bar, bar line, baroque, bass, bebop, berceuse, bitonality, blues, boogie woogie, brevis, buffa, cadence, cadenza, calypso, cantata, chamber music, chamber orchestra, chord, clef, coda, colpo, concerto, consort, cross rhythm, demisemiquaver, discord, dissonance, duet, echo, elegy, embouchure, ensemble, etude, fanfare, fantasia, finale, flat, fughetta, fugue, glissando, half note, hemidemisemiquaver, hootenanny, house, hymn, improvisation, incidental music, interlude, intermezzo, interval, intonation, jam, key signature, lament, libretto, lullaby, lyric, maestoso, maestro, measure, medley, melisma, melody, meter, minuet, modulation, motif, movement, natural, nocturne, notation, octave, octet, ode, opera buffa, operetta, opus, oratorio, ornaments, overture, paraphrase, pasticcio, pastoral, pedal tone, philharmonic, pitch, polyrhthmic, portamento, quarter note, quarter rest, quartet, quintet, ragtime, refrain, reprise, rest, retrograde, rhapsody, riff, score, secondo, seimiquaver, septet, serenade, sextet, sharp, sightreading, signature, sonata, sonatina, spiritual, staff, stanza, suite, symphonic poem, symphony, syncopation, time signature, toccata, tonguing, transpose, treble, tremolo, trill, vamp, virtuoso, vivace, whole note

musicals: *Annie Get Your Gun, Anything Goes, Avenue Q, Barnum, The Beautiful Game, Blood Brothers, Bombay Dreams, The Boyfriend, Brigadoon, Buddy, Cabaret, Call Me Madam, Camelot, Can-Can, Carmen Jones, Carousel, Cats, La Cava, Chicago, Company, Dreamgirls, Evita, The Fantasticks, Fiddler On the Roof, Follies, For Me and My Gal, 42nd Street, Fosse, Gigi, Godspell, Grease, Guys and Dolls, Gypsy, Hair, Hello Dolly!, In the Heights, Jersey Boys, Jesus Christ Superstar, Joseph and the Amazing Technicolour Dreamcoat, The King and I, Kismet, Kiss Me Kate, La Cage Aux Folles, The Lion King, A Little Night Music, Little Shop of Horrors, Mamma Mia!, Man of La Mancha, Les Misérables, Miss Saigon, My Fair Lady, Napoleon, Notre-Dame de Paris, Oklahoma!, Oliver!, The Pajama Game, The Phantom of the Opera, Porgy and Bess, Rent, The Rocky Horror Show, Salad Days, Showboat, The Sound of Music, South Pacific, Spring Awakening, Starlight Express, Sunset Boulevard, Sweeney Todd, Sweet Charity, West Side Story, Wicked*

musicals adapted from films (or inspired by their source): *Beauty and the Beast, Big, Billy Elliot, Breakfast at Tiffany's, Brighton Rock, Carrie, Catch Me if You Can, The Color Purple, Dance of the Vampires* (based on Polanski's *The Fearless Vampire Killers*), *Desperately Seeking Susan, Dirty Dancing, Dirty Rotten Scoundrels, Don Juan DeMarco, Evil Dead: The Musical, Flashdance, Footloose, 42nd Street, The Full Monty, Ghost, Gone With the Wind, Hairspray, Harold and Maude, High Fidelity, Kiss of the Spider Woman, Legally Blonde, The Lion King, A Little Night Music* (adapted from Ingmar Bergman's *Smiles of a Summer Night*), *Little Shop of Horrors, The Lord of the Rings, Love Story, A*

Man of No Importance, Martin Guerre, Mary Poppins, A Matter of Life and Death, Meet Me in St. Louis, Monsoon Wedding, My Favorite Year, Nine to Five, The Opposite of Sex, Passion (adapted from Ettore Scola's *Passione d'Amore*), *Peggy Sue Got Married, Poseidon! An Upside Down Musical, Priscilla Queen of the Desert: The Musical, The Producers, Ragtime, The Red Shoes, Saturday Night Fever, Seven Brides for Seven Brothers, Shrek the Musical, Spamalot* (adapted from *Monty Python and the Holy Grail*), *Sugar* (adapted from *Some Like it Hot*), *Sunset Boulevard, Sweet Smell of Success, Tarzan, Thoroughly Modern Millie, Urban Cowboy, The Wedding Singer, Whistle Down the Wind, The Witches of Eastwick, Woman of the Year, Young Frankenstein, Zorba*

musicians, patron saints of: Cecilia, Dunstan

musicologists: Sir William Hadow, Antony Hopkins, Hans Keller, Albert Schweitzer

musk deer, adjective: moschine

musk ox, adjective: bovine

musketeers: Aramis, D'Artagnan, Athos, Porthos

muskrat, adjective: cricetid

Muslim book: Koran (or Qur'an)

Muslim church: mosque

Muslim cleric: Abu Hamza (removed from his position as imam at London's Finsbury Park mosque)

Muslim coat (worn by men): jibba

Muslim crier: muezzin

Muslim curtain (to screen women from the sight of male strangers, etc): purdah

Muslim fast: Ramadan

Muslim harem: seraglio

Muslim nymph: houri

Muslim pantaloons: shintiyan

Muslim record of God's revelation to Muhammad: Koran (or Qur'an)

Muslim religion: Islam

Muslim robe: jilbab

Muslim singer: Yusuf Islam (formerly Cat Stevens; before that: Steve Adams; before that: Steven Demetre Georgiou)

Muslim spirit: djinn, ifrit

Muslim student: softa

Muslim term for non-Muslim: Kafir (pejorative use)

Muslim turret: minaret

Muslim veil: burqa (or burka), niqab, yashmak (or yashmac)

muslin: butter muslin, mousseline, mull, organdie, tarlatan, tiffany

mute, famous: Harlequin

mutineer: Fletcher Christian

Myanmar: republic in South-East Asia formerly known as Burma (see)

Mycenae, king of: Agamemnon

My Lai massacre: 16 March 1968

mystery explainer: hierophant

mystery writer: Agatha Christie
- see crime writers, detective writers, etc

mystics: William Blake, Helena Blavatsky, Jakob Boehm, Carlos Castaneda, Eleazar of Worms, Nicholas Ferrar, Margery Kempe, Padre Pio, Pythagoras, Grigori Rasputin, Thomas Traherne

mystics, patron saint of: John of the Cross

mythographer: Joseph Campbell

N

NAAFI: No Ambition and Frigging Interest
naïve art, father of: Henri Rousseau
naïve artists: Edward Hicks, L. S. Lowry, Grandma Moses, Nykifor, Henri Rousseau, Alfred Wallis
naked, the act of imagining someone: apodyopsis
nakedness, fear of: gymnophobia
NALGO: Not a lot going on
name, adjective: onomastic
name adopted by a word: eponym (see)
name spelled backwards: ananym
nameless: innominate
namer: nomenclator
names, aversion to: nomatophobia
names, inability to remember: anomia
Namibia: country in southern Africa, formerly known as German Southwest Africa (until 1919)
    capital: Windhoek
    currency: Namibian dollar (NAD); South African rand
    language: English (official), Afrikaans, German
    religion: animist (majority), Christian
nanny: Mary Poppins
napalm victim: Kim Phuc (nine-year-old South Vietnamese girl who was bombed in June 1972, her agony caught by the camera of Vietnamese photographer Nick Ut)
Naples, adjective: Neapolitan
Naples, ancient name: Neapolis
Naples, birthplace of: the pizza; also the birthplace of Gian Lorenzo Bernini, Enrico Caruso, Farinelli (born Carlo Broschi), Domenico Scarlatti
Napoleon of Crime: Moriarty (nemesis of Sherlock Holmes)
Napoleon's retreat from Moscow: 1812
Napoleonic Wars: 1800–1815
Napster creator: Shawn Fleming
narcolepsy: sleeping disorder that affects 2,500 people in Britain and 150,000 Americans
narrowness, fear of: anginophobia
NASA: National Aeronautics and Space Administration (or, after the Challenger catastrophe of 28 January 1986: Need Another Seven Astronauts)
National Security Agency, nickname: No Such Agency
Native American Indians: Black Hawk, Joseph Brant (aka Thayendanegea), Chato, Cochise, Crazy Horse, Geronimo, Chief Joseph, Hiawatha, Russell Means, Minnehaha (aka Laughing Water), Pocahontas, Pontiac, Popé, Powhatan, Buffy Sainte-Marie, Sitting Bull, Kateri Tekakwitha, Jim Thorpe (raised as Wa-Tho-Huk), Tiger Lily (from *Peter Pan*)
Native American Indian activist: Russell Means
Native American Indian authority: Clark Wissler
Native American Indian chief: sachem, sagamore
Native American Indian scout: Buffalo Bill (aka William Cody)
Native American Indian spirit: Thunderbird
Native American Indian tribes: Alabama-Coushatta, Algonquin, Apache, Arapaho, Assiniboine, Blackfoot, Caddo, Cherokee, Cheyenne, Chickahominy, Chickasaw, Chiricahua Apache, Choctaw, Comanche, Creek, Delaware, Havasupai, Hidatsa,

Hopi, Illinois, Iroquois, Kiowa, Klamath, Kootenay, Lakota, Lenape, Maidu, Mandan, Menominee, Micmac, Miwok, Mohawk, Mohican, Muscogee, Narragansett, Natchez, Navajo, Nez Percé, Oglala, Ojibwa, Oneida, Onondaga, Osage, Ottawa, Paiute, Pamunkey, Patwin, Pawnee, Pomo, Potawatomi, Pueblo, Rappahannock, Seminole, Shawnee, Shoshone, Sioux, Spokane, Umatilla, Upper Mattaponi, Ute, Walla Walla, Wampanoag, Wintun, Wiyot, Yakama, Yurok

Native American Indians, painter of: George Catlin

Native American Indians, victim of: General George Armstrong Custer

NATO Phonetic Alphabet: A for Alpha, B for Bravo, C for Charlie, D for Delta, E for Echo, F for Foxtrot, G for Golf, H for Hotel, I for India, J for Juliet, K for Kilo, L for Lima, M for Mike, N for November, O for Oscar, P for Papa, Q for Quebec, R for Romeo, S for Sierra, T for Tango, U for Uniform, V for Victor, W for Whiskey, X for X-ray, Y for Yankee, Z for Zulu

naturalists: Sir David Attenborough, Sir Joseph Banks, Thomas Bell, Sabin Berthelot, Alfred Brehm, George-Louis Buffon, Charles Darwin, Gerald Durrell, Philip Henry Gosse, Mariano de la Paz Graells, Ernst Haeckel, Alexander von Humboldt, Jean-Baptiste Lamarck, Georges-Louis Leclerc (Comte de Buffon), Carolus Linnaeus, Pliny the Elder, René Antoine Ferchault de Réaumur, Sir Peter Scott, Sir Hans Sloane, Georg Steller, Nicolaus Steno, Robert Swinhoe, Charles Waterton

natural world, killing of: ecocide

Nauru: island republic in the south-west Pacific, a United Nations Trust Territory administered by Australia; formerly known as Pleasant Island
capital: Yaren
currency: Australian dollar
language: Nauruan, English
religion: Christian

naval commanders – see admirals

naval officers: Captain Ahab, Prince Louis Battenberg, Sir David Beatty, Captain William Bligh, James Cook, Jacques Cousteau, Horatio Hornblower, John Paul Jones, Captain William Kidd, Captain Hans Langsdorff, Lord Jim, Earl Louis Mountbatten, Matthew Perry, Sir Walter Raleigh, Yamamoto Isoroku (who masterminded the attack on Pearl Harbor)
- see admirals

navel: belly button, little man in the boat, omphalos, umbilicus

navel, adjective: omphaloid

navel contemplation: omphaloskepis

navigation, adjective: nautical

navigators: Vitus Bering, John Cabot, James Cook, William Dampier, John Davis, Sir Martin Frobisher, Vasco da Gama, Sir John Hawkins, Sir Richard Hawkins, Ferdinand Magellan, Nathaniel Palmer, Pytheas, George Vancouver, Giovanni da Verrazano

navy, adjective: naval

Nazis: Klaus Barbie, Werner von Blomberg, Martin Bormann, Wernher von Braun, Adolf Eichmann, Friedrich Flick, Reinhard Gehlen, Paul Joseph Goebbels, Hermann Goering (founded the Gestapo), Amon Goeth, Rudolf Hess, Reinhard Heydrich, Heinrich Himmler, Adolf Hitler, Josef Mengele, Vidkun Quisling, Joachim von Ribbentrop, Erwin Rommel, Alfred Rosenberg, Albert Speer, Karl Wolff

Nazi apologist: David Irving

Nazi hunter: Simon Wiesenthal

Nazi marching step: goose step
Nazi newspaper: *Voelkische Freiheit*
Nazi symbol: swastika
NC: postcode for North Carolina
NCD: No claims discount (insurance term for motorists)
ND: postcode for North Dakota
NE: postcode for Nebraska
Neapolis: ancient name for Naples (see)
Nebraska, 37th state (1867), Cornhusker State
    capital: Lincoln
    state bird: western meadowlark
    state flower: goldenrod
    state tree: cottonwood
    birthplace of: Fred Astaire, Warren Buffett, Dick Cheney, Montgomery Clift,
        Henry Fonda, Gerald R. Ford, Harold Lloyd, Malcolm X, Nick Nolte,
        Hilary Swank
    motto: 'Equality before the law'
    tourist attractions: state capitol, Lincoln; Joslyn Art Museum, Omaha;
        Pioneer Village; Chimney Rock historic site
neck, adjective: cervicle
neck-like: colliform
necromancer: George Faust
need: "Our chief want in life is someone who will make us do what we can" -
    Ralph Waldo Emmerson
needle, adjective: acicular
needle and pin case: étui
needle-shaped: aciform
needles, fear of: belonephobia, blenophobia
negotiation: "The minute you settle for less than you deserve, you get even less
    than you settled for" - Maureen Dowd; "Negotiation is the art of letting them
    have your way" – Italian diplomat Daniele Vare
negro: black person, brother, coloured person, ghetto pimp, juba (American), jungle
    bunny, Mandingo, monkey, nigga, nigger, shiney, Uncle Tom
Neighbours: long-running Australian soap opera exploring the lives and relationships
    of the residents of Ramsay Street in Erinsborough. Filmed in the outer suburbs of
    Melbourne, the TV show – Australia's most popular – has managed to transform
    a number of little-known actors into international stars
    created by Reg Watson
    first broadcast: 1985 on the Seven Network (who dropped the series after a
        few months, when it was picked up by Ten Network)
    cast: Ian Smith (Harold Bishop), Tom Oliver (Lou Carpenter), Alan Fletcher
        (Greg Cooper/Karl Kennedy), Jackie Woodburne (Susan Smith/Kennedy),
        Kym Valentine (Elizabeth 'Libby' Kennedy/Kirk), Ryan Moloney (Jarrod
        'Toadfish'/'Toadie' Rebecchi), Shane Connor (Joe Scully), Jason Donovan
        (Scott Robinson), Deborra-Lee Furness (Linda Fielding), Russell Crowe
        (Kenny Larkin), Natalie Imbruglia (Beth Brennan/Willis), Craig McLachlan
        (Henry Mitchell), Kylie Minogue (Charlene Mitchell/Robinson), Guy
        Pearce (Mike Young), Radha Mitchell (Catherine O'Brien), Holly Valance
        (Felicity 'Flick' Scully), Delta Goodrem (Nina Tucker)
neighbour whose house is on fire: ucalegon

Neoclassical painters: Jacques David, Gavin Hamilton, Anton Mengs, Joseph Vien, Johann Winckelmann
neo-Nazi party, in Britain: Combat 18
neo-Nazi party, in Germany: People's Party (DVU), which won its first seats in a state parliament in April 1998, voted for by a quarter of the under-25s
Nepal: former kingdom in southern Asia now known as the Federal Democratic Republic of Nepal (since 28 May 2008)
    capital: Katmandu
    currency: Nepalese rupee
    language: Nepali
    mountains: Everest, Mount Kangchenjunga
    population: Gurkhas; minorities: Sherpas ('eastern people', more than half of whom now live off tourism and mountaineering), Rai, Tamang
    religion: Hinduism, Mahayana Buddhist (minority)
    history: the country only opened its borders in 1949
Nepalese soldier: Gurkha
nerve/nervous system, adjective: neural
nerve gas: cyclosarin, GV, sarin, soman, tabun
nerve inflammation: neuritis
nerve pain: neuralgia
nervous system, doctor of: neurologist
nervous system, study of: neurology, neuropathology
net, adjective: retiary (rare), retiform
Netherlands, The: kingdom in north-west Europe
    capital: Amsterdam; government seat: The Hague
    currency: euro, formerly: guilder
    language: Dutch
    religion: Christian (majority), Protestant, Roman Catholic
    patron saint: Willibrord
    fact: the first country in the world to give legal recognition to gay marriages - see Dutch and famous
Netherlands Guiana: former name for Suriname
nettles, adjective: urticacous
nettles, use of in sexual stimulation: urtication
nettle-rash: urticaria
neuro-biologists: David Hubel, Torsten Wiesel
neurologists: Jean-Martin Charcot, George Huntington, Hermann Rorschach
neurophysiologists: John Eccles, Stephen Kuffler
neurosurgeon: Harvey Cushing
Nevada, 36th state (1864), Battle Born State, Sagebrush State, Silver State
    capital: Carson City
    state bird: mountain bluebird
    state flower: sagebrush
    state tree: single-leaf piñon
    birthplace of: André Agassi, Curtis Hanson (filmmaker), Jena Malone (actress)
    motto: 'All for our country'
    quote: "Nevada is a sandbox for adults with too much money" - Jon Tenney in the 1997 film *Fools Rush In*
    tourist attractions: Bristlecone Pines (the oldest living things in the world), Hoover Dam, Lake Tahoe, Las Vegas, Reno
    fact: receives less rain than any other state

fact: the only state in which prostitution is legal

New Age gurus: Deepak Chopra, Gary Zukav

New Age therapy: Reiki

New Amsterdam: former name for New York City (until 1664)

Newcastle upon Tyne, birthplace of: Donna Air, Cheryl Cole, Cardinal Basil Hume, Janet McTeer, Tony Scott, Sting, Bill Travers (actor), Greg Wise (actor)

Newcastle upon Tyne beer: Newcastle Brown Ale

Newcastle upon Tyne river: Tyne

Newcastle upon Tyne statue: The Angel of the North (on a hill overlooking the city), designed by Antony Gormley

New France: former name for Canada

New Hampshire, 9th state (1788), Granite State

  capital: Concord

  state bird: purple finch

  state flower: purple lilac

  state tree: white birch

  birthplace of: John Irving, Mandy Moore (actress/singer), Franklin Pierce (14th president of the USA), Daniel Webster (lawyer)

  motto: 'Live free or die'

  tourist attractions: Mount Washington, Shaker Village in Canterbury

  fact: New Hampshire was the first state to set up its own government

  fact: the state still uses hanging as a mode of capital punishment

New Hebrides: former name for Vanuatu (until 1980)

New Jersey, 3rd state (1787), Garden State

  capital: Trenton

  state bird: Eastern goldfinch

  state flower: purple violet

  state tree: red oak

  birthplace of: Buzz Aldrin, Jason Alexander (actor), Count Basie, Jason Biggs (actor), James Fenimore Cooper, David Copperfield, Stephen Crane (writer), Billy Crudup (actor), Sandra Dee, Michael Douglas, Kirsten Dunst (actress), Donald Fagen (musician), James Gandolfini (actor), Allen Ginsberg, Ed Harris, Lauryn Hill, Whitney Houston, Jerry Lewis, Norman Mailer, Ricky Nelson, Jack Nicholson, Shaquille O'Neal, Queen Latifah, Dennis Rodman, Norman H. Schwartzkopf, Paul Simon, Frank Sinatra, Kevin Spacey, Kevin Smith (filmmaker), Bruce Springsteen, Martha Stewart, Meryl Streep, John Travolta, Dionne Warwick

  motto: 'Liberty and prosperity'

  tourist attractions: Atlantic City, Miss America Pageant, Cape May Historic District, Princeton University, Liberty State Park

  fact: the world's first professional baseball game was played in Hoboken (in 1846)

New Mexico, 47th state (1912), Land of Enchantment

  capital: Santa Fe

  state bird: roadrunner

  state flower: yucca

  state tree: piñon

  motto: 'Crescit Euundo' ('It grows as it goes')

  tourist attractions: Carlsbad Caverns, White Sands National Monument, Pueblo ruins (dating from 100 AD)

birthplace of: John Denver, Demi Moore, Popé (Native American leader), Kim
Stanley (actress)

fact: the oldest building in the USA is the Palace of the Governors in Santa Fe
(built in 1610)

New Orleans: Louisiana city founded by the French in 1718; nicknamed The Big Easy

New Orleans, birthplace of: jazz, Louis Armstrong, Truman Capote, Kitty Carlisle
(singer), Fats Domino, Lillian Hellman, Mahalia Jackson, Dorothy Lamour,
Elmore Leonard, Wynton Marsalis, Jelly Roll Morton, Lee Harvey Oswald,
Tom Petty & The Heartbreakers, Godfrey Reggio (filmmaker)

New Orleans, fact: named the fattest 'major' city in the USA, where 37.55% of the
city's population are obese

New Orleans flooding disaster: 29 September 2005

newness, fear of: neophobia

news: "News is something someone is trying to hide. Everything else is just
advertising" – William Randolph Hearst

news anchors – see TV newscasters

newscasters - see TV newscasters

News of the World: British tabloid Sunday newspaper founded by John Browne
Bell on 1 October 1843

newspaper; first published (regularly): *Nieuwe Tijdinghen* in 1605 in Antwerp;
followed, in January of 1609, by the German publications *Aviso Relation oder
Zeitung* and *Relation: Aller Fürnemmen und Gedenckwürdigen Historien*

newspaper; first British daily: *Daily Courant*, founded 11 March 1702

newspapers: "Never argue with people who buy ink by the gallon" - H.L. Mencken

newspapers, fact; country with most daily publications: India

newspapers, fact; English-language newspaper with largest circulation: *The Sun*

newspaper tycoons: Max Beaverbrook, Malcolm Forbes, James Goldsmith, Alfred
Harmsworth (later Lord Northcliffe), William Randolph Hearst, Charles Foster
Kane (played by Orson Welles in *Citizen Kane*), Robert Maxwell, Rupert
Murdoch, Adolph Simon Ochs, Sir Frank Packer, Kerry Packer, Joseph Pulitzer

newspaper-speak, short news item: squib; even shorter: vignette

newsreaders – see TV newscasters

newt: eft (archaic), triton

newt, young: tadpole

New Year's Eve: hogmanay

New York, 11st state (1788), Empire State

  capital: Albany

  state bird: bluebird

  state flower: rose

  state tree: sugar maple

  motto: 'Excelsior' ('Ever upward')

  tourist attractions: Great Lakes, Niagara Falls, Saratoga Springs

  birthplace of: Christina Aguilera, Woody Allen, James Baldwin, Lucille Ball,
  Billy the Kid (aka William Bonney), Humphrey Bogart, James Cagney,
  Al Capone, Tom Cruise, Kirk Douglas, George Gershwin, Ira Gershwin,
  Mel Gibson, Jennifer Lopez, Barry Manilow, Groucho Marx, Herman
  Melville,Arthur Miller, Henry Miller, Franklin D. Roosevelt, Theodore
  Roosevelt, Adam Sandler, Danielle Steel, Mike Tyson, Luther Vandross,
  Denzel Washington, Sigourney Weaver, Walt Whitman

fact: New York was the first capital of the emerging United States

New York City: The Big Apple, Gotham; formerly: New Amsterdam (until 1664, when King Charles II took over and named the town after his brother, James, Duke of York)

New York City boroughs: Manhattan, The Bronx, Queens, Brooklyn, Staten Island (formerly Richmond)

New York City buildings: American International Building, Bloomberg Tower, Chrysler Building, Citigroup Center, CitySpire, Conde Nast Building, Empire State Building, Flatiron Building, G.E. Building, MetLife, One Chase Manhattan Plaza, Rockefeller Center, Seagram Building, The Trump Building (aka 40 Wall Street), Trump World Tower

New York City cemetery: Potters Field on Hart's Island, New York, for the down-and-out and unclaimed dead

New York City newspapers: *The New York Daily News, New York Post, The New York Times, The Wall Street Journal*

New York City river: Hudson

New York City statue: Statue of Liberty (originally called Liberty Enlightening the World) (see)

New York Police Department (NYPD), fact: a force that is better funded than the North Korean army

New Yorker of Puerto Rican descent: Nuyorican

New York Times, The: newspaper founded in 1851

New York Times, The; rogue reporter: Jayson Blair

New Zealand: independent dominion comprising the North Island, the South Island and several smaller islands, in the south-east Pacific

    capital: Wellington

    currency: New Zealand dollar

    language: English and Maori

    religion: Christian, atheist, Maori

    famous Kiwis: Martin Campbell (filmmaker), Jane Campion (filmmaker), Russell Crowe, Neil Finn, Tim Finn, Kerry Fox, Maurice Gee (novelist), Sir Edmund Hillary, Keri Hulme, Peter Jackson, Michael Jones (rugby player), Roy Kerr (mathematician), Jonah Lomu (rugby player), Katherine Mansfield (writer), Dame Ngaio Marsh, Sam Neill, Anna Paquin, Ernest Rutherford ('father of nuclear physics'), Lee Tamahori (film director), Dame Kiri Te Kanawa, Hayley Westenra

    groups: The Clean, Crowded House, The Datsuns

    nickname: EnZed

New Zealand, fact: first sighted by the European Abel Janszoon Tasman in 1642

New Zealand, fact: taken posession of by Captain James Cook on behalf of Great Britain in 1769, although the country wasn't formerly recognised until 75 years later

New Zealand, fact: with the exception of two species of bat, no indigenous mammals are native to New Zealand

New Zealand, fact: in the summer of 2001, NZ's environmental minister Pete Hodgson proposed a 'flatulence tax,' a scheme that would cost farmers $39 for each cow or sheep they own

New Zealand prime ministers: Helen Clark, Robert Muldoon, Richard Seddon, Jenny Shipley (first female PM of NZ)

NFSP: National Federation of Subpostmasters (in the UK)

ng: speech sound (as in si*ng*) known as an agma

NH: postcode for New Hampshire

Nicaragua: republic in Central America
  capital: Managua
  currency: córdoba
  language: Spanish
  religion: Roman Catholic
  birthplace of: Ernesto Cardenal (poet), Rubén Darío (poet), Bianca Jagger, Daniel Ortega
  patron saint of: James the Greater
Nicaraguan political leaders: Anastazio Somoza Debayle, Daniel Ortega
niceness: "It's often niceness that causes all the trouble. Niceness is a killer really. Niceness settles for mediocrity" - George Walden
nicknames: America's Sweetheart (Mary Pickford), Auntie (BBC), Bambi (Tony Blair), the Bard (William Shakespeare), the Bear (football coach Paul Bryant), the Beau (Duke of Wellington), the Beeb (BBC), Big Apple (New York), the Big Easy (New Orleans), the Body (Elle Macpherson), Bony (Napoleon Bonaparte), Boobs from Brazil (Gisele Bündchen), the Boy Wonder (Robin, Batman's sidekick), Brazilian Bombshell (Carmen Miranda), Buffalo Bill (William F. Cody), Caped Crusader (Bruce Wayne aka Batman), Comical Ali (Mohammed Saeed al-Sahhaf), Dapper Don (John Gotti), Da Schnozz (Jimmy Durante), Desert Fox (Erwin Rommel), Dirty Digger (Rupert Murdoch), Dubya (George W. Bush), il Duce (Benito Mussolini), the Duke (John Wayne), Dutch (Ronald Reagan), El Cordobés (Manuel Benítez), Evita (Eva Duarte de Perón), the Galloping Gourmet (Graham Kerr), Gentleman Jim (James L. Corbett), the Good Book (The Bible), Good Time Charlie (King Charles II), the Great Profile (John Barrymore), the Great Stone Face (Buster Keaton), the Great White Way (Broadway), the Green Goddess (Diana Moran), Hanoi Jane (Jane Fonda), Hollywood Madam (Heidi Fleiss), Ike (Dwight D. Eisenhower), Iron Chancellor (Otto von Bismarck), Iron Duke (Duke of Wellington), the Iron Lady (Margaret Thatcher), J.Lo (Jennifer Lopez), the King (Elvis Presley), the Kingmaker (Richard Neville, Earl of Warwick), La Lollo (Gina Lollobrigida), Leadbelly (Huddie William Ledbetter), Macca (Paul McCartney), Madge (Madonna), Maid of Orleans (Joan of Arc), Man of a Thousand Faces (Lon Chaney), Man of Steel (Clark Kent aka Superman), Master of Suspense (Alfred Hitchcock), Muscles from Brussels (Jean-Claude Van Damme), Ol' Blue Eyes (Frank Sinatra), Old Blood and Guts (General George Patton), Old Man River (Mississippi River), Papa Doc (François Duvalier), Pineapple Face (Manuel Noriego), Pizza Face (Manuel Noriego), Plum (P.G. Wodehouse), Queen of Mean (Leona Helmsley), Red Ken (Ken Livingstone), Satchmo (Louis Armstrong), Scarface (Al Capone), Slick Willie (Bill Clinton), the Smoke (London), Sultan of Sleaze (Jerry Springer), Sundance Kid (Harry Longbaugh), Supermac (Harold Macmillan), the Teflon Don (John Gotti), Tin Lizzie (Henry Ford's Model T car), Titan of Trash (Jerry Springer), Tricky Dickie (Richard M. Nixon), Trout Pout (Leslie Ash), Virgin Queen (Elizabeth I), Johnny Wadd (John C. Holmes), the Worm (Dennis Rodman), Xtina (Christina Aguilera), Yorkshire Ripper (Peter Sutcliffe) - see alter egos
nicknaming, the act of: prosonomasia
NICO: National Insurance Contributions Office
Nietzschean killers: (Nathan) Leopold and (Richard) Loeb
Niger: landlocked republic in West Africa, the second poorest country in the world
  capital: Niamey
  currency: franc

language: French

religion: Muslim

fact: where it is reported that there are still 870,364 slaves in captivity

Nigeria: republic in West Africa

    capital: Abuja

    currency: naira

    language: English (official), Hausa, Ibo, Yoruba

    religion: animist, Muslin, Christian

Nigerian novelists: Chinua Achebe, Buchi Emecheta, Ben Okri, Wole Soyinka

Nigerian singers: Sunny Ade, Fela Kuti, Femi Kuti

night, adjective: nocturnal

night, attack by: camisade (noun)

night, fear of: nyctophobia

night, god of: Hödur

night, goddess of: Freya (Norse mythology), Nyx (Greek), Nox (Roman)

Night at the Opera, A (1935 film), famous lines: Otis B. Driftwood (Groucho Marx) to Mrs Claypool (Margaret Dumont): "When I invite a woman to dinner, I expect her to look at my face. That's the price she has to pay"; Otis (going over contract): "'If any of the parties participating in this contract is shown not to be in their right mind, the entire agreement is automatically nullified.' That's in every contract. That's what they call a sanity clause." Fiorello (Chico Marx): "Ha-ha-ha! You can't fool me. There ain't no Sanity Clause!"

night-blindness: nyctalopia

nightclub: dancing pharmacy (rave club)

nightclubs, famous: Copacabana (New York), 54 (New York), Haçienda (Manchester), Tramp (London), Viper Room (West Hollywood, Los Angeles)

nightclub, gay: Heaven (in London)

nightclub manager: Tony Wilson (Haçienda)

nightingale, adjective: philomelian

nightingale, collective noun: watch

nightingale, sound: pipe, jug-lug, warble

nightingale, young: chick

nightmare: Freddy Krueger

nightshade fruit: capsicum, tomato

nightshade vegetable: potato

Nile, adjective: Nilotic

Nimby: Not In My Backyard

nine, pertaining to: novenary

nine, group of: ennead, nonet

nine-sided plane figure: enneagon, nonagon

nine-sided solid figure: enneahedron

nine muses – see muses

Nineteen Fifties, fads, fashions and movements: abstract expressionism, action painting, Angry Young Man, Beat Generation, big hair, Pat Boone, Marlon Brando, Chelsea boot, crew cut (hairstyle), cruising (in cars), James Dean, drag racing, flat-top (hairstyle), folk music, hot-rodding, hula hoop, jive, Jerry Lewis, Dean Martin, New Wave (aka *nouvelle vague*), pencil skirt, Elvis Presley, quiff, Frank Sinatra, Tommy Steele, Teddy boys

Nineteen Sixties: "If you can remember anything about the sixties, you weren't really there" – Paul Kantner

Nineteen Sixties, fads, fashions and movements: acid rock, Afro hairstyle, Julie Andrews, Angel Delight, Arts Lab, The Beach Boys, The Beatles, beehive (hairstyle), Black Panthers, Black Power, bovver boots, The Byrds, Michael Caine, Chelsea boot, cinéma vérité, Conceptual Art, Sean Connery, cruising (in cars), Sandra Dee, drag racing, encounter groups, Existentialism, Fleetwood Mac, flower power, folk music, fringe theatre, frisbee, Gonk troll, Green movement, *Hair*, herpes, hippies, The Hollies, I-Ching, Jesus boots, Jesus freaks, Tom Jones, kaftan, kipper tie, Martin Luther King, kinky boots, lava lamps, loon pants, Low Riders, LSD, macrobiotics, maxi-skirt, midi (skirt), minimalism, miniskirt, mods, monkey boots, Op Art, ponytail on men, Pop Art, post-modernism, Elvis Presley, protest songs, psychedelia, Mary Quant, Radio Caroline, Jim Reeves, rockers, The Rolling Stones, The Shadows, Simon & Garfunkel, skinheads, TaB (diet cola), therapy, *Thunderbirds*, transactional analysis, Twiggy

Nineteen Seventies, fads, fashions and movements: acupuncture, alternative comedy, animal rights movement, aromatherapy, Austin Allegro, Bay City Rollers, Bhangra music, David Bowie, braids, break dancing, bumbags, CB radio, Clackers (fetish toy), clogs, Conceptual Architecture, consumerism, Cornish Pasty (shoe), cruising (in cars), Disco music, Doc Martens, drag racing, dreadlocks (or 'locks), Dub music, Clint Eastwood, Electro Pop, Farrah Fawcett, flares (trousers), Fleetwood Mac, funk, Gloria Gaynor, geodesic domes, ghetto-blaster, glam rock, gobbing, gonzo journalism, hot pants, jellies, Jesus freaks, jogging, Elton John, lava lamp, Led Zeppelin, loon pants, LSD, Mohican (hairstyle), mountain bikes, The Muppets, the New Man, Newton's cradle (executive toy), Jack Nicholson, nouvelle cuisine, *Oh! Calcutta!*, Al Pacino, Performance Art, pet rocks, Pink Floyd, platform soles, pogo dancing, porno chic, Elvis Presley, preppies, punk rock, Queen, rap music, Burt Reynolds, roller disco, Diana Ross, Demis Roussos, Rubik's Cube, runes, The Sex Pistols, shagpile, Silver Jubilee (see), Simon & Garfunkel, skateboards, Smurfs, soap-on-a-rope, The Specials, Status Quo, Rod Stewart, Barbra Streisand, Tab cola, Teasmade, John Travolta

Nineteen Eighties, fads, fashions and movements: acid house, aerobics, Band Aid, base-jumping, BMX bikes, break dancing, bungy-jumping, Cabbage Patch Dolls, chaos theory, Charter 88, the Chippendales, combat games, cruising (in cars), crystals (used in the focus of cosmic energy), cyberpunk, dwarf throwing, Ecstasy, Essex boys, Filofax, foodies, Garage music, Gobots, Gonk, House music, Industrial music, jellies, karaoke, lager louts, lambada, Madonna, Meat Loaf, moshing, My Little Pony, New Age, New Romantics, nouvelle cuisine, organic architecture, pixie boots, political correctness, power dressing, Elvis Presley, Queen, raves, virtual reality

Nineteen Nineties, fads, fashions and movements: Beanie Babies, bungy-running, Charter 88, crop circles, crop top, cyberporn, Death Metal, Ecstasy, Essex girls, fanny packs, friendship bracelets, Furbies (interactive toys), Goths, grunge (fashion statement), heroin chic, hotting, Jello shots, karaoke, lambada, Madonna, Meat Loaf, Napster, Pokemon, political correctness, push pops, rollerblading, Spice Girls, Swatch, Take That, Tamagotchi virtual pets, Tickle Me Elmo (toy), tracksuit, Wonderbra

ninety, adjective: nonagenarian
ninety-year-old: nonagenarian
nipple, adjective: mamillate
nipple erection: thelerethism
nipple-shaped: mastoid
nipples, sexual arousal caused by: thelerethism

Nirvana: US rock band formed in Aberdeen, Washington, in 1986; comprised of Kurt Cobain (guitar, vocals; died: 5 April 1994), Chris Novoselic (bass), Chad Channing (drums) and Jason Everman (guitar). In 1990 Channing was replaced by Dave Grohl and Nirvana disbanded in 1994

nitrogen gas: discovered by Joseph Priestley and Lewis Morris Rutherdorf (independently) in 1772

NJ: postcode for New Jersey

NLF: National Liberation Front

NM: postcode for New Mexico

NMD: National Missile Defence

Noah's Ark, resting place: Great Ararat (in east Turkey)

Nobel Prize: established in 1901 per the instructions of Alfred Nobel's will

Nobel Prize, youngest recipient: Professor Richard Bragg, awarded the Nobel Prize for Physics in 1915 - at the age of 25

nodding, adjective: nutant

noise, hatred of: phonophobia

noisy: strepitant, strepitous

nom de plumes – see pen names

Noah's sons: Ham, Japheth, Shem

nobility: "All that is beautiful and noble is the result of reason and calculation" - Charles Baudelaire

Norfolk, administrative centre: Norwich

Norfolk Island: island in the South Pacific discovered by Captain Cook in 1774

Norfolk Island, fact: along with Tasmania, Norfolk Island was the British Empire's most remote penal colony

normality: "The state in which one is able to disguise one's neuroses" - anonymous; "The only normal people are the ones you don't know very well" - comedian Joe Ancis

Norman conquest of England: 1066

Norman kings of England: William I, William II, Henry I, Stephen Count of Blois

Normandy beaches invaded on 6 June 1944: Juno, Omaha, Utah, Sword, Gold

Norn goddesses: Urdr, Verdandi and Skuldr, i.e. Fate, Being and Necessity, or Past, Present and Future (Norse mythology)

Norse deities: Aegir, Ask, Balder, Bragi, Eir, Embla, Forseti, Frey, Freyja, Frigg, Hel, Hödur, Idun, Loki, Odin, Sif, Skuld, Thor, Tyr, Urd, Verdandi

Norse warrior: berserker, Sigurd

north, adjective: boreal

North American Indian chief: sachem, sagamore

North American Indian tribes – see Native American Indian tribes

North Carolina, 12th state (1789), Tar Heel State, Old North State
    capital: Raleigh
    state bird: cardinal (a state bird it shares with Illinois, Indiana, Kentucky, Ohio, Virginia and West Virginia)
    state flower: dogwood
    state tree: pine
    motto: 'Esse Quam Videri' (To be rather than to seem')
    birthplace of: Tori Amos, Ben Folds Five (musical trio), John Coltrane, Jennifer Ehle (actress), Roberta Flack, Ben Folds, Ava Gardner, Richard Gatling (inventor), Billy Graham (evangelist), Pam Grier (actress), Jesse Helms, Jesse Jackson, Andrew Johnson (17th president of the US), Dolley Madison (society hostess), Thelonious Monk, Julianne Moore, Edward R. Murrow

(journalist), James K. Polk (11th president of the US), Doc Watson, Thomas
Wolfe (novelist), Evan Rachel Wood (actress)
  tourist attractions: Cape Hatteras and Cape Lookout, Great Smoky
    Mountains, Wright Brothers National Memorial at Kitty Hawk
  fact: the first aeroplane flight in the world was successfully launched by the
    brothers Orville and Wilbur Wright at Kitty Hawk (17 December 1903)
  fact: North Carolina was the first colony to vote for independence from
    England
North Dakota, 39th state (1889), Peace Garden State
  capital: Bismarck
  birthplace of: Lynn Anderson (singer), Angie Dickinson (actress), Louis
    L'Amour (novelist), Peggy Lee (singer), Bobby Vee, Lawrence Welk
    (bandleader)
  motto: 'Liberty and union, now and forever, one and inseparable'
  state bird: Western meadowlark
  state flower: wild prairie rose
  state tree: American elm
  tourist attractions: North Dakota Heritage Center, Fort Union Trading Post
    National Historic Site
  fact: fires have been burning in underground coal beds even before records
    were taken
Northamptonshire, administrative centre: Northampton
Northern Ireland, counties: Antrim, Armagh, Down, Fermanagh, Londonderry,
    Tyrone
northern lights: aurora borealis
northern lights, fear of: Aurorophobia
Northern Rhodesia: former name for Zambia (until 1964)
North Korea: republic in north-east Asia officially known as the Democratic
    People's Republic of Korea
  capital: P'yŏngyang
  currency: won
  language: Korean
  religion: Buddhist, Confucianist
North Korean dictators: Kim-Il Sung, Kim Jong-il
Northumberland, administrative centre: Newcastle upon Tyne
Norway: kingdom in north-west Europe
  capital: Oslo
  currency: krone
  language: Norwegian
  religion: Evangelical Lutheran
  patron saint of: Olaf
  fact: where the law states that all gravestones have to be the same height
  fact: comprises the world's most northerly town, Hammerfest (which was also
    the first town in Europe to benefit from electric street lighting)
Norwegian and famous: a-ha, Karin Fossum (crime novelist), Edvard Grieg, Knut
    Hamsun (Nobel Prize-winning novelist), Sonja Henie, Thor Heyerdahl, Henrik
    Ibsen, Marius Lie (mathematician), Edvard Munch, Fridtjof Nansen (explorer),
    Vidkun Quisling, Erik Rotheim (inventor of the aerosol), Liv Ullmann
nose: beak, beeze, honker, hooter, schnoz, schnozzle, snoot
nose, adjective: nasal, rhinal
nose; the bone between the nostrils: vomer, nasal septum
nose, emptying of (blowing, picking, etc): emunction

nose, endowed with a flat, upturned one: simous (adjective)

nose, endowed with a large one: nasute (adjective), Cyrano de Bergerac (noun)

nose, endowed with a long one: leptorrhinian (adjective)

nose, plastic surgery of: rhinoplasty

nose, runny: rhinorrhea

nose, study of the: nasology

nose and pharynx combined, adjective: rhinopharyngeal

nose inflammation (of the mucous membrane): rhinitis

nose job: rhinoplasty

nose types: aquiline, button, celestial, cogitative, Greek, hawk, Nubian, retroussé, Roman, snub

nose-like: nasutiform

nosebleed: epistaxis

nosebleed, died from: Attila the Hun

nosebleeds, fear of: epistaxiophobia

nostalgia: "Enjoying something you didn't like the first time" - anonymous

nostril, adjective: narial, rhinal

nostril bone: vomer

nostril hair: vibrissa

nostrils: nares

notoriety: "Celebrity with mud on its face" - Roy Hattersley

Nottingham, birthplace of: Viv Anderson (footballer), Kenneth Clarke, Christopher Dean, Robert Harris (novelist), Michael Jayston (actor), Samantha Morton, Su Pollard, Alan Sillitoe, Jayne Torvill

Nottingham river: Trent

Nottinghamshire, administrative centre: Nottingham

nougat: sweet first recorded in 1701, in Montelimar, France

noun most commonly used in the English language: time; second most common: person

nourishment, adjective: alimentary

Nova Scotia: birthplace of Sarah McLachlan, Anne Murray, Ellen Page, Joanna Shimkus

novel focusing on the protagonist's early life: Bildungsroman

novels by women, best loved (as conducted in a poll by Orange): 1) *Pride and Prejudice*, by Jane Austen; 2) *Jane Eyre*, by Charlotte Brontë; 3) *Wuthering Heights*, by Emily Brontë; 4) *Middlemarch*, by George Eliot; 5) *Rebecca*, by Daphne du Maurier; 6) *Persuasion*, by Jane Austen; 7) *Frankenstein*, by Mary Shelley; 8) *Emma*, by Jane Austen; 9) *Unless*, by Carol Shields; 10) *To Kill a Mocking Bird*, by Harper Lee

novelty, fear of: kainolophobia

novelty, love of: neophilia

Now, Voyager (1942 film), famous line: Charlotte Vale (Bette Davis): "Oh, Jerry, don't let's ask for the moon. We have the stars!" [last line]

NPOV: neutral point of view

NSAID: non-steroidal anti-inflammatory drug

nuclear fission: discovered by Otto Frisch and his aunt Lise Meitner in 1939

nuclear physicists: Sir John Cockcroft, Igor Kurchatov, Robert Oppenheimer, Andrei Sakharov

nuclear physics, father of: Ernest Rutherford

nuclear reactor, first; built by: Enrico Fermi in 1942

nuclear weapons, dread of: nucleomitophobia

nudist: gymnosophist

nudists: Lady Godiva, Stephen Gough (who, over seven months in 2003, walked stark naked from Land's End to John O'Groats)

nudity, dread of: gymnophobia, gymnotophobia (rare)

nudity, photographer of: Spencer Tunick

nuns: Sister Wendy Beckett (art authority), Saint Bernadette, Saint Clare of Assisi, Frances Dominica (pioneer of the hospice movement), Sister Emmanuelle ('the ragpicker of Cairo'), Elsie Ethrington (aka The Flying Nun, Sister Bertrille), Sister Jeannine Gramick (who advocated the acceptance of homosexuals in the Catholic church), Isabella (from Shakespeare's *Measure for Measure*), Saintt Scholastica, Soeur Sourire (aka Sister Smile, the Singing Nun), Mother Teresa (aka Agnes Gauxha Bojaxhiu and Teresa of Calcutta), Maria von Trapp, Mary Ward

nuns, patron saints of: Scholastica and Brigid of Kildare

nursery rhyme characters: Bobby Shafto, Cock Robin, Georgie Porgie, Humpty Dumpty, Jack Sprat, Little Jack Horner, Little Miss Muffet, Little Tommy Tucker, Mother Goose, Old King Cole, Old McDonald, Old Mother Hubbard, Peter Piper, Solomon Grundy, Tom Tom the Piper's Son, Wee Willie Winkie

nurses: Clara Barton (founder of the US Red Cross), Nurse Betty (from the film of the same name), Vera Brittain, Edith Cavell, Deborah (Rebecca's nurse, in the Old Testament), S. Emma E. Edmonds (American Civil War), Kerry Griffiths (who was hailed as an angel of mercy after she saved the life of a man injured in the Staten Island Ferry accident of 2003), Sister Elizabeth Kenny, Florence Nightingale, Nurse (from *Romeo and Juliet*), Caroline Petrie (suspended for offering to pray for a patient), Mildred Ratched (from *One Flew Over the Cuckoo's Nest*), Mary Seacole (Jamaican healer who tended the wounded on the Crimean front line), Harriet Tubman

nurses, patron saints of: Camillus de Lellis, John of God and Agatha

nut, adjective: nucal

nut-eating: nucivorous

nut-shaped: nuciform

Nutcracker, The: ballet composed by Pyotr Tchaikovsky, first performed in St Petersburg in 1892

nutriment, adjective: alimentative

nutrition, adjective: alimentary, trophic

nutritionist: Gillian McKeith

NV: postcode for Nevada

NWA: Niggaz Wit' Attitude, Northwest Airlines

NY: postcode for New York state

Nyasaland: former name for Malawi (until 1964)

nymphs: Arethusa, Callisto, Calypso, Chloris, Daphne, dryad, Echo, Eurydice, Galatea, hamadryad, Hesperides, houri, Hyades, naiad, Nereid, Oceanid, Oenone, oread, siren, Syrinx

nymphet: Lolita (from the novel by Vladimir Nabokov)

nymphomaniacs: Catherine the Great, Rosemary West
    - see femmes fatale, women of ill repute, etc

NYPD: New York Police Department

O

oak, adjective: quercine

oar, small-handled: scull

Oasis: guitar-driven, UK rock band formed in Burnage, Manchester, in 1991; comprised of Noel Gallagher (guitar, songwriter), Liam Gallagher (younger brother of Noel; vocals), Paul 'Bonehead' Arthurs (rhythm guitar), Paul 'Guigsy' McGuigan (bass) and Tony McCarroll (drums). McCarroll left the band in 1995 and was replaced by Alan White, while Arthurs parted in 1999 and was succeeded by guitarists Andy Bell and Gem Archer. In 2005, the band recruited a new drummer, Zak Starkey – son of Ringo Starr

oath, doctor's: Hippocratic

oath, evidence under: deposition

OBE: Officer of the Order of the British Empire

obesity: a condition defined by 20% excess of body weight

obesity, British city with worst case of: Stoke-on-Trent, where 24.5% of its citizens are obese

obesity, place with worst case of: Hawaii (72% of women, 70% of men)

Obie: Off-Broadway and Off-Off Broadway award, administered by New York's *Village Voice* publication

obligation, adjective: deontic

Observer, The: Britain's oldest national Sunday newspaper, founded 1 December 1791; "written by Germans for blacks" – Nancy Astor

obstetricians, patron saint of: Raymond Nonnatus

obstructive speech: filibuster

occultists: Alessandro Cagliostro, Aleister Crowley, Georgei Gurdjieff, Colin Wilson

occupation, adjective: vocational

ocean, adjective: marine, pelagic

ocean, fact: seas cover 70% of the earth's surface, 60% of which is more than one mile deep – only six submersibles in the world can dive more than one mile down

ocean, largest in the world: Pacific; second largest: Atlantic

ocean, original: Panthalassa (that which enveloped the entire globe)

ocean depths, adjective: abyssal

oceanographers: Robert Ballard, Jacques Cousteau

octopus, adjective: octopine

octopus, fact: the creature has three hearts

octopus, female: hen

octopus, reproductive organ: hectocotylus (generally the third right arm of the male)

Odin's maidens: Valkyries

odours, particular fear of: osmophobia

Office, The: hugely popular BBC sitcom set in the Slough branch of the Wernham Hogg paper merchants
>   **created by** Ricky Gervais and Stephen Merchant
>   **broadcast:** 9 August 2001–27 December 2003
>   **cast:** Ricky Gervais (David Brent), Martin Freeman (Tim Canterbury), Mackenzie Crook (Gareth Keenan), Lucy Davis (Dawn Tinsley), Emma Louise Manton (Emma). An American spin-off featured Steve Carell, Rainn Wilson, John Krasinski and Jenna Fischer

off-licences: Bottoms Up, Jeroboams, Majestic Wine, Nicolas, Oddbins, Thresher, Unwins, Victoria Wine, Wine Rack

OFT: Office of Fair Trading
ogre: Shrek
OGT: obviously gay trait
OH: postcode for Ohio
Ohio, 17th state (1803), Buckeye State
    capital: Columbus
    state bird: cardinal (a state bird it shares with Illinois, Indiana, Kentucky, North Carolina, Virginia and West Virginia)
    state flower: scarlet carnation
    state tree: buckeye
    birthplace of the hot dog and ice cream cone
    birthplace of: Neil Armstrong, Ambrose Bierce, The Cramps, Clarence Darrow, Thomas A. Edison, Clark Gable, James A. Garfield (20th president), John Glenn (astronaut), Ulysses S. Grant (18th president), Zane Grey (novelist), Warren G. Harding(29th president), Benjamin Harrison (23rd president), Rutherford B. Hayes (19th president), Jon Hendricks (jazz legend), John C. Holmes (aka Johnny Wadd), William McKinley (25th president), Toni Morrison, Paul Newman, Pontiac, Martin Sheen, Steven Spielberg, William Howard Taft (27th president), Ted Turner, Orville Wright
    motto: 'With God, all things are possible.'
    tourist attractions: The Top Thrill Dragster in Cedar Point (the world's fastest and tallest rollercoaster ride), Neil Armstrong Air and Space Museum, Jack Nicklaus Sports Center
    fact: the law states that pets have to carry lights on their tails at night
oil, adjective: oleaginous
oil painting: painting technique whose development was originally credited to the Flemish artist Jan van Eyck - until the discovery of oil in the eighth century painting of stone and glass
oil tycoons: Roman Abramovich, John Paul Getty, John D. Rockefeller
oil-yielding: oleiferous
OK: postcode for Oklahoma
Oklahoma, 46th state (1907), Sooner State
    capital: Oklahoma City
    state bird: scissor-tailed flycatcher
    state flower: mistletoe
    state tree: redbud
    birthplace of: Garth Brooks, Ralph Waldo Ellison, The Flaming Lips James Garner, Woody Guthrie, John Hinckley Jr., S.E. Hinton, Ron Howard, Mickey Mantle, Brad Pitt, Tony Randall, Will Rogers, Jim Thorpe
    motto: 'Labor Omnia Vincit ('Labor conquers all things')
    tourist attractions: Will Rogers Memorial, National Cowboy Hall of Fame
    fact: where more people are executed per capita than in China or Iran
    fact: where it is illegal to catch whales or get fish drunk, even though it is an inland state
Oklahoma City, birthplace of: Johnny Lee Bench (baseball player), Lon Chaney, Jr, Ralph Waldo Ellison, The Flaming Lips
Oklahoma City bombing: 19 April 1995; death toll: 168; injured: over 800; culprits: Timothy McVeigh and his accomplice Terry Nichols
okra: bhindi (in Indian cuisine), gumbo (in the USA)
Ol' Blue Eyes: nickname for Frank Sinatra
old: ancient, antediluvian, crinkly, mature, passé, rusty, wrinkly
old age: "Old age will only be respected if it fights for itself, maintains its rights, avoids dependency on anyone, and asserts control over its own to its last

breath" – Marcus Cicero; "I am in the departure lounge of life. My only hope is that my plane will be delayed" - Sir Robin Day

old age, adjective: geratic, senile

old age, scientific study of: gerontology

Old Bailey: informal name given to the Central Criminal Court in London EC1, taken from the street in which it is situated. The building, which was designed by E.W. Mountford, was opened in 1907 by King Edward VII on the site of the old Newgate Prison

Old Blood and Guts: nickname for General George Patton

oldest elected official: the 104-year-old Emma Schweer, who was re-elected as city tax collector in Crete, Illinois, in April 2001

Old Glory: nickname for the Stars and Stripes

Old Hickory: nickname for Andrew Jackson, seventh president of the United States

Old Ironsides: nickname for Oliver Cromwell

old man: Methuselah (who lived to 969)

Old Man River: nickname for the Mississippi River

Old Testament books: Genesis, Exodus, Leviticus, Numbers, Deuteronomy, Joshua, Judges, Ruth, First Book of Samuel, Second Book of Samuel, First Book of Kings, Second Book of Kings, First Book of Chronicles, Second Book of Chronicles, Ezra, Nehemiah, Esther, Job, Psalms, Proverbs, Ecclesiastes, Song of Songs, Song of Solomon, Canticles, Isaiah, Jeremiah, Lamentations, Ezekiel, Daniel, Hosea, Joel, Amos, Obadiah, Jonah, Micah, Nahum, Habakkuk, Zephaniah, Haggai, Zechariah, Malachi

Old Vic Theatre, London: founded in 1818, when it was known as the Royal Coburg Theatre

Old World, adjective: gerontogeous

Olympic Games (aka The Olympics): established in Athens in 1896

Olympic Games, period of four years between: Olympiad

Omaha, Nebraska, birthplace of: Fred Astaire, Marlon Brando, Montgomery Clift, Gerald Ford, Malcolm X, Dorothy McGuire, Nick Nolte, Andy Roddick (tennis player), Ed Ruscha

Oman: sultanate in south-east Arabia; formerly known as Muscat and Oman (until 1970)
　　capital: Muscat
　　currency: rial
　　language: Arabic
　　religion: Muslim

omen reader: augur, auspex (particularly in ancient Rome), clairvoyant, haruspex (from the entrails of animals), oracle, prophet, soothsayer, sibyl

one-upmanship authority: Stephen Potter

oneself, fear of: autophobia

onion, adjective: alliaceous

onion, collective noun: rope

onion, cooked with: lyonnaise (adjective)

onion dish: lyonnaise

onion sauce: soubise

Only Fools and Horses: enduringly popular BBC1 sitcom about a South London opportunist
　　created by John Sullivan
　　broadcast: 8 September 1981–25 December 2003
　　cast: David Jason (Derek 'Del Boy' Trotter), Nicholas Lyndhurst (Rodney Charlton Trotter) Lennard Pearce (Grandad), Buster Merryfield (Uncle

Albert), Roger Lloyd Pack (Trigger), Tessa Peake-Jones (Raquel Trotter), Gwyneth Strong (Cassandra Louise Trotter), Paul Barber (Denzil)

ONS: Office for National Statistics

On the Waterfront (1954 film), famous line: Terry Malloy (Marlon Brando): "I coulda had class. I coulda been a contender. I coulda been somebody – instead of a bum, which is what I am"

open countryside, adjective: campestral

open spaces, fear of: agoraphobia

opening words of medieval manuscript: incipit

opera composers: Ludwig van Beethoven, Vincenzo Bellini, Hector Berlioz, Georges Bizet, Aleksandr Borodin, Luigi Cherubini, Aaron Copland, Claude Debussy, Léo Délibes, Frederick Delius, Antonín Dvořák, Manuel de Falla, George Gershwin, Mikhail Glinka, Christoph Willibald Gluck, Charles Gounod, George Frideric Handel, Hans Werner Henze, Scott Joplin, Jean Baptiste Lully, Pietro Mascagni, Jules Massenet, Giacomo Meyerbeer, Claudio Monteverdi, Wolfgang Amadeus Mozart, Modest Mussorgsky, Jacques Offenbach, Carl Orff, Giovanni Battista Pergolesi, Sergey Prokofiev, Giacomo Puccini, Henry Purcell, Maurice Ravel, Nikolay Rimsky-Korsakov, Gioacchino Rossini, Camille Saint-Saëns, Alessandro Scarlatti, Arnold Schoenberg, Dmitry Shostakovich, Bedrich Smetana, Richard Strauss, Igor Stravinsky, Peter Ilich Tchaikovsky, Ralph Vaughan Williams, Giuseppe Verdi, Richard Wagner, Carl Maria von Weber, Kurt Weill

opera directors: Sir Peter Hall, Sir Jonathan Miller, Peter Sellars, Franco Zeffirelli

opera glasses (endowed with a long handle): lorgnette (from the French *lorgner*, meaning "to squint")

opera hat: gibus

opera houses: Bolshoi (Moscow), Colon Theatro (Buenos Aires), Deutsche Oper (Berlin), Estates Theatre (Prague), La Fenice (Venice), Festspielhaus (Bayreuth), Komische Oper (Berlin), London Coliseum, Marinsky Theatre (St Petersburg) (formerly Kirov Theatre), Metropolitan Opera House (New York), Monte Carlo Opera House, National Theatre (Prague), Paris Opera House, Royal Opera House (Covent Garden, London), Royal Opera House (Stockholm), Royal Theatre (Copenhagen), La Scala (Milan), Sydney Opera House, Teatro di San Carlo (Naples), Theatre dell'Opera (Rome), Theatro Municipal (Rio de Janeiro)

opera patron: John Christie

opera singers: Roberto Alagna, Dame Janet Baker, Dame Josephine Barstow, Cecilia Bartoli, Kathleen Battle, Isabel Bayrakdarian, Andrea Bocelli, Montserrat Caballe, Maria Callas, Ann Cargill, José Carreras, Enrico Caruso, David Daniels, Placido Domingo, Sir Geraint Evans, Maria Ewing, Wilhelmenia Fernandez, Renée Fleming ("the greastest lyric soprano of her generation"), Lesley Garrett, Angela Gheorghiu, Filippa Giordano, Dame Gwyneth Jones, Simon Keenlyside, Sylvia McNair, Dame Nellie Melba, Grace Moore, Jessye Norman, Adelina Patti, Luciano Pavarotti, Dame Margaret Price, Lisa Saffer (Lulu), Dame Kiri Te Kanawa, Bryn Terfel, Floria Tosca, Dawn Upshaw, Willard White, Ying Huang - see sopranos, tenors

operatic song: aria, ariette

operatic realism: verismo

operettas, writers of: W.S. Gilbert and Arthur Sullivan, Victor Herbert

opinion, adjective: doxastic

opinions, loathing for: allodoxaphobia

opium: big O, bird's eye, brick gum, brown stuff, Chinese tobacco, dream wax, gee, God's own medicine, gow, midnight oil, mira, mud, pen yan, tar

opium, fact: in ancient Egypt opium was used as an anaesthetic before surgery

opportunists: Elmer Gantry, Derek 'Del Boy' Trotter (from TV's *Only Fools and Horses*)

opposite: flip side, Yin and Yang

optician: Dollond & Aitchison, ocularist (a person who makes artificial eyes), oculist, ophthalmologist, optometrist

optimist: cheerleader, Pollyanna, positivist, scoutmaster

optimists, in literature: Wilkins Micawber (from Dickens' *David Copperfield*), Pangloss (from Voltaire's *Candide*), Mark Tapley (from Dickens' *Martin Chuzzlewit*)

OR: postcode for Oregon

orange: citrus fruit native to China and south-east Asia

orange (fruit), adjective: aurantiaceous

oranges: Bergamot (bitter), blood orange (sweet), clementine, Jaffa (sweet), Navalina, navel, Ortanique, satsuma, Seville (bitter), Spanish, sweet orange, tangerine, Valencia (sweet)

orange segment: lith

orange seller: Nell Gwynn

orang-utan, famous: Clyde (as featured in the films *Any Which Way You Can* and *Every Which Way But Loose*)

orang-utan, slang: pongo

orators: Sir Winston Churchill, Marcus Cicero, William Gladstone, Henry Grattan, Isocrates, Martin Luther King, Abraham Lincoln, Pericles, Leon Trotsky, Daniel Webster

orators, patron saint of: John Chrysostom

orbit's extremity (of a satellite, planet, etc): apsis

orchardist: Maria Ann Smith

orchards, goddess of: Pomona (Roman mythology)

orchestras: Academy of St. Martin in the Fields, BBC Symphony Orchestra, Berlin Philharmonic Orchestra, Boston Symphony Orchestra, Camerata de' Bardi (in Pavia, Italy), CBC Radio Orchestra, Chicago Symphony Orchestra, Czech Philharmonic Orchestra, Detroit Symphony Orchestra, Gothenburg Symphony Orchestra (in Sweden), Israel Philharmonic Orchestra, London Philharmonic Orchestra, London Symphony Orchestra, New York Philharmonic, Orchestra of La Scala (in Milan), Royal Philharmonic Orchestra, St. Petersburg Philharmonic Orchestra, Stuttgart Radio Symphony Orchestra, Sydney Symphony Orchestra, Toronto Symphony Orchestra, Vienna Philharmonic Orchestra

orchestra, the four sections: strings, wood-wind, brass-wind, percussion

orchid, collective noun: coterie

order, goddess of: Themis (Greek mythology)

Order of the Garter: English structure of chivalry founded by King Edward III in 1348

ordinary: bog standard, exoteric, garden variety

Oregon, 33rd state (1859), Beaver State

    capital: Salem

    state bird: Western meadowlark

    state flower: Oregon grape

    state tree: Douglas fir

    birthplace of: Raymond Carver, Matt Groening, Tonya Harding, Chief Joseph (Nez Percé warrior), Jane Powell, Steve Prefontaine, John Reed

    motto: 'She flies with her own wings'

tourist attractions: Crater Lake National Park, Oregon Caves National
   Monument, Shakespearean Festival in Ashland, Portland Rose Festival,
   Evergreen Aviation Center in McMinville (housing Howard Hughes'
   Spruce Goose – see)
fact: the world's largest living thing, the *Armillaria ostoyae* (or honey
   mushroom), is in Oregon and covers 2,200 acres, mostly underground
fact: Oregon was the first state in the USA to legally facilitate euthanasia,
   courtesy of the Death with Dignity Act of 1994
organ, largest belonging to the human body: skin
organ solo: voluntary (usually played in church)
organs: brain, ear, eye, gall bladder, heart, intestine, kidney, liver, lung, nose,
   pancreas, penis, skin, spleen, stomach, tongue, uterus, womb
organs, illegally collected by: Dutch pathologist Dick van Velzen (who, from 1988
   to 1995, amassed a collection of 6,900 organs and body parts, supposedly for
   medical research)
organists: Leon Battista Alberti, Johan Sebastian Bach, Wilhelm Friedemann Bach,
   E. Power Biggs, William Boyce, Frantisek Xaver Brixi, Anton Bruckner,
   Dietrich Buxtehude, William Byrd, Walter Carlos (who later became Wendy
   Carlos), François Couperin, Marcel Dupré, Maurice Duruflé, Sir Edward Elgar,
   Gabriel Fauré, César Auguste Franck, Girolamo Frescobaldi, Giovanni Gabrieli,
   George Handel, Richard 'Groove' Holmes, Rued Immanuel Langgaard, Olivier
   Messiaen, Thomas Morley, Johann Pachelbel, Giovanni Pierluigi da Palestrina,
   Henry Purcell, Jean Philippe Rameau, Giovanni Battista Sammartini, Albert
   Schweitzer, Jimmy Smith, Antonio Soler, Leopold Antoni Stanislaw Stokowski,
   Sir Arthur Sullivan, Jan Pieterszoon Sweelinck, Thomas Tallis, John Taverner,
   Sarah Vaughan, Fats Waller, Charles Marie Widor, Sir Henry Wood
orgasm, fear of: orgasmaphobia
orgasm, inability to achieve/reach: anorgasmia
orgasm, quick: tachorgasmia (noun)
orgasm, simultaneous (by both partners): synorgasmia
orgasm experts: Steve and Vera Bodansky
orgasmic disorder: persistent sexual arousal syndrome (PSAS)
orgy: cluster-fuck
Oriental person: chopstick (derog.)
orifice, adjective: stomatic
origin, adjective: genetic
origins, science of: epistemology, etiology
oriole, adjective: icterine
ornithologists: John James Audubon, James Bond (after whom the secret agent was
   named), George Gray, Roger Tory Peterson, Sir Peter Scott, Henry Seebohm,
   Alexander Wilson
orphans: Annie (aka Little Orphan Annie), Roman Abramovich (once the richest
   man in Britain), Babe (a pig), Batman, Klaus, Sunny and Violet Bauedelaire
   (from *Lemony Snicket's A Series of Unfortunate Events*), Lyra Belacqua (from
   Philip Pullman's *His Dark Materials*), Coco Chanel, Sara Crewe (from Frances
   Hodgson Burnett's *A Little Princess*), Daredevil, Artful Dodger (aka Master
   John Dawkins), Jude Fawley (from *Jude the Obscure*), Heathcliff, James Bond,
   Jane Eyre, Huckleberry Finn, Heidi, Jor-El (aka Superman), Kim (from Rudyard
   Kipling's 1901 novel), Hannibal Lecter, Fra Filippo Lippi, Stuart Little, Sally
   Lockhart (from Philip Pullman's *The Ruby in the Smoke*, etc), W. Somerset
   Maugham, Marilyn Monroe, Saparmyrat Niyazov, Samantha Parkington (doll),

Philip 'Pip' Pirrip (from *Great Expectations*), Edgar Allan Poe, Roman Polanski, Harry Potter, Jean Racine, Buffy Sainte-Marie, Becky Sharp, Tom Sawyer, Esther Summerson (from Charles Dickens' *Bleak House*), Superman, Swee'pea, Tarzan, Oliver Twist, Bruce Wayne (aka Batman), Homer Wells (from John Irving's *The Cider House Rules*), Mary Yelland (from *Jamaica Inn*)

orphans, patron saint of: Jerome Emiliani

orthopaedic surgeon: Sir John Charnley

Orwell, George; terms coined by: Big Brother, doublethink, memory hole, newspeak, Room 101, thought police, unperson

Oscar: nickname for the Academy Award of the Motion Picture Arts and Sciences

Oscar fact; percentage of votes needed for a film or person to win: 21%

Oslo, patron saint of: Halivard

osteopath: Stephen Ward (who became embroiled in the Profumo scandal)

ostrich, adjective: ratite, struthious

ostrich, fact: a bird whose eye is bigger than its brain

ostrich, famous: Oswald (introduced on BBC TV's *For the Children*)

Otello: opera by Gioacchino Rossini, first produced in Naples in 4 December 1816; opera by Giuseppe Verdi, first produced in Milan 5 February 1887

Ottawa, birthplace of: Paul Anka, Margaret Atwood, Dan Aykroyd, Simon Dee, Alanis Morissette

otter, adjective: lutrine

otter, collective noun: family, romp

otter, famous: Tarka

otter, habitat: holt

otter, young: whelp

otter faeces: spraint

otters, fear of: lutraphobia

Ottoman emperor: Süleyman (or Suleiman) the Magnificent

Outer Mongolia: former name for Mongolia (until 1924, from which time – until 1992 - the nation was known as the Mongolian People's Republic)

outlaws: Ben Hall, Robin Hood, Frank James, Jesse James, Ned Kelly, Little John, Rob Roy (aka Robert Roy MacGregor), Friar Tuck, Dick Turpin

outspokenness: parrhesia

Ovaltine: malt drink invented in 1904 in Berne, Switzerland, by Dr George Wander, when it was originally known as Ovomaltine (a clerical error later altered it to Ovaltine and the name stuck)

overdose, death from: Kenneth Allsop, Jean-Michel Basquiat, John Belushi, Lenny Bruce, Tim Buckley (musician), Dorothy Dandridge, Nick Drake (musician), John Entwistle, Brian Epstein (ruled as accidental death), Chris Farley, Rainer Werner Fassbinder, Judy Garland, Tim Hardin, Margaux Hemingway, Jimi Hendrix, Billie Holiday, Brian Jones, Janis Joplin, Heath Ledger, Sonny Liston (reportedly), Bela Lugosi, Frankie Lymon (musician), Aimee Semple McPherson (radio evangelist), Marilyn Monroe (allegedly), Keith Moon, Jim Morrison, Gram Parsons (musician), Robert Pastorelli (actor), River Phoenix, Elvis Presley, Dee Dee Ramone (musician), Edie Sedgwick (actress/model), Sid Vicious, Kenneth Williams, Paula Yates

over-drinking nausea: crapulence

over-eating nausea: crapulence

overlap: imbricate

overweight, fear of being: adipophobia

ovum, fertilised: oosperm, zygote

owl, adjective: strigine

owl, collective noun: parliament, stare

owl, sound: hoot, screech, wail

owl, young: owlet

ox, adjective: bovine

ox, belief in being an: boanthropy

ox, collective noun: drove, herd, team, yolk

ox, famous: Babe (companion of Paul Bunyan)

ox, female: cow

ox, male: bullock

ox, plural: oxen

ox, sound: bellow, low

ox, young: steer

Oxford, adjective: Oxonian

Oxford, birthplace of: Nell Gwyn (reportedly), Stephen Hawking, Hugh Laurie, Yasmin Le Bon, Jacqueline du Pré, Dorothy L. Sayers, Philip Toynbee

Oxford and Cambridge boat race; starts: Putney Bridge; ends: Mortlake; distance: four-and-quarter miles

Oxford Dictionary of National Biography, The: sixty-volume biographical reference begun in 1882, first published in 1884; intitially edited by Leslie Stephen. The second edition, published in 2004, was edited by H.C.G. Matthew and Brian Harrison, and comprises 54,922 entries

Oxford English Dictionary: created and edited by James Murray between the years 1879 and 1928 (but not completed until after Murray's death)

Oxford library: Bodleian Library

Oxford nickname: City of dreaming spires (coined by the poet Matthew Arnold)

Oxford river: The Isis (a ten-mile stretch of the Thames)

Oxfordshire, administrative centre: Oxford

oxygen: gaseous element identified by Joseph Priestley in August 1774

oxygen, lack of: anoxia

oxymorons (or oxymora): accurate estimate, act naturally, airline food, almost exactly, alone together, British fashion, business ethics, butt-head, child-proof, Christian scientist, clearly misunderstood, definite maybe, exact estimate, found missing, general consensus, genuine imitation, good grief, government organisation, Great Britain, Great Depression, greatest weakness, growing smaller, happily married, hay fever, healthy tan, living dead, Microsoft Works, military intelligence, new classic, passive aggression, peace force, perfect gentleman, pretty ugly, resident alien, same difference, sanitary landfill, silent scream, small crowd, soft rock, sweet sorrow, taped live, tight slacks, twelve-ounce pound cake, working vacation

oyster, adjective: ostracine, ostreiform, ostreoid

oyster, collective noun: bed

oyster, fact: traditionally only eaten in a month with the letter 'R' in it (March, December, etc)

oyster, offspring: spat

oyster bed (artifical): stew

oyster breeding: ostreiculture

oyster farm: parc

oyster-eating: ostreophagous (adjective)

oysters wrapped in bacon slices: angels-on-horseback

ozone layer, chemicals responsible for depletion of: CFCs

P

PA: postcode for Pennsylvania

pacifists: Alfred Fried, Mahatma Mohandas Gandhi, Henry Kissinger, Jeannette Rankin, Rosika Schwimmer

paediatricians: Dr Benjamin Spock, Helen Taussig

paedophile ring: Wonderland Club

paedophiles (suspected or otherwise): Lord Robert Baden-Powell, J.M. Barrie, Benjamin Britten, Lewis Carroll, Arnold Friedman, Eric Gill, Gary Glitter, General Charles George Gordon, Humbert Humbert, Jonathan King, Michael Jackson (officially exonerated), Chris Langham (officially exonerated), Laurie Lee, L.S. Lowry, Viscount Bernard Law Montgomery, Wilfred Owen, John Ruskin, Dr Ralph Underwager

page, adjective: paginal

page, left-hand side: verso

page, right-hand side: recto

Page Three girls: Debee Ashby, Sam Cooke, Samantha Fox, Jordan (aka Katie Price), Keeley Hazell, Linda Lusardi, Melinda Messenger

pain, fear of: algophobia

pain, receiving sexual gratification from: algolagnia

pain relief, patron saint of: Madron

painkillers: acetaminophen, Advil, Anadin, anaesthetic, Aspro, Bextra (withdrawn because of unpleasant dermal side effects), Celebrex, Co-proxamol, Demerol (strong), diclofenac, Disprin, Disprol, Fentanyl, Hedex, Ibuprofen, ketamine, laudanum, morphine, Nurofen, Panadol, Paracetamol, Rennie, Tylenol, Valium, Vicodin, Vioxx (withdrawn because of cardiovascular complications, such as heart attacks and strokes)

paint: acrylic, Day-Glo, distemper, emulsion, enamel, gouache, matt, oil, poster paint, watercolour

paint applied thickly (to canvas, etc): impasto

painter, collective noun: curse, illusion

painters, patron saint of: Luke

painters of the twentieth century: Francis Bacon, Leonora Carrington (surrealist and former lover of Max Ernst), Beryl Cook (specialised in fat women), Salvador Dalí, Lucian Freud, Sir Terry Frost, Patrick Heron, David Hockney, Jasper Johns, Anselm Kiefer, Edward Kienholz, Franz Kline, Dame Laura Knight (specialised in scenes of the ballet, circus and gypsy life), Roy Lichtenstein, L(aurence) S(tephen) Lowry, Alexandra Nechita (ten-year-old girl who sold at least 250 paintings for between £5,000 and £40,000), Ben Nicholson, Georgia O'Keeffe, Marla Olmstead (abstract painter who became a star at the age of four), Robert Rauschenberg, Gerhard Richter, Mark Rothko, Jenny Saville, David Siqueiros (Mexican muralist), Sir Stanley Spencer (specialised in Biblical scenes transposed to Cookham), Cy Twombly, Graham Sutherland, Jack Vettriano (born Jack Hoggan, in Fife), Andy Warhol - see modern artists

painters of portraits – see portrait painters

painters, female: Vanessa Bell, India Jane Birley, Cecily Brown, Leonora Carrington, Judy Cassab, Mary Cassatt, Beryl Cook, Marlene Dumas, Natalia Goncharova, Gwen John, Frida Kahlo, Dame Laura Knight, Berthe Morisot, Alexandra Nechita, Georgia O'Keeffee, Marla Olmstead, Jenny Saville, Melissa Scott-Miller, Daphne Todd, Élisabeth Vigée-Lebrun

painters, Western: Frederic Remington, James Reynolds, Charles M. Russell, Frank Tenney-Johnson

painting: "Painting is the pattern of one's nervous system being projected on the canvas" – Francis Bacon

painting, circular: tondo (noun)

painting styles: abstract, baroque, chiaroscuro (use of shadow delineation), conceptual, cubism, expressionism, impasto (where you can actually see the brush strokes), impressionism, naïve, neoplasticism, pointillism, postmodernism, pre-Raphaelite, surrealism
- see also art terms

pair, without: azygous (as in "an azygous sock") (adjective)

pair up: geminate (verb)

paired: didymous (adjective)

Pakistan: republic in south Asia
    capital: Islamabad
    currency: rupee
    language: Urdu
    religion: Muslim

Pakistani presidents: Mohammad Zia ul-Haq (1978–1988), Muhammad Rafiq Tarar (1998–2001), Pervez Musharraf (2001–2008), Asif Ali Zardari (2008–)

Pakistani prime minister: Benazir Bhutto

Pakistani singer: Nusrat Fateh Ali Khan

Pakistani writer: Salmon Rushdie

palaeobotanist: Marie Stopes

palaeontologists: Mary Anning, Edward Cope, Raymond Dart, Ross Geller (played by David Schwimmer in *Friends*), Don Johanson, Louis Leakey, Mary Leakey, Richard Leakey, Gideon Mantell, Sir Richard Owen

Palaeozic periods: Cambrian (600 million years ago), Ordovician (500m), Silurian (440m), Devonian (400m), Carboniferous (350m), Permian (270m)

palate, adjective: palatine

Palestinian activist: Leila Khaled

Palestinian leader: Yasser Arafat

Palestinian militant groups: Fatah, Hamas, Islamic Jihad

palm, adjective: palmar, volar (as of a hand)

Pan, home of: Arcadia

Panama: republic in Central America
    capital: Panama City
    currency: balboa
    language: Spanish (official), English
    religion: Roman Catholic

Panama, birthplace of: Rubén Blades, John McCain, Manuel Noriega

pancreas, adjective: pancreatic

pancreas, inflammation of: pancreatitis

panda: mammal formerly classified as a member of the raccoon family but now considered a true bear. The giant panda belongs to the subfamily Ailuropodinae in the family Ursidae, order Carnivora. It is classified as *Ailuropoda melanoleuca*

panda, famous: Bao-Bao, Chi-Chi, Ming Ming, Pe-Pe (nicknamed El Macho), Po (from DreamWorks' *Kung Fu Panda*), Soo (girlfriend of Sooty)

panther, famous: Bagheera (from *The Jungle Book*)

panting: anhelation (shortness of breath)

pantomime, muse of: Polyhymnia

Papa Doc: nickname for the Haitian dictator François Duvalier
papal court: Curia
papal court, adjective: Curial
papal envoy: nuncio
papal letter: encyclical
paparazzi: fourth estate, media, press, stalkerazzi
paper: invented by the Chinese in the second century AD (bold estimates put the
    date to between 104 and 104 AD and credit the eunuch Zai Lun as the inventor)
paper decoration (particulalrly using paper cut-outs): découpage
paper folding, art of: origami
paper types: A4, A3, bond paper, laid paper, papyrus, parchment, ream, vellum,
    wove paper
paperback: credited to the publisher Allen Lane who was instrumental in launching
    the first set of Penguin paperbacks in the summer of 1935 (when each edition
    cost sixpence)
Papua New Guinea: country in the south-west Pacific
    capital: Port Moresby
    currency: kina; formerly sea shells (abolished in 1933)
    language: English (official), also Tok Pisin (English creole), Motu
    religion: Christian
parachute: concept first devised in 1495 by Leonardo Da Vinci, although an
    actual parachute jump was not attempted until 1783 when the Frenchman
    'Le Normand' jumped out of a house while holding onto an umbrella with a
    30-inch diameter. Officially, the parachute was patented in October of 1802 by
    another Frenchman, André-Jacques Garnerin, who used it to land in London's
    Grosvenor Square in September of 1802
Paradise: Arcady, Avalon (in Arthurian legend), Eden, Garden of Eden,
    Nephelococcygia, Shangri-La
paradise, adjective: paradisal
Paradise, nymph of: houri
paraffin: invented by James Young in 1847
Paraguay: landlocked republic in South America
    capital: Asunción
    currency: guarani
    language: Spanish, Guarani (both official)
    religion: Roman Catholic
    patron saint: Our Lady of the Assumption
Paraguayan leader: Alfredo Stroessner
paralysis, patron saint of: Osmund
paranoid, a: "Someone who knows a little of what is going on" – William S.
    Burroughs
paranormal investigators: John Constantine (from the adult-orientated comic
    book), Fox William 'Spooky' Mulder (from *The X-Files*), James Randi, Dana
    Scully (from *The X-Files*)
paraplegics: Cristy Brown, Roald Dahl, Jacqueline du Pré, Michael Flanders, Larry
    Flynt, Dame Tanni Grey-Thompson, Stephen Hawking, Ron Kovik, Yitzhak
    Perlman, Christopher Reeve, Franklin D. Roosevelt, George Wallace, Robert
    Wyatt (singer)
parakeet, adjective: psittacine
parakeet, famous: Onan (companion to Dorothy Parker, so named because he kept
    spilling his seed)

parasites: candiru (Amazonian parasite that swims up a man's urine flow and lodges itself inside the penis), hookworm, leech, mistletoe, mosquito, ringworm, trypanosome

parasite, adjective: supercrescent

parasite, fear of: acarophobia

parasites, science of: parasitology

parent, murder of: parricide

parenthood, patron saint of: Rita of Cascia

Paris airport: Charles de Gaulle

Paris buildings: Eiffel Tower (wrought-iron tower built in 1889), Notre Dame cathedral (completed in 1330), Pompidou Centre, Sacré-Coeur basilica (completed in 1914)

Paris museum: Musée du Louvre

Paris nickname: City of Light, The Mother of New Orleans

Paris prisons: Bastille, La Santé

Paris riots: May 1968

Paris river: Seine

Paris thoroughfare: Champs Elysees

Paris university: Sorbonne

Paris, birthplace of: Isabelle Adjani, Charles Aznavour, Brigitte Bardot, Simone de Beauvoir, Jean-Paul Belmondo, Juliette Binoche, Georges Bizet, Maurice Chevalier, Jacques Chirac, Catherine Deneuve, Rudolf Diesel, Sacha Distel, Georges Feydeau (playwright), Jean Gabin, Paul Gaugin, Françoise Hardy, Isabelle Huppert, Édouard Manet, W. Somerset Maugham, Claude Monet, Edith Piaf, Roman Polanski, Marcel Proust, Jean Renoir, Auguste Rodin, Marquis de Sade, George Sand, Georges Seurat, Jacques Tati, François Truffaut, Maurice Utrillo, François Villon

Paris, fact: 10,000 Parisian women are actresses

Paris, patron saint of: Genevieve

Paris, red-light district: Place Pigalle

Parisian schoolgirl: Gigi

Parisian slum dweller: Gervaise (from Emile Zola's novel *L'Assommoir*)

parish churches in the Church of England, number of: 16,000

park shelter: gazebo

Parkinson's disease, famous sufferers: Mohammed Ali, Sir John Betjeman, Johnny Cash, Salvador Dalí, Michael J. Fox, Francisco Franco (Spanish dictator), Billy Graham (televangelist), Katharine Hepburn, Adolf Hitler, Pope John Paul, Pauline Kael (film critic), Deborah Kerr, Dudley Moore (suffered from the related disease of PSP), Kenneth More, Enoch Powell, Vincent Price, Michael Redgrave, Janet Reno (former US Secretary of Justice), Terry-Thomas, Pierre Elliott Trudeau (former prime minister of Canada), Margaret Bourke White (photojournalist)

parkours (or 'free runners'): David Belle, Sebastien Foucan

parliament, oldest in the world: Althing of Iceland

parrot: Polly, popinjay (archaic term)

parrot, adjective: arine (rare), psittacine

parrot, collective noun: company, flock, pandemonium

parrot, sound: talk

parrot, young: chick

parrots, famous: Captain Flint (from *Treasure Island*), Paulie (eponymous blue crown conure in the 1998 film), Polly, Polynesia (friend of Doctor Dolittle)

parrot fever: psittacosis

partridge, adjective: perdicine

partridge, collective noun: covey

partridge, young: cheeper

Partridge Family, The: highly popular but retrospectively kitsch ABC TV sitcom about a single mother and her children who form a rock 'n' roll band. Records of *The Partridge Family* sold in their millions, although only Shirley Jones and David Cassidy contributed to the vocals, along with hand-picked studio musicians

    broadcast: 25 September 1970–31 August 1974

    cast: Shirley Jones (Shirley Renfrew Partridge), David Cassidy (Keith Douglas Partridge), Susan Dey (Laurie Partridge), Danny Bonaduce (Jimmy Partridge), Jeremy Gelbwaks and Brian Forster (Chris Partridge), Suzanne Crough (Tracy Partridge), Dave Madden (Reuben Kincaid), Ricky Segall (Ricky Stevens), Alan Bursky (Alan)

party: bash, bender, binge, rage, rave, shindig, soiree

Parsifal: opera by Richard Wagner first produced in Bayreuth 26 July 1882

Passover, adjective: paschal

Passover festival: Pesach

Passover lamb: paschal lamb

Passover ritual: Seder

Passover wafer: matzo

past events, the act of dwelling upon: alethia

past vision (the act of seeing or finding oneself in a former time): retro cognition

pasta: agnolini, anolini, bavette, bigoli, bombolotti, bucati, bucatini, cannelloni, capelli d'angelo ('angel's hair'), capelletti, capellini, conchiglie, farfalle, fettucine, fusilli, laksa, lasagne, lingue di passero ('sparrows' tongues'), lumache, macaroni, maccheroni alla chitarra, maltagliati, noodles, orzo, penne, ravioli, rigatoni, rotolo, sedani, spaghetti, tagliatelli, tortellini, vermicelli

Pastoral Symphony: Beethoven's nickname for his *Symphony No. 6*, first performed in 1808

pastry: choux, Danish, filo, flaky, puff pastry, shortcrust

pasture, adjective: pascual

pathologist, collective noun: body

pathologists: Christiaan Eijkman, Gunther von Hagens, Dr Samantha Ryan (from TV's *The Silent Witness*), Kay Scarpetta (c/o Patricia Cornwell), August von Wassermann

patience: "Another word for doing nothing" - Alexander Ossipon in Joseph Conrad's *The Secret Agent*; "Beware the fury of a patient man" – John Dryden; "Patience is the virtue of the unadventurous" - Una Pope Hennessy

patient man: Job

patriarchs of Israel: Abraham, Isaac and Jacob

patriotism: "Patriotism is the conviction that this country is superior to all other countries because you were born in it" - George Bernard Shaw

patriots: Sir Roger Casement, Michael Collins, Éamon de Valera, Giuseppe Garibaldi, George Mason, Giuseppe Mazzini, Ignacy Paderewski, Paul Revere, Cola di Rienzo, Scanderbeg, Hannah Sheehy-Skeffington, William Tell, William Wallace, Ziaur Rahman

Patton (1970 film), famous line: George S. Patton (George C. Scott): "I want you to remember that no bastard ever won a war by dying for his country. He won it by making the other poor dumb bastard die for his country"

pawnbroker, slang: pop-shop
pawnbrokers: Harvey & Thompson (Britain's biggest), Albemarle & Bond (Britain's second biggest)
pawnbrokers, patron saint of: Nicholas
PBAB: Please Bring A Bottle
PDA: Public Display Of Affection, Public Display Of Anger
PDSA: People's Dispensary for Sick Animals
pea, adjective: leguminous, pisiform
peace, adjective: pacific
peace, goddess of: Irene (Greek mythology), Pax (Roman)
peace, home of: Shanti Nilaya (Sanskrit)
peace pipe: calumet
peace proposal: eirenicon
peach skin: epicarp, exocarp
peacock, adjective: pavonine
peacock, collective noun: muster, ostentation
peacock, female: hen, peahen
peacock, male: peacock
peacock, sound: scream
peacock, young: chick
peacock, the eye in the tail: ocellus (c/o Argus, a Greek giant with a hundred eyes)
peanut, fact: it is one of the ingredients of dynamite
peanut allergy, fact: from which seven people in the UK die each year and one in 200 are affected by
Peanuts characters (from the comic strip by Charles M. Schulz): Charlie Brown, Eudora, Franklin, Frieda, Linus van Pelt, Lucy van Pelt, Marcie, Patty, Peppermint Patty, Pigpen, Rerun van Pelt, Sally Brown, Schroeder, Shermy, Snoopy, Spike, Violet, Woodstock
pear, fact: throughout the world there are over 5,000 varieties of pear
pear cider: perry
pear varieties: Abbé, Anjou, Bartlett, Beurre, Clapp Favorite, Comice, Conference, Glou Morceau, Jargonelle, Josephine de Malines, Kaiser, Louise Bonne de Jersey, Olivier de Serres, Packham's Triumph, Passe crasanne, Seckel, Wardens, Williams, Winter Nelis
Pearl Harbor, attack on: 7 December, 1941; death toll: 2,400
pear-shaped: pyriform (as in "it's all gone pyriform")
pearl, substance of: nacre
pearl of high quality: orient
Pears' soap, slogan: 'Cleanliness is next to Godliness'
pebble-shaped: calciform
pedants: Holofernes (from *Love's Labour's Lost*), Lynne Truss
pedlar, collective noun: malapertness
peerage, book on: Debrett's Peerage of England, Scotland and Ireland (see)
Pekingese, collective noun: pomp
pelican, adjective: pelecanid
pelican, collective noun: raft (when on water), squadron (in flight)
pelican, famous: Nigel (from *Finding Nemo*)
pen: ballpoint, Bic, biro, felt-tip, fountain pen, Pentel, quill, roller pen, rollerblade, uni-ball
pen name, borrowed: allonym
pen names: Alain-Fournier (for Henri-Alban Fournier), Richard Allen (for James Moffat), Richard Bachman (for Stephen King), Boz (for Charles Dickens),

Anthony Burgess (for John Burgess Wilson), Lewis Carroll (for Charles
Dodgson), Colette (for Sidonie-Gabrielle Colette), Joseph Conrad (for Jozef
Korzeniowski), Marie Corelli (for Mary Mackay), Elia (for Charles Lamb),
George Eliot (for Mary Ann Evans), O. Henry (for William Sydney Porter),
Hergé (for Georges Prosper Remi), James Herriot (for James Alfred Wight),
Jeffrey Hudson (for Michael Crichton), Sophie Kinsella (for Madeleine
Wickham), John Lange (for Michael Crichton), John Le Carré (for David
Cornwell), Victoria Lucas (for Sylvia Plath), J.J. Marric (for John Creasey),
Molière (for Jean Baptiste Poquelin), George Orwell (for Eric Arthur Blair),
Phiz (for Hablot K. Browne), Ellery Queen (for Frederick Dannay and Manfred
Lee), Pauline Réage (Dominique Aury, author of *The Story of O*), Frank
Richards (for Charles Hamilton), A.N. Roquelaure (for Anne Rice), Saki
(for Hector Hugh Munro), George Sand (for Amandine Aurore Lucie Dupin),
Dr Seuss (for Theodor Seuss Geisel), Stendhal (for Henri Marie Beyle), Mark
Twain (for Samuel Clemens), Barbara Vine (for Ruth Rendell), Voltaire (for
François Marie Arouet)

pendulum, move like a: oscillate (verb)

penguin, collective noun: colony, parcel, rookery

penguin, habitat: rookery

penguin, sound: bleat

penguin, speed in water: 25 mph

penguin, young: chick

Penguin chocolate biscuit, slogan: 'P-P-P-Pick up a Penguin'

penguins, famous: Chilly Willy, Mumble (from *Happy Feet*), Pablo Penguin (c/o
Disney), The Penguin (from *Batman*), Peregrine (introduced on BBC TV's *For
the Children*), Pingu

penicillin: discovered by Dr Alexander Fleming in 1928

penis: "Something that's unattractive when limp and threatening when erect" –
anonymous; "The problem is God gives men a brain and a penis, but only
enough blood to run one at a time" - Robin Williams

penis: abraham, affair, agate (small), almond rock (CRS), bacon, bacon bazooka,
bald-headed hermit, baloney, banana, bazooka, beef truncheon, beeze, big
daddy, big rig, blow torch, bolt, bone phone, business, cannon, charley, chicken,
choad, cock, cockpit, crank, crow bar, cucumber, dick, dingus, dipstick,
divining rod, dong, donger (Australian), donkey dick (a large one), doodle
(Australian), dork, drill, drumstick, engine, father confessor, finger of love,
flapper, fuck muscle, German helmet, gigglestick (CRS), goober, gutstick,
hairy wheel (English slang from 1870 onwards), hammer, Hampton Wick, hand
tool, hardware, hickory, honk, horn, hose, Jack Hammer, jigger, Jim Dog, john,
Johnny, Johnson, John Thomas, joint (black slang), joint knob, joystick, kidney
wiper, knob, lingam (Hindi), little gentleman in a pink polo neck sweater, lob,
log, loom (archaic), love muscle, maleness, manhood, man-root, man Thomas,
member, the member for Cockshire, membrum virile, mickey (Irish slang),
middle leg, Mr Happy, nail, nimrod, 900-millimeter lens, one-eyed trouser
snake, pecker, pee-pee, pencil, pencil pipe, percy, pestle, Peter, phallus,
pikestaff, pile-driver, pintel, pintle, pisser, pistol, pizzle (of a large animal),
plonker, plow, plug, pole, poperine pear, pork sword, power tool, prick, pry bar,
pud, pump, ramrod, Rector of the Females, rod, root, Saint Peter, salami,
sausage, shaft, shank, sixteen ton jack, skin flute, slug, snake, the Solicitor
General, stick, stick shift, straight six engine, tadger, tail, tape measure, todger,
tubesteak, virga, weenie, willy, wooter, yang, yoyo, yutz (Yiddish)

penis, adjective: penile, phallic

penis, downward curve during arousal (a painful condition): chordee, phallocamposis

penis, notable curve during arousal: Pyronie's disease (or the Pyronie bend)

penis, plastic surgery of: balanoplasty

penis, removal of: penectomy, peotomy

penis amputee: John Wayne Bobbitt

penis chopper: Lorena Bobbitt

penis piercings: ampallang, apadravya, dolphin, dydoe, frenum, lorum, Prince Albert

Pennsylvania, 2nd state (1787), Keystone State

    capital: Harrisburg

    state bird: ruffed grouse

    state flower: mountain laurel

    state tree: hemlock

    motto: 'Virtue, liberty and independence'

    birthplace of: Maxwell Anderson (playwright), Samuel Barber, James Buchanan (15th US President), Daniel Boone, Bill Cosby, Richard Gere, Newt Gingrich, Alexander Haig, Edward Hicks, Gene Kelly, Grace Kelly, Jamie Kennedy (actor/comedian), Mario Lanza, Harry Longbaugh (aka the Sundance Kid), Jayne Mansfield, Tom Mix, Pink, Will Smith, Gertrude Stein, Sharon Stone, John Updike, Bobby Vinton, Andrew Wyeth

    tourist attractions: Independence Hall and National Historic Park (in Philadelphia), Philadelphia Museum of Art

    fact: the world's first oil well was drilled in Pennsylvania; the largest chocolate factory in the world is in the city of Hershey

Penthouse: adult magazine launched in 1969 by Bob Guccione

people: "You learn most about people not from the things they say but from the questions they ask" - Viv Groskop

people, aversion to: anthropophobia

peppers: ancho (mild), bell pepper, Californian (medium), chilli, chipotle (very hot), fresno (pretty hot), green pepper, guero (medium), hontaka (very hot), jalapeno (fairly hot), malagueta (very hot), mulato (hot), pasilla (pretty hot), pimiento (tame), piquin (very hot), poblano (mild), red pepper, serrano (ferociously hot), sweet pepper

percussion instruments: bass drum, bell lyra (a portable glockenspiel), bongos, campanella, carillon, castanets, Chinese crash cymbal, Chinese wood block, claves, cowbell, crescent, cymbal, drum, glockenspiel, gong, grelots, guiro, jingling Johnnie, kettledrum, maraca, marimba, mridanga, naker, roto toms, snare drum, steel drum, tablas, tambourine, tampon (double-headed drumstick designed to produce a drum roll), tam-tam, timpani, tom-toms, triangle, tubular bells, vibraphone, washboard, xylophone

percussionists: Dame Evelyn Glennie

    - see drummers

peregrine, male: tiercel

perforations along the side of old-fashioned computer paper: microperf

performance artists: Laurie Anderson, Chris Burden, Karen Finley, Gilbert (Proesch) and George (Passmore), Miranda July, Yves Klein, Yoko Ono, Annie Sprinkle, Survival Research Laboratories

perfume - see scent

perfumers, patron saints of: Mary Magdalene and Nicholas of Myra

period: Aunt Flo, the curse, menstruation, monthly, on the rag, Pride and Prejudice (period drama), that time of the month

Persia: former name for Iran (until 1935)

Persian king: Xerxes
Persian polymaths: Avicenna, Abū Rayhān al-Bīrūnī
Persian prophet: Zoroaster
Persian queens: Esther, Soraya
Persian Wars: 490–479 BC
persimmon: black sapote (Mexican), kaki (Japanese), velvet-apple (Filipino)
person, type of: airhead, anorak, big girl's blouse, bitch, bloke, chap, chick, dude,
	fart, fellow, fox, geek, geezer, girl, git, guy, harlot, hombre, individual, jock,
	John, lad, man, mate, party animal, party girl, sad-sack, sort, tosser,
	trainspotter, wanker, wildcat, wimp, woman
perspective: "The further backward you look, the further forward you can see" -
	Winston Churchill
perspective bender: Maurits Escher (artist)
perspiration: hidrosis
perspiration in excess: hyperhidrosis
Peru: republic in South America
	capital: Lima
	currency: nuevo sol
	language: Spanish, Quechua, Aymara
	religion: Roman Catholic
	fact: bus crashes are a national hazard, from which some 700 people die every year
Peru; guerrilla organisation: The Shining Path (Sendero Luminoso), with a
	membership estimated to be 200 armed militants
Peru; lost city of the Incas: Machu Picchu
Peruvian and famous: Carlos Castaneda (mystic), José Santos Chocano (poet),
	Juan Diego Flórez (opera singer), Mario Vargas Llosa (novelist), Ricardo Palma
	(writer), Yma Sumac (soprano), Mario Testino (photographer)
perversions: undinism
pessimism: "Smile. Tomorrow will be worse" - Woody Allen
pessimist: Jeremiah
pessimistic outlook: Weltschmerz
pet, genetically modified; first: tropical zebra fish (the glowing red variety)
pet, politically correct term: animal companion, household nonhuman animal
pet hates: accidentally dropping the loo roll down the pan, automated telephone
	services, funny mobile ring tones, junk mail, magazine inserts, misplaced
	modifiers, muzak, other people's burglar alarms, speed bumps, pedestrians
	who text, themed pubs, wasted time
pet name, adjective: hypocoristic
Peta: People for the Ethical Treatment of Animals
petal; adjective for having narrow petals: stenopetalous
Peter Grimes: opera by Benjamin Britten first produced in London on 7 June 1945
Petrograd: former name for St Petersburg (1914–1924)
petroleum jelly: petrolatum, Vaseline
petticoat, hooped: farthingale
PGA: parental guidance agreement
PGD: pre-implantation genetic diagnosis
pharaohs: Akhenaten, Cheops, Hatshepsut, Khufu, Rameses, Tutankhamen
pharmacists, patron saints of: Cosmas and Damian
pharmacologists: John Hughes, Otto Loewi
phat (hip-hop acronym for pussy, hips, ass, tits): excellent, fit, great, def, hot, sexy
pheasant, adjective: phasianid

pheasant, collective noun: bouquet, eye, nide, nye
pheasant, female: hen
pheasant, male: cock
pheasant, young: chick
Philadelphia, birthplace of: Ethel Barrymore, John Barrymore, Lionel Barrymore,
   Bill Cosby, Richard Gere, Alexander Haig, Grace Kelly, Mario Lanza, Will
   Smith, Robert Venturi (architect)
Philadelphia, fact: established by the Swedish in 1636; named Philadelphia in 1682
Philadelphia river: Delaware
philanthropist: bleeding heart, do-gooder, humanitarian
philanthropists: Thomas John Barnardo, Michael Bloomberg, Thomas Bray,
   Eli Broad (building tycoon), George Cadbury, Andrew Carnegie, Cedric the
   Entertainer (aka Cedric Kyles), Prince Charles, Leonard Cheshire, Esmond
   de Beer, Dorothea Dix, Jean Henri Dunant, George Eastman, Michael Eisner,
   Mark Firth, Henry Ford, Bill Gates, David Geffen, Bob Geldof, Sir J. Paul
   Getty, Sir Thomas Gresham, Armand Hammer, Edward Harkness, Phoebe
   Hearst, Frederick Hervey 4th Earl of Bristol, Sir Edmund Hillary, Chris Hohn,
   Robin Hood, Johns Hopkins, Sir Tom Hunter (who committed £1 billion of his
   company's money to charity), Mrs Jellyby (from Charles Dickens' *Bleak
   House*), Sir Elton John, Jeffrey Katzenberg, Kirk Kerkorian, Zell Kravinsky
   (who made $45 million on the stock exchange and gave it all to charity, then
   donated a kidney to save a complete stranger), Li Ka-shing, James Lick, Sir
   Edwin Manton, Sir Josiah Mason, Paul Mellon, Sir Moses Montefiore, Gordon
   Moore, Peter Moores (Littlewoods heir), J. P. Morgan, Alfred Nobel, James
   Oglethorpe, George Peabody, John Rockefeller, Joseph Rowntree, Haim Saban
   (TV mogul), Earl of Shaftesbury, Lawrence Sheriff, George Soros, Steven
   Spielberg, Leland Stanford, Henry Sugar (from Roald Dahl's *The Wonderful
   Story of Henry Sugar*), Ted Turner, George Weston, Dick Whittington, William
   Wilberforce, Oprah Winfrey
Philippines: republic in South-East Asia; officially known as the Republic of the
   Philippines
   capital: Manila
   currency: peso
   fact: divorce is still illegal
   language: Filipino, English
   religion: Roman Catholic
   native: Filipino
   famous Filipinos: Ferdinand Marcos, Imelda Marcos
philologists: Mark Abley, Alexander Ellis, Frederick Furnivall, Jacob and Wilhem
   Grimm, Francis March, Sir James Murray, Sir John Rhys (Celtic authority),
   J.R.R. Tolkien, Richard Trench, Michael Ventris, William Whitney, Joseph Wright
   - see lexicographers
philosophers: Peter Abelard, Theodor Adorno, Samuel Alexander, Louis Althusser,
   Saint Thomas Aquinas, Aristippus, Aristotle, Augustine of Hippo, J.L. Austin,
   Sir Alfred Ayer, Francis Bacon, Edmund Burke, Albert Camus, Rudolf Carnap,
   Noam Chomsky, Cleanthes, Arthur Collier, Confucius, Benedetto Croce, Gilles
   Deleuze, Jacques Derrida, René Descartes, John Dewey, Denis Diderot, Ralph
   Waldo Emerson, Empedocles, Friedrich Engels, Epicurus, Ludwig Andreas
   Feuerbach, Michel Foucault, Erich Fromm, Galileo Galilei, Kurt Gödel,
   Gotama, A.C. Grayling, Jürgen Habermas, Georg Hegel, Martin Heidegger,
   Robert Hooke, David Hume, Hypatia of Alexandria, Immanuel Kant, Søren

Kierkegaard, Julia Kristeva, Thomas Kuhn, Imre Lakatos, Laozi, Gottfried Leibniz, Bernard-Henri Lévy, John Locke, Jean-François Lyotard, Ernst Mach, Niccolò Machiavelli, Karl Marx, Mencius, Maurice Merleau-Ponty, John Stuart Mill, Ernest Nagel, Sir Isaac Newton, Friedrich Nietzsche, Robert Nozick, Robert M. Pirsig (author of *Zen and the Art of Motorcycle Maintenance*), Plato, Plutarch, Karl Popper, Proclus, Protagoras, Pythagoras, Willard van Orman Quine, John Rawls, Ernest Renan, Richard Rorty, Jean-Jacques Rousseau, Josiah Royce, Bertrand Russell, Gilbert Ryle, Jean-Paul Sartre, Friedrich Schelling, Arthur Schopenhauer, Albert Schweitzer, Lucius Annaeus Seneca, Shankaracharya, Peter Singer, Adam Smith, Socrates, Herbert Spencer, Thales (the first philosopher), Swami Vivekananda, James Ward, Simone Weil, Ludwig Wittgenstein, Xenophanes, Zeno of Citium, Zeno of Elea, Zhuangzi

philosophers, patron saints of: Albert the Great, Albertus Magnus and Catherine of Alexandria

Phiz: nickname for the illustrator Hablot Knight Browne

phonetician: Daniel Jones

photograph: anaglyph, autoradiograph, candid photo, close-up, daguerreotype, encephalogram (X-ray of the brain), ferrotype (old-fashioned), glossy, half-plate, hologram (three-dimensional), micrograph (produced by a microscope), microphotograph (a very small reproduction), monochrome, mugshot, panorama, photogram (archaic), photomicrograph (produced by a microscope), picture, pin-up, Polaroid, print, quarter-plate, shadowgraph, shot, snap, snapshot, tintype (old-fashioned), X-ray

photograph, first: taken by Joseph Nicéphore Nièpce in 1826 of his courtyard in Gras, France, featuring a pigeon-house, pear tree and barn

photographer: lenser, paparazzo, shutterbug, snapper

photographers: Berenice Abbott, Ansel Adams, Eddie Adams (specialising in pictures of war), Nobuyoshi Araki, Diane Arbus, Eve Arnold, Richard Avedon, David Bailey, Sir Cecil Beaton, Harry Benson (celebrity specialist), Guy Bourdin, Margaret Bourke-White, Bill Brandt, Gyula Brassaï, Julia Margaret Cameron, Henri Cartier-Bresson, Robert Capa, Dickey Chapelle (war photographer; real name: Georgette Louise Meyer), Larry Clark, Anton Corbijn, Nick Danziger, Robert Doisneau, Terence Donovan, Elliott Erwitt, Frederick Evans, Walker Evans, Bernard Faucon, Robert Frank, Nan Goldin, Fergus Greer, Philippe Halsman, David Hamilton, Frank Horvat, Yousuf Karsh, André Kertész, William Klein, Josef Koudelka, David LaChapelle, Dorothea Lange, Annie Leibovitz, Gemma Levine (leading British portrait photographer), David Levinthal, Alexander Liberman, Patrick Lichfield, O. Winston Link, Loretta Lux, Sally Mann, Robert Mapplethorpe, Mary Ellen Mark, Don McCullin (war photographer), Gideon Mendel, Duane Michals, Lee Miller (lover of Man Ray), Tina Modotti, Tracey Moffatt, László Moholy-Nagy, Lewis Morley, Arnold Newman, Helmut Newton, Paul Outerbridge, Norman Parkinson, Gordon Parks, Irving Penn, Jack Pierson, Man Ray, Leni Riefenstahl, Herb Ritts, Andres Serrano, Cindy Sherman, Sandy Skogland, Antony Snowdon, Koo Stark, Edward Steichen, Alfred Stieglitz, Frank Sutcliffe, Oliviero Toscani, Spencer Tunick (specialising in public urban nudes), Nick Ut (most famous photograph: 'Children fleeing an American napalm strike'), Julie Ward (murdered in a Kenyan game park), Andy Warhol, Albert Watson, Bruce Weber, Weegee (real name: Arthur Fellig), Edward Weston, Joel-Peter Witkin
- see war photographers

photographer, collective noun: phalanx

photography, pioneers of: Gerolamo Cardano, Louis Jacques Daguerre, Thomas
    Dallmayer, René Descartes, George Eastman (invented the roll of film and
    Kodak box camera), William Henry Fox-Talbot, Sir John Herschel (who coined
    the term 'photography'), Gabriel Lippmann, Joseph Nicéphore Nièpce (who
    took the very first photograph), Dr Johann Heinrich Schultz, H.D. Taylor
photography prize: Deutsche Börse
photojournalists: Margaret Bourke-White, Eugene Smith
phrase misconstrued: mondegreen
phrase newly coined: neologism
physicians: Dannie Abse, Elizabeth Garrett Anderson, Sir Frederick Banting,
    Josef Breuer, J.L.H. Down, Havelock Ellis, Galen, William Gilbert, Herophilus,
    Hippocrates, Oliver Holmes, Edward Jenner (who officially discovered
    vaccination), Leo Kanner, Carolus Linnaeus, John Macleod, Maria Montessori,
    Nostradamus (aka Michel de Notredame), Walter Reed, Peter Roget, John
    Snow, Andreas Vesalius
    - see doctors
physicists: Ernst Abbe, André-Marie Ampère, Anders Jonas Ångström, Sir Edward
    Appleton, Archimedes, Francis William Aston, Alexander Graham Bell, John
    Stewart Bell, Hans Bethe, Felix Bloch, Niels Bohr, Robert Boyle, Sir William
    Bragg, Louis-Victor Broglie, Sadi Carnot, Henry Cavendish, Sir James
    Chadwick, Jacques Charles, Georges Charpak, Sir John Cockcroft, Arthur
    Compton, Allan Cormack, Clyde Cowan, Francis Crick, Sir William Crookes,
    Marie Curie, Pierre Curie, Clinton Davisson, Peter Debye, Lee De Forest,
    Christian Doppler, Albert Einstein, Joseph F. Engelberger, Gabriel Daniel
    Fahrenheit, Michael Faraday, Enrico Fermi, Richard Feynman, William Fowler,
    Ilya Frank, Dennis Gabor, George Gamow, Murray Gell-Mann, William
    Gilbert, Donald Glaser, Michael Green, Stephen Hawking, Victor Francis Hess,
    James Hey, James Hillier, Robert Hooke, Frédéric Joliot-Curie, Irène Joliot-
    Curie, James Joule, William Thomson Kelvin, Willis Lamb, Sir Oliver Lodge,
    Fritz London, Heinz London, Hendrik Lorentz, Ernst Mach, Guglielmo
    Marconi, Bernd Matthias, Sir Isaac Newton, Wolfgang Pauli, Auguste Piccard,
    Max Planck, Cecil Frank Powell, Ilya Prigogine, John Rayleigh, John Ernest
    Rutherford, Sir Martin Ryle, Andrei Sakharov, John Schwarz, Thomas Seebeck,
    Edward Teller, Evangelista Torricelli, Charles Townes, John Tyndall, James Van
    Allen, Alessandro Volta, Steven Weinberg, Eugene Wigner, Charles Wilson,
    Chen Ning Yang, Yukawa Hideki, Pieter Zeeman
physics: aerodynamics, hydraulics, hydrodynamics, magnetism, mechanics,
    propulsion, velocity
physics, father of: Sir Isaac Newton
physiologists: Walter Cannon, Henry Dale, Herophilus, Walter Hess, John Macleod
physiotherapist: F. Matthias Alexander (who established the Alexander Technique)
pianists: Claudio Arrau, Vladimir Ashkenazy, Count Basie, Leonard Bernstein,
    Victor Borge, Alfred Brendel, Yefim Bronfman, Dave Brubeck, Alan Bush,
    Ray Charles, Frédéric Chopin, Cy Coleman, Russ Conway, Chick Corea,
    Johann Cramer, Karl Czerny, Fats Domino, Eddy Duchin, Georges Enesco, Bill
    Evans, Gil Evans, Walter Gieseking, Emil Gilels, Glenn Gould, Percy Grainger,
    Buddy Greco, Hélène Grimaud, Sir Charles Hallé, David Helfgott (played by
    Geoffrey Rush in *Shine*), Dame Myra Hess, Earl Hines, Josef Hofmann,
    Vladimir Horowitz, Dr John, Sir Elton John, Scott Joplin, Eileen Joyce, Alicia
    de Larrocha, Tom Lehrer, James Levine, Liberace, John Lill, Franz Liszt,
    Little Richard, Jay McShann, Thelonious Monk, Dudley Moore, Gerald Moore,

Bennie Moten, Guiomar Novaes, John Ogdon, Ignace Paderewski, Bud Powell, André Previn, Sergei Rachmaninoff, Maurice Ravel, Sviatoslav Richter, Anton Rubinstein, Artur Rubinstein, Camille Saint-Saëns, András Schiff, Artur Schnabel, Clara Schumann, Rudolf Serkin, Giovanni Sgambati, Nina Simone, Wladyslaw Szpilman, Art Tatum, Billy Taylor, Cecil Taylor, Dame Mitsuko Uchida, Fats Waller, Marguerite Wolff, Yanni (aka John Yanni Christopher)

piano: invented by Bartolomeo Cristofori in 1709

piano: apple and banana (CRS), baby grand, Bechstein, Blüthner, Bösendorfer (the Rolls Royce of pianos), Bösendorfer grand, concert grand, Fazioli, goanna (Australian slang), grand, honky-tonk, joanna (CRS), piano organ, pianoforte, pianola, player-piano, spinet, square piano, Steinway, transposing piano, upright

piano keys, number of: 88

piano music: bagatelle, ballade, boogie-woogie, five-finger exercise, honky-tonk, lied, nocturne, novelette, prelude, ragtime, sonata

piano parts: action, balance pin, capstan screw, case, damper, escapement, escapement lever, frame, hammer, jack, key, keyboard, lever, loud pedal, natural (a white key), pedal, soft pedal, soundboard, string plate, strings, whippen, wrest-block, wrest-plank, wrest-pin

piano playing: pianism

piano practice, someone who hates: misodoctakleidist

piano sound: arpeggio (an ascending and descending figuration of chords used in practise), mode, portamento, run

piano tuning key: wrest

Piccadilly Circus statue: Anteros, although commonly referred to as Eros, and less commonly as the Shaftesbury Memorial, or the Angel of Christian Charity. Anteros was the younger brother of Eros and his statue the first to be cast in aluminium

pickle relish: piccalilli

pickpockets: Artful Dodger (aka Master John Dawkins), Autolycus (from *The Winter's Tale*)

Pictures at an Exhibition: piano suite composed by Petrovich Mussorgsky in 1874

Piers Plowman: allegorical poem by William Langland written in alliterative verse and properly known as *The Vision of Piers Plowman*. Comprising 15,000 verses, the epic was written at some point in the fourteenth century

pig: "Dogs look up to us, cats look down on us and pigs look on us at equals" - Winston Churchill

pig: porker

pig, adjective: porcine

pig, British breeds: Berkshire, Cumberland, Essex, Gloucester Old Spots, Landrace, Large Black, Large White, Middle White, Saddleback, Tamworth, Welsh, Yorkshire

pig, collective noun: litter, herd, swine

pig, female: sow

pig, male: boar

pig, sound: grunt, squeak, squeal

pig, young: farrow, piglet, shoat, suckling

pig, fact: a pig's orgasm can allegedly lasts 30 minutes

pig, fact: wild pigs in Britain became extinct by the end of the 17th century

pig diarrhoea: scour

pig feet: trotters

pig food: hogwash, mast, swill, truffle

pig intestine (for cooking): chitterling
pig meat: bacon, ham, pork
pigs, famous: Arnold Ziffel (the smartest pig in Hooterville, from CBS TV's *Green Acres*), Babe, Butch and Sundance (the Tamworth Gingers that captured the media's attention when they escaped from a Wiltshire slaughterhouse in 1998), the Empress of Blandings (c/o P.G. Wodehouse), Hamm (from *Toy Story*), Miss Piggy, Napoleon (from *Animal Farm*), Olivia, Piglet (from *Winnie the Pooh*), Pinky and Perky (string puppets who first appeared in 1957 on BBC TV), Porky Pig (Warner Brothers' creation whose famous line was 'Th-th-th-th-that's all, folks'), St Anthony's pig, Snowball (from *Animal Farm*), the Three Little Pigs, Wilbur (from *Charlotte's Web*)
pigeon: capuchin, carrier pigeon, collared dove, dove, fantail, jacobin, ring-dove, rock-dove, roller, stock dove, tumbler pigeon, turtle dove, wood pigeon
pigeon, adjective: columbaceous, peristeronic
pigeon, collective noun: flight, flock
pigeon, famous: Valiant
pigeon, female: hen
pigeon, male: cock
pigeon, sound: coo
pigeon, young: squab, squeaker
pigeon-toed: varus
piles: haemorrhoids
pilgrim: haji, palmer
pilgrimage attractions: Lourdes, Mecca
pill – see drugs
pillars of wisdom – see Five Pillars of Wisdom
pilots: Buzz Aldrin, Douglas Bader, Biggles, William Bishop, George Bush, Dan Dare, John Travolta, Chuck Yeager
    - see fighter pilots
PIN: personal identification number
pin, split: cotter pin
pine forest: taiga
Pineapple Face: nickname for Manuel Noriego
pink eye: conjunctivitis
Pink Floyd: psychedelic rock group formed in London in 1965; comprised of Syd Barrett (vocals, lead guitar, songwriter; died: 7 July 2006), David Gilmour (guitar, vocals), Roger Waters (bass), Nick Mason (drums) and Richard Wright (keyboards; died: 15 September 2008). Formerly known as Pink Floyd Sound. Disbanded in 1995
pink ribbon: symbol of Breast Cancer Awareness
pins, fear of: blenophobia
pin-up girls: Christina Aguilera, Jessica Alba, Pamela Anderson, Ursula Andress, Theda Bara, Brigitte Bardot, Halle Berry, Clara Bow, Christie Brinkley, Louise Brooks, Gisele Bündchen, Naomi Campbell, Cindy Crawford, Marion Davies, Bo Derek, Angie Dickinson, Farrah Fawcett, Jane Fonda, Samantha Fox, Betty Grable, Deborah Harry, Cheryl Ladd, Veronica Lake, Hedy Lamarr, Lillie Langtry, Gypsy Rose Lee, Jennifer Lopez, Sophia Loren, Madonna, Jayne Mansfield, Marilyn Monroe, Bettie Page, Jane Russell, Claudia Schiffer, Jean Shrimpton, Jessica Simpson, Jaclyn Smith, Britney Spears, Dorothy Stratten, Cheryl Tiegs, Lana Turner, Raquel Welch, Mae West, Esther Williams, Fay Wray
pioneers: Jim Bowie, John Chapman (aka Johnny Appleseed)

pipe, for smoking: brier, calabash, calumet (peace pipe), chibouk (Turkish), clay pipe, corncob, cutty (short pipe), hookah (oriental), meerschaum, narghile (oriental), peace pipe

piped music, campaign against: Pipe Down

piper, collective noun: skirl

piper, famous: John D. Burgess

PIPPY: Person Inheriting Parents' Property (also called a Pippy)

pirates: Khaireddin Barbarossa (aka Redbeard), Uruz Barbarossa (Khaireddin's brother), Barbossa (played by Geoffrey Rush in *The Pirates of the Caribbean),* Black Bart (aka Bartholomew Roberts), Blackbeard (aka Edward Teach), Black Dog, Captain Peter Blood, Bloody Bill (from Ballantyne's *The Coral Island),* Billy Bones, Anne Bonny, Calico Jack (aka John Rackham), Cut-Throat Jake (as featured in *Captain Pugwash),* William Dampier, Captain Flint (*Treasure Island),* Captain Hook, Captain William Kidd, Jean Lafitte, Long John Silver, Sir Henry Morgan, Pew, the Pirate King (from *The Pirates of Penzance),* Captain Pugwash, Redbeard (aka Khaireddin Barbarossa), Bartholomew Roberts (aka Black Bart), Captain Jack Sparrow (played by Johnny Depp in *The Pirates of the Caribbean),* Edward Teach (aka Blackbeard), Thomas Tew

pirate flags: black flag, Jolly Roger, skull and crossbones

Pirates of Penzance, The: operetta by W.S. Gilbert and Arthur Sullivan, first produced in Paignton, Devon, in 1879

pitch (tar), adjective: piceous

Pittsburgh, birthplace of: Mary Cassatt, Erroll Garner, Jeff Goldblum, Martha Graham, Gene Kelly, Dan Marino (footballer), William Powell, David O. Selznick, Andy Warhol

Pittsburgh rivers: Allegheny, Monongahela and Ohio

pizza, birthplace of: Naples; first appearing around the year 1000

Pizza Face: nickname for Manuel Noriego

pizza ingredients: American sausage, anchovies, Balti chicken, barbeque chicken, barbeque sauce, black olives, chicken satay, Chinese chicken, crispy bacon, garlic sauce, green pepper, ham, jalapeno peppers, mushrooms, onion, pastrami, pepperoni, pineapple, prawns, red onion, red pepper, salami, smoky sausage, spicy beef, spicy pork, sweet & sour sauce, sweetcorn, tuna

places, fear of: topophobia

place name: toponym

place name, commonest in UK: 1) Newton; 2) Black Hill/Blackhill; 3) Mount Pleasant/Mountpleasant; 4) Castle Hill/Castlehill; 5) Wood Side/Woodside

place names, fictitious: Ambridge, Atlantis, Barchester, Bedrock, Brobdingnag, El Dorado, Elrond, Emerald City, Gondor, Lilliput, Narnia, Ruritania, Shangri-La (since adopted by a settlement in Tibet), Utopia, Wessex, Xanadu

place names, study of: toponymics, toponymy

place names of interest: Aberllynfi Three Cocks (Brecon Beacons), Bastad (Sweden), Beaver (Alaska, Kansas, Oklahoma, Oregon, Pennsylvania, Utah, Washington, West Virginia, Wisconsin), Bonar Bridge (Scottish Highlands), Brown Willy (Cornwall, England), Buggerru (Sardinia), Chinaman's Knob (Australia), Climax (Saskatchewan, Canada), Cockermouth (Cumbria), Cunter (Switzerland), Dildo (Newfoundland, Canada), Fucking (Austria), Fuku Island (Japan), Half Way Inn (Devon, England), Lickey End (Worcestershire, England), Little Dix Bay (West Indies), Pishill (Oxfordshire), Prickwillow (Cambridgeshire), Six Mile Bottom (Cambridgeshire), Titsey (Surrey), Tossor (Kyrgyzstan), Twatt (Orkney Islands, Shetland Islands), Ugley (Essex), Upper

Dicker (East Sussex), Upperthong (West Yorkshire), Wankie (Zimbabwe), Wetwang (East Riding of Yorkshire), Windpassing (Austria)

placebo: mind-body medicine, psychoneuroimmunology

plagiarism: "Copy from one, it's plagiarism; copy from two, it's research" - Wilson Mizner

plagues: Black Death (or bubonic plague) (killed 25 million people), Great Plague of 1665 (killed one in seven Londoners), Spanish Flu of 1918–19 (killed 40–70 million), White Death of 1992 (outbreak of tuberculosis in New York), measles (affected around 800,000 people, mostly children, in 1960s Britain), Ebola (identified in 1976, currently kills 80% of those infected), Aids (first identified in 1981)

plague, adjective: loimic

plane, famous: *The Spirit of St Louis*

plane, adjective: planar

plane crash, odds of being killed in: 1 in 1,000,000

plane crash, killed in: Aaliyah, Patsy Cline, Jim Croce, John Denver, Yuri Gagarin, Graham Hill, Buddy Holly, Leslie Howard, Lech Kaczyński (Polish president), John F. Kennedy Jr, Carole Lombard, Rocky Marciano, Glenn Miller, Grace Moore, Audie Murphy, Ricky Nelson, Wiley Post, Otis Redding, Will Rogers, Robert Smithson (American sculptor), Mike Todd (film producer), Ritchie Valens, John Walton, Orde Wingate

plane-spotters: in 2002, 12 British plane-spotters in Greece were jailed for six weeks, then acquitted on appeal after a year-long legal fight against convictions for spying

planet, adjective: planetary

planets, the eight major planets known to revolve around the Sun are (in order of increasing distance from it): Mercury, Venus, Earth, Mars, Jupiter, Saturn, Uranus and Neptune. Pluto was stripped of its planetary status on 24 August 2006 when members of the general assembly of the International Astronomical Union voted it out. For a while, there seemed to be twelve major planets revolving around the Sun (including Pluto, Ceres, Charon and 2003 UB313) before the shuffling of goalposts

plant, fastest growing in the world: bamboo

plant growing on another plant: epiphyte

plant stand or pot: jardinière

plant-eating: phytivorous

plants, dissection of: phytotomy

plants, largest family of: orchid (said to comprise as many as 22,000 species)

plants, science of: botany

Plantagenet king, first: Henry II

Plantagenet king, last: Richard III

plaque, blue: the first blue plaque was erected in 1867 to commemorate the birthplace of Lord Byron in Holles Street, London. The current plaque is now a 19 $\frac{1}{2}$ inch-diameter blue and white circle made from glazed earthenware (and its subject must have been dead for at least 20 years)

plates – see pottery

platinum: figure denoting 300,000 units of a single record sold or 600,000 units of an album sold (in the UK); figure denoting two million units of a single or album sold (in the US) - see gold

platypus, adjective: monotremal

play (as in playful), adjective: ludic

Playboy, first issue: December 1953

playboys: Warren Beatty, Oleg Cassini, Nick Charles, Errol Flynn, Hugh Hefner, Howard Hughes, Aly Kahn, John F. Kennedy Jr., Jack Nicholson, Stavros Niarchos (ship-owner), Aristotle Onassis, Roman Polanski, Porfirio Rubirosa, Gunther Sachs, Peter Stringfellow, Roger Vadim

Playboy centrefolds: Pamela Anderson, Kimberley Conrad (later Mrs Hugh Hefner), Erika Eleniak, Claudia Jennings, Jayne Mansfield, Jenny McCarthy, Patti McGuire (wife of tennis star Jimmy Connors), Marilyn Monroe, Cynthia Myers, Bettie Page, Anna Nicole Smith, Stella Stevens, Dorothy Stratten, Shannon Tweed, Victoria Vetri

Playboy pin-ups: Pamela Anderson, Ursula Andress, Brigitte Bardot, Kim Basinger, Barbi Benton, Barbara Carrera, Joan Collins, Bo Derek, Bambi Lin Finney (a Marine who was thrown out of the service after her photographs were published), Mariel Hemingway, Margot Kidder, Vikki La Motta, Jayne Mansfield, Victoria Principal, Anna Nicole Smith, Suzanne Sommers, Sharon Tate, Raquel Welch - see pin-up girls

playful: lusory

playing card, collective noun: hand, flush, suit, trick playwrights - see American playwrights, Australian playwrights, British playwrights, French playwrights, German playwrights, Irish playwrights, Italian playwrights, Russian playwrights

Pleasant Island: former name for the island republic of Nauru

please, new speak: puh-leeze

pleasure: "Most men pursue pleasure with such breathless haste that they hurry past it" – Søren Kierkegaard

pleasure, chemical released from the brain that produces a sense of happiness: serotonin

pleasure, fear of: hedonophobia

pleasure, god of: Bes (Egyptian)

pleasure, goddess of: Bastet (Egyptian)

pleasure, inability to experience: anhedonia

pleasure region of the brain: dorsal striatum

PLO leader: Yasser Arafat

plover, collective noun: congregation

Plum: nickname for P.G. Wodehouse

plum brandy: slivovitz

plumage: ptilosis

plumbers: Thomas Crapper (who invented the ballcock and, incidentally, the manhole cover), Cyril Hoskins (novelist also known as Lobsang Rampa), Luigi (from the video game *Super Mario Bros.*), Mario (from the video game *Super Mario Bros.*)

plume, as worn on a headress: aigrette

poem: acrostic, anacreontic, ballad, clerihew, eclogue, elegy, epic, epithalamium, epode, epyllion, haiku, idyll, limerick, nursery rhyme, ode, palinode, prothalamium, sestina, sonnet, tanka, triolet, tristich, villanelle, virelay

poem of three lines: tristich

poets: Gerrit Achterberg, Al Alvarez, Maya Angelou (the Clinton inaugural poet), Reinaldo Arenas, John Ashbery, W.H. Auden, Pam Ayres, Chaim Bialik, Charles Baudelaire, Hilaire Belloc, John Berryman, Sir John Betjeman, Elizabeth Bishop, William Blake, Alexander Blok, Bertolt Brecht, Joseph Brodsky, Rupert Brooke, Robert Browning, Charles Bukowski, Robert Burns,

Lord Byron, T.P. Cameron-Wilson, Giosuè Carducci, Lewis Carroll, Raymond
Carver, Willa Cather, Paul Celan, Geoffrey Chaucer, G.K. Chesterton, José
Santos Chocano, Sophus Claussen, Leonard Cohen, Samuel Taylor Coleridge,
Wendy Cope, Gregory Corso, Robert Creeley, e.e. cummings, Dante Alighieri,
Rubén Darío, Cecil Day-Lewis, Walter de la Mare, Sir John Denham, Emily
Dickinson, John Donne, Rita Dove (former US Poet Laureate), Michael
Drayton, John Dryden, Carol Ann Duffy, T.S. Eliot, Ralph Waldo Emerson,
Lawrence Ferlinghetti, Edward Fitzgerald, Robert Frost, Federico García Lorca,
John Gay, Allen Ginsberg, Lorna Goodison, Günter Grass, Robert Graves,
Thomas Gray, Joy Gresham, Thom Gunn, Peter Handke, Seamus Heaney, Sir
A.P. Herbert, Zbigniew Herbert, Robert Herrick, Geoffrey Hill, Homer, Thomas
Hood, Langston Hughes, Ted Hughes, Linton Kwesi Johnson (black reggae
poet), John Keats, Rudyard Kipling, Philip Larkin, Edward Lear, Vachel
Lindsay, Thomas Lodge, Henry Wadsworth Longfellow, Robert Lowell (at
the height of his career regarded as the greatest poet in the English language),
Sir David Lyndsay, Louis MacNeice, Christopher Marlowe, John Masefield,
Christopher Matthew, William McGonagall (known as the world's worst),
Roger McGough, Michelangelo Buonarroti, Spike Milligan, Czeslaw Milosz
(Polish Novel laureate), John Milton, Viggo Mortensen, Ogden Nash, Thomas
Nashe, Pablo Neruda, Charles Olson, Omar Khayyám, Ovid, Wilfred Owen,
Octavio Paz, Francesco Petrarca Petrarch, Sylvia Plath, Edgar Allan Poe,
Alexander Pope, Ezra Pound, John Pudney, Jean Racine, Sir Walter Raleigh,
Adrienne Rich, Arthur Rimbaud, Rainer Maria Rilke, Theodore Roethke,
Christina Rossetti, Dante Gabriel Rossetti, Sir Thomas Sackville, Vita
Sackville-West, Sappho, Siegfried Sassoon, Christian Schubart, Delmore
Schwartz, Vikram Seth, William Shakespeare, Percy Bysshe Shelley, Dame
Edith Sitwell, Stevie Smith, Solon, Sophocles, Sir Stephen Spender, Edmund
Spenser, Robert Louis Stevenson, Torquato Tasso, Thespis, Dylan Thomas, R.S.
Thomas (allegedly Britain's greatest living poet), John Updike, Paul Verlaine,
François Villon, Virgil, Edmund Waller, Walt Whitman, William Williams,
William Wordsworth, Sir Thomas Wyatt, W.B. Yeats, Xenophanes, Yevgeni
Yevtushenko, Benjamin Zephaniah
- see English poets, Greek poets, Roman poets, Russian poets, Scottish poets, etc
poet, undistinguished: poetaster
poetry: "Shorthand of the heart" – John Betjeman; "Imaginary gardens with real
toads in them" – Marianne Moore (American poet)
poetry, god of: Apollo (Greek and Roman), Bragi (Norse)
poetry, loathing of: metrophobia
poetry, muse of: Erato
Poets Laureate: John Dryden (1668–1688), Thomas Shadwell (1688–1692),
Nahum Tate (1692–1715), Nicholas Rowe (1715–1718), Laurence Eusden
(1718–1730), Colley Cibber (1730–1757), William Whitehead (1757–1785),
Thomas Wharton (1785–1790), Henry James Pye (1790–1813), Robert Southey
(1813–1843), William Wordsworth (1843–1850), Alfred, Lord Tennyson
(1850–1892), Alfred Austin (1896–1913), Robert Bridges (1913–1930), John
Masefield (1930–1967), Cecil Day-Lewis (1968–1972), Sir John Betjeman
(1972–1984), Ted Hughes (1984–1998), Sir Andrew Motion (1999–2009),
Carol Ann Duffy (from May 2009)
points, fear of: aichurophobia
pointillist: Georges Seurat

poison: aconitine, aflatoxin (a cancer agent), antimony, arsenic, blister gas, curare, neurotoxin, poison gas, poison ivy, poison oak, ricin, rodenticide, thallium, toxin, venom, warfarin

poison, adjective: toxic

poison, fear of: iophobia, toxiphobia

poison, science of: toxicology

poisoners: Barabas, Marie Besnard, Lucrezia Borgia (allegedly), Claudius, Mary Anne Cotton, Catherine Deshayes, Hamlet, Medea, Thomas Wainewright, Mary Wilson, Graham Young

poisonous snakes: thanatophidia

poker champions: Doyle Brunson, Amarillo Slim, Jennifer Tilly, Stuey 'The Kid' Ungar

poker player: Doc Holliday

Poland: republic in central Europe
    nickname: Land of the Plain-dwellers
    capital: Warsaw
    currency: zloty
    language: Polish (official), German
    patron saint: Casimir
    religion: Roman Catholic

polar bear, collective noun: pack

polar bear, young: cub

polar explorers: Tom Avery, Robert Peary, Robert Scott, Sir Ernest Shackleton

Polaroid camera: invented in 1947 by Edwin Land; launched in November of 1948

polecat, female: jill

police, adjective: constabulary

police, slang: bacon, blue meanies, Bobbies, boy scouts, boys in blue, cops, fuzz, peelers (after Sir Robert Peel, founder of the Metropolitan Police), pigs, Smokey, warbs (Elizabethan slang)
- see policeman

Police, The: UK rock group formed in London in 1977; comprised of Sting (vocals/bass; real name: Gordon Sumner), Stewart Copeland (drums) and Andy Summers (guitar). The Police officially disbanded in 1984 but have had several reunion concerts since then

police chiefs: Sir Ian Blair (Metropolitan Police), Bill Bratton (who introduced the concept of zero tolerance in New York), Sir Paul Condon (Metropolitan Police), Sir John Stevens (Metropolitan Police)

police codes, numerical: 10-0 (use caution), 14 (ambulance en route), 15 (citizen holding suspect), 18 (traffic incident), 19 (drunk), 20 (auto accident), 23 (traffic congestion), 29 (death), 30 (homicide), 34 (aggravated battery), 42 (aggravated rape), 43 (simple rape), 51b (bomb threat), 64 (armed robbery), 82 (prostitution), 93 (cruelty to juvenile), 94 (illegal use of weapon), 100 (hit-and-run), 148 (resisting arrest), 187 (homicide), 261 (rape), 390 (drunk), 1272 (an animal attack)

police detective, first: Eugène François Vidocq, 1812, head of the French Sûreté

police force, first: independent Paris body established in 1667

police informer: Eugène François Vidocq

police terms: bust, John Doe (an unidentified corpse), siege, stakeout, zero tolerance

policeman: bear (US), beck (old fashioned), bill, Bobby, chota (Latino slang), constable, cop, copper, detective, flatfoot, fuzz, grab (1950s' slang), peeler, peter jay (US black slang), pig, plod, sheriff, state trooper, 'tec, the Garda Siochana (Irish Republic police force)

policemen: Lavrenti Beria, Sir Ian Blair (Metropolitan Police Commissioner), PC Keith Blakelock (victim of the 1985 Broadwater Farm riot), Jimmy 'Popeye' Doyle (played by Gene Hackman in *The French Connection*), PC Steve Guscott (convicted for assault in 1994 after hitting a youth for disturbing pensioners by ringing their doorbells), Richard King (fined £150 for assaulting 19-year-old David Hobbs who had threatened to throw his baby out of a train window), Inspector Lestrade (c/o Arthur Conan Doyle), Sir John Stevens (former Metropolitan Police Commissioner)

policemen, children of: Binnie Barnes, Pope Benedict XVI, Edward Burns, Linda Lovelace, Roger Moore, Eddie Murphy, Queen Latifah

policemen, fictitious: Frank Bullitt, 'Dirty' Harry Callahan, Steve Carella (c/o Ed McBain), Inspector Jacques Clouseau, George Dixon (of Dock Green), Dogberry (from *Much Ado About Nothing*), Inspector Javert (from *Les Miserables*), Inspector Thomas Lynley, Jules Maigret (c/o Georges Simenon), Lieutenant Theo Kojak, Mr Plod
- see detectives

policewoman: Carol Shaya (New York policewoman fired for posing for Playboy)

policewoman, first: Alice Stebbins Wells, who joined the Los Angeles Police Department in 1910

policewomen, fictitious: Chris Cagney, Mary Beth Lacey

policewomen killed on duty in Britain: Alison Armitage, Sharon Beshenivsky, Angela Bradley, Yvonne Fletcher, Nina Mackay, Nisha Patel-Nasri (a special constable)

polio sufferers: Alan Alda (in childhood), Ben Bradlee (former editor of *The Washington Post*), Sir Arthur C. Clarke, Judy Collins, Francis Ford Coppola, Claudius (emperor of Rome), Mia Farrow, Michael Flanders, Joni Mitchell, Jack Nicklaus, J. Robert Oppenheimer, Itzhak Perlman, Franklin D. Roosevelt, Sir Walter Scott, Dinah Shore, Lord Snowden, Neil Young
- see paraplegics

Polish and famous: Sholem Asch (later a naturalised American), Marie Curie (later French), Frédéric Chopin, Joseph Conrad (later British), Nicolaus Copernicus, Felix Dzerzhinsky (police chief), Edward Gierek (politician), Samuel Goldwyn (film tycoon who later became American), Ignacy Jan Paderewski (pianist and prime minister), Wojciech Jaruzelski, Pope John Paul II, Tadeusz Kantor (theatre director), Krzysztof Kieslowski (filmmaker), Stanislaw Lem (writer), Daniel Libeskind, Pola Negri, Arthur Schopenhauer (Polish-born), Isaac Bashevis Singer (later American), Andrzej Wajda (filmmaker), Lech Walesa

Polish composers: Frédéric Chopin, Henryk Górecki, Witold Lutos awski, Ignacy Jan Paderewski, Carol Szymanowski

politeness: "Politeness is half good manners and half good lying" - Mary Wilson Little

political activists: Angela Davis, Charles Coughlin, Eugene Dennis, Bernardine Dohrn, Rudi Dutschke, Abbie Hoffman, George Jackson, Bertrand Russell, Jean-Paul Sartre, Benjamin Spock
- see activists

political advisors: Alastair Campbell, James Carville, John Dean, Walt Whitman Rostow, George Stephanopoulos

political commentators: William Buckley, Edmund Burke, Sir Robin Day, Robert Harris, Anthony Howard, Zhores Medvedev, Leonardo Sciascia, John Sergeant, Aleksandr Solzhenitsyn, Hugo Young

political philosophers: Herbert Hart, Karl Marx

political satirist: Art Buchwald

political theorists: Nikolai Bukharin, Edmund Burke, Eldridge Cleaver, Anthony Crosland, Régis Debray, Ronald Dworkin, Karl Marx, Juliet Mitchell, Jean-Jacques Rousseau, Léopold Senghor, Leo Strauss

political thinkers: Hannah Arendt, Raymond Aron, James Burnham, Frantz Fanon, Marcus Garvey, Aleksandr Herzen, Eric Hobsbawm, Henry Kissinger, Herbert Marcuse, Karl Marx, Michael Oakeshott, E.P. Thompson, Alexis de Tocqueville

politician: "A statesman who approaches every question with an open mouth" – Adlai Stevenson

politicians: "Politicians and diapers have one thing in common: They should both be changed regularly and for the same reason" - anonymous

politicians as novelist: Sir Norman Angell, Jeffrey Archer, Winston Churchill (who penned one novel, *Savrola*), Edwina Currie, Benjamin Disraeli (who was awarded the biggest financial advance in the 19th century), Iain Duncan Smith, Gary Hart, Roy Hattersley, Douglas Hurd, Andre Malraux, Chris Mullin, Ann Widdecombe

politics: "Politics is the art of looking for trouble, finding it whether it exists or not, diagnosing it incorrectly, and applying the wrong remedy" - publisher Ernest Benn; "Politics is showbiz for ugly people" - Christopher Buckley, *National Review*; "A promising young man should go into politics so that he can go on promising for the rest of his life" - Robert Byrne; "Politics is the accomplishment of what would have happened anyway" - Hans Magnus Enzensberger

pollster: George Horace Gallup

pollution, fact: one quarter of the world's greenhouse gas emissions are produced by the United States

pollution, types: Asian Brown Haze (a cloud two miles thick, extending over Asia and the India Ocean and which can travel halfway round the world in a week, cutting off 15% of the world's sunlight and causing up to 40,000 premature deaths a year); global warming (see); greenhouse effect

polo player: Adolfo Cambiaso

polo session: chukka

polo stick: hammer

Poltergeist (1982 film), famous line: Carol Anne Freeling (Heather O'Rourke): "They're he-e-e-e-re!"

polygamist: Fela Kuti

polyglots: Alexander Arguelles, Cleopatra, James Joyce, Mary Queen of Scots, J.R.R. Tolkien

polymaths, famous: Aristotle, Archimedes, Stephen Fry, Fred Housego, Johann Goethe

Polynesian god of sea monsters: Paikea

Pompeii, destruction of (by the eruption of Mount Vesuvius): 79 AD

pool (of the aquatic variety), adjective: lacuscular

pool player: Minnesota Fats (from the 1961 film *The Hustler*)

Pools winner: Viv Nicholson, who won £150,000 in 1961 (motto: "spend, spend, spend")

poorest country in the world: Sierra Leone, followed by Niger

pop artists: Peter Blake, Christo, David Hockney, Richard Hamilton, Keith Haring, Jasper Johns, Allen Jones, Roy Lichtenstein, Marco, Lisa Milroy, Claes

Oldenburg, Sir Eduardo Paolozzi, Gerhard Richter, Bridget Riley, Ed Ruscha, Andy Warhol

pop group, first: The Bluecaps, a Nashville quintet whose first recordings – *Be-Bop-a-Lula* and *Woman Love* – were released in June of 1956 by Capitol Records

Pop Idol **judge:** Simon Cowell

pop impresarios: Simon Fuller (the man behind The Spice Girls, S Club 7, TV's *Pop Idol*, etc), Jonathan King, Malcolm McLaren, Andrew Loog Oldham (the man behind The Rolling Stones, The Righteous Brothers, Marianne Faithfull, etc), Larry Parnes, Phil Spector, Tony Wilson

pop programmes on TV: *CD: UK; The Dick Clark Show; Disco 2; The Ed Sullivan Show; Hit Parade; Juke Box Jury; Later...With Jules Holland; The Old Grey Whistle Test; Pop World; Ready, Steady, Go!; Rock Goes to College; The Smash Hits Chart; So It Goes; Soul Train; Thank Your Lucky Stars; Top of the Pops; The Tube; Unplugged; The Word*

Pope: SP, Summus Pontifex (Latin), Supreme Pontiff

pope, adjective: papal, pontifical

pope, ambassador of: nuncio

pope, English: Adrian IV (originally Nicolas Breakspear), 1100–1159

Pope Benedict XVI: the 265th Pope since St Peter (real name: Joseph Ratzinger)

Pope John Paul II: the 264th Pope since St Peter (real name: Karol Jozef Wojtyla)

population, fact: the world's most populous city is Mumbai (Bombay); the world's most populous urban area is Tokyo–Yokohama

population, world: 6.7 billion

population, United Kingdom: 61.8 million

pop video, first: The Beatles' *I Feel Fine*, made in 1966

porcelain: Arita, celadon, china, Crown Derby, Dresden china, eggshell, *famille*, hard-paste, imari, ko, Limoges, mandarin, Meissen, Ming, Minton, Satsuma, Sèvres, Spode, Royal Worcester

porcelain, glazed and decorated: faience

porcupine, collective noun: prickle

porn, purveyors of: Danni Ashe, Nic Cramer, Gerard Damiano, Richard Desmond, Ben Dover, Larry Flynt, David Friedman, Al Goldstein (publisher of *Screw* magazine), Bob Guccione, Hugh Hefner, Steve Hirsch, Jenny Jameson, Radley Metzger, Russ Meyer, Harry H. Novak, Bill Osco, Charles Prast, Paul Raymond, Jim South, David Sullivan, Carlos Tobalina, Chuck Traynor

porn films, ground-breaking: *Behind the Green Door* (1972), *Deep Throat* (1972), *The Devil in Miss Jones* (1973), *Caligula* (1979) - see sex films, ground-breaking

porno chic: term coined by Vincent Canby, critic for *The New York Times*

porn stars: Peter Berlin, Marilyn Chambers, 'La Cicciolina' (aka Ilona Staller), Veronica Hart, John C. Holmes (aka Johnny Wadd), Darren James (diagnosed with HIV in 2004), Jenna Jameson, Ron Jeremy, Traci Lords, Linda Lovelace (born Linda Boreman), Gina Lynn, Kitten Natividad, Peter North ('the Loadmaster'), Harry Reems, Seka, Serenity, Rocco Siffredi, Georgina Spelvin, Annie Sprinkle, Lexington Steele

porpoise, adjective: delphine

porpoise, collective noun: herd, pod, turmoil

porridge, adjective: pultaceous

Porto Rico: former name for Puerto Rico (until 1932)

portrait painters: Andrea del Sarto, Sofonisba Anguissola, Pietro Annigoni, Robert Beckett, Gentile Bellini, India Jane Birley, Sandro Botticelli, Agnolo Bronzino, Karl Bryullov, Judy Cassab, George Catlin, Philippe de Champaigne, Giorgio de Chirico, Jean Clouet, John Singleton Copley, Jean-Baptiste-Camille Corot, Imogen Cunningham, Jacques-Louis David, Sir William Dobell, Sir Anthony van Dyck, Robert Feke, Thomas Gainsborough, Frans Hals, Nicholas Hilliard, Hans Holbein (the Younger), John Hoppner, Jean Auguste Dominique Ingres, Augustus John, Marie-Claire Kerr, Sir Godfrey Kneller, Oskar Kokoschka, Wyndham Lewis, Hans Memling, Howard Morgan, Bryan Organ, Sir William Orpen, Charles Willson Peale, Jean Baptiste Perronneau, Sir Henry Raeburn, Rembrandt Harmenszoon van Rijn, Pierre-Auguste Renoir, Sir Joshua Reynolds, Hyacinthe Rigaud, George Romney, John Singer Sargent, Melissa Scott-Miller, Gilbert Stuart, Thomas Sully, Graham Sutherland, Daphne Todd, Cosimo Tura, Diego Velázquez, Élisabeth Vigée-Lebrun, George Frederic Watts, Benjamin West, Antony Williams (whose 1996 painting of the Queen caused considerable controversy), Joseph Wright of Derby, Anders Leonhard Zorn

Portugal: republic in south-west Europe
  capital: Lisbon
  currency: euro; formerly: escudo
  language: Portuguese
  religion: Roman Catholic

Portuguese and famous: Joaquim de Almeida (actor), António Lobo Antunes (writer), Marcelo Caetano (politician), Luis de Camoëns (poet), José Maria de Eça de Queiros (novelist), Silva Ferreira da Eusebio (footballer), Luis Figo (footballer), Vasco da Gama (explorer), Ferdinand Magellan (explorer), Mariza (fado singer born in Mozambique), Maria de Medeiros (actress and filmmaker), Carmen Miranda (actress and singer born near Lisbon but raised in Rio de Janeiro), José Mourinho (football manager), Eduardo Souto de Moura (architect), Carlos de Oliveira (writer), Manoel de Oliveira (filmmaker), Fernando Pessoa (poet), Marquês de Pombal (statesman), Dame Paula Rego (painter), Amália Rodrigues (fado singer), Cristiano Ronaldo (footballer), António de Oliveira Salazar (dictator), José Saramago (writer), Álvaro Siza Vieira (architect), Mário Soares (statesman), Gil Vicente (playwright)

Portuguese colonies: East Timor, Goa, Macau, Mozambique

Portuguese Timor: former name for East Timor, the Democratic Republic of Timor-Leste (from 1596 to 1975)

possessive determiners: her, his, its, my, our, their, your

possessive pronouns: hers, his, its, mine, ours, theirs, yours

postage stamp: invented by Sir Rowland Hill in 1840

postage stamps, sheet of: pane

postcard, saucy seaside; creator of: Donald Gill

postcard collector: deltiologist

post-impressionist painters: Pierre Bonnard, Paul Cézanne, Paul Gauguin, Camille Pissarro, Henri Rousseau, Georges Seurat, Henri de Toulouse-Lautrec, Vincent Van Goch, Édouard Vuillard

postman: Postman Pat

potato: aloo, murph, murphy, Spanish waiter (CRS), spud, tater, tatur

potato, fact: a vegetable member of the nightshade family

potato, introducer of: erroneously attributed to Sir Walter Raleigh, the potato was introduced to Europe – from its home in South America – by an anonymous Spaniard

potato, types of: anya, Arran Pilot, Craig Royal red, Cyprus new potato, Desiree, Duke of York, golden wonder, Home Guard, Kerr's Pink, King Edward, kumara, Majestic, Maris Piper, mashed, new potato, Pentland Crown, Pentland Dell, Pentland Hawk, Pentland Dell, Pentland Squire, pratie, Ratte, Red Craig's Royal, Red King, Redskin, Russet Burbank, Shepody, Smash, sweet potato, yam

potato fork: graip

potato promoter: Antoine Parmentier (who convinced Louis XVI of the tuber's nutrional value)

potato stalk: haulm

potency pills: Cialis (which allows men to achieve an erection up to 24 hours after ingestion), Viagra

Potsdam Conference: 17 July to 2 August 1945 (attended by Joseph Stalin, Winston Churchill and Harry S. Truman - and later by Clement Attlee)

potters: Alan Caiger-Smith, Michael Cardew, Clarice Cliff, Hans Coper, Hamada Shoji, Bernard Leach, Thomas Minton, William Murray, Kathleen Pleydell-Bouverie, Dame Lucie Rie, Josiah Spode, William Taylor, Josiah Wedgwood

potter, adjective: ceramean

pottery: delft, English Delftware, Jasperware, Minton Ware, Portmeirion, Royal Doulton, Spode, Wedgwood

pottery, adjective: ceramic, fictile

pound sterling: banana (Australian), quid

pout: moue

poverty, fear of: peniaphobia

PR gurus: Alastair Campbell, Max Clifford, Lynne Franks

practical jokers – see pranksters

Prague, birthplace of: Rudolf Friml (composer and pianist), Václav Havel, Franz Kafka, Martina Navratilova, Rainer Maria Rilke, Prince Rupert

Prague opera house: National Theatre

Prague square: Wenceslas Square

Prague river: Vltava

praising others, the practice of (in the hope of making them happy): macarism

pranksters: Banksy, Pierre Brassard (Canadian disc jockey who quizzed the British Queen on the radio), George Clooney, Noel Edmonds, Sir John Falstaff, Dom Joly, Paul Krassner, Ashton Kutcher, Loki, Chris Morris

prawn: Dublin Bay prawn, king prawn, nipper, Norway lobster, yabby

prayer book: missal

prayer summons: adhan

preacher, collective noun: converting

preachers: Omar Bakri Mohammed (banned from Britain in August of 2005), Henry Beecher, John Bunyan, Jesus Christ, Marjoe Gortner, Billy Graham, Benny Hinn, Jesse Jackson, John the Baptist, Jim Jones, Martin Luther King, David Lloyd-Jones, Ian Paisley, Billy Sunday
- see evangelists

preachers, patron saint of: John Chrysostom

preaching, adjective: homiletic, kerygmatic, pulpitarian

preaching, study of: homiletics

precipices, fear of: cremnophobia

precipitation, continent with least: Antarctica

predatory animal, adjective: raptorial

prefabricated bands: All Angels, Boyzone, The Monkees, S Club 7, Spice Girls

pregnancy: cyesis

pregnancy, adjective: antenatal
pregnancy, fear of: maieusiophobia
pregnancy, study of: cyesiology
pregnancy line (the dark vertical line on the distended abdomen): linea nigra
pregnancy occurring outside the womb: ectopic pregnancy
pregnant: enceinte (archaic), expecting, gravid, in the family way, knocked up, with a bun in the oven
pregnant women, lust for: cyesolagnia
prehistorian: Vere Gordon Childe
prehistoric organisms, ecology of: palaeoecology
premature ejaculation: tachorgasmia
Pre-Raphaelite painters: Ford Madox Brown, Sir Edward Burne-Jones, Arthur Hughes, William Holman Hunt, Sir John Everett Millais, Dante Gabriel Rosetti, John William Waterhouse
Presbyterian: anagram for "best in prayer"
presents, the compulsive urge to give: doromania
president: "When I was a boy I was told that anybody could become president. I'm beginning to believe it" – Clarence Darrow
President: chief executive, commander in chief
Presidents of the United States: 1. George Washington (1789–1797); 2. John Adams (1797–1801); 3. Thomas Jefferson (1801–1809); 4. James Madison (1809–1817); 5. James Monroe (1817–1825); 6. John Quincy Adams (1825–1829); 7. Andrew Jackson (1829–1837); 8. Martin Van Buren (1837–1841); 9. William Henry Harrison (1841); 10. John Tyler (1841–1845); 11. James Polk (1845–1849); 12. Zachary Taylor (1849–1850); 13. Millard Fillmore (1850–1853); 14. Franklin Pierce (1853–1857); 15. James Buchanan (1857–1861); 16. Abraham Lincoln (1861–1865 - assassinated); 17. Andrew Johnson (1865–1869); 18. Ulysses S. Grant (1869–1877); 19. Rutherford B. Hayes (1877–1881); 20. James Garfield (1881 - assassinated); 21. Chester Alan Arthur (1881–1885); 22. Grover Cleveland (1885–1889); 23. Benjamin Harrison (1889–1893); 24. Grover Cleveland (1893–1897); 25. William McKinley (1897–1901 - assassinated); 26. Theodore Roosevelt (1901–1909); 27. William H. Taft (1909–1913); 28. Woodrow Wilson (1913–1921); 29. Warren G. Harding (1921–1923); 30. Calvin Coolidge (1923–1929); 31. Herbert Hoover (1929–1933); 32. Franklin D. Roosevelt (1933–1945); 33. Harry S. Truman (1945–1953); 34. Dwight D. Eisenhower (1953–1961); 35. John F. Kennedy (1961–1963 - assassinated); 36. Lyndon B. Johnson (1963–1969); 37. Richard M. Nixon (1969–1974); 38. Gerald Ford (1974–1977); 39. Jimmy Carter (1977–1981); 40. Ronald Reagan (1981–1989); 41. George Bush (1989–1993); 42. Bill Clinton (1993–2001); 43. George W(alker) Bush (2001–2009); 44. Barack Obama (2009–
press: media, paparazzi, stalkerazzi
press barons – see media tycoons, newspaper tycoons, publishers
pressure, measurement of: tasimetry
Pret A Manger founders: Jeremy Metcalfe and Sinclair Beecham
pretence: "We are what we pretend to be, so we must be careful what we pretend to be" - Kurt Vonnegut Jr
prickly: lappaceous
priest, adjective: clerical, hieratic, sacerdotal
priest's assistant: curate
priest's cap: biretta (Roman Catholic)

priests: Aaron (Old Testament), David Beaton, St Thomas à Becket, Henry Beecher, George Berkeley, John Bunyan, Don Camillo (see), Edmund Cartwright (also invented the power loom), Giacomo Casanova, Father Ted Crilly (played by Dermot Morgan in TV's *Father Ted*), Eli (of Shiloh), Ezra (Old Testament), Dimitri Gallitzin, Geraldine Granger (played by Dawn French in TV's *The Vicar of Dibley*), Reverend Al Green, Imhotep (high priest of Ptah), William Ralph Inge, John Keble, Martin Luther King, Father Merrin (played by Max Von Sydow in *The Exorcist*), John Newton, Rev. Mervyn Noote (played by Derek Nimmo in TV's *All Gas and Gaiters*), Titus Oates, Sinéad O'Connor (ordained in 1999), Desmond Tutu, Chad Varah, Edward Young

priests, directory of: Crockford's Clerical Directory

priests, fear of: hierophobia

prime ministers, British: Sir Robert Walpole (1721–1742); Earl of Wilmington (1742–1743); Henry Pelham (1743–1754); Duke of Newcastle (1754–1756); Duke of Devonshire (1756–1757); Duke of Newcastle (1757–1760; 1760–1762); Earl of Bute (1762–1763); George Grenville (1763–1765); Marquis of Rockingham (1766); Earl of Chatham (1766–1768); Duke of Grafton (1766–1769); Lord North (1770–1782); Marquis of Rockingham (1782); Earl of Shelburne (1782–1783); Duke of Portland (1783); William Pitt (1783–1801); Viscount Sidmouth (1801–1804); William Pitt (1804–1806); Lord Grenville (1806–1807); Duke of Portland (1807–1809); Spencer Perceval (1809–1812 - assassinated); Earl of Liverpool (1812–1827); George Canning (1827); Viscount Goderich (1827); Duke of Wellington (1827–1830); Earl Grey (1830–1834); Viscount Melbourne (1834); Sir Robert Peel (1834–1835); Viscount Melbourne (1835–1837); Viscount Melbourne (1837–1841); Sir Robert Peel (1841–1846); Lord John Russell (1846–1852); Earl of Derby (1852); Earl of Aberdeen (1852–1855); Viscount Palmerston (1855–1858); Earl of Derby (1858–1859); Viscount Palmerston (1859–1865); Earl Russell (1865–1866); Earl of Derby (1866–1868); Benjamin Disraeli (1868); William Gladstone (1868–1874); Benjamin Disraeli (1874–1880); William Gladstone (1880–1885); Marquis of Salisbury (1885–1886); William Gladstone (1886); Marquis of Salisbury (1886–1892); William Gladstone (1892–1894); Earl of Rosebery (1894–1895); Marquis of Salisbury (1895–1901); Marquis of Salisbury (1901–1902); Arthur J. Balfour (1902–1905); Sir Henry Campbell-Bannerman (1905–1908); Herbert Asquith (1908–1916); David Lloyd George (1916–1922); Andrew Bonar Law (1922–1923); Stanley Baldwin (1923–1924); James Ramsay MacDonald (1924); Stanley Baldwin (1924–1929); James Ramsay MacDonald (1929–1935); Stanley Baldwin (1935–1937); Neville Chamberlain (1937–1939); Winston Churchill (1940–1945); Clement Attlee (1945–1951); Sir Winston Churchill (1951–1955); Anthony Eden (1955–1957); Harold Macmillan (1957–1963); Sir Alec Douglas-Home (1963–1964); Harold Wilson (1964–1970); Edward Heath (1970–1974); Harold Wilson (1974–1976); James Callaghan (1976–1979); Margaret Thatcher (1979–1990); Sir John Major (1990–1997); Tony Blair (1997–07); Gordon Brown (2007–2010), David Cameron (2010–)

prime minister, youngest in Britain: William Pitt the Younger (in office 19 December 1783, aged 24 – 14 March 1801 and then again 10 May 1804 – 23 January 1806)

prime number, largest: 213,466,917–1

Prime Suspect: critically esteemed, award-winning TV drama featuring the hard-nosed police inspector Jane Tennison who not only solves grisly murder cases but fights sex discrimination within her own ranks. Following the enormously

popular first, four-hour edition, the show was followed by *Prime Suspects* 2,3,4,5,6 and *The Final Act*
created by Lynda La Plante
broadcast: 7 April 1991–15 October 2006 on Granada TV
cast: Helen Mirren (Det. Supt. Jane Tennison), John Benfield (Supt. Mike Kernan)
primitive painters: Edward Hicks, Henri Rousseau
princess, Australian: Mary Donaldson (a former estate agent from Hobart) aka Her Royal Highness Crown Princess Mary Elizabeth
Princess Consort: Camilla Parker Bowles
printers: John Baskerville, William Caxton, Étienne Dolet, Johannes Gutenberg
printing blur/smudge: mackle (noun)
printing press: (probably) devised in 1423 in Germany, by Johannes Gutenberg
printmakers: Thomas Bewick, Patrick Caulfield, Frank Stella
prison: bagnio (Oriental), bastille, big house, bird, bridewell, calaboose, can, choky (Anglo-Indian), clink, clinkerum, freezer, gib, gladiator school, glasshouse (military), gow, gulag, hoosegow, joint, limbo, municipal farm, pen, pokey, skookum house (Canadian), slammer, statesville, stir, stockade (military)
prison, adjective: custodial
prison, first female governor of an all-male maximum security British facility: Hilary Banks
prison, Iraqi: Abu Ghraib
prison camp: Guantanamo Bay
prison camp, German: stalag
prison management, study of: penology
prisoners, patron saint of: Dismas and Joseph Cafasso
prisons, demolished (or destroyed): Bastille (Paris), The Fleet (London), Marshalsea (London), Newgate (London), Spandau (Berlin)
prisons, London: Belmarsh, Brixton, Feltham, Holloway, Latchmere House, Pentonville, Wandsworth, Wormwood Scrubbs
prisons, UK: Broadmoor, Everthorpe (North Humberside), Parkhurst (Isle of Wight), Strangeways, Winson Green (Birmingham)
prisons, USA: Alcatraz (closed in 1963), Attica, Auburn, Folsom, San Quentin, Sing Sing, Supermax (The Administrative Maximum Facility of the Florence Correctional Institution, in Colorado), The Tombs
prisons, USA; state with largest prison population: California
Prisoner, The: weird, cutting-edge British TV series featuring Patrick McGoohan as the enigmatic Number Six, an ex-secret agent who is imprisoned in a Welsh village in order for his secrets to be wormed out of him. In spite of running for only seventeen episodes the show gained a huge cult following
broadcast: 29 September 1967–4 February 1968
created by George Markstein and Patrick McGoohan
cast: Patrick McGoohan (The Prisoner/Number Six), Angelo Muscat (the butler), Peter Swanwick (supervisor), Christopher Benjamin (Number Two's assistant), Alexis Kanner (Number Forty-Eight), Leo McKern (Number Two)
prisoner, collective noun: pity
prisoners, famous – see jailed and famous
prisoners, patron saints of: Dismas and Joseph Cafasso
private detective, first: François Vidocq
Private Eye: satirical magazine founded in 1962 by Peter Cook and Willie Rushton
private eyes: Lew Archer, Mike Hammer, Lew Harper (played by Paul Newman on screen), Barnaby Jones, Philip Marlowe, Jim Rockford (from TV's *The Rockford Files*), Sam Spade
- see detectives, etc

professors: Cuthbert Calculus (from the Tintin comic books), Henry Higgins (from *Pygmalion* and *My Fair Lady*), Robert Langdon (from *The Da Vinci Code*)

programming language: Visual Basic (Microsoft)

progress: "Progress would be wonderful if only it would stop" - Robert Musil

prolific: philoprogenitive

promiscuous (of a woman): horizontally accessible (PC)

promiscuous woman (especially an ugly one): munta (modern slang)

promiscuous women, famous: Sarah Bernhardt, Catherine the Great, Valeria Messalina
 - see prostitutes and women of ill repute

pronunciation, poor: cacology

pronunciation, study of: ortheopy

property tycoons: Steve Bing, Sean Mulryan, Donald Trump

prophecy: "The art of prophecy is very difficult, especially with respect to the future" – Mark Twain

prophecy, adjective: mantic, vatical

prophecy, god of: Apollo (Greek and Roman)

prophesy: hariolate (verb)

prophet, murder of: vaticide

prophets: Amos, Balaam, Cassandra (but nobody believed her), Deborah, Eli, Elijah, Elisha, Ezekiel, Habakkuk, Haggai, Hosea, Isaiah, Jeremiah, Job, John the Baptist, Jonah, Mani, Micah, Mohammed, Mormon, Moses, Nathan, Nostradamus (aka Michel de Notredame), Obadiah, sibyl, Solomon, Tiresias, Zarathustra, Zoroaster

prostate cancer, fact: in the United Kingdom, seventy per cent of men over seventy develop prostate cancer

prostitute: academician (18th century slang), alley cat, arse peddler, bangster, call girl, chicken rancher, compensated dater, graduate, hooker, moll, pavement princess, piece of trade, rumper, sex care provider (PC), snatch peddler, soap (plural), streetwalker, tackle (17th century slang), whore, working girl

prostitute, adjective: meretricious

prostitute, child of: Georges Feydeau (playwright)

prostitute, sex with: cypripareunia

prostitute killers: Jack the Ripper, William Suff, Peter Sutcliffe, Steve Wright

prostitutes and women of ill repute: Divine Brown, Carmen, Mary Magdalene, Moll Flanders, Heidi Fleiss, Fanny Hill, Billie Holiday (who took to the streets aged 13), Xaviera Hollander, Jezebel, Manon Lescaut (c/o Abbe Prevost), Maggie May, Nana (from the novel by Emile Zola), Rhopopis (who was in such demand in Egypt that she built a pyramid from her takings), Annie Sprinkle

prostitution: compensated dating

protective clothing: biohazard suit

protein: actin, albumin, aleurone, antibody, capsid, casein, collagen, enzyme, factor VIII (aka factor eight), fibrin, fibrinogen, fibroin, flavoprotein, gelatin, globulin, gluten, haemocyanin, haemoglobin, histone, immunoglobulin, interferon, keratin, lectin, lipoprotein, mycoprotein, myoglobin, myosin, prion, protamine (predominantly found in fish sperm), Quorn, scleroprotein, transferrin, tuberculin, TVP (textured vegetable protein), vitellin, zein

protest singers: Joan Baez, Johnny Cash, The Clash, Bob Dylan, Steve Earle, Woody Guthrie, Janet Jackson, John Lennon, Pete Seeger, Sting

protesters: Margaret Beckett, Guy Fawkes, Otis Ferry (who, in September 2004, burst into the House of Commons to oppose the anti-fox hunting bill), Jane Fonda, Ben Hartley, Brian Haw (who, armed with anti-war placards and a

sleeping bag, camped outside the Palace of Westminster for five years),
Emmeline Pankhurst, Martin Sheen, Swampy (aka Daniel Hooper)

proud and famous: Niobe (whose children were slaughtered by Apollo and Artemis to punish her conceit)

Prussian kings: Frederick II, Frederick the Great

Prussian military leaders: Gebhard Leberecht von Blücher, Carl von Clausewitz

psalmist: David

pseudonyms – see pen names

PSP: phenolsulphonphthalein (disease suffered by Dudley Moore)

psychiatric doctor: analyst, psychiatrist, psychoanalyst, psychologist, shrink, therapist

psychiatrists: Alfred Adler (author of *Study of Organ Inferiority and its Psychical Compensation*, 1907), Pierre Deniker, Sigmund Freud (author of *The Interpretation of Dreams*, 1900), Carl Gustav Jung (author of *The Psychology of the Unconscious*, 1911–12), R.D. Laing, Wilhelm Reich, Hermann Rorschach, Thomas Szasz

psychiatrist's bible: The Diagnostic and Statistical Manual (DSM)

psychiatrist's oath: Hippocratic oath

psychiatrist's talk: psychobabble

psychiatrist's test with ink blots: Rorschach test

psychic: Jeane Dixon
 - see mediums

psychic performer: Uri Geller

Psycho (1960 film), famous line: Norman Bates (Anthony Perkins): "A boy's best friend is his mother"

psychoanalysis, father of: Sigmund Freud

psychoanalysts: Bruno Bettelheim, John Bowlby, Erik Erikson, Sigmund Freud, Erich Fromm, Heinz Hartmann, Melanie Klein, Heinz Kohut, Julia Kristeva, Jacques Lacan, Wilhelm Reich

psychologists: Alfred Adler, Eric Berne, Jerome S. Bruner, Cyril Burt, Edward Francis de Bono, Hans Eysenck, Gustav Fechner, Erich Fromm, Arthur Jensen, Timothy Leary, Kurt Lewin, A.R. Luria, Jean Piaget, Eleanor Rosch, Dorothy Rowe, B.F. Skinner, Wilhelm Wundt

psychologist, collective noun: complex

psychotherapist: Fritz Perls

psychotherapy, father of: Galen (aka Claudius Galenus; ?130–?200 AD)

ptarmigan (bird), adjective: tetraonid

ptarmigan, collective noun: covey

pub, most popular names in the UK: 1) The Red Lion; 2) The Crown; 3) The Royal Oak; 4) The White Hart

pubs, famous: Jamaica Inn, The Queen Vic (from *EastEnders*), Rovers Return (from *Coronation Street*)

pub landlords: Al Murray, Jack and Annie Walker (of the Rovers Return)

puberty, adjective: hebetic

pubic hair: beard, bird's nest, bush, fleece, grass, G-Wax (the strip of hair above the vulva left over from a Brazilian waxing), lawn, merkin (pubic wig), mink, short and curlies

pubic hair, trimming of: Beckham (UK), Brazilian (US), depilation, Hollywood (complete shave), Sphynx (complete shave)

pubic wig: merkin

public opinion pollster: George Horace Gallup

publican, collective noun: glozing
publicists: Phineas T. Barnum, Max Clifford, Lynne Franks
Public Enemy: radical, confrontational, controversial and highly politicised rap group formed in Hempstead, New York, in 1982; comprised of Chuck D (real name: Carlton Ridenhour), Hank Shocklee, Flavor Flav (real name: William Drayton) and Terminator X (on turntable; real name: Norman Rogers)
public school, fact: in the UK, public school is attended by seven per cent of the country
publishers: Helen Gurley Brown, Robert Chambers, Archibald Constable, John Debrett, Lawrence Ferlinghetti, Larry Flynt, Malcolm Forbes, Maurice Girodias, John Harris (children's books), Hugh Hefner, Sir Edward Hulton (founded *Picture Post*), Harvey Kurtzman (comic strips), Sir Allen Lane, Alexander Liberman, George Maciunas, Tom Maschler, Sir Algernon Methuen, Richard Neville, John Newbery (children's books), Adolph Simon Ochs (turned *The New York Times* into a world-class newspaper), Phyllis Pearsall, Generoso Pope Jr., Paul Raymond, Theodor Roszack, Axel Springer, Gloria Steinem, Dewitt Wallace, George Weidenfeld, Joseph Whitaker
  – see newspaper tycoons
publishers, fact: there are 20,000 publishers in Britain, but only 180 recognised by The Publishers Association
publishers' emblem (found on a book): colophon
publishing trade journal: *The Bookseller*
puddings: apple charlotte, banoffee pie, cabinet pudding, charlotte, Christmas pudding, college pudding, cream caramel, crème brûlée, duff, jam roly-poly, milk pudding, nesselrode, parfait, pavlova, plum duff, plum pudding, queen of puddings, roly-poly, semolina, sponge pudding, spotted dick, suet pudding, summer pudding, tapioca, tart, tiramisu, zabaglione
pudendum wig: merkin
Puerto Rico: self-governing Caribbean commonwealth (linked with the United States), formerly known as Porto Rico (until 1932)
  capital: San Juan
  currency: US dollar
  language: Spanish
  religion: Roman Catholic (85%), Protestant
  famous citizens: Marc Anthony, Chayanne, Benicio Del Toro, José Feliciano, Luis Guzman (character actor), Jennifer Lopez (extraction only), Ricky Martin, Joaquin Phoenix (born there only)
pulp, adjective: pultaceous
Pulp Fiction (1994 film), famous lines: Mia (Uma Thurman): "That's a little bit more information than I needed, Vince, but go right ahead" (after Vince announces that he's off to relieve himself); Marsellus (Ving Rhames): "I'm gonna get Medieval on your ass"; Fabienne (Maria de Medeiros): "Who's Zed?" Butch Coolidge (Bruce Willis): "Zed's dead, baby, Zed's dead"; Jules (Samuel L. Jackson) to Brett, after shooting Brett's friend to kingdom come: "Oh, I'm sorry. Did that break your concentration?"; The Wolf (Harvey Keitel) to Vince: "Pretty please, with sugar on top, clean the fucking car!"
pulp novelist: Richard Allen (real name: James Moffat)
  - see crime writers, detective writers, thriller writers, etc
pulse (as of the heart), adjective: sphygmic
pun: paronomasia

pun, adjective: biverbal

punch: body blow, bunch of fives, hook, jab, kidney punch, knockout blow, knuckle sandwich, left hook, rabbit killer (Australian), rabbit punch, right hook, slug, upper-cut

Punch, or The London Charivari: weekly satirical periodical founded in 1841 by Henry Mayhew, Joseph Stirling Coyne and Mark Lemon. The magazine folded in 1992 when its circulation plummeted to 33,000, down from the lucrative 175,000 of the 1940s

Punch and Judy show: first recorded in the UK in 1662

punctuality: "Punctuality is the virtue of the bored" - Evelyn Waugh

punishment, adjective: penal

punishment, fear of: poinephobia

punishment, goddess of: Nemesis (Greek mythology)

punk bands: Blondie, The B52's, The Buzzcocks, Chelsea, The Clash, The Cramps, The Damned, Devo, Generation X, New York Dolls, Penetration, Pere Ubu, Ramones, The Rezillos, The Sex Pistols, The Stooges, Subway Sect, Television

puppets: Archie Andrews, Basil Brush, Bill and Ben, Lord Charles, Emu, Flat Eric (spokespuppet for Levi's), Lady Penelope, Lamb Chop (c/o Shari Lewis), Charlie McCarthy, Muffin the Mule, Orville the Duck, Petrushka, Pinocchio, Punch and Judy, Punchinello, Sooty, Sweep, Thunderbirds
- see hand puppets

puppet on a string: marionette

puppet theatre: Bunraku (from Japan)

puppeteers: Gerry Anderson, Jim Henson, Frank Oz

purchase obsession: oniomania

purple, aversion to: porphyrophobia

pus, adjective: purulent, pyoid

puzzles: brain-teaser, Chinese puzzle, crossword, jigsaw, rebus, Rubik's cube (invented by the Hungarian teacher Dr Erno Rubik), Sudoku, tangram (Chinese), wordsearch

PVS: persistent vegetative state

PWA: People With Aids, Person With Aids

pygophilia: arousal derived from anything relating to buttocks

pyramid, longest in world: Huaca Larga (a structure in Túcume, Peru, which is half a mile long)

pyramid builder: Cheops (aka Khufu)

Q

Qatar: state in eastern Arabia
  capital: Dohar
  currency: riyal
  language: Arabic
  religion: Muslim (Sunni)

QBE: qualified by experience

QED: quod erat demonstrandum (Latin for: 'which was to be proved'), Quite Easily Done

Q-tips: invented in 1927

quadriplegics: Hilary Lister (who, paralysed from the neck down, sailed across the English Channel in August 2005), Christopher Reeve, Ramon Sampedro (Spanish writer)

quail, adjective: gallinaceous
quail, collective noun: bevy, covey
quail, female: hen
quail, male: cock
quail, young: cheeper, chick
Quakers, founded by: George Fox
qualification: QBE (qualified by experience)
quantum theory: proposed in 1900 by Max Planck
quarry: Carrara (where Michelangelo got his white marble)
Queen, mode of verbal address: Your Majesty
Queen: UK rock band formed in London in 1971; comprised of Freddie Mercury
    (real name: Farrokh Bulsara; died: 24 November 1991) (vocals), Brian May
    (guitar), John Deacon (bass) and Roger Taylor (drums)
Queen of Mean: nickname for Leona Helmsley
Queer as Folk: eight-part, ground-breaking TV drama series following the lives of
    three men in Manchester's gay village around Canal Street. It was later adapted
    into an American-Canadian series (2000–2005) set in Pittsburgh
    created by Russell T. Davies
    broadcast: 23 February 1999–22 February 2000 on Channel Four
    cast: Aidan Gillen (Stuart Alan Jones), Craig Kelly (Vince Tyler), Charlie
        Hunnam (Nathan Maloney)
question: The $64,000 question
question, adjective: interrogative
question mark, first featured in a British publication: in Sir Philip Sidney's *Arcadia*
quizmasters: Art Fleming, Bamber Gascoigne, Gilbert Harding, John Humphrys,
    Henry Kelly, Magnus Magnusson, Jeremy Paxman, Anne Robinson, Robert
    Robinson, Chris Tarrant, Alex Trebek
qv: quod vide (see which, as in a cross-referenced word or feature, etc)

R

'r' rolled, adjective: hirrient
R & B: rhythm and blues
rabbis: Eleazar of Worms, Sir Jonathan Sacks
rabbit: bunny, cottontail, hare (in America)
rabbit, adjective: lapine, leporid
rabbit, collective noun: bury, colony, nest
rabbit disease: myxomatosis
rabbits, famous: Benjamin Bunny (Beatrix Potter), Bigwig (from *Watership Down*),
    Brer Rabbit, Bugs Bunny, Dylan (from *The Magic Roundabout*), Easter Bunny,
    Fiver (from *Watership Down*), Flopsy (Beatrix Potter), Harvey, Hazel (from
    Watership Down), Jessica Rabbit, Miffy, Mopsy, Flopsy and Cotton-tail, Rabbit
    (from *Winnie the Pooh*), Peter Rabbit (Beatrix Potter), Roger Rabbit, Thumper
    (from *Bambi*), the Velvetine Rabbit, White Rabbit (from *Alice's Adventures in
    Wonderland*)
rabbit, home: burrow, nest, warren
rabbit, male: buck
rabbit, female: doe
rabbit, tail: scut
rabbit, young: bunny
rabies, fear of: lyssophobia

rabies; first man to die from rabies in England for over 100 years: naturist painter and volunteer bat conservationist David McRae (died 10 September, 2010)

raccoon, adjective: procyonine

raccoon, collective noun: nursery

raccoon, young: cub

raccoons, famous: Clyde (from TV's *The Beverly Hillbillies*), Jasper (from TV's *Little House on the Prairie*), Meeko (from Disney's *Pocahontas*), Rascal (from Donna Braymer's *The Adventures of Rascal Raccoon*), Rascal (from Sterling North's autobiographical novel of the same name and the Disney film adapted from it)

race, mixed: Cablinasian (part Caucasian, part black, part American Indian, part Asian - à la Tiger Woods), marabou, mulatto, octoroon, quadroon

racecourses: Aintree, Ascot, Belmont Stakes (USA), Cheltenham, Epsom, Goodwood, Kempton Park, Kentucky (USA), Lingfield Park, Newbury, Newmarket, Preakness (USA)

racehorses: Amberleigh House, Best Mate, Bindaree, Denman, Desert Orchard, Devon Loch (the Queen Mother's horse which collapsed at the end of the Grand National immediately after the commentator announced 'he can't lose now'), Foinavon (100–1 winner of the Grand National), High-Rise, Kahyasi, Kauto Star, Lammtarra (fastest horse in the Epsom Derby), Lord Gwyllene, Mahmoud, Mariah's Storm, Mon Mome (100–1 winner of the Grand National), Monty's Pass, Mr Frisk, Phar Lap, Red Rum, Reference Point, Rock of Gibraltar, Rough Quest, Royal Athlete, Seabiscuit, Shergar, Troy, War Admiral, Whistlejacket (painted by George Stubbs), Windsor Lad

racing drivers: Fernando Alonso, Alberto Ascari, Sir Jack Brabham, Martin Brundle, Jenson Button, Sir Malcolm Campbell, Jim Clark, David Coulthard, Juan Manuel Fangio, Emerson Fittipaldi, Dario Franchitti, Mika Hakkinen, Lewis Hamilton, Mike Hawthorn, Johnny Herbert, Damon Hill, Graham Hill, James Hunt, Jacky Ickx, Eddie Irvine, Niki Lauda, Nigel Mansell, Felipe Massa, Sir Stirling Moss, Barney Oldfield, Nelson Piquet, Alain Prost, Kimi Räikkönen, Michael Schumacher, Ayrton Senna, Sir Jackie Stewart, John Surtees, Jacques Villeneuve

racists: Mark Fuhrman (O.J. Simpson trial witness), Nick Griffin (chairman of the BNP), Abu Hamza, Adolf Hitler, Jack London, General William C. Westmoreland (who went on record to explain that American lives were more important than 'Oriental' ones), Ann Winterton (Tory MP expelled from parliament for cracking a joke at the expense of the Chinese)

racist bands: Rahowa, Skrewdriver

racist magazine: *Stormer*

racist organisation: Ku Klux Klan

racist singing duo: Prussian Blue (fronted by Lynx and Lamb Gaede)

raconteurs: Alan Bennett, Gyles Brandreth, Quentin Crisp, Barry Cryer, Charles Dickens, Sir Clement Freud, Stephen Fry, Denis Healey, Richard Ingrams, Garrison Keillor, Baron Munchhausen, George Bernard Shaw, Sir Peter Ustinov, Gore Vidal, Oscar Wilde
- see orators

RADA: Royal Academy of Dramatic Art, pre-eminent acting school founded by Sir Herbert Beerbohm Tree on 25 April 1904 at His Majesty's Theatre in the Haymarket, London. The academy received a royal charter in 1920 and in 2000 Queen Elizabeth II opened a £32m new headquarters in Gower Street, a complex that includes three new theatres, an exhibition space and cabaret stage.

RADA students: Richard Attenborough, Alan Bates, Kenneth Branagh, Joan
  Collins, Tom Courtenay, Laura Dern, Anthony Edwards, Trevor Eve, Ralph
  Fiennes, Albert Finney, John Gielgud, Iain Glen, Ian Holm, Anthony Hopkins,
  Jane Horrocks, John Hurt, Glenda Jackson, Charles Laughton, Mike Leigh,
  Vivien Leigh, Paul McGann, Peter O'Toole, Clive Owen, Jonathan Pryce, Alan
  Rickman, Diana Rigg, Eric Roberts, Flora Robson, Mark Rylance, Fiona Shaw,
  Michael Sheen, Juliet Stevenson, John Thaw
radar: acronym for 'radio detecting and ranging'
radar: perfected in 1935 by the Scottish physicist Sir Robert Watson-Watt
radio: invented in 1901, by Guglielmo Marconi
radio: citizens' band, Roberts (popular make), wireless
radio operator: Odette Sansom
radio presenters: Richard Baker, Zoë Ball, Art Bell, Tony Blackburn, Sara Cox,
  Chris Evans, Alan Freeman, Mark Goodier, Rush Limbaugh, Humphrey
  Lyttelton, Simon Mayo, Chris Moyles, Dave Pearce, John Peel, Mark Radcliffe,
  Sir Jimmy Savile, Howard Stern, Studs Terkel, Jo Whiley, Sir Terry Wogan,
  Sir Jimmy Young
  - see disc jockeys
radio telescope, largest in the world: the Arecibo telescope in Puerto Rico
radiochemist: Otto Hahn
Radiohead: UK alternative rock group formed in Oxford, England, in 1988;
  comprised of: Thom Yorke (vocals, guitar), Jonny Greenwood (guitar), Colin
  Greenwood (bass), Ed O'Brien (guitar, backing vocals) and Phil Selway (drums)
radiologists, patron saints of: Michael, Gabriel and Raphael
radium: element discovered in 1898 by Pierre Curie and his wife Marie
RAF pilot: Sir Douglas Bader
raft, famous: Kon Tiki (on which Thor Heyerdahl crossed the Pacific in 1947)
rag-and-bone men: Krook (from Charles Dickens' *Bleak House*), Albert Steptoe,
  Harold Steptoe
railroad gauge, standard US and UK: 4 feet, 8.5 inches, derived from the original
  specifications for an Imperial Roman war chariot, itself made just wide enough
  to accommodate the back ends of two war horses
railways, fear of: siderodromophobia
railway engineers: Matthew Boulton, Thomas Russel Crampton, William Murdock,
  Thomas Newcomen, George Stephenson, Richard Trevithick, James Watt
rain, adjective: hyetal, pluvial, pluvious
rain, fear of: ombrophobia
rain, god of: Tlaloc (Aztec mythology)
rain, goddess of: Tefnut (Egyptian mythology)
rain, love of: ombromania
rain, study of: ombrology
rain cloud: nimbostratus, nimbus
rain gauge: pluviometer
rainbows, goddess of: Iris (Greek)
rainfall, study of: hyetography
rainfall chart: hyetograph
rainfall measure: hyetograph
raisin: "A humiliated grape" – as described by Mary Stuart Masterson in the 1993
  film *Benny & Joon*
raja, wife of: ranee
rakes, famous: Alfie Elkins, Henry Bellingham (from Elizabeth Gaskell's *Ruth*),
  Lord Darlington (from *Lady Windermere's Fan*), Don Juan, James Hewitt,
  Lothario, Barry Lyndon (from the novel by Thackeray)

RAM: random-access memory

ram, adjective: arietine

ram, castrated: wether

ram-headed god: Amen, Ammon, Khnum (all Egyptian mythology)

Ramones, The: punk rock band formed in 1974 in the Forest Hills suburb of New York; comprised of Joey Ramone (aka Jeff Hyman; vocals), Johnny Ramone (aka Johnny Cummings; guitar), Dee Dee Ramone (aka Douglas Colvin; bass) and Tommy Ramone (aka Tommy Erdelyi; drums). Disbanded in 1996

rancher, politically correct term: cattle murderer

rap music, father of: Melvin Van Peebles

rap/hip-hop artists: Akon (real name: Aliaune Thiam), Mary J. Blige, Kurtis Blow (real name: Curtis Walker), Chuck D (real name: Carlton Douglas Ridenhour), Common (real name: Lonnie Rashid Lynn Jr), Sway Dasafo, Diddy (real name: Sean Combs; formerly known as Puff Daddy, Puffy and P. Diddy), Dizzee Rascal (real name: Dylan Mills), DMX (real name: Earl Simmons), Dr Dre (real name: Andre Young), Eminem (real name: Marshall Mathers), Estelle (full name: Estelle Fanta Swaray), 50 Cent (real name: Curtis Jackson), GZA (aka The Genius) (real name: Gary Grice), Lauryn Hill, Ice Cube (real name: O'Shea Jackson), Ice-T (real name: Tracy Morrow), Ja Rule (real name: Jeffrey Atkins), Jay-Z (real name: Shawn Corey Carter), Kool Mo Dee (real name: Mohandas DeWese), KRS-One (real name: Kris Parker), Kurupt (real name: Ricardo Brown), Lil' Kim (real name: Kimberly Jones), LL Cool J (real name: James Todd Smith), Ludacris (real name: Christopher Bridges), Master P (real name: Percy Miller), Method Man (real name: Clifford Smith), Mos Def (real name: Dante Smith), The Notorious B.I.G. (real name: Christopher Wallace), O.D.B. (Ol' Dirty Bastard) (real name: Russell T. Jones), Queen Latifah (real name: Dana Owens), Rah Digga (real name: Rashiya Fisher), Redman (real name: Reggie Noble), Busta Rhymes (real name: Trevor Smith, Jr), RZA (aka the Abbot and Bobby Digital) (real name: Robert Diggs), Snoop Doggy Dogg (real name: Calvin Broadus), Tupac Shakur (aka 2Pac), The Streets (aka Mike Skinner), Vanilla Ice (real name: Robert Van Winkle), Kanye West, Will.i.am (aka William Adams Jr)
   - see gangsta rap acts

rap/hip-hop groups: Arrested Development, Beastie Boys, De La Soul, Digital Underground, Eric B. & Rakim, The Fat Boys, Grandmaster Flash & The Furious Five, Jurassic 5, N.W.A., OutKast, Public Enemy, The Roots, Run DMC, TLC, A Tribe Called Quest, Wu Tang Clan
   - see gangsta rap acts

rape, fact: in the US, a woman is raped every two minutes

rape, sexual arousal derived from the act of: biastophilia, raptophilia

rape capital of the world: South Africa, where a woman is raped every 26 seconds

rape victims, patron saint of: Agnes of Rome

rapist: nonce (prison slang)

rapists: Oscar De La Hoya ('Golden Boy' of American boxing), Josef Fritzl, Andrew Luster (heir to the Max Factor fortune who drugged and then videoed his victims during sex), Owen Oyston (worth £40m, although he believes his property interests are worth £90m; jailed for six years), Mike Tyson

rappers – see rap/hip-hop artists

Rastafarians, famous: Bob Marley, Sinéad O'Connor (even though she was ordained as a Catholic priest in 1999), Maxi Priest, Benjamin Zephaniah

Rastafarian Messiah: Emperor Haile Selassie of Ethiopia

Rastafarianism, based on: the ideas of Marcus Garvey

rat, adjective: murine, rattine

rat, collective noun: hoard, mischief, pack, swarm

rat, fact: seven per cent of house fires in the UK are caused by rats biting through electric cables

rat, fear of: musophobia

rat (a rodent), rhyming slang: cabbage hat (USA)

rat (an informer), rhyming slang: cocked hat (USA)

rat, young: pinky, pup

rat disease (transmitted by rat fleas): murine typhus

Rat Pack: informal name coined by *Time* magazine to describe the show business entourage of Frank Sinatra, whose members included Dean Martin, Sammy Davis Jr, Peter Lawford and Joey Bishop. The entertainers also appeared together in a handful of films, notably *Ocean's Eleven* (1960)

rat's den: midden

rats, famous: Ben (eponymous star of the film), Ratbert, Ratty (from *Wind in the Willows*), Rémy (c/o *Ratatouille*), Rizzo the Rat (Muppet), Roland Rat, Samuel Whiskers ((c/o Beatrix Potter), Scabbers (from *Harry Potter*), Splinter (Teenage Mutant Ninja), Templeton (from *Charlotte's Web*), Willard (star of the eponymous film)

rattle-snake, adjective: crotaline

rattle-snake, collective noun: rhumba

raven, adjective: corvine

raven, collective noun: unkindness

raven, famous: Grip (from Dickens' *Barnaby Rudge*)

raven, sound: croak

raw flesh, eating of: omophagy

ray, adjective: actinoid, radial

read, inability to: alexia

Reader's Digest: American magazine with a broad appeal, founded as a mail-order magazine in 1922 by Dewitt Wallace and his Canadian wife, Lila Bell Acheson

reading, fact: the average British child spends 15 minutes a day reading books

real estate: "Buy land. They aren't making it any more" - Mark Twain

realism in art or literature: verism

reality: "Reality is an illusion that occurs due to lack of alcohol" – anonymous; "Reality is that which, when you stop believing in it, doesn't go away" - Philip K. Dick; "I don't mistrust reality, of which I know next to nothing. I mistrust the picture of reality conveyed to us by our senses" - Gerhard Richter

reality, adjective: ontal

Rebecca (1938 novel by Daphne du Maurier), opening line: "Last night I dreamt I went to Manderley again"

rebels: Barabbas, Jane Fonda, Owen Glendower, Spartacus, Sid Vicious - see activists

rebirth, god of: Nefertum (Egyptian mythology)

recession: "It's a recession when your neighbour loses his job; it's a depression when you lose yours" - Harry S. Truman

recluses: Neil Armstrong, Count Balthasar Balthus (French painter), Syd Barrett, Samuel Beckett, Marlon Brando, Dan Brown, Clive Calder, Eileen Chang, Homer Collyer, Charles Darwin (semi), Emily Dickinson, Sir John Ellerman (in real terms, the richest British businessman of all time), Agnetha Fältskog, Robert Frank (photographer), Greta Garbo, Glenn Gould, Thomas Harris, Miss Havisham (from *Great Expectations*), Howard Hughes, Ted Kaczynski (aka

the Unabomber), Stanley Kubrick, Harper Lee, Ludwig II, Terrence Malick
(filmmaker), Chris Morris (TV comedy writer), Sir Isaac Newton, Grigori
Perelman, Cole Porter (in his later years), Thomas Pynchon, Paul Raymond,
Sviatoslav Richter (pianist), Paul Robeson (in his last years), Axl Rose, J.D.
Salinger, Phil Spector, Sly Stone, Douglas Thompson (co-founder of the
fashion company Esprit), Brian Wilson (between the years 1973 and 1975,
when he locked himself in his bedroom)

record executives: Clive Calder, Miles Copeland, Kim Fowley, David Geffen, Berry
Gordy Jr
- see music executives

record producers: John Culshaw, Clive Davis, David Geffen, George Martin, Jack
Nitzsche, Sam Phillips, Phil Ramone, Mark Ronson, Rick Rubin, Phil Spector,
Timbaland (born Timothy Z. Mosley), Don Was (born Donald Fagenson),
Kanye West

recording engineer: Lee 'Scratch' Perry

rectum: back way, Cadbury alley, ying-yang [sic]

rectum, adjective: proctal

rectum, doctor of: proctologist

rectum, science of: proctology

Red Ken: nickname for Ken Livingstone

redheads: Tori Amos, Gillian Anderson, Ann-Margret, Ginger Baker, Lucille Ball,
Princess Beatrice, Boris Becker, Sarah Bernhardt, Paul Bettany, Anne Boleyn,
Lizzie Borden, Clara Bow, Belinda Carlisle, David Caruso, Winston Churchill,
Cleopatra, Christopher Columbus, Robin Cook, Oliver Cromwell, General
George Armstrong Custer, Steve Davis, Carol Decker, Kiki Dee, Emily
Dickinson, Isla Fisher, Charlie Dimmock, Kirsten Dunst, Queen Elizabeth I,
Chris Evans, Angie Everhart, Sarah Ferguson, Art Garfunkel, Greer Garson,
Mitzi Gaynor, Nell Gwynne, Daryl Hall, Geri Halliwell, Lady Emily Hamilton,
Prince Harry, Susan Hayward, Noddy Holder, Ron Howard, Mick Hucknall,
Charles Kennedy, Deborah Kerr, Nicole Kidman, Neil Kinnock, Cyndi Lauper,
Rod Laver, Lindsay Lohan, Shirley MacLaine, Shirley Manson (of Garbage),
Malcolm McLaren, Debra Messing, Bette Midler, Julianne Moore, Napoleon
Bonaparte, Jack Nicklaus, Pippi Longstocking, Red Pollard (jockey), Molly
Ringwald, Julia Roberts, Anne Robinson, Ginger Rogers, Susan Sarandon, Eric
Stoltz, Tilda Swinton, Mark Twain, Vincent Van Gogh, Esther Williams, Kate
Winslet, Fay Wray

reed, adjective: ferulaceous

reflection (of light), adjective: catadioptric

reflexes, study of: reflexology

reformed criminals: Tim Allen, Jimmy Boyle, John McVicar, Johnny Vaughan
- see jailed and famous

reformers: Vinoba Bhave, Martin Bucer, John Calvin, Johnny Cash, Joaquín Costa,
Miles Coverdale, Dorothea Dix, William Lloyd Garrison, Thomas Wentworth
Higginson, Ebenezer Howard, Thomas Hughes, Toyohiko Kagawa, Hugh
Latimer, Martin Luther, Robert Owen, Elizabeth Palmer Peabody, Eleanor
Rathbone, James Redpath, George Ripley, Samuel Smiles, William Wilberforce,
Victoria Woodhull, John Wycliffe, Huldreich Zwingli (aka Ulrich Zwingli)

refuse produced annually – see rubbish

reggae acts: Big Youth, Dennis Brown, Burning Spear, Jimmy Cliff, Eddy Grant,
Inner Circle, Gregory Isaacs, Bob Marley, Freddie McGregor, Ras Michael,

Augustus Pablo, Lee 'Scratch' Perry, Shabba Ranks, Shaggy (real name: Orville Burrell), Peter Tosh

reggae poet: Linton Kwesi Johnson

rehabilitation hospital: Craiglockhart War Hospital, Edinburgh

reign, adjective: regnal

reindeer, Santa Claus's: Dasher, Dancer, Prancer, Vixen, Comet, Cupid, Donner, Blitzen and Rudolph

relationship, good: "A contest of generosity" - Madonna

relative, murder of: parricide (also applies to the murder of a parent or king)

relativity theorist: Albert Einstein

relics, writer specialising in: lipsanographer

religions – see faith systems

religious cults: Aum Shinri Kyo, Branch Davidians, Children of God, Church of the Sub-Genius (formed in 1978), Concerned Christians, Fundamentalist Church of Jesus Christ of Latter-Day Saints, Heaven's Gate, Kabbalah, Movement for the Restoration of the Ten Commandments of God (in Uganda), the People's Temple, Rastafarianism, Solar Temple

religious festivals: *Chinese*: Lunar New Year; *Christian*: Ash Wednesday, Good Friday, Easter Day, Ascension Day, Whit Sunday, Corpus Christi, Advent Sunday, Christmas Day (December 25); *Hindu*: Holi, Navratri, Diwali; *Jewish*: Pesach (Passover), Shavuot (Pentecost), Rosh Hashanah (Jewish New Year), Yom Kippur (Day of Atonement), Succot (Tabernacles), Hanukkah

religious pretender: Tartuffe

religious thinker: Xenophanes

REM: rapid-eye-movement in sleep

R.E.M.: iconic US rock group formed in Georgia in 1980; comprised of Michael Stipe (lead vocals), Peter Buck (guitar), Mike Mills (base) and Bill Berry (drums). The group became a threesome in 1979 when Berry left to pursue a life of agriculture

remedy: elixir, nostrum (usually mythological), panacea

repetition of words spoken by another: echolalia

reporters – see journalists

reproduction, adjective: genetic

reptile, adjective: ophidian

reptile, largest in the world: saltwater crocodile

reptiles, fear of: batrachophobia, herpetophobia

reptiles, use of in sexual stimulation: ophidicism

residences of the famous – see homes of the famous

resin, adjective: abietic (particularly of fir trees)

resistance fighters: Yasser Arafat, Charlotte Gray, Sophie Scholl, Lise Villameur

responsibility: "No snowflake in an avalanche ever feels responsible" – Stanislaw Jerzy Lec

responsibility, fear of: hypegiaphobia

restaurant: bistro, brasserie, café, cafeteria, carvery, diner, eatery, greasy spoon, grill, luncheonette, pit stop, pizzeria, rotisserie, steakhouse, taverna, trattoria

restaurant, first known: Sobrino de Botín, which opened in Madrid in 1725, although some sources list the Champ d'Oiseau, which opened in 1770 in Paris (however, restaurants were believed to be in existence in medieval times, both in Alexandria and Jerusalem)

restaurant, first in London: Rules, which opened in Maiden Lane in 1798

restaurant critics: A.A. Gill, Fay Maschler, Ruth Reichl, Michael Winner

restaurant guides: Egon Ronay, Harden's, Michelin

retail executives: Mohamed Al-Fayed, Philip Green

retirement: "When you stop living at work and start working at living" – saying

retribution, goddess of: Nemesis (Greek mythology)

revolutionaries: Simón Bolívar, Nikolai Bukharin, Georges Cadoudal, Lazare
    Carnot, Fidel Castro, Chauvelin (from *The Scarlet Pimpernel*), Georges
    Danton, Éamon de Valera, Felix Dzerzhinsky, Luigi Farini, Giuseppe Garibaldi,
    Ernesto 'Che' Guevara, He Xiangning, Sergey Kirov, Henry Laurens, Vladimir
    Ilyich Lenin, Jean Paul Marat, Comte de Honoré Gabriel Mirabeau, Velestinlis
    Rigas, Maximilien Robespierre, Bobby Sands, Antonio López de Santa Anna,
    Joseph Stalin, Leon Trotsky, Pancho Villa, Emiliano Zapata, Grigori Zinoviev
    - see patriots

revolutionary theorist: Amilcar Cabral

Reykjavik, birthplace of: Björk, Magnus Magnusson, Sigur Røs (alternative music
    group)

rhea, adjective: struthious

rheumatic disease, science of: rheumatology

rheumatism, patron saint of: James the Greater

rhinoceros, adjective: ceratorhine

rhinoceros, collective noun: crash

rhinoceros, female: cow

rhinoceros, male: bull

rhinoceros, sound: grunt, growl, snort, whistle

rhinoceros, young: calf

Rhode Island, 13th state (1790), Little Rhody, Ocean State
    capital: Providence
    state bird: Rhode Island red
    state flower: violet
    state tree: red maple
    birthplace of: Blu Cantrell, Marilyn Chambers (porn star), George M. Cohan,
        Nelson Eddy, Spalding Gray, Van Johnson, H. P. Lovecraft
    motto: 'Hope'
    tourist attraction: Narragansett Indian Fall Festival
    fact: Rhode Island is the smallest state in the USA

Rhodesia: former name for Zimbabwe (1964–1979), prior to which the country was
    known as Southern Rhodesia

Rhodesian prime minister: Ian Smith

Rhodesian writer: Doris Lessing

rhubarb: edible plant that originated in Tibet

rhyming game: crambo

rhythm and blues acts: Babyface, Anita Baker, Brandy, Chris Brown, James
    Brown, Ruth Brown, James Carr, Ray Charles, Chic, The Coasters, D'Angelo,
    Terence Trent D'Arby, Bo Diddley, Fats Domino, The Drifters, Earth, Wind &
    Fire, The Four Tops, Aretha Franklin, Marvin Gaye, Al Green, Anthony
    Hamilton, Isaac Hayes, Janet Jackson, Etta James, R. Kelly, Alicia Keys,
    Gladys Knight, Beyoncé Knowles, Kool & the Gang, Lemar, Leona Lewis,
    Manfred Mann, Curtis Mayfield, Harold Melvin, Ms Dynamite, Ne-Yo, Pink,
    Prince, Smokey Robinson, Diana Ross & the Supremes, Jill Scott, The
    Shirelles, Percy Sledge, Sly & the Family Stone, Joss Stone, The Temptations,
    Irma Thomas, Usher, Luther Vandross, Dionne Warwick, Kanye West, Barry
    White, Jackie Wilson, Bobby Womack

RI: postcode for Rhode Island

rib, adjective: costal

rib-shaped: costate

rice: Arborio, basmati, boiled rice, brown rice, carnaroli, coconut rice, copra kana, egg-fried rice, kesar chaval, long grain, makhani chaval, mattar pilau, narial ka chaval, nimbu ka chaval, Patna rice, pilau, pongal, Thai fragrant, Uncle Ben's

rice dish: a la riojana (Spanish), biriani (Indian), copra kana (Indian), huo tuei dan chao fan (Chinese), Paella (Spanish), pilau

Rice Krispies' slogan: 'Snap! Crackle! Pop!'

rice-eating: oryzivorous

riches, god of: Mammon (Syrian mythology)

riches, worship of: mammon

rickshaw: cyclo, pedicab (pedal-operated), trishaw

ridicule, fear of: catagelophobia, karagalophobia, katagelophobia

riding school: manège

rifle: AK-47, carbine, elephant gun, Enfield, express rifle, Kalashnikov, musket, SLR, Winchester
- see gun

right: "I disapprove of what you say, but I will defend to the death your right to say it" – Voltaire

right, adjective: dextral (see left)

right angles, adjective: orthogonal

right-hand page of a book or magazine: recto

right-handed: dextral (compare sinistral)

Rigoletto: opera by Giuseppe Verdi first produced in Venice on 11 March 1851

Ring, The: series of four operas by Richard Wagner, first produced in their entirety in Bayreuth in 1876

ring, adjective: annular

ring-shaped: annular, circinate, cingular

ringing noise (in head): acouasm

rings, adjective: armillary

Rio de Janeiro, birthplace of: Paulo Coelho, Oscar Niemeyer, Ronaldo

Rio de Janeiro concert/sports arena: Maracaña Municipa Stadium

Rio de Janeiro landmark: Sugarloaf Hill

Rio de Janeiro opera house: Theatro Municipal

Rising Damp: British sitcom set in a run-down townhouse featuring the penny-pinching and scruffy landlord Rupert Rigsby; adapted from the 1971 stage play *The Banana Box* by Eric Chappell. It was later adapted for the big screen in 1980
    created by Eric Chappell
    broadcast 2 September 1974 – 9 May 1978 on ITV
    cast: Leonard Rossiter (Rupert Rigsby), Frances de la Tour (Ruth Jones), Richard Beckinsale (Alan George Moore), Don Warrington (Philip Smith)

river, adjective: potamic, riverine

river, longest in Europe: the Danube

river, longest in Great Britain: the Severn

river, longest (wholly) in England: the Thames

river, longest in the United States: the Missouri-Red Rock

river bank, adjective: riparian

river mouth: embouchure

river nymph: naiad

river of forgetfulness: Lethe (Greek mythology)

rivers, British: Aire, Avon, Clyde, Great Ouse, Humber, Isis, Mersey, Nene, Severn, Spey, Tay, Thames, Trent, Tyne, Wye

rivers, fear of: potamophobia

rivers, largest in the world (ranked by drainage area): 1) Amazon (South America); 2) Paraná (South America); 3) Congo (Africa); 4) Nile (Africa); 5) Mississipp-Missouri (USA); 6) Ob-Irtysh (Russia); 7) Yenisey (Siberia); 8) Lena (Russia); 9) Yangtze (China); 10) Niger (Africa)

rivers, longest in the world: 1) Amazon (South America) or the Nile (Africa) – depending on various definitions (the Amazon wins hands down if the Brazilian claim is correct that the source of their river starts at the top of the Nevado Mismi mountain in Peru); 3) Mississipp-Missouri (USA); 4) Yenisey (Siberia); 5) Yangtze (China); 6) Yellow River (China); 7) Ob-Irtysh (Russia); 8) Paraná (South America); 9) Congo (Africa); 10) Amur-Argun (China)

rivers, study of: potamology

roach, adjective: blattid

road rage victim: Stephen Cameron (killed in 1996 by Kenneth Noye on the M25, London)

road spikes: caltrops, crows' feet

roadrunner, adjective: cuculid

robbers – see thieves

robber, collective noun: band

robbery, biggest in Britain: 22 February 2006, when £53 million in cash was stolen from a Securitas depot in Tonbridge, Kent

robbers, fear of: harpaxophobia

robbery, fear of: harpagophobia

robin, adjective: turdine

robot: word coined by the Czech writer Karel Capek (from the Czech word *robota*, meaning 'forced labour')

robot, first recorded design of a humanoid automaton: in 1495 by Leonardo Da Vinci

robots: android, Mr Chips (from TV's *Catchphrase*), Rodney Copperbottom (from the film *Robots*), C-3PO, cyborg (see), Dalek, Gort (from *The Day the Earth Stood Still*), K9 (robotic canine in *Doctor Who*), Adam Link (from Isaac Asimov's *I, Robot*), Maria (as played by Brigitte Helm in the 1926 film *Metropolis*), Robby the Robot (from *Forbidden Planet*), R2-D2, Sonny (from the 2004 film *I, Robot*), Stepford wife, Wall-E
- see androids

rock, adjective: petrean, petrous

rock dating: geochronology

rock formation: petrogenesis

rock (music) journalists: Lester Bangs, Julie Burchill, Mick Farren, Nick Kent, Greil Marcus, Richard Meltzer, Paul Morley, Charles Shaar Murray, Tony Parsons
- see film critics, journalists, music critics, etc

rock (music) publications: *The Face, Melody Maker, Mojo, NME (New Musical Express), Q, Rolling Stone, Spin, Sounds*

rock salt: halite

rock-dwelling (adjective): saxatile, saxicolous

rocks (living on or in), adjective: rupestrine

rocks, science of the composition and origin of: petrology

rocks, study of the characteristics of: lithology
rocket scientists: Sergei Korolev, Wernher von Braun
rod, adjective: vergate, vergiform
rod-shaped: bacilliform
rodent, adjective: glirine, rosorial
roe deer, collective noun: bevy
ROFLMAO: Rolling On Floor Laughing My Ass Off
rogue, adjective: picaresque
rogue traders: Jérôme Kerviel, Nick Leeson
rolled 'r', adjective: hirrient
Rolling Stone magazine, founded by: Jann S. Wenner
Rolling Stones, The: UK rock group formed in London in 1962; group members:
    Mick Jagger (vocals), Brian Jones (guitar; died: 3 July 1969), Keith Richards
    (guitar), Bill Wyman (bass) and Charlie Watts (drums); former member: pianist
    and maraccas player Ian Stewart (who dropped out to become the group's
    manager)
Roman Catholic president of the US: John F. Kennedy
Roman Catholic priest, house of: presbytery
Roman Catholic priest, skullcap of: zucchetto
Roman dramatists: Livius Andronicus, Plautus, Lucius Pomponius, Lucius
    Annaeus Seneca
Roman emperors: Augustus, Caligula, Claudius I, Lucius Commodus, Constantine
    the Great, Publius Gallienus, Hadrian, Heliogabalus, Jovian, Julian the Apostate,
    Justinian I, Marcus Aurelius, Nero (full name: Nero Claudius Cæsar Augustus
    Germanicus), Marcus Nerva, Marcus Otho, Romulus Augustulus, Tiberius,
    Trajan, Titus Vespasian, Aulus Vitellius
Roman empress: Drusilla Livia
Roman enemy: Hannibal
Roman fountain: Trevi
Roman generals: Titus Andronicus, Julius Caesar, Gaius Marcius Coriolanus,
    Marcus Claudius Marcellus, Pompey, Scipio Aemilianus Africanus (aka Scipio
    the Younger), Scipio Africanus (aka Scipio the Elder), Tiberius
Roman magistrate: aedile
Roman numerals: 1: I, 2: II, 3: III, 4: IV, 5: V, 6: VI, 7: VII, 8: VIII, 9: IX, 10: X, 11:
    XI, 12: XII, 13: XIII, 14: XIV, 15: XV, 16: XVI, 17: XVII, 18: XVIII, 19: XIX,
    20: XX, 21: XXI, 30: XXX, 40: XL, 49: XLIX, 50: L, 60: LX, 70: LXX, 80:
    LXXX, 90: XC, 99: XCIX, 100: C, 101: CI, 144: CXLIV, 200: CC, 400: CD (or
    CCCC), 500: D, 900: M (or DCCCC), 1000: M, 1900: MCM (or MDCCCC),
    1995: MCMXCV, 1999: MCMXCIX, 2000: MM
Roman omen reader: augur, auspex
Roman orators: Cicero, Gaius Pliny the Younger
Roman poets: Horace, Livius Andronicus, Ovid, Virgil
Roman scholar: Gaius Pliny the Elder
Roman soldier: Gaius Marcius Coriolanus
    - see Roman generals
Roman steam bath: sudatorium
Romania: republic in south-eastern Europe
    capital: Bucharest
    currency: leu
    language: Romanian (official); also Hungarian, German
    religion: Romanian Orthodox (80%), Roman Catholic (6%)

mountains: Carpathian Mountains, Transylvanian Alps
river: Danube
Romanian and famous: Constantin Brancusi (sculptor), Nicolae Ceauşescu
(dictator), Paul Celan (poet), I.A.L. Diamond (screenwriter), Georges Enesco
(composer), Angela Gheorghiu, Ion Iliescu, Bela Lugosi, Ilie Nastase (tennis
player), Eugène Ionesco, Edward G. Robinson, Saul Steinberg (cartoonist)
romantic novelists: Maeve Binchy, Barbara Taylor Bradford, Sandra Brown,
Barbara Cartland, Jackie Collins, Shirley Conran, Catherine Cookson, Marie
Corelli, Catherine Coulter, Celeste DeBlasis, Cynthia Freeman, Julie Garwood,
Olivia Goldsmith, Victoria Holt, Susan Isaacs, Judith Krantz, Judith Michael
(pseudonym of Judith Barnard and Michael Fain), Fern Michaels, Nora
Roberts, Anne Rivers Siddons, LaVyrle Spencer, Danielle Steel, Jacqueline
Susan, Phyllis A. Whitney
Romantic painters: William Blake, Eugène Delacroix, Caspar David Friedrich,
Henry Fuseli, Théodore Géricault, John Martin, J.M.W. Turner
Romantic sculptor: François Rude
Rome, birthplace of: Marcus Aurelius, Julius Caesar, Sophia Loren, Roberto Rossellini
Rome, nickname: the Eternal City; the City of the Seven Hills
Rome, river: Tiber
Rome, tourist attractions: Colosseum, Tivoli Gardens, the Trevi Fountain (which
took 39 years to construct)
rook, collective noun: building, clamour
rook, sound: caw
room temperature: 70°F (21°C)
roommates, famous - see flatmates of yore
rooster, young: cockerel
root, adjective: radical, rhizoid
root beer ingredients: ginger, sarsaparilla, sassafras, spikenard, spruce, sugar, wild
cherry, wintergreen
root-producing: rhizocarpous
rope, adjective: funicular
rope ladder: étrier
rope-walker: funambulist
Rose, Axl: lead singer of the US rock band Guns N' Roses (see) and an anagram
for "oral sex"
Roseanne: enduring, ground-breaking ABC TV sitcom which uncharacteristically
focused on a white, working-class family, headed by the real-life, working-class
Roseanne Barr in the title role
created by Matt Williams
broadcast: 18 October 1988–20 May 1997
cast: Roseanne Barr (Roseanne Conner), John Goodman (Dan Conner), Laurie
Metcalf (Jackie Harris), Sara Gilbert (Darlene Conner-Healy), Tom Arnold
(Arnie Thomas), Ned Beatty (Ed Conner), Sandra Bernhard (Nancy
Bartlett), George Clooney (Booker Brooks), Johnny Galecki (David Healy),
Martin Mull (Leon Carp)
Rough Guide travel books, founders: Mark Ellingham, Natania Jansz and John
Fisher
Rough Guide travel book, top-selling title: *The Rough Guide to Spain*
rounded: bombous
row backwards: back water (verb)
rowanberry liqueur: alisier

rowers: James Cracknell, Sir Matthew Pinsent, Sir Steve Redgrave (winner of gold
  medals at four Olympics)
Rowntree's Fruit Gums, slogan: 'Don't forget the fruit gums, Mum'
Royal Exchange of London: founded by Sir Thomas Gresham in 1568
royal intruders: Aaron Alexandra Barscak (a self-styled comedy terrorist, who
  gained entry into Prince William's 21st birthday party at Windsor Castle on
  21 June 2003 and reputedly kissed the prince on both cheeks), Michael Fagin
  (who was found sitting on the end of the Queen's bed)
Royal Philharmonic Orchestra: founded in 1946 by Thomas Beecham; played its
  first concert in Croydon, London, on 15 September 1946
royal reporters: Jennie Boyd, Clive Goodman (disgraced for illegally tapping into
  telephone messages from the Princes William and Harry)
RSI: repetitive strain injury
rubber bands: patented on 17 March 1845 by Stephen Perry of London
rubbish produced annually by the average British household: one ton's worth
rudeness: "Rudeness is the weak man's imitation of strength" – Socrates
ruffle on shirt: jabot
rug: hearthrug, kilim, mat, maud, numdah, throw rug
rugby coaches: Sir Ian McGeechan, Sir Clive Woodward
rugby event: Six Nations
rugby players: Rob Andrew, Bill Beaumont, Serge Blanco, Naas Botha, David
  Campese, Will Carling, Dan Carter, Sébastien Chabal, Lawrence Dallaglio,
  Matt Dawson, Gareth Edwards, Danie Gerber, Ellery Hanley, Gavin Henson,
  Dickie Jeeps, Barry John, Martin Johnson, Michael Jones, Sean Lamont, Jonah
  Lomu, Willie John McBride, Sir Ian McGeechan, Colin Meads, Frederic
  Michalak, Lewis Moody, Brian Moore, François Pienaar, Hugo Porta, Andy
  Ripley, Jason Robinson, Jim Sullivan, Mike Tindall, Jonny Wilkinson
  (England's all-time top points scorer and 'winner' of the 2003 World Cup),
  J.P.R. Williams
ruin, fear of: atephobia
rule, adjective: hegemonic
rum: Bacardi, Captain Morgan's Parrot Bay, grog, Lamb's, mur (slang), myrrh
  (slang)
rum drink: daiquiri
rump, adjective: pygal
runners: Harold Abrahams, Atalanta, Roger Bannister (officially the first man to run
  a mile in less than four minutes, in 1954), Abebe Bikila, Usain Bolt, Leroy
  Burrell, Bob Brown, Dwain Chambers, Linford Christie, (Lord) Sebastian Coe,
  Steve Cram, Brendan Foster, Terry Fox, Frankie Fredericks, Dame Kelly Holmes
  ("the greatest British female Olympian of all time" who became the first British
  woman to win two gold medals at the Olympics, in Athens, 2004), Icarius, Ben
  Johnson, Alberto Juantorena, Carl Lewis, Eric Liddell, Lord Andrew Lindsay,
  Paavo Nurmi, Steve Ovett, James Parrot (unofficially the first man to run the
  four-minute mile, in 1770 - according to the historian Peter Radford),
  Pheidippides (who ran the first marathon, from Marathon to Athens to announce
  the Greek victory over the Persians), Asafa Powell, Steve Prefontaine, Paula
  Radcliffe, Frank C. Shorter, Lasse Virén, Allan Wells, Emil Zátopek
running, adjective: cursorial
rush (plant), adjective: juncaceous
Russia: largest country in the world; full name: Russian Federation
  capital: Moscow

currency: rouble
language: Russian
religion: aetheist, Russian Orthodox Christian
patron saints of: Andrew, Basil the Great, Casimir, Joseph and Nicholas
Russian airline: Aeroflot
Russian alphabet: Cyrillic
Russian composers: Aleksandr Borodin, Mikhail Glinka, Aram Khatchaturian,
    Modest Mussorgsky, Sergei Prokofiev, Sergei Rachmaninov, Nikolai Rimsky-
    Korsakov, Aleksandr Scriabin, Dmitri Shostakovich, Igor Stravinsky, Pyotr
    Ilyich Tchaikovsky
Russian dancers: Mikhail Baryshnikov, Michel Fokine, Alexander Godunov,
    Natalia Makarova, Vaslaw Nijinsky, Rudolf Nureyev, Anna Pavlova
Russian doll: babushka, Marusia
Russian empress: Catherine the Great
Russian film directors: Sergei Bodrov, Sergei Bondarchuk, Sergei Eisenstein, Elem
    Klimov, Andrei Konchalovsky, Nikita Mikhalkov, Alexander Sokurov, Andrei
    Tarkovsky
Russian leaders: Alexander III (1881–1894), Yuri V. Andropov (1982–1984), Leonid
    I. Brezhnev (1964–1982), Catherine II the Great (1762–1796), Konstantin U.
    Chernenko (1984–1985), Mikhail S. Gorbachev (1985–1991), Ivan IV the
    Terrible (1533–1584), Nikita S. Khrushchev (1958–1964), Vladimir Ilyich
    Lenin (1917–1924), Georgi M. Malenkov (1953–1955), Vyacheslav Molotov
    (1930–1941), Nicholas II (1894–1917), Peter I the Great (1682–1725), Vladimir
    Putin (2000–), Joseph Stalin (1941–1953), Boris Yeltstin (1991–1999)
Russian painters: Ivan Aivazovsky, Wassily Kandinsky, Kazimir Malevich,
    Vladimir Tatlin
Russian pancake: blini
Russian parliament: the Duma
Russian peasant: muzhik
Russian playwrights: Anton Chekhov, Nikolai Gogol, Vladimir Mayakovsky,
    Vladimir Sorokin, Ivan Turgenev
Russian poets: Velimir Khlebnikov, Boris Pasternak, Yevgeni Yevtushenko
Russian police chief: Lavrentiy Beria
Russian politicians: Lavrentiy Beria, Mikhail Suslov
    – see Russian leaders
Russian pop duo: t.A.T.u.
Russian reform: glasnost, perestroika
Russian soprano: Anna Netrebko
Russian soup: bortsch, shchi
Russian tennis players: Anna Kournikova, Maria Sharapova
Russian writers: Anton Chekhov, Fyodor Dostoevsky, Nikolai Gogol, Maxim
    Gorky, Andrey Kurkov, Vladimir Nabokov, Boris Pasternak, Viktor Pelevin,
    Alexander Pushkin, Ayn Rand, Mikhail Sholokhov, Aleksandr Solzhenitsyn,
    Vladimir Sorokin, Leo Tolstoy, Ivan Turgenev
Russo-Japanese War: 1904–05
rust, adjective: ferruginous
rust, fear of: iophobia
Rutland, administrative centre: Oakham
Rwanda: republic in central Africa
    capitol: Kigali
    currency: Rwanda franc

language: Rwandan, French, English
religion: Roman Catholic, African Protestant, Muslim, animist
fact: in less than 100 days during 1994, more than 800,000 Rwandans were
murdered (mostly in churches) by fellow countrymen

S

sable, adjective: zibeline
sable fur: zibeline
sacred dance, muse of: Polyhymnia
sacred things, fear of: hierophobia
sacrifice by fire: immolation
SAD: seasonal affective disorder (from which 10 million Americans suffer)
saddle, woman's: pillion
saddle flap: skirt
saddle girth: cinch
saddle loop: tug
saddle pad: numnah
saddle projection (at the back): cantle
saddle projection (at the front): pommel
saddle strap: crupper
safe-breaker: peterman (slang)
safe-breaker, famous: Eddie Chapman
Saga: company that provides a range of benefits for people aged 50 and over, such
as financial and insurance services
sail, adjective: velic
sailor, adjective: nautical
sailor, collective noun: crew, deck, watch
sailors, famous – see yachtsmen and women
sailors, patron saints of: Brendan, Constabilis, Elmo and Francis of Paola
Sainsbury's: supermarket chain that began life in 1869 as a small dairy shop in
Drury Lane, London, selling butter, milk and eggs
saint, biography of: hagiography
Saint Kitts-Nevis: independent state in the East Caribbean
capital: Basseterre
currency: East Caribbean dollar
language: English
religion: Protestant
Saint Lucia: island state in the Caribbean
capital: Castries
currency: East Caribbean dollar
language: English
religion: Roman Catholic
Saint Patrick's Day: 17 March
Saint Petersburg, ballet company: Ballet of the Marinsky Theatre (aka the Kirov)
Saint Petersburg, leading film studio: Lenfilm
Saint Petersburg river: Neva
Saint Vincent and the Grenadines: island state in the Caribbean
capital: Kingstown
currency: Caribbean dollar
language: English

religion: Protestant (majority)

sake, fact: there are more types of sake in Japan than there are wines in France

salad: Caesar, Greek, green, Niçoise, Russian, side salad, tabbouleh (Arab), Waldorf

salesmen: Arthur Daley (from TV's *Minder*), Elmer Gantry, Willy Loman (from Arthur Miller's *Death of a Salesman*)

saliva, adjective: sialic, sialoid

saliva, agent or thing that promotes salivation (i.e. chocolate, Angelina Jolie): sialogogue

saliva, fact: during a lifetime, the average human being generates 10,000 gallons of saliva

saliva, lack of: aptyalism

salmon, after spawning: kelt

salmon, female: hen

salmon, male: cock

salmon, swimming speed: 25 mph

salmon, young: fingerling, fry, grilse (in its second year), parr, smolt

Salome: opera by Richard Strauss first produced in Dresden in 1905

salsa, queen of: Celia Cruz

salt: monosodium glutamate (MSG)

salt, adjective: haloid, saline

salt removal: desalination

Salvadorian archbishop: Oscar Romero

Salvadorian Civil War: 1980–1992

salvation, adjective: soterial

salvation (theologically speaking), adjective: soteriological

Salvation Army: Christian organisation dedicated to social work and helping the poor, founded by William and Catherine Booth in 1865

Salzburg airport: Mozart

Samaritans, The: charity founded in 1953 by Chad Varah

sameness: homogeneity

Samoa: independent state comprising nine islands (five of them uninhabited) in South Pacific archipelago

    capital: Apia

    currency: tala

    language: Samoan, English

    religion: Christian

samurai: Oda Nobuyuki, Ryoma Sakamoto (19th century warrior who packed a six-shooter revolver and had an airport in Kochi, Japan, named after him)

samurai code of honour: bushido

samurai outlaw: ronin

samurai suicide: hara-kiri

sand, adjective: arenoid, arenaceous, sabulous, sabulose, sabuline

sand-loving: ammophilous

sandals: chappal (Indian), espadrille, flip-flop, jelly, Jesus boot, Springer, zori (Japanese)

sandalwood perfume: chypre

sandpiper, adjective: tringoid

sandpiper, collective noun: fling

sandstone: psammite (rare)

sandstone, adjective: arenilitic

Sandwich Islands: former name for Hawaii

San Francisco, birthplace of: Bill Bixby, Mel Blanc, Counting Crows, Clint Eastwood, Robert Frost (poet), Jerry Garcia, Grateful Dead, Josh Hartnett, William Randolph Hearst, Steve Jobs, Jack London, Robert McNamara, O.J. Simpson, Irving Stone

San Francisco, fact: "between 1969 and 1973, at least 9,000 gay men moved to San Francisco" (c/o Randy Shilts)

San Francisco, gay quarter: Castro district

San Francisco, red light district: Market Street

San Francisco, tourist attractions: Coit Memorial Tower on Telegraph Hill, Fisherman's Wharf, Golden Gate Bridge, Transamerica Pyramid Building

San Francisco ballet company: San Francisco Ballet

San Marino: very small republic within eastern-central Italy
    capital: San Marino
    currency: euro; formerly: lira
    language: Italian
    religion: Roman Catholic

Santa's reindeer: Dasher, Dancer, Prancer, Vixen, Comet, Cupid, Donner, Blitzen and Rudolph

Santiago, Chile, airport: Arturo Marino Benitez

São Tomé and Principe: republic in the Gulf of Guinea
    capital: São Tomé
    currency: dobra
    language: Portuguese
    religion: Roman Catholic

São Paulo, birthplace of: Ayrton Senna

São Paulo sports stadium: Estadio Morumbi

Sarajevo, bridge: The Bridge of Brotherhood and Unity

sardine, collective noun: family

Sars: severe acute respiratory syndrome

SAS, former Commander of Special Forces: Sir Peter de la Billiere

SAS novelist: Andy McNab

SAT: standard assessment test

Satan: Antichrist, Archfiend, Auld Hornie, Azazel, Beelzebub, Belial, Clootie, Day-star Son of the Dawn (Hebrew translation of Helel ben-Shahar), The Deuce, The Devil, Diabolus, the Dickens, fallen angel, Father of Lies, God of This World, God's prosecution lawyer, Helel ben-Shahar (Hebrew), hellion, Lucifer, Mephisto, Mephistopheles, Miffy, Old Gentleman, Old Harry, Old Ned, Old Nick, Old Scratch, Prince of Darkness, Prince of This World, proud angel, The Serpent, Son of the Morning (Isaiah)

Satan, fear of: Satanophobia

Satchmo: nickname for Louis Armstrong

satellites falling, fear of: keraunothnetophobia

satirists: Clive Anderson, Aristophanes, John Barclay, Roberto Benigni, Ambrose Bierce, Sebastian Brant, Craig Brown, Thomas Brown, Lord Byron, Peter Cook, Alan Coren, William Donaldson (aka Henry Root), Eminem, Dario Fo, Jaroslav Hašek, William Hogarth, William Hone, Horace, Clive James, Juvenal, Paul Krassner, Tom Lehrer, John Marston, Jean de Meung, Michael Moore, Thomas Nashe, P.J. O'Rourke, Thomas Love Peacock, Alexander Pope, Jacques Prévert, François Rabelais, Mort Sahl, Ronald Searle, Lucius Annaeus Seneca, Ned Sherrin, Jonathan Swift, James Thurber, Nathanael West, John Wolcot

Saturday Night Live: experimental TV comedy revue produced by NBC which became an unexpected breeding ground for comic genius and movie stars.

first broadcast: 11 October 1975
cast regulars: Dan Aykroyd, Jim Belushi, John Belushi, Albert Brooks, Dana
  Carvey, Chevy Chase, Billy Crystal, Jane Curtin, Joan Cusack, Jimmy
  Fallon, Chris Farley, Will Ferrell, Tina Fey, Anthony Michael Hall, Phil
  Hartman, Victoria Jackson, Chris Kattan, Norm Macdonald, Steve Martin,
  Tim Meadows, Garrett Morris, Eddie Murphy, Bill Murray, Mike Myers,
  Laraine Newman, Joe Piscopo, Amy Poehler, Randy Quaid, Gilda Radner,
  Chris Rock, Charles Rockett, Maya Rudolph, Andy Samberg, Adam
  Sandler, Rob Schneider, Molly Shannon, Martin Short, David Spade,
  Ben Stiller, Julia Sweeney, Robert Townsend, Damon Wayans
sauce: aïoli, avgolémono, béarnaise, béchamel, bolognaise, bordelaise, brown sauce,
  catsup, chocolate sauce (sweet), Cumberland sauce, custard (sweet), espagnole,
  fumet, glace de viande, gravy, guacamole, hollandaise, HP, ketchup,
  mayonnaise, mole (Mexican), mousseline, pesto, ragú (Bolognese), ravigote
  (French), rouille (French), romesco, skorthalia, stock, tarator, travelling sauce,
  velouté, vinaigrette, white sauce
saucer-shaped, adjective: pateriform
Saudi Arabia: kingdom in South-West Asia
  capital: Riyadh (royal), Jidda (administrative)
  currency: riyal (subdivided into 100 halala)
  language: Arabic
  religion: Muslim (Sunni)
sausage: andouillette, beef, bierschinken, birnenformige salami, black pudding,
  boudin, bratwurst, butifara, cervelat, chipolata, cotechino, country style salami,
  crépinette, Cumberland, Danish salami, edel salami, extrawurst, farmer-style
  salami, felinetti, frankfurter, French herb, French pepper, Genoa salami,
  German salami, Greek, hot dog, Hungarian salami, katenrauchwurst, kielbasa,
  knackwurst, knoblauchwurst, land salami, lap cheong, Luganeghe, Merguez,
  mettwurst, Milano salami, Morcilla, mortadella, Napoli salami, netz salami,
  paprika, peperoni/pepperoni, pfeffer plockwurst, pork, pork and beef, salami,
  salamelle, salsiccie casalinga, saucisson fume aux herbes, saveloy, schinken
  jagdwurst, schinken kalbfleischwurst, schinkensulzwurst, skinless, smoked,
  spiced English, spiced French, teewurst, toscana, Toulouse, venison, Wall's,
  zampone, zungenwurst
sausage, adjective: allantoid
sausage, slang: banger, snag (Australian)
sausage-shaped: allantoic, allantoid
saviours: Christ (see), John Rabe, Oskar Schindler, Raoul Wallenberg
Savoy Hotel, culinary creation: peach Melba
saxophone: invented by Adolphe Sax in 1846
saxophonists: Albert Ayler, Sidney Bechet, Benny Carter, Ornette Coleman, John
  Coltrane, Eric Dolphy, Jimmy Dorsey, Stan Getz, Benny Green, Coleman
  Hawkins, Illinois Jacquet, Steve Lacy, Gerry Mulligan, Charlie Parker, Evan
  Parker, Courtney Pine, Don Redman, Sonny Rollins, Pharoah Sanders, Ronnie
  Scott, Lester Young
SC: postcode for South Carolina
scale-like: ganoid
scalpel: bistoury
scaly anteater: pangolin
scampi prawn: Dublin Bay prawn, Norway lobster

scar, adjective: uloid
Scarborough playhouse: The Stephen Joseph Theatre
scare: "A good scare is worth more to a man than good advice" – Edgar Watson Howe
scarecrow: Worzel Gummidge
scarf: ascot (type of cravat), babushka, boa, comforter, cravat, foulard, headscarf, headsquare, Hermès, mantilla (Spanish), muffler, puggaree, square, stole, wrap
scarf, choked to death by: Isadora Duncan (when her ubiquitous stole caught in the wheel of her open-topped car)
Scarface: nickname for Al Capone
scent: eau de parfum, perfume
scent, some brands: Aqua Allegoria Tutti Kiwi (Guerlain), Brut (Fabergé), Cacherel Amor Amor Eau Fraiche, Casmir (Chopard), CKOne (Calvin Klein), Clive Christian, Coco (Chanel), Dior Addict, Escada Eau De Parfum, Evelyn Rose (Crabtree & Evelyn), Femme (Boss), Ghost Serenity, Island (Michael Kors), Just Cavalli Her (Roberto Cavalli), Lovely Prism (Givenchy), MAC Creations, Miracle (Lancôme), Miss Sixty Elixir, Moments, Must (Cartier), No 5 Chanel, Opium (Yves St Laurent), Oscar de la Renta, Paloma Picasso, Paris (Yves St Laurent), Safari (Ralph Lauren), Sun Moon Stars (Lagerfeld), Tommy Girl 10 (Tommy Hilfiger), Touch of Pink (Lacoste), Valentino, Vendetta (Valentino), Very Sexy For Her (Victoria's Secret)
scent bottle: flacon
schemer: Jezebel
schizophrenics: Shirley Ardell Mason (the model for Sybil Isabel Dorsett, the subject of Flora Rheta Schreiber's book *Sybil*), Dr Jekyll, Sybil Isabel Dorsett (as played by Sally Field in the TV movie *Sybil*)
Schlitz beer slogan: 'The Beer that made Milwaukee famous'
school, adjective: scholastic
school, fear of: scholionophobia
school attendance, fear of: didaskaleinophobia
school types: athlete, bully, cheerleader, dweeb, goth, homecoming queen, jock, mathlete, nerd, queen bee, swat, swot, wannabe
schoolboys: Tom Brown, William Brown (of *Just William* fame), Billy Bunter, Adrian Mole, nigel molesworth [sic], Harry Potter, Tom Sawyer, Mick Travers (as played by Malcolm McDowell in *If...*)
schools, British: Bedford, Brentwood, Charterhouse, Eton, Gordonstoun (see), Harrow, King's School (Canterbury), King's School (Rochester), Lancing, Merchant Taylor's, Radley College, Roedean, Rugby, St Albans, St Paul's, St Peter's (York), Sherborne, Shrewsbury, Tonbridge, Uppingham, Westminster, Winchester, Wolverhampton
- see girls' schools, UK
schoolteacher: "A schoolteacher is a disillusioned woman who used to think she liked children" - anonymous
science: "Science without religion is lame; religion without science is blind" – Albert Einstein
science fiction award: Hugo (named after the sci-fi publisher Hugo Gernsback)
science fiction writers: Douglas Adams, Brian W. Aldiss, Roger MacBride Allen, Kevin J. Anderson, Poul Anderson, Piers Anthony, Isaac Asimov, J.G. Ballard, Iain M. Banks, Stephen Baxter, Greg Bear, Gregory Benford, Alfred Bester, Michael Bishop, James Blish, Ray Bradbury, John Brunner, Edgar Rice Burroughs, Anthony Burgess, Jack L. Chalker, Sir Arthur C. Clarke, Michael Crichton, Philip K. Dick, Harlan Ellison, Philip José Farmer, William Gibson,

Robert A. Heinlein, Frank Herbert, Sir Fred Hoyle, L. Ron Hubbard, Aldous Huxley, Ursula H. Le Guin, Stanislaw Lem, Barry N. Malzberg, Richard Matheson, Paul J. McAuley, Ian McDonald, Michael Moorcock, Larry Niven, Andre Norton, Paul Park, Frederick Pohl, Kim Stanley Robinson, Robert Silverberg, John T. Sladek, Olaf Stapledon, Bruce Sterling, Theodore Sturgeon, James Tiptree Jr., Jack Vance, Jules Verne, A.E. van Vogt, Kurt Vonnegut, H.G. Wells, Kate Wilhelm, Gene Wolfe, John Wyndham, Roger Zelazny

science philosopher: Ernest Nagel

science writers: Bill Bryson, Richard Dawkins, Jared Diamond, Stephen Jay Gould, Stephen Hawking, Steve Jones, Eric Kandel, Fred Pearce, Roger Penrose, Matt Ridley, Simon Singh

scientist: prof, propeller head, nanotechnologist

scientists: George Wells Beadle, Prof. Baruch Blumberg, Robert Boyle, Wernher von Braun, Professor Challenger (from Conan Doyle's *The Lost World*), Sir William Congreve, Nicolaus Copernicus, Marie Curie, Thomas Edison, Paul Ehrlich, Albert Einstein, Sir Martin Evans (the first scientist to isolate stem cells from mouse embryos), Baron Frankenstein, Benjamin Franklin, Galileo Galilei, William Gilbert, Stephen Hawking, Sir John Herschel, Albert Hofmann, Robert Hooke, Edward Jenner, Donald F. Jones, Michio Kaku, Immanuel Kant, Johannes Kepler, Edwin H. Land, James Lovelock, Gregor Mendel, Sir Isaac Newton, Robert Oppenheimer, Paracelsus, René Antoine Ferchault de Réaumur, Frederick Sanger, C.P.Snow, Kip Thorne, Sir William Watson
- see biochemists, chemists, physicists, etc

scientists, patron saint of: Albert the Great

scientific name: onym

Scientology: movement founded in 1948 by the science-fiction writer L. Ron Hubbard

Scientology members: Kirstie Alley, Anne Archer (film actress), Beck, Chick Corea, Tom Cruise, Jenna Elfman (actress and comedienne), Isaac Hayes, Michael Jackson, Nicole Kidman (lapsed), Jason Lee, Demi Moore, Lisa Marie Presley, Kelly Preston, Giovanni Ribisi, Mimi Rogers (lapsed), John Travolta

scimitar-shaped: acinaciform

scissor-shaped: forficiform

scorpion, adjective: pedipalpous, scorpioid

Scotch: Bailie Nicol Jarvie, Ballantine's, Bell's, Cutty Sark, Famous Grouse, Grant's, J&B Rare, Johnnie Walker

Scotland, adjective: Caledonian

Scotland, nickname: Marmalade Country (19th century music hall slang)

Scotland, patron saints of: Andrew and Margaret

Scotsman, The: Scottish newspaper founded 25 January 1817 by the lawyer William Ritchie

Scottish beret: tam-o'-shanter

Scottish groups: Altered Images, The Average White Band, Aztec Camera, Bay City Rollers, Belle & Sebastian, The Beta Band, Big Country, The Blow Monkeys, Blue, The Blue Nile, BMX Bandits, Cocteau Twins, Deacon Blue, Del Amitri, Dogs Die in Hot Cars, Fairground Attraction, Franz Ferdinand, The Fratellis, Hue and Cry, The Jesus and Mary Chain, Marmalade, Midge Ure, Mogwai, Orange Juice, The Proclaimers, Simple Minds, Snow Patrol, Strawberry Switchblade, Texas, Travis, The View, Wet Wet Wet

Scottish inventions: bicycle, insulin, kaleidoscope, overdraft, penicillin, pneumatic tyres, radar, steam engine, telephone, television, transistor

Scottish mayor: provost

Scottish patriots: Ian Hamilton, Robert the Bruce, Sir William Wallace (played by Mel Gibson in *Braveheart*)

Scottish poets: Blind Harry, Robert Burns, Sir Arthur Conan Doyle, Ivor Cutler, George MacDonald, William McGonagall, Edwin Muir, Sir Walter Scott, Robert Louis Stevenson

Scottish regions: Borders, Central, Dumfries and Galloway, Fife, Grampian, Highland, Lothian, Strathclyde, Tayside; island areas: Orkney, Shetland, Western Isles

scout master: Lord Robert Baden-Powell

scratched, fear of being: amychophobia

screen door, Japanese: shoji

screenplays, fact: 30,000 screenplays are registered with The Writers Guild of America annually

screw: invented by Archimedes of Syracuse (287–212 BC)

scrivener: Bartleby (from Melville's *The Piazza Tales*)

scroll ornament (in decoration and architecture): cartouche

scrotum, adjective: oscheal

scuba (acronym): Self-Contained Underwater Breathing Apparatus

sculptors: Wäinö Aaltonen, Carl André, Jean Arp, John Bacon, Frédéric-Auguste Bartholdi, Gian Lorenzo Bernini, Gutzon Borglum (famous for his carving of four US presidents on Mount Rushmore), Louise Bourgeois, Constantin Brancusi, Antonio Canova, Sir Anthony Caro, Alexander Calder, Judy Chicago, Christo, Camille Claudel, Tony Cragg, Jules Dalou, Richard Deacon, Willem de Kooning, Donatello, Sir Jacob Epstein, Dame Elisabeth Frink, Alberto Giacometti, Grinling Gibbons, Eric Gill, Antony Gormley, Maggi Hambling, Duane Hanson ("puts Madame Tussauds to shame"), Dame Barbara Hepworth, Donald Judd, Anish Kapoor, Jeff Koons, Jannis Kounellis, Leonardo Da Vinci, Alexander Liberman, Jacques Lipchitz, Richard Long, David Mach, Aristide Maillol, Michelangelo Buonarroti, Kate Millett, Henry Moore, Ron Mueck, Louise Nevelson, Isamu Noguchi, Claes Oldenbourg, Pheidias, Praxiteles, Marc Quinn, Auguste Rodin, Richard Serra, David Smith, Robert Smithson, Veit Stoss, Andrea del Verrocchio, Rachel Whiteread

sculptors, patron saints of: Claude and Luke the Apostle

sculptures: *Angel of the North* (66ft figure of an angel in Gateshead, Tyne and Wear, by Antony Gormley), *The Burghers of Calais* (Rodin), *David* (Michelangelo), *Ebbsfleet Landmark* (164tf steel white horse in Kent, the brainchild of Mark Wallinger), *Falling Man* (Giacometti figure that sold for $18.5 million in 2007), *The Kiss* (Rodin), *Little Mermaid* (bronze statue in Copenhagen sculpted by Edvard Erichsen), *Mannekin-Pis* (Brussels statue of a urinating boy originally sculpted by Jerome Duquesnoy, but now replaced by a copy), Mount Rushmore (see), *Pietà* (Michelangelo), *Prospero and Ariel* (Eric Gill), *Stations of the Cross* (Eric Gill), *The Thinker* (Rodin), *Venus de Milo* (once thought to have been hewn by Praxiteles, but now attributed to an anonymous artist) (see) - see statues

scurvy, adjective: scorbutic

scythe-shaped: drepaniform

SD: postcode for South Dakota

sea, adjective: marine, maritime, thalassic (especially of inland seas)

sea, fear of: thalassophobia

sea, god of: Aegir (Norse mythology), Neptune (Roman), Poseidon (Greek)

sea, goddess of: Amphitrite (wife of Poseidon), Ran (Norse)

sea, obsession with: thalassomania

sea, open; adjective: pelagic

sea, original: Panthalassa (that which enveloped the entire globe)

sea captains: Ahab, William Bligh, Peter Blood, James Cook, Hook, William Kidd, Hans Langsdorff, Wolf Larsen (from Jack London's *The Sea Wolf*), Pugwash (see, under Captain Pugwash), Jack Sparrow (played by Johnny Depp in *The Pirates of the Caribbean*)
- see admirals, explorers, naval officers, pirates, etc

sea devil: Davy Jones

sea horse, adjective: hippocampine

sea monster: hippodame, kraken, leviathan (Biblical)

sea monsters, god of: Paikea (Polynesian mythology)

sea nymphs: Galatea, Nereid

sea spray: spindrift

sea swell, fear of: cymophobia

sea without a coast: Sargasso Sea (in the North Atlantic)

seagull, adjective: laroid

seagull, collective noun: colony

seagull, sound: squawk

seagull, young: chick

seal (of the secure kind), adjective: sphragistic

seal (the mammal), adjective: phocine

seal, collective noun: colony, herd, pod

seal, female: cow

seal, male: bull

seal, young: pup

seals, study of: sphragistics

seamen, adjective: nautical

seamstress: Betsy Ross

seasickness: mal de mer, naupathia

seaside postcards, artist of: Donald McGill

seasons, goddesses of: the Horae (Greek mythology)

seat belts; first made compulsory in: Czechoslovakia, in January 1969

Seattle, ballet company: Pacific Northwest Ballet

Seattle, birthplace of: Paul Allen, Carol Channing, Judy Collins, Frances Farmer, Bill Gates, Gypsy Rose Lee, Jimi Hendrix

Seattle, fact: consumes more coffee than any city in the USA

Seattle, groups: Alice in Chains, Foo Fighters, Heart, Nirvana, Pearl Jam, Soundgarden, Supersuckers

Seattle, landmark: Space Needle

Seattle, nickname; formerly: Jet City (because Boeing had its headquarters there)

seaweed eater: fucivore

Second Amendment: the right to keep and bear arms

Second City: nickname for Chicago

Second World War: 1 September 1939–2 September 1945

secrets: Atlantis (location of), Deep Throat (identity of - later revealed as FBI agent W. Mark Felt), Holy Grail (location of), King Solomon's Mines (opening of), Rosetta Stone, the Vatican's Fatima secret, the anonymous Watergate whistle-blower, the identity of the subject of the Carly Simon song *You're So Vain*

secret agents: Cody Banks, Modesty Blaise, James Bond, John Drake (from TV's *Danger Man*), Derek Flint, Matt Helm, Illya Kuryakin (from TV's *The Man*

From U.N.C.LE.), G. Gordon Liddy, Angus MacGyver (from TV's *MacGyver*),
W. Somerset Maugham, Lady Penelope (c/o TV's *Thunderbirds*), Maxwell
Smart, Napoleon Solo (from TV's *The Man From U.N.C.LE.*), Adolph Verloc
(hero of Joseph Conrad's *The Secret Agent*)
- see spies
secretaries, patron saint of: Genesius of Arles
sect leaders: Warren Jeffs, Jim Jones, David Koresh
sects: Adventists, Albigenses, Amish, black Muslims, Diggers, Donatism, Druze,
Fundamentalist Church of Jesus Christ of Latter Day Saints, Hare Krishna,
Heaven's Gate (see 'suicide, mass'), Jehovah's Witnesses, Levellers, Mennonites,
Moonies, Muggletonians, Nazarenes, Nizari, Pharisees, Rastafarianism, Seventh-
Day Adventists, Shakerism, Sikhism, United Society of Believers in Christ's
Second Appearing, Wahabi, Worldwide Unification Church, Zealots
security guard: Frank Wills (who, in the early hours of 17 June 1972, discovered a
burglary at the Watergate Hotel in an office leased to the Democratic National
Committee. In the words of the crusading journalist Bob Woodward, Frank
Wills was "the only one in Watergate who did his job perfectly")
seductress, politically correct term: seductron
seed, adjective: seminiferous
seed coating: testa
seeds, study of: carpology, spermology
seers – see soothsayers
Seinfeld: hugely popular TV sitcom in which the stand-up comic Jerry Seinfeld
played a variation of himself, mixing his comedy routines with domestic
sketches featuring a handful of regular fictitious characters
    created by Jerry Seinfeld and Larry David
    broadcast: 31 May 1990–14 May 1998
    cast: Jerry Seinfeld (Jerry Seinfeld), Jason Alexander (George Costanza), Julia
        Louis-Dreyfus (Elaine Benes), Michael Richards (Cosmo Kramer), Wayne
        Knight (Newman), Estelle Harris (Estelle Costanza), Jerry Stiller (Frank
        Costanza), Patrick Warburton (David Puddy)
self-deceit: "Nothing is easier than self-deceit. For what each man wishes, that he
also believes to be true" - Demosthenes
self-help authorities: Stephen Potter, Gary Zukav
self-help books: *The Art of Making Friends*; *The Be Happy Attitudes*, by Robert H.
Schuller; *The Break-up Survival Kit* (by Pam Spurr); *Breast is Best*;
A Father's Legacy to His Daughters (1774; by Dr John Gregory); *Feel the
Fear and Do It Anyway* (by Susan Jeffers); *Guide to Getting It On* (by
Paul Joannides); *He's Just Not That into You* (by Greg Behrendt and Liz
Tuccillo); *How to Talk So Kids Will Listen & Listen So Kids Will Talk*
(by Adele Faber and Elaine Mazlish); *How to Win Friends and Influence
People* (by Dale Carnegie, first published in 1937); *The Joy of Sex: A Gourmet
Guide To Lovemaking* (1972; by Alex Comfort); *The Little Book of Calm* (by
Paul Wilson); *Men Are from Mars, Women Are from Venus* (by John Gray);
Organizing From the Inside Out (by Julie Morgenstern); *The Power of Positive
Thinking* (by Norman Vincent Peale); *Power Through Constructive Thinking*
(by Emmet Fox); *The Purpose-Driven Life* (by Rick Warren); *Queen Bees and
Wannabes: Helping Your Daughter Survive Cliques, Gossip, Boyfriends and
Other Realities of Adolescence* (by Rosalind Wiseman); *The Real Rules* (by
Barbara de Angelis); *The Road Less Traveled* (by M. Scott Peck); *The Secret*
(by Rhonda Byrne); *Self-Help; with Illustrations of Character and Conduct*

(by Samuel Smiles); *Self Matters* (by Dr Phil McGraw); *The Sermon on the Mount: The Key to Success in Life* (by Emmet Fox); *The Seven Habits of Highly Effective People* (by Stephen R. Covey); *Status Anxiety* (by Alain de Botton); *Women's Pleasure* (by Rachel Swift); *Zen and the Art of Motorcycle Maintenance* (by Robert M. Pirsig)

self-knowledge: autognosis

self-worship: autolatry

semen: come, cream, cum, jism, love juice, maria monk (rhyming slang), milt, protein, seed, sperm, splooge, spunk

semen, adjective: seminal

semicolon: first used in print by Aldus Manutius in 1494

Senegal: republic in West Africa
    capital: Dakar
    currency: African franc
    language: French
    religion: Muslim

Senegalese and famous: Akon (full name: Aliaune Damala Bouga Time Puru Nacka Lu Lu Lu Badara Akon Thiam) (of Senegalese descent), Baaba Maal (singer), Youssou N'Dour (musician), Ousmane Sembene (filmmaker), Léopold Senghor (poet)

senility, study of: nostology

sense, adjective: sensory, sensorial

sensorial duplication (by which a person can appreciate colours, words or sounds with two or more senses simultaneously, a condition found in one of 2,000 people): synaesthesia

sentence containing all the letters of the alphabet: pangram

sentence of one word (in English): monepic

sentimentality: "What we call the sentiment we don't share" - Grahan Greene; "Sentimentality is the emotional promiscuity of those who have no sentiment" - Norman Mailer

Serbia: republic of the former Yugoslavia
    capital: Belgrade
    currency: Serbian dinar
    language: Serbian (95%), Albanian
    religion: Orthodox (65%), Muslim (19%), Roman Catholic, Protestant

Serbian secret police: MUP

Serendip: medieval name for Sri Lanka

serial killer: term coined by FBI agent Rex Ressler in 1978

serial killer capital: Rostov, in southern Russia (the size of Manchester and home to 30 serial killers)

serial killers: Donato Bilancia (nicknamed the 'Riviera Killer,' who confessed to 17 murders), Ian Brady and Myra Hindley (who abused and murdered five children in the 1960s), Ted Bundy, John Bunting (the 'Snowtown killer'), Andrei Chikatilo (a travelling salesman who confessed to the murder of 56 boys), John Christie (who lived at 10 Rillington Place), Jeffrey Dahmer, Albert DeSalvo (aka The Boston Strangler), Michel Fourniret (the 'Ogre of Ardennes'), Ed Gein, Fritz Haarmann (murdered teenage boys to sell as meat), Anthony Hardy (Camden Town killer), Colin Ireland (the 'Gay Slayer'), Jack the Ripper (killed five prostitutes in 1888), Richard Kuklinski (who confessed to killing over 200 people), Peter Kürten (nicknamed the 'Monster of Düsseldorf'), Henri-Desire Landru (nicknamed 'Bluebeard'), Henry Lee Lucas (confessed to the murder of

600 people), Charles Manson, Ivan Milat (murdered seven backpackers in the Australian Outback), Dennis Nilsen (strangled or drowned at least 15 students and homeless men), Anatoly Onoprienko (Ukrainian responsible for at least 52 murders), Dr Marcel Petiot (confessed to the murder of 63 people during the Second World War), Alexander Pichushkin (known as the 'Chessboard Killer' and convicted of 48 murders), Dennis Rader (aka 'the BTK killer'), Gary Ridgway (dubbed the 'Green River killer'; in November 2003, in Seattle, he pleaded guilty to murdering 48 women), Jean-Claude Romand (as chronicled in the film *L'emploi du temps*), Harold Shipman GP (Britain's most prolific serial killer of the 20th century, credited with at least 215 murders), Roberto Succo, Peter Sutcliffe (the 'Yorkshire Ripper'), Jack Unterweger (also a playwright and author of children's stories), Frederick West (accused of murdering 12 young women, then committed suicide on 1 January 1995), Steve Wright (the 'Suffolk Strangler'), Aileen Wuornos (a prostitute who killed six of her clients and is reportedly the world's first female serial killer)

sermon, adjective: homiletic

sermons, art of writing: homiletics

serpent, adjective: serpiginous

serums, science of: serology

servants: Bunter (for Lord Peter Wimsey), Launcelot Gobbo (for Shylock), Mrs Hudson (for Sherlock Holmes), Reginald Jeeves (for Bertie Wooster), Miss Lemon (for Hercule Poirot), Sancho Panza (for Don Quixote), Passepartout (for Phileas Fogg)
- see also butlers, housekeepers and slaves

servants, patron saint of: Zita of Lucca

sesame oil: gingili

sesame paste: tahini

Sesame Street: influential, hugely popular children's show which blended education, entertainment, songs, puppets, animation and celebrity guests in an irresistible package. Aimed at inner-city pre-schoolers, the show was based on the eponymous city street but proved popular to children (and adults) of every denomination.
created by: Joan Ganz Cooney, executive director of the Children's Television Workshop
first broadcast: 10 November 1969
cast: Loretta Long (Susan), Matt Robinson and Roscoe Orman (Gordon), Bob McGrath (Bob), Will Lee (Mr Hooper), Northern J. Calloway (David), Emilio Delgado (Luis), Sonia Manzano (Maria). Of equal importance (if not more so) where the puppets created by Jim Henson: Bert, the Cookie Monster, Ernie, Grover, Oscar the Grouch and Big Bird
(see **Big Bird**)

SETI: Search for Extra-Terrestrial Intelligence

seven, adjective: septenary

seven deadly sins: pride, covetousness (or greed), lust, envy, gluttony, anger and sloth

Seven Dwarfs (as featured in Disney's *Snow White and the Seven Dwarfs*): Bashful, Doc, Dopey, Grumpy, Happy, Sleepy and Sneezy

seven virtues: faith, fortitude, hope, justice, love (charity), prudence, temperance

Seven Wonders of the Ancient World: Colossus of Rhodes, The Great Pyramid of Giza, The Hanging Gardens of Babylon, Mausoleum at Halicarnassus, Pharos of Alexandria, The Statue of Zeus at Olympia, Temple of Artemis at Ephesus

Seven Wonders of the Modern World (drawn up in July 2007, based on over 100 million votes): Chichén Itzá in Mexico, Christ the Redeemer in Rio de Janeiro, the Great Wall of China, Machu Picchu in Peru, the Petra archaeological site in Jordan, the Roman Colosseum in Italy, the Taj Mahal in India

Seven Years War: 1756–1763

seven-hundredth anniversary: septcentenary

seven-sided figure: heptagon

seven-sided solid figure: heptahedron

Seventies – see Nineteen Seventies

seventy-year-old: septuagenarian

Seville: capital of tapas

Seville, birthplace of: Paz Vega (actress), Diego Velázquez

sewing case: étui

sewing machine: invented in 1846 by Elias Howe (USA)

sex: humpy-pumpy, nookie, rumpy-pumpy, skin theatre
- see copulation

sex: "Love is the answer, but while you're waiting for the answer, sex raises some pretty good questions" - Woody Allen; "Sex is like air. It's not important unless you aren't getting any" – anonymous; "Christianity has done a great deal for love by making it a sin" – Anatole France; "Sex is one of the most beautiful, wholesome, natural things that money can buy" – Steve Martin; "Sex is the only mysticism offered by materialism" – Malcolm Muggeridge

sex, average times a year for a homo sapien: 103 (according to the 2005 global Durex Sex Survey)

Sex and the City: exceedingly popular (and controversial) TV series focusing on four single New York women and their candid observations of the mating game. An enormously successful film of the show was released in 2008
written by Candace Bushnell
broadcast: 6 June 1998–22 February 2004
cast: Sarah Jessica Parker (Carrie Bradshaw), Kim Cattrall (Samantha Jones), Kristin Davis (Charlotte York), Cynthia Nixon (Miranda Hobbes), Chris Noth (Mr Big), David Eigenberg (Steve), Willie Garson (Stanford Blatch)

sex, craving for: erotomania

sex, fear of: erotophobia, genophobia

sex, god of: Min (Egyptian)

sex, without passion: acokoinonia

sex films, ground-breaking: *I Am Curious – Yellow* (1967), *Last Tango in Paris* (1972), *Emmanuelle* (1974), *Ai No Corrida* (aka *In the Realm of the Senses*), *Romance* (1998), *9 Songs* (2004)
- see porn films, ground-breaking

sex guru: Annie Sprinkle

sex manual: *The Joy of Sex: : A Gourmet Guide To Lovemaking* (1972), by Alex Comfort

sex patch (for women): Intrinsa

Sex Pistols, The: UK punk band formed in 1975; comprised of Johnny Rotten (vocals; real name: John Lydon), Steve Jones (guitar), Glen Matlock (bass) and Paul Cook (drums). In 1977 Matlock was replaced by Sid Vicious (real name: John Simon Ritchie, who died of a heroin overdose in 1979)

sex symbols, male: David Beckham, Orlando Bloom, George Clooney, Tom Cruise, James Dean, Johnny Depp, Leonardo DiCaprio, David Duchovny, Ganymede,

Gareth Gates, Josh Hartnett, Ronan Keating, Narcissus, Orion, Brad Pitt, Keanu Reeves, Justin Timberlake, Rudolph Valentino, Will Young

sex symbols, female: Brigitte Bardot, Cheryl Cole, Farrah Fawcett, Angelina Jolie, Madonna, Kate Moss, Jessica Simpson, Raquel Welch, Mae West
- see pin-up girls, supermodels, etc

sex therapist: Dr Ruth Westheimer

sexologists – see sexperts

sexperts: Steve and Vera Bodansky (orgasm specialists), Alex Comfort, Havelock Ellis, Shere Hite, Alfred Kinsey, Masters and Johnson (i.e. William Masters and Virginia Johnson), Dr Ruth Westheimer

sextant: navigational instrument invented in 1550 by Tycho Brahe

sexual abuse, fear of: agraphobia

sexual daydreaming: emeronaria

sexual desire, in the morning: matutolagnia

sexual desire for elderly women: anililagnia

sexual desire for younger women: neanirosis

sexual dysfunction: agrexophrenia (inability to perform due to fear of being overheard), anorgasmia (inability to reach orgasm)

sexual frustration (from the premature climax of one's male partner): artamesia

sexual gratification derived from using scatological language: coprolalia

sexual harassment claimant: Anita Hill

sexual harassment defendant: Clarence Thomas

sexual intercourse, adjective: coital, copulative

sexual intercourse, fear of: coitophobia

sexual interest in faeces: coprophilia

sexual promiscuity, fact: in the UK, six per cent of 13-year-old girls have had sexual intercourse

sexuality, goddess of: Aphrodite (Greek mythology), Astarte (Phoenician), Venus (Roman)

sexually potent in unusual circumstances: paravalent, paraphilic

sexually transmitted diseases, science of: venereology

sexy: attractive, babelicious, bacon (university use), erotic, foxy, sensuous, steamy
- see beautiful

sexy but ugly, state of being: cacocallia

Seychelles: group of islands in the Indian Ocean
    capital: Victoria
    currency: rupee
    language: creole, English, French
    religion: Roman Catholic

shade, providing: umbriferous

shading in drawing, art of: sciagraphy

shadow, adjective: umbrageous

Shadows, The: incredibly successful UK instrumental group formed in 1959. Comprised of Hank Marvin (real name: Brian Rankin) (lead guitar), Bruce Welch (guitar), Jet Harris (real name: Terry Harris) (bass) and Tony Meehan (drums). Marvin and Welch formerly backed Cliff Richard as The Drifters but changed their name to avoid confusion with America's R&B Drifters

shadows, fear of: sciophobia

Shakespeare, William (1564–1616): wrote 37 plays and (arguably) two extra plays in collaboration with John Fletcher: *Two Noble Kinsmen* (1612) and *Henry VIII* (1612)

Shakespeare, fact: he referred to America once, in *The Comedy of Errors*

Shakespeare; phrases contributed to the English language: be cruel to be kind, be in a pickle, beggar all description, blinking idiot, budge an inch, cold comfort, dead as a doornail, fast and loose, flesh and blood, foregone conclusion, foul play, green-eyed monster, in my mind's eye, method in my madness, milk of human kindness, more in sorrow than in anger, more sinned against than sinning, mum's the word (as in "seal up your lips, and give no words but mum" from *Henry VI, Part 2*), one fell swoop, play fast and loose, poisoned chalice, pomp and circumstance, pound of flesh, remembrance of things past, salad days, sound and the fury, to thine own self be true, tower of strength, vanish into thin air, with bated breath

Shakespeare; words contributed to the English language: 2,000, including abstemious, antipathy, assassination, barefaced, countless, critical, dwindle, eventful, excellent, extract, frugal, gloomy, gust, hereditary, hint, horrid, indistinguishable, leapfrog, lonely, mountaineer, radiance, reclusive, schoolboy, skimmed milk, summit, tranquil, unlock, untie, unveil, vast, well-read, zany

Shakespeare's longest play: *Hamlet*

Shakespeare's lost plays: *Cardenio* and *Love's Labour's Won*

Shakespeare's shortest play: *The Comedy of Errors*

Shakespeare's plays, in chronological order: *Henry VI, Part II, Henry VI, Part III, Henry VI, Part I, Richard III, Comedy of Errors, Titus Andronicus, Taming of the Shrew, Two Gentlemen of Verona, Love's Labour's Lost, Romeo and Juliet, Richard II, A Midsummer Night's Dream, King John, The Merchant of Venice, Henry IV, Part I, Henry IV, Part II, Much Ado About Nothing, Henry V, Julius Caesar, As You Like It, Twelfth Night, Hamlet, The Merry Wives of Windsor, Troilus and Cressida, All's Well That Ends Well, Measure for Measure, Othello, King Lear, Macbeth, Antony and Cleopatra, Coriolanus, Timon of Athens, Pericles, Cymbeline, The Winter's Tale, The Tempest, Henry VIII, The Two Noble Kinsmen* (co-written with John Fletcher)

Shakespeare's vocabulary: different sources cite Shakespeare's word power as being between 21,000 and 33,000 words (compared to Milton's 8,000 or the 3,000–4,000 of today's Oxbridge graduate), while he used 20,000 different words in his plays

Shakespearean actors: John Barrymore, Kenneth Branagh, Richard Burbage, Dame Judi Dench, Maurice Evans, Edwin Forrest, David Garrick, Sir John Gielgud, Sir Alec Guinness, Greg Hicks, William Hutt, Sir Henry Irving, Edmund Kean, Dame Madge Kendal, Kevin Kline, William Macready, Sir Laurence Olivier, Al Pacino, Samuel Phelps, Christopher Plummer, Sir Ralph Richardson, Simon Russell Beale, Mark Rylance, Sarah Siddons, William Shakespeare, Dame Ellen Terry, Peg Woffington

Shakespearean character with most dialogue: Hamlet

Shakespearean library: the Folger Shakespeare Library in Washington

Shakespearean portrait: the famous engraving by Droeshout which prefaces the first folio

Shakespearean pretenders: Sir Francis Bacon, Ben Jonson, Christopher Marlowe, Thomas Middleton, Sir Henry Neville, Sir Walter Raleigh, Edward de Vere, John Webster

Shakespearean verse style: blank verse, iambic pentameter

shape, adjective: figural

shark: marine fish that first appeared on earth 400 million years ago

shark, adjective: carcharinid, selachian
shark, collective noun: school, shiver
shark, dread of: selachophobia
shark, fact: there are now 350 species
shark, fact: the first creatures in evolutionary history to develop an immune system
shark, fact: the only fish that can blink with both eyes
shark, fact: are extremely sensitive to electromagnetic signals, posessing a 'sixth
     sense' that lets them home in on another fish's heartbeat
shark, fact: have a low incidence of disease in general and extremely low rates of
     cancer
shark, fact: each year between 30,000,000 to 100,000,000 sharks are caught for
     their meat, fins, hides, jaws and internal body parts (the latter to be made into
     lubricants, cosmetics and 'health' products); for each shark caught deliberately,
     one is accidentally killed
shark, fact: each human who dies in the jaws of a shark is avenged roughly six
     million-fold. However, sharks take two decades to reach sexual maturity, have a
     long gestation period and bear only a few young at one time. Killing a relatively
     small number of females can dramatically limit the reproductive potential of an
     entire species
shark, famous: Bruce (from *Finding Nemo*, voiced by Barry Humphries), Don Lino
     (from *Shark Tale*, voiced by Robert De Niro), Lenny (from *Shark Tale*, voiced
     by Jack Black)
shark, young: cub, pup
shark attacks, fact: as many as 100 shark attacks can be recorded in a single year,
     approximately 15–30 of which can be fatal (however, far more people are killed
     by bees and elephants)
shark scale, adjective: placoid
shark skin: shagreen
sharon fruit: persimmon
sharp objects, fear of: belonophobia
She Done Him Wrong (1933 film), famous line: Lady Lou (Mae West): "When
     women go wrong, men go right after them." Lady Lou: "I wasn't always rich.
     No, there was a time I didn't know where my next husband was coming from."
     Incidentally, the line, "Is that a pistol in your pocket or are you just glad to see
     me?" attributed to the film, isn't actually in it
sheep, adjective: ovine
sheep, castrated: wether
sheep, collective noun: flock
sheep, famous: Dolly (the first cloned mammal), Lamb Chop, Louise (introduced on
     BBC TV's *For the Children*), Shaun (c/o Nick Park and Aardman Animation)
sheep, female: ewe
sheep, god of: Pan (Greek mythology)
sheep, male: ram
sheep, sound: baa, bleat
sheep, young: cosset, lamb, lambkins
sheep breeds: Awassi, Cardy, Cheviot, Chios, Corriedale, Dorset Horn, Exmoor
     Horn, Fries Melkschaap, Gotland, Hebridean, Herdwick, Jacob, Karakul,
     Lacaune, Lleyn, Longmynd, Longwools, Lonk, Manx Loghtan, Masham,
     Merino, Morfe, Mule, Oldenberg, Poll Dorset, Polwarth, Portland, Romney,
     Rough Fell, Scottish Blackface, Shetland, Soay, Suffolk, Swaledale, Teeswater,
     Texel, Welsh Mountain, Wensleydale, Whitefaced Woodland, Wiltshire Horn

sheep disease: louping-ill
sheep's wool covered in excrement: dag
sheep's wool grease: suint
Sheffield, birthplace of: Gordon Banks, Josephine Barstow, Sean Bean, David Blunkett, Malcolm Bradbury, Alastair Burnet, A. S. Byatt, Marti Caine, Jarvis Cocker, Joe Cocker, Margaret Drabble, Roy Hatteresley, Jimmy Jewel, Michael Palin, Peter Stringfellow, Roger Taylor (tennis player)
Sheffield groups: ABC, The All-Seeing I, Arctic Monkeys, Cabaret Voltaire, Def Leppard, Heaven 17, The Human League, Moloko, Pulp, Thompson Twins
Sheffield river: Don
Sheffield theatre: Crucible Theatre
shell, adjective: conchoid
shell-shaped: conchiform
shell shock: post-traumatic stress disorder
shells, study of: conchology
shellfish: abalone, clam, cockle, crab, limpet, lobster, mollusc, paua (New Zealand), prawn, scallop, winkle
shellfish, spawn of: spat
shellfish dish: tempura
shellfish measure: pint
shellfish soup: bisque
shepherds: Abel, David, Endymion, Faustulus (who discovered Romulus and Remus)
shepherds, god of: Pan (Greek mythology), Faunus (Roman)
shepherdess: Chloe
sheriff, adjective: shrieval
sheriff, collective noun: posse
Sherlock Holmes: modelled on Dr Joseph Bell
Sherlock Holmes, address: 221B Baker Street, London
Sherlock Holmes, author: Sir Arthur Conan Doyle
Sherlock Holmes, best friend: Dr John Watson
Sherlock Holmes, brother: Mycroft Holmes
Sherlock Holmes, drug of choice: a seven-per-cent solution of cocaine
Sherlock Holmes, first novel: *A Study in Scarlet* (1887)
Sherlock Holmes, habit: a seven-per-cent solution of cocaine
Sherlock Holmes, hat: deerstalker
Sherlock Holmes, housekeeper: Mrs Hudson
Sherlock Holmes, musical instrument: violin (Stradivarius)
Sherlock Holmes, nemesis: Professor Moriarty
Sherlock Holmes, played by: Hans Albers, Tom Baker, John Barrymore, Carlyle Blackwell, Jeremy Brett, Clive Brook, Peter Cook, Benedict Cumberbatch, Peter Cushing, Robert Downey Jr, Rupert Everett, Martin Fric, Stewart Granger, Bruno Guttner, Ronald Howard, Christopher Lee, John Longden, Radovan Lukavsky, Raymond Massey, Roger Moore, Alwin Neuss, John Neville, Eille Norwood, Reginald Owen, Christopher Plummer, Jonathan Pryce, Basil Rathbone, Robert Rendel, Ian Richardson, Richard Roxburgh, H.A. Sainsbury, Hermann Speelmans, Robert Stephens, Alan Wheatley, Geoffrey Whitehead, Nicol Williamson, Douglas Wilmer, Arthur Wonter
Sherlock Holmes, violin: Stradivarius

Sherpa guide: Tenzing Norgay
She Wore a Yellow Ribbon (1949 film), famous line: Captain Nathan Brittles (John
    Wayne): "Don't apologise. It's a sign of weakness."
sherry: Amontillado, Fino, Manzanilla, Oloroso, Tio Pepe
sherry glass: copita
shield, god of: Ull (Norse mythology)
shield border: bordure
shield centre: boss, umbo
shield-shaped: aspidate
shilling: tater-pillin' (CRS)
shin bone: tibia
shin bone, adjective: cnemial
ship, adjective: marine, maritime, nautical
ship, collective noun: armada, fleet, flotilla (a small fleet)
ships, famous: Adventure (James Cook), Argo (Jason), Arizona (supposedly the
    first US battleship sunk at Pearl Harbor), Beagle (Charles Darwin), Belfast,
    Bismarck, Black Pig (Captain Pugwash), Bounty (Captain William Bligh),
    Britannia (Royal Yacht, laid to rest in 1997), Canberra (used as a hospital ship
    during the Falklands' war), Challenger, Cutty Sark, Discovery (Captain Robert
    Scott), Endeavour (James Cook), Endurance (Sir Ernest Shackleton), Estonia
    (Swedish ferry which sank in 1994), Flying Dutchman (ghost ship), General
    Belgrano (Argentinean cruiser torpedoed by the British in the Falklands' war),
    Exxon Valdez, Golden Hind (Sir Francis Drake), Gypsy Moth IV (Sir Francis
    Chichester), Hispaniola (from *Treasure Island*), Kon Tiki (Thor Heyerdahl),
    Lively Lady (Sir Alec Rose), Lusitania (torpedoed in 1915 by the Germans),
    Marchioness (pleasure steamer sunk on the Thames), Marie Celeste, Mary
    Rose, RMS Mauretania, Mayflower, Missouri, Morning Cloud (Sir Edward
    Heath), Nimrod (Sir Ernest Shackleton), Niña, Noah's Ark, Nonsuch (Hudson's
    Bay Trading Company), Pequod (Captain Ahab), HMS Pinafore, Pinta, Queen
    Elizabeth, QEII, Queen Mary, Rainbow Warrior (Greenpeace), Santa Maria
    (Christopher Columbus), Terra Nova (Scott of the Antarctic), Titanic, Ventura,
    Victoria, Victory (Horatio Nelson)
    - see submarines
shipping, adjective: maritime
shipwrecks, chief discoverer of: Robert Ballard (who found the Titanic, the
    Bismarck and five Roman wrecks in the Mediterranean between Sicily and
    Tunisia - the largest concentration of shipwrecks ever found, in August of 1997)
Shirazi: former name for Zanzibar
shirt: belly top, blouse, boob tube, crop top, dashiki, kurta, middy, sark, tank top,
    T-shirt, vest
shock, dread of: hormephobia
shoe: alpargata, balmoral, batt, bootee, bovver boot, brogue, brothel creeper,
    Church's brogue, buskin, chopine, clog, clodhopper, Cornish Pasty, desert boot,
    Doc Marten, earth shoe, espadrille, flattie, flip-flops, jellies, Jesus boot, Jimmy
    Choo, kinky boots, lace-up, loafer, Manolo Blahnik, moccasin, Oxford, patten,
    pedary, platform shoe, plimsole, plimsoll, pump, sabot (with wooden sole),
    sandal, slingback, sneaker, stiletto, tennis shoe, trainer, veldskoen, wedge,
    winklepicker (with pointed toes)
shoe bombers: Saajid Badat, Richard Colvin Reid
shoe cap: blakey
shoe collector: Imelda Marcos

shoe designers: Manolo Blahnik, Jimmy Choo
- see shoemakers
shoe fetish: retifism
shoe frame: last (as used by a shoemaker on which to shape and repair a shoe)
shoe parts: blakey, broguing, counter, front, heel, instep, outsole, quarter, shank, tongue, vamp, waist, welt, wing tip
shoe rim: welt
shoe-shaped: calceiform
shoelace eyelet: grommet
shoelace tip: aglet
shoemakers: Carl Franz Bally, Manolo Blahnik, Jimmy Choo, Patrick Cox, Daniel Day-Lewis (just for a while), Guccio Gucci, Tokio Kumagai, Guido Pasquali, Steve Pateman, Walter Steiger, Vivienne Westwood
shoemaker, collective noun: blackening
shoemakers, patron saint of: Crispin
shoguns: Minamoto Yoritomo, Minamoto Yoshinaka, Oda Nobunaga, Tokugawa Ieyasu, Toyotomi Hideyoshi
shop worker's union: Usdaw (The Union of Shop, Distributive and Allied Workers)
shopaholism: oniomania
shops in New York: Bergdorf Goodman, B&H Photo Video, Bloomingdale's, Commodore Music Shop, FAO Schwarz, Macy's, Saks Fifth Avenue, Strand Bookstore (secondhand books), Tiffany & Co., Zabar's (fancy food)
shopkeeper's union: Acas
shoplifter, famous: Winona Ryder
shoplifter, politically correct term: nontraditional shopper
shopping: "A woman who is tired of shopping has finally got a life" - Angela Mollard
shore, adjective: littoral
short and famous: Alexander the Great, Woody Allen (5'6"), Tammy Faye Bakker (4'11"), Honoré de Balzac (5'2"), Napoleon Bonaparte (5'6$^1/_2$"), Mel Brooks (5'4"), Jimmy Clitheroe (4'3"), Gary Coleman (4'8"), Ronnie Corbett (5'1"), Sammy Davis Jr (5'3"), Warwick Davis (2'11"; actor), Danny DeVito (5'), Bob Dylan (5'6"), Sheena Easton (5'1"), Bernie Ecclestone (5'4"), Charles Forte (5'4"), Michael J. Fox (5'4"), Saint Francis of Assisi (5'1"), Yuri Gagarin (5'2"), Mahatma Mohandas Gandhi (5'3"), Joel Grey (5'5"; Oscar-winning actor), Joaquin 'El Shorty' Guzman (5'), Hirohito (5'5"), Dustin Hoffman (5'6"), William Hogarth (5'), Bob Hoskins (5'5$^1/_2$"), Harry Houdini (5'5"), Linda Hunt (4'9"; Oscar-winning actress), King Hussein of Jordan (5'3"), Joan of Arc (4'11"), John Keats (5'), Nikita Khrushchev (5'3"), Olga Korbut (4'11"), Alan Ladd (5'4$^1/_2$"), T.E. Lawrence (of Arabia) (5'5$^1/_2$"), Doris Lessing (5'), James Madison (at 5'4" the shortest president of the USA), Gustav Mahler (5'4"), Charles Manson (5'5"), Bette Midler (5'1"), Kylie Minogue (5'1"), Margaret Mitchell (4'11$^3/_4$"), Dudley Moore (5'2"), George "Baby Face" Nelson (5'4$^3/_4$"), Horatio Nelson (5'5$^1/_2$"), Aristotle Onassis (5'5"), Bonnie Parker (4'10"), Dolly Parton (5'), Joe Pesci (5'5"), Edith Piaf (4'8"), Pablo Picasso (5'4"), Roman Polanski (5'4"), Alexander Pope (4'6"), Prince (5'2$^1/_2$"), Lou Reed (5'5"), Debbie Reynolds (5'1"), Mickey Rooney (5'3"), Marquis de Sade (5'6"), Nicolas Sarkozy (5'5"), Martin Scorsese (5'3"), Willie Shoemaker (4'11"; jockey), Paul Simon (5'2"), Joseph Stalin (5'6"), Charles Stratton (aka General Tom Thumb) (40 inches), Gloria Swanson (4'11"), Mother Teresa (4'10"), Henri de Toulouse-Lautrec (4'11"), King Tutankhamen (5'6"), Verne

Troyer (2'8"; plays 'Mini-Me' in the *Austin Powers* films), Queen Victoria (5'),
Herve Villechaize (3'2"; played 'Tattoo' on TV's *Fantasy Island*), Voltaire
(5'3"), Dr Ruth Westheimer (4'7"), Paul Williams (5'1"; songwriter and actor),
Sir Norman Wisdom (5'4"), Pia Zadora (5')

short, politically correct term: vertically challenged, vertically constrained

short-sighted character: Mr (Quincy) Magoo

short-story writers: Alain-Fournier, Maya Angelou, H.E. Bates, Charles Bukowski,
A.S. Byatt, Albert Camus, Truman Capote, Angela Carter, Raymond Carver,
John William Cheever, Anton Chekhov, G.K. Chesterton, Colette, Roald Dahl,
Philip K. Dick, Dame Daphne du Maurier, Andre Dubus, James T. Farrell, F.
Scott Fitzgerald, Paul Gallico, L.P. Hartley, Ernest Hemingway, O. Henry,
M.R. James, James Joyce, Rudyard Kipling, Mary Lavin, Stephen Leacock,
Katherine Mansfield, W. Somerset Maugham, Guy de Maupassant, Ian
McEwan, Herman Melville, Toni Morrison, Alice Munro, Edna O'Brien,
Dorothy Parker, Luigi Pirandello, Edgar Allan Poe, V.S Pritchett, Damon
Runyon, Saki (born: Hector Hugh Munro), J.D. Salinger, Delmore Schwartz,
Helen Simpson, Isaac Bashevis Singer, James Thurber, Leo Tolstoy, William
Trevor, Mark Twain, John Updike, H.G. Wells, Angus Wilson, P.G. Wodehouse

shorthand (as in writing): tachygraphy

shorts: baggies, Bermuda shorts, boyshorts (boxers for girls), capris (that reach
below the knee), cargo shorts, cut-offs, cycling shorts, hotpants, jorts (jean
shorts), lederhosen, pedal pushers, shants (baggy and long), stubbies, three
quarter pants

shoulder, adjective: humeral

shoulder blade: scapula

shoulder blade, adjective: scapular

ShoWest: the annual convention for the National Association of Theater Owners in
the USA

showjumpers: Princess Anne, David Broome, Colonel Piero d'Inzeo, Lucinda
Green, Harry Llewellyn, Zara Phillips, Nick Skelton, Harvey Smith, Pat
Smythe, Hans Günter Winkler

showmen: P(hineas) T(aylor) Barnum, George M. Cohan, Billy Rose, Charles
Stratton (aka General Tom Thumb)
- see theatre impresarios

Shredded Wheat, slogan: 'Bet you can't eat three...'

shrew, adjective: soricid, soricine

shrimp, adjective: macruran

shrine keeper: pheretrer

Shropshire, administrative centre: Shrewsbury

shrub, adjective: frutescent, fruticose

shy: verecund (adjective)

Siam: former name for Thailand (until 1939 and then 1945–1949)

Siamese twins, first: Chang and Eng (although they were Chinese, but born in
Siam)

Siamese twins, famous: the Corsican Brothers

Siberia, birthplace of: Roman Abramovich, Irving Berlin, Rudolf Nureyev, Maria
Sharapova, Alexander Sokurov (filmmaker), Maxim Vengerov

siblings, famous: LaVerne, Maxene and Patti Andrews (singers); Antonio and
Prospero (from *The Tempest*); Alexis, David, Patricia and Rosanna Arquette
(actors); David and Richard Attenborough; Alec, Daniel, Stephen and William

Baldwin; John and Michael Banim (novelists); Khaireddin and Uruz Barbarossa (pirates); Ethel, John and Lionel Barrymore; Warren Beatty and Shirley MacLaine; Daniel and Natasha Bedingfield; Vanessa Bell and Virginia Woolf; James and John Belushi; Maria Bethânia and Caetano Veloso (Brazilian singers); Babs, Joy and Teddy Beverley (singing trio); Lili and Nadia Boulanger (composers); John and Roy Boulting (filmmakers); Moya Brennan and Enya (singers); Beau and Jeff Bridges; Anne, Charlotte and Emily Brontë; Jeb and George W. Bush; A.S. Byatt and Margaret Drabble (novelists); Cain and Abel; Anna and Jane Campion (filmmakers); Josef and Karel Čapek; Karen and Richard Carpenter; David, Keith and Robert Carradine; David and Shaun Cassidy (half-brothers); Dinos and Jake Chapman (artists); Bobby and Jack Charlton (footballers); Claudio and Isabella (from Shakespeare's *Measure for Measure*); Betty and Rosemary Clooney; Ethan and Joel Coen (filmmakers); Jackie and Joan Collins; Tom Conway and George Sanders (actors); Andrea, Caroline, Jim and Sharon Corr (singers); Kieran, Macaulay and Rory Culkin (actors); Joan and John Cusack (actors); Niamh, Sinead and Sorcha Cusack (actors); Dave and Ray Davies (pop stars); Olivia De Havilland and Joan Fontaine; Lord Delfont and Lew Grade; Catherine Deneuve and Françoise Dorléac; Dido (singer) and Rollo (of the dance band Faithless); David and Jonathan Dimbleby (broadcasters); Jennie and Rosie Dolly (vaudeville dancers); Jimmy and Tommy Dorsey (bandleaders); Sir Alec and Sir William Douglas-Home; Haylie (singer) and Hilary Duff (actress/singer); Allen Welsh Dulles (intelligence officer) and John Foster Dulles (Republican politician); Gerald and Lawrence Durrell (writers); Emilio Estevez and Charlie Sheen; Don and Phil Everly (singers/guiarists); Bobby and J.R. Ewing; Bobby and Peter Farrelly (filmmakers); Joseph, Martha and Ralph Fiennes; Neil and Tim Finn (musicians); Dave and Max Fleischer (cartoonists); Jane and Peter Fonda; Edward and James Fox; Lucien and Mario Franchi (the Corsican brothers); Bella (fashion designer) and Esther Freud (novelist); Clement and Lucian Freud; Liam and Noel Gallagher; George and Ira Gershwin (songwriters); Barry, Robin and Maurice Gibb; Edmond and Jules de Goncourt (French novelists); Graham and Hugh Greene (writers); Jacob Ludwig and Wilhelm Carl Grimm; Hansel and Gretel; Dan and Justin Hawkins (from the metal band The Darkness); Caroline and William Herschel (astronomers); Nicky and Paris Hilton; Brian and Edward Holland (Motown songwriters); Mycroft and Sherlock Holmes; Aldous and Sir Julian Huxley, Enrique and Julio (Jr) Iglesias; Kelly, Ronald, Rudolph and Vernon Isley (singers); La Toya, Marlon, Michael, Randy and Tito Jackson; Frank and Jesse James (outlaws); Augustus and Gwen John (painters); Ashley and Wynonna Judd; Alyosha, Dmitrí, Ivan and Smerdyakov Karamazov; Charles, John Philip and Stephen Kemble and Sarah Siddons (actors); Gary and Martin Kemp; Edward, John F. and Robert Kennedy; Andy and Liz Kershaw (broadcasters); Juan, José and Vincente Lladro (porcelain makers); Andrew and Julian Lloyd Webber; Ambrogio and Pietro Lorenzetti (Sienese painters); Michael and Virginia Madsen (actors); Ron and Russell Mael (singers, of Sparks fame); Jo, Amy, Beth and Meg March (from *Little Women*); Forrest, John and Jacqueline Mars (confectionary billionaires); Chico, Groucho, Gummo, Harpo and Zeppo Marx (comedians); Albert and David Maysles (documentary filmmakers); Joe, Mark, Paul and Stephen McGann (actors); Anna and Kate McGarrigle (singers); David and Ed Miliband (politicians); Hayley and Juliet Mills; Dannii and Kylie Minogue; Jacques and Joseph Montgolfier (hot air balloonists); Shiva and Sir V.S. Naipaul (writers); Aaron, Arthur, Athelga, Charles and Cyril Neville (singers); Gary and Phil Neville (footballers); David and Thomas Newman (composers); Anne, Bernadette, Coleen, Denise, Linda and Maureen Nolan (singers); Alan, Donny, Jay, Jimmy, Marie, Merrill and Wayne Osmond (singers); Christopher and Sean Penn (actors); Joaquin, Liberty, Rainbow, River and Summer Phoenix (actors); Anita, Bonnie, June and Ruth Pointer (singers); Prospero and Antonio (from Shakespeare's *The Tempest*); Jorn and Kirsten Rausing (billionaire tycoons); Corin, Lynn and Vanessa Redgrave (actors); Joely and Natasha Richardson (actors); Albert, Alfred, Charles, John and Otto Ringling (circus performers and impresarios); Eric and Julia Roberts; Jonathan and Paul Ross (film critics); Christina Georgina and Dante Gabriel Rossetti (poets); Albert and Michel Roux (chefs); Charles and Maurice Saatchi (advertising tycoons); Peter and Robin Sarstedt singers); Maria and Maximilian Schell (actors); Michael and Ralph Schumacher (racing drivers); Ridley and Tony Scott (filmmakers); Anthony and Peter Shaffer (playwrights); Jacob, Lee and Sam Shubert (theatre owners); Ashlee and Jessica Simpson (entertainers); Isaac Bashevis and Israel Joshua Singer (writers); Dick and Tom Smothers; Gilbert and Sir Stanley Spencer (artists); Leon and Michael Spinks (boxers); Paolo and Vittorio Taviani (filmmakers); Del Boy and Rodney Trotter (TV characters); Theo and Vincent Van Gogh; Gianni and Donatella Versace; Larry and Andy Wachowski (filmmakers); Martha and Rufus Wainwright (singers); Alec and Evelyn Waugh (writers); Bob and Harvey Weinstein (film tycoons); Serena and Venus Williams (tennis players); Brian and Dennis Wilson (of The Beach Boys); Luke and Owen Wilson (actors); Bernie and Mike Winters (comedians); Virginia Woolf and Vanessa Bell; Orville and Wilbur Wright (aviation pioneers); David and Jerry Zucker (filmmakers) – see twins

sibling, murder of: fratricide

sick bed, adjective: clinical

sickle, adjective: drepaninoid

sickle, earliest discovery of: 6000 BC

sickle-shaped: drepaniform, falcate, falciform

sickness, from overindulgence in food and/or drink: crapulence

Siegfried: opera – the third work of Richard Wagnmer's *Ring* cycle – first performed at the Bayreuth Festspielhaus in 1876, as part of the first complete presentation of *The Ring*

Sierra Leone: West African republic founded by Granville Sharp
  capital: Freetown
  currency: leone
  language: English
  religion: Muslim (official), animist
  fact: the poorest country in the world
  fact: one of the world's largest producers of diamonds
  fact: holds vast untapped reserves of titanium and gold

sieve, adjective: cribriform

sight disorders: amaurosis, glaucoma, hypermetropia, myopia (short-sightedness), presbyopia (loss of focus)

Sikh book of prayer: Granth

Sikh leaders: Guru Nanak, Guru Gobind Singh

Sikh temple: gurdwara

silent film comedians: Fatty Arbuckle, Charlie Chaplin, Charley Chase, Oliver
    Hardy, Buster Keaton, Harry Langdon, Stan Laurel, Harold Lloyd, Mack
    Swain, Ben Turpin
silent film stars: George Arliss, Mary Astor, Theda Bara, John Barrymore, Richard
    Barthelmess, Wallace Beery, Clara Bow, Louise Brooks, Francis X. Bushman,
    Lon Chaney, Jackie Coogan, Joan Crawford, Bebe Daniels, Marion Davies,
    Douglas Fairbanks, Greta Garbo, John Gilbert, Dorothy Gish, Lillian Gish,
    William S. Hart, Brigitte Helm, Emil Jannings, Florence Lawrence, Bessie
    Love, Mae Marsh, Tom Mix, Colleen Moore, Mae Murray, Alla Nazimova,
    Pola Negri, Mabel Normand, Ramon Novarro, Ivor Novello, Mary Pickford,
    Norma Shearer, Gloria Swanson, Norma Talmadge, Rudolph Valentino, Conrad
    Veidt, Erich Von Stroheim, Pearl White
silk capital of the world: Lyon
silk fabrics: chiffon, damask, dupion, gauze, gazar, lutestring, marquisette, moire,
    mousseline, ninon, organza, panne, peau-de-soie, pongee, samite, satin, shot,
    surah, tussah, voile
silk painting: kakemono
silk production: sericulture
silkworm, adjective: bombic
silkworm-breeding: sericulture
silver, adjective: argent
Silver Jubilee: 25th anniversary of The Queen's accession (6 February 1952),
    celebrated throughout the United Kingdom and the Commonwealth in 1977
silver poisoning: argyria
silversmith: Georg Jensen
simplicity: "Simplicity is the outcome of technical subtlety" - Maurice Saatchi
Simpsons, The: cult prime-time cartoon show (set in Springfield), that began life in
    1987 as a 30-second spot on *The Tracey Ullman Show*. The movie version
    arrived in 2007
    created by Matt Groening
    first broadcast: 14 January 1990 on Fox TV
    voice cast: Nancy Cartwright (Bart Simpson), Dan Castellaneta (Homer), Julie
        Kavner (Marge), Yeardley Smith (Lisa), Harry Shearer (various)
sin, fear of: hamartophobia
sing, inability to: amusia
Singapore, Republic of: independent city-state in southeastern Asia, comprising one
    major island and more than 50 small adjacent islets, located off the southern tip
    of the Malay Peninsula
    capital: Singapore
    currency: Singapore dollar
    language: Chinese, Malay, English, Tamil
    religion: Buddhist, Taoist, Muslim, Hindu, Sikh, Confucianist
    fact: In 1992 chewing gum was banned, the penalty for smuggling it from
        abroad amounting to a year in jail or a fine of S$5,500
singer, adjective: cantatory
singers of the Second World War: Alma Cogan, Gracie Fields, Vera Lynn, Ann
    Shelton
singing, adjective: cantative, cantatory
singing, muse of: Polyhymnia
single (biologically speaking), adjective: haploid
single, top-selling globally of all time: *White Christmas*, by Bing Crosby (over 50m
    units)

single, top-selling UK of all-time: *Candle in the Wind 1997*, by Elton John
(4,770,000 units)

sinning, fear of: peccatophobia

sinning, sexual arousal derived from: pecattiphilia

Sinn Féin leaders: Michael Collins, Éamon de Valera

Sinn Féin president: Gerry Adams

sinus, adjective: antral, sinal

Sirius, adjective: canicular

sister, adjective: sororal

sisters, famous – see siblings

sister-killing: soricide

sitar player: Ravi Shankar

sitting, abnormal interest in: kathisomania

sitting, adjective: sedentary

sitting, fear of: cathisophobia

sitting still, aversion to: akathisia

six, adjective: senary

six, group of: hexad

six years, adjective: sexennial

six-hundredth anniversary: sexcentenary

six-year period: sexennium

Sixth Sense, The (1999 film), famous line: Cole Sear (Haley Joel Osment): "I see
dead people"

Sixties: "If you can remember anything about the sixties, you weren't really there"
(famous saying by Paul Kantner)
- see Nineteen Sixties

sixteen, adjective: sexadecimal

sixty, adjective: sexagenary, sexagesimal

sixty-year-old: sexagenarian

size; delusion that parts of one's body are bigger than they actually are:
macromania

ska bands: Bad Manners, Madness, The Specials

skateboarding stars: Tony Alva, Tony Hawk, Stacy Peralta, Mark 'Gator' Rogowski

skaters – see ice skaters

skeleton, adjective: osteal, skeletal, skelic

ski jumper: Matti Nykaenen

skiers: Graham Bell, Jean-Claude Killy, Ingemar Stenmark

skiing, killed by: Sonny Bono (after crashing into a tree), Natasha Richardson

skiing race: slalom

skiis, god of: Ull (Norse mythology)

skin, adjective: cutaneous (particularly regarding the surface), dermal, dermoid

skin, aversion to: dermatophobia

skin, doctor of: dermatologist

skin, inner layer: corium (aka derma and dermis)

skin, outer layer: epidermis

skin, science of: dermatology

skin abrader: exfoliant, exfoliator

skin conditions: achromasia, acne, albinism, blackheads, boils, carbuncle, chloasma
(brown patches), contact dermatitis, corn, dermatitis, eczema, erythema,

herpes, hives, keratosis, nettle-rash, pimple, rash, ringworm, serpigo, shingles, tetter, tinea, urticaria, verruca, wart

skin diseases: dhobi itch, erysipelas, framboesia (aka yaws), herpes, impetigo, leprosy, lupus, (tuberculosis of the skin), mange, prurigo, psoriasis, scabies

skin diseases, fear of: dermatopathophobia, dermatophobia, dermatosiophobia

skin fold: plica

skin grafting: first performed in the 17th century by the Boiani, a family of Italian surgeons

skin infection: athlete's foot, ringworm, tinea

skin inflammation: dermatitis, eczema

skin markings, study of: dermatoglyphics

skin reddening: erythema

skin spot: freckle, lentigo, liver spot, macula

skull: cranium

skull, adjective: cephalic, cranial

skull, pointed: acrocephalic (adjective)

skull, science of: craniology

skull saw: trepan, trephine

skunk, collective noun: surfeit

skunk, famous: Commander St. John (from the TV cartoon *Sonic the Hedgehog*), Flower (from *Bambi*), Mamselle Hepzibah (from the Pogo comic strip)

skunk, young: kit

sky, god of: Horus (Egyptian), Uranus (Greek)

sky goddesses: Hathor (Egyptian mythology), Mut (Egyptian), Nut (Egyptian)

skyscraper, first (in the true sense of the word): Wainwright Building in St Louis (1890), designed by Dankmar Adler and Louis Sullivan

slander: calumniate (verb)

slave dealers: Sir John Hawkins, Simon Legree (from *Uncle Tom's Cabin*), John Newton

slavery critics: Abraham Lincoln, William Wilberforce

slaves: Aesop, Aida, Androcles, Celie (from *The Color Purple*), Henri Christophe (later king of Haiti), Denmark Vesey, Olaudah Equiano (later an influential abolitionist), Esther (c/o *Ben-Hur*), Hagar, Jim (friend of Huckleberry Finn), Joseph, Kunta Kinte, Mammy (from *Gone With the Wind*), Prissy (from *Gone With the Wind*), Uncle Remus, Ignatius Sancho (later an influential abolitionist), Spartacus, Dred Scott, Harriet Tubman, Nat Turner, Booker T. Washington

sleep: "Nature's soft nurse" – William Shakespeare (*Henry IV, Part II*)

sleep; average length a Briton sleeps: 7.9 hours a day

sleep, abnormal interest in: hypnomania

sleep, act of falling: dormition

sleep, adjective: somnolent

sleep averages: working women, aged 16 to 59: 8hrs 22mins
    working men: 8hrs 10mins
    women out of work: 9hrs 1min
    men out of work: 8hrs 56mins (figures: Office for National Statistics)

sleep, Cockney rhyming slang (noun): Bo Peep; Botany Bay (from 'hit the hay')

sleep, deep: sopor (noun)

sleep, fact: in 1910, the average adult in industrialised countries slept 10 hours a night

sleep, fear of: hypnophobia

sleep, god of: Hypnos (Greek), Somnus (Roman)

sleep, inability to wake up fully after: dysania
sleep, science of: hypnology
sleep, words connected with:
    the act of yawning and stretching: pandiculation
    that which drives sleep away: agrypnotic (such as coffee or worry)
sleep-abating drugs: eugeroic, modafinil, ProVigil
sleep disturbance: hypnophrenosis
sleep expert: somnologist
sleep inducing: somniferous, somnific (adjective)
sleep learning: hypnopaedia
sleep patterns: paradoxical sleep, rapid-eye-movement sleep, slow-wave sleep
sleep talking: somniloquy
sleep walking: somnambulism
Sleeping Beauty: ballet composed by Pyotr Tchaikovsky, first performed in
    St Petersburg in 1890
sleeping in the nude: hypnudism
sleeping pills, herbal: Natrasleep, Restful Night, Slumber, Somnus
sleeping policeman: speed hump, speed ramp
sleeplessness: agrypnia
sleepwalker: somnambulist
sleepwalking, patron saint of: Dymphna
sleepy heads: Silas Marner (a cataleptic), Ronald Reagan, Buck Rogers (who was
    put to sleep for 500 years by a radioactive gas), Sleeping Beauty, Sleepy
    (dwarf), Rip Van Winkle
sleeve types: dolman, mandarin, oversleeve, raglan, virago
sleuths – see detectives, detectives in fiction
Slick Willie: nickname for Bill Clinton
slide, in swimming pool: flume
slime, fear of: blennophobia
slip of the tongue: lapsus linguae
slipper-shaped: calceolate
slope-measuring instrument: clinometer
slot machines: anagram of "cash lost in me"
sloth, adjective: xenarthral
Slovakia: country in central Europe
    capital: Bratislava
    currency: euro; formerly: koruna
    language: Slovak
    religion: Roman Catholic
Slovenia: republic in south-central Europe
    capital: Ljubljana
    currency: euro; formerly: tolar
    language: Slovene
    religion: Roman Catholic
Slovenian and famous: Martin Strel (who swam the length of the Amazon,
    Mississippi, Yangtze and Danube rivers)
slow musical tempos: adagio, largo, lento
slug, adjective: limaceous, limacine
Sly and the Family Stone: psychedelic pop-funk band formed in San Francisco in
    1966. Comprised of: Sly Stone (born: Sylvester Stewart) (vocals, keyboards,
    guitar), Cynthia Robinson (trumpet), Jerry Martini (sax), Rosie Stone (vocals,

piano), Freddie Stone (guitar), Greg Errico (drums) and Larry Graham (bass). Disbanded in 1979

smallpox: variola

smallpox, adjective: varioloid, variolous

smegma: cock cheese

smell, adjective: olfactory

smell, aversion to: olfactophobia

smell, brain part that deals with: rhinencephalon

smell, inability to: anosmesia, anosmia (noun)

smell, sense of: olfaction

smell, sexual arousal derived from: olfactophilia, ozolagnia

smell, study of: osmology

smelling, act of: osmesis

smelling bad: mephitic

Smith, W.H.: newsagent which first opened in 1848 as a bookstall at London's Euston station

Smiths, The: UK rock group formed in Manchester in 1982; comprised of Steven Morrissey (vocals), Johnny Marr (guitars), Mike Joyce (drums) and Andy Rourke (bass)

Smoke, the: nickname for London

smoke, aversion to (from cigarettes, cigars, etc): misocapny

smokers' rights group: Forest

smoking (cigarettes, pipes, etc), act of: capnosis

smoking, adjective: fumatory

smoking habit: capnodulia

smooth-haired: leiotrichous, liotrichous, lissotrichous

smooth-skinned: glabrous

smother to death: burke (verb)

smothering, fear of: pnigerophobia

smuggler: Billy Hayes

smugglers, fictitious: Joss Merlyn (from *Jamaica Inn*), Dr Syn

smuggling gang: Snakeheads (specialising in the traffic of Chinese emigrants)

snafu (acronym): Situation Normal, All Fucked Up

snail, famous: Brian (from *The Magic Roundabout*)

snake, adjective: anguine, colubrine, ophidian, serpentine - see reptile

snake, collective noun: bed, nest, pit, rave

snake, famous: Kaa (from *The Jungle Book*)

snake, longest in the world: reticulated python (reaching record lengths of over 32 ft)

snake, most poisonous in the world: 1) fierce snake (Australia); 2) brown snake (Australia); 3) Malayan krait (Southeast Asia); 4) taipan (Australia); 5) tiger snake (Australia); 6) beaked sea (Southeast Asia); 7) saw scaled viper (Middle East Asia); 8) coral snake (North America); 9) boomslang snake (Africa); 10) death adder (Australia)

snake, sound: hiss

snake, young: hatchling, snakelet

snake-bite capital, Burma, where an average 1400 people are killed by snakes every year

snake experts: Steve Irwin, Joe Slowinski (killed by a multi-banded krait on 11 September 2001)

snakes, fear of: ophiophobia, ophidiophobia

snakes, passion for: ophidiomania

snakes, study of: ophiology

snakes, use of in sexual stimulation: ophidicism
snapper (fish), adjective: lutjanid
sneeze: sternutation
sneeze, adjective: sternutatory, sternutative
sneeze causing (of substance): errhine, ptarmic, sternutatory
snipe, collective noun: walk, wisp (in flight)
sniper: franc-tireur
snipers of Washington DC: John Allen Muhammad, 41, and John Lee Malvo, 17 (who used a .233 rifle to kill their victims)
SNL: Saturday Night Live (TV show) - see
snooker players: Joe Davis, Steve Davis, Stephen Hendry, Alex 'Hurricane' Higgins, John Higgins, Paul Hunter, Ronnie O'Sullivan, Ray Reardon, Matthew Stevens, Mark Williams
snooze alarms: anagram for "alas, no more z's"
snow, adjective: nival, niveous
snow, fear of: chionophobia
snow, gust of: flurry
snow, obsession for: chionomania
snow area, adjective: nival
snow culture: nivenclature
snow blindness: chionablepsia
snow pea: mangetout, sugar snap
snow slide: glissade
Soap: groundbreaking American TV sitcom that dared to tackle such taboo subjects as adultery, impotence and transsexualism. As protest groups bombarded ABC TV with complaints, the nation settled in with the Tate and Campbell families (of Dunn's River, Connecticut) to its collective glee. The show spawned the successful spin-off *Benson* (1979–1986) starring Robert Guillaume
    broadcast: 13 September 1977–20 April 1981
    created by Susan Harris
    cast: Katherine Helmond (Jessica Tate), Robert Mandan (Chester Tate), Jennifer Salt (Eunice Tate), Diana Canova (Corinne Tate), Jimmy Baio (Billy Tate), Robert Guillaume (Benson, the family's cook), Cathryn Damon (Mary Campbell), Richard Mulligan (Burt Campbell), Ted Wass (Danny Campbell), Billy Crystal (Jodie Dallas Campbell), Richard Libertini (The Godfather), Robert Urich (Peter), Roscoe Lee Browne (Saunders)
soap, adjective: saponaceous
soap, fact: soap was known to exist in Mesopotamia in 2500 BC
soap, fact: in Britain soap was a taxed luxury until 1853
soap remnant: sloover (soap too small to use but too big to throw away)
social climbers: Hyacinth Bucket (from TV's *Keeping Up Appearances*), Miss Piggy, Becky Sharp
social critic: Ivan Illich
social historian: Studs Terkel
social reformers: Grace Abbott, Muhammad Abduh, Jane Addams, Felix Adler, Amelia Bloomer, John Bright, Dorothy Day, Rowland Hill, Toyohiko Kagawa, John Stuart Mill, Robert Owen, Eva Perón (aka Evita), Elizabeth Cady Stanton, Joseph Stephens, Beatrice Webb, Sidney Webb
socialites: Betsy Bloomingdale, Georgiana Cavendish, Margaret Eaton, Gertrude (from *Hamlet*), Holly Golightly, Vivienne Haigh-Wood, Prince Harry, Paris Hilton, Elizabeth Hurley, Tara Palmer-Tomkinson, Nicole Richie, Wallis

Simpson, Donald Ogden Stewart, Jessica Tate (played by Katherine Helmond in TV's *Soap*), Sunny von Bülow

society, fear of: anthropophobia

sociologists: Ralf Dahrendorf, Emile Durkheim, Erving Goffman, C. Wright Mills, Lewis Mumford, Talcott Parsons, Herbert Spencer, Richard Titmuss, Alexis de Tocqueville, Max Weber

soften: macerate (by soaking), pour oil on troubled waters, soft-pedal

soil, adjective: edaphic, telluric

soil, study of: edaphology

soil management, science of: agronomy

solar system, mechanical model of: orrery

soldier: Anzac, askari, berserker, carabineer, cavalryman, Chelsea pensioner, commando, companion-in-arms, condottiere, cuirassier, dogface, fencible, foot soldier, fugleman, fusilier, GI, Green Beret, grenadier, guardsman, gunner, Gurkha, hoplite (of ancient Greece), hussar, infantryman, kern (Irish foot soldier), lancer, lansquenet, leatherneck (marine), legionary, man-at-arms, marine, mercenary, musketeer, Navy SEAL, officer, para, pikeman, pistoleer, poilu, pongo, private, ranger, ranker, rapparee, redcoat, regular, rifleman, sabre, sapper, SAS, sentry, sepoy, spearman, Spetnaz, standard-bearer, Tommy, trooper, Turco, Wren, Yankee

soldiers, famous: Sir Ralph Abercromby, Sir Harold Alexander of Tunis, Sir Edmund Allenby, Antigonus ('the one-eyed'), Mark Antony, Sir Claude Auchinleck, Lord Robert Baden-Powell, Robert Blake, Werner von Blomberg, Gebbard Blücher, General Omar N. Bradley, General Braxton Bragg, Lt. General Frederick 'Boy' Browning, Count Friedrich von Bülow, Ambrose Burnside, Sir Colin Campbell, Miguel de Cervantes, Carl von Clausewitz, Gaius Marcius Coriolanus, Oliver Cromwell, Moshe Dayan, Richard Deane, Emilio De Bono, Charles De Gaulle, Alfred Dreyfus, Robert Essex, Harry Feversham, Harry Flashman, Henry Fleming (from Stephen Crane's *The Red Badge of Courage*), Sir John French, Baron Werner von Fritsch, Leopoldo Galtieri, Giuseppe Garibaldi, Beau Geste, Field Marshal Douglas Haig, Hannibal, Andrew Jackson, Admiral Husband Kimmel, Horatio Herbert Kitchener, Stephanus Paulus Kruger, T.E. Lawrence, General Douglas MacArthur, Louis-Joseph de Montcalm, Simon de Montfort, (Bernard) Montgomery of Alamein, Marquis of Montrose (James Graham), Baron Munchhausen, Nearchus, Michel Ney, James Oglethorpe, Juan Domingo Perón, Philippe Pétain, Pompey, Colin Powell, Ptolemy I, Erwin Rommel, Karl Rundstedt, Sir Edward Sabine, Antonio López de Santa Anna, H. Norman Schwarzkopf, Scipio Aemilianus Africanus (aka Scipio the Younger), Scipio Africanus (aka Scipio the Elder), William Sherman, Myles Standish, John Sullivan, Sergeant Francis Troy (from Thomas Hardy's *Far from the Madding Crowd*), Sir Tomkyns Turner, Sir William Waller, Anthony Wayne (aka 'Mad Anthony'), William Westmoreland, Orde Wingate, Xenophon
- see military leaders

soldier's ammunition bag: pouch

soldier's coat: trench coat

soldier's headwear: balaclava

soldier's helmet: bascinet, casque, pickelhaube, sallet

sole (of the foot), adjective: plantar, volar

solitude, fear of: eremophobia

Solomon Islands: independent state in the South-West Pacific

capital: Honiara
currency: Solomon Islands dollar
language: English
religion: Christian
Somalia: republic in north-eastern Africa
capital: Mogadishu
currency: Somali shilling
language: Arabic, Somali
religion: Sunni Muslim
birthplace of: Waris Dirie (supermodel), Ayaan Hirsi Ali (now a Dutch MP)
Some Like it Hot (1959 film), famous line: Jerry/Daphne (Jack Lemmon): "Osgood, I'm going to level with you. We can't get married at all... I'm a man." Osgood E. Fielding III (Joe E. Brown): "Well, nobody's perfect." [last line]
Somers Islands: former name for Bermuda
Somerset, administrative centre: Taunton
son, adjective: filial
son, murder of: filicide
son killers: Abraham, Joseph Goebbels, Hercules, Ivan the Terrible, Medea, Peter the Great
Son of God: Jesus Christ (see Jesus, other names for), David Icke (self-proclaimed)
song: air, aria, ditty, doodle, glee, golden oldie, hymn, lament, madrigal, number, phrase, torch song, track, tune
song, adjective: melic
songbird, adjective: oscine
songwriters: Peter Allen, Paul Anka, Burt Bacharach, Marilyn Bergman, Irving Berlin, Leslie Bricusse, Hoagy Carmichael, George M. Cohan, Elvis Costello, Noël Coward, Bob Dylan, Stephen Foster, George Gershwin, Ira Gershwin, Ray Henderson, Jerry Herman, Brian and Edward Holland, Sir Elton John, (Bert) Kalmar and (Harry) Ruby, Jerome Kern, Carole King, Frank Loesser, Johnny Mercer, Stephen Merritt, Joni Mitchell, Ivor Novello, Cole Porter, Carole Bayer Sager, Neil Sedaka, Stephen Sondheim, Bernie Taupin, Diane Warren, Hank Williams, Paul Williams
songwriting teams: Burt Bacharach and Hal David, Gerry Goffin and Carole King, Ellie Greenwich and Jeff Barry, Elton John and Bernie Taupin, John Kander and Fred Ebb, Jerry Leiber and Mike Stoller, John Lennon and Paul McCartney, Alan Jay Lerner and Frederick Loewe, Andrew Lloyd Webber and Tim Rice, Barry Mann and Cynthia Weil, Doc Pomus and Mort Shuman, Richard Rodgers and Oscar Hammerstein II, Richard Rodgers and Lorenz Hart, Neil Sedaka and Howie Greenfield
Son of Star Wars: National Missile Defence system of the USA
Sony Walkman: portable hi-fi devised by Nobutoshi Kihara and launched in Japan in 1979
soot, adjective: fuliginous
soothing: demulcent
soothsayers: Jeane Dixon, Jeremiah Horrocks, Nostradamus (aka Michel de Notredame) - see clairvoyants
sopranos: Marie Angel, Martina Arroyo, Florence Austral, Lillian Bailey, Dame Isobel Baillie, Dame Josephine Barstow, Kathleen Battle, Isabel Bayrakdarian, Barbara Bonney, June Bronhill, Montserrat Caballé, Maria Callas, Lynne Dawson, Natalie Dessay, Dorothy Dow, Maria Ewing, Wilhelmenia Fernandez, Renée Fleming, Amelita Galli-Curci, Lesley Garrett, Angela Gheorghiu, Dame

Joan Hammond, Soile Isokoski, Florence Foster Jenkins, Katherine Jenkins, Dame Gwyneth Jones, Emma Kirkby, Marjorie Lawrence, Lotte Lehmann, Jenny Lind, Victoria de Los Angeles, Dame Felicity Lott, Valerie Masterson, Sylvia McNair, Dame Nellie Melba, Julia Migenes, Grace Moore, Anna Netrebko, Birgit Nilsson, Jessye Norman, Felicity Palmer, Adelina Patti, Lily Pons, Rosa Ponselle, Lucia Popp, Leontyne Price, Dame Margaret Price, Lisa Saffer, Elisabeth Schumann, Elisabeth Schwarzkopf, Honor Sheppard, Beverly Sills, Yma Sumac, Dame Joan Sutherland, Dame Kiri Te Kanawa, Anna Tomowa-Sintow, Dawn Upshaw, Johanna Wagner, Sophie Wyss, Ying Huang

soprano, male: Giusto Tenducci

Sopranos, The: highly-praised, award-winning TV series focusing on Mob boss Tony Soprano and his domestic and criminal families

created by David Chase for HBO

broadcast: 10 January 1999–10 June 2007

cast: James Gandolfini (Tony Soprano), Edie Falco (Carmela Soprano), Lorraine Bracco (Dr Jennifer Melfi), Aida Turturro (Janice Soprano), Jamie-Lynn Sigler (Meadow Soprano), Nancy Marchand (Livia Soprano), Michael Imperioli (Christopher Moltisanti), Dominic Chianese ('Junior'), Tony Sirico (Paulie Walnuts), Steve Van Zandt (Silvio Dante), Drea de Matteo (Andrea La Cerva), Vincent Pastore (Salvatore 'Big Pussy' Bonpensiero), Joe Pantoliano (Ralph Cifaretto), Steve Buscemi (Tony Blundetto)

Sorbonne: the most prestigious university in France, founded as a theological institute in 1253 by Robert de Sorbon. By the time the facility was rebuilt in 1885, the Sorbonne had become the University of Paris

sorcerers: Simon Magus, Sauron (from *The Lord of the Rings*) - see wizards

sorcerer's textbook: grimoire

sorceress: Circe, Medea

sorrel, adjective: oxalidaceous

sorrow, goddess of: Mara

soul: anima (in Jungian psychology)

soul, adjective: pneumatic

soul, godfather of: James Brown

soul, queen of: Aretha Franklin

soul duo: Righteous Brothers

soul groups: Booker T and the MGs, The Chi-Lites, The Commodores, The Drifters, Earth Wind & Fire, The Four Tops, Harold Melvin & The Bluenotes, The O'Jays, Smokey Robinson & the Miracles, Rose Royce, The Spinners, The Stylistics, The Temptations

soul singers: Adele, William Bell, Bobby Bland, Mary J. Blige, James Brown, Solomon Burke, Ray Charles, Sam Cooke, Lee Dorsey, Aretha Franklin, Gabrielle (born: Louise Gabrielle Bobb), Marvin Gaye, Al Green, Roy Hamilton, Etta James, Eddie Kendricks, Alicia Keys, Ben E. King, Beverley Knight, Gladys Knight, Little Willie John, Curtis Mayfield, Clyde McPhatter, Sam Moore, Aaron Neville, Wilson Pickett, Corinne Bailey Rae, Otis Redding, Smokey Robinson, Percy Sledge, Candi Staton, Joss Stone, Levi Stubbs, The Supremes (see), Joe Tex, Irma Thomas, Rufus Thomas, Luther Vandross, Jackie Wilson, Stevie Wonder

sound, adjective: acoustic, audio, sonic

sound, fear of: akousticophobia

sound, study of: acoustics

sound wave, adjective: sonic

sound wave, transmitting: phonophorous

sounds in speech: accent, agma, alliteration, anaptyxis, articulation, cacology, click, consonant, continuant, diphthong, drawl, enclitic, euphony, gibber, glide, haplology, lallation, lilt, lisp, nasality, palatalization, phoneme, plosive, pronunciation, snuffle, splutter, sputter, stammer, stutter, vowel

soup: bird's nest soup, bisque, bortsch (beetroot soup), bouillabaisse (fish and vegetable, flavoured with spices), broth, chlodnik (a cold soup from Poland), chowder, cock-a-leekie (Scottish soup of chicken and leeks), consommé, cullen skink (Scottish fish soup), dal, gazpacho, Heinz, lentil, matelote, minestrone, mock turtle soup, mulligatawny, onion, oxtail, portable, potage, Scotch broth, shchi (Russian cabbage soup), shark's fin, vichyssoise (a chilled potato and leek cream soup)

soured milk, adjective: clabrous

sourness, aversion to: acerophobia

South Africa: republic occupying the southern spread of the African continent
    capital: Cape Town (legislative), Pretoria (administrative), Bloemfontein (judicial)
    currency: rand
    language: Afrikaans, English, Ndebele, Pedi, South Sotho, Swazi, Tsonga, Tswana, Venda, Xhosa, Zulu
    religion: Christian (majority)

South African and famous: Dr Christiaan Barnard, Sister Wendy Beckett, Steve Biko, Louis Botha, Naas Botha, Pieter Willem Botha (president), André Brink (novelist), Zola Budd (athlete), Mangosuthu Buthelezi (Zulu prince), J(ohn) M(ichael) Coetzee, Hansie Cronje (cricketer), Marlene Dumas (painter), Athol Fugard, Danie Gerber (rugby player), Nadine Gordimer (novelist), Richard Hannay (creation of John Buchan), F.W. de Klerk, Stephanus Paulus Kruger, Winnie Madikizela-Mandela, Miriam Makeba, Nelson Mandela, Hugh Masekela, Thabo Mbeki, Alan Paton, Francois Pienaar, Gary Player, Olive Schreiner (writer and feminist), Shaka, Sir Antony Sher, Walter Sisulu, Gillian Slovo (writer), Jan Smuts, Helen Suzman (anti-apartheid activist), Janet Suzman, Oliver Tambo, Charlize Theron, Desmond Tutu, Jamie Uys (filmmaker), Hendrik Verwoerd (prime minister)

South African gambling mecca: Sun City, aka Sin City, devised by Sol Kerzner

South African murder rate: it has been estimated that 44 out of every 100,000 people are murdered

South African music: marabi (popular in the 1930s)

South African organisation: The New Partnership for Africa's Development (Nepad), set up so that South Africa may receive aid from donors in return for demonstrating good governance

South African park: Kruger National Park

South African soldier: Stephanus Paulus Kruger

Southampton, birthplace of: Craig David, The Delays, Charlie Dimmock, Benny Hill, Sir John Jellicoe, Howard Jones, Sir John Everett Millais, Ken Russell, Isaac Watts (hymn writer)

South Carolina, 8th state (1788), Palmetto State
    capital: Columbia
    state bird: Carolina wren
    state flower: yellow jessamine
    state tree: palmetto
    motto: 'Dum Spiro Spero' ('While I breathe, I hope')

birthplace of: Mary McLeod Bethune, James Brown, Chubby Checker, Joe Frazier, Dizzie Gillespie, Lauren Hutton, Andrew Jackson, Jesse Jackson, 'Shoeless' Joe Jackson, Eartha Kitt, Andie MacDowell, Chris Rock, Vanna White

tourist attractions: historic Charleston, Charleston Museum (established in 1773, the oldest musuem in the USA), Myrtle Beach, Hilton Head Island

fact: more battles during the American Revolution were fought in South Carolina than in any other state

South Dakota, 40th state (1889), Coyote State, Rushmore State

    capital: Pierre

    state bird: ring-necked pheasant

    state flower: pasqueflower

    state tree: Black Hills spruce

    motto: 'Under God, the people rule'

    birthplace of: Tom Brokaw, Chief Crazy Horse, Hubert H. Humphrey, Cheryl Ladd, George McGovern, Russell Means, Chief Sitting Bull

    tourist attractions: Black Hills, Mount Rushmore, Needles Highway, Badlands National Park, Wind Cave

    fact: South Dakota boasts the world's largest sculptured portrait, a 90-foot high carving of the head of the Sioux chief Crazy Horse, which stares out of the Black Hills. The portrait was started in 1939 by Korczak Ziolkowski and was completed in 2004. The rest of Crazy Horse – his arms, legs and horse – is expected to be finished by 2054

southeast Asia, adjective: Oriental

southern: austral

Southern Rhodesia: former name for Zimbabwe (1911–1964)

South Korea: republic in North-East Asia

    capital: Seoul

    currency: won

    language: Korean

    religion: Buddhist, Confucianist, Shamanist, Chondokyo

South Korean nationalist: Syngman Rhee

South Pole: first reached by the Norwegian explorer Roald Amundsen (in 1911)

sovereign, murder of: regicide

Soviet police chief: Lavrentiy Beria

    - see Russians

space, adjective: cosmic, galactic, intergalactic, interstellar, spatial

space and time, adjective: spatiotemporal

space, first creature in: the fruit fly

space shuttles: Atlantis (docked with Mir on 29 June 1995, at 17,500 mph), Columbia (disintegrated on re-entry in 2003)

space station, Russian: Mir

space theorist: Konstantin Tsiolkovsky

space travellers: Arthur Dent (from *The Hitchhiker's Guide to the Galaxy*), Flash Gordon, James Tiberius Kirk, Buck Rogers, Luke Skywalker, Han Solo, Mr Spock
    - see astronauts

space walk, first: carried out by Alexei Leonov on 18 March 1965

spacecraft; the first man-made object to leave the solar system: Pioneer 10 (launched 2 March 1972 on what was expected to be a 21-month journey; sent its farewell message in March 2003, 31 years after its launch, 7.6. billion miles from home)

spade-shaped: palaceous
Spain: kingdom in south-west Europe
   capital: Madrid (see)
   currency: euro; formerly the peseta
   language: Castilian Spanish; also Catalan, Galician, Basque
   religion: Roman Catholic
Spain, fact: country with the lowest birth rate in the world: 1.2 per couple
Spanish Armada, defeat of: 1588 (by the English)
Spanish artists: Ferrer Bassa, Bartolomé Bermejo, Alonso Cano, Claudio Coello, Salvador Dalí, Mariano Fortuny, Fernando Gallego, Antonio López García, Francisco Goya, El Greco (albeit born in Crete), Juan Gris, Jaume Huguet, Bernat Martorell, Joan Miró, Luís Morales, Bartolomé Esteban Murillo, Francisco Pacheco, Pablo Picasso, Jusepe (José) de Ribera, Antonio Saura, Santiago Sierra, Antoni Tàpies, Master of Taüll, Diego Velázquez, Francisco de Zurbarán
Spanish Civil War: 1936–39
Spanish composers: Manuel de Falla, Joaquín Rodrigo, Martin Sarasate, Joaquín Turina
Spanish film directors: Pedro Almodóvar, Alejandro Amenábar, Vicente Aranda, Luis Bunuel, Alex de la Iglesia, Victor Erice, Bigas Luna, Julio Medem, Carlos Saura
Spanish flu: 1918–1919; infection that killed more than 20 million people across the world
Spanish Inquisition: founded in the kingdom of Castile in 1478 by King Ferdinand V and Queen Isabella and formally abolished in 1820
Spanish Inquisitor: Tomás de Torquemada
Spanish novelists: Mateo Alemán, Miguel de Cervantes, Federico García Lorca, Garcilaso de la Vega
Spanish playwrights: Federico García Lorca, Lope de Vega
Spanish racing driver: Fernando Alonso
Spanish rivers: Douro, Ebro, Guadalquivir, Guadiana, Tagus
Spanish sausage: chorizo
Spanish song: *Que Séra, Séra* (aka *Whatever Will Be, Will Be*)
Spanish tennis player: Rafael Nadal
Spanish warrior: El Cid (real name: Rodrigo Diaz de Vivar)
Spanish words adopted by the English language: adobe, adios, aficionado, banderillero, bolas, bolero, bonanza, burro, camino real, cedilla, chaparral, conquistador, corral, desperado, embargo, fandango, fiesta, flamenco, gaucho, gringo, guerrilla, hacienda, hasta la vista, incommunicado, junta, machete, macho, marijuana, mascara, matador, mesa, pampas, patio, peccadillo, picador, pinto, pistachio, poncho, pronto, rodeo, savannah, sierra, siesta, sombrero, supremo, tequila, tilde, toreador, tortilla, vigilante
sparrow, adjective: passerine
sparrow, collective noun: flight, host
sparrow, sound: chirp
sparrow, young: chick
Spartacus revolt: 73–71 BC
Spartan king: Menelaus
Spartan queen: Helen, Leda
spasm sufferers, patron saint of: John the Baptist
speaking, fear of: halophobia

speaking in tongues: glossolalia
speaking out loud, fear of: phonophobia
spear, magic: Gungnir (Norse mythology)
spear carrier, sculpture of: doryphorus
spear handle: haft
spear mounted with a battleaxe: halberd
spear-shaped: hastate
Spears, Britney: anagram for "Presbyterians"
Special K slogan: 'Can't pinch an inch on you'
specialist: wonk
spectacles (glasses): first recorded in 1268
Spectator, The: weekly radical periodical founded by Robert Stephen Rintoul in 1828; Rintoul edited the first edition and stayed in charge until 1958. An earlier publication, also called *The Spectator*, was founded in 1711 by Sir Richard Steele and Joseph Addison. Published daily, the periodical's circulation peaked at 3,000 and folded in 1712
speech: "Speech was given to man to disguise his thoughts" – Charles Talleyrand
speech, aversion to: lalophobia
speech, disruption of (as in 'um' or 'er'): disfluency
speech, inability to comprehend: asemia
speech impaired, patron saint of the: Drogo
speech impediments: lallation (pronouncing an 'r' like an 'l'), lisp, stammer, stutter
speech sounds: accent, agma, alliteration, anaptyxis, articulation, cacology, click, consonant, continuant, diphthong, drawl, enclitic, euphony, gibber, glide, haplology, lallation, lilt, lisp, nasality, palatalization, phoneme, plosive, pronunciation, snuffle, splutter, sputter, stammer, stutter, vowel
speech sounds, study of: phonology
speech therapy: logopaedics
speed (drug): amphetamine, Benzedrine, dexies, methamphetamine, purple heart, upper
speed (of motion), fear of: tachophobia
speed (of motion), measurement of: tachometry
speed camera (UK): Gatso, PIPS Spike, Specs
speed of sound: Mach number 1
speed readers: Andrew Marr, H.L. Mencken, John Stuart Mill, Theodore Roosevelt
spelling, adjective: orthographic
spelling, bad: cacography
spelling, conventional: orthography
spelling, study of: orthography
sperm: baby gravy, blockers, cream, cum, face cream, French dressing, go-getters, home brew, jack, jam, jism, jizz, protein, semen, splooge, spunk
sperm, fact: the world's largest sperm belongs to the fruit fly, which reaches 2.3 inches long, 20 times the length of its body and making up 11 per cent of its body weight
sperm, adjective: seminal, seminiferous, spermatic
sperm, fact: the average man will produce 14 gallons of sperm over the course of his life
sperm, inability to produce during ejaculation: aspermia
sperm count, average in the British male: 62 million per millilitre (down from 87 million per millilitre in 1989)

spermatoza: male sex cell discovered by Anthony van Leeuwenhoek in 1679

Sphinx-like: Sphingine

spice: acitrón, agar wood, ajmud, ajowan, alexanders, allspice, angelica, anise, anise-pepper, annatto, asafoetida, Ashanti pepper, balsam, bay, basil, borage, caper, caraway, cardamom, cassia, cayenne pepper, celery seed, chervil, chilli, Chinese five-spice powder, cinnamon, clove, corianda, cumin, curcuma, cury powder, dill seed, fennel seed, fenugreek, galangal (or galingale), garam masala (mixture), garlic, ginger, grains of Paradise, horseradish, juniper, mace, mustard, nigella, nutmeg, paprika, pepper, pickling spice, poppy, pumpkin seed, saffron, sesame seed, star anise (star-shaped spice), sunflower seed, tamarind, tarragon, thyme, turmeric, vanilla, wormwood
- see herbs

spice, most expensive: saffron

Spice Girls, The: phenomenally successful UK girl band prefabricated in London in 1993; comprised of Geri Estelle Halliwell (aka Sexy Spice and Ginger Spice), Melanie Janine Brown (aka Scary Spice, Mel B and Mel G), Victoria Adams (aka Posh Spice, later known as Victoria Beckham), Melanie Jayne Chisholm (aka Sporty Spice and Mel C) and Emma Lee Bunton (aka Baby Spice). Having answered an advertisement requesting five 'lively girls,' the Spice ensemble almost immediately dumped their first manager and set off on their own. However, it would be two years before the girls finally secured a recording contract – with Virgin Records – whereupon they hunted for a manager. They found Simon Fuller near the end of 1995 and launched their first single, *Wannabe*, in the summer of 1996. It went straight to No. 1, the first debut single by an all-female band to do so (in England). Their next five songs also shot to No. 1. Geri Halliwell left the group in 1998 and in 2008 the others officially called it quits

spider, adjective: arachnid

spider, collective noun: cluster, clutter

spider, famous: Charlotte

spider, most venemous: Brazilian wandering huntsman

spider, young: spiderling

spider maiden: Arachne (Greek mythology)

spiders, study of: arachnology

spiders, fear of: arachnophobia

spider's vagina: epigynum

spider's web, adjective: araneous

spies: Aldrich Ames, Elyesa Bazna (aka Cicero), Aphra Behn, Michael Bettany (MI5 officer jailed for 23 years in 1984 for passing information to the Soviet Union), George Blake, Anthony Blunt, Guy Burgess, Giacomo Casanova, Juanita Castro, Anna Chapman, Eddie Chapman, Olga Chekhova (allegedly), Janet Chisholm, 'La Cicciolina' (aka Ilona Staller), Cicero (aka Elyesa Bazna), Eli Cohen, Roald Dahl, Daniel Defoe, Denis Donaldson (veteran Sinn Féin figure who spied for the British), Emma E. Edmonds, Frank Foley, Klaus Fuchs, Oleg Gordievsky (KGB officer working for MI6), S. Günter Guillaume, Robert Hanssen, Helen Kroger, Peter Kroger, Alexander Litvinenko (poisoned in London in November 2006 by a large dose of polonium-210), Gordon Lonsdale, Donald Maclean, Christopher Marlowe, Mata Hari (allegedly), James Mossman, Melita Norwood (87-year-old grandmother from Bexleyheath who spied for the Soviet Union for 40 years), Arthur Owens, Oleg Penkovsky, Kim Philby, Vladimir Putin, Sidney Reilly, Stella Rimington, Ethel and Julius

Rosenberg, David Shayler (former intelligence officer who blew the whistle on MI5 incompetence and subsequently went to prison), Richard Tomlinson (accused of posting a list of 117 M16 officers on the Internet), Mordechai Vanunu (revealed Israel's nuclear secrets to the world), Stanislaw Wielgus (the very brief Archbishop of Warsaw), Greville Wynne
- see traitors

spies, fictitious: James Bond, Ethan Hunt (from *Mission: Impossible*), Barry Lyndon (from the novel by Thackeray), Number Six, Austin Powers, George Smiley
- see secret agents

spike, adjective: spicate

spikes, used in warfare: caltrops (spikes designed to be scattered on roads), caltrop chain (ditto), cheval-de-frise: (a log set with spikes), crows' feet (spikes designed to be scattered on roads)

spin doctors: Tim Bell, Alastair Campbell

spinach, adjective: spinaceous

spinal column: vertebrae

spine, adjective: dorsal, spinous

spine doctor: orthopaedist

spiny anteater: echidna

spiny-backed: notacanthous

spiral, adjective: spiroid

spirits, fear of: demonophobia

spiritualists – see mediums, mystics

spleen, adjective: splenetic, splenic

spokesperson: prolocutor

sponge-like: cancellous

spontaneous human combustion: first recorded in literarature by Charles Dickens in *Bleak House* (1852), in which the rag-and-bone dealer Krook was burned to a cinder

spoon: first recorded in 1490 BC (and mentioned in The Old Testament, Numbers vii, 26)

spoon bender: Uri Geller

sport: "Sports do not build character. They reveal it" - Heywood Hale Broun

sport: American football, archery, athletics, badminton, baseball, basketball, battledore, biathlon, billiards, bobsleigh, bowling, bowls, boxing, bullfighting, canoeing, carriage driving, chess, cricket, croquet, curling, cycling, darts, discus, diving, fencing, figure skating, football, frisbee, golf, gymnastics, hammer, handball, harness racing, high jump, hockey, horse racing, hunting, hurdling, ice hockey, javelin, judo, lacrosse, long jump, luge, marathon (running), motocross, motor cycling, motor racing, mountaineering, orienteering, paintball, pelota, pentathlon, ping pong, pole vault, polo, powerboating, racket tennis, racquetball, rallying, rodeo, rowing, rugby, Rugby League, Rugby Union, running, scuba diving, shooting, shot put, show jumping, skin diving, skating, skiing, skydiving, soccer, speed skating, skiing, snooker, Speedway, squash, sumo wrestling, surfing, swimming, synchronised swimming, table tennis, tennis, thoroughbred racing, tobogganing, triathlon, triple jump, volleyball, wakeboarding, walking, water polo, water skiing, weightlifting, windsurfing, wrestling, yachting

sports car designer: Donald Healey

sports commentators: Henry Blofeld (cricket), Heywood Hale Broun, Harry

Carpenter, David Coleman, Bob Costas, Brian Johnston, Craig Kilborn, Tony
Lewis, Desmond Lynam, David Vine
sports tycoons: Roman Abramovich, Malcolm Glazer
sportswear: Adidas, Lacoste, Nike, Puma AG, Reebok, Speedo
spots, adjective: liturate
spouse, adjective: spousal
spray can: invented in 1926 by the Norwegian Erik Rotheim
spring, adjective: vernal
spring, goddess of: Hebe (Greek), Juventas (Roman)
springs (of the mineral variety), adjective: crenitic
spring onion: scallion
sprinkling receptacle (for salt, sugar, etc): castor
sprinters: Usain Bolt, Dwain Chambers, Carl Lewis, Jesse Owens, Asafa Powell
  - see runners
Spruce Goose: nickname given to the H-4 Hughes Flying Boat, also known as
  The Hercules. The biggest aircraft ever built (it has a wingspan of 320 feet and
  could accomodate 700 troops), the ship was created to ferry supplies and
  soldiers from the United States to Europe during the Second World War. It was
  the brainchild of Henry Kaiser and Howard Hughes, and was largely made out
  of birch wood (not spruce), but failed to meet its war-time deadline. It was
  finally launched on 2 November 1947 – with Howard Hughes at the helm – and
  flew one mile in less than a minute at a top speed of 80 mph. It was then placed
  in storage and never flew again. Today, it is a popular tourist attraction at the
  Evergreen Aviation Center in McMinnville, Oregon
spur, adjective: calcarine
spur wheel: rowel
spur-shaped: calcarine
spy: mole, operative, plant, secret agent, snark, spook (see spies)
squash player: Susan Devoy
squid, fried: calamary, calamari
squint (noun): cyclophoria, strabismus
squirrel, adjective: sciurine, sciuroid
squirrel, collective noun: dray, scurry
squirrels, famous: Mr Bushytail (from Howard R. Garis's *Uncle Wiggily's Stories to
  Read Aloud*), Eddie the Squirrel (TV cartoon), Goody Tiptoes (from Beatrix
  Potter's *Tale of Timmy Tiptoes*), King Maximillian Acorn (from TV's *Sonic the
  Hedgehog*), Melvin (from TV's *The Simpsons*), Ratatosk (Norse mythology),
  Rocky (Bullwinkle's friend), Secret Squirrel, Silvertail (Beatrix Potter),
  Squirrel Nutkin (Beatrix Potter), Timmy Tiptoes (Beatrix Potter), Wirral (c/o
  Paul McCartney, Geoff Dunbar and Philip Ardagh)
squirrel, young: pup
squirrel's nest: drey
Sri Lanka, Democratic Socialist Republic of: republic in southern Asia, previously
  known as Taprobane and Serendip (in Medieval times) and Ceylon (up until
  1972)
  capital: Colombo (administrative), Sri Jayawardenepura Kotte (legislative)
  currency: Sri Lankan rupee
  language: Sinhalese, Tamil, English
  nickname: Blessed Island
  religion: Hinayana Buddhism, Hinduism, Christianity and Islam
  majority people: Sinhalese (religion: Theravada Buddhism)

Sri Lanka, average annual fatality from snake bites: 800
Sri Lankan Civil War: 1983–1988
Sri Lankan king: Ravana (Hindu mythology)
S-shaped: annodated
SS: SchutzStaffel (Nazi police)
SSRI: selective serotonin reuptake inhibitor (anti-depressant)
SSSI: site of special scientific interest
stabbing in the leg: juking
Staffordshire, administrative centre: Stafford
stag, sound of: bell (particularly in the rutting season)
stage designers: John Byrne, Edward Gordon Craig, Giacomo Torelli
stage directors – see theatre directors
stain with blood: imbrue
stained-glass artists: Stephen Adam, Daniel Cottier
staircase, exterior: perron
stairway to river: ghat
stalking disorder: De Clerambault's syndrome
stammer, fact: speech disorder affecting approximately one in every 100 people
stammerers, famous: Aesop, Aristotle, Ed Balls, Thomas Becket, Arnold Bennett,
    Anthony Blanche (from Evelyn Waugh's *Brideshead Revisited*), Elizabeth Bowen,
    Lewis Carroll, King Charles I, Sir Winston Churchill, Charles Darwin, Margaret
    Drabble, Gareth Gates, King George VI, Hotspur (from Shakespeare's *Henry IV
    Part 1*), Sandra Howard (wife of Michael Howard, Britain's former Conservative
    party leader), Leigh Hunt, Aldous Huxley, Henry James, Harvey Keitel, Charles
    Kingsley, Philip Larkin, Larry the Lamb, W. Somerset Maugham, Marilyn
    Monroe (in her childhood), Moses, Sir Isaac Newton, Mervyn Noote (as played
    by Derek Nimmo in TV's *All Gas and Gaiters*), Wilfred Owen, Porky Pig, Nevil
    Shute, Carly Simon, JMW Turner, John Updike, Virgil, Bruce Willis (in his
    childhood), Tiger Woods
    - see lispers, famous
stamp collecting: philately
stamp collector: philatelist
stamp collectors, patron saint of: Gabriel the Archangel
stamps, sheet of: pane
Standard, The: London newspaper founded in 1827 (later became *The Evening
    Standard*)
standing up, fear of: stasiphobia
standing up, making love: stasivalent
star, adjective: asterial, stellar, stellular
star, brightest: Sirius (in the Canis Major constellation)
star-shaped: stellate
stars, fear of: siderophobia
star signs: Libra (24 September - 23 October), Scorpio (24 October - 22 November),
    Sagittarius (23 November - 21 December), Capricorn (22 December - 20
    January), Aquarius (21st January - 19th February), Pisces (20 February - 20
    March), Aries (21 March - 20 April), Taurus (21 April - 21 May), Gemini (22
    May - 21st June), Cancer (22 June - 23rd July), Leo (24th July - 23rd August),
    Virgo (24th August - 23rd September)
stars, adjective: sidereal
starch, consisting of: farinaceous
stared at, aversion to being: ophthalmophobia

starfish, adjective: actinoid, asteroidean

starling, adjective: sturnine

starling, collective noun: murmuration

starling, fact: can mimic the sound of other birds, frogs, mammals and even machinery (such as mobile phones), weaving the sound into their song

starship: Enterprise (from *Star Trek*)

Starsky and Hutch: popular one-hour TV crime show about a pair of undercover cops working in a metropolis called 'Bay City'

    created by William Blinn

    broadcast: 10 September 1975–21 August 1979

    cast: Paul Michael Glaser (Dave Starsky), David Soul (Ken 'Hutch' Hutchinson), Bernie Hamilton (Captain Harold Dobey), Antonio Fargas (Huggy Bear)

Star Trek: eternally beloved sci-fi series set in the twenty-third century and featuring the civilised and racially harmonious crew of the Starship *Enterprise*, whose mission is "to boldly go where no man has gone before." Such was the success of the series (whose popularity dramatically increased during reruns and syndication), that it spawned eleven big-screen versions (1979–2009), a cartoon edition (*Star Trek*, 1973–1975) and the small-screen spin-offs *Star Trek: The Next Generation*, *Star Trek: Deep Space Nine* and *Star Trek: Voyager*, not to mention some phenomenal merchandising, fan conventions and spoofs. Interestingly, the series' pilot, starring Jeffrey Hunter, was never aired

    created by Gene Roddenberry

    broadcast: 8 September 1966–2 September 1969

    cast: William Shatner (James Tiberius Kirk), Leonard Nimoy (Mr Spock), DeForest Kelley (Dr Leonard 'Bones' McCoy), James Doohan (Montgomery 'Scotty' Scott), Nichelle Nichols (Lt. Uhura), George Takei (Mr Sulu), Majel Barrett (Christine Chapel), Walter Koenig (Ensign Pavel Chekov)

Star Trek, famous line: Mr Spock: "It's life, Jim, but not as we know it."

Star Trek fan: Trekker, Trekkie

Star Wars (1977 film), opening line (written on-screen): "A long time ago in a galaxy far, far away…"

Star Wars characters: Queen Amidala (aka Padmé Naberrie), C-3PO, Chewbacca, Jar Jar Binks, Lando Calrissian, Count Dooku, General Grievous, Qui-Gon Jinn, Obi-Wan Kenobi, Darth Maul, Darth Vader, Bail Organa, Leia Organa, Senator Palpatine, R2–D2, Anakin Skywalker, Luke Skywalker, Han Solo, Mace Windu, Yoda

stars, adjective: sidereal

Stars and Stripes: Old Glory

Stars and Stripes Forever, The: military march composed in 1897 by John Philip Sousa

starve: abstain, diet, dine with Duke Humphrey, fast, go without

starving people, patron saint of: Anthony of Padua

states of North America: Alabama (AL), Alaska (AK), Arizona (AZ), Arkansas (AR), California (CA), Colorado (CO), Connecticut (CT), Delaware (DE), Florida (FL), Georgia (GA), Hawaii (HI), Idaho (ID), Illinois (IL), Indiana (IN), Iowa (IA), Kansas (KS), Kentucky (KY), Louisiana (La., LA), Maine (ME), Maryland (MD), Massachusetts (MA), Michigan (MI), Minnesota (MN), Mississippi (MS), Missouri (MO), Montana (MT), Nebraska (NE), Nevada (NV), New Hampshire (NH), New Jersey (NJ), New Mexico (NM), New York (NY), North Carolina (NC), North Dakota (ND), Ohio (OH), Oklahoma (OK), Oregon (OR), Pennsylvania (PA), Rhode Island (RI), South Carolina (SC), South Dakota (SD), Tennessee (TN), Texas (TX), Utah (UT), Vermont (VT), Virginia (VA), Washington (WA), West Virginia (WV), Wisconsin (WI),

Wyoming (WY)

stasivalent: the unusual condition of only being able to make love by standing up

stately homes, number owned by National trust: 300

statesman: "A politician who has been dead ten or 15 years" – Harry S. Truman

statesmen, patron saint of: Thomas More

stations, types of: action, comfort, dressing, panic, petrol, railway, relay, Underground

statistician: "Someone who is good with numbers, but lacks the personality to be an accountant" - anonymous

statistician, famous: Herman Hollerith

Statue of Liberty: 306ft, 8in (93.5 metres) statue standing on Liberty Island in the harbour of New York City. Designed by the French sculptor Frédéric-Auguste Bartholdi, the monument – originally called Liberty Enlightening the World – was a present from France to the United States to commemorate the centennial of U.S. independence. It was dedicated by President Grover Cleveland on 28 October 1886. One of the largest statues in the world, the body alone is 152ft 2in tall and the head 10ft wide

statues: Angel of the North, Christ the Redeemer (in Rio de Janeiro), Colossus of Rhodes, David (c/o Michelangelo), Eros, Galatea (c/o Pygmalion), Little Mermaid (in Copenhagen), Manneken Pis, Sphinx, Statue of Liberty, Statue of Zeus at Olympia
- see sculptures

statue, pedestal of: acropodium

St. Bartholomew's Day Massacre: 1572 (when the French Huguenots were slaughtered by Charles IX)

STD: sexually transmitted disease

steak: chateaubriand, contre-filet, entrecôte, faux filet, filet mignon, fillet, minute steak, pope's eye, porterhouse steak, rump steak, T-bone, tournedos

steal: blag, cop, lift, nick, pinch, rob, snatch, swipe

stealing, aversion to: kleptophobia

stealing, sexual excitement derived from: kleptolagnia

steel magnate: Lakshmi Mittal

steering device on aeroplane: joystick

St Elsewhere: critically lauded TV drama series set at St Eligius, a civic hospital in Boston. The institution acquired its nickname, 'St Elsewhere,' because of its reputation as a 'dumping ground'
broadcast: 26 October 1982–25 May 1988
created by Joshua Brand and John Falsey
cast: Ed Flanders (Dr Donald Westphall), William Daniels (Dr Mark Craig), Ed Begley Jr (Dr Victor Ehrlich), David Morse (Dr Jack Morrison), Howie Mandel (Dr Wayne Fiscus), Christina Pickles (nurse Helen Rosenthal), Denzel Washington (Dr Philip Chandler), Norman Lloyd (Dr Daniel Auschlander), David Birney (Dr Ben Samuels), Cynthia Sikes (Dr Annie Cavanero), Mark Harmon (Dr Bob Calswell), Alfre Woodard (Dr Roxanne Turner), France Nuyen (Dr Paulette Klein), Patricia Wettig (Joanne McFadden), Ronny Cox (Dr John Gideon)

stepmother, adjective: novercal

steps, average taken each day by a human being: between 8,000 and 10,000

steps leading to river: ghat

Steptoe and Son: eternally popular and poignant TV sitcom featuring the grotesque and cantankerous Albert Steptoe and his son Harold, who together operate a rundown junkyard. Developed from a half-hour TV play, *The Offer* (1962), the series was translated into the American sitcom *Sanford and Son* (1972–77) and

spawned two big-screen spin-offs, *Steptoe and Son* (1972) and *Steptoe & Son Ride Again* (1973)
created by Alan Simpson and Ray Galton
broadcast 14 June 1962–10 October 1974 on BBC1
cast: Wilfred Brambell (Albert Steptoe), Harry H. Corbett (Harold Steptoe)
sterile: antiseptic, axenic, disinfected, impersonal, nebulous, nondescript, sanitary, sterilised
sterility in females: acyesis
stew: bouillabaisse, carbonnade, cassoulet, chilli con carne, daube, Fanny Adams, goulash, gumbo, hotchpotch, Irish stew, jambalaya, matelote, olio, pottage (archaic), slumgullion
STI: sexually transmitted infection
still life painters: Jacopo de' Barbari (considered the first still life painter), Georges Braque, Jan Brueghel, Paul Cézanne, Jean Baptiste Chardin, Juan Gris, Henri Matisse, Piet Mondrian, Jean Baptiste Oudry, Pablo Picasso, Frans Snyders, Chaïm Soutine, Vincent Van Gogh
stillness, fear of: eremophobia
stilton, fact: the blue cheese, granted protected status by the European Commission, can only be produced by seven dairies in the world, all situated in the English counties of Derbyshire, Leicestershire and Nottinghamshire
stimulants: adrenalin, amphetamine, Benzedrine, caffeine, coca, cocaine, coffee, Dexedrine, ecstasy, julep, khat, methamphetamine, methylenedioxymethamphetamine, pep pill, purple heart, speed, stomachic, strychnine, upper, valerian
stings, fear of: cnidophobia
stinging nettles, adjective: urticacous
stirrup cup: deoch an doris
St John's wort (flowering shrub): hypericum
stock-car racing driver: Richard Petty
Stockholm, birthplace of: Benny Andersson (of Abba fame), Bo Bergman (poet), Ingrid Bergman, Neneh Cherry, Greta Garbo, Lena Olin (actress), August Strindberg
Stockholm, nickname: Venice of the North
Stockholm river: Norrström
stocking seller: hosier
Stoicism, philosophers of: Chrysippus of Soli, Cleanthes of Assos, Epictetus, Marcus Aurelius Antoninus, Lucius Seneca, Zeno of Citium (founder)
stomach: beer belly, belly, gut, paunch, pot, pot belly, six-pack, tummy, washboard
stomach, adjective: gastric, stomachic
stomach, science of: gastrology
stomach, surgical removal of: gastrectomy
stomach; having a big one: ventricose (adjective)
stomach doctor: gastroenterologist
stomach pain: gastrodynia
stomach rumbling: borborygmus
stomach stapling (cosmetic surgery): gastroplasty
stomachs of the cow and other ruminants: rumen (first), reticulum (second), psalterium or omasum (third), abomasum (fourth)
stone, adjective: lapidary, lithic, lithoid(al)
stone, turn into: lapidify
Stone Age (early), adjective: palaeolithic

Stone Age (middle), adjective: mesolithic
Stone Age (later), adjective: neolithic
stone circles: Avebury (Wiltshire), Boscawen-un (near St Burian), Men-an-Tol, Ring of Brodgar (in the Orkneys), Stonehenge
stone cutter: lapicide, lapidary
stone engraver: lapicide
stone to death: lapidate
stoned, politically correct term: chemically inconvenienced
stoning: lapidation
Stooges – see Three Stooges, The
stooping, fear of: kyphophobia
stork, adjective: ciconine, pelargic
stork, collective noun: mustering
storm, adjective: procellous
storm, fact: in the Great Storm of October 1987, Britain lost 15 million trees
stowaway: Billy Crocker (from *Anything Goes*)
stowaways, fact: in June of 2000, 58 Chinese corpses were found trapped inside a sealed lorry container at Dover (there were only two survivors)
Strand cigarette, slogan: 'You're never alone with a Strand'
stranger: "A friend you don't know" - advertisement for Ericsson communications
strangers, fear of: xenophobia
Strasbourg, fact: city noted for its production of pâté de foie gras
Strasbourg river: Ill
Stratford-upon-Avon theatres: Royal Shakespeare Theatre, Shakespeare Memorial Theatre (destroyed by fire), Swan Theatre
stratosphere: atmospheric layer that stretches from seven to 30 miles in altitude
straw, adjective: stramineous
straw turner (machine): tedder
straw-coloured: festucine
stream, dried up: arroyo, wadi
street: alley, avenue, back alley, boulevard, byway, close, court, crescent, cul-de-sac, high street, lane, main drag, side street, terrace, wynd (a very narrow one)
street lamps, gas: first installed in 1807, in London, along Pall Mall
street vendor: costermonger
stress: computer rage (aka technology-related anxiety), road rage, technology-related anxiety, trolley rage
stress factors: 1: death; 2: divorce; 3: holidays; 4: family Christmas; 5: row with the in-laws
stress hormone: cortisol
stretch-marks: striae
strife, god of: Loki (Norse mythology)
string, fear of: linonophobia
string puppet: marionette
string theory: conceived by Edward Witten
stringed musical instruments: aeolian harp, archlute, balalaika, banjo, cello, citole, double bass, fiddle, gittern, guitar (see), harp, kanoon, koto (Japanese), lute (see), lyre, mandolin, pentachord, psaltery, rebec, sarangi (Indian), sitar (Indian), tamboura (Indian), tetrachord, theorbo, viol, viola, violin, violoncello, Welsh harp, zither
stringed musical instrument, adjecive: fidicinal
stringed musical instrument maker: luthier

stripe painter: Barnett Newman

stripper: cock tease, ecdysiast (facetious term), exotic dancer, lap dancer, minge winker (slang), pole dancer, table dancer

strippers, famous: Josephine Baker, Marilyn Chambers, Colette (also a famous writer), Catherine D'Lish, Carol Doda, Dixie Evans, Gypsy Rose Lee, Sally Rand, Fiona Richmond, Salome, Blaze Starr, Lili St. Cyr, Stella Vine (also a famous painter), Dita Von Teese

stroke (/), as used in fractions and written alternatives (such as in 'and/or'): solidus (plural: solidi)

stronghold: fastness, hedgehog (well-fortified; military term), keep

strong girl: Pippi Longstocking

strong men: Charles Atlas, Paul Bunyan, Geoff Capes, Lou Ferrigno, Hercules, the Hulk, Steve Reeves, Dwayne 'The Rock' Johnson, Arnold Schwarzenegger

structure, science of: morphology

student: freshman, sophomore, junior, senior

students, patron saint of: Albert the Great and Gabriel of Our Lady of Sorrows

stumble: "A stumble may prevent a fall" – Thomas Fuller

stun gun: Taser

stuntmen: Vic Armstrong, Rod Cameron, Yakima Canutt, Eddie Kidd, Evel Knievel, Cliff Lyons, Jock Mahoney, Paul Mantz, George Montgomery, George O'Brien, Eric Scott (who hovered over London wearing a Rocketbelt for a record 26 seconds), Colt Seavers (of TV's *The Fall Guy*), Richard Talmadge

stupid, equally: unasinous

sturgeon, adjective: acipenserine

stutter: logospasm

stuttering, fear of: laliophobia

stutterers – see stammerers, famous

style gurus: Carole Caplin (linked with Cherie Blair and Peter Foster), Don Johnson, Martha Stewart, Gok Wan

submarine: first design drawn up by Leonardo Da Vinci in 1495 (approximately). The first practical version – a wooden rowboat encased in leather - was built in 1624 for James I by the Dutch inventor Cornelius Drebbel

submarine, German: U-boat

submarine, parts of: ballast tanks, conning tower, diving planes, galley, hull, periscope, pressure hull, snorkel, sonar room, torpedo

submarine, nuclear: Polaris, Trident

submarine, slang: tin fish

submarine, small: submersible

submarines, famous: *American Turtle* (the first submersible used in warfare), *Dreadnought* (Britain's first nuclear submarine), *Nautilus* (from Jules Verne's *20,000 Leagues Under the Sea*, also the name of the world's first nuclear-powered submarine)

submarine tragedy: Kursk, in which all its occupants perished in August 2000

success: "The ability to go from one failure to another with no loss of enthusiasm" – Winston Churchill; "The secret of success is honesty and fair dealing. If you can fake those, you can fake anything" – Groucho Marx; "Success has many parents, but failure is an orphan" – old saying

success, goddess of: Felicitas (Roman mythology)

sucking (as in having a sucking proboscis), adjective: haustorial

Sudan: republic in north-east Africa

capital: Khartoum
currency: Sudanese dinar
language: Arabic
religion: Muslim (official), Christian, animist
fact: Sudan is the largest country in Africa
Sudanese leader: Omar al-Bashir
Sudanese religious leader: The Mahdi (aka Mohammed Ahmed)
Suffolk, administrative centre: Ipswich
suffragettes: Susan B. Anthony, Harriot Stanton Blatch, Amelia Bloomer, Dame
    Kathleen Courtney, Emily Davison, Crystal Eastman, Adela Pankhurst, Dame
    Christabel Pankhurst, Emmeline Pankhurst, Sylvia Pankhurst, Mary Richardson
    (who repeatedly slashed Velázquez' *The Rokeby Venus* at the National Gallery
    in protest of Emmeline Pankhurst's imprisonment), Anna Howard Shaw,
    Elizabeth Cady Stanton, Flora Tristan (grandmother of the painter Gauguin)
Sugababes, The: harmonious all-girl British pop trio formed in 1998. Comprised
    of school friends Keisha Buchanan and Mutya Buena, along with Siobhan
    Donaghy. In 2001, Donaghy was replaced by Heidi Range, from the original
    line-up of Atomic Kitten
sugar: first recorded in 325 BC, in Western India (by the Macedonian general
    Nearchus)
sugar: aspartame, Canderel, caster sugar, corn syrup, custard, demerara,
    deoxyribose, disaccharide, fructose, galactose, golden syrup, granulated sugar,
    HFCS (six times sweeter than sugar, it preserves biscuits and cakes almost
    indefinitely but does not break down in the human body), honey, icing sugar,
    invert sugar, lactose, low-cal, lump sugar, maltose, maple sugar, milk sugar,
    monosaccharide, muscovado, ribose, saccharin, soft sugar, Sweet 'n' low, syrup,
    treacle, trisaccharide, sweetener
sugar, adjective: saccharine
sugar snap: mangetout (aka snow pea)
suicide, fact: an estimated one person commits suicide every 40 seconds in Britain,
    now the biggest single cause of death of men aged 25 to 34
suicide, fact: one third of all English murderers commit suicide (and about half
    attempt it), compared with only 4% of American killers
suicide, god of: Omisto (Japanese mythology)
suicide, mass: Heaven's Gate sect (whose 39 members, in March of 1997, ate apple
    sauce laced with poison), based in a San Diego suburb
suicide, most common method worldwide: overdose; second most common:
    hanging, strangulation or suffocation
suicide, obsession with: automania
suicide, slang: Dutch act (US prison term), OD, solitaire, taking a rope
suicide bomber: shaheed
suicide capital of England: Hastings (briefly eclipsed in 2007 by the village of
    Gnosall in South Staffordshire and then, more dramatically, by the Welsh
    town Bridgend, where 23 young people hanged themselves within the space
    of 17 months)
suicide charity: Dignitas, a Swiss company founded in 1998 by Ludwig Minelli, a
    lawyer and former journalist, which offers assisted suicide
suicide committed to seek attention: parasuicide
suicide pioneers: Diane Pretty (who, suffering from motor neurone disease, fought
    for the right to assisted suicide), Debbie Purdy, Ramón Sampedro, Kelly Taylor,
    Dr Anne Turner
suicide site, most popular in the world: the Golden Gate Bridge in San Francisco

suicides, famous: Nick Adams (actor), Aïda, Ajax, Alcyone, Salvador Allende
   (president of Chile), Mark Antony, Diane Arbus, Andreas Baader, Cliff Baxter
   (Enron executive), Jill Bennett (actress), John Berryman (poet), Bruno
   Bettelheim (psychoanalyst), Martin Bormann, Boudicca, Emma Bovary,
   Charles Boyer, Eva Braun, Brutus, Jeff Buckley, Bernard Buffet (French
   painter), Donald Cammell (filmmaker), Capucine, Juliet Capulet, Dora
   Carrington, Cassius, Robert Castlereagh, Iris Chang, Thomas Chatterton (poet),
   Leslie Cheung (Hong Kong film star), Cleopatra, Lord Robert Clive of India,
   Kurt Cobain, Hart Crane (poet), Ian Curtis (lead singer of Joy Division),
   Terence Donovan, Sir Edward Downes, Brian Epstein, Richard Farnsworth,
   Vincent Foster, Hedda Gabler, Paul Joseph Goebbels, Hermann Goering,
   Goneril (from *King Lear*), Thomas Hamilton, Tony Hancock, Hannibal, Ernest
   Hemingway, Margaux Hemingway, Heinrich Himmler, Adolf Hitler, Abbie
   Hoffman, Juzo Itami (Japanese filmmaker), Randall Jarrell (poet and suspected
   suicide case), Jason (of the Argonauts), Inspector Javert (from *Les Miserables*),
   Jim Jones, Miss Julie, Juliet (Capulet), Sarah Kane (British playwright), Anna
   Karenina, Yasunari Kawabata (Japanese writer), Dr David Kelly, John Toole
   Kennedy, Heinrich von Kleist (playwright and poet), Arthur Koestler,
   Konstantine (from *The Seagull*), Lakmé, Hans Langsdorff (German naval
   commander), Primo Levi, Bernard Loiseau (chef), Willy Loman, Malcolm
   Lowry (arguably), Madame Butterfly, Guy de Maupassant (cut his own throat),
   Vladimir Mayakovsky (Russian poet and playwright), Alexander McQueen,
   Ulrike Meinhof, Marilyn Monroe, Romeo Montague, James Mossman,
   Narcissus, Nero, Ophelia, Otello, Othello, Emperor Marcus Otho, Jan Palach,
   Cesare Pavese (Italian poet and novelist), Phaedre, Sylvia Plath, Melvin Purvis
   (FBI agent), Pyramus, Thich Quang-Duc (Vietnamese monk who set himself
   on fire in July of 1963), Roy Raymond (founder of Victoria's Secret), Romeo
   (Montague), Erwin Rommel, Mark Rothko, Crown Prince Rudolf of Austria,
   Michael Ryan, Salome, George Sanders, Bobby Sands, Jean Seberg, Lucius
   Annaeus Seneca, Del Shannon, Harold Shipman, Elliott Smith, Margaret
   Sullavan, Screaming Lord Sutch (aka David Edward Sutch), Thisbe, Hunter S.
   Thompson, Tosca, Anne Turner, Vincent Van Gogh, Getúlio Vargas, Stephen
   Ward, Frederick West, Virginia Woolf, Wozzeck, Paula Yates, Mishima Yukio
sulphurous vent: solfatara
Sultan of Sleaze: nickname for Jerry Springer
Sumerian king: Gilgamesh
summer, adjective: aestival, estival
sumo wrestler: Koki Taiho
sumo wrestling tournament: basho
Sun, The: tabloid British newspaper founded in 1911
sun, adjective: helioid, solar, soliform
sun, fear of: heliophobia
sun, god of the: Helios (Greek), Horus (Egyptian), Sol (Roman), Surya (Hindu)
sun, poetic word for: Sol
sun god: Ra (Egyptian mythology)
Sun King: nickname for Louis XIV of France
sun spot: facula
sun worship: heliolatry
Sundance Kid: nickname for Harry Longbaugh
Sunday, adjective: dominical
Sunday Express, The: British Sunday newspaper founded in 1918

Sunday Mirror, The: British Sunday tabloid newspaper founded in 1915
Sunday People, The: British Sunday tabloid newspaper founded in 1881
Sunday Telegraph, The: British Sunday newspaper founded in 1961
Sunday Times, The: British Sunday newspaper founded in 1821
sundial pin (that which casts the shadow): gnomon
sunglasses: Gotrocks, Oakley, Alain Mikli, Police, Ray-Ban, shades, Speedo
sunset, adjective: acronical, acronychal
Sunset Boulevard (1950 film), famous line: Joe (William Holden): "Wait a minute, haven't I seen you before? I know your face… You're Norma Desmond. Used to be in silent pictures. Used to be big." Norma Desmond (Gloria Swanson): "I *am* big. It's the pictures that got small."
sunspot centre: umbra
sunstroke: heliosis, siriasis, touch of the sun
superheroes: Captain America, Atom Smasher, Batman (see), the Black Panther, Blade, James Bond (see), Dan Dare, Daredevil, Judge Dread, Gilgamesh, Flash Gordon, the Green Hornet, He-Man, Heracles, Hercules, Iron Man, Indiana Jones, Kick-Ass, Captain Marvel, Perseus, the Phantom, Plastic Man, the Punisher, Robin Hood, Doc Savage, Spider-Man, Supergirl, Superman (see), Tarzan, Wolverine, Zorro
- see comic strip heroines
Supermac: nickname for the British prime minister Harold Macmillan
superman: Übermensch
Superman, aka: Clark Kent, Jor-El, the Man of Steel (partly based on pulp hero Doc Savage, whose first name was also Clark)
   city: Metropolis
   created by: Jerry Siegel and Joseph Shuster
   newspaper: *The Daily Planet*
   planet: Krypton
   publisher: DC Action Comics
supermarkets (UK): Aldi, Asda, Bejam, Budgens, the Co-op, Costcutter, Fine Fare, Iceland, Lidl, Marks & Spencer, Morrisons, Safeway, Sainsbury's, Somerfield, Tesco, Waitrose
supermodels: Sophie Anderton, Tyra Banks, Christie Brinkley, Carla Bruni, Gisele Bündchen ('The Boobs from Brazil'), Naomi Campbell, Caprice, Gia Carangi, Laetitia Casta ('Marianne, the face of France'), Helena Christensen, Cindy Crawford, Agyness Deyn, Waris Dirie, Linda Evangelista, Jenna Fisher, Jerry Hall, Shalom Harlow, Marie Helvin, Eva Herzigova (of Wonderbra fame), Gabriel Hill, Kirsty Hume, Lauren Hutton, Jordan (aka Katie Price), Adriana Karembeu, Jodie Kidd, Carmen Kass ("the richest girl from Estonia"), Rachel Kirby (started at 12-years-old), Heidi Klum, Karolina Kurkova, Adriana Lima, Angela Lindvall, Elle Macpherson ('The Body'), Kate Moss, Karen Mulder, Carolyn Murphy, Fabiane Nunes, Erin O'Connor, Tatjana Patitz, Paulina Porizkova, Lisa Ratliffe (former dental nurse from High Wycombe), Caroline Ribeiro, Ines Rivero, Georgianna Robertson, Nakiesha Robinson, Rebecca Romijn-Stamos, Isabella Rossellini, Claudia Schiffer, Stephanie Seymour, Brooke Shields (Revlon's 'Charlie girl'), Jean Shrimpton (aka The Shrimp), Anna Nicole Smith, Vivien Solari, Talisa Soto, Fernanda Tavares, Niki Taylor, Stella Tennant, Christy Turlington, Twiggy, Amber Valletta, Veruschka (aka Countess Vera von Lehndorff), Gianne Vicente, Natalia Vodianova, Rachel Williams
Superwomen: Shirley Conran, Katherine Garrett-Cox (£1m-a-year fund manager dubbed 'Katheine the Great'), Nicola Horlick (dubbed 'Superwoman' for

juggling a lucrative career with SG Asset Management – where she handled £6.6 billion worth of assets –while raising six children)

Supremes, The: phenomenally successful female vocal group formed in Detroit in 1961; comprised of Diana Ross (real name: Diane Earle), Mary Wilson and Florence Ballard, all of whom came from the Brewster housing project. Originally called The Primettes, when Barbara Martin was also a member. In 1967 Ballard was replaced by Cindy Birdsong (Ballard, on welfare, died ten years later), when the group's name was changed a second time, to Diana Ross & The Supremes. However, Ross left in 1970 and was replaced by Jean Terrell, leaving the group to struggle on until disbanding in 1977

Sureté: undercover police unit created in 1811 by François Vidocq

surface, adjective: acrotic

surfers, female: Megan Abubo, Rochelle Ballard

surfers, male: Tom Carroll, Laird Hamiton

surgeons: Dr Christiaan Barnard, James Barry (disguised as a man throughout her military career, Barry is now believed to be the first British woman to become a qualified medical doctor), Dr Peter Barton (from TV's *ER*), Alexis Carrell, Sir John Charnley, Dr Mark Craig (from TV's *St Elsewhere*), Henry Gray, Sir William Gull, Lemuel Gulliver, John Hunter (responsible for the first transplant), Jack the Ripper, Dr Richard Kimble (from TV's *The Fugitive*), Joseph Lister, Sean McNamara (from TV's *Nip/Tuck*), Captain Benjamin Franklin 'Hawkeye' Pierce (from *M*A*S*H*), Walter Reed, Christian Troy (from TV's *Nip/Tuck*), Yury Zhivago
- see doctors, physicians

surgeons, patron saint of: Luke the Apostle

surgery, types of: blepharoplasty, colostomy, colotomy, cosmetic, cryosurgery, electrolysis, endoscopy, enterostomy, exploratory, facelift, fenestration, keyhole, liposuction, microsurgery, neurosurgery, open-heart, photocoagulation, plastic, psychosurgery, rhinoplasty, stereotaxis, stitch, synthesis, taxis, transplant

surgical instruments: curet, curette, dermatome, dilater, dilator, gouge, haemostat, hemostat, laparoscope, photocoagulator, probang, probe retractor, scalpel, snare, speculum, surgical knife, syringe, trepan, trephine, trocar

surgical operations, fear of: ergasiophobia (suffered by the doctor, not the patient)

Suriname: republic in north-eastern South America; formerly known as Dutch Guiana
  capital: Paramaribo
  currency: guilder
  language: Dutch (official), English
  religion: Hindu, Christian, Muslim
  former names: Dutch Guiana, Netherlands Guiana

surnames, most common in the world: Chang and Chen

Surrealists: Luis Buñuel, Giorgio de Chirico, Salvador Dalí, Paul Délvaux, Marcel Duchamp, Max Ernst, Charlie Kaufman (screenwriter), Paul Klee, René Magritte, André Masson, Joan Miró, Man Ray, Yves Tanguy

Surrey, administrative centre: Kingston upon Thames

Sussex, East, administrative centre: Lewes

Sussex, West, administrative centre: Chichester

sustenance, adjective: alimentary

Svalbard: Norwegian archipelago in the Arctic Ocean; also known as Spitsbergen
  capital: Longyearbyen
  currency: Norwegian krone

language: Russian, Norwegian
SWAG: Scientific Wild-Assed Guess
SWAK: Sealed With a Kiss
swallow (bird), adjective: hirundine
swallow, collective noun: flight
swallow greedily: glop (verb)
swallowing, act of: deglutition, glutition
swallowing, fear of: phagophobia
swallowing difficulty: dysphagia
swan, adjective: cygneous, cygnine
swan, collective noun: bevy, mustering
swan, famous: Fionnuala (who in Irish legend was actually the daughter of Lir, later
    turned into a swan), the Ugly Duckling
swan, female: pen
swan, god disguised as: Zeus
swan, male: cob
swan, sound: bark, cry, hiss
swan, young: cygnet
Swan Lake: ballet composed by Pyotr Tchaikovsky, first performed in St
    Petersburg in 1895
swashbucklers: Alan Breck (from Stevenson's *Kidnapped*), Miguel de Cervantes,
    Edmond Dantes (aka the Count of Monte Cristo)
    - see pirates, swordsmen
swastika: gammadion cross (as it is known in Christian and Byzantine art)
Swaziland: kingdom in southern Africa
    capital: Mbabane (administrative), Lobamba (legislative)
    currency: lilangeni
    language: Swazi, English
    religion: Christian (majority)
    birthplace of: Richard E. Grant (actor/writer)
swearing: "I swear too much. My mother gave me a good hint. She said the 'f'
    word is good as an exclamation mark, but not as a comma" - Ben Elton
swearing: coprolalia
swearing, the act of, to let off steam: catarolysis (noun)
sweat: hidrosis, perspiration
sweat, adjective: sudatory, sudoriferous
sweat, foul-smelling: bromidrosis, kakidrosis
sweat-impeding: anhidrotic
sweat-inducing: diaphoretic
sweat-producing: sudorific (particularly said of a drug)
Sweater Girl: sobriquet applied to both Lana Turner and Jane Russell
sweating, the act of: diaphoresis
sweating in excess: hyperhidrosis
Sweden: kingdom in north-western Europe
    capital: Stockholm
    currency: krona (subdivided into 100 öre)
    language: Swedish
    religion: Church of Sweden (Lutheran)
Swedish and famous: Abba, Ann-Margret, Bo Bergman (poet), Ingmar Bergman,
    Ingrid Bergman, Hans Blix (diplomat), Björn Borg, The Cardigans, Queen
    Christina, Stefan Edberg, Anita Ekberg, Sven-Göran Eriksson, Greta Garbo,

Lasse Hallström (filmmaker), Andreas Johnson (pop singer), Ingvar Kamprad (founder of Ikea), Pär Lagerkvist (playwright and novelist), Selma Lagerlöf (novelist), Carl Larsson (artist), Stieg Larsson (novelist), Astrid Lindgren (children's author), Anna Lindh (Swedish foreign minister, assassinated in 2003), Carolus Linnaeus (botanist), Henning Mankell (crime writer), Alfred Nobel, Robyn (born: Robin Carlsson), Stellan Skarsgård (actor), Peter Stormare (actor), August Strindberg, Ann-Sofie von Otter, Max Von Sydow, Raoul Wallenberg (diplomat), Bo Wilderberg (filmmaker)

Swedish groups: Abba, Ace of Base, The Ark, The Cardigans, The Hives, The Radio Dept., Roxette, The Sounds, The Soundtrack of Our Lives, Teddybears, The Wannadies

Swedish inventions: ball bearing, dynamite, the Nobel Prize, safety match, styrofoam

Swedish prime minister, murdered in 1986: Olof Palme

Sweeney, The: tough, highly popular crime series featuring a pair of officers from Scotland Yard's Flying Squad, developed from a single show, *Regan*, in 1974. Fifty-three episodes were filmed, along with two big-screen spin-offs, *Sweeney!* (1976) and *Sweeney 2* (1978). A third film was being planned in 2009
  broadcast: 2 January 1975–28 December 1978 on Thames TV
  created by Ian Kennedy Martin
  cast: John Thaw (Det. Insp. John Albert 'Jack' Regan), Dennis Waterman (Det. Sgt. George Hamilton Carter), Garfield Morgan (Chief Insp. Frank Haskins), John Alkin (Det. Sgt. Tom Daniels)

sweeten: dulcify, edulcorate

swelling, adjective: nodal

swift, collective noun: flock

swift, fact: over the course of its lifetime, the bird will cover 2.8 million miles, a distance equivalent to 100 times around the Earth or six round-trips to the moon

swimmers: Buster Crabbe, Sharron Davies, Gertrude Ederle (first woman to swim the English Channel), Janet Evans, Dawn Fraser, Mille Gade (first mother to swim the English Channel), Duncan Goodhew, Annette Kellerman, Kevin Murphy (who swam the English Channel 34 times), Henry Myers, Kristin Otto, Michael Phelps, Alexander Popov, Lewis Gordon Pugh (British-born lawyer who undertook the longest-ever swim in Polar waters and the only man to carry out endurance swims in all five oceans), Mark Spitz, Alison Streeter, Martin Strel (who swam the length of the Amazon, Mississippi, Yangtze and Danube rivers), Henry Taylor, Ian Thorpe, Captain Matthew Webb (the first man to swim the English channel), Johnny Weissmuller, Esther Williams

swimming: natation (noun)

swimming, adjective: natatorial, natatory

swimming pool slide: flume

swindlers: Kenneth L. Lay and Jeffrey Skilling (see Enron), Bernie Madoff
  - see forgers, inside traders, etc

swine, adjective: suine

swine, collective noun: doylt, drift, sounder

swine, young: piglet

swing, king of: Benny Goodman

Swiss and famous: Jacob Amman (Mennonite bishop whose followers founded the Amish sect), Ursula Andress, Arnold Böcklin (painter), Adolf Busch (violinist), Jean Dunant (philanthropist), Friedrich Dürrenmatt (novelist and playwright),

Roger Federer (tennis player), Bruno Ganz (actor), Alberto Giacometti (sculptor), H.R. Giger (graphic artist), Claude Goretta (filmmaker), Heidi (orphan), Martina Hingis (tennis player), Albert Hofmann (scientist), Carl Jung, Gottfried Keller (poet), Marthe Keller (actress), Paul Klee, Elisabeth Kübler-Ross (a naturalised American from 1961), Auguste Piccard (physicist), Hermann Rorschach, Alain Tanner (filmmaker), William Tell, Marie Tussaud (wax modeller), Erich von Däniken, Alfred Werner (chemist), Huldreich Zwingli (reformer)

Switzerland: federal republic in west-central Europe
    capital: Bern
    currency: Swiss franc
    language: German, French, Italian, Romansch (all official)
    religion: Protestant, Roman Catholic
    fact: the country has no prime minister but is represented by four main parties whose duty is to find a compromise on every issue

sword: adya katti (short, heavy-bladed Indian sword), barong (Philippine), bilbo, broadsword, campilan, choora (Khyber knife), claymore, curtana (ceremonial), cutlass, dao, dha (Burmese), épée, falchion, firangi, flyssa, foil, glaive, kaskara, kastane (Sri Lankan), katana (Japanese), ken (Japanese), khanda, kilij (Turkish sabre), kindjal, kirpan (ceremonial), klewang, kora, kukri, mandau (used by the head hunters of Borneo), noklang (two-handed sword from Assam), parang pandit (Malay), pata, quaddara, ram dao (sword used for sacrifices in Nepal and northern India), rapier, sabre, saif (curved Arab sword), scimitar, shamshir (Persian sabre), shashqa, shotel (Ethiopian), sosun pattah, tachi (Japanese), takouba, talibon (Philippine), talwar, tanto (Japanese), toledo, tulwar, yataghan (Turkish), zafar takieh (Indian)

sword, adjective: xiphoid

swords, famous: Arondight (of Lancelot), Caliburn (another name for Excalibur), Curtana (of Edward the Confessor), Damocles (Sword of), Delphic, Excalibur, Flamberge (of Charlemagne), Joyeuse (of Charlemagne), Sanglamore (of Braggadochio), Tizona (of El Cid)

sword maker: Andrea Ferrara

sword parts: blade, edge, cross-guard, fuller, grip, guard, hilt, point, pommel, rain guard, scabbard

sword-shaped: ensate, ensiform

swordfish, adjective: xiphioid

swordsmen: Aramis, D'Artagnan, Athos, Cyrano de Bergerac, Oda Nobuyuki, Porthos, Scaramouche, Zorro

swordsmiths, patron saint of: Dunstan

swordplay and chivalry art form: wuxia

SWS: slow-wave sleep

Sydney, birthplace of: Toni Collette (actress), John Howard, Natalie Imbruglia, Hugh Jackman, Clive James, Thomas Keneally, Elle Macpherson, Sam Sparro

Sydney beach: Bondi Beach

Sydney Opera House: multiple-shell-shaped building erected in 1973 on the edge of Sydney Harbour by the Irish structural engineer Peter Rice. Originally designed by the Danish architect Jørn Utzon in 1966, the project was completed without him

syllable; last of a word: ultima

syllables; word having few: oligosyllable

symbols, list of (in a book): sigla

symbol used to represent an entire word ($ for dollar, etc): logogram, logograph

symbologist: Robert Langdon (from *The Da Vinci Code*)

symmetry, abnormal interest in: symmetromania
symphony, first recorded: Beethoven's Fifth
symptoms, without: asymptomatic
synagogue, largest in the world: Temple Emanu-El on Fifth Avenue at 65th Street, New York City (although the religious structure of Angkor Wat in Cambodia is bigger)
synchronised swimmers: Sylvie Fréchette, Estella Warren
syphilis: the pox
syphilis, died from: Charles Baudelaire, Ludwig van Beethoven (allegedly), Al Capone, Christopher Columbus, Alphonse Daudet, Frederick Delius, Gaetano Donizetti, Gustave Flaubert, Paul Gaugin, Henry VIII, Ivan the Terrible (allegedly), Scott Joplin, Vladimir Ilyich Lenin, Édouard Manet, Guy de Maupassant, William Orpen, Franz Schubert, Robert Schumann, Bedrich Smetana, Paul Verlaine
Syracuse tyrants: Agathocles, Dion, Dionysius the Elder, Dionysius the Younger, Gelon, Hiero I, Hiero II
Syria: republic in western Asia
    capital: Damascus
    currency: Syrian pound
    language: Arabic
    religion: Muslim
Syrian sultan: Saladin
SYS: see you soon

T

table: bench, card table, coffee table, console table, desk, dining table, dressing table, duchesse, dumb waiter, gaming table, gateleg, high table, lazy Susan, loo table, lowboy, occasional table, operating table, pedestal table, Pembroke table, piecrust table, pier table, side table, slab (in a mortuary), teapoy, toilet table, trestle-table, triclinium, tripod, trivet table, vanity, work table
table, adjective: mensal
table tennis champion: Fred Perry
tabletop football: Subbuteo
tact: "The ability to describe others as they see themselves" – Abraham Lincoln
Tahiti: island in the South Pacific; formerly known as King George II Island
    capital: Papeete
Tahitian artist: Paul Gauguin
tail, without: acaudal, acaudate
tailless: acaudal, acaudate, anurous
tailor, adjective: sartorial
tailor, collective noun: disguising
tailors, patron saint of: Homobonus
Taiwan: island in South-East Asia, off the coast of China; formerly known as Formosa
    capital: Taipei
    currency: new Taiwan dollar (TWD)
    language: Mandarin (official), Taiwanese and various Hakka dialects
    religion: Buddhist, Confucian and Taoist mixture (93%), Christian (4.5%)
Taiwanese and famous: Hou Hsiao-Hsien (filmmaker), Ang Lee (filmmaker)
Taj Mahal: majestic domed mausoleum in Agra, India, built by the Mughal

emperor Shah Jahan (1632–1648) as a memorial to his wife, Mumatz Mahal. With its white marble walls inlaid with semiprecious gemstones and its four minarets, it has become a symbol of India. Its name, 'Taj Mahal,' is Urdu for 'crown of buildings'

Tajikistan: republic in central Asia
    capital: Dushanbe
    currency: rouble
    language: Tajiki
    religion: Muslim

Tale of Two Cities, A (1859 novel by Charles Dickens); opening line: "It was the best of times, it was the worst of times, it was the age of wisdom, it was the age of foolishness, it was the epoch of belief, it was the epoch of incredulity..."

talent: "Talent comes from God. If you have been given some, then value it, cultivate it, work it and develop it" – Denzel Washington; "Talent is really rather common. What is rare, dear, is the combination of talent and the character to look after it" – literary agent Peggy Ramsay

talent spotter: Simon Cowell

Taliban leader: Mullah Mohammed Omar

talk show hosts: Clive Anderson, Johnny Carson, Craig Ferguson, David Frost, Russell Harty, Clive James, Jay Leno, David Letterman, Michael Medved, Graham Norton, Conan O'Brien, Michael Parkinson, Alan Partridge, Regis Philbin, Maury Povich, Geraldo Rivera, Jonathan Ross, Frank Skinner, Jon Stewart, Oprah Winfrey, Sir Terry Wogan

Talking Heads: trendy, ironic New Wave New York-punk band formed in Rhode Island in 1975; comprised of: David Byrne (vocals, guitar), Chris Frantz (drums), Tina Weymouth (bass) and Jerry Harrison (keyboards); later augmented (in the 1980s) by Cherry Jones (bass), Bernie Worrell (keyboards), Steven Scales (percussion) and Adrian Belew (guitar). The group disbanded in 1991

talking in one's sleep, someone prone to: somniloquist

tall; politically correct term: vertically inconvenienced

tall and famous: Kareem Abdul-Jabbar (7'2"), Maya Angelou (6'), John Cleese (6'4^3/$_4$"), Michael Crichton (6'9"), Peter Crouch (6'7"), Lindsay Davenport (6'2^1/$_2$), Tamara Dobson (6'2"; actress), Clint Eastwood (6'5"), Lou Ferrigno (6'5"), Mick Fleetwood (6'5"), Penn Jillette (6'6"), Fred Gwynne (6'5"), Jerry Hall (6'), Miranda Hart (6'1"), Penn Jillette (6'6"), Jodie Kidd (6'1"), Christopher Lee (6'5"), Abraham Lincoln (almost 6'4" – very tall for his time), Mariel Hemingway (6'), Janet McTeer (6'1"), Brigitte Nielsen (6'1"), Shaquille O'Neal (7'1"), Sergei Rachmaninov (6'6"), Janet Reno (6'1"), Tim Robbins (6'5"), Dwayne 'The Rock' Johnson (6'5"), Maria Sharapova (6'), Howard Stern (6'5"), Vince Vaughn (6'5"), Venus Williams (6'1^1/$_2$)

talon, adjective: ungual

tambourine: timbrel

Tamla Motown: record label launched by Berry Gordy Jr in 1959

Tamworth Two, The: Butch and Sundance, the Tamworth Ginger pigs that captured the media's attention when they escaped from a Wiltshire slaughterhouse in 1998

tank battle: Kursk: (4 July–23 August 1943)

Tannhäuser: opera by Richard Wagner, first produced in Dresden 19 October 1845

Tanzania: republic in East Africa; originally formed in 1964 by the unification of Tanganyika and Zanzibar
    capital: Dodoma
    currency: Tanzananian shilling

language: Swahili and English (both official)
religion: Christian, Muslim, animist
fact: boasts the largest population of elephants in the world
fact: the highest peak in Africa is the country's Mount Kilimanjaro
Tanzanian mountain: Mount Kilimanjaro
Tanzanian national park: Serengeti
tap dancers: Fred Astaire, Hinton Battle, Savion Glover, Gregory Hines, Ruby
    Keeler, Gene Kelly, Ann Miller, Donald O'Connor, Eleanor Powell, Ginger
    Rogers, Tommy Tune
    - see dancers
tapestry: arras, Bayeux, Bruges, Gobelin
tapir, adjective: pachydermoid
tar and feathering, adjective: plumeopicean
tarantula, adjective: theraphosid
tarantula expert: Rick West
Tardis: acronym for Time And Relative Dimension In Space (as featured in the
    TV series *Doctor Who*)
tarsier, adjective: lemuroid
Tasmania: island and Australian state in the South Pacific, formerly known as
    Van Diemen's Land (until 1855)
    capital: Hobart
    nickname: Apple Isle
    fact: along with Norfolk Island, Tasmania was the British Empire's most
        remote penal colony
Tasmania, birthplace of: Simon Baker (actor), Errol Flynn, Eileen Joyce (pianist)
taste: "My tastes are very simple. The best is good enough for me" – Oscar Wilde
taste, adjective: gustatory, saporific
taste, fear of: geumatophobia
tasting, act of: gustation
tattoo, earliest: found on the skin of a frozen corpse ('Ötzi the Iceman) c. 3300 BC
tautological expressions - see oxymorons
taverner, collective noun: closing, glozing
tax collector: Levi
tax dodgers: Spiro Agnew, Al Capone, Ken Dodd, Heidi Fleiss, Leona Helmsley,
    Paul Hogan, J.P. 'Jack' Morgan (banker), Willie Nelson, Pete Rose
taxation: "For a nation to try to tax itself into prosperity is like a man standing
    in a bucket and trying to lift himself up by the handle" – Winston Churchill
taxi: cab, Fairway (London make)
Taxi: American TV sitcom set in and around the Sunshine Cab Company in
    New York
    created by: Ed Weinberger, David Davis, Stan Daniels and James L. Brooks
    broadcast: 12 September 1978–20 July 1983
    cast: Judd Hirsch (Alex Reiger), Jeff Conaway (Bobby Wheeler), Tony Danza
        (Tony Banta), Randell Carver (John Burns), Marilu Henner (Elaine Nardo),
        Danny DeVito (Louie DiPalma), Andy Kaufman (Latka Gravas), Christopher
        Lloyd ('Reverend' Jim Ignatowski), Carol Kane (Simka Gravas)
Taxi Driver (1976 film), famous line: Travis Bickle (Robert De Niro), to his
    reflection in the mirror: "Are you talkin' to me? Well, I'm the only one here.
    Who the fuck do you think you're talking to?"
taxi drivers: Travis Bickle, Fred Housego (1980 winner of the TV quiz game
    Mastermind)

taxi drivers, patron saint of: Fiacre

taxonomist: Lionel Walter Rothschild

TBC: to be confirmed

tea: Assam, bamboo, bohea (Chinese), camomile, Ceylon, char, congou, Darjeeling, Earl Grey, fan yong, Formosa oolong, green, hibiscus, hyson, jasmine, kanoy, keemun, lapsang souchong, orange pekoe, pekoe, PG tips, Red Label, silver needle white, souchong, Tetley, Twinings, Typhoo, Whittard

tea, fact: the drink dates back to 2737 BC

tea, fact: first introduced to Europe from China by the Dutch East India Co. in 1609

tea, iced: invented in the United States at the 1893 Chicago Colombian Exposition, when an Englishman with a tea stand (who was losing business during a heat wave) poured his tea over ice

tea, oldest brand in the UK: Twinings

tea-drinking nation, top: Ireland, followed by the United Kingdom and then Turkey

teabag: first produced around 1920 by Joseph Krieger, but at the time was almost exclusively used by caterers – until the fad caught on with the American public in 1935

teabag: first produced for retail in Britain in 1952

tea leaf reading: foliomancy

tea plant, adjective: theaceous

teachers: Aristotle, Jean Brodie, Simon Casey (played by Andrew Lincoln in TV's *Teachers*), Charles 'Mr Chips' Chipping, Andrew Crocker-Harris (from *The Browning Version*), Eli (of Shiloh), Charles Handy, Bernard Hedges (played by John Alderton in TV's *Please Sir!*), Isocrates, Gwen Mayor (the teacher shot in the Dunblane massacre), Plato, Protagoras, Socrates, Wackford Squeers (from *Nicholas Nickleby*), Mark Thackeray (played by Sidney Poitier in *To Sir, with Love*)

teacher, adjective: pedagogical

teacher accused of having sex with her students: Amy Gehring

teaching: "To teach is to learn twice" – Joseph Joubert

teal, collective noun: spring

tear (drop), adjective: lacrimal, lachrymal, lachrymatory

tear duct: lacrimal duct

tearful and famous – see cry-babies

tears, adjective: lachrymal

technology, adjective: technoid

technophobe: Luddite

teddy bears: Aloysius (from *Brideshead Revisited*), Mohammed (so named by Gillian Gibbons, who was subsequently imprisoned in Sudan for defaming the prophet), Pudsey (mascot for Children in Need), SuperTed, Winnie the Pooh

teddy bear collector: arctophile

teenagers, fear of: ephebiphobia

teeth: canines, china, choppers, chops, crockery, fangs, gummers, incisors, ivories, molars, nutcrackers, pearly whites

teeth, drilling of: odontotrypy

teeth, fear of: odontophobia

teeth, first depicted in a painting: self-portrait by Louise Vigee-Le Brun (1791)

teeth, gap between: diastema

teeth, having few: oligodontous

teeth, in possession of: dentigerous

teeth, number in adult human: 36

teeth, science of: dentistry
teeth, sexual arousal derived from: odontophilia
teeth, study of: odontology
teeth decay: saprodontia
teeth grinding: bruxism
teething (in babies): odontiasis
telephone: patented by Alexander Graham Bell on 9 March 1876
telephone, Cockney Rhyming Slang: Molly Malone
telephone, first private call made in the UK: between Queen Victoria and Sir
    Thomas Biddulph, on 14 January 1878
television: "Chewing gum for the eyes" – American critic John Mason Brown;
    "A medium of entertainment which permits millions of people to listen to the
    same joke at the same time, and yet remain lonesome" – T.S. Eliot; "A form of
    organised indifference" – Arthur Miller
television; the first demonstration of a television image was provided by John Logie
    Baird in 1926
television, patron saint of: Clare of Assisi
television executives: Andy Allen, John Birt, Sir Christopher Bland, Sam Chisholm,
    Gavyn Davies, Greg Dyke, Michael Grade, Marmaduke Hussey, Peter Salmon,
    Mark Thompson, Jane Tranter, Alan Yentob
television producers: Steve Bochco, Rod Serling
television regulator, UK: Ofcom (Office of Communications)
television scriptwriters: Paul Abbott, Alan Bennett, Alan Bleasdale, Daniel Boyle,
    Jim Cartwright, Alan Clarke, Dick Clement and Ian La Frenais, David Croft,
    Richard Curtis, Andrew Davies, Russell T. Davies, Ray Galton, David E.
    Kelley, Nigel Kneale, Lynda La Plante, Tony Marchant, Philomena McDonagh,
    Jimmy McGovern, Kay Mellor, Paula Milne, Peter Morgan, Terry Nation,
    Simon Nye, Jimmy Perry, Alan Plater, Stephen Poliakoff, Dennis Potter, Jack
    Rosenthal, Rod Serling, Alan Simpson, Johnny Speight, John Sullivan, Charles
    Wood
temperature, adjective: thermal
tempo, adjective: agogic
Temptations, The: highly influential all-singing, all-dancing Motown quintet
    formed in Detroit, Michigan, in 1960. Originally called The Elgins, the group
    initially comprised Otis Williams (second tenor/baritone), Elbridge 'Al' Bryant
    (first tenor), Melvin Franklin (bass), Eddie Kendricks (first tenor/falsetto) and
    Paul Williams (second tenor/baritone). Other members over the years have
    included G.C. Cameron, Dennis Edwards, Damon Harris, Theo Peoples, David
    Ruffin, Richard Street, Ron Tyson and Ali-Ollie Woodson. Most recently they
    have included Cameron, Tyson, Joe Herndon, Terry Weeks and Otis Williams
ten, adjective: denary
ten million billionth of a second: attosecond
Ten Commandments: 1) Thou shalt have no other gods; 2) Thou shalt not make any
    graven images; 3) Thou shalt not take the Lord's name in vain; 4) Remember the
    Sabbath day; 5) Honour thy father and mother; 6) Thou shalt not kill; 7) Thou
    shalt not commit adultery; 8) Thou shalt not steal; 9) Thou shalt not bear false
    witness against thy neighbour; 10) Thou shalt not covet thy neighbour's house…
    nor anything that is his
ten million: crore (Hindi word)
ten years, adjective: decennial
ten-faced solid figure: decahedron

ten-sided plane figure: decagon
ten-year period: decade
tendrils, in possession of: cirrate
Tennessee, 16th state (1796), Volunteer State
    capital: Nashville
    state bird: mockingbird
    state flower: iris
    state tree: tulip poplar
    motto: 'Agriculture and commerce'
    birthplace of: James Agee, Chet Atkins, Davy Crockett, Morgan Freeman, Aretha Franklin, Arthur Golden, Al Gore, Isaac Hayes, Andrew Jackson (7th president), Andrew Johnson (17th president), Kings of Leon, Dolly Parton, James K. Polk (11th president), Cybill Shepherd, Dinah Shore, Justin Timberlake, Tina Turner, Dawn Upshaw
    tourist attractions: Memphis, Nashville, the Grand Old Opry, Graceland (home of Elvis Presley), Lookout Mountain, Chattanooga, Great Smoky Mountains National Park
tennis elbow: epicondylitis
tennis players, male: Andre Agassi, Vijay Amritraj, Arthur Ashe (black player who won Wimbledon in 1975), Henry Wilfred 'Bunny' Austin, Jeremy Bates, Boris Becker, Björn Borg, Jean Borotra, Don Budge, Michael Chang, Jimmy Connors, Jim Courier, Barry Cowan, Stefan Edberg, Roy Emerson, Roger Federer, Guy Forget, Vitas Gerulaitis, Tim Henman, Lewis Alan Hoad, Goran Ivanisevic, Richard Krajicek, Rod Laver, Ivan Lendl, John Lloyd, Todd Martin, John McEnroe, Andrei Medvedev, Andy Murray, Rafael Nadal, Ilie Nastase, John Newcombe, Fred Perry, Pat Rafter, William Renshaw, Bobby Riggs, Andy Roddick, Ken Rosewall, Greg Rusedski, Pete Sampras, Michael Stich, William (Bill) T. Tilden, Guillermo Vilas, MaliVai Washington (in 1996 became the first black player to reach the Wimbledon final since Arthur Ashe)
tennis players, female: Sue Barker, Louise Brough, Maria Bueno, Evonne Cawley (aka Evonne Goolagong), Margaret Court, Lindsay Davenport, Jelena Dokic (16-year-old Serb-born Australian who beat Martina Hingis in her debut at Wimbledon), Chris Evert, Gigi Fernandez, Althea Gibson (first black Wimbledon champion), Evonne Goolagong, Steffi Graf, Martina Hingis, Billie Jean King, Anna Kournikova, Suzanne Lenglen, Conchita Martinez, 'Gorgeous' Gussie Moran, Martina Navratilova, Jana Novotna, Mary Pierce, Gabriela Sabatini, Arantxa Sanchez-Vicario, Brenda Schultz, Monica Seles, Maria Sharapova, Pam Shriver, Helena Sukova, Virginia Wade, Maud Watson (the first Wimbledon champion: 1884), Hazel Wightman, Serena Williams, Venus Williams, Helen Wills Moody
tennis tournaments: Australian Open, Compaq Grand Slam Cup, Davis Cup, Federation Cup, French Open, Hopman Cup, Paris Open, Rogers Cup, US Open, Wimbledon
tenors: Roberto Alagna, Andrea Bocelli, José Carreras, Enrico Caruso, José Cura, Placido Domingo, Juan Diego Flórez, Beniamino Gigli, Ben Heppner, Joseph Hislop, Mario Lanza, John McCormack, Lauritz Melchior, Luciano Pavarotti, Sir Peter Pears, Russell Watson
    - see opera singers, sopranos
tent: bell tent, big top (circus), ger (Mongolian), kibitka (Tartar), marquee, pavilion, tabernacle, tepee, Wendy house, wigwam, yurt (Russian)

tentacle, adjective: tentacular

tequila: Casa Noble, Corzo, Cuervo Especial, José Cuervo, Sauza

Terminator, The (1984 film), famous line: Terminator (Arnold Schwarzenegger): "I'll be back"

Terminator 2: Judgment Day (1991 film), famous line: Terminator T-800 (Arnold Schwarzenegger): "Hasta la vista, baby"

termite, adjective: termitine

termite, collective noun: colony

Terracotta Warriors: literally 7,000 life-size warriors made from terracotta, fashioned after the imperial guard and their horses and chariots of the Qin Dynasty (211–206 BC). Discovered by peasants in 1974, the site is now encompassed by a museum 1.5 kilometers east of Emperor Qin Shi Huang's Mausoleum in Lintong County, Shaanxi province, China

terrorists: James Aitken (aka John the Painter), Ali Mohmed Al Megrahi (convicted of planting the bomb on board the Pan Am Boeing 747 that crashed at Lockerbie in 1988), Baader-Meinhof gang, Carlos the Jackal (real name: Ilich Ramirez Sanchez), Osama bin Laden, David Copeland (Nazi sympathiser and homophobe who built nail bombs from instructions on the Internet), Patrick Magee (Brighton bombing), Timothy McVeigh (Oklahoma bombing), Imad Mughniyeh (Hizbollah security chief), Terry Nichols (Oklahoma bombing), Abu Nidal (radical Palestinian), Richard Reid (the 'shoe bomber'), Veerappan (Tamil terrorist who murdered 120 people and kidnapped the famous Indian film star Rajkumar), Abu Musab al-Zarqawi (aka 'the Z-man')

terrorist attack on Bali: 12 October 2002 (which killed 202 people)

terrorist attack on London: 7 July 2005 (when 52 people were killed, along with the four suicide bombers)

terrorist attack on Madrid: 11 March 2004 (which killed 191 people and wounded 1,800)

terrorist attack on Mumbai: 26–29 November 2008 (which killed 172 people)

terrorist attack on New York: 11 September 2001 (which killed 2,974 people)

terrorist leaders: Renato Curcio, Osama bin Laden

terrorist organisations: Afghan Mujahidin, al-Qa'eda (Muslim), Baader-Meinhof Group (aka the Red Army Faction), Eta, Farc (The Revolutionary Armed Forces of Colombia), Fenians, Hamas (fundamentalist Islamic militants), Hezbollah, IRA, Jemaah Islamiyah (Muslim), Lashkar-e-Taiba (responsible for the November 2008 attacks on Mumbai which killed 173), Lord's Resistance Army (responsible for a two-decade campaign of bloodshed in Uganda), Mau Mau, Provisional Irish Republican Army, Red Brigade (Italy), Symbionese Liberation Army, Tamil Tigers

Tesco, slogan: 'Every little helps'

testicle, having only one: monorchid (adjective)

testicle inflammation: orchitis

testicle muscle (that which draws the testicles closer to the body when cold): cremaster

testicle pouch: scrotum

testicles: balls, bollocks, cajones, clinkers, family jewels, flowers and frolics (RS), gonads, goolies, nuts, rocks

testicles, abnormal interest in: orchidomania

testicles, person without: anorchus

testicles, without: anorchous (adjective)

testicles; condition of being exceptionally small: microorchidism

test tube baby, first: Louise Brown

testosterone, creature with highest level of: bull shark
Texan fortress: The Alamo (besieged in 1836 by Mexican forces)
Texas, 28th state (1845), Lone Star State
    capital: Austin
    state bird: mockingbird
    state flower: bluebonnet
    state tree: pecan
    motto: 'Friendship'
    birthplace of: Lance Armstrong, Gene Autry, Clyde Barrow, Carol Burnett, Cyd
        Charisse, Joan Crawford, Hilary Duff, Dwight D. Eisenhower, Jamie Foxx,
        Jennifer Garner, Ben Hogan, Buddy Holly, Howard Hughes, Lyndon B.
        Johnson, Tommy Lee Jones, Janis Joplin, Scott Joplin, Beyoncé Knowles,
        Steve Martin, Roger Miller, Willie Nelson, Roy Orbison, Bonnie Parker,
        Dan Rather, Tex Ritter, Andy Roddick, Usher, Barry White, Owen Wilson
    tourist attractions: Big Bend, Guadalupe Mountains national parks, The Alamo
    fact: in 1997 an average of one prisoner a week was executed
TFT: thin-film transistor (used in liquid crystal displays)
TGIT: Thank God it's Friday
Thai and famous: Tony Jaa (martial arts star), Thaksin Shinawatra (prime minister
    deposed in 2006)
Thailand: kingdom in south-east Asia, formerly known as Siam (until 1939 and
    1945–1949) and nicknamed Land of the Free
    capital: Krung Thep, commonly referred to as Bangkok in the West
    currency: baht
    language: Thai
    religion: Buddhist (Hinayana)
    fact: in the 1970s, the average Thai woman bore five children; by the 21st
    century the average had fallen to two
thank you: arigato (Japanese), dank (Yiddish), danke schön (German), dank u
    (Dutch), dziekuje (Polish), gracias (Spanish), grazie (Italian), merci (French),
    obrigada/o (Portuguese), spasibo (Russian), tack (Swedish), terima kasih
    (Malay), xie xie (Mandarin)
Thanksgiving: American holiday celebrated on the fourth Thursday in November
thatched properties in England, number of: 30,000
the: definite article
theatre, art of: dramaturgy
theatre critics: James Agate, Clive Barnes, Thomas Barnes, Robert Benchley,
    Harold Clurman, Sheridan Morley, Dorothy Parker, Frank Rich, Kenneth Tynan
    - see film critics, journalists, rock critics, etc
theatre directors: Lindsay Anderson, Antonin Artaud, Michael Bennett, Ingmar
    Bergman, Michael Blakemore, Matthew Bourne, Michael Boyd, Bertolt Brecht,
    Peter Brook, Sir Lewis Casson, Harold Clurman, Edward Gordon Craig,
    Stephen Daldry, Howard Davies, George Devine, Frank Dunlop, Sir Richard
    Eyre, Jill Fraser, Peter Gill, Rupert Goold, Harley Granville-Barker, Andre
    Gregory, Jerzy Grotowski, Sir Tyrone Guthrie, Sir Peter Hall, Terry Hands,
    Sir Nicholas Hytner, Tadeusz Kantor, Joan Littlewood, Yuri Lyubimov, Sam
    Mendes, Mike Nichols, Adrian Noble, Sir Trevor Nunn, Antoinette Perry, Robin
    Phillips, Harold Prince, Max Reinhardt, Martin Ritt, Mark Rylance, Peter
    Sellars, Max Stafford-Clark, Konstantin Stanislavski, Peter Stein, Julie Taymor,
    Deborah Warner, Arnold Wesker
theatre impresarios: Bernard Delfont, Fred Karno, Cameron Mackintosh
theatre managers: Binkie Beaumont, John Drinkwater, David Garrick, Oscar

Hammerstein, Philip Henslowe, Sir Johnston Forbes-Robertson, Roger Kemble, William Macready, Max Reinhardt, Lee Shubert, Sir Herbert Beerbohm Tree, Sir Donald Wolfit, Florenz Ziegfeld

Thebes, goddess of: Wosret (Egyptian mythology)

theft, dread of: harpaxophobia

theft in Britain, fact: 85% of all thefts are committed by opportunists

theme parks, UK: Alton Towers, Chessington World of Adventures, Legoland Windsor, Longleat Safari Park, Pleasure Beach Blackpool, Thorpe Park

theme parks, US: Astroland (New York), Disney World (Orlando), Disneyland (California), Knott's Berry Farm (California), Magic Mountain (California), Neverland Ranch (California), Water Country USA (Virginia)

theologians: Jacobus Arminius, Hans Urs von Balthasar, William Barclay, Karl Barth, the Venerable Bede, Dietrich Bonhoeffer (who attempted to assassinate Hitler), John Calvin, Arthur Collier, Thomas Erastus, Nikolai Grundtvig, Gustavo Gutiérrez, Ole Hallesby, Carl Henry, Charles Hodge, Richard Hooker, Benjamin Jowett, Søren Kierkegaard, Hans Küng, Eric Mascall, Increase Mather, Luis de Molina, Martin Niemöller, Rudolf Otto, Pelagius, Peter Roget, Philip Schaff, Albert Schweitzer, Nicolaus Steno, Pierre Teilhard de Chardin, Helmut Thielicke, Paul Tillich, John Wesley, John Wycliffe

theoretical chemist: Charles Coulson

theoretical physicists: Paul Dirac, Werner Heisenberg, John Archibald Wheeler

theorists: Amílcar Cabral, John Cage

theremin player: Lydia Kavina

thicken: inspissate (verb)

thief: Aladdin, Ali Baba, Autolycus (Greek mythology), Barabbas, Clyde Barrow, Ronald Biggs, Fay Cheyney, D.B. Cooper, Moll Flanders, Joan Hannington, Robin Hood, Loki, Arsène Lupin, Bonnie Parker, A.J. Raffles, Sciron (Greek mythology), Sinis (Greek mythology), Jemmy Twitcher (from *The Beggar's Opera*), Jean Valjean (from *Les Miserables*)
- see bank robbers, burglars, jewel thieves, train robbers

thieves, dread of: harpaxophobia

thigh, adjective: crural, femoral

thighs, sexual arousal derived from: merophilia

thighs, between: interfemoral (adjective)

thinker: Georgei Gurdjieff – see philosophers

thinking, abnormal interest in: phronemomania

thin person: bag of bones, beanpole, broomstick, gangleshanks, spindleshanks, stick insect, toothpick, turkey legs

third eye, mark on forehead: bindi (adopted by women only), tilak

Third Reich marching step: goose step

thirteen, dread of the number: triskaidekaphobia

thirty, adjective: tricenary

Thirty Years' War: 1618–1648

thirtysomething: critically celebrated, much talked-about TV series featuring seven baby boomers struggling with contemporary life in Philadelphia
   broadcast: 29 September 1987–3 September 1991
   created by Ed Zwick and Marshall Herskovitz
   cast: Mel Harris (Hope Murdoch), Ken Olin (Michael Steadman), Timothy Busfield (Elliot Weston), Patricia Wettig (Nancy Weston), Polly Draper (Ellyn Warren), Melanie Mayron (Melissa Steadman), Peter Horton (Gary Shepherd)

This is Your Life: enduring television show (a precursor to reality TV), which gestated on American radio in 1948. Ralph Edwards hosted the original radio version and then presented it on NBC TV in 1952. The BBC borrowed the format in 1955 and hired Eamon Andrews to surprise various celebrities with the blood-freezing words, "this is your life!" And so a string of fellow luminaries, aunts, uncles and long-forgotten friends traipsed into the studio to add a note of cringing nostalgia. Later, Michael Aspel took over as the BBC presenter.

This Life: cult, influential and provocative BBC TV series about a group of young lawyers who live in the same shabby London house
  created by first-time screenwriter Amy Jenkins
  broadcast: 18 March 1996–7 August 1997
  cast: Jack Davenport (Miles Stewart), Amita Dhiri (Milly Nassim), Jason Hughes (Warren Jones), Andrew Lincoln (Edgar 'Egg' Cook), Daniela Nardini (Anna Forbes)

thistle motif: acanthus (used in architecture)
thorn, adjective: spinous
thorn-shaped: aculeiform
thousand (years), adjective: chilial
thousand, group of: chiliad
thousand million years: aeon
thousand years: chiliad
thousand-sided figure: chiliagon
thread, adjective: filar
thread, loosely coiled: skein
three, adjective: ternary, treble, tripartite, triple
Three Day Event champion: Lucinda Green
Three Degrees, The: singing trio formed in Philadelphia in 1965; comprised of Fayette Pinkey, Shirley Porter and Linda Turner. All in all, twelve singers have represented the trio, who are currently made up of Cynthia Garrison, Valerie Holiday and Helen Scott
three hundred years, adjective: tercentenary
three hundredth anniversary: tercentenary
Three Kings (also known as the Magi): Caspar, Melchior and Balthasar
Three Stooges, The: trio of comics whose knockabout routines were enormously popular in vaudeville and later in two-reeler shorts from the 1930s through to the 1950s. They were comprised of Larry Fine, Moe Howard and his brother Jerry, also known as Curly. Curly was eventually replaced by his brother Shemp Howard who, on his death in 1955, was succeeded by Joe Besser. Besser himself was replaced by Joe de Rita in 1959
three times a day: terdiurnal
three-way sex: troilism
three-year period: triennium
Three Wise Men (also known as the Magi): Caspar, Melchior and Balthazar
threesome: ménage à trois (usually in a romantic or sexual context), trifecta, trio, triumvirate
threshold, adjective: liminal
thriller writers: Eric Ambler, Peter Benchley, Dan Brown, Tom Clancy, Richard Condon, Michael Connolly, Robin Cook, Patricia Cornwell, Michael Crichton, Clive Cussler, Len Deighton, Colin Dexter, James Ellroy, Ian Fleming, Frederick Forsyth, Dick Francis, John Grisham, Donald Hamilton, Thomas Harris, James Herbert, Jack Higgins, Patricia Highsmith, Stephen King, Dean Koontz, John Le Carré, Ira Levin, Robert Ludlum, Ross Macdonald, Alistair MacLean, Ed McBain, James Patterson, Ian Rankin, Kathy Reichs, R.L. Stine,

Scott Turow, Minette Walters, Donald E. Westlake
- see crime writers, detective writers

throat, adjective: gular, gutteral, jugular

throat armour: gorget

thrush (as in the bird), adjective: musicapine, turdiform, turdoid

thrush, collective noun: mutation

thumb: pollex

thumb, adjective: pollical

thunder, adjective: tonitruous

thunder, fear of: brontophobia, tonitrophobia

thunder, gods of: Jupiter (Roman mythology), Susanowa (Japanese), Thor (Norse), Zeus (Greek)

thunder, study of: brontology

thunder and lightning, adjective: fulminous, fulmneous

Thunderbirds: cult British TV series filmed in 'supermarionation', using string puppets as the courageous protagonists of International Rescue. Such was the popularity of the series, that it spawned innumerable toys, two supermarionation theatrical features (*Thunderbirds Are Go* and *Thunderbirds 6*), a stage production and a full-scale, live-action movie (2004) starring Bill Paxton (as Jeff Tracy) and Ben Kingsley (as the villainous 'The Hood')
   created by Gerry and Sylvia Anderson
   broadcast: 30 September 1965–25 December 1966
     lead characters: Jeff Tracy and his five sons (Scott, Virgil, Alan, Gordon and John Tracy), Brains, Lady Penelope Creighton-Ward and Aloysius Parker (her chauffeur)

Tiananmen Square massacre: 3–4 June, 1989

Tibet, fact: original source of rhubarb

Tibetan Buddhism: Lamaism

Tibetan Buddhist monastery: lamasery

Tibetan Buddhist monk: lama

Tibetan ruler: Dalai Lama

Tibetan scroll painting: tanka

tibia, adjective: cnemial

Tichborne Claimant: Arthur Orton

tick (arachnid), adjective: acarian, acaroid

ticks, study of: acarology

tickle: vellicate (verb)

tickled with feathers, dread of being: pteronophobia

tide, adjective: tidal

tide, types of: high, low, neap

tiger, collective noun: ambush, streak

tiger, famous: Hobbes (of the strip-cartoon Calvin and Hobbes), Shere Khan (from *The Jungle Book*), Tigger

tiger, female: tigress

tiger, male: tiger

tiger, sound: growl, roar

tiger, young: cub, whelp

tightrope walker: equilibrist, funambulist

tightrope walkers, famous: Charles Blondin (real name: Jean François Gravelet), Elvira Madigan, Philippe Petit

tiles, to overlap with: imbricate (verb)

TILF: teacher I'd like to fuck

Till Death Us Do Part: notorious, long-running sitcom featuring a working-class family – headed by the opionated bigot Alf Garnett – in London's dockland area. The show inspired the American remake *All in the Family* (1971–1983) and spawned two films, *Till Death Us Do Part* (1968) and *The Alf Garnett Saga* (1972)

    created by Johnny Speight

    broadcast: 22 July 1965–16 December 1975 on BBC1

    cast: Warren Mitchell (Alf Garnett), Dandy Nichols (Else Garnett), Anthony Booth (Mike, Alf's son-in-law), Una Stubbs (Rita), Patricia Hayes (Min Reed), Alfie Bass (Bert Reed)

time: "Nature's way of keeping everything from happening all at once" – anon.; "The most important thing we haven't got" – anon; "Time is a great teacher. Unfortunately, it kills all its pupils" – Hector Berlioz; "Anything lost can be found again. Except time" – Sam (played by Samuel L. Jackson) teaching his son the value of time in Boaz Yakin's 1994 film *Fresh*; "Time makes more converts than reason" – Tom Paine; "A psychological construct for organising the world" – anon.

time, adjective: temporal

time, study of: horology

Time magazine: periodical founded in 1923 by Henry Luce

time measurement, study of: horology

Time Out: opinionated listings magazine for London founded in 1968 by Tony Elliott

time travel: "closed time-like curves" (technical jargon), temporal divergence

time travel, Stephen Hawking's theory on: that space and time are closely related and that both are affected by gravity. Thus, enormous gravitational fields could reverse the flow of time

time travellers: Sam Beckett, Bill and Ted, Arthur Dent, Captain James T. Kirk, Connor MacLeod, Dr Leonard 'Bones' McCoy, Marty McFly, Captain Jean-Luc Picard, Austin Powers, Commander William T. Riker, Hank Smith, Spock, the Terminator, Terminator T-800, etc, the Time Traveller (H.G. Wells' unnamed eponymous hero), Dr Who

Times, The: newspaper founded in 1785 by John Walter. Originally known as *The Daily Universal Register* (its name was changed to *The Times* in 1788)

Times Literary Supplement, The: weekly literary periodical which, in 1902, was published with *The Times*, then in 1914 became an independent publication

tin, adjective: stannic

Tin Lizzie: nickname given to Henry Ford's Model T car

tin mine: stannary

tinnitus, fact: a disorder suffered globally by 20 million people

tin-opener: tool invented in 1858

tipster: the Lemon Drop Kid (c/o Damon Runyon)

tipsy: half-rats, half-rinsed, half-tore, squiffy

    - see drunk

tiredness, fear of: kopophobia

tiredness curing: acopic (adjective)

tissue, study of: histology

title, adjective: titular

titmouse, adjective: parine

TLAM: Tomahawk Land Attack Missile

TLC: tender loving care

TMPR: Too Much Positive Reinforcement

TN: postcode for Tennessee

toad, adjective: batrachian

toad, collective noun: knot

toad, young: tadpole, polliwog

tobacco companies: RJ Reynolds (second largest cigarette maker in the USA), Brown & Williamson Tobacco Corporation (third largest cigarette maker in the USA), American Tobacco Company, Liggett Group Inc. (fifth largest cigarette maker in the USA), Lorillard Tobacco, Philip Morris USA (largest cigarette maker in the USA), Reemtsma (the world's fourth-largest cigarette company), US Tobacco

tobacco, introducer of: Jean Nicot (*not* Sir Walter Raleigh)

tobacco, the juice or spittle from chewing: ambeer

tobacco smoke, adverse to: misocapnic (adjective)

today, adjective: hodiernal

toenail, adjective: onychoid

toes, without: adactylous (adjective)

Tofi: thin outside, fat inside (said of a person who looks healthy on the outside but has dangerous levels of interior fat)

Togo: republic in West Africa
    capital: Lomé
    currency: African franc
    language: French
    religion: animist

toilet paper: first manufactured in 1857

toilet paper, fact: the average American uses 57 sheets of toilet paper a day and more than 20,805 sheets a year

Tokelau: group of islands in the South Pacific annexed by New Zealand

Tokyo, birthplace of: Joan Fontaine, Takeshi Kitano, Akira Kurosawa, Yoko Ono, Takashi Shimura (actor), Liv Ullmann, Emperor Yoshihito

tomato: "In four hundred years the Italians have turned the tomato into the basis for the best cooking in the world. In the same period the Americans have turned it into ketchup" – Miles Kington

Tonga: kingdom in the south-west Pacific, occupying an archipelago of more than 150 islands; also known as the Friendly Islands
    capital: Nuku'alofa
    currency: pa'anga
    language: Tongan, English
    religion: Christian

tongue, adjective: glossoid, glossal, lingual

tongue, removal of: glossectomy

tongue, without: aglossal

tongue; endowed with a thick one: crassilingual

tongue inflammation: glossitis

tongue pain: glossalgia

tongue restraint (Medieval device): brank

tonsils, adjective: amygdaloid

tools: adze, auger, awl, axe, bevel, billhook, bolt cutters, bradawl, chainsaw, chisel, chopper, circular saw, cleaver, clippers, crowbar, dibble, drill, edge trimmer, electric drill, fork, gimlet, hoe, jemmy, jenny, lathe, machete, mattock, monkey wrench, nail gun, paint scraper, pickaxe, pitchfork, pliers, pruners, pruning hook, sander, saw, scalpel, scissors, screwdriver, scythe, secateurs, shears, shovel, sickle, spade, spanner, Stanley knife, strickle, strimmer, swage, trowel, tweezers, wire cutters, wrench

tooth, drilling of: odontotrypy

tooth-edged: dentate

tooth-like: odontoid

toothache: dentagra, odontalgia

toothache, patron saint of: Apollonia

toothbrush: invented in China in 1498

> **first nylon toothbrush:** Dr West's Miracle Tuft Toothbrush, marketed in the USA from September 1938

> **electric toothbrush:** first manufactured in 1961

toothless (literally): edentulate, edentulous

Top of the Pops: TV chart show originally broadcast from the BBC studio in Dickenson Road, Manchester. The first episode, aired on New Year's Day in 1964, was presented by Jimmy Savile and featured The Rolling Stones, Dusty Springfield, The Dave Clark Five, The Hollies, The Swinging Blue Jeans and The Beatles. The Beatles, miming to *I Want To Hold Your Hand*, were the first group to be featured in the number one spot. The show ran for 42 years, ending 30 July 2006

Toronto, birthplace of: John Candy, Cowboy Junkies, David Cronenberg (filmmaker), Gil Evans (jazz pianist), Percy Faith, Bonnie Fuller ('queen of the newsstand'), Frank Gehry, Mary Pickford, Christopher Plummer, Robbie Robertson, Neil Young

tortoise, adjective: testudinal

tortoise, famous: Frank (Aardman creation), George (from TV's *Blue Peter*), Lonesome George (Galapagos giant who refused to mate during 36 years in captivity, then finally changed his mind)

tortoise, sound: grunt

torture victims, patron saint of: Julitta

Tosca: opera by Giacomo Puccini first produced in Rome in 1900

touch, adjective: haptic

touch, aversion to: aphenphosmphobia, haphephobia, haptophobia

Tourette's sufferers: Pete Bennett, Samuel Johnson (allegedly)

tourist: "The traveller sees what he sees, the tourist sees what he came to see" – G.K. Chesterton

tower of ice: serac

tower-shaped: pyrgoidal

towers, study of: pyrgology

town, adjective: civic, opidan, oppidan, urban

town, most northerly in the world: Hammerfest in Norway

toxins, science of: toxicology

toy shops: Hamleys, Toys R Us

Toy Story (1995 film), famous lines: Buzz Lightyear [the voice of Tim Allen], to Woody: "You are a sad, strange, little man. You have my pity. Farewell." Buzz Lightyear: "To infinity and beyond!"

toys: balloon, Barbie Doll, beanbag doll, Biker Mice From Mars, Chatter Telephone, deely-bobbers (imitation antennae), Disco-ball, doll, Etch A Sketch, flannelboard, frisbee, fuds, furby, Game Boy, Gobots, gyroscope, hobby horse, hula-hoop, jack-in-the-box, jumping jack, kaleidoscope, kazoo, kite, Lego, Lolobal, marble, Meccano set, The Mighty Morphin' Power Rangers (inc. Megazord, Tommy and Kimberley), My Lover (virtual lover from Hong Kong), Noddy, pea-shooter, playhouse, pogo stick, popgun, puzzle, Robosapien, Slinky, spacehopper,

Tamagotchi computer pet, teddy bear, Teenage Mutant Ninja Turtle, tin soldier, top, Trimball, tumbler, virtual pet, water pistol, whirligig, yo-yo, zoetrope

TPO: tree preservation order

tractor, famous: Terence the Tractor

trade, patroness of: Athene (Greek), Minerva (Roman)

trade union leaders: Ernest Bevin, Bob Crow, Brenda Dean, Jimmy Hoffa, George Meany, Arthur Scargill, Norman Willis

Trafalgar Square, London, statues of: King George IV, Horatio Nelson, Sir Henry Havelock, Sir Charles Napier; and previously: Alison Lapper

traffic control: ramp, sleeping policeman, stinger spike (a six-inch wide plastic lattice-work with small spikes, used by police to throw in the path of runaway vehicles in order to deflate tyres), traffic light

traffic jam: bottleneck, gridlock, logjam, traffic-jam-from-hell

traffic technology: sat-nav, Trafficmaster

traffic lights, first: erected at the corner of Bridge Street and New Palace Yard off Parliament Square in London, England, which first turned red on 10 December 1868 (red indicated 'stop' and green 'caution'); the lights were actually a revolving lantern illuminated by gas

tragic heroines: Fantine (from *Les Miserables*), Anna Karenina, Amy Robsart (from Walter Scott's *Kenilworth*)

train crashes, in Britain: Clapham Junction, Hatfield, Ladbroke Grove, Potters Bar, Selby (north Yorkshire)

train robbers: Ronald Biggs, Butch Cassidy, Buster Edwards, Jesse James, Bruce Reynolds, the Sundance Kid
- see Great Train Robbery

trainers: Converse all star, gym shoes, New Balance, Nike, plimsolls, Reebok, sneakers, tennis shoes

trains, famous: America, Arrow, Atlantic, Atlantic Coast Express, Best Friend of Charleston, Blucher, Brighton Belle, Bristolian, Britannia, Catch-me-who-can, Cornwall, Decapod, Devonian, De Witt Clinton, Duke of Gloucester, Duplex, Elizabethan, Evening Star, Flying Scotsman (first train to travel non-stop between London and Edinburgh), Globe, Golden Arrow, Great Bear, Green Arrow, Ivor the Engine (from the children's TV series), James the Red Engine, Kentish Belle, Lancashire Witch, Liverpool, Locomotion, Lord Nelson, Lord of Isles, Mallard, No. 1, Novelty, Old Ironsides, Orient Express, Planet, Rocket, Royal George, Royal Scot, Sanspareil, South Carolina, Stourbridge Lion, Thanet Belle, Thomas the Tank Engine, 3:10 to Yuma, Tom Thumb, Tootle, Union of South Africa

Trainspotting (1996 film), famous line [opening speech]: Mark Renton (Ewan McGregor): "Choose life. Choose a job. Choose a career. Choose a family. Choose a fucking big television, choose washing machines, cars, compact disc players and electrical tin openers...Choose your future. Choose life. But why would I want to do a thing like that? I chose not to choose life: I chose something else. And the reasons? There are no reasons. Who needs reasons when you've got heroin?"

traitors: Anthony Blunt, Guy Burgess, Anatoly Golitsyn, Lord Haw-Haw (real name: William Joyce), Judas, Vidkun Quisling, Julius and Ethel Rosenberg, David Shayler (who leaked MI5 documents), Mordechai Vanunu (who revealed Israel's nuclear secrets to the world)

tramps: Charlie Chaplin, Davies (from Harold Pinter's *The Caretaker*), Estragon (from *Waiting for Godot*), Jean Genet, Jack London, 'Simon' (whose drawings were exhibited at Tate Britain and who was then given a home - a £30,000

of Diana, Tree of Liberty, Tree of the Universe, Tree of Wisdom, Tyburn Tree, Yggdrasil (Norse mythology)

trees, fear of: dendrophobia

trees, goddess of: Pomona (Roman mythology)

trees, number of species native to Europe: 85

trembling, fear of: tremophobia

tribute bands: Alike Cooper, Antarctic Monkeys, Bjorn Again (for Abba), The Bootleg Beatles, The Counterfeit Stones, Crowded Scouse, Dread Zeppelin, Oashish

tribute band festival: Glastonbudget, in Leicestershire

trickery: jiggery-pokery

trickster: Loki (Norse mythology)
  - see pranksters

tri-coloured: trichromatic

trident (for spearing fish): leister

Trinidad and Tobago: independent republic in the Caribbean
  capital: Port of Spain
  currency: Trinidad and Tobago dollar
  language: English
  religion: Christian (majority), Hindu

Trinidadian cricketer: Lord (Learie) Constantine of Maraval and Nelson

Trinidadian novelist: Sir V.S. Naipaul

Trojan king: Priam

Trojan princes: Hector, Paris

Trojan queen: Hecuba

Trojans: Antigone, Cassandra, Clytius, Cressida, Ganymede, Troilus

Trojans, The, two-part opera by Hector Berlioz, *The Taking of Troy* first produced in Karlsruhe, Germany, in 1890 (after the composer's death), while the second part, *The Trojans at Carthage*, was produced in Paris in 1863 (before his death)

Trojan Wars: c.1200 BC

trombonists: Vic Dickenson, Tommy Dorsey, J.J. Johnson, Glenn Miller, Jack Teagarden (real name: Weldon Leo Teagarden)

trouble: "If you don't learn to laugh at trouble, you won't have anything to laugh at when you're old" - Edgar Watson Howe

trousers: bell-bottoms, bloomers, breeches, Capris, chinos, chuddies, corduroys, culottes, drainpipes, ducks (white and sporting), dungarees, flannels, flares, galligaskins, hipsters, knee-breeches, Oxford bags, pantalets, pantaloons, pants, pedal pushers, salopettes, slacks, slops (worn by sailors), spongebags, sweatpants, Zouaves

trouser strap: belt, bowyang, braces

Trout, The: name given to quintet (D.956) for piano, violin, viola, cello and double-bass, composed by Franz Schubert in 1819

trout, adjective: truttaceous

trout, collective noun: hover

trout, swimming speed: 23 mph

trout, young: fingerling, fry

Trucial States: former name for the United Arab Emirates (until 1971)

truffle: black truffle, Perigord truffle (one of France's most expensive food items), Terfezia, white truffle

truffle, largest: a four-pound (2 kg) specimen dug up in 1951 near Alba, in Italy. It was sold for 130,000 lire (the quivalent of over £3,000 today) and was allegedly presented to President Harry S. Truman by a wealthy Italian businessman

trumpet, adjective: buccinal

trumpet, to blow the: tubicinate (verb)

trumpeters: Herb Alpert, Louis Armstrong, Kenny Ball, Alison Balsom, Benny Carter, Buck Clayton, Miles Davis, Billy Eckstine, Roy Eldridge, Dizzy Gillespie, Ernest Hall, Håkan Hardenberger, Philip Jones, Humphrey Lyttelton, Wynton Marsalis, Red Nichols, John Solomon, Anton Weidinger

trust, adjective: fiduciary

truth: "Never believe anything until it has been officially denied" - old newspaper maxim; "There are only two ways of telling the complete truth – anonymously and posthumously" - Thomas Sowell; "Truth - like art - is in the eye of the beholder. You choose what you believe and I'll choose what I know" – Jim Williams (played by Kevin Spacey) in the 1997 film *Midnight In the Garden of Good and Evil*

truth, lover of: philalethist

truth drug: Pentothal, thiopentone

tsar, first: Ivan the Terrible

T-shaped cross: Saint Anthony

tsunami disaster: Boxing Day catastrophe that claimed the lives of 224,495 people (but relatively few animals) on the rim of the Indian Ocean on 26 December 2004

tuberculosis, adjective: consumptive

tuberculosis, dread of: tuberculophobia

Tudor monarch, first: Henry VII

Tudor monarch, last: Elizabeth I

tugboat, famous: Scuffy

tumours, doctor dealing with: oncologist

tumours, study of: oncology

tumour extraction: enucleation

tumour treatment: oncology

tuning fork: invented in 1711 by John Shore (who called it a 'pitch fork')

Tunisia: republic in North Africa
>   **capital:** Tunis
>   **currency:** dinar
>   **language:** Arabic (official), French
>   **religion:** Muslim

Tunisian and famous: Hannibal

Turandot: opera by Giacomo Puccini, first produced in Milan in 1926

turban: puggaree

turf: AstroTurf, divot, grass, greensward, sod, sward

turf, adjective: cespitous

turf plot: turbary

Turkey: republic both in south-eastern Europe and western Asia
>   **capital:** Ankara
>   **currency:** Turkish new lira
>   **language:** Turkish, Kurdish, Arabic
>   **religion:** Muslim

turkey (bird), adjective: meleagrine

Turkey (country), adjective: Turkish

turkey (bird), collective noun: rafter

turkey (bird), head or throat appendage of: wattle

turkey (bird), male: jake, stag, tom

Turkish concubine: odalisque

Turkish hostel: imaret

Turkish volcano: Great Ararat (extinct)

Turkish writer: Orhan Pamuk
Turkmenistan: republic in central Asia
  capital: Ashkhabad
  currency: manat
  language: Turkmen
  religion: Muslim, Christian orthodox
  famous Turkman: Saparmyrat Niyazov (aka Turkmenbashi the Great)
Turner Prize winners: Richard Wright (2009), Mark Leckey (2008), Mark
  Wallinger (2007), Tomma Abts (2006), Simon Starling (2005), Jeremy Deller
  (2004), Grayson Perry (2003), Keith Tyson (2002), Martin Creed (whose only
  exhibit at Tate Britain was an empty room with lights that flicked on and off
  every five seconds, 2001), Wolfgang Tillmans (2000), Steve McQueen (1999),
  Chris Ofili (1998), Gillian Wearing (1997), Douglas Gordon (1996), Damien
  Hirst (1995), Antony Gormley (1994), Rachel Whiteread (1993), Grenville
  Davey (1992), Anish Kapoor (1991)
Turn of the Screw, The: opera by Benjamin Britten first produced in Venice in
  1953; adapted from the novel by Henry James
turnip-shaped: napiform
turret, adjective: turrical
turtle, adjective: anapsid, testudinal
turtle, breeding ground: rookery
turtle, collective noun: bale, turn
turtle, young: hatchling
turtle meat: calipash (the greenish part), calipee (the yellow part)
turtle plate: scute
turtles, famous: Donatello (mutant), Franklin, Leonardo (mutant), Michelangelo
  (mutant), Raphael (mutant), Skipperdee (from Kay Thompson's *Eloise*), Yertle
  (c/o Dr Seuss)
turtledove, collective noun: pitying
Tuscany: "Chiantishire" (nicknamed by John Mortimer)
Tuscany horse race: the Palio (held in Siena)
Tuvalu: country in the south-west Pacific, formerly known as Lagoon Islands,
  Ellice Islands
  capital: Funafuti
  currency: Australian dollar, Tuvalu dollar
  language: English, Tuvaluan
  religion: Christian
TV newscasters: George Alagiah, Fiona Armstrong, Mark Austin, Richard Baker,
  Carol Barnes, Reginald Bosanquet, Tom Brokaw, Fiona Bruce, Micheal Buerk,
  Alastair Burnet, Andrea Catherwood, Katie Couric, Walter Cronkite, Katie
  Derham, Robert Dougall, Anna Ford, Bryant Gumbel, John Humphrys, Peter
  Jennings, Natasha Kaplinsky, Kenneth Kendall, Martyn Lewis, Sian Lloyd,
  Trevor McDonald, Dermot Murnaghan, Edward R. Murrow, Nicholas Owen,
  Dan Rather, Angela Rippon, Selina Scott, Peter Sissons, Jon Snow, Moira
  Stuart, Nicholas Witchell, Kirsty Young
TV presenter: anchor, anchorman, anchorwoman, autocutie (female), himbo
TV presenters: Eamonn Andrews, Michael Aspel, Dani Behr, Frank Bough, Fiona
  Bruce, Terry Christian, Jeremy Clarkson, Jill Dando (convicted killer of:
  Barry George), Amanda de Cadanet, Angus Deayton, David Dickinson, David

Dimbleby, Jonathan Dimbleby, Chris Evans, Judy Finnigan, Hughie Green, Rolf Harris, John Humphrys, Ulrika Jonsson, Matthew Kelly, Richard Madeley, Graham Norton, Jack Paar, Jeremy Paxman, Jeff Probst, Anne Robinson, Jon Ronson, Gaby Roslin, Nick Ross, June Sarpong, Jimmy Savile, Selina Scott, Melanie Sykes, Chris Tarrant, Louis Theroux, Alan Titchmarsh, Anthea Turner, Johnny Vaughan, Sir Terry Wogan

TV reporters: Kate Adie, Sandy Gall, Brian Hanrahan, John Simpson
- see broadcasters, war correspondents, etc

Twain, Mark; words coined by: bathtub, boom (the verb), nifty

twelve plus one: anagram for "eleven plus two"

twelve-sided plane figure: dodecagon

twelve-sided solid figure: dodecahedron

twentieth century: "The 20th century story is one of gradual addiction to the cinema, then the television, then the computer screen" - Nicholas Wapshott

twenty, adjective: vigesimal, vicenary

twenty years, happening every: vigentennial

24: cult, innovative and dynamic TV series in which federal agent Jack Bauer faces a crisis played out in real time over a 24-hour period, unveiled in 24 one-hour episodes
created by: Joel Surnow and Robert Cochran
first broadcast: 6 November 2001
cast: Kiefer Sutherland (Jack Bauer), Dennis Haysbert (David Palmer), Elisha Cuthbert (Kimberly Bauer), Leslie Hope (Teri Bauer), Penny Johnson Jerald (Sherry Palmer), Sarah Clarke (Agent Nina Myers), Carlos Bernard (Tony Almeida), William Devane (Secretary of Defense James Heller), Alberta Watson (Erin Driscoll)

twice-yearly: biannual (once every two years is biennial)

twigs, adjective: vimineous

twilight, adjective: crepuscular

Twilight Saga fan: Twihard, Twilighter

Twin Peaks: surreal TV serial created by David Lynch and Mark Frost, later expanded into the 1992 movie *Twin Peaks: Fire Walk with Me*
broadcast: 8 April 1990–10 June 1991 on ABC TV (29 episodes)
cast: Kyle MacLachlan (Dale Cooper), Michael Ontkean (Harry S. Truman), Mädchen Amick (Shelly Johnson), Dana Ashbrook (Bobby Briggs), Richard Beymer (Benjamin Horne), Sherilyn Fenn (Audrey Horne), Lara Flynn Boyle (Donna Frost), Peggy Lipton (Norma Jennings), Ray Wise (Leland Palmer), Joan Chen (Jocelyn 'Josie' Packard), Piper Laurie (Catherine Martell), Russ Tamblyn (Dr Lawrence Jacoby), Sheryl Lee (Laura Palmer/Madeleine)

twins: Antipholus and Dromio (from *The Comedy of Errors*), Apollo and Diana, Artemis and Apollo, Sir David and Sir Frederick Barclay (tycoons), Belus and Agenor, Castor and Pollux (Greek mythology), Dan and Dean Caten (fashion designers), Frank and Ronald de Boer (Dutch footballers), Dupont et Dupond (from the Tintin comic-book), Lamb and Lynx Gaede (singers/instrumentalists, of Prussian Blue), Maurice and Robin Gibb (singers), Luke and Matt Goss (singers, formerly of Bros), He-Man and She-Ra, Johnny and Luther Htoo (Burmese guerrilla fighters), Jacob and Esau, Jedward (singing siblings John and Edward Grimes), Lech and Jaroslaw Kaczyński (the president and prime minister of Poland respectively), Ronnie and Reggie Kray, Norris and Ross

McWhirter (founders of the Guinness Book of Records), Ann Landers and
Pauline Phillips (rival columnists aka Abigail Van Buren and Dear Abby),
Princess Leia Organa and Luke Skywalker, Ashley and Mary-Kate Olsen, The
Petrona Towers (in Kuala Lumpur), Auguste and Jean Felix Piccard
(balloonists), Michael and Mark Polish (filmmakers), The Proclaimers (Charlie
and Craig Reid), Nicholas and Stephen Quay (animators), Romulus and Remus,
Anthony and Peter Shaffer, Thomson and Thompson (from the Tintin comic-
book), Tweedledee and Tweedledum, The Twin Towers (World Trade Center),
Viola and Sebastian (from Shakespeare's *Twelfth Night*)

twins, fact: "Two American brothers, separated at birth, discovered, on being
reunited at 39, that they had both married a woman called Linda, divorced her,
remarried one called Betty and had a child called James. Both owned a dog
called Toy and both chain-smoked Salem cigarettes"

twist: circumvolute (verb)

twists and turns, adjective: anfractuous

two-faced: Janiform

TX: postcode for Texas

tycoons: Andrew Carnegie, Sir John Ellerman (in real terms, the richest British
tycoon of all time), Sir James Goldsmith, Hugh Hefner, Soichiro Honda, Howard
Hughes, John de Lorean, John Rockefeller, Sir Alan Sugar, Donald Trump
- see billionaires, business executives, entrepreneurs, etc

Tyne and Wear, administrative centre: Newcastle

typefaces: agency FB, Albertus, Algerian, arial, arial black, arial narrow,
AvantGarde Bk BT, batang, Belwe Bd BT, book antiqua, bookman old style,
clarendon, comic sans MS, courier new, Fraktur, Garamond, gautami, Georgia,
gill sans, goudy old style, heading sans-serif, heading serif, helvetica neue,
italic, macabre, Ming, mystical, pictorial, pixel, Song, tahoma, techno, text
sans-serif, text serif, times new roman, verdana, zapfino

typeface designers: Giambattista Bodoni, Adrian Frutiger

typeface, plain: roman

typewriters: anderson shorthand writing machine (available from 1914),
blickensderfer, corona, hammond multiplex Typewriter, IBM Model D, L.C.
Smith and Corona, Lexicon 80, Monroe, Noiseless Typewriter, Oliver Standard
Visible Writer, Olivetti, Princess, Remington Standard, Royal Typewriter,
Selectric, Sholes and Glidden Machine (1874; the first commercial type-
writer), Smith-Corona, Underwood, Valentine

typewriter roller: platen

typing, fact: 56% of typing is performed by the left hand

typing, fact: the longest word typed with only the left hand is 'stewardesses'

typographers: John Baskerville, Claude Garamond, Eric Gill, Stanley Morison

tyrants: Jean-Bédel Bokassa, Simon Legree
- see dictators

tyre manufacturer: André Michelin

tyres: Dunlop, Firestone, Goodyear, Michelin, Pirelli

U

U2: post-punk Irish pop group formed in Dublin in 1977; comprised of: Bono (real
name: Paul Hewson; vocals), Adam Clayton (bass), Larry Mullen (drums) and
The Edge (real name: David Evans; guitar)

Ubangi-Shari: former name for Central African Republic (until 1958)

UFO: unidentified flying object; term coined by Charles Fort (1874–1932)
UFO sites: Rachel, Nevada; Roswell, New Mexico (1947); Varginha, Brazil (1996)
Uganda: republic in East Africa
    capital: Kampala
    currency: Ugandan shilling
    language: English
    religion: Christian
Ugandan and famous: Idi Amin (former president), Princess Elizabeth of Toro (diplomat and model), Bernard Kabanda (musician), Milton Obote (former president), John Sentamu
Ugandan Civil War: 1978–1979
Ugandan drink: malwa
Ugandan mountain: Mount Margherita, Mount Stanley
ugliness: "Ugliness is much better than beauty; it lasts longer" - Serge Gainsbourg
ugliness, fear of: cacophobia
ugly: cosmetically different (PC)
ugly, fear of being: dysmorphophobia
ugly, the condition of feeling: body dysmorphic disorder
ugly but sexy, the state of being: cacocallia
ugly woman: munta (modern slang)
UHT: ultra-heat treated (of milk)
ukulele player: George Formby
Ukraine: republic in south-eastern Europe
    capital: Kiev
    currency: hryvna
    language: Ukrainian
    religion: Christian
ulcers, study of: helcology
um or er (in speech): disfluency
Unabomber: Ted Kaczynski
uncle, adjective: avuncular
undercover agent: Odette Sansom
    - see secret agents, spies
understand?: capeesh? (Italian-American slang), collar the jive?
undertakers: Basil Bulstrode (from TV's *That's Your Funeral*), Nate Fisher (from TV's *Six Feet Under*), Sowerberry (from *Oliver Twist*)
undertaker, collective noun: unction
undertakers, patron saints of: Joseph of Arimathea and Nicodemus
underwater: subaquatic
underwater explorer: Jacques Cousteau
underwear, female: basque, bodice, bra, camisole, conical bra, corset, knickers, push-up bra, stockings, suspenders, tanga, thong
underwear, male: boxer briefs, boxer shorts, Hanes, Jockey shorts, thong, Y-fronts
Underworld, adjective: chthonian, chtonic
underworld, gods of: Dis Pater (Roman mythology), Hades (Greek), Orcus (Roman), Osiris (Egyptian), Pluto (Roman)
underworld, goddess of: Hecate (Greek), Proserpina (Roman)
underworld, queen of: Persephone
undressing, dread of: gymnophobia
UNESCO: United Nations Educational, Scientific, and Cultural Organisation

unexpected: inopinate
UNICEF: United Nations Children's Fund (originally known as the United Nations International Children's Emergency Fund)
unicorn: monoceros
unicorn, collective noun: blessing
union leaders: César Chávez, James Hoffa, Arthur Scargill
    - see trade union leaders
United Arab Emirates: nation of seven emirates in south-west Asia, consisting of Abu Dhabi, Dubai, Sharjah, Ajman, Umm al Qaiwain, Ras el Khaimah and Fujairah; formerly known as the Trucial States (until 1971)
    capital: Abu Dhabi
    currency: dirham
    language: Arabic
    religion: Muslim
United Artists: film company founded in 1919 by Charlie Chaplin, Douglas Fairbanks, D.W. Griffith and Mary Pickford
United Kingdom: kingdom in north-western Europe
    capital: London
    currency: pound sterling
    language: English; Gaelic, Welsh (with over 100 minority languages)
    religion: Christian
    dependencies: Ascension Island, Bermuda, British Antarctic Territory, British Virgin Islands, Cayman Islands, Diego Garcia (in the British Indian Ocean Territory), Falkland Islands, Gibralta, Montserrat, Pitcairn, South Georgia, St Helena, Tristan da Cunha, Turks and Caicos Islands
    exports: The Beatles, English language, Fergie, Harry Potter, Internet, Shakespeare, The Spice Girls, Jerry Springer, Prince William
    rivers: Avon, Clyde, Humber, Mersey, Severn, Spey, Thames, Tyne, Wye
United Nations: international organisation set up in 1945 to help promote world peace. The headquarters, on Manhattan's East Side in New York, on land donated by John Rockefeller Jr, comprises four buildings: the Secretariat, the General Assembly, the Conference building and the Dag Hammarskjöld Library. The complex was designed by a panel of architects, including Charles Le Corbusier, Oscar Niemeyer and Walter H. Harrison.
United Nations agencies: FAO (Food and Agriculture Organisation), UNESCO (United Nations Educational, Scientific, and Cultural Organisation), UNICEF (United Nations Children's Fund), UNRWA (United Nations Relief and Works Agency)
United States of America: America, Babylon (Afro-American), Land of the Free and Home of the Brave (as lifted from *The Star-Spangled Banner*), the New Land, the New World, the States, Uncle Sam, the US, the US of A, Yankee land
United States of America: federal republic predominantly in North America
    capital: Washington, D.C.
    currency: dollar
    language: English, Spanish
    religion: Christian
    fact: two thirds of Americans are overweight and one third clinically obese
    flag: Old Glory, Stars and Stripes
    guns: according to a 1998 study, one person dies by gunshot every 18 minutes
    murder rate: 5.5 people in 100,000 are murdered

number of lawyers: 800,000
presidential residence: White House
presidential jet: Air Force One
presidents elected at the start of a decade:
    1840: William Henry Harrison (died in office)
    1860: Abraham Lincoln (assassinated)
    1880: James A. Garfield (assassinated)
    1900: William McKinley (assassinated)
    1920: Warren G. Harding (died in office)
    1940: Franklin D. Roosevelt (died in office)
    1960: John F. Kennedy (assassinated)
    1980: Ronald Reagan (survived assassination attempt)
    2000: George W. Bush
rivers: Colorado, Columbia, Hudson, Mississippi, Ohio, Rio Grande, Snake
United States of America: Alabama, Alaska, Arizona, Arkansas, California,
    Colorado, Connecticut, Delaware, Florida, Georgia, Hawaii, Idaho, Illinois,
    Indiana, Iowa, Kansas, Kentucky, Louisiana, Maine, Maryland, Massachusetts,
    Michigan, Minnesota, Mississippi, Missouri, Montana, Nebraska, Nevada, New
    Hampshire, New Jersey, New Mexico, New York, North Carolina, North Dakota,
    Ohio, Oklahoma, Oregon, Pennsylvania, Rhode Island, South Carolina, South
    Dakota, Tennessee, Texas, Utah, Vermont, Virginia, Washington, West Virginia,
    Wisconsin, Wyoming
United States of America, largest: 1) Alaska; then 2) Texas; 3) California; 4) Montana;
    5) New Mexico; 6) Arizona; 7) Nevada; 8) Colorado; 9) Wyoming; 10) Michigan
universe: "My suspicion is that the universe is not only queerer than we suppose,
    but queerer than we *can* suppose" – J.B.S. Haldane
university, adjective: academal
universities, patron saint of: Blessed Contardo Ferrini
university, largest in the world: University of Paris
university, oldest in Britain: University of Oxford, whose University College was
    founded in 1249
university, oldest in North America: Harvard (established in 1636)
upper lip: philtral dimple, philtral ridge, philtrum, snuffle-trough (informal)
Upper Peru: former name for Bolivia (until 1825)
Upper Volta: former name for Burkina Faso (until 1984)
Upstairs, Downstairs: enormously popular, award-winning series chronicling the
    lives of the aristocratic, Edwardian Bellamy family at 165 Eaton Place in
    London's Belgravia, as well as the parallel affairs of their servants. London
    Weekend Television also produced a spin-off series, *Thomas and Sarah* (1979)
    created by: Jean Marsh and Eileen Atkins
    broadcast: 10 October 1971–21 December 1975
    cast: Gordon Jackson (Angus Hudson), David Langton (Richard Bellamy), Jean
        Marsh (Rose Buck), Angela Baddeley (Mrs Kate Bridges), Pauline Collins
        (Sarah Moffat), Lesley-Anne Down (Georgina Worsley), Rachel Gurney
        (Lady Marjorie Bellamy), George Innes (Alfred Harris), Christopher Beeny
        (Edward Barnes), Jenny Tomasin (Ruby Finch), Simon Williams (James
        Bellamy), Jacqueline Tong (Daisy Barnes), Patsy Smart (Maud Roberts),
        Meg Wynn Own (Hazel Bellamy), Nicola Pagett (Elizabeth Kirkbridge),
        John Alderton (Thomas Watkins), Hannah Gordon (Virginia Bellamy), Joan
        Benham (Lady Prudence Fairfax), Raymond Huntley (Sir Geoffrey Dillon),
        Ian Ogilvy (Lawrence Kirkbridge), Gareth Hunt (Frederick Norton)

Uruguay: republic in South America, on the Atlantic coast
    capital: Montevideo
    currency: peso
    language: Spanish
    religion: Roman Catholic
    patron saints of: Philip and James
urban: civic, inner-city
urinary bladder: vesica
urinate: drain the main vein, hit or miss (CRS), micturate (urinate frequently), pass water, pee, piss, pop a squat (female), relieve oneself, shake the dew off the lily (male), slash, take a leak, tinkle, water the flowers, waz (male), wee
urinating involuntarily, the act of: enuresis
urination: emiction, micturition (medical terminology)
urination; inability to control during sleep: enuresis
urination, affecting: uretic (adjective)
urination, painful: dysuria
urine: mickey (CRS for Mickey Bliss), number one, piddle, piss, wee
urine, adjective: uric, urinary, urinous
urine, involuntary discharge of (especially while asleep): enuresis
urine, one aroused by the smell of: renifluer (noun)
urine, sexual interest in: undinism (rare), urolagnia, urophilia
urine, that which produces: diuretic, emictory (adjective)
urine of cattle: stale
urine of horse: stale
URL (in computing): Universal Resource Locator
Urundi: former name for Burundi (until 1962)
USB (in computing): universal serial bus
USDAW: The Union of Shop, Distributive and Allied Workers
uselessness, adjective: otiose
UT: postcode for Utah
Utah, 45th state (1896), Beehive State, Mormon State
    capital: Salt Lake City
    state bird: seagull
    state flower: sego lily
    state tree: blue spruce
    motto: 'Industry'
    birthplace of: Roseanne Barr, Frank Borzage (filmmaker), John Moses Browning (gunsmith), Butch Cassidy, John Gilbert (actor), Donny Osmond, Marie Osmond, Ivy Baker Priest (politician), James Woods, Loretta Young
    tourist attractions: Bryce Canyon, Great Salt Lake, Lake Powell, Timpanogos Cave
    fact: the water in the Great Salt Lake is more than four times saltier than any ocean
    fact: it is illegal to hunt for whales, even though Utah is completely land-locked
Uzbekistan: republic in central Asia
    capital: Tashkent
    currency: sum
    language: Uzbek
    religion: Muslim

V

V-1 bomb: doodlebug

VA: postcode for Virginia

vaccination: officially first carried out by the English physician Edward Jenner on 14 May 1796. However, in spite of the widely held belief in Jenner's ground-breaking triumph, the Dorset farmer Benjamin Jesty appears to have beaten him to it. Indeed, in the graveyard of St Nicholas in Worth Matravers, Dorset, there is a gravestone that attests to this fact, Benjamin Jesty being a "man particularly noted for having been the first Person (known) that introduced the Cow Pox by Inoculation... in the Year 1774." Even so, other sources credit a Mr Downe, a surgeon from Bridport, Dorset, for performing the first vaccination in 1771

vacillation: "Vacillation is the blood of life. A mind made up is a dead mind" - Alan Sillitoe, *Raw Material*

vacuum cleaner: invented in 1901 (in England) by H.C. Booth

Vacuum cleaner entrepreneur: Sir James Dyson

vacuum flask: invented in 1906 by the Scottish chemist Sir James Dewar

vagina: bacon sandwich, bearded clam, beaver, bite, biter, bit on a fork, black hole, bottomless pit, brasole, breadwinner (a prostitute's), bung (US slang), canyon, cock (Southern US), cunt, dumb glutton, female pudend, fireplace, free fishery, front attic, front bottom, front door, front doormat, front garden, front-gut, front parlour, front room, front window, fur, furburger, furry hoop, futy, fuzz burger, fuzzy cup (US black use), gash, gazon maudit, gib teenuck (19th century slang, referring to a particularly large vagina), ginch, glory hole, groceries, hair burger, hair pie, hairy oracle, hairy ring, hairy wheel, happy valley, Holiday Inn, honeypot, hoop, jam, jelly roll, manhole, man trap, mick (Australian slang), mickey (Australian slang), mill town, mill village, minge, money, oracle, pintle-case, pisser, poes (South African), poke-hole, porthole, princock, princox, promised land, pudendum, pum-pum, punaany, pussy, quiff, quim, scat (black slang), skincoat (16th century), skin-the-pizzle, snapper, snatch, tuna town, twait, twat, vertical smile, vicious circle, yoni (Hindi)

vaginal discharge: leucorrhoea, 'whites'

vaginal dryness: colpoxerosis

vaginal instrument for opening/widening (primarily for medical inspection): speculum

vagrants – see tramps

valets: Figaro (from Mozart's *The Marriage of Figaro*), Jean (from Strindberg's *Miss Julie*), Jeeves, Kato (from *The Green Hornet*), Kato (c/o Inspector Clouseau), Passepartout (c/o *Around the World in 80 Days*) - see butlers

Valium: tranquiliser known as "mother's little helper;" invented by Leo Sternbach and introduced in 1963

value (philosophically speaking), adjective: axiological

vampire bat, adjective: desmodontid

vampire hunters: Blade (aka The Daywalker), Anita Blake, Jack Crow, Carl Kolchak, Captain Kronos, Dr Strange, Buffy Summers, Abraham Van Helsing, Dr Van Meer

vampires: Angel (from the TV series), Edward Cullen (from the *Twilight* series), Count Dracula, Lestat de Lioncourt, Nosferatu

Vancouver, birthplace of: Yvonne De Carlo, James Doohan ('Scotty' in *Star Trek*), Ryan Reynolds, Seth Rogen, Dorothy Stratten (Playboy centrefold), Margaret Trudeau

Vancouver, nickname: Hollywood North

Vancouver river: Fraser River

Van Diemen's Land: former name for Tasmania (until 1855)

Van Gogh, only painting sold in his lifetime (allegedly): *Red Vineyard, Arles* (1888)

Van Halen: metal rock band formed in Pasadena, California, in 1974; comprised of Michael Anthony (bass), David Lee Roth (vocals), Eddie Van Halen (guitar) and Alex Van Halen (drums). Formerly known as Mammoth and Rat Salade

vanished and and famous – see disappearances

Vanuatu: republic consisting of a group of islands in the West Pacific; formerly known as New Hebrides (until 1980)

>   **capital:** Vila
>   **currency:** vatu
>   **language:** Bislama, French, English
>   **religion:** Christian

Variety newspaper, famous headline: Sticks Nix Hicks Pix

Variety newspaper, words coined by: baloney, bimbo, chick, cliffhanger, corny, high-hat, hype, sex appeal, showbiz, soap opera, whodunit

Vassy massacre: 1562 (in which the Huguenots were defeated by Francis de Guise)

Vatican City: independent state, being an enclave in Rome

>   **currency:** euro; formerly: Vatican City lira; Italian lira
>   **language:** Latin (official), Italian
>   **newspapers:** *Acta Apostolicae Sedis*, *L'Osservatore Romano*
>   **Pope's residence:** Vatican Palace
>   **population:** 900
>   **religion:** Roman Catholic
>   **fact:** Vatican City is the world's smallest state

vaudevillians: Fred Allen, Gracie Allen, Josephine Baker, Jack Benny, Milton Berle, Fanny Brice, George Burns, James Cagney, Eddie Cantor, Charlie Chaplin, Jimmy Durante, Ruth Etting, Gracie Fields, W.C. Fields, George Formby, Eddie Foy, Will Hay, Bob Hope, Al Jolson, Buster Keaton, Sir Harry Lauder, Dan Leno, Marie Lloyd, the Marx Brothers (see), Helen Morgan, Will Rogers, Eric Sykes, the Three Stooges (see), Sophie Tucker

veal, adjective: vituline

veal, slice of: schnitzel

vegetable, oldest known: broad bean (also known as the fava and horsebean)

vegetables, fear of: lachanophobia

vegetarian, collective noun: sprig

vegetarianism taken to extremes: veganism

vegetarians: fruitarian (only eats fruit and vegetables classified as fruit), lacto vegetarian (eats dairy products), ovo lacto vegetarian (eats eggs and dairy products), pescetarian (fish-eating vegetarian), pescevegetarian (another name for pescetarian), pecto-vegetarian (fish and poultry-eating vegetarian), vegan (avoids all animal-related foods)

vegetation, god of: Dionysus (Greek)

vehicles, fear of: amaxophobia

veil: chador, mantle, shroud, weeper (worn by widows), yashmac, yashmak (worn by Muslim women in public)

veil, adjective: velar

vein, adjective: venous

vein inflammation: phlebitis

veins, adjective: venous
veins, study of: phlebology
velvet, adjective: velvet
Velvet Underground, The: phenomenally influential experimental rock group
that experienced little commercial success during its own epoch. The band
formed in 1965 in New York, but disbanded in 1971, only to reform in 1992
and disband in 1995. They were comprised of: Lou Reed (vocals, guitar),
Sterling Morrison (guitar), John Cale (vocals, bass, viola), Maureen 'Moe'
Tucker (drums) and Nico (vocals). When John Cale left the band in 1968 he
was replaced by Doug Yule
veneral disesase, fear of: cypridophobia
venereal disease, patron saint of: Fiacre
Venetian coin: sequin
Venetian leader: Enrico Dandolo
Venetian merchants: Antonio (from *The Merchant of Venice*), Marco Polo
Venetian moneylender: Shylock
Venetian official: doge
Venetian painters: Gentile Bellini, Antonio Canaletto, Tintoretto, Titian
Venetian traveller: Marco Polo
Venezuela: republic in South America
    capital: Caracas
    currency: bolívar
    language: Spanish
    religion: Roman Catholic
    patron saint: Our Lady of Coromoto
    river: Orinoco
    waterfall: Angel Falls
Venezuelan and famous: Simón Bolívar (liberator), Carlos the Jackal, Hugo
Chávez (president), Gustavo Dudamel (conductor)
vengeful and famous: Captain Ahab, Batman, Hera, Montezuma II, Pied Piper,
Shylock, Titus Andronicus
Venice, birthplace of: Tomasso Albinoni, Giovanni Bellini, Canaletto (aka Giovanni
Antonio Canal), Giacomo Casanova, Antonio Vivaldi
    bridges: Bridge of Sighs, Rialto Bridge
    bridges, number of: 400
    buildings: The Doges Palace, St Mark's Cathedral, San Giorgio Maggiore
        (church and monastery)
    canals, number of: 150
    cathedral: San Marco (St Mark's)
    islands, number of: 118
    nickname: Bride of the Sea, City of Canals
    patron saint: Mark
ventriloquists: Ray Alan, Edgar Bergen, Peter Brough, Terry Hall, Keith Harris, Jay
Johnson, Shari Lewis
Venus: planet discovered in 1611
Venus de Milo: iconic statue of Venus (minus arms), discovered in 1820 on the island
of Milos (in the South Aegean Sea) by a French naval officer. A year later, the
statue was installed at the Louvre in Paris, where it has remained to this day
verb functioning as a noun: gerund
verb most commonly used in the English language: to be; second most common:
to have

verbal diarrhoea: logorrhoea
Vermont, 14th state (1791), Green Mountain State
    capital: Montpelier
    state bird: hermit thrush
    state flower: red clover
    state tree: sugar maple
    motto: 'Freedom and unity'
    birthplace of: Chester Alan Arthur (21st president of the USA), Ted Bundy, Calvin Coolidge (30th president of the USA), Admiral George Dewey, John Dewey (philosopher), Stephen A. Douglas (judge), James Fisk (financial speculator), Rudy Vallee (singer and actor), Brigham Young
    tourist attractions: Bennington Battle Monument, Rock of Ages Tourist Center, Shelburne Museum, Vermont Marble Exhibit
vermouth: Cinzano, Martini, Noilly Prat
Versailles, Château de: 700-room palace outside Paris, conceived by Louis XIV and established as the royal court of France – and government seat – in 1682. The original chateau was constructed in 1624 but considerably expanded on by the architect Louis Le Vau and the landscape artist André Le Nôtre. The palace boasts 2,000 windows, 1,250 fireplaces, 67 staircases and the famous 240-foot long Hall of Mirrors
versatility, adjective: pancratic, versatile
vertabrae inflammation: spondylitis
vertical growth: orthotropism
veterinarians, famous: Dr Dolittle, Siegfried Farnon, James Herriot
veterinarians, patron saint of: Eligius
Viagra: sildenafil (generic name)
vicar's assistant: curate
viceroy of India: Earl Louis Mountbatten
Vichy statesmen: Pierre Laval, Philippe Pétain
victory: "Once you hear the details of victory, it is hard to distinguish it from a defeat" - Jean-Paul Sartre
victory, goddess of: Nike (Greek), Victoria (Roman)
video, fact: videos are approximately 4% shorter than a celluloid film due to the differing number of frames per second
video artists: Matthew Barney, Nam June Paik, Sam Taylor-Wood, Bill Viola
video game apparatus: joypad, joystick
Vienna, birthplace of: Otto Frisch, Gustav Klimt, Hedy Lamarr, Fritz Lang, Marie Antoinette, Wolfgang Pauli, Otto Preminger, Maximilian Schell, Arnold Schoenberg, Franz Schubert, Erich von Stroheim, Billy Wilder, Ludwig Wittgenstein, Fred Zinnemann, Stefan Zweig (playwright)
Vienna Circle: philosophical group who congregated in Vienna between 1929 and 1934, comprising Rudolf Carnap, Philip Frank, Kurt Gödel, Otto Neurath, Karl Popper, Moritz Schlick, Ludwig Wittgenstein, Edgar Zilsel and others
Vietnam: republic in South-East Asia, officially known as the Socialist Republic of Vietnam
    capital: Hanoi
    city: Ho Chi Minh City (formerly Saigon)
    currency: dong
    language: Vietnamese
    religion: Buddhist

tribal people: the Montagnards (from the central highlands, much persecuted by their government)

Vietnam war: 1954–1975; cease-fire agreed at Paris peace talks: January 1973; final death toll: 900,000 North Vietnamese and members of the National Liberation Front; more than 180,000 South Vietnamese; 56,226 American servicemen

Vietnamese military leader: No Nguyen Giap

Vietnamese political leader: Ho Chi Minh

Viking, The: nickname given to the darts champion Andy Fordham

villains: John Bindon, Ernst Blofeld (nemesis of James Bond), Fagin, Casper Gutman (from *The Maltese Falcon*), Ian Huntley (killer of Holly Wells and Jessica Chapman), Iago, Judas Iscariot, Emilio Largo (from Ian Fleming's *Thunderball*), Nick Leeson ('rogue trader,' who brought down Barings' bank), Simon Legree (from *Uncle Tom's Cabin*), Harry Lime (from *The Third Man*), Ming the Merciless (from *Flash Gordon*), Moriarty ("the Napoleon of crime"), Pontius Pilate, Bill Sikes, Winston Silcott (convicted of the murder of PC Keith Blakelock, but exonerated in 1991), Anakin Skywalker (aka Darth Vader)
- see serial killers, terrorists, etc

vine disease: phylloxera

vines, adjective: vineatic

vinegar, adjective: acetic, acetous

vineyard owners: Carole Bouquet, Francis Ford Coppola, Gérard Depardieu, Sam Neill, Greg Norman, Cliff Richard, Dick Smothers, Tom Smothers, Alex Trebek

vintners, patron saint of: Amand

viola players: Yuri Bashmet, Frank Bridge, William Primrose (considered to be the greatest player of the 20th century)

violence: "The last refuge of the incompetent" – Isaac Asimov

violet-coloured: violaceous

violin: Cremona, fiddle, fiedel, Guadagnini, hardinger (Norwegian fiddle), Hill, kit (obsolete), lira da braccio, rebec, Stradivarius, viele

violin; fact: the instrument is constructed of maple or sycamore, except for the soundboard, which is made of pine or spruce

violin; number of strings: four, tuned a fifth apart to the notes g, d', a' and e"

violin; sound produced by plucking with fingers: pizzicato

violin makers: Andrea Amati, Nicolò Amati, Guarnenius Josef Filius Andreae, Gasparo da Salò, Giuseppe Guarneri del Gesù, Nicolas Lupot, Giovanni Paolo Maggini, Antonio Stradivari, David Tecchler, Jean-Baptiste Vuillaume

violin periodical: *The Strad*

violin plucking (with the fingers): pizzicato

violinists: Maria Bachmann, Joshua Bell, Adolf Busch, Arcangelo Corelli, James Ehnes, Georges Enesco, Clio Gould, Stephane Grappelli, Chlöe Hanslip, Jascha Heifetz, Joseph Joachim, (Nigel) Kennedy, Fritz Kreisler, Linda Lampenius, Sir Neville Marriner, Yehudi Menuhin, Nathan Milstein, Wolfgang Amadeus Mozart, Anne-Sophie Mutter, Nero, David Oistrakh, Nicolò Paganini, Julian Rachin, Vadim Repin, Nadja Salerno-Sonnenberg, Pablo de Sarasate, Louis Spohr, Johann Strauss the Elder, Johann Strauss the Younger, Henryk Szeryng, Jacques Thibaud, Vanessa-Mae, Maxim Vengerov, Henri Vieuxtemps, Giovanni Viotti, Antonio Vivaldi, Eugène Ysaÿe, Efrem Zimbalist

viper, collective noun: generation, nest

viper, young: snakelet, neonate

virgin: canned goods, cherry, maid, maiden, nun, old maid, prude
virgin, adjective: parthenian
virgin birth: parthenogenesis
virgin goddess: Athene
Virgin Islands: group of islands (approximately one hundred) in the Caribbean, including the Virgin Islands of the United States and, in the east, the British Virgin Islands
Virgin Queen: Elizabeth I
virginal: chaste, hymenally challenged, virgo intacta
Virginia, 10th state (1788), Old Dominion
> **capital:** Richmond (formerly Jamestown and Williamsburg)
> **state bird:** cardinal (a state bird it shares with Illinois, Indiana, Kentucky, North Carolina, Ohio and West Virginia)
> **state flower:** flowering dogwood
> **state tree:** dogwood tree
> **motto:** 'Sic Semper Tyrannis' ('Thus always to tyrants')
> **birthplace of:** Arthur Ashe, Warren Beatty, Sandra Bullock, Willa Cather, Joseph I, Missy Elliott, Ella Fitzgerald, William H. Harrison (ninth president of the USA), Thomas Jefferson (third president of the USA), Robert E. Lee, Shirley MacLaine, James Madison (fourth president of the USA), James Monroe (fifth president of the USA), George C. Scott, Nat Turner, Cy Twombly (abstract painter), John Tyler (tenth president of the USA), Booker T. Washington, George Washington (first president of the USA), Woodrow Wilson (28th president of the USA), Tom Wolfe
> **tourist attractions:** Colonial Williamsburg, Arlington National Cemetery, Mount Vernon (home of George Washington), Yorktown, Jefferson's Monticello in Charlottesville, Blue Ridge Parkway, Virginia Beach
> **fact:** out of the 4,000 battles fought during the American Civil War, 2,200 were fought in Virginia
> **fact:** the American celebration of Thanksgiving was first held in Virginia, in 1619
virgins (or late starters): Saint Agnes, Saint Apollonia, Artemis, Athena, Jane Austen, Saint Bernadette, Doris Day (apocryphal), Elizabeth I, Havelock Ellis (until his marriage), Hestia, Adolf Hitler (until late in life), Hypatia of Alexandria, Isabella (from *Measure for Measure*), Immanuel Kant, Alfred Kinsey (who lost his virginity at 27, on his honeymoon), Mary (mother of Jesus), Walter Matthau (late starter), William Pitt the Younger, Beatrix Potter, Rosie Reid (Bristol University student who sold her virginity on eBay for £8,400), John Ruskin, George Bernard Shaw, Siddhartha Gautama, Britney Spears, Marie Stopes, Mark Twain, Ann Widdecombe, Kenneth Williams
virgins; number of in paradise (according to some interpretations of Islam): 72
virgins, patron saint of: Agnes of Rome
virologist: Jonas Salk
virus: Aids, anthrax, avian influenza, bacteriophage, bird flu, computer virus, cytomegalovirus, echovirus, enterovirus, Epstein–Barr virus, fowl pest, hepatitis, herpes, herpes simplex, HIV, influenza, mosaic disease, myxovirus, parvovirus, pathogen, pox, retrovirus, rubella, Sars (severe acute respiratory syndrome, a deadly pneumonioa that started mid-November 2002 in the Guangdong province of China), slow virus, staphylococcus aureus (aka golden Staph, SA – probably the most common human infectious agent – carried by about a third of the population at any given time), swine flu, tobacco mosaic virus, tuberculosis, typhus, yellow fever, zoonosis (an animal disease that can spread to humans)

virus, adjective: viral

viruses: "Humans are not so bright. They think about lots of things, but bugs only think about one thing: surviving. They are always at least one step ahead." Professor Gary French, head of microbiology at St Thomas's Hospital, London; "Molecular sharks, a motive without a mind" – Richard Preston, *The Hot Zone*

viruses, computer: Bagle-A, Code Red (affected 300,000 computers in July 2001), Conficker (aka Kido and Downandup, it affected 15 million computers in 2009), GoKar, Loveletter (aka the Love Bug and responsible for an estimated £3.2 billion worth of damage worldwide), Lovgate, macro virus, Melissa, MyDoom A., Mydoom.O, Netsky, Netsky-B, Netsky-C, Netsky-D, Netsky-P, Netsky-Z, Pathogen, Phatbot, Queeg, Sasser, Slammer, Sober-C, Sobig.F (believed to have infected tens of millions of computers), trojan, trojan horse, worm, Zafi-B

viruses, lethal: Aids, bird flu, Congo fever, Ebola, Hanta, Lassa fever, Marburg, Sars, streptococcus, West Nile (mosquito-borne disease)

viruses, specialist in: virologist

viscount, mode of verbal address: Your Lordship

viscountess, mode of verbal address: Your Ladyship

vision, correct; adjective: orthoptic

vision dimming: amblyopia

visionaries: Joan of Arc, Bernadette Soubirous

Vision of Piers Plowman, The – see Piers Plowman

vitamin A: retinol

vitamin A, found in: broccoli, butter, carrots, cheese, egg yolk, fish-liver oil, kale, liver, milk, squash, spinach and sweet potatoes

vitamin B^1: thiamine

vitamin B^1, found in: berries, brewer's yeast, cereals (whole or enriched), eggs, heart, kidney, lean meats, legumes, liver, nuts, pork, vegetables (leafy green) and wheat germ

vitamin B^2: riboflavin

vitamin B^2, found in: bread, cereals (whole grain and enriched), liver, meat, milk, mushrooms, pasta and vegetables (dark green)

vitamin B^3: niacin

vitamin B^3, found in: beans (dried), cereals (whole grain and enriched), liver, meat, nuts, peas, poultry, salmon (canned) and tuna (canned)

vitamin B6: pyridoxine

vitamin B6, found in: avocadoes, bananas, bread, cereals, grains (whole), green beans, liver, and spinach

vitamin B12: cobalamin

vitamin B12, found in: eggs, fish, kidneys, liver, meat and milk

vitamin C: ascorbic acid

vitamin C, found in: broccoli, Brussels sprouts, cabbage, cantaloupe, citrus fruits, green peppers, guava, kale, pineapple, spinach, strawberries, tomatoes and turnips

vitamin D, found in: egg yolk, liver and tuna

vitamin D2: calciferol

vitamin D3: cholecalciferol

vitamin E: tocopherol

vitamin E, found in: liver, vegetables (leafy green), vegetable oils and wheat germ

vitamin G: riboflavin (i.e. another term for vitamin B2)

vitamin H: biotin (a vitamin of the B complex)

vitamin K, found in: alfalfa, egg yolk, fish livers, liver, soybean oil and vegetables (leafy green)
vitamin K1: phylloquinone
vitamin K2: menaquinone
vitamin P: citrin, bioflavonoid
VJs: Steve Blame, Russell Brand, Ray Cokes, Cat Deeley, Davina McCall, Alex Zane
vocabulary, adjective: lexical
vocabulary; language with the largest: English, containing 490,000 words, with another 300,000 technical terms. Including new street slang, foreign words used in English and homonyms, the English language is said to include more than one million words
vocabulary; total in a language: lexis
vocal loss: aphonia
vodka: Absolut, Popov, Seagram's, Smirnoff, Stolichnaya, Vladivar
Vogue: fashion magazine published in 16 international editions, launched in 1910 as a bi-monthly by the young publisher Condé Nast
Vogue editors: Grace Mirabella, Alexandra Shulman, Diana Vreeland, Anna Wintour
voice: "The muscle of the soul" – quoted on Radio 4
voice artist: Rasel ("ask him to do a soap bubble and he can do it" – Björk)
voice-over artists: Joss Ackland, Patrick Allen, Alexander Armstrong, Peter Barkworth, Sanjeev Bhaskar, Richard Briers, Tom Conti, Mariella Frostrup, Stephen Fry, Michael Gambon, Jon Glover, Hannah Gordon, Ian Holm, John Hurt, James Earl Jones, Dervla Kirwan, Don LaFontaine (dubbed 'the Voice of God'), Hugh Laurie, Joanna Lumley, Felicity Montagu, Geoffrey Palmer, Sean Pertwee, Robert Powell, Anton Rodgers
voices, fear of: phonophobia
volcanic glass: obsidian
volcanic vent: fumarole, solfatara
volcano, produce of: basalt, fissure, geyser, lahar (volcanic mudflow, a flood of rain-soaked ash), lava, magma (molten rock contained beneath the earth's surface), pumice, pyroclastic flow (a ground-hugging, incandescent cloud of super hot gases, ash and rock fragments), tephra (the solid material ejected by volcanoes)
volcanoes: Cumbre Vieja (unstable volcano on Las Palmas in the Canary Islands which could produce a tsunami capable of engulfing the USA), Eyjafjallajökull (Icelandic volcano that disrupted European air travel in 2010), Great Ararat (Turkey), Krakatau (erupted 1883), Miyi-Yama (Java, erupted 1793, killing 53,000), Pinatubo (Phillipines; erupted June 15, 1991), Mount Etna (Sicily), Mount St Helens (Washington, erupted 1980), Tambora (Indonisia; erupted 1815, claiming 92,000 lives), Vesuvius (erupted 79 AD)
volcanoes, fact: there are 550 known active volcanoes on earth (with 500 million people living close to them)
vole, adjective: microtine
volleyball player: Ekaterina Gamova
vomit (noun): technicolour yawn
vomit (verb): barf, chunder, honk, puke, spew, spule, throw up, upchuck
vomit, adjective: emetic
vomit, black in colour: melaena (noun)
vomit on: bespew
vomiting: emesis
vomiting, fear of: emetophobia
vomiting, sexual arousal derived from: emetophilia

vomiting, study of: emetology
vomiting blood: haematemesis
voodoo doll: poppet
vorticism: art movement pioneered in 1913 by Wyndham Lewis in which cubism was expanded to embrace machinery in a human form
vote for women first introduced in the United Kingdom: 1918
voting: "It's not how people vote that matters, it's who counts the votes" - Joseph Stalin
vow, adjective: votive
vowel omission: elision
VPH: virtual physiological human
VPL: visible panty line
VT: postcode for Vermont
vulgarity: "What is vulgarity but beauty that does not give a fig for restraint?" – Adam Nicholson
vulture, adjective: vulturine
vulture, collective noun: wake
vulture-goddess: Nekhbet (goddess of Upper Egypt)
vultures, famous: John, Paul, George and Ringo (from Disney's *The Jungle Book*)

W

WA: postcode for Washington state
Waco siege: 28 February-19 April 1993 (when the FBI stormed the Branch Davidian ranch at Mount Carmel, nine miles east-northeast of Waco, Texas, resulting in 89 deaths)
wading birds, adjective: grallatory
Wagner, Richard; of whose music Mark Twain once said, "is better than it sounds"
wagon maker: wainwright
waiter: cold potato (Cockney Rhyming Slang), garçon, soup jockey
waitress, politically correct term: dining room attendant, waitperson, waitron
Wake Island: atoll in the Pacific, claimed by the United States in 1899
waking drugs: eugeroic, modafinil, ProVigil
waking up: pandiculation (the act of stretching and yawning)
Wales: principality and a part of Great Britain
    capital: Cardiff
    Latin name: Cambria
    patron saint: David
    Welsh name: Cymru
    - see Welsh and famous, Welsh counties
Wales, adjective: Cambrian
walk (verb): amble, clump, dawdle, go by Shank's pony, hike, hotfoot, jaywalk, sashay, saunter, schlep, step, stride, stroll, strut, swagger, toddle, traipse, tramp, trek, yomp
walker: ambler, flâneur, hiker, stroller
walkers, famous: Stephen Gough and Melanie Roberts (who strode the 874 miles from Land's End to John O'Groats in the nude, taking nine months between 2005 and 2006), Ffyona Campbell (the first woman to walk round the world), Ed Stafford (who walked the entire length of the Amazon)
walking: "I like long walks. Especially when they're taken by people who annoy me" - Fred Allen
walking, adjective: ambulatory, pedary (rare)

walking, dread of: basophobia
walking, obsession for: ambulomania
walking stick cap/end piece: ferule
walking upright: plantigrade (adjective)
Walkman – see Sony Walkman
wall, adjective: mural
Wall Street (1987 film), famous line: Gordon Gekko [Michael Douglas]: "Greed, for lack of a better word, is good. Greed is right. Greed works. Greed clarifies, cuts through, and captures the essence of the evolutionary spirit. Greed, in all of its forms - greed for life, for money, for love, knowledge - has marked the upward surge of mankind. And greed - you mark my words - will not only save Teldar Paper, but that other malfunctioning corporation called the USA. Thank you very much"
Wall Street crash: 1929
Wall Street Journal: New York business newspaper founded in 1889
Wal-Mart, founder: Sam Robson Walton, who opened his first Wal-Mart outlet in 1962
walrus, adjective: obenid
walrus, female: cow
walrus, male: bull
Waltons, The: fondly remembered CBS TV series about a solid Virginian family braving the Depression
    created by: Earl Hammer Jr (who based the series on his own experiences)
    broadcast: 14 September 1972–20 August 1981
    cast: Michael Learned (Olivia Walton), Ralph Waite (John Walton), Richard Thomas (John 'John-Boy' Walton Jr), Jon Walmsley (Jason Walton), Judy Norton (Mary Ellen Walton), Eric Scott (Ben Walton), Mary Elizabeth McDonough (Erin Walton), David W. Harper (James Robert 'Jim-Bob' Walton), Kami Cotler (Elizabeth Walton), Will Geer (Zeb Walton), Ellen Corby (Esther Walton)
waltz: valse
wander aimlessly: obambulate
war: "War is God's way of teaching Americans geography" - Ambrose Bierce
war: jihad or jehad (a Muslim holy war waged against infidels)
war, adjective: bellicose, martial
war, god of: Ares (Greek), Khonsu (Egyptian), Mars (Roman), Montu (Egyptian), Tyr (Norse), Upuaut (Egyptian), Wepwawet (Egyptian)
war, goddess of: Athena (Greek mythology), Ishtar (Babylonian), Mut (Egyptian), Neith (Egyptian), Sekhmet (Egyptian)
war, shortest in history: between Zanzibar and England in 1896, when Zanzibar surrendered after 38 minutes
war correspondents: Martin Bell, Jeremy Bowen, Ed Bradley, Dickey Chapelle (real name: Georgette Louise Meyer), Sir Winston Churchill, Stephen Crane, Oriana Fallaci, Martha Gellhorn (ex-wife of Ernest Hemingway), Sir Max Hastings, Ernest Hemingway, Michael Herr, Lee Miller, John Pilger, John Reed, Whitelaw Reid, Frederic Remington, Damon Runyon, Sydney Schanberg, John Simpson, Aleksey Tolstoy
war hospital: Craiglockhart (in Edinburgh)
War of American Independence: 1775–1783
War of the Austrian Succession: 1740–1748
War of the Grand Alliance: 1689–1697

War of the Roses: 1455–1485

War of the Spanish Succession: 1701–1714

war photographers: Eddie Adams, Dmitri Baltermants, Larry Burrows, Robert Capa, Dickey Chapelle, Horst Faas, Philip Jones Griffiths, Bert Hardy, Don McCullin, Lee Miller, Nick Ut

warming up: calescent (adjective)

warmth, causing: calefacient

warmth, giving: calefactory

warrior queen: Boudicca (sometimes spelled Boadicea)

Warsaw, birthplace of: Marie Curie, Samuel Goldwyn, Dame Marie Rambert

warship: aircraft carrier, battleship, bireme (ancient Greek), corvette, cruiser, destroyer, frigate, ironclad, long ship (Viking), monitor, pocket battleship, sloop, submarine, three-decker, torpedo boat

warthog, famous: Pumbaa (from Disney's *The Lion King*)

Warwickshire, administrative centre: Warwick

washing machine, cycles: rinse, spin, wash

washing powders: Ariel, Ark, Bold, Comfort, Daz, Dreft, Ecover, Fab, Lenor, Lux, OMO, Persil, Surf, Tide, Woolite

Washington, 42nd state (1889), Evergreen State

    capital: Olympia

    state bird: willow goldfinch

    state flower: rhododendron

    state tree: Western hemlock

    motto: 'Alki' ('by and by')

    birthplace of: Paul Allen, Dyan Cannon, Carol Channing, Kurt Cobain, Judy Collins, Bing Crosby, Bob Crosby, Merce Cunningham, Frances Farmer, Bill Gates, Jimi Hendrix, Gypsy Rose Lee, Kenny Loggins, Hank Ketcham, Mary McCarthy, Adam West

    tourist attractions: Mount St Helen's, Puget Sound, Seattle Space Needle, Spokane's Riverfront Park

    fact: the state still uses hanging as a mode of capital punishment

    fact: it is the only state named after a president

Washington DC, birthplace of: Edward Albee, Carl Bernstein, Tracy Chevalier, Duke Ellington, Marvin Gaye, Goldie Hawn, J. Edgar Hoover, Samuel L. Jackson, Marjorie Kinnan Rawlings (novelist), Henry Rollins, Pete Sampras

Washington Post, The: newspaper founded in 1877 by Stilson Hutchins, the first daily paper of the US capital

wasp, adjective: vespine, vespoid

wasps, fear of: spheksophobia

wasps, killing of: vespacide

wasps' nest: vespiary

watch: Gucci, Omega, Patek Philippe, Pulsar, Rolex, Seiko kinetic, stem-winder, Swatch, TAGHeuer, Timex, Timex Indiglo

watchmaker: horologist

watchmakers, famous: Louis Cartier, Maurice Lacroix

water; fact: in Victorian London a family could typically afford nine buckets of water a week

water, adjective: aquatic, aqueous; and: brackish, murky, salty

water, bottled: Abbey Well, Agua Vida, Buxton, Dasani (c/o Coca Cola), Evian, Highland Spring, Malvern, Perier, Spa, Strathmore, Volvic

water, fear of: aquaphobia, hydrophobia

water, science of: hydrology

water clock: clepsydra

water divining: bletonism

water intoxication: hyponatremia, polydipsia

Water Music – see Handel's Water Music

water of life: aqua vita

water slide: flume

watercolour painters: Paul Cézanne, John Constable, John Cotman, David Cox, John Cozens, Raoul Dufy, Thomas Girtin, Winslow Homer, Paul Klee, John Marin, Paul Nash, Emil Nolde, Sir William Russell Flint, Paul Sandby, John Singer Sargent, Paul Signac, Philip Steer, Joseph Mallord William Turner, David West, Peter de Wint

waterfall, highest in the United Kingdom: Eas Coul Aulin in Scotland (658 feet)

waterfall, highest in the world: Angel Falls in Venezuela (3,212 feet)

Waterloo, Battle of: 18 June 1815

watertight chamber: caisson

wave: boomer, bore, bow, breaker, comber, dumper, roller, tsunami, white horse, whitecap

wave motion, dread of: cymophobia

wave motion, study of: kymatology

wavy: ondoyant, sinuate

wax, adjective: ceraceous

wax artist: Marie Tussaud

wax modelling, adjective: ceroplastic

weakness, fear of: asthenophobia

wealth: "Wealth unused may as well not exist" – Aesop

wealth, study of: chrematistics

weapons: biological warfare, chainsticks, chemical (see), CS gas sprays, cudgel, electromagnetic pulse gun (which can destroy information stored on enemy computer files from a space satellite), electrothermal chemical weapons, flame-thrower, gun (see), logic bombs (weapons that target microchips), machete, nerve gas (see), nunchucks, poleaxe, spear, sword (see), trebuchet (Medieval machine used for hurling rocks)

weapons inspector: Dr David Kelly

weapon-carring: armiferous (adjective)

weasel, adjective: mustelid, musteline

weasel, collective noun: gam

weasel, famous: Biff (comic book character), Leroy (comic book character), Nack the Weasel (c/o *Sonic the Hedgehog*)

weasel, young: kitten

weather, adjective: meteorological

weather; the introduction of records in the UK: 1697

weatherman: Michael Fish

weather map line: isobar

weavers: Bottom (from *A Midsummer Night's Dream*), Silas Marner

weavers, patron saint of: Anthony Claret

weaving, adjective: textrine

web, adjective: retiary (rare)

web-footed: palamate, palmiped

weblish: the shorthand form of English that is used in text messaging and internet chat rooms; examples: A3 (anytime, anywhere, any place), ATB (all the best),

BBL (be back later), GAL (get a life), HAND (have a nice day), IYKWIMAITYD (if you know what I mean and I think you do), KISS (keep it simple, stupid), LOL (laugh out loud)

websites for music: Gnutella, Grokster, iTunes, Kaazaa, Limewire, Napster, Shareaza, Soulseek, Spotify, Wippit

wedding: "A wedding is just a funeral where you can smell your own flowers" - Victor Lewis-Smith

wedding, adjective: bridal, nuptial

Wedding March: 1826 composition by Felix Mendelssohn, written when he was seventeen as the overture to *A Midsummer Night's Dream*. Three years later Mendelssohn decided on a career in music

weddings, god of: Hymen (Greek mythology)

weddings, most popular venues in England: 1) London Eye; 2) Lanesborough Hotel, London; 3) Epsom race course, Surrey; 4) Institute of Contemporary Arts; 5) Pennyhill Park & Spa, Surrey; 6) Hanbury Manor Hotel, Herts; 7) Rowton Castle, Shrewsbury; 8) Brookfield Manor, Derbyshire; 9) Allerton Castle, North Yorkshire; 10) Linthwaite Hall, Cumbria

wedding anniversaries, UK: 1st: cotton; 2nd: paper; 3rd: leather; 4th: fruit or flowers; 5th: wood; 6th: sugar; 7th: wool or copper; 8th: bronze or pottery; 9th: pottery or willow; 10th: tin; 11th: steel; 12th: silk or linen; 13th: lace; 14th: ivory; 15th: crystal: 20th: china; 25th: silver; 30th: pearl; 35th: coral; 40th: ruby; 45th: sapphire; 50th: gold; 55th: emerald; 60th: diamond; 65th: blue sapphire; 70th: platinum; 75th: diamond

wedge, adjective: cuneate

wedge-shaped: cuneiform, sphenic

weed: chickweed, cocklebur, crabgrass, darnel, dock, Good King Henry, groundsel, jimson (very poisonous), knotgrass, mayweed, nipplewort, ragwort, scentless mayweed, shepherd's needle, shepherd's purse, spurrey, stinking mayweed, tare, wall-barley, wall rocket, water hyacinth, wild oat

weed, common garden: buttercup, chickweed, daisy, dandelion, ground elder, lady's-smock, sun spurge

week: sennight (archaic)

week, adjective: hebdomadal

Weekly World News: sensational US tabloid founded in 1979; famous headlines: Blind Man Regains Sight and Dumps Ugly Wife!, Elvis is Alive!, 12 US Senators are Aliens!

weeping, adjective: lachrymal

weevil, adjective: coleopterous, curculionid

weird: "When the going gets weird, the weird turn professional" – Hunter S. Thompson

Welsh and famous: Laura Ashley, Sir Stanley Baker, Christian Bale, Black Bart (pirate), Dame Shirley Bassey, Rob Brydon, Richard Burton, Joe Calzaghe (boxer), Catatonia, Charlotte Church, Roald Dahl, Timothy Dalton, Saint David, Richard Deacon (sculptor), Duffy (full name: Aimee Anne Duffy), Gareth Edwards (rugby player), Caradoc Evans (writer and novelist), Sir Geraint Evans, Feeder, Catrin Finch, Owen Glendower (chieftain and rebel), Dame Tanni Grey-Thompson, Ioan Gruffudd, Sir Anthony Hopkins, John Humphrys, Rhys Ifans, Katherine Jenkins, Roy Jenkins, Augustus John, Barry John (rugby player), Gwen John, Tom Jones, Glenys Kinnock, Neil Kinnock, T.E. Lawrence, Tony Lewis (cricket commentator), David Lloyd George, Arthur Machen (novelist), Manic Street Preachers, Cerys Matthews, Ray Milland, Ivor Novello, Robert Owen (reformer), Arthur Owens (double agent), Jonathan Pryce, Griff

Rhys Jones, Bertrand Russell, Harry Secombe, Michael Sheen, Stereophonics, Shakin' Stevens (real name: Michael Barratt), Super Furry Animals, Arthur Symons (poet), Bryn Terfel, Dylan Thomas, Bonnie Tyler, Sarah Waters (novelist), Emlyn Williams, Richard Wilson (landscape painter), Ian Woosnam (golfer), Hedd Wyn, Catherine Zeta-Jones

Welsh counties: Clwyd, Dyfed, Gwent, Gwynedd, Mid Glamorgan, Powys, South Glamorgan, West Glamorgan

Welshman: Taffy

Wembley Stadium: football stadium in Wembley, London, the world's largest with a covered roof. Originally built by Sir Robert McAlpine for the British Empire Exhibition of 1924, its lengthy reconstruction between 2000 and 2007 drew enormous controversy when, due to a series of setbacks, its final cost totalled £757 million

werewolf: lycanthrope

werewolf, adjective: lycanthropic

west, adjective: occidental

Western Samoa: former name for Samoa (until 1997)

Western Union Phonetic Alphabet: A for Adams, B for Boston, C for Chicago, D for Denver, E for Easy, F for Frank, G for George, H for Henry, I for Ida, J for John, K for King, L for Lincoln, M for Mary, N for New York, O for Ocean, P for Peter, Q for Queen, R for Roger, S for Sugar, T for Thomas, U for Union, V for Victor, W for William, X for X-ray, Y for Young, Z for Zero

West Indies: archipelago off Central America; also referred to as the Caribbean

West Indies, patron saint of: Gertrude

West Midlands, administrative centre: Birmingham

West Virginia, 35th state (1863), Mountain State

　　capital: Charleston

　　state bird: cardinal (a state bird it shares with Illinois, Indiana, Kentucky, North Carolina, Ohio and Virginia)

　　state flower: rhododendron (a state flower it shares with Washington)

　　state tree: sugar maple

　　motto: 'Montani Semper Liberi' ('Mountaineers Are Always Free')

　　birthplace of: Pearl S. Buck, Joanne Dru, Thomas Stonewall Jackson, Don Knotts, John Forbes Nash, Jr, Mary Lou Retton, Blaze Starr, Bill Withers, Chuck Yeager

　　tourist attractions: Charleston, Harpers Ferry National Historic Park, Williamstown

　　fact: to this day West Virginia has not been legally recognised as an independent state either by Virginia or the Supreme Court

West Wing, The: TV series produced by NBC and Warner Bros. TV, created by Aaron Sorkin

　　broadcast: 22 September 1999–14 May 2006

　　cast: Martin Sheen (President Josiah Bartlet), Rob Lowe (Sam Seaborn), John Spencer (Leo McGarry), Bradley Whitford (Josh Lyman), Moira Kelly (Madeline Hampton), Richard Schiff (Toby Ziegler), Allison Janney (C.J. Cregg), Stockard Channing (Abigail Bartlet), Janel Moloney (Donna Moss), Tim Matheson (John Hoyle), Dule Hill (Charlie Young), John Goodman (House Speaker Walkman)

Western film, first: Thomas Edison's *Cripple Creek Bar-Room Scene*

whale, adjective: cetacean (also includes dolphins and porpoises)

whale, collective noun: pod, school

whales, famous: Keiko, Moby Dick, Shamu, Willy

whale, female: cow

whale, male: bull

whale food: krill

whale hunter: Captain Ahab

whalebone carving: scrimshaw

wheat: bulgar, durum, einkorn, emmer, spelt, tabbouleh

wheat, adjective: triticoid

wheat disease: bunt, cockle

wheel, earliest surviving evidence of: from the Sumerian civilisation 3,500 years ago

wheel clamp: invented by Frank Marugg in 1953. Marugg was a violinist for the Denver Symphony Orchestra and his immobiliser was nicknamed the 'Denver boot'

wheel for a pulley block: sheave

wheel wedge (to prevent movement): chock

When Harry Met Sally (1989 film), famous line: Woman in restaurant (Estelle Reiner), to waiter: "I'll have what she's having" [referring to Sally, who's just faked a very public orgasm]

whisky: Ballantine's, Bell's, bourbon, Campbeltowns malt, Canadian, corn, Grouse, Haig, home rule (slang), hooch, Irish, Islay malt, J&B Rare, Jim Beam (Kentucky Straight Bourbon Whiskey), Johnnie Walker, Lowland malt, malt, Highland malt, Penderyn (Welsh), red-eye (cheap), rye, Scotch (see), usquebaugh, whisky (any Scotch whiskey), White Horse

whisky liqueur: Drambuie

whisper: siffilate (verb)

whist authority: Edmond Hoyle

whistle-blowers: Marta Andreasen (the EU's former chief accountant who was suspended in 2002 for saying that the European budget was "an open till waiting to be robbed"), Julian Assange (director of the WikiLeaks website), Ivan Boesky (aka 'Ivan the Terrible,' assisted the US Justice Department in exposing corruption on Wall Street), Deep Throat (anonymous source who was instrumental in bringing down the Nixon administration – see), Mark Felt (aka 'Deep Throat'), Katherine Gunn (leaked classified memos from the US National Security Agency to the press), David Shayler, Edmund Waller, Sherron S. Watkins (vice-president for Corporate Development for Enron), John Wick (who leaked British MPs' outrageous abuse of their expenses), Mark Whitacre (exposed the price fixing of his company, ADM), Jeffrey Wigand (exposed corruption in the tobacco industry)
- see spies

whistler: siffleur

whistler, famous: Roger Whittaker

Whit Sunday: Pentecost

Whitaker's Almanack: annual reference book of factual data established in 1868 by Joseph Whitaker

White Horse whisky, slogan: 'You can take a White Horse anywhere'

White House address: 1600 Pennsylvania Avenue, Washington D.C.

white person: honky, ofay (derogatory)

White Supremacist singing group: Prussian Blue

whiten: blanch (verb)

Who, The: English rock group formed in London in 1964, when they were known as The Detours, then The High Numbers; members include: Pete Townshend (rhythm guitar), Keith Moon (drums; who replaced Dougie Sandon in the first year; died: 7 September 1978, was then replaced by Kenny Jones), John Entwhistle (bass) and Roger Daltrey (vocals, lead guitar)

whooping cough: pertussis

WHT: wandering hands trouble

WI: postcode for Wisconsin

W.I.: Women's Institute

widescreen in film; first use of: in *The Corbett-Fitzsimmons Fight* (1897)

widow, collective noun: ambush

widow's veil: weeper

widows, patron saint of: Clotilde, Frances of Rome, Julitta and Paula

wife: ball and chain, better half, missis, missus, old woman, other half

wife, adjective: uxorial

wife, collective noun: impatience

wife, killing of: uxoricide

wife killers: Bluebeard, Hawley Crippen

wig: periwig, peruke, sheitel, toupee

wig for the pudendum: merkin

Wikipedia: on-line encyclopaedia established in 2001 by Jimmy 'Jimbo' Wales

wild animals, fear of: agrizoophobia

wild boar, collective noun: sounder

wildcat, collective noun: destruction, dout

wildlife photographer: Julie Ward (murdered in a Kenyan game park)

wilf (an approximate acronym applied to Internet browsing): What Was I Looking For?

will, adjective: volitional, voluntary

will-o'-the-wisp: ignis fatuus

willow shoot/sprig: osier

Wiltshire, administrative centre: Trowbridge

Wimbledon: leading centre of lawn tennis in south London, which began in 1877 with Spencer W. Gore winning the first final

Wimbledon record holders: William Renshaw and Pete Sampras, both of whom have won the singles final seven times

wind, adjective: aeolian, eolian

wind, fear of: anemophobia

wind, god of: Aeolus (Greek mythology), Vayu (Norse mythology)

wind, instrument for measuring: anemograph, anemometer

wind, spirits of: Harpies

wind-borne (adjective): aeolian

wind harp: aeolian harp

wind instruments: bagpipes, bugle, clarinet, cor anglais, cornet, cornetto, didgeridoo, English horn, euphonium, flugelhorn, flute, French horn, harmonica, helicon, horn, krummhorn, oboe, ocarina, ophicleide, pipe, recorder, sarrusophone, saxophone, serpent, shawm, sousaphone, trombone, trumpet, tuba, Wagner tuba, whistle

wind measurement: anemometry

windmill blade: vane

windmill chaser: Don Quixote

winds: antitrade wind, berg wind, bora, boreas (northerly), breeze, brickfielder, chinook, cordonazo, crosswind, easterly, föhn, gale, gust, headwind, hurricane, khamsin (oppressively hot), levanter (Mediterranean), mistral (cold and northerly), monsoon, northeaster, norther, northerly, northwester, pampero

Winnipeg, birthplace of: Bachman–Turner Overdrive, Crash Test Dummies, Deanna Durbin, Anna Paquin

winter, adjective: brumal, hibernal, hiemal

Wire, The: critically acclaimed HBO TV crime series set in the city of Baltimore, Maryland

  created by David Simon

  broadcast: 2 June 2002–9 March 2008

  cast: Dominic West (Jimmy McNulty), John Doman (Deputy Police Commissioner William Rawls), Idris Elba (Russell 'Stringer' Bell), Frankie Faison (Police Commissioner Ervin H. Burrell), Larry Gilliard, Jr (D'Angelo Barksdale), Wood Harris (Avon Barksdale), Deirdre Lovejoy (Rhonda Pearlman), Wendell Pierce (Bunk Moreland), Lance Reddick (Cedric Daniels), Andre Royo ('Bubbles'), Sonja Sohn (Shakima 'Kima' Greggs), Clarke Peters (Lester Freamon), Jim True-Frost (Roland 'Prez' Pryzbylewski)

wireless pioneer: Guglielmo Marconi

Wisconsin, 30th state (1848), Badger State

  capital: Madison

  state bird: robin

  state flower: wood violet

  state tree: sugar maple

  motto: 'Forward'

  birthplace of: Don Ameche, Willem Dafoe, Tyne Daly, Chris Farley, Heather Graham, Woody Herman, Tom Hulce, ice cream sundae, Liberace, Alfred Lunt, Fredric March, Jackie Mason, Georgia O'Keeffe, Charles and John Ringling, Gena Rowlands, Tom Snyder, Spencer Tracy, Orson Welles, Thornton Wilder, Frank Lloyd Wright

  tourist attractions: Circus World Museum, Lake Winnebago, Noah's Ark in Wisconsin Dells (the country's largest water-themed park)

  fact: Wisconsin is home to the first Barbie doll, Harley Davidson motorcycles, the first Ringling Brothers circus and, er, Swiss cheese

Wisden Cricketers' Almanac: first published by John Wisden in 1864

wisdom: "Wisdom is the reward you receive for a lifetime of listening when you'd rather have been talking" – Aristotle; "Knowledge consists of knowing that a tomato is a fruit, and wisdom consists of not putting it in a fruit salad" - Miles Kington

wisdom, adjective: sapiential

wisdom, god of: Thoth (Egyptian mythology)

wisdom, goddess of: Athena (Greek), Minerva (Roman)

wit: "Educated insolence" – Aristotle

witches: Baba Yaga, Dorrie (in the stories of Patricia Coombs), Hag Dowsabel (in the stories of Lorna Wood), Jadis (from *The Lion, The Witch and the Wardrobe*), Lamia, Madame Mim (from *The Sword in the Stone*), Morgan le Fay (sister of King Arthur), Sylvia Daisy Pouncer (from John Masefield's *The Midnight Folk*), Sabrina the Teenage Witch (as played by Melissa Joan Hart on TV), sibyl, Samantha Stephens (as played by Elizabeth Montgomery on TV's *Bewitched*)

witches, good – see fairy godmothers

witch lynching; last incident recorded in England: 1945

witchcraft: necromancy, obeah, obi, sortilege, voodoo, Wicca

witchcraft, adjective: necromantic

wits: Ambrose Bierce, Winston Churchill, Peter Cook, Noël Coward, Quentin Crisp, Stephen Fry, Groucho Marx, Dorothy Parker, Mark Twain, Voltaire, Oscar Wilde, John Wilkes

Wizard of Oz, The (1939 film), famous line: Dorothy (Judy Garland): "Toto, I've a feeling we're not in Kansas anymore"

wizards: Albus Dumbledore, Gandalf, Merlin, Harry Potter, Voldemort

WMD: Weapons of Mass Destruction

wolf, adjective: lupine

wolf, collective noun: route

wolf, famous: Akela (from *The Jungle Book*), Skoll (Norse mythology), Loopy De Loop, White Fang (offspring of an Indian wolfdog and wolf)

wolf, female: bitch

wolf, male: dog

wolf, young: whelp

woman: babe, bellibone (old-fashioned), bitch, bombshell, broad, cherry (old-fashioned), cupcake, dish, fish, floozie, hellcat, homoney (old-fashioned), jane, lesbian, Miss Right, 'one of the boys', sister, skinny (Australian), vamp, wench, whore, wildcat
- see girl

woman: "A woman is like a tree. You must judge it not by its flowers, but by its fruit" - Sarel Bok in the 1993 film *A Far Off Place*; "Women make the best psychoanalysts. Until they fall in love. Then they make the best patients" - Michael Chekhov in Alfred Hitchcock's *Spellbound* (1945)

woman, adjective: female, gynaecoid

woman (very old), adjective: anile

woman, collective noun: gaggle (derog.)

woman, killing of: femicide, gynecide, gynaecide

woman who has never given birth: nullipara

womanisers: Warren Beatty, Bluebeard, James Bond, Russell Brand, Giacomo Casanova, George Clooney, Don Juan, John Donne, Alfie Elkins (as played by Michael Caine, Alan Price and Jude Law), 'Pal' Joey Evans, Genghis Khan, William Hazlitt, Henry VIII, Howard Hughes, Victor Hugo, Mick Jagger, Tom Jones, John F. Kennedy, Fela Kuti, Lothario, Mao Tse-tung, Jack Nicholson, Pablo Picasso, Brad Pitt, Georges Simenon, Rod Stewart, H.G. Wells, John Wilmot (2nd Earl of Rochester)

womb: uterus

womb, adjective: matric(al), uterine

wombat, adjective: vombatid

wombat, collective noun: mob

Wombles, The: rubbish-collecting creatures from Wimbledon Common, created by Elisabeth Beresford. Successfully transposed to television (in 1973, on BBC1), the furry animals were later relocated to the big screen, the stage and the record charts. Main Wombles include Great Uncle Bulgaria, Bungo, Orinoco, Tobermory and Wellington

women, fear of: gynophobia

women, hatred of: misogyny

women, government headed by: gynocracy

women of ill repute: Divine Brown, Carmen, Moll Flanders, Heidi Fleiss, Fanny Hill, Jezebel, Manon Lescaut (c/o Abbe Prevost)
- see femmes fatale, prostitutes, etc

Wonderbra, slogan: 'Hello Boys'

wonders of the world (unofficial): Angkor Wat, Channel Tunnel, Eiffel Tower, Empire State Building, Forth Railway Bridge, Golden Gate Bridge, Grand Canal in Venice, Great Wall of China, Machu Picchu, Panama Canal, Statue of Liberty, Sydney Opera House, Taj Mahal, Viceroy's House in New Dehli - see Seven Wonders of the Ancient World

wood, adjective: ligneous, ligniform, xyloid

wood (forest), adjective: sylvan

wood engraver: Thomas Bewick

wood engraving, art of: xylography

wood knot: knag, knar, knur, knurr

wood-eating: xylophagous

woodcarvers: Grinling Gibbons, Veit Stoss

woodchuck: groundhog

woodchuck, collective noun: fall

woodcutter: Ali Baba

wooden characters: Noddy, Pinocchio

wooden household utensils: treen, treenware

woodpecker, adjective: picine

woodpecker, collective noun: descent

woodpecker, famous: Woody

woods, god of: Pan (Greek), Silvanus (Roman)

Woodstock: iconic rock festival of the summer of 1969 held in Bethel, New York. Featured acts included Joan Baez, Joe Cocker, Canned Heat, Country Joe & the Fish, Crosby Stills & Nash, Arlo Guthrie, Richie Havens, Jimi Hendrix, Jefferson Airplane, Janis Joplin, Sly & the Family Stone, and The Who

woodworm powder: frass

wool fat: lanolin

wool-bearing: laniferous

woolly: lanate

Woolworth Building: sixty-storey Manhattan skyscraper that, in its day, was the tallest building in the world. Designed by Cass Gilbert, the neo-Gothic, 760-foot structure was completed in 1913 and served as the corporate headquarters for Frank W. Woolworth

Worcestershire, administrative centre: Worcester

word, adjective: verbal

word, long: sesquipedalian

word, newly coined: neologism

word, used but once: hapax legomenon

word blindness: alexia

word from which its last letters have been omitted (as in admin and curio): apocope

word lover: logophile

word lover whose enthusiasm for words surpasses his knowledge of them: logastellus (coined in 1970 but not officially recognised by any reference source)

word maniac: logolept

word named after a person: eponym

word repetition: echolalia

word sounding the same but spelled differently: homophone

word that use body parts: anatonym (i.e. to face the music, to finger the suspect, to foot the bill, etc)

word types: acronym, anatonym (see), antonym, aptronym, autonym, capitonym, charactonym, consonym, contronym, domunym, eponym, euonym, exonym,

heteronym, homonym, malonym, meronym, metonym, patronym, pseudonym, retronym, synonym, tautonym
word with a number of alternative meanings: polysemy
word words:
    habit of frequently repeating favourite words or expressions: verbigeration
    inability to recall the right word: onomatomania
    mania for trying to recall forgotten words: loganamnosis
    symbol used to represent an entire word ($ for dollar, etc): logogram/logograph
    worship of words: logolatry
words: "When ideas fail, words come in very handy" – Johann Goethe
words, addition of in order to clarify meaning: epexegesis
words, aversion to: logophobia
words, battle of: logomachy
words, condition of forgetting: lethologica, logamnesia
words, enthusiasm for that outstrips a knowledge of them: logastellus
words, fascination for: logofascination
words, fear of: verbaphobia
words, forgotten: abracadabrant (marvellous or stunning), aflunters (in a state of disorder), chimble (to gnaw like a rat), clointer (make noise with feet – especially with metal-shod shoes), expede, fatigate, quanked (overpowered by fatigue), raw-gabbit (speaking confidently on a subject of which one is ignorant)
words, inability to comprehend: asemia
words, overuse of: circumlocution, pleonasm
work: "There are only two kinds of work: work for money, and work for love. Any other kind of work should be spurned" – Ewen Brownrigg; "I like work; it fascinates me. I can sit and look at it for hours" - Jerome K. Jerome
work, dread of: ergophobia
work, lover of: ergophile
work of one day: darg (Scottish, Australian)
work to little purpose: ploiter (verb)
workaholism, official word for: ergomania
workers, patron saint of: Joseph
workshop, adjective: banausic
world, complete destruction of: mundicide
World Trade Centre: New York, bombed in 1993; completley destroyed 11 September, 2001, when 2,974 people died
World Trade Centre rubble spot: Ground Zero
worm, adjective: helminthic, vermian, vermicular, vermiculate
Worm, The: nickname for basketball player Dennis Rodman
worms, fear of: helminthophobia
worm of the intestine, adjective: helminthic
worry: "Worry is interest paid on trouble before it falls due" – William Ralph Inge
worsening (disease, etc): ingravescent (adjective)
wounds, patron saints of: Aldegundis, Marciana of Mauretania, Rita of Cascia
wren, adjective: troglodytine
wren, female: jenny-wren
wrestlers: Big Daddy (Shirley Crabtree), Randy Couture, Hulk Hogan, Milo of Croton, Dwayne 'The Rock' Johnson
wrestling school: palaestra

Wrigley's Doublemint chewing gum, slogan: 'Double your pleasure, double your fun'
wrinkles, dread of: rhytiphobia
wrinkling of the skin, prematurely: acrogeria
wrist muscles: extensor carpi radialis, extensor carpi ulnaris, extensor carpi radialis, flexor carpi ulnaris
writer: "A writer is someone for whom writing is harder than it is for other people" – Thomas Mann
writer, collective noun: worship
writers – see African-American writers, children's writers, cookery writers, crime writers, detective writers, food writers, Indian writers, Irish writers, Japanese writers, Lake District writers, Russian writers, science fiction writers, short-story writers, thriller writers, travel writers, etc
writers, fact: in 1982 the average annual income of full-time writers in America was $4,700 (as discovered in a University of Columbia survey of 10,000 people claiming to be full-time writers)
writers, patron saint of: Francis de Sales
writer's block: "Writer's block is nature's way of telling you you're not a writer" - Rupert Cornwell
writer's block: agraphia (resulting from a lesion on the brain)
writer's cramp: graphospasm
writing: "Most writers, like oysters, need only minor irritants to get them going" – Al Alvarez; "Writing is turning one's worst moments into money" - J.P. Donleavy; "Authorship is a rat race in which you never get to meet the other rats" - Gabriel Fielding (novelist); "Writing is a misery isn't it? I used to think it was all about wearing brocade dressing gowns and getting up at 11am, doing the crossword and having a little Madeira before writing a few hundred words. It was nothing like that. The isolation was terrible. I'd sit at my desk until 3am, smoking far too many cigarettes, drinking too much coffee and becoming morose and embittered. I'd spend whole days wondering if I should put in a comma or a full stop, and then I would hate it all so much that I would randomly change all the names of the characters" - Hugh Laurie; "Never write about what you know; use your imagination. Whenever you use the imagination you are taking risks, and writing must be full of experimenting. Everything is an experiment, whether people would say this or that, and if somehow or other you set off with an idea and you don't let it develop imaginatively, or if you are not relaxed in some way, it is unlikely to work. You must be relaxed when you hit the typewriter so that it does not feel as if it is at all important" - William Trevor
writing, aversion to: graphophobia
writing, goddess of: Seshat (Egyptian mythology)
writing, oldest known form of: cuneiform script (from the Sumerian civilization)
WV: postcode for West Virginia
WWF: World Wildlife Fund (now the Worldwide Fund for Nature), World Wrestling Federation
Wyoming, 44th state (1890), Equality State
    capital: Cheyenne
    state bird: meadowlark
    state flower: Indian paintbrush
    state tree: cottonwood
    motto: 'Equal Rights'
    birthplace of: Tom Horn, Jackson Pollock

tourist attractions: Yellowstone National Park, Grand Teton National Park, National Elk Refuge, Fort Laramie, Buffalo Bill Museum in Cody
fact: the first state to give women the right to vote
fact: boasts the lowest population of all fifty US states

X

X-Files, The: cult TV series in which FBI agents Fox Mulder and Dana Scully investigate cases of unexplained phenomena; adapted for the big screen in 1998 and 2008
  created by Chris Carter
  broadcast: 10 September 1993–19 May 2002
  cast: David Duchovny (Fox William 'Spooky' Mulder), Gillian Anderson (Dana Scully), Mitch Pileggi (assistant director Walter Skinner), William B. Davis (The Cigarette-Smoking Man), John Neville (The Well-Manicured Man)
X-Files fan: X-phile
X-Men: Marvel Comics series created by Stan Lee in 1963
X-Men characters: Professor Charles Francis Xavier, Angel, Beast, Cyclops, Jean Grey, Iceman,Magneto, Marvel Girl, Rogue, Storm, Wolverine
X-rays, study of: radiology
X-rays, specialist in: radiologist
X-shaped: decussate
Xerox: copying machine invented by Chester Carlson in 1937
Xtina: nickname for the singer Christina Aguilera
xylophone-like musical instrument: balafon (from West Africa)

Y

yacht, royal: Britannia (sailed the high seas between 1953 and 1997)
yachts, famous: Gypsy Moth IV, Lively Lady, Maiden, Morning Cloud
yachting trophies: Admirals Cup, America's Cup, Britannia Cup, Camrose Trophy, Prince of Wales Cup, Seawanhaka Cup, Sir William Burton Trophy
yachtsmen and women: Tony Bullimore (rescued on the 9th of January, 1997, from his upturned yacht *Global Exide Challenger*), Dee Caffari (the first woman to sail solo non-stop the 'wrong' way around the world), Sir Francis Chichester (sailed around the world solo in his yacht *Gypsy Moth IV*, 1966–1967), Denis Conner, Tracy Edwards, Clare Francis (the first woman to make a solo crossing of the Atlantic), Pete Goss, Francis Joyon, Dame Ellen MacArthur, Sir Robin Knox-Johnston (the first person to sail solo and non-stop around the world, in his yacht *Suhaili*, 1968–1969), Michael Perham (at 14 the youngest person to sail solo across the Atlantic, docking in Antigua 3 January 2007; then sailed around the world solo, aged 17), Leslie Powles (who completed his third solo round-the-world voyage at the age of 70 on 6 July, 1996), Sir Alec Rose, Zac Sunderland (in 2009, aged 17, was the youngest person to sail solo around the world – until his record was beaten by the UK's Michael Perham, and then by Australia's Jessica Watson), Jessica Watson (in 2010, aged 16, became the youngest person to sail around the world solo)
yak, female: dri, nak
Yalta Conference: 4 February 1945–11 February 1945 (attended by Joseph Stalin, Winston Churchill and Franklin D. Roosevelt)

Yankee: American; the word possibly derives from Jan Kees ('John Cheese'), a
   Dutchman who happened to live in America
yard: measurement first standardised by King Henry I (of England), as the length
   of his arm
yawn, adjective: oscitant
yawn, the act of yawning and stretching: pandiculation
yawning: oscitance (noun)
YBA: Young British Artist
year, a terrible one: annus horribilis
year, a wonderful one: annus mirabilis
yellow: amber, flaxen, gold, jaundiced, luteous (with a greenish tint), mustard, sandy
Yemen: republic in south-west Arabia, officially known as the Yemen Republic
   capital: Sana'a
   currency: riyal
   language: Arabic
   religion: Muslim
   biggest crop: qat (a green leaf which gives a pleasant high when chewed)
   birthplace of: Eddie Izzard
Yeomen of the Guard, The: operetta by W.S. Gilbert and Arthur Sullivan, first
   produced in London in 1888
Yes: extravagant British rock group formed in London in 1968; comprised of Jon
   Anderson (vocals), Chris Squire (bass/vocals), Peter Banks (guitar) – replaced
   by Steve Howe in 1971 - Bill Bruford (drums) – replaced by Alan White in
   1973 - and Tony Kaye (keyboards) - replaced by Rick Wakeman in 1972. In
   1980 Anderson was replaced by Trevor Horn and Wakeman by Geoff Downes,
   and in 1997 Billy Sherwood came on board
Yes Minister: much loved TV sitcom chronicling the political machinations in and
   around Downing Street; followed by *Yes, Prime Minister* (1986–1988)
   created by Antony Jay and Jonathan Lynn
   broadcast: 25 February 1980–25 November 1982 (on BBC2)
   cast: Paul Eddington (James Hacker), Nigel Hawthorne (Sir Humphrey Appleby),
      Derek Fowlds (Private Secretary Bernard Woolley)
yesterday, adjective: hesternal
Yiddish writers: Isaac Bashevis Singer, Israel Joshua Singer
yoghurt; first recorded: in biblical times, when Abraham was recommended the
   dish by an angel
yoghurt, world's largest consumer of: France
yolk, being without: alecithal (said of an ovum)
York river: Ouse
Yorkshire, North, administrative centre: Northallerton
Yorkshire, South, administrative centre: Barnsley
Yorkshire, West, administrative centre: Wakefield
Yorkshire Ripper: nickname for the seiral killer Peter Sutcliffe
Your Show of Shows: highly influential live TV variety show which was a Satuday
   night fixture in the USA for four years
   broadcast: 25 February 1950–5 June 1954
   produced by Max Liebman and co-written by Mel Tolkin, Lucille Kallen, Mel
      Brooks, Larry Gelbart, Woody Allen, Sam Denoff, Bill Persky and Neil Simon
   starring Sid Caesar, Imogene Coca, Carl Reiner, Howard Morris and a slew of
      guest hosts
youth: "You are only young once but you can stay immature indefinitely" - adage
youth, goddess of: Hebe (Greek mythology), Juventas (Roman), Renpet (Egyptian)

youth, patron saints of: Aloysius Gonzaga, Maria Goretti and John Bosco
youthful appearance (especially in older people): agerasia
youths, fear of: ephebiphobia
YouTube: video sharing website launched in a Californian garage in February 2005 by Chad Hurley and Steve Chen
Y-shaped: cruciate
Yugolsavian and famous: Milovan Djilas (politican and writer), Emir Kusturica (filmmaker and musician), Slobodan Milosevic (statesman), Josip Broz Tito (statesman)
Yuppie flew: aka Chronic fatigue syndrome, ME (see)
Yuppie flew, fact: a syndrome from which an estimated 150,000 people in the UK suffer

Z

Zaïre: former name for the Democratic Republic of the Congo
Zaïre dictator: Mobutu Sese Seko
Zambia: republic in southern Africa; gained its independence from the British in 1964 (when it was known as Northern Rhodesia)
   capital: Lusaka
   currency: Zambian kwacha
   language: English (official); Bemba, Kaonda, Lozi, Lunda, Luvale, Nyanja, Tonga, and around 70 other native tongues
   religion: Christian, Muslim, Hindu
   birthplace of: Kenneth Kaunda (first president), Thandie Newton (actress)
Zanzibar, birthplace of: Freddie Mercury
Z Cars: realistic, long-running BBC TV series that was the first to show the grim, tedious reality of day-to-day police work. Set in the northern English estate of Newtown, the show documented casebook stories partly provided by former CID Chief Superintendent Cecil Lindsay. The series produced two spin-offs, *Softly, Softly* and *Barlow at Large*
   broadcast: 2 January 1962–20 September 1978
   created by: Troy Kennedy Martin
   cast: Jeremy Kemp (PC Bob Steele), James Ellis (PC Herbert 'Bert' Lynch), Joseph Brady (PC John 'Jock' Weir), Brian Blessed (PC William 'Fancy' Smith), Terence Edmond (PC Ian Sweet), Colin Welland (PC David Graham), Stratford Johns (Det. Chief Insp. Barlow), Frank Windsor (Det. Sgt. John Watt), Paul Angelis (PC Bannerman), Dudley Foster (Det. Insp. Dunn), Leslie Sands (Det. Superintendent Miller), Dorothy White (Janey Steele), John Woodvine (Det. Insp. Alan Witty), Leonard Rossitor (Det. Insp. Bamber), John Slater (Det. Sgt. Tom Stone), Alison Steadman (WPC Bayliss)
zebra, adjective: hippotigrine, zebrine
zebra, collective noun: cohort, herd, stripe (jocular), zeal
zebra, famous: Stripes
zebra, female: mare
zebra, male: stallion
zebra, young: foal
zebra types: Burchell's zebra, Grévy's zebra, mountain zebra, true quagga
Zeebrugge disaster: 6 March 1987, in which a British ferry capsized off the Belgian coast, killing 193

zero tolerance: uncompromising crackdown on crime introduced in New York by police chief William J. Bratton; now a routine practice carried out in many corners of the world

Zimbabwe: country in south-east Africa; formerly known as Southern Rhodesia (until 1964) and Rhodesia (until 1979)
capital: Harare
currency: Zimbabwe dollar
language: English, Shona, Ndebele
religion: Christian

Zimbabwe Rhodesia: former name for Zimbabwe (1979–1980)

Zimbabwean and famous: Canaan Banana, Robert Mugabe, Morgan Tsvangirai

zither players: Gertrud Huber, Anton Karas (who composed and performed the score of the 1949 film *The Third Man*)

zodiac signs: Archer (Sagittarius), Bull (Taurus), Crab (Cancer), Fish (Pisces), Lion (Leo), Ram (Aries), Scales (Libra), Scorpion (Scorpio), Sea-goat (Capricorn), Twins (Gemini), Virgin (Virgo), Water Carrier (Aquarius)

zoologists: Karl Ernst von Baer, Sir Gavin de Beer, Iain Douglas-Hamilton, Sir James Gray, John Gray, Alfred Kinsey, Carolus Linnaeus, Desmond Morris, Sir Richard Owen, Nathaniel Rothschild, Sir Peter Scott, William Thorpe, Nikolas Tinbergen

Zulu chief: Albert Luthuli

Zulu kings: Cetshwayo, Goodwill Zwelethini kaBhekuzulu, Shaka

Zulu composer: Solomon Linda (whose *Mbube* was popularised as *The Lion Sleeps Tonight*)

Zulu warrior, collective noun: impi

Zurich, birthplace of: Felix Bloch (physicist), Max Frisch (novelist and playwright), Bruno Ganz (actor), Robert Frank (photographer), Henry Fuseli (painter), Hermann Rorschach

Zurich river: Limmat

Lightning Source UK Ltd.
Milton Keynes UK
16 February 2011

167595UK00002B/59/P

9 781907 652455